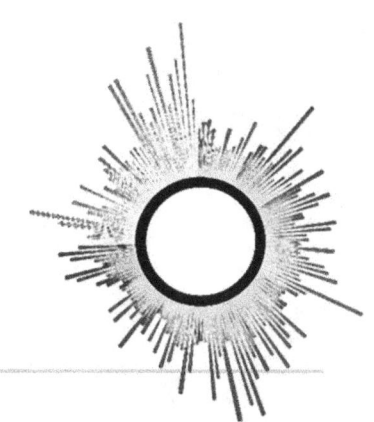

Alma Mater A Workbook for the Astrological Manipulation of Events

Ajani Abdul-Khaliq

Social Arts &
Technical Alliance

Copyright © 2021 by Ajani Abdul-Khaliq

All rights reserved. This book or any portion thereof may not be reproduced or used in any manner whatsoever without the express written permission of the publisher except for the use of brief quotations in a book review or scholarly journal.

First Printing: 2021

ISBN 978-1-955275-01-9

Social Arts & Technical Alliance, LLC
San Antonio, TX 78223

Table of Contents

Preface to the Print Edition x

Chapter 44. Dimensional Sight — 1
    About This Book 4
    On Applied Spirituality 4
    Who is This Book For? 4
    A Map of Our Journey 5

Chapter 45. The Worlds — 9
    Testing Out the Worlds 12
    The Realm of Instincts (Aries) 12
        Introductory Exercise 13
        Detailed Exercise 13
    The Realm of Identity Mirrors (Taurus) 16
        Introductory Exercise 16
        Detailed Exercise 17
    The Realm of Internal Monologue (Gemini) 19
        Introductory Exercise 20
        Detailed Exercise 21
    The Realm of Want (Cancer) 25
        Introductory Exercise 26
        Detailed Exercise 27
    The Realm of Show (Leo) 30
        Introductory Exercise 31
        Detailed Exercise 32
    The Realm of Joining (Virgo) 36
        Introductory Exercise 37
        Detailed Exercise 37
    The Realm of Exchanging (Libra) 39
        Introductory Exercise 39
        Detailed Exercise 40
    The Realm of Influence (Scorpio) 41
        Introductory Exercise 42
        Detailed Exercise 42
    The Realm of Foreign Actors (Sagittarius) 46
        Introductory Exercise 47
        Detailed Exercise 49
    The Realm of Authorities (Capricorn) 52
        Introductory Exercise 54
        Detailed Exercise 55
    The Realm of Surrounding Information (Aquarius) 58
        Introductory Exercise 58
        Detailed Exercise 61
    The Realm of the Call (Pisces) 66
        Introductory Exercise 68
        Detailed Exercise 69
    A Quick Pass Through the Twelve Worlds 73
    Conclusion 74

Chapter 46. The Embodiment — 83
- Revisiting the 4-Cycle: For Interactions — 85
- The Body Wheels — 100
- Controlling Your Inputs — 106
- Conclusion — 106

Chapter 47. The Resonance — 107
- The Normal Senses — 111
- The "Psychic" Senses — 115
  - Clairaudience — 115
  - Clairsentience — 116
  - Projection — 120
  - Claircognizance — 127
  - Clairvoyance — 130
  - Telepathy — 134
  - Conclusion — 140

Chapter 48. The Sphere — 143
- Spheres of Effect — 144
- The Other Spheres Which Your Sphere Bonds To — 147
- Curious Holes — 151
- Slot Holders — 152
- It's Their Fault...Until It Keeps Happening...Then It's Probably You — 156
- Conclusion — 158

Chapter 49. The Conflict — 163
- We Will Put Conflict to Use — 163
- Dissection of the Conflict Factors — 165
- A Case Study in Planets: Chiron — 169
- A Case Study in Angles: Squares — 170
- A Case Study in Life Areas: Battles Between People — 172
  - Final thoughts on conflict rewriting — 179
- A Case Study in Character Combinations: Sun-Juno — 179
  - Two kinds of karmic reflection — 180
- A Case Study in General Stressors: Pax — 181
- Table of Energy Stressors — 184
- Delila and Other Items That Go Against Your Principles — 189
- Conclusion — 193

Chapter 50. The Rift — 197
- Clearing Voices — 197
- Determining the Endings — 198
  - Identify your better endings — 199
  - Ask if the trouble travels with them, but don't dwell too much on this — 199
  - Let's practice intuition: the best decision-making for your own growth — 199
- An Aftermath — 206

Chapter 51. The Spirits — 209
- 100%+ Relationships — 209
  - An Example of an Under 100% Relationship — 209
  - An Example of a 100%+ Relationship — 210
- The Actual Workings of an Ideal Tribe — 214
- Splits and Merges — 216

- Basic Types of Spirits 224
  - How Table 51-2 Was Created 226
  - Working with Negative Spirits 227

Chapter 52. The Role — 231
- What Feels Like Fate: A Story 233
- An Introduction to the Role Beyond Yourself 234
- Let No Door Be Considered Closed 235
- The Real Story 241
  - Handling these questions 241
- Your Beneficiaries 251

Chapter 53. The Friends and Their Paths — 258
- Friends Have Partly Different Paths 266
- Intuition Begins with Affinities 274
- Friends and Clairvoyance 276
  - Another warning against pre-punishment 277
  - Fast-forwarding 278
- The Talent for Connecting 279
- Conclusion: Your Friends Are Your First Test 280

Chapter 54. The Foresight — 281
- An Important Note about the Psychic Senses 283
- A Senses Scale 284
- Developing Projection 287
  - Dream projection 289
  - Astral projection 303
- Developing Clairsentience 327
  - A clairsentience hypothesis 328
  - Touch clairsentience 329
  - Charged objects 335
  - Vision-cognitive clairsentience 340
  - Empathic clairsentience 343
- Developing Clairvoyance 346
  - Unassisted clairvoyance 346
  - Assisted clairvoyance 348
- Developing Clairaudience 358
- Developing Claircognizance 362
- Developing Telepathy 364
- Conclusion 371

Chapter 55. The Asteroid — 373
- A Review of the Chart 373
  - Table 55-1 [17-3]: What the signs do (simple) 375
  - Table 55-2 [16-6]: The harmonics (angle families) 1-36 376
  - Table 55-3 [16-2]: What the houses do 379
  - Table 55-4 [16-3]: What the main planets, asteroids, and points do 380
  - Table 55-5 [54-2] Additional bodies 381
- The Two Rules of Astrological Potential (Individual) 384
- A Clock for all Wheels 390
- The Two Rules of Astrological Potential (Relationships) 390
  - Is this relationship legit? 391

    How will this relationship play out?......393
    How do I get the most out of this relationship, given the doubts have begun? A hypothesis......399
  A Brief Recap of Three Kinds of Relationship Astrology......401
  Telepathy and the Asteroid......402
    An example of three triggers......404
    What waking humans couldn't say......414
    Square process......419
  Conclusion......423

Chapter 56. The Star   425

  How to Read the Following Sections......426
  56-1 Pisces......427
  56-2 Aquarius......428
  56-3 Capricorn......429
  56-4 Sagittarius......430
  56-5 Scorpio......430
  56-6 Libra......431
    Relationship quirks and the squares to Libra......432
  56-7 Virgo......435
  56-8 Leo......436
  56-9 Cancer......438
    On Cancer and riches......440
    Easier said than done?......443
    Breaking into a sign......443
  56-10 Gemini......445
  56-11 Taurus......447
  56-12 Aries......448
  Universal Access......449
  Conclusion......450

Chapter 57. The Nickname   451

  Challenge: The *Other* Role Group......454
  Square Roles (Ajani's Observations)......456
  A Master Plan......461
  Moving On......462

Chapter 58. Some Background on This Book   463

  Using This Book for Calculated Life Path Hacking......464
  Final Thoughts......468

Appendix I: True Signs   470

  The General 12-Cycle, Senses, and the True Signs......473
    Table I-2: Sidereal Duodecanates......473
  So What Does Each Sidereal Signs Actually Represent?......478

Appendix II: Completed Sample of the Body Wheels   480

Appendix III: Ajani's Answer to Question 48.3   483

Appendix IV: Ajani's Answer to Question 49.3   484

Appendix V: Ajani's Answer to Question 49.7   485

Appendix VI: Ajani's Answer to Question 57.14   486

Index 490

Before we begin, I'll summarize this book on the whole: Although I don't like using this hocus-pocus word, for simplicity, **Alma Mater is a textbook for teaching "psychicism."** Given that you are now aware, you'll need to bear with its many strange corners. Read through everything, even the sections that seem negative or uncalled for. They are a necessary part of the training. Skipping them (especially the conflict chapters) is the reason many people keep their sights blind. Failing to practice is the main reason people never develop their talents beyond the accidental or coincidental. This book is *full* of practice. It will help you develop your intuition to a high level, <u>but you absolutely MUST do the exercises</u>. If you try to read through everything without doing the exercises, things will get very difficult very quickly. If you skip sections you'll find that the practice isn't nearly as effective. The content is dense, and is much easier to absorb if you do the exercises in between. *Alma Mater* is a serious book for serious intuitive development. And almost none of it is *actually* psychic-based. It's just behavior, just attention.

You don't have to believe in magic, God, or even "psychicism" in order to develop strong non-normative senses. I didn't. That may or may not change by the time you are finished with the book, but as long as you do the exercises, you will develop at least one of the senses anyway.

Read the chapters, even the awkward ones. If you can't do awkward, don't expect to see much beyond your own comfort.

You may want to skip to your favorite senses. Okay, but your results will likely be capped.

If you find my examples distracting, cover them up. You can't imagine how much harder it would be for people to persist through all of this book's activities with vast stretches of blank lines to greet them on every other page. The examples are there to show you *exactly* what I'm asking you to do... and to discourage you from giving the kinds of short, lazy answers so typical of our age. We'll need more practice than that. (Practice is the real reason *Alma* is more likely to advance your development.)

If you finish the book in less than two months and haven't gotten anything out of it, there is a good chance you cut corners. Don't do that.

I repeat again: Do the exercises in earnest, get the results.

Preface to the Print Edition

A few years ago I purchased a book online about a subject I was interested in for which there was little information. The book was, by publishing standards, pretty terrible—so terrible, in fact that it irritated me for a moment how well the book seemed to be doing. The feeling didn't last long, however. The more I progressed through that book, the more I respected the author for being brave enough to put *something* out there in his own voice. Back when I was still a college instructor, the thing that disappointed me most was my students' hesitation to *try*. 90% of the time, when you presented something new or complicated—something that brought the risk of a mark other than the easy A—there would be pushback. I get it. I knew even then that part of the occasionally rough road I experienced in my classes stemmed from my own refusal to meet the students in their language. The catch is, my colleagues and I in General Education always got the subjects people had *not* come to college for. Environmental Science at a fashion school? College Algebra and Physical Anthropology? Of course there are plenty of teachers who could come out of that with rave reviews, but if you're a teacher in the modern American education system, you know that those rave reviews almost always come at someone's expense—often your students…long after they've graduated.

About a month before releasing this book, I think back to the one person who started the journey with me, though we were unable to complete it together. I've described her in another book as the worst exchange I've ever had with a human, hands down. But of all the people I've ever met in four decades, there is no one whom I respect more highly. Despite having had *a lot* of doors closed in my face over the years—by her as well—she was, like me, someone with a unique spirit which refused to be diverted. When larger systems left us with nowhere else to go, we started our own business, opened its service to others the best way we knew at the time, and did it in a way that didn't require compromise. It hasn't made us millionaires yet, but the blue flame stays lit.

All of my books, both in and out of the *Full Spectrum Astrology* series, have been lone works. I've done all the writing, editing, copyrighting, and formatting myself, published it myself through the company my former partner and I started, with no reviewers available to me and no help besides that of Victoria Ward, who produced two of my covers, and Keith Hayden, my middle brother, who indulged my crazy ideas along the way and recently helped me greatly in tying the series together online. The distribution, the ISBNs, eBook transformation (which took forever), indexing and all the macro programming that comes with it (which also took forever), the re-reading and re-reading and re-reading—despite the grand difficulty in catching everything in a 2000-page series—have all just been me, since other publishers wouldn't take these books. Where there was research or theory to be learned, I studied it and included it in order to help others address the same questions I was having as I wrote it. Where there was no accepted explanation for something, I reasoned out what made practical sense and presented that as a hypothesis. Accordingly, I've put a lot of work into these books, and challenged my own "hogwash" more than any anyone. Hopefully the result is a thorough treatment that won't make you look like a fool when you talk to people about the topics herein.

Anyone who calls you a fool for studying this spiritual stuff should probably read what it consists of first. While I was writing *Full Spectrum Astrology*, I was still a little concerned that the work needed a second eye as a kind of level-setting for the book. The funny thing is, however, though people would *say* you needed to do such and such as part of the idea-publishing process, they never had "time," and never cared to read it after all. It was too long, too abstract. Many couldn't understand it, but still managed to have an opinion on the whole thing. When it came time to help shape the work to their liking, they were nowhere to be found. I say this to you the reader not to cloud your day, but to establish something early on: It's okay to seek others' contributions to what you're doing, but if they don't give it, that's your cue to keep going without them. *Alma Mater* and its companions are—thanks to limited help—works in my own voice. They aren't the end-all be-all for their subjects, but I couldn't be prouder of them. *Your* works in your own voice may also arise in situations where you will find little help. Yet, the things you create in those places will truly be your own, and will say everything about who you are when there is no other crutch to define you. Take pride in those works. They are the clearest reflection of the people whose lives you're here to change and the tools you'll use to accomplish that change in its purest form. I truly believe that limited help can be a blessing for the creative. Read on and you'll see.

I've written this preface in order to say two things. First, I am truly, immeasurably grateful to my original business partner, and the mother of our unique enterprise. For any readers out there who have ever fought someone in order to build something great in the process, I hope you realize just how valuable that "enemy" is. While others may not have the time or interest in your dreams, your apparent opponent will task you to stand strongly where you were meant to stand. As long as you don't take your eyes off your goal, your opponent may be the only person who ensures you get there.

Secondly, don't be afraid to *try*. If you have something within that you wish to share with the world, then share it. After you're gone, this will be the thing you left behind. Otherwise, you might risk letting the comfortable bubble of others' sideline opinion prevent you from having any legacy of your own. It's okay to try. The people who want to understand you, just like regular friends, will get your point. Those who judge you are not worth holding back for anyway. Just try. Make sure it doesn't harm others. Then try the next. It's a role you were put on this earth to play and play fully.

All that said, I hope this book will make it safe for you to finally do the impossible.

Chapter 44. Dimensional Sight

Alma Mater began as a lesson I channeled about multidimensionality—the idea that we can be in two places at once. Of course, your hands and your feet already know this, but do you? Your stance on the floor and your reach for the door happen in two different places, but can you appreciate that idea? And then again, your stance is not the same as your feet. Your gaze is not the same as your eyes. One lives in the action dimension, the other in the physical dimension. But do you have the presence of mind to imagine these separate dimensions as worlds all their own?

In the talk with my guardians about multidimensionality, I was reminded that my physical body is an illusion, just like the drawing of an atom as being circular. Atoms aren't really circular; they aren't even a single thing, but a collection of forces spending their time around certain other collections packed into a region. Zoomed in, my neurons don't touch at their synapses. My clothes float over my skin on a miniscule layer of repulsion forces. The me who writes this is now thousands of miles away from the me who wrote the last page as he sits upon a spinning Earth sliding around the sun, rendering me an exotic mouse trail—an animation with no memory of even its closest antecedent keyframe.

Our solid world is mostly empty space. Things in one place—by virtue of being things at all—have a length or at least a duration. Thus they are located at least in the two places that constitute their beginning and their end. Physical things now become memories later, have patterned experiences tied to them, and pass back and forth as constructs in the minds of those who reference them. When you consider these phenomena alongside those listed in the previous paragraphs, you arrive at a set of truths which are easy to accept in theory but difficult to make use of in fact. For those of us who claim to demonstrably apply such theoretical truths to the viewable world, our abilities can take on a kind of otherworldliness similar to the sight of an airplane to a medieval man. For all its wonder outside of the scientific inquiry of the time, our otherworldly talents are rendered fantastic, earning them status as a kind of calculated magic.

Our science of complementary dimensions can be trained, but for that training to work, you'll need to accept at least one idea early on:

> For any one thing you can name, there exist at least
> three other worlds in which that same thing lives.

The tree in the woods has its physical tree-ness, its communicated idea-ness, its "in the woods" existence, and its influence on your next moment of thinking now that its concept has been raised from the sea of other potential concepts. All you'll need to do for now is accept that any event which is claimed to happen must 1) exist as a claim, 2) be claimed, 3) be an event, 4) and happen. We'll call these worlds 1) air, 2) earth, 3) fire, and 4) water respectively. Even *you* have at least four dimensions: physical self, the self's behavioral pattern, the other-environment effector, and additional identity labels against which you are compared.

Consider the following: I am a man in event fire. I write ideas in air. You, reader, are my earth whose reading proves that I have written. The effect of reading this upon you is my water. Even if you never meet me as a perceivable human "event," at least three of my other worlds have already tangled with yours via something that one of us has written.

To complicate matters further, there is the story I tell you about myself, the story you tell or don't tell yourself about me, and the story a third party would tell about all of it. Thus, for every four dimensions, there are at least three more: the self, the other, and the world. This gives us 12 possible dimensions for anything conceivable.

- It's a physically *plastic box* unto itself.
- To the world it's *a phone*.
- To you it's *your phone* with your customizations on it. And these are just the earth physical worlds.
- It *runs commands* unto itself.
- To the world it *rings*.
- To you it *makes demands on your attention* in fire.
- It feels *heat* as it spends memory running its call command.
- You feel *your mood* as you note that a caller is there.
- Others in the world feel *their feelings about your mood* as you appear to respond or tell the story of your response. These are the water dimensions.
- It passes a *file* across its memory.
- You hear that certain *ringtone*.
- The world says that someone is using it to *call* you. The information traded depends on whose air you're looking at.

☞ Now, take two minutes to think only of the demands on your attention these days. Set your phone timer for two whole minutes if you want real clarity. But here's the catch: Don't think AT ALL about anything else. Not about the things' images. Not about who or what those things "are." Don't dwell AT ALL on how you feel about those things. Or how you relate to those things. Just pay attention to how your attention goes from thing to thing for the next two minutes. If you do it right, you'll learn something insightful about who the real "stars" of your subconscious show are. (But don't do this activity if you know the content will upset you.)

Take two minutes now. I will too while writing this.

We'll call this the Leo dimension: Other-Fire. My attention moved from my face to the top left of my head. I thought of Duran Duran – View to a Kill. The Alumni Center at my former place of work. And just before my timer sounded, the voice of a soon-to-be exiting colleague said "Ajani!" Notable for me though was what was not on my attention: any number of to-dos that people might think I was concerned about. In the Leo dimension, don't feel obligated to fixate on something just because society suggests you should. If you don't care you don't care. The attention-grabbing dimension is where you get to "squirrel" out on things that interest you just because they do. This is its own world. Now let me show you how different from each other two of your very own worlds can really be.

☞ Take two minutes to pay attention to the messages you are currently sending to anything around you. These are breathing noises, thoughts, attitudes, seating or posture positions, mannerisms. They include the way in which you're mashing down the chair, heating up the air with your breath, casting the evil eye on that device that doesn't work and is about to get tossed, or scaring the spiders in the corner with your colossal magnificence. Don't think about anything else. Just pay attention to ANY information that you are currently throwing out to anything anywhere directly around you. Don't think about the targets themselves though, just your own messages to them. Set your timer for two minutes. (But don't do this activity if you know the content will upset you.)

Start your two minutes now. I will too.

Perhaps because I am currently writing this book, the only feeling I got was that of being larger than life. I filled up the whole room with a sense of command towards no target in particular. What signals did you send? We'll call this the Gemini dimension: Self-Air. Perhaps you noticed differences between this world and your Leo world. My Leo was all about comfortable daring while my Gemini clearly involved command. If you had to summarize these two worlds in a word or a phrase only, how would you describe yours?

Can you imagine what it would be like if, through a shift in attention like this, you could push negative experiences away from your life and invite favorable ones in?

There are actually many more than 12 worlds. Just as countries have regions which have cities which have blocks, there are worlds within worlds for as grand or as microscopic as your attention is able to conceive. You can feel the other-water surprise in another's microexpression or send your self-air outlook towards an entire human race. The first rule of our magic will be this:

> Whatever world you specialize in, don't stay in one that brings pain or disharmony to yourself or the key aids for your expression.

Key aids could be other people, your environment, your health, an attitude, a physical tool, a type of opportunity, a beneficial challenge or rival, or anything whatsoever. If you need it in order to be a better version of yourself, be prepared to accept it, even if it doesn't accept you. You'll outgrow it once you learn to seek better versions of its lessons. But if it is currently a necessary part of your world, know that if you break it you may have to start all over with a meaner version of it. As if the next one holds a piece of the previous one's memory. For our magic to work, we need to stay in places with the fewest impediments to its use. Disharmony with your teachers is disharmony with reflections of yourself. It is your psychology. Thanks to your being stuck in your own perspective for life, the golden rule upon your own understanding is very real.

About This Book

Alma Mater, Full Spectrum Astrology 5, represents a return to the original conceptualist nature of the first book in the series, laying out a foundation for applied spirituality. Unlike the rest of the series, however, *Alma's* roots lie in my more philosophical works, particularly *Analytical Essays (AE), Black Male Feminism (BMF), Gamified Spirit (GS), Sex in 12 Dimensions (S12)*, and two unpublished works (*Embodiments* and *The Sphere*). While I will be using astrology to provide the framework for what we'll call "calculated magic," we'll lean heavily on the *BMF/S12* concept of the body as a package of announcements mainly for other viewers to respond to. (Fire) internal you is not as you appear, rather your outward appearance (earth) is largely meant to be a trigger for anyone who sees you. We'll also lean on the *GS/AE* idea that you come equipped with weighted "stats" that compel you towards certain paths over others. Learn to love your character's stats and the quest alongside those who challenge those stats, and much of your life may easily transform into an enjoyable game. It is just as the Chan (Zen Buddhist) masters depicted it to be. The new bit of astrology in this book consists of 1) further exploration of the first 1000 numbered asteroids introduced in *FSA 4: Laurentia* and 2) a much more precise look at the astrological circle as we divide *it* into 144 sections—"worlds" if you will.

On Applied Spirituality

The central aim of *Alma* is to help you develop intuition—so that you can call favorable things into your life while removing unfavorable ones. This is not quite the same as calling the events you "want" into your life, because as we'll see, people "want" on many different levels. In line with *AE*, our aim is actually to *stop* wanting more and more, and to start loving the entire lives we've built instead. There are trained wants and then there are the smooth states we actually prefer. To summarize *Alma*, by learning and appreciating which states are which, then separating the less perfected ones from the perfected ones, we can more easily follow a path towards perfecting them all. Not pie in the sky perfection, but the kind of "I'm living my best at every moment" perfection. Using a well-studied framework like astrology for turning our attention to certain facets of our lives over others, we can do all of that psychological reprogramming that the motivational speakers have been telling us about for years. As with the other *FSA* books, though, you don't have to believe in astrology in order to use *Alma*. We will cover many more topics relevant to applied spirituality which will definitely make practical sense regardless your level of ability in picturing those topics in action. Many of those topics consist of new perspectives on the basic science already familiar to us.

Who is This Book For?

Alma is for anyone wishing to develop their intuition in any way. It can be used by beginners and advanced intuitives alike, and presents many useful ways for understanding the possible science behind several spiritual techniques. Once we understand these techniques as rooted in a set of laws rather than fancy, making use of them becomes easy. This is similar to the power one gains once they realize the effects of dressing a certain way. It's amazing how a change in clothing can cause certain doors to open or close without your doing anything else. A change in facial expression, attention, attitude, a sense of what is limiting, an expectation, a meaning made, an impulse, or a tuned-in information source can also change your opportunities. None of this is new. We'll just use astrology and the sphere to organize it.

Although *Alma* is for everyone, there are certain easy ways to get very little out of it. As in all of my books, I take a more investigative approach towards spirituality here. You can be skeptical. But if you won't look at the science for how physics actually works, if you won't try the activities, if all you're doing is flipping through pages until you're convinced of something you want to hear—something that affirms it was all bullshit—you'll be disappointed at every turn. *Alma* wasn't written for the arrogant. I won't make any attempt to convince you. Most of the talk of proofs, imaginary numbers, orbit densities, and general astronomy was already done in the previous four books, so we're long past that. Readers who need to be convinced should read *Laurentia* instead. *Alma* is for people who want to make their own perspectives better, not those who want to make other's perspectives worse. The practices in this book are fairly simple and will work if you try them. They can't work if you don't.

Because of the nature of the topics we'll be covering, this book has A LOT of practice activities. Many of those activities come with my own examples on the side, for reasons that I explain a couple of times in the book. To give you an idea of why the examples are necessary though, you might just try doing a few of the exercises with the examples covered up. A vast sea of blank lines will await you—not a good incentive for you to get the practice you need or to answer the prompts as they were intended. Throughout the book we will be approaching esoteric topics like telepathy and clairaudience through the lens of regular logic, with no frills, no crazy claims, and no requirement that you believe in any particular spiritual doctrine. At least some of the activities have a high likelihood of working for you but, again, it will be essential that you play along and do the practice for that to happen. If the examples get in your way, you can always cover them up. Not having them at all, however, will have made the book several orders of magnitude more difficult for readers to get through. Many of the questions require a great deal of thought—where the terse, one-line, autocompleted answers our modern society has trained us to give won't be sufficient at all. Do the practice for the practice, not just to power through the activities. Additionally you'll find, as you progress through the book, that there is a certain level of honesty regarding your perceptions that will be essential to top-notch intuitive development. Face the questions as you would a live trainer. The examples are meant to show you what's expected.

A Map of Our Journey
In order to become good at this book's forms of "calculated magic," we'll need to become proficient in four key areas:

- Objects as embodiments of interactions (Fires)
- The 12 major worlds (Earths)
- Spheres of patterned relating (Airs)
- Attraction and repulsion towards consequences (Waters)

The four key areas are actually divisible into three sub-areas—self, other, and world—so that we'll really be looking at 12 key areas:

- Objects of your interaction as embodiments of *your attention* (Leo, Other Fires)
    - Cultures and collections of *objects known for their behavioral patterns* (Sagittarius (Saj), World Fires)

- Your impulses, genes, and personality as interactions against *your own internal* state (Aries, Self Fires)
- The 12 major *boundary-defining* worlds (Capricorn, World Earths)
    - The worlds you use to *describe your own* (Taurus, Self Earths)
    - The worlds you *attach to others' worlds*; making meaning (Virgo, Other Earths)
- Spheres of patterned relationships *with you* (Libra, Other Airs)
    - Spheres of patterned exchanges of relationships *around you* (Aquarius, World Airs)
    - Spheres of patterned relating *from yourself* (Gemini, Self Airs)
- Attraction and repulsion towards *consequences for yourself* (Cancer, Self Waters)
    - Attraction and repulsion of others towards consequences for those *relating to you* (Scorpio, Other Waters)
    - Attraction and repulsion of exchanges of others towards consequences *around you* (Pisces, World Waters)

For reasons I've talked about in previous books, there seems to be a natural order to these which has everything to do with cycles in mathematics. I learned these in such an order, and will cover them in *Alma* the same way.

- **The Worlds** of attention form our starting place. We need to know that the dimensions of attention and intention are out there before we can practice picking wisely from among them. Here we'll practice visiting different faces of the same reality—the 12 worlds.

- **The Embodiment**. Once we know what worlds can be chosen from, we can get a better appreciation for how all things that exist in form tend to "prefer" certain worlds over others. We'll investigate our own embodiments and the embodiments of the key things we keep around us at all times, learning to understand what patterns of action they represent.

- **The Resonance**. Now that we know what we embody and understand how our embodiments intentionally match certain aspects of our worlds, we can learn how our process of preferentially combining ideas can show our daily paths in the world. Here we take a first look at the psychic senses as complements to our normal ones.

- **The Sphere**. Our daily paths consist of connecting situations beyond ourselves to ends beyond themselves; this is a kind of service. But we'll need to form certain kinds of partnerships to do this regularly. Here we'll stop looking at ourselves as selves and start looking at ourselves as spheres. We'll see how atomic-us loves to orbit around a few major atomic people-types, places, and attitudes. Also, we'll learn what to do when the spaces we orbit are not so healthy.

- **The Conflict**. Many of the occupants of our sphere do not appear to be our friends, yet they form some of the strongest motivators for us to move forward. Why do we need conflict? Because conflict compels us to use the world of force which all things possess. All things have certain events attached to them which threaten, impose fear, or unsettle others emotionally. These could be death (others or their own), addiction, a loss of power, certain secrets or mysteries which the person isn't ready to hear, or anything else which foists emotional turns onto others. Whatever these things are for you, they have analogies in a world all their own. In this chapter we'll learn to look at the kinds of conflict we gravitate towards, the asteroids which indicate that conflict, and how to put such scenarios under our own positive control.

- **The Spirits**. Once we have tamed our realm of conflict, our lives may take on a very different character. We've fought every major battle. We've learned to attend to the right worlds which match us. Now is the time to find our tribe—not just in this life but in realms beyond. The Spirits are those personality-like patterns which are not us, but are essential for our effective navigation of the worlds beyond ourselves.

- **The Role**. We've fought. We've won. We've listened. Now the world is ready to give us a stable label that we ourselves can also agree with. This may be the label which stays with us after we die, so it is important that we choose the boundaries of our self-definition rather than having them chosen for us. In this chapter we will determine our larger role across a window spanning both directions, before and after our earthly lives. It's about here where our unique style of calculated magic becomes much easier to determine.

- **The Friends and Their Paths**. When your intuition becomes very strong, so too will the situations you affect. Your friends can serve as some of the most effective practice partners when it comes to testing your skills—particularly those involving psychic communication and aligned timing. What once may have seemed like esoteric nonsense should be old hat to you by now as you practice your skills alongside others. It will be more important than ever to choose your communication partners wisely.

- **The Foresight**. With your calculated magic now determined and your intuitive modes introduced, you can now develop a systematic view of brand new experiences. The more we know about the kinds of relationship patterns we're in—be they with people, worlds, or ourselves—the more we can predict the behaviors of the other participants in those relationships—be they people, worlds, or ourselves. You don't need to understand the object of your prediction. You only need to be richly plugged into the *type* of bond you have with that object or any self, other, or world like it. The Foresight is the central chapter of *Alma Mater*; here we fully investigate all six psychic senses, a possible standard scientific basis for each, and how to train such senses regardless of what you believe about how it works. Even if you don't believe in spirituality at all, you can still practice the psychic senses anyway using the activities in this chapter.

- **The Asteroid**. At this point in our intuitive training it may be helpful to revisit a more formal system for matching ourselves to scenarios that are easy to plug into. Following a brief review of basic astrology, we investigate—for the first time—the relative chart: the synastry of merged energies. A quick look at the relative chart can show us what a basic interaction between ourselves and another is built upon. This makes it much easier for us to determine how easy it will be to engage the other using any of the senses discussed in this book.

- **The Star**. By looking at worlds within worlds, we no longer have to be vague about where we're using our skills. Rather, arranging the descriptions of those worlds around the astrological wheel allows us an interesting portrait of multidimensionality. Building on the idea that astrological bodies ("asteroids") are just oscillators of different frequency bounded on two ends by the center and edge of the solar system (and then the galaxy), we can scale those oscillation relationships down to our own biological cycles in order to assign stable meaning to each section of the astro wheel. The Star assigns a question which each of our 144 sections of the wheel is capable of answering. This gives us a more reliable framework for knowing when we're using certain behaviors over others.

- **The Nickname**. The nickname is your summary for people and things you interact with in your life after you've figured out what they represent, why they are there, and what each one calls you to do. Nicknaming is very easy. Once you've done it, absorbing the skills of the things you've named becomes even easier. We'll use grand crosses in astrology to argue that you always have four choices of mask when engaging anything. It turns out that summoning what you want in life shouldn't have been that hard after all. You just needed to know which traits constituted which families.

Chapter 45. The Worlds

This book is intended to help you develop and practice a kind of "calculated magic." When we think of magic we often assume either the showman's kind, the occultist's kind, or the fantastic kind, but there is at least one more with which we are almost all familiar: the future technology kind. Just as person from the 1500s might have seen our commercial airliners as a type of magic, just as a person from the 1800s might have seen our touch screen monitors or our creation of new elements on the periodic table as magic, there are certain technologies which people from the 2200s might use which would strike us in the same way. Using implanted chips to project holograms of ourselves into parties on another planet? Drawing hearts in the air to send an "I love you" message to someone whose pain we just felt miles away? Placing a device on a tree which allows it to give you its opinion regarding the state of the land? None of these are magic of the Merlin type, but each of them has an otherworldly quality that lives comfortably in a world beyond our current one. To us in the early 21st century they might seem astounding, but their magic will surely have been calculated based on natural laws we've essentially figured out already. **Calculated magic** isn't actual magic, but **a kind of technology based on laws incomprehensible to the average observer to produce effects whose origins few of those observers can easily explain.**

There are many sources of future technology which we know about, but have not yet been able to harness in a commonplace way. Using sunlight to power certain organ systems, locking objects together across billions of miles using gravity, perpetual-like motion of particle-sized energy carriers, even the mood changes transmitted from one facial expression to the eyes of the other who views it… These represent already known sources of future technology which our commonly available inventions have not yet encapsulated. But they will. If nature displays it, surely we can replicate it, but until we do, people who seem to be able to mimic these kinds of sources without any known invention will continue to strike us as phenomenal. Until then, using "light hands" to heal organ systems, locking thoughts together through telepathy, perpetual recordkeeping through astral travel, and mood transmission through clairvoyance will all be seen as much more fantastic than their physics-based analogs.

Still, despite our lack of familiarity with certain human tricks, the rules governing small nature and big nature are the same throughout. Parallel dimensions such as those of mother, daughter, bill payer, citizen, audience member, and resident can all be held by the same person at the same time with different levels of harmony and discord entirely. It depends on what you pay attention to. Some of these dimensions seem to constantly cost us. Others may be tied to laws which are far too tangled for the average person to understand. For one to command the complex laws and co-opt them with ease is for that person to be an alien.

But if we all hold a similar basis for the same set of worlds as everyone else, and if we all live in a shared dimension which constantly intrudes upon every one of those worlds, how useful is it to live only in the physical realm while leaving the others to chance? Are you *really* okay with letting public media write your world of information exchange for you? Has living on the latest post brought you closer to the life you dreamed? If it has, then good for you. But what if you want to take control of those worlds yourself? A baby eventually grows and learns how to ask for food, move herself around, and summon her toys on purpose. Until she matures, others will choose when these options are available to her and all she can do is cry or googoo to convey what she thinks about it. As adults we are very similar. Some of us learn to take control of our political responsibilities, the quality of our friendships, the environments we frequent or the effectiveness of our work lives. Until we mature, others will choose when these options are available to us and all we can do is cry or googoo to convey what we think about it. These worlds are separable from our family and hobby lives, and real enough to alter our personalities when we engage them. So when we talk about multiple worlds, we are really talking about separate realms of attention. If only we had a way to organize these worlds, they might be easier to clean up.

As I've discussed in several previous books, the astrological signs provide us with 12 types of experience for describing the same life. These types of experience color the character of the bodies located within them, based less on their inherent "powers" and more on their order along a trigonometric cycle with respect to a more obvious section 1.

Signs covered in *FSA* and *HBS*			
♈	♉	♊	♋
Aries spontaneous behaving	**Taurus** experiencing things you value or identify yourself against	**Gemini** communicating your ideas or instinctual movement; thinking or talking to or for yourself	**Cancer** paying attention to how you feel or how you're reacting to things
0°-30°	**30°-60°**	**60°-90°**	**90°-120°**
♌	♍	♎	♏
Leo playing, enjoying leisure time, having fun, broadcasting yourself	**Virgo** working, making meaning, doing daily duties and maintenance tasks	**Libra** socializing, talking in conversation with others, engaging in 1:1 feedback activities like playing instruments or video games	**Scorpio** using your power over others, over information, or over situations broadly
120°-150°	**150°-180°**	**180°-210°**	**210°-240°**
♐	♑	♒	♓
Sagittarius leaving an impression among strangers	**Capricorn** being associated with certain formal classes of people	**Aquarius** being talked about	**Pisces** performing default actions
240°-270°	**270°-300°**	**300°-330°**	**330°-360° (0°)**

Table 45-1: Signs covered in FSA & HBS

Since we live our lives in cycles (daily, monthly, yearly, relationally, task-based, want-satiation, interest-boredom, etc....), it pays to have some reasonable means of counting steps along a circular cycle in general. In *Laurentia* I explained how 6 *would be* a perfectly good count for the number of sub-worlds associated with any cycle...

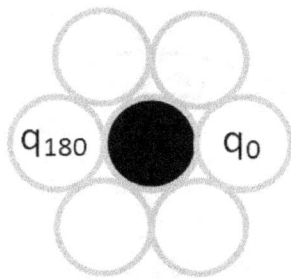

Figure 45-1: A hexagonal arrangement of cycles

…except that 6 leaves no room for up-down (potential, 90°, 270°) dimensions which we know have to be there. It only leaves room for the left-right (real, 0°, 180°) dimensions. Thus we need 12 dimensions for geometric and real-potential energy reasons, not least of which is the idea that a good cycle should be geometrically divisible by 6 and x-y axially divisible by 4. 12 is the least common denominator…

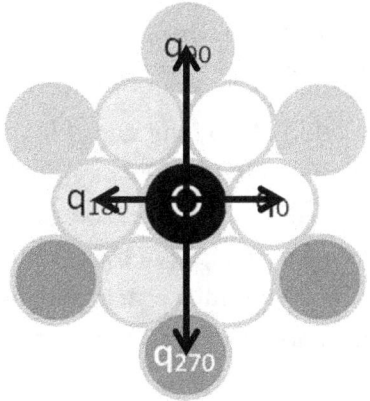

Figure 45-2: A snowflake arrangement of cycles

…and to make a long story short, you can see how this gives rise to 12 different stable divisions of a circle which all hold the same amount of information as the inner circle itself.

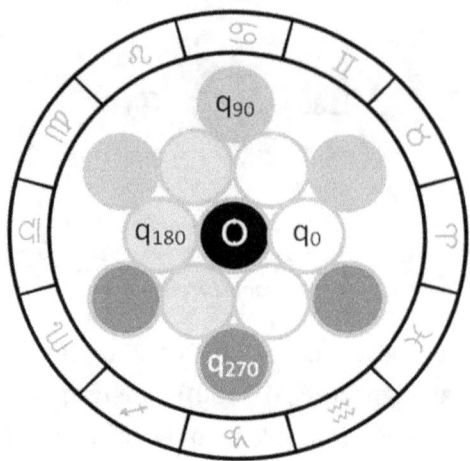

Figure 45-3: The 12 signs are analogies for where we are on any kind of real-potential energy cycle given an initial starting region.

I'll spare you Chapter 37's[1] gory explanation of why the signs hold the character that they do. But the summary is in Table 37-1 if you care to look at it. We'll just say that the 12 "worlds" are mathematically meaningful in the same way that your organ systems are biologically meaningful to your whole body. They overlap, talk to each other, do different things as a byproduct of how they originally differentiated themselves from each other in biochemical-potential space, and feel differently as you pay attention to them. Accordingly, you can also break up how you handle them.

Testing Out the Worlds

From here on, our plan is to develop our special talents in intuition and "effect-causing" using an organized pattern of attention to the different dimensions in our lives. We already know how to divert our attention from realms like work on the job to realms like traveling. There is also some mixing of the realms that occurs. But we'll need a really strong sense of how each of these worlds differs from the others in order to use them along the way, so let's take a tour of what each of them consists of.

The Realm of Instincts (Aries)

There is a world which consists entirely of the you who gets things started. That world includes why you start things, how, under what attitude, your motivations for doing so, and several other factors involved with your style of initiation. Oftentimes you will find that this realm does not need to complete or even

---

[1] The *FSA* series has four books prior to this one whose chapters stack in order: *Full Spectrum Astrology* (1-15), *Hayden's Book of Synastry* (16-25), *All 144 Aspects* (26-35), and *Laurentia* (36-43).

sustain its intended goal. It only needs to begin. If you don't know what this side of yourself looks like, there is a fairly easy way to find out.

As with all of the following exercises, don't follow any steps that will bring you disharmony.

Introductory Exercise
This exercise requires 4 minutes of absolute stillness, so make sure you're in a quiet enough space.

☞ Take 2 minutes to hold yourself completely still. Don't move. Don't think of anything. **Don't focus on anything.** If any thoughts come to mind while you're doing this, just exhale and allow them to go away. They waited this long, they can wait for two more minutes. See if you can manage to do absolutely nothing at all for 2 whole minutes. Then, when the timer goes off, <u>start it for 2 more minutes</u>. *Right after* you've started it again, you can read the next paragraph…

…imagine what you feel like doing right now. Picture yourself talking to whomever, going wherever, doing whatever is on your instinct. Pay particular attention to why you feel like doing it. BUT DON'T MOVE. This is important.

Detailed Exercise
Preventing yourself from moving during the Instinct activity helps amplify your desire to do something. Anything. If you gained even two impressions of your instincts here, then good for you. You did well. Write down what you experienced in the space below.

☞ Question 45.1.1 (Instinctual starter): Based on this brief exercise, how would you describe yourself as an instinctual starter?

	Example
	Wanted to contact a friend of mine
	Had Peabo Bryson – "If Ever You're in My Arms Again" playing
	I'm a sharer of happiness, like to make others feel good

That small activity was only a glimpse. What we really want is to identify those factors which help us start the things we want.

☞ **Question 45.1.2 (Major starts):** Keeping in mind your answers from the previous activity, take a moment to think about 3–5 major-ish things you have started in life. You may or may not have finished them. List them here.

	Example
	Creative Business
	Save our College Campaign
	Engineering Club (reboot)
	That one major relationship with that girl
	Written books

☞ **Question 45.1.3 (Involved in the start):** What, if applicable, were the common factors underlying how you began these things?

	Example
	A lone wolf, rebellious partner with a vision. They were brilliant, misunderstood. I had high respect for them. Get cooperation. Seen as equals. Mutual listening.
	A cause worth fighting for, academic setting
	The push for free expression, to be recognized

☞ **Question 45.1.4 (Evolved from the start):** (Important) Once you got out of the starting phase, which of the common factors above also stopped applying? These form a key part of your motivation.

	Example
	~~A lone wolf~~. The partner gets a partner. ~~with a vision~~. Their vision diverges from mine. ~~Misunderstood~~. The partner suddenly "understands" everything. ~~Get cooperation. Seen as equals. Mutual listening.~~ Foists it on me/everyone. ~~A cause worth fighting for~~, the people we serve don't care

☞ **Question 45.1.5 (Start reaction): How would you describe your behavior towards these (important) start-motivators above?**

	Example
	I try to offer reassurance, shared vision. But am generally more rebellious / unpredictable than my partner. I think I'm listening, but am probably immovable in my views. The fight is all-important. True partnership is not. Probably better not starting things on my own, unless they are one-sided (like books).

☞ **Question 45.1.6 (Start's aftermath):** On the other side of the above, which of your common factors (45.1.3) seem to remain successful even after you've finished with the starting phase? These form the overall "point" of your starting things, even if they don't finish.

	Example
	My own vision usually gains a platform. The partner is still brilliant. Respect for the partner basically remains. The academic contribution remains. The quest to be free and be recognized is almost always successful for both of us.

☞ **Question 45.1.7 (Why you begin):** Now, take your answers from 45.1.4, 45.1.5, and 45.1.6 and fill in the following cocktail:

In order to highlight my Instinct realm, I should pay attention to the [45.1.4s] in my life, get ready to [45.1.5] towards them, so that I can ultimately produce a [45.1.6] result.

	Example
	In order to highlight my Instinct realm, I should pay attention to the [visionary lone wolves in my life with whom I share a cause worth fighting for], I'll be [an immovable, fight-focused, source of surprises] towards them, so that I can ultimately [give my own, usually free-expressing academic vision a permanent platform].

Of course, we won't know much about the specific result or how you attract these conditions until we visit other realms, but this is the catalyst for your realm of new beginnings.

Interestingly, the earlier degrees of Aries are related to your race. Does your summary from 45.1.7 remind you of others' stereotypes of you based on how you look?

If you ever want to get something major started, look for situations that mirror your 45.1.7. They won't always show up in the form you expect, but later on as we study embodiments and spheres, you'll learn how to recognize them any way they arrive.

The Realm of Identity Mirrors (Taurus)

When you describe yourself, what kinds of labels do you use? A daughter or son? A successful someone? One who is quick-witted? A visual learner? All of these will be constructs which you use in order to provide yourself with valuable definition both to yourself and to others. The Identity realm has the interesting property of describing not only your various labels, but also your perfect reflection-partner— that kind of person who keeps showing up in your life even though you keep dumping them. Or maybe you don't. Reflection partners—unlike life-loves, twin flames, comrades-in-arms, better halves, or karmic connections—are valuable sources of hard facts about the kinds of labels you adopt. You'll tend to keep getting them for as long as you need in order to learn what exactly it is you are representing through your chosen labeling system. In the end, unless you truly know and love your own reflection, reflection partners and identity mirrors are often undesirable to *really* "marry" until you have nicknamed them properly, understood yourself as reflected by them, accepted yourself, and signed up to stay with your same identity for the long haul.

Introductory Exercise

☞ This one doesn't require a timer. Take a moment to write down a brief description of yourself using any labels which are most fitting for you. They could be physical, behavioral, relational, contextual, affiliation or group based, citizenship based, skill based, talent related, hobby-centered, or anything. Here's the catch: Only write down labels that you're prepared to be stuck with for the rest of your life. If you must note temporary things, be sure to add "for now" to the label. This will prevent your list from getting unnecessarily long.

_____
_____
_____
_____
_____

Even though you label yourself against the above things, it doesn't mean that you gravitate towards others who have those things, or that you gravitate towards the things themselves. Some identity labels are very much a product of the world that raised you. Others are simply bags that you reluctantly yet proudly carry, Hercules-style. Given these caveats, the main role of the Identity realm is for you to know exactly who you are, who you are not, and what you should allow yourself to be measured against. Will you find money (tradeable value), success (prosocial elevation), or fame (noteworthiness) among these labels? Our society suggests you should hope so. Now we'll find out whether you and society are on the same page in that department.

Let's use the realm of Identity to determine the *actual* basis of your highest worth.

Detailed Exercise

☞ Question 45.2.1 (Self-description): How did you describe yourself in the introductory exercise?

	Example
	Oldest brother, writer, black, free-scholar, system structurer, listener, diplomatic, amorous

It's too bad we haven't studied embodiments yet. Labels like "oldest brother" should really be converted into patterns like "goes out front among a group of same-emotional-background-asserters into the unknown." "Writer" should become "prefers ideas to have a permanent, public, path-traceable, status." If you can translate your list now then good for you, though it isn't really necessary this early in our studies.

☞ Question 45.2.2 (A key partner): Have you noticed that certain types of key people in your life—girlfriends, boyfriends, bosses, etc.…—seem to keep getting recycled even after you've ended it with their previous clone? (Actually, this will happen with *many* of your relationships.) Pick the one which is closest to a life partner, romantic partner, or best friend forever (bff) for you.[2] If you already have one, consider any people similar to them who preceded them. Keeping in mind that reflection-partners tend to have a high failure rate in a world of endless striving for more "worth," write down the characteristics of this kind of person. If there are no people who fit this, describe a type of *event* which qualifies.

	Example
	Hypersexual with a dirty streak, arrogant, but really wants to do good for others, critical and bullying, alone with her creation / child and doesn't understand why; prefers high worldly status partners, but also weak-willed partners (servants), conveyor belt dumper, unforgiving, easily deeply hurt. Super-magnetic allure.

---

[2] The priority goes: life partner, romantic partner, bff, in that order. Just in case you can't think of anyone on a higher priority level.

Your identity mirrors are the others against which your actions are compared. They are not necessarily meant to be your friends. Instead, they are the types of personalities who are best designed to view you as a person. They are your audience, your judge, and (perhaps reluctantly) your fan base. They may love you or hate you, but they will keep showing up to tell the rest of the world about what you did, for they saw it up close. Will you accept their assessment or tell them what to do with themselves? Let's find out.

☞ Question 45.2.3 (Do you complement?): Take the traits from 45.2.1 and match them up with those from 45.2.2. If the traits support each other, put a ✓. If they oppose each other, put an ✗. See if you can match them all.

		Example
	hypersexual, magnetic	✓ amorous
	arrogant	✗ oldest brother
	wants to do good	✓ free-scholar
	critical, bullying, unforgiving	✗ diplomatic
	critical, bullying, unforgiving	✓ writer
	alone, doesn't know why	✓ listener
	wants high status partners	✗ system structurer
	wants high status partners	✗ free-scholar
	wants weak-willed partners	✓ black[3]
	conveyor belt dumper	✓ free-scholar
	easily deeply hurt	✓ black[3]

Oftentimes you will not see the societally trained values anywhere on your list. But again, we'll need to study embodiments before we can form any conclusions. Regular values aside, there are definitely some things worth noting.

It turns out that your reflection partner encapsulates all of the lessons you need for building your *actual* (as opposed to societally suggested) worth. Some of their traits are exactly what you would want. Others are traits you are really being compelled to value *against*. For example, my books are invariably anti-judgment, anti-imposition of [rich-pretty-judgmental-hide your uniqueness in a closet] values. You can favor all of these things, but it's the imposition of all that on others which I write against. It wasn't until after I wrote *Sex in 12 Dimensions* that I finally stopped attracting the more damaging version of my reflection partner. And it wasn't until I owned up to my "oldest brother"-pattern responsibilities to others that I finally stopped making room for the arrogant version of my reflection partner (something about using your first-rank in a way that doesn't cut down others.) And what does this mean for you? Do your work. Build your worth properly. That way you may lose the need to have others force your work out of you.

Despite the cleanup, there is still an extent to which your reflection partners will reflect you. I may not feel arrogant, but still appear so among people who've just met me. I may not feel like a bully, but the

---

[3] See my discussion of the asteroid 26 Proserpina in *Laurentia*, Chapter 3 in *Black Male Feminism*, or Chapter 1 of *Gamified Spirit* for why I've made this equivocation.

immovability from my Aries surely makes me look like one. What do you do once you've cleaned up your worth engine, only to find yourself guilty of everything your reflection-partner showed to you? Try "sublimating the negative." Arrogance has a positive counterpart called self-assuredness. Being unforgiving has a positive counterpart called "recordkeeping accountability." If you are called to display these traits but haven't, and if your non-display of them somehow negatively affects your world's advancement, your world will present the negative version of these traits through your reflection partner. We won't really practice sublimating the negative until much later in the book, but for now we might note the following about building real value in the world:

> ***If there is something you are supposed to measure your worth against and you're not doing so,***
> ***If your not doing so negatively affects your world's progress,***
> ***Your reflection partner may very well hold that worth for you. Negatively.***

That's about all we can say regarding this realm for now. To master Identity, we'll need to get comfortable with a number of other topics throughout the book first. As a kind of preview to the later chapter on conflict, the guardians leave me with this additional message:

> *For any character trait which you hate in the world, you are tasked to stand against it while conflict still suits you. Once you grow beyond conflict and into the union of your own psychology with everything else you perceive, you will be tasked to adopt that very trait in its positive form.*

The Realm of Internal Monologue (Gemini)

Most of us are very familiar with the Gemini realm. This is the world of internal monologue, our real opinions of things, our mannerisms and our style of navigating spaces full of strangers (like traffic). Unfortunately, the vain Western world places a premium on the value of one's own thoughts about anything we can imagine, such that everyone's opinion, no matter how useless, is given some seat at most tables viewable to the public eye. I heard somewhere, "If you want something done right, don't tell anybody you're doing it," a not so subtle critique, I suppose, of the hindrances posed by a rampant opinionating culture.

When we air our internal monologue, we invariably air our "movements" through terrains full of other expressions—the motivations of which are largely unknown to us. The Gemini realm says, "I don't know who everyone is in this kitchen, but I'm going to throw this here pie anyway. Truly, we can tell the health of a culture by the peace or aggressiveness with which its people communicate against it. Relatedly, your Gemini realm is less useful as a look at your own vanity, and much more useful as a look at the culture you call home.

In *Black Male Feminism* I wrote about how I still use the N-word, F-words, MF-words, and others because I was raised in a context that rendered these fun and pro-social from people who look like me. I was also raised that the N-word's use by people who don't look like me is typically a bad thing. Yes it's a double standard, and no I won't typically use it among non-blacks, but no one can tell me that it "keeps me and my people down." As a reflection of my own view of my own culture, it still shows—more than anything else—how much fun I have being in my own skin.

Your realm of Internal Monologue betrays both 1) how you view your world and 2) how you communicate towards that world for the purposes of self-improvement. You'd like to associate with spaces where the words you use are words you *want* to use, not words you know are bad for you. Earlier today during the writing of this book for example, I used the word "hate" a couple of times in conversation with my friend, and I used it to describe the excessively crowded space in which we were meeting. *Hate* is a word I really avoid using to describe anything, but in the place where I used it there was a "culture" pattern that wasn't fit for me. Your words and manner tell you whether you are where you want to be. Do you use the same kinds of words that are music to your own ears, or do you use words which you know you ought to abandon?

Introductory Exercise

☞ Here's something neat. We can use your own words to find out your ideal culture. Take two minutes to imagine yourself in conversation with a special machine. This machine is going to record your personality perfectly so that it can transport your data faithfully to a beautiful new settlement on another planet. The only thing is, you must be your complete and true self during the recording. Otherwise you'll be transported with injuries and errors. Set your timer for 8 minutes and tell the machine about the following:

- the best experience you've ever had in your life
- the worst experience you've ever had in your life
- the most questionable thing you've ever done in your life
- the most questionable thing you've ever wanted in your life

We won't write any of this down in the exercises afterwards, but do keep note of the kinds of words you use to describe these items. Spend about two minutes on each. (I'll be using my recorder.)

What was your general attitude towards these topics? Did your attitude change? Were you critical? Did certain topics have special words associated with them? Take a moment to write down any words or [attitudes] that came with your accounts above.

Experience		Example
Best		Intimate, gray, sharing, time together, peace
Worst		Glo-bus (non-voluntary, competition, pressure), stress, assignment [slangish] [more curse words]
Questionable Deed		(none) [matter of fact], [analytical]
Questionable Want		(an unhealthy exchange) [matter of fact] [slangish]

In general, your ideal culture or environment enables your [best], is free of your [worst], may need to be monitored if you perceive [questionable wants], while you may seek a second opinion on your own actions when you are approaching [a questionable decision] on your own. While in that culture, you are tasked to represent your 45.2.1 traits.

Detailed Exercise

When a person knows his internal monologue, he also gains access to command of the messages he sends, physically and communicatively. Imagine the kind of body awareness that a dancer or athlete must have. Your internal monologue and your subsequent style of opinion giving are your main route to directly giving others personal information about yourself. Thus, this realm is important for knowing how and when to control the messages you send, and is one of the most important realms for earning or avoiding blame for those messages. A good grasp of your monologue can convince you of your own innocence in any matter, define and sustain the issues you deem important in any matter and, most of all, reinforce the "truths" of any issue placed before your understanding.

The more you use certain types of words or reactions to reinforce certain topics, the more those topics become permanently defined by those words or reactions.

For this next exercise, we will work on developing an emotional sensitivity to the unfitting words you use, as well as an early way to abandon those words when you catch yourself using them.

The general rule is that words act as a billboard for holding their associated ideas in front of you. Indeed, when the brain loads and processes a word, your representation systems are employed for reminding yourself of the various ideas that come with that word. This is called contextual memory; it is the same mechanism behind our being unable to recall something until we can recall another set of things associated with it. When you load, read, hear, or speak words which to you yourself are negative, you hold a brief dosage of negative temporarily in front of your thoughts. This is like standing in your kitchen, pulling arsenic off the shelf, removing the cap for a moment, then putting it back on the shelf. Words of love are like pulling roses. Words of power are like pulling something pungent. You can imagine, though, that the more times you pull arsenic or cyanide, the greater the dosage of poison you infuse into your own communications.

Some words—derogatory, vulgar, or diminishing—are good for us but bad for others. They may fuel our pride or our identity, but when used in the presence of others only serve to subtract from those others' worlds. There are multiple ways to handle such words besides eliminating them from your vocabulary: You can use them in fun, teaching others that they are not really harmful; you can use them in strength, teaching others that such words are a testament to your skill as a fighter or expert; you can use them in defense, teaching others that you are not to be trifled with. But if you only use them to belittle the idea you're referencing, you have only belittled your own notion of the reference—your own thoughts about the thing. The thing, however, may not only refuse your opinion, it MUST—less it grant *you* the power to break itself apart completely.

In *Gamified Spirit* I defined **respect** as "**treating a thing in the way that it (or its circumstances) suggest it be treated.**" I defined honor as "thinking of (or treating) something as though it deserves willing, voluntary respect." Key to both respect and honor is the idea that others should see you as you are claimed. Since we might assume that most people truly do the best they know how, the best they feel capable of, or the things that they prefer over other options (even if they say they don't) at any moment, words that defy this such as "stupid," "useless," or "hate" respectively will automatically foster disrespect towards the described thing in the mind of the describer. But my disrespect for you—my treatment of you as *other than* you claim to deserve—harms me more than it harms you. Not because God or the Bible or some other authority says so, but because I am the one who has put in the energy to 1) load the idea of you, 2) claim that the idea I just loaded is *not* you, and, 3) dedicate my precious thoughts to a waste, and 4) do a thing that your continued life (despite me) definitely renders wrong. It's something like showing my anger towards my neighbor by dumping my own trash can in my own yard. I can call you stupid all day, but you'll go home and make your stupid decisions anyway—except to you and everyone else who remains in your corner, your "stupid" decisions will make perfect sense regardless of my mighty opinion. And you'll keep making them long after I'm gone. Oh, the metabolic energy I've wasted.

☞ Question 45.3.1 (The once disrespected): Think about someone whom you seriously, knowingly disrespected (if applicable). List BOTH 1) the kinds of words you used to describe them AND 2) the kinds of emotions you felt towards them at the time. There does not need to be a distinction between these two sets of words.

	Example
	stupid, flaky, irresponsible, selfish, hedonistic, angry, pissed, used, weak, unreliable, powerful but…, all about [themselves], difficult [personality], ignorant

Congratulations, you have discovered a class of words which travel together in your own psychology in a quest to keep your mood negative. The negativity stays almost entirely with you when you use these words, though some of it may come out as communication towards the other. Or worse, towards your friends in your talk about the other. Your friends will then hold onto this little mob of words as a kind of posse which you are known to recruit whenever you are poised to bring negativity into your exchanges with them. And while those friends will usually not hold this against you (that's why they're friends), they *will* find you slightly harder to believe should you decide to change one day. Slightly harder every time you bring them another negative report. "My friend's files on this are *always* negative. Why would they change all of a sudden? Although I don't mean to, I struggle to (subconsciously) affirm their efforts to improve." Does that make sense?

45.3.1 represents your class of "disrespect words." When you use any one of them to describe anything, your chances of loading the others goes up. If you have used these words multiple times towards different people, it is much more likely that it's not the people you were describing, but a "type" which lives in your psychological-emotional library, which you think should be less eligible for treatment as claimed. These are deletions from your own smooth path as a relater more than they are any means to really change the person you're dissecting. Your disrespect of others is psychological baggage that *you* must carry, not them.

☞ Question 45.3.2 (Respected words): **given your disrespect words' role as anti-claimers, let's see what they are "anti-" against. List the words which in your mind are the opposite of each of your disrespect words.**

	Example
	~~stupid~~ smart, ~~flaky~~ reliable, ~~irresponsible~~ responsible, ~~selfish~~ selfless, ~~hedonistic~~ caring, ~~angry~~ serene, ~~pissed~~ excited, ~~used~~ serving, ~~weak~~ strong, ~~unreliable~~ reliable, ~~powerful but...~~ humble, ~~all about [themselves]~~ responsible to others, ~~difficult [personality]~~ easygoing, ~~ignorant~~ wise

These are the values which are closer to the respect side of your outlook. Remember that last note in the Taurus realm? Though we have not yet addressed what you would want to be respected for, these "respect words" form a class of traits which, if you display, will help others (and you yourself) see you in the way that you or your circumstances claim you deserve. Show these traits while playing out your desired role, and others will have an easier time agreeing that such a role indeed belongs to you.

☞ Question 45.3.3 (A respected person): **Suppose now that you want to attract something into your life, a new supporter of your truest skilled efforts, for example. (We could all use that, right?) Take a moment to think about a time when someone who fit the above traits in 45.3.2—that is, someone whom you respected—also supported your skill. What words describe the behavior that this person displayed towards you?**

	Example
	faith, excitement, action, comfort with position, confidence, wide command of others

As with the previous word families, this latest set forms a class of ideas that travel together, this time for "encouraging [your] mastery." Things you do which raise these ideas, whether they come from you or from someone else towards you, will more likely bring you further support for your unique talents.

One more. In order to transition from negative words to supportive ones, we need a way of turning down the volume on the negative. No amount of additional negative words will defeat a negative outlook. Positive words will only add a smooth covering to a still rough terrain. Instead, the best way to reduce negative messages is to grow tired of or indifferent towards them—to exhaust the energy for using them. Here we defer to the same 1-2-3-4 cycle cited so many times in previous books:

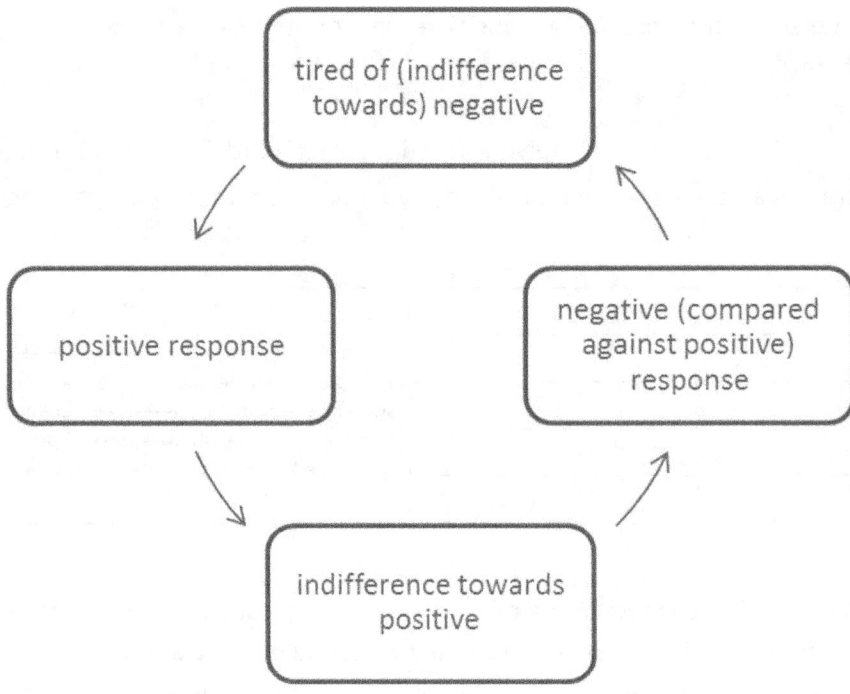

Figure 45-4. A real-antipotential-antireal-potential (4-cycle) for responding to events

All repeating cycles go through the same four phases of real energy→ spent real (anti-potential) energy→ complementary (anti-real) energy→ spent complementary (potentially real) energy. Again, <u>all repeating cycles</u>, no matter what they involve, do this. Day and night, inhalation and exhalation, hiring and leaving, Big Bang and Big Crunch,… whatever. It's part of the reason why these worlds have the order that they do. We notice, though, that it's not reasonable to go straight from a thing to its opposite. It's more efficient to pass through the *turning down* of the first thing first. Much of what we're taught about instantly replacing negative thoughts with positive ones is oversimplified. Before we make such a replacement, we usually benefit from turning down the source of the negative thoughts first. Then we insert the positive.

☞ Question 45.3.4 (Transition words): **Think of those occasions when you're simply tired of fighting, stressing out, or worrying about something. Write down a typical set of sentences which you might say in order to convey this, then circle the key phrases which you think are most important for shutting down the conflict.**

	Example
	Anyway, whatever.
	Not to waste any more energy on this.
	You know what, it doesn't even matter.
	They're gonna do whatever they're doing; who knows what they're deal is.
	F#ckin' sh*theads.
	I swear.
	No need to get all tangled up in that.

	Craziness, man.

If you had your own personal linguist, he might have a field day with this. I noticed that my own words consistently rendered the issue either 1) so confused as to be not worth solving or 2) worthy of a new insight. Since I identify as a scholar by identity, solvability makes all the difference in whether or not I stay on something. "You know what," in particular, was the strongest phrase I had available—probably because it does double duty as both an unproductive-subject dropper (tired of negative) and an insight raiser (newly positive). Did you notice if some of your "negative volume down" words were related to the actions you use for building your worth? Use these words whenever your disrespect class gets out of hand. It's stronger than reaching directly for the positive when you're not really in the mood to mean it.

The Realm of Want (Cancer)

Our worlds of want are some of the most assaulted worlds in our entire space of attention. What the Buddhists call endless striving or deeming desire involves that stream of nonstop drops of good placement in search of greener grass. More money, more status, eventual retirement, more posted happiness, more opinion weigh in, newer tech, newer gifts, the latest news, and so on…though our pattern for responding to the new things when we get them is rarely new at all. There is a "way" in which we want, a way in which we start anew. And though the various catalysts for that new experience may change, *we* don't really.

The Want world is both tricky and exciting. On the one hand, it is the realm most strongly associated with "exhaustion of real energy." That is, on a 12-cycle like the astrological wheel or in a complex math space like the real-imaginary axis—the 90° mark (where want/Cancer is located)—the [real event we were just looking at] becomes→ [entirely potential] for the thing which looks at us. Not only have we finished taking our turn, but the game also sits in that in-between state where the other is about to take their turn. So we won't be back around for a while. Accordingly, our realm of Want includes all of the things we haven't finished doing with our own Start, Identity, or Monologue—serving as a great place placeholder for all of the ways in which we can be clingy and insecure.

The good part of Want is that it anticipates the next moves of your complement. We can see this if we turn the cycle around by 180°. Consider how people's public labels for us (Capricorn, 270°; also known as the *world's overall treatment* of us) will form the optimum predictor of what we can be publicly interpreted as doing next (Aries, 0°). Relatedly, our ~~wants~~ inclinations (Cancer, 90°) will form the optimum predictor of what we see our respondents doing next. So it is Cancer/the want Realm which is most heavily associated with premonition.[4]

What we want often (but not always) comes with disharmony with what we have. Forcing socially suggested standards onto how you want is a very good way to *never* develop your intuition, as well as never develop peace with your own natural direction. It is common for intuitive parents to deactivate their gifts for the sake of their children, but the tradeoff is that the empathy associated with the child's path is also reduced. Where there is intuition there is an inherent plug-in to those who are set to respond to you. Control whose responses you consider and you control the ability of others to flood you with their emotional energy. Silence your ability to predict those responses altogether and you lose a valuable gauge for viewing the emotional consequences of your own actions.

Introductory Exercise

☞ In order to get a handle on the world of Want, we first need to separate it into four subsections: 1) Wanting, 2) Inclining Towards, 3) Expecting, and 4) Feeling. These are more or less associated with 1) giving your potential to an object, 2) giving your potential as a process without an object, 3) receiving potential regarding an object, and 4) receiving potential as a process in light of an object respectively. As a general rule, it requires more energy to give out than to receive (obviously). It requires more energy to interpret than to simply feel without interpretation. So Wanting and Inclining cost more than Expecting and Feeling; Wanting and Expecting cost more than Inclining and Feeling. Once in the realm of Want, you have two choices to make: to give potential or receive it, to translate the information you get or simply describe it. None of these are better than the other, but in a course on intuition development, you're encouraged to practice describing more and translating less. The current society teaches us to translate our wants into achievements enough already.

We won't really get into the nuances of Want until much later in the book, since we really need the Star in order to break this world up into manageable pieces. For now we'll get started with a simple exercise that will be useful towards your Sphere: Let's find out which characters in the world are currently essential to your "plot line."

☞ Question 45.4.1 (Places you "live" in): **Places:** Name any of the main places AND situations where you can generally be easily found during most of these days. These are places (not necessarily just home) where some might say you "live."

	Example
	home, my office at the college, on Knime (software), on Microsoft Word (software; writing this book), on an advocacy project

---

[4] Cancer is associated with *premoni*tion, predicting events from the perspective of the self. Scorpio is associated with *project*ion, putting energy onto others. Pisces is associated with *in*tuition, reading environments in the world.

☞ Question 45.4.2 (Central plot-advancing characters): **People:** What people are currently playing critical roles in advancing your "character's story" in the world?

	Example
	C, D, M, S, J, E, M, H, B, L, M, J, S

☞ Question 45.4.3 (Central plot activities): **Projects:** What ongoing projects or tasks occupy most of your focus these days?

	Example
	job investigation, life path project, ACEs, *Alma Mater*, publishing tasks, Knime nodes

If you imagine yourself to be a sphere which floats between your current places, with logos being absorbed into it indicating your current situations, logos radiating out of it indicating any work you are regularly producing, and logos spinning around it indicating any tools or tasks you are on—if you imagine dots located at all of the people whom you listed in 45.4.2, and co-orbits with all of the strongest connections among that same group, you get a basic image of yourself as a "Sphere." If the gods were to take a microscope to the Earth and study you as a particle, they wouldn't necessarily see your body. They would see your mixed frequency pattern consisting of the answers you listed. Notice how much easier you are to describe—how much clearer your most important objectives appear—when you eliminate the unnecessary details.

Detailed Exercise

When I first tried communicating with others psychically, I wasn't very successful. Later I learned that so-called psychic phone calls require more than two willing and able interactants. These calls also require a shared language, concentration on the actual exchange, and an ability to recognize the unique ways in which each person understands their halves of the signal. A friend of mine, for example, calls with her 12th realm (Pisces). I call with my 4th (Cancer). She calls with authority. I usually call with lust or (more G-rated) interruptions. How you call depends on which asteroids live in certain sections of your chart. Who you can get away with calling depends on who tolerates your style of dialing. I have asteroids like 99 Dike, 126 Velleda, and 79360 Sila-Nunam in my calling region of Cancer, so the people who "pick up" my calls (purposeful or accidental) tend to be lusty, playful, and body-centric women. Like you, however, almost all of my calls are accidental. (It's a lot of work to coordinate things like this on purpose.) You can look up the meanings of the first 1000 numbered asteroids in *Laurentia*. But on the issue of psychic attunement,

You can use your Want realm to call people or events, as long as

- the receiver is inclined to respond to you,
- the receiver is disinclined to hide major parts of themselves from you (that's a big one),
- the receiver likes getting your calls, and
- <u>you are capable of **easily** going back and forth from Inclining to Feeling (from intuitive "speaking" to intuitive "listening") as you receive the conversation on the whole</u>

Remember, the Want realm is a potential realm. It makes less sense to force translation of it (Wanting or Expecting) into a real world conversation. Describing as it flows is the key. Given that you'll need to let it flow, your earliest practice in intuitive communication should be with people or events <u>who want you around</u>—who'd have as good a time talking to you as you would to them. I probably couldn't talk to Money or Success as easily as I could talk to Knime or my friend Jackie. I couldn't talk to people who were guarded against my crossing a particular line (especially with Velleda) as easily as I could to a shameless person. So how do you know what kinds of people or events are more likely to give you their psychic phone number? For those of us who like to call Cancer-style (the things which readily respond to us), here's what you can do:

Critical Exercise
THE PLAYLIST

Trains: Empathy, Clairaudience

☞ Question 45.4.4 (Good call reception): **Take a few hours to assemble a playlist of songs which reflect the kinds of things you are inclined to want in your life. Put together any songs which you could see yourself playing in your mansion, with your partner, during retirement, in great health, around friends, after the award ceremony, or whatever. Afterwards, group the songs by the type of inclination involved. The personalities of these songs will resemble the personalities of your easiest callers. List a few of your songs along with their personality categories and, if applicable, any person who fits this personality that you may have successfully "psychically" called before or regularly dreamt of below. (I've also put a couple of asteroids from my Cancer section which support each kind of call in here, but you won't be able to find such specific information about your call style until The Asteroid chapter.)**

	Example

	Epic J-Pop {Relationships}
	    Description: light communication, ultra-intensity, body-comfort / sensuality, futurist immersion
	    Examples: Akino Arai–Unknown Vision, Ilaria Graziano–Christmas in the Silent Forest, George Michael–Father Figure, The Fat Rat–Mayday.
	    People: JG, MB
	    Asteroids: 391 Ingeborg, 126 Velleda, 261 Prymno
	
	Wise Gangsta {Status}
	    Description: Graduated past little conflicts, more boss than ever
	    Examples: Storm–Will I Rize; Mr. Mike–Where is Your Love
	    People: ES, BO, CC
	    Asteroids: 142 Polana, 623 Chimaera, 790 Pretoria
	
	Philosophical Acoustic {Self-Actualization}
	    Description: peaceful relational, natural, reflective
	    Examples: Chris Thile, Aoife O-Donovan, et al…–Here and Heaven, Poets of the Fall–The Poet and The Muse, John Mayer–Gravity.
	    People: SB
	    Asteroids: 795 Fini, 65 Cybele, 737 Arequipa, 390 Alma

Now I know you didn't actually spend the hours like I suggested. Instead, you came straight to this paragraph. But if you plan on calling anyone psychically, you should get used to spending actual time doing actual listening to the person on the other end. In the same way that most of us wouldn't just fast forward our friends in conversation, most of us really will need to practice tuning into the feeling of being called by the kinds of people we prefer. One of the quickest ways to identify this family of feelings (and thus the personalities who simulate them) is to put the "gotta do the next thing next" behavior aside, chill the hell out, and listen. Accordingly, we'll stop the Want section right here. If you want to find out which energies are actually interested in your call or interested in calling you back—which events are calling you towards them and which ones you are truly calling to you, independent of all other suggested noise—you'll take the time to build the playlist, observe the character of its songs, then fill out the blanks in 45.4.4. <u>Don't expect to get any farther in your psychic calls until those blanks are filled in</u>. I'm serious.

Our society teaches us to rush even important things towards an instant answer. The conversations we love, however, are exactly the ones we don't want to rush. Don't rush 45.4.4. Don't skip it (if you intend to add premonitory communication as one of the skills you get from this book). Only you can know which patterns of feeling make for a good phone call with you. Do yourself a favor and build your psychic contact list the right way.

The Realm of Show (Leo)

I spent some time thinking about the realm of Show, wondering why I wasn't so enthusiastic to write about it. During a break from writing, however, my guardians explained why this was the case: The realm of Show is more or less our regular 3D world. The only difference is that Show by itself is flattened into a single stream called attention, and is not constrained to the limits of human perception. This is like taking a video game and smashing it into a wifi signal—taking our Sun-centered solar system and limiting what can be perceived to what the perceiver is able to cast the light of his attention onto. The Show realm is all about that which is visible. The things that shine in this realm are things that are obvious, famous, noteworthy, fun, and beautiful. Anything that captures attention and holds it can be found here. This also includes egos, spotlight addiction, childishness, and colossal mistakes.

(Technical note; if you've read *Laurentia*)

When I asked why the Show dimension appears in 3D rather than some other form, the guardians corrected me, told me that it was four physical (other seeable) dimensions—three of space and one of time—and that these were the same four dimensions involved in any basic cycle.

- Closer-farther shows what you are viewing (anti-real to you), but to everyone else shows you as a doer (real to them).
- Spinning in a circle shows what *can* be real to you (potential real to you).
- Vertical pitch shows what influences are being donated to you or what you are interacting with as an actor (anti-real meaning put upon you), but to everyone else shows what you are doing (real you to them).
- Time-energy stacking shows what the next state of all three of the above will be for you (anti-potential you).

These are the r_B, θ_B, ϕ_B, t (Leo, Virgo, Libra, Cancer) dimensions I talked about in *Laurentia*.

As for the self-seeable and world-seeable dimensions among the 12 in *Laurentia*, not surprisingly they can also be seen in the body by the self and world respectively. The next actual dimension in the sequence, tau (τ) / Scorpio is indeed your lifespan. The world sees this one very easily. The dimension that goes in a circle around you, de (Д, differential energy) / Capricorn is akin to the "auric structure"—a reflection of your species and health in comparison to the average creature like you; this is also viewable by the world. Temperature, beta (β, within and about you) / Aquarius is something like your energy output, effort, or surroundings to which you respond. Combined with technology on our ears and screens in our faces, it is viewable by the world as raising the Earth's frequency broadly. Those are just some examples. None of these additional dimensions are naturally visible to other people like you, but we'll talk more about all this in the next chapter on Embodiments. 🔧

Thus, the Show dimension, though pretty familiar by normal human standards, still has much to teach us. Namely, what you pay attention to in this dimension is THE basis for what is projected as real to others in the physical world. Your Gemini dimension, on the other hand, is the basis for what's real to you. By selecting wisely what you pay attention to, you can shape the story that others tell about everything you are.

Introductory Exercise

This one is *really* easy. Many people talk as though we can simply pay attention to whatever we want and miraculously manifest our dreams. The reason it doesn't work that way, though, is because there are at least 12 different ways to "pay attention." Unlike many of my friends, I am not a visual learner. No matter how many times you show it to me, I won't believe it until I 1) hear it and 2) know that it's okay interacting with me. This second basis for "seeing" something as real is the work of my Scorpio Sun. The first basis is the result, I believe, of my Aquarius Ascendant. As the representative (ruler) of Leo, the Sun in your astro chart shows how you make things known and consider them broadly knowable. The Sun in Scorpio knows what it can successfully influence. As the starting point for how you approach events in the world, the Ascendant shows how and why you introduce yourself to things. An Ascendant in Aquarius approaches through the information surrounding a thing. Don't know your Sun or Ascendant? Here is your exercise:

☞ Go onto astro.com and obtain a free astrology chart. Read it. Look for the Asc, ☉, and anything else you're interested in. Don't forget to save it. We will use this later as the book progresses.

Signs and their common associations		
Aries instinct, assertion, bravery, pressure to BE, spontaneity, creation, existence	**Leo** ego, attention, good standing, leadership, reliability, pride	**Sagittarius (Saj)** fun, exploration, journey, success, importance, luck, politics, fame, expansiveness
Taurus self-image, money, confidence, body, sensation, self-value (ideas that you build your identity against)	**Virgo** meaning, comparative health, analytical nature, rules of order	**Capricorn** rules, karma, old age, time, built structures, wealth as security, law, history, authority, respect
Gemini internal thoughts, ideas, dexterity, driving, talking	**Libra** fairness, affinity, friendship, sharing, manners	**Aquarius** sociable detachment, society, rumors, peer groups, technology, humane ideals, renown
Cancer subconscious, feeling, dreaming, wants, connection, emotionality, the home, mothery-ness	**Scorpio** sex, death, others' money, psychology, power, the occult	**Pisces** humane feeling, intuition, illusion, escape, the hidden, art, abstraction

Table 45-2 (17-3): Basic sign characteristics

Though many of us would *like* to pay attention really hard to $100 million and suddenly get it, we can't do this any more than we can just plop an extra floor onto the top of our homes. Realities need to be rewritten; new dynamics need to match old ones; the potential (purchasing power) energy inherent in $100 million needs to be properly gathered from wherever you plan to get it. All of your life dynamics will need to be reprogrammed around the sudden change—including the original dynamic that made you crave $100 million that you *didn't have* in the first place. More fundamentally, fewer of us subconsciously care about all that than we're taught to expect. Many of us would be really happy finding $100 on the street. Most of us haven't prioritized the public dream all that much; few of us can naturally know this kind of object through our regular Sun lens. Despite the public dream, some objects of attention just aren't us.

Detailed Exercise

As with Want, you'll find it easier to pay attention to things which hold your favorable interest. Parties whose interest you hold will find it easier to make you real in their lives. This is as true for institutions and causes as it is for people. So busy trying to obtain our own wants, we don't often think of the people who have *manifested us* in their lives. Yet sometimes we have those people whose presence in our worlds we just can't explain. We end up around them, doing things for them and communicating with them without really knowing what the point of it all happens to be. How can you tell if someone has manifested you—summoned you in order to answer a dilemma they sought to resolve? To answer this we need to use a well-known staple of standard science:

>Just because two things occur together does not mean that one caused the other.

>For A to cause B,
>A and B need to be associated with each other, A needs to precede B,
>and there can't be other confounding factors involved.

With humans this is more complicated because we never really know which of A or B's relevant personality or situational needs came "first." Still, we can ask basic questions like *Who came to whom? Who keeps coming to whom? Who keeps the conversation going? Who does the asking?* Most importantly we can ask, *If the two were to be separated, which of them would be stuck and have to start all over again?*

Now, because of the way energy tangles (spheres) work, it often doesn't matter who called. Once the molecule is assembled, who cares? EXCEPT, sometimes you and the other person aren't really meant to be equal buddies. One will have been contracted to donate a skill while the other will have summoned the first for her skill. Try as you might, the relationship may keep wanting to veer off into some space other than friendship or mutual support, into a kind of practical-sometimes thing. Maybe you'd love for the exchange to take a definitive turn, but neither you nor the other know how to speed this up.

In this exercise we are going to determine who, between you and another person, has summoned the other, what the summoner wants, and why the summoned one is set to provide it. We cannot determine how or when at this point. Let's begin with a basic question.

☞ Question 45.5.1 (How did I get here?): **Name a person or situation that you're currently involved with, where the basis for your exchange with them is a mystery. You'd like to know what the point of the exchange is, and how each party contributes to that script.** _____

(From here on I'll assume your other is a person.)

☞ Question 45.5.2 (Reasons for the summon): **Use the table below to help yourself identify the summoner.**

Who initiated contact?	
Who keeps the contact going?	
Who asks more of the other?	
Who has benefitted more from the exchange *in the visible world*?	
Who would lose the most if the two of you were unpaired?	

If you were summoned by the other

As is typical for me, I found myself taking an interest in a particular other who clearly summoned me for something other than what I ended up wanting to give. (How's that for a political correctness?) In cases like that you may find that, while there is a clear summoner, there is no longer a clear beneficiary. They manifested you for some reason X. You gave it. And now you want them to stay around for your own reason Y. Will this work out? Usually not, unless you communicate the change in plans with them. The problem is easier to see if you are the original summoner. You want them to help you get a job done.

They do. Now they want you to help them through their personal issue. Do you want to? How uncomfortable.

So I'm going to recommend something that might be difficult for those of us humans who prefer to be needed AND accepted: Don't impose new conditions on the person who asked for you. They were already in need to begin with. Try not to make them pay for seeking help from the most reasonable person who had it. Person-to-person help works differently from financial transactions.

If you were the summoner

It will typically be easier for you to know what the person offers you, as you may be all too eager to put them right into whatever role that may be. But there are still protocols for cases like this. In the case where you have attracted a stranger into your life, don't impose your urgency on them before they know what you really called them for. If possible, tell them (in non-spooky ways) what you called them for as early as you can. See how comfortable they are with the idea.

In both cases:

For the good of your exchange and for greater clarity in your intuition development, don't tangle agendas with the people who summoned you. Romances are different. But for jobs, projects, and partnerships, this rule of thumb can spare you much complication later.

Generally, if you know exactly what you want them to do for you, it's as good as your having summoned them. If you're more focused on understanding what you're supposed to do for them, it's as good as them having summoned you. Maybe you called each other. But now, what if you're clear on what's supposed to happen next while they aren't?

☞ Question 45.5.3 (You've been briefed, they haven't): **When the person communicates with you, what do they talk about? Specifically, what is changing in their lives and how are they handling that change?**

_____
_____
_____
_____

☞ Question 45.5.4 (Providing for the one who doesn't know): **In response to 45.5.3, is there something you can provide which will make their path easier?**

_____
_____
_____
_____

The reason this matters is because we often ask for things subconsciously without consciously knowing that we asked for them. In order to become aware of another's role, it helps if we learn to want that person around. Path clearing is part of the trust process. Trust is one of the steps for having the other person connect more strongly to your sphere. If you know why you're in their life but they don't know, they may need to trust you more before they listen to you as an actor in their lives. In effect you're saying, *I'm removing barriers to our exchange so that you'll be open to understanding why I'm actually here.* The reason is rarely limited to superficial roles. The sooner you can trade the superficial for the actual the sooner everyone can move forward.

And what if you don't care enough to remove any barriers? Then maybe, despite your knowledge of the proper path alongside their lack of knowledge, you're not the one for the job. Let them find someone else to answer their call.

☞ Question 45.5.5 (Why they called): **Assuming you have determined it by now, why did the summoner make their call?**

_____
_____
_____
_____

☞ Question 45.5.6 (Bonus) (Other motivations): **Is there anything else that the summoner was missing which you think may be connected to their original request?**

_____
_____
_____
_____

☞ Question 45.5.7 (Bonus 2) (Other uses): **Is the summoned person willing and able to answer this request as well?**

_____
_____

The last question is not answerable through astrology or any of the Worlds, because it involves a sequence of events. Astrology only does snapshots.

Question 45.5.8: How can the summoned person complete the summoner's request in the best, most thorough way possible?

We *can* answer this question, but only after we've gotten familiar with The Spirits, and then The Asteroid.

When we call people into our lives in the visible world, we are asking for them to serve as the most powerful kind of attention grabber the Show as to offer: a visible form. Shown things have the effect of diverting our intent from less salient objects onto themselves, thereby rearranging our normally weighted behavioral patterns to fit the new thing we're staring at. We can get a broad idea of what a visible object wants us to do by comparing its form to other similar forms we have observed in the past. We may even learn what it wants us to do specifically by looking at the ways in which it asks us to make each successive move.

The unfortunate issue surrounding the realm of Show is that is possesses a poor capacity for time as well as those processes that went into producing any one image. Processes are more likely to be invisible, so it's much harder to know why the latest spotlight getter chose to be there. It's harder to know how long they intend to stay around. Even if we know what the form wants, we often don't know how to give it to them. Or whether they will be satisfied when they get it. To answer these questions we'll need to go beyond astrology for a while and explore more dynamic types of insight. Until then, the world of Show, though apparently obvious in its structure, will remain one of the most secretive worlds of all.

The Realm of Joining (Virgo)

Whereas the Identity realm joins other concepts to you, the Joining realm joins other concepts to other concepts. This appears as meaning making when done in our minds, as daily tasks when done as part of our life routine, as health when done to match our physical states with some desired stable point, and as service when done in a regulated pattern for another party's benefit. Like the realm of Want, then, Joining really needs to be divided in order to be understood. The good news is that this realm's principles are the same as those describing Dimension 6 in *Sex in 12 Dimensions*. If you can find the right cause, person, or lifestyle for framing the things you continually join together, your usefulness to (and often your acceptance by) the world is guaranteed. Our styles of meaning making are our work. Our work is our identity as a thing experienced directly by others. Just as we don't have to dread the processes of shaping ourselves in our own eyes, we don't have to dread the process of shaping ourselves in others' eyes. The aim is to target work that isn't odious to us, and see that work through to its highest end.

Introductory Exercise

☞ **Question 45.6.1 (The fixation): Take a moment to imagine something you are extremely curious about OR something you are determined to make work.** This will be an area you could fixate on all day in order to figure out, turn around, and make sense of in your head or in your actions. What is that area?

	Example
	the physical human and its systems as embodiments of natural laws

☞ Question 45.6.2 (The problem statement): **Write down the main question that you seek to answer or issue that you seek to work on regarding this area.** The issue can be simple or abstract, but do try to pose one.

	Example
	the physical human and its systems as embodiments of natural laws: how can we simulate it and evolve it as a technology?

If the above issue somehow guided all of your broad performance of meaningful tasks in your life, you would have found your work calling.

Detailed Exercise

Your work calling, unlike the job life you may have been trained to hate, is a space that you can evolve throughout life, produces its own rewards, and from which you may never want to retire. Some callings change form with age—athlete to commentator, actress to artist, elected representative to public benefactor, manager of employees to matriarch in a family—but even if its physical representation will change, the process which that calling embodies doesn't have to.

Callings don't have to happen through a formal job. Some people play out their calling in the space between simultaneous jobs. Some callings can be adhered to anywhere as long as the person following them displays a certain attitude or perspective. The main thing is, if you did answer question 45.6.1 but find yourself not integrating it into your work or daily life—if you answered question 45.6.2 but have partners, friends, or circumstances that don't help you advance its aim—your realm of Joining might be compromised. Time is not an excuse. It will never stop for you. It will remain through death and beyond. It will never wait for you to answer something only you can address.

☞ Question 45.6.3 (Room for the calling): **Are you currently making room for your calling from 45.6.1 in your daily life?** _____

☞ Question 45.6.4 (Aligned actions): **Have you adopted any activities, hobbies, or other practices which enable you to address the issue in 45.6.2? That is, do you perform any actions towards 45.6.2?**

_____
_____

☞ Question 45.6.5 (Align THIS week!): **Since you have picked up this book and have made it to this question, I assume you are interested in a certain kind of self-development. Write down one thing which you can do <u>this week</u>, <u>using ONLY the currently accessible resources in your life</u>, which will address your 45.6.2.**

_____
_____

Unless acquiring a certain new resource is part of your calling, no new meetups, relationships, purchases, trips, or web research is allowed. Do with what you have. If your answer included "go to/visit/join/buy/look up…anything not <u>currently</u> in your sphere," *go back and change it* unless it's absolutely a part of your 45.6.2. Joining is mostly about your service through a pair of ideas. There is a good chance there are already people or situations around you which will allow this. Don't give in to the new and shiny. This is extra important if you are to wean yourself off of the popular idea that all worthwhile great things require plugging into some new dude's crap.

Critical Exercise
TOWARDS AN ANSWER

Trains: Claircognizance, Telepathy

☞ Question 45.6.6 (Do 45.6.5): **Sometime this week, do the thing in 45.6.5. Check here ____ once it's done.**

Of course your 45.6.6 won't be a permanent solution. This isn't a problem to solve, it's a <u>life calling</u>. And we're not looking for permanence since your calling is ongoing, remember? Instead, we are looking for you to make room for the kind of "work" that will always reward you, ideally with or without pay, with or without external validation, with or without approval from other intruders upon your schedule. Just as exercise 45.4.4 was a gatekeeping exercise for anyone wishing to further develop their psychic communication, exercise 45.6.6 is a gatekeeping exercise for anyone wishing to attract (manifest) grand support for their unique worth in what they do for a living. Related to "work-worth" is greater clarity in the kinds of things we spend our meaning-making energy on—our daily stress. Love your work, decrease your stress (at least compared to someone who hates the same work). The realm of Joining is our route to contentment with what we do in the world. Society's occasional noise and rampant dissatisfaction will affect us A LOT less as we get deeper into the habit of serving it in ways we know to be our most effective, and ways that we know we love.

The Realm of Exchanging (Libra)

In astrology, Venus is typically associated with love and beauty; Libra, the sign associated with Venus, holds a similar character but is less relational and more practical. Libra is associated with balance, "the iron hand in the velvet glove." When you remove all of the human reframings for this dimension, however, you are left with Venus and Libra as representatives of back and forth exchange: the conversation between any two things which keep giving and responding to feedback from the other. Beautiful things, things we love, games we participate in, instruments we play, conversations and friendships all have this in common. You take a turn, I take a turn that responds to your turn. The object makes a sound, I play the next note which acknowledges that the first sound has been made. There had to be some world which held this property of "other interaction;" the seventh world is it. When we learn how to tune into the realm of Exchange we ultimately enter that space full of other objects, situations, people, and things that we continually talk to and that continually talk back to us. It is here where we can find our truly matched partnerships. Even if those partnerships are with people who attach strongly to us as enemies.

Introductory Exercise

The goal of the Exchange realm is to contain our trades' influence. As we talk to our favorite interlocutors, we absorb their characteristics. It goes for enemies and topics we dwell on as well. It should be obvious why we tend to mirror the habits of our five closest friends, think in terms of our two or three favorite subjects, and believe in line with our favorite information sources, but of course we often miss all this. The more dollars I give you in exchange for more favors that you give me, the more your bank account consists of my dollars; the more my experiences consist of your favors. We build more and more of our own meaning upon each other's contributions, which is one of the reasons why Venus is also frequently associated with Taurus identity as well. But don't get it confused. What you trade with me isn't *completely* me, and I have the right to leave you if what you give me is harmful. So we treat the Exchange realm as separate from other realms and instead think of it in terms of whom (or what) we can easily influence rather than who (or what) we are.

Let's define a **musical instrument** as an **object which can receive an organized pattern of input to produce a reliably mapped pattern of output to that input, mainly for the purpose of creating organized patterns using that output.** By this definition, a violin can be thought of as a musical instrument, but so can a glass of water (if sound is the mode of pattern you want). So can a paintbrush (if pressured strokes form the pattern you want). A lover's body can be a musical instrument if their perceived sensation is the pattern you want, and you can perceive that music if that person adopts a reliable means of showing you what they feel. On the other side of all this, however, there are also instruments which damage. Every time you goad a perceived enemy into doing something you know you want to punish them for, you use them as an instrument for your own discord. The music is their pattern of unsettling acts, triggered by you for your own reinforced discontentment. The result is, of course, more of your own discontentment.

In order to pick our favorite sounding experiential "instrument," we'll first need to settle on the type of patterns we like. This exercise may seem odd to some, but you may gain insight from it.

☞ Question 45.7.1 (Patterns you like): Do you prefer patterns which are disjointed (boom, boom, boom) or patterns which flow together (woooiiishh)? _____ (Mine was flowing.)

☞ Question 45.7.2 (Directed patterns): Which do you prefer more: Patterns you can perceive directly or patterns which you can't perceive directly (through the basic senses)? _____ (Mine was directly.)

☞ Question 45.7.3 (Pattern heights): Do you prefer high patterns (compared to your own voice), low patterns, very high patterns, or very low patterns? _____ (Mine was higher, but not too high.)

☞ Question 45.7.4 (Favored senses): Which of the six senses is most likely to get you hooked on what you perceive there? (The senses are touch, taste, smell, sight, hearing, and internal feeling) _____ (Mine was hearing.)

☞ Question 45.7.5 (Abstract) (You as an instrument): If we considered your identity to be the pattern of music you make through your experiences, which of your traits from 45.2.1 do you most enjoy reinforcing in yourself? _____ (Mine were listening, writer.)

☞ Question 45.7.6 (Abstract) (Them as a musician): If we considered your identity to be the pattern of music you make through your experiences, which of the traits from 45.2.1 do you most enjoy reinforcing in your preferred interaction partner? _____ (Mine was amorous, diplomatic.)

☞ Question 45.7.7 (Abstract) (Your music): If we considered your identity to be the pattern of music you make through your experiences, which of the traits from 45.2.1 do you most enjoy reinforcing *in the overall shared situation* you prefer to be in? _____ (Mine was amorous, system structuring, writer, free-scholar.)

☞ Question 45.7.8 (Abstract) (The sounds made): Do any of your music types from 45.4.4 support your answers above? _____ (Yes, Epic J-Pop from the interactant / 45.7.6, Reflective Acoustic from me / 45.7.5.)

Detailed Exercise

☞ Question 45.7.9 (Abstract, Challenge) (Your overall best "instrument"): See if you can pick an "instrument" which enables ALL of the above. This instrument will produce your preferred music, and will be the basis of some of your most enduring, most expression-supportive communication. _____ (I had two: 1) peaceful-day model-building / art creation, and 2) sensual, easy-to-get-along-with female voices.)

Although I had originally omitted my own answers as examples, I decided that it would be easier to point you towards greater abstraction if you saw where I ended up from where I started. Not everyone is a musical musician. Many of us are relationship builders, caretakers, designers, game players, or anything else you might name. In particular, in order to produce "peaceful-day model-building" as one of my instruments, I thought about my answer to 45.7.4 (what gets me hooked), what it meant to prefer sounds higher than mine but not too high (situations that are bigger than me but which I can still feel a part of), what my favorite sense was (hearing is VERY close to internal monologue thinking), and what I liked to reinforce in my interactant (where amorousness and diplomacy from non-human things produces something like increased connectedness under a want for my influence). Maybe you didn't go this far in your answer. After we discuss embodiments in the next chapter, you'll be able to.

In order to travel different worlds, you'll need to practice focusing on different aspects of the same thing. Every human has a non-human object-like summary (their 390 Alma), a skill or expert attribute they provide (their [White Moon] Selene), a role they tend to be pushed towards (their 79 Eurynome), and a fundamental truth they reflect about something (their 490 Veritas). Identifying which of these non-them sides of their lives is most relevant to yours is the basis of your Nickname for them, and through the rest of our studies throughout this book we will work on seeing things in ways that let us perceive far beyond the notion of a basic human-style conversation. Music isn't just a thing made by human hands for human ears. Wave patterns are wave patterns whatever the case. It's up to the perceiver to claim such as music. Relatedly, high and low frequencies, voices, or tones, percussive or flowing characteristics all have equivalents in human, object, idea, and process-based spaces. The more easily you can identify your favorite musical instruments in forms other than the physical, the easier it will be to make that feedback-for-feedback music all the time simply through your behavior. If you had a hard time with this one, don't worry about it. There's no rule against trying it again. We'll develop the skills for abstraction as the book goes on.

The Realm of Influence (Scorpio)

There exists a realm where you specialize in extracting the inclinations from the things you interact with. This is the same realm as the one you use to manipulate your interactants. The world of influence is accessible mainly by means of those things or people who bow to your will by default. If you can take note of the things you do in order to trigger such responses then you are that much closer to realizing the proper form of that power you most successfully use to compel. BUT...

Many of us are unaware of our unique ability to compel events. One of the reasons for this, I believe, lies in our natural and healthy need to protect ourselves. Others may feel your mojo, but aren't likely to show you how you have affected them because it's just not safe to be so vulnerable like that. In order to realize your special brand of influence, you'll not only need to identify it first, you'll also need to practice it, and you'll also need to be around things or people who let you practice on *them*. While we are taught in the West that manipulation and intentional influence lie at the root of power, there is an increasing realization among those who study leadership that the "servant" or spokesperson often wields the most power of all. The greater the *portion* of the population that a president speaks for, the greater the president. The greater the dependence on the Administrative Assistant, the greater the assistant. Not only will the CEO of a company serve at the behest of her board, her entire role consists of channeling the machinery of the company below her into a natural order; she is its caretaker. What kinds of people, then, are most likely to let you practice your power on them? The people whom you serve. Contrary to the macho society many of us have been raised in, people you manipulate, bully, or exercise your laws on are not likely to *keep* following you willingly, but tend to bow towards the next most convenient source of pressure as soon you turn your back—hence the need of the "powerful" to keep having to start all over again. The pride we take in having to force somebody three, four, five… times to do something they wouldn't willingly do otherwise is odd when you think about it. I'm more powerful if I simply represent what you always want to do automatically. You want to be effective, appreciated, acknowledged, and satisfied with certain events. If I serve these ends broadly for you, the two of us will align in a way far more thorough than a more forced arrangement—even if the short term force produces more dramatic-looking (but fleeting) results.

Introductory Exercise

Scorpio isn't typically associated with service, but it is associated with uncovering others' depths. One way we can do this is by serving as channel through which others may offload that which burdens them. The best boss I ever had taught me many important lessons, one of which was asking her team at the end of meetings, "What can I do for you? Are there any barriers I can help remove?" This is the kind of influence we'll practice now.

Think of someone whom you would be glad to do things for or give a certain behavior to. Make sure they are the kind of person who, if you served them, would not burden you with demands that you couldn't handle. Also make sure that your giving to the person builds up something in you, just because you gave it, *regardless of what they might ask you to give*. Don't do anything with this person just yet. We're going to strengthen your capacity for influence relationships by doing this same exercise in a more formal way.

☞ Just pause your reading for a few seconds to think about the above.

Detailed Exercise

☞ Question 45.8.1 (Where you would faithfully serve): **Take a moment to list any people, situations, or causes in your life which you would be glad to serve under, be a servant to, or give to (just because you enjoy doing so). List EVERYTHING OR EVERYONE whom you would serve <u>without hesitation</u>, even if this person or thing is your "enemy."** Just pretend that the apocalypse was happening, where the enemy suddenly corrected themselves and joined your side. (The "enemy" / "non-ally" listing takes considerable maturity on your part, but will have benefits which you will surely see throughout the rest of the book. On the other hand, even your closest friends may not make this list because *service* may not be the basis of your friendship with them.)

	Example
_____	I would serve under:
_____	
_____	People: J, C, B, I
_____	Situations: astrology studies, the human experience, the non-human earth (animals and plants), novel data for analysis
_____	Causes: good societal systems, my "Ghost in the Shell" set of projects, my life path project, my writings
_____	
_____	

Notice that my own example includes personal projects unique to me as well as big generic situations.

The people listed above tend to be involved in your more intensely felt relationships, for better or worse. Mine include one distant acquaintance, one boss, one very dear friend, and one outright "enemy." We'll talk more about enemies in the chapter on conflict.

☞ Question 45.8.2 (Uneasy service): Draw a line through any items or people in the above list who would burden, drain you or mistreat you if you did try to serve them. This includes those whom you think 1) would ask too much of you if you gave them the chance, as well as those whom 2) in real life you'd currently have to go through a lot of trouble to *actually* serve and 3) simply wouldn't accept your service. This doesn't mean you won't serve them at all (you probably still will). It's just that doing so underline{directly} may not be optimal for you right now. Relatedly, be sure to put today's date next to your list so you can come back later and revise things if you need to.

	Example
_____	(7/12/2019)
_____	People: ~~J~~, ~~C~~, ~~B~~, I
_____	Situations: ~~astrology studies~~, the human experience, ~~the non-human earth (animals and plants)~~, novel data for analysis, my regular day job
_____	Causes: good societal systems, ~~my "Ghost in the Shell" set of projects~~, ~~my life path project~~, my writings
_____	
_____	
_____	

☞ **Question 45.8.3 (The rewards of service):** Of the items that are not lined through on your list, note any qualities that you feel would be built up <u>in you</u> through your service to them. Again, this list is only valid for the present, not necessarily for the future.

	Example
	(7/12/2019)
	People: I (my capacity for devotion, the overall quality of all relationships I enter)
	Situations: the human experience (my sense of role in the world), novel data for analysis (my scholarship), my regular day job (my creativity, my 302 Clarissa [asteroid of one's accepted place in the world])
	Causes: good societal systems (my current contribution to everyone else), my writings (my longstanding contribution to everyone else)

☞ **Question 45.8.4 (Service extractors):** If any of the items on your list are particularly good at extracting your willing service to them, put a * by them. If you're simply addicted to them and know that you probably shouldn't be (but they hijack your service anyway) put an ✕ over them. Hopefully all of your potential ✕s went away at question 45.8.2. If not, don't worry about it. Just note it.

	Example
	(7/12/2019)
	People: *I (my capacity for devotion, the overall quality of all relationships I enter)
	Situations: **the human experience (my sense of role in the world), **novel data for analysis (my scholarship), **my regular day job (my creativity, my 302 Clarissa [asteroid of one's accepted place in the world])
	Causes: *good societal systems (my current contribution to everyone else), *my writings (my longstanding contribution to everyone else)

Critical Exercise
BEGIN TO SERVE

Trains: Claircognizance, Telepathy

Question 45.8.5 (Time to bring out your power): **Make a list of all of the items that remain and also have *s under your 45.8.4. Within the next week,**

- For people: (If you can) contact them and ask them in whatever way makes sense for you, *What can I do for you?*

- For causes: Put yourself in a position to advance those causes, then observe which skill you yourself have which you can use to support them, while building up the quality you listed in 45.8.4. It could be writing a letter, encouraging someone, working on a little project, learning more, having a productive discussion with someone in a better position to actually affect the cause positively (not just any know-it-all online), or any other useful action that will increase your sense of effectiveness towards a thing you actually believe in. Not a sense of powerlessness towards a thing you don't believe in, can't affect, or don't healthily understand.

- For situations: Put yourself in the situation and do anything which will appropriately advance the quality you listed in 45.8.4.

	Example
	1. Message I (devotion)
	2. Calculate new astro stuff (scholarship)
	3. Go to work (creativity)
	4. Write something about the human experience, that helps build a good societal system (role, current and long term contribution)

Do them all within one week.

If it's possible to do these in one week, but you don't do them, plan to do <u>them all</u> AGAIN the next week. The point of this is to build up a whole-lifestyle habit. No piecemealing allowed.

You might be surprised to find that this exercise is a gatekeeper for the "intuitive gifts/telepathy" series of talents. It will compel you to put aside those topics which are psychobiologically noisy to you and keep only the areas which build you up in calculated influence where you are actually effective. If you're not already where you want to be in your intuition and can't manage to do this activity, don't be surprised if you still aren't where you want to be a week from now.

- Your list shouldn't include anything that you need to command three, four, five,… times in order to get moving.

- It shouldn't include anything that frustrates you to work with

- or anything that you don't enjoy engaging.

- It shouldn't include anything that pulls effort from you without your willing, consensual, mutually beneficial, permission. Sexy-only stuff, socially pressured stuff, friended favorites, and anything else which simply obligates your drool but does not grow you in return <u>should not be on this list</u>.

- Your list shouldn't include anything or anyone who simply expects your service and spits in your eye if you don't give it. Scratch those off your list if they're still there.[5]

Notice how even though we are servants in this exercise, we are in full control of the context and the standards therein. Anyone who calls you weak for serving must not want your service. Jobs, relationships, belief systems, and objects of worldly value all obey this rule. If the acquisition of money, for example, doesn't build me up personally, I shouldn't bend over backwards to serve it. If the security which that money buys is the thing that actually builds me up instead, I might serve that quest for security, as long as I understand that belonging, efficacy, and identity (for example) are the actual pieces which that security is made of. There is no need to give your all to an ingrate. Serve something with a better sense of fairness towards you. See how much more easily you'll grow your sense of your own power.

The Realm of Foreign Actors (Sagittarius)

Paul Simon's "You Can Call Me Al" contains images of a man in a foreign land, and in my mind is one of those songs which says more about the effects of one's surroundings on a person than it does the person himself. We don't often think of the lands we dwell in as being described by a particular class of personalities, but indeed we engage our foreign society-mates as a collective class all the time. We talk to them through our beliefs and learning, suggest rules for them through our politics, suggest order through our laws, and enter group discussions with them through our choice of commitment partners. Seen this way, the culture in which you dwell behaves as a kind of alter-you. When it obeys a

---

[5] I didn't tell you to do this before, now we're eliminating these types at the last hour. This is similar to the way it happens in real life: I love you or like you enough to serve you. You love getting my service. But it doesn't seem to bother you *really* that my serving you costs me. It's not a big deal now, but eventually…someday, maybe not today… I'll grow tired of being taken for granted, and may not always be around.

"personality" you don't agree with you respond via your politics, learnings, commitments, and beliefs in the same way that you would respond communicatively to a person like that. But unlike another person, society won't usually back down. You'll just have to stay mad at it. Or learn to cooperate with it in as self-empowered a way as you can. Your society will respond to you in the same way that the specific people in your life who embody that society will respond. But have you figured such people out yet?

I've described in a couple of previous books my relationships with volatile Latinas. My native society is San Antonio, and this particular kind of woman has always embodied the society I call home. At its worst, my relationship to San Antonio as a source of jobs, social acceptance for blacks, options for economic and educational equality for non-Northsiders, and in-group mobility for non-collectivist thinkers was very bad; and my relationship to the handful of volatile Latinas in my life—though basically a constant in my life—was equally bad. The various women I interacted with at the time were classic examples of the kind of "embodiment" which we'll discuss in the next chapter, but you should know that we all tend to have such representative people in our lives.[6]

There is a certain type of person, culture, situation, or ideological environment which will keep returning no matter where you move to, how often you dump them, how many jobs you change, or how many groups you join to remove them. Sagittarius is the complement of Gemini; foreign actors are the complement of your internal monologue. If your monologue is impatient, your foreigners will be slow. If your monologue is chill and accepting, your foreigners may be volatile and judgmental by comparison. At least until you master the Conflict chapter later on. Until then, expect certain kinds of cultures to piss you off with ease. The irony is that these same cultures are also the ones most poised to acknowledge your accomplishments in the world.

Introductory Exercise

☞ **Question 45.9.1 (The upsetters):** Take a moment to list every class of people or situations which has an easy time upsetting you. Be honest. It won't do you any good as a student of intuition to lie to yourself.

	Example
_____	flaky-without-a-care communicators; critical, judgmental people; people who need you, but put up walls whenever they come to you
_____	
_____	San Antonio gentrification; most real estate culture; go getter / motivation speaking culture, "professional" culture; leaders or institutions who leave their people to die, or leaders who pick favorites and leave the rest to fend for themselves; sales pressure
_____	
_____	

---

[6] At its best, by the way, my relationship with San Antonio and this same "avatar"—the volatile Latina—in my life has been excellent. The thing to note is that a type of person in your life can embody a whole situation. I talk a lot about this in GS and S12. When your relationship to the situation is bad or good, your relationship to this type/class of people will follow. We will revisit this this several times throughout the book (including the MAJOR activity 48.3, whose example you can find the Appendix.)

	liars
	any situation which plays games with me, my time, or my group's time, giant egos inflated through their own system of non-listening

This exercise is similar to the one in Dimension 4 of *Sex in 12 Dimensions*, but here we're going to give it a realm 9 spin.

A Reminder to the Reader: In case you've asked yourself why I include my own examples in most of the exercises, it's not because I have a grand ego or aim to patronize you. I actually have two reasons: 1) as a former teacher, I'm used to working through examples for the class so that the audience knows what kinds of answers I'm asking them to produce. Without the examples, we have a bunch of abstract questions with a bunch of blank lines, and not a lot of context for even *starting* the exercises. 2) If you read the end of *S12* you know that writing (along with talking into my recorder) is my main mode of channel (clairaudience). Whenever I write, the information comes through as if some other brain is thinking of what I'm typing while I myself am more like a listener to it, so I tend to need examples *for myself* in order to know what kinds of questions a reader might have next. It's not like writing with an outline or a plan. I don't normally have those. It's more like going on a tour through a kind of library. (Erwin Schrödinger—ES in 45.4.4—has made several teaching appearances in my dreams.) I either ask for clarification via an example right now or otherwise never pass this way again. It's also the reason why the specific topics of my books progressively elaborate the ones before them. Through writing, my guardians teach me. My aim is to be told each book's lesson only once. Without the examples (or detailed theory chapters in books like *Laurentia*), I won't remember how to tell you what I meant at the time if you should ever ask me later.

And why do you care about this? Maybe you don't. But once you've settled on your own style of intuition, you too will develop habits that sometimes may warrant explanation. Including myself in the examples was one of those things. By asking myself to do what I'm asking you to do, I learn a lot more about what kinds of questions you might have next.

Ideally you will have a culture which serves as your home base for making your public image known. The classes of people who upset you also comprise your audiences of blank faces for watching your monologue come to life. You will convey your monologue to that audience; then it is THEY who will tell your story to everyone else not in attendance.

And you thought all that talk of yours stopped at your friends. Nope.

What you post, your friends' friends see. What you do, your friends' friends experience as part of your bio. The more you tell it, the more attached it becomes to how people who've never met you believe that you think. Your foreign audiences are a much bigger part of your sphere than you imagined. The good news is, you can also use this phenomenon to hear messages from any guiding spirits that you might believe in.

I presented a theory of spirits in *Analytical Essays*, *144*, *Laurentia*, and *S12*, and won't repeat it here. Ignoring the occult for a while, we'll just say that spirits are your personifications of "abstract personality packets" which urge you in certain directions. If you are an actor whose diction is unpolished, then one of your spirits might urge you towards clearer speech. If you are a natural leader whose default is to be stepped on, one of your spirits may have a character which urges you to be less of a doormat. Perhaps you can see how we don't need to believe in gods or anything fantastic in order to make use of spirits.

1. You display behaviors towards others.
2. Those others tell the rest of the world.
3. The rest of the world (associates of your associates) holds a broadly generic opinion of what it has heard about you. It also has a broad box of suggestions for how you might better advance yourself in that world's esteem.
4. You hear about that foreign world via *the issues that your friends bring back to you from that world*. The politics they bring, the ideologies they convey, and ESPECIALLY the outgroups they reference (those Democrats, those Mexicans, those Corporations, those Friends of So and So...) will be the groups before whom your deeds will be encouraged to matter. I invite you to consider why this is true psychologically. The chain of cognitive frames can get pretty involved, so we won't elaborate here.

The bottom line is that your most natural out-groups—those people or situations that you expressly DO NOT belong to, but for whom you have bothered to build up a significant framework and a significant response, whose desires are clarified through your friends' reports—*are* your foreign audience, and the group before whom you are charged to make your image known. You may be charged to fight that group, but unless you're playing sports, they'll almost certainly be back. So much for your personal efficacy. Even if you used your army to exterminate them completely, there is a high chance you will not exterminate what they embody. So if you wiped out the communists over there, you won't wipe out the collectivizing social welfare, public law, and open source cultures in here. You can wipe out Republicans but never wipe out individual-liberty centrism/unified morality as a desire. You can erase Democrats but never erase collective-social quality centrism/individual morality as a desire. Your outgroup embodies what you are charged to engage, not usually (in times of peace) what you are charged to rant against. Your rants won't make you more effective as a person or an organization. They will grant increased imminence to an enemy of your own making.

Detailed Exercise
Almost every crime has a positive story associated with it—usually in the mind of the one who committed it at the time. That story is the secret to turning those foreigners into friends. In this exercise we'll identify your proper foreign audience by sharpening and reframing your answers from 45.9.1.

☞ Question 45.9.2 (The upsetters who actually exist): **Copy the items you listed in 45.9.1 EXCEPT for those groups which are so not-you that you don't even have a framework for them.** If, to your knowledge, they don't show up anywhere in your world or in your natural outgroups, do not include them in your copied list. These excluded groups are essentially ones you don't recognize as being what they claim. They get a big "whatever" from you. You have a zero tolerance policy for their class on the whole. Even if you have dozens of friends who have this quality as individuals, it's not really an item you have the behavioral vocabulary for. Only copy the items that you set aside brain time to think about.

	Example
	critical, judgmental people; people who need you, but put up walls whenever they come to you
	San Antonio gentrification;
	any situation which plays games with me, my time, or my group's time
	giant egos inflated through their own system of non-listening

☞ Question 45.9.3 (Transitioning from the nonexistent upsetters): **Now 1) copy every item from 45.9.1 which you left out of 45.9.2. 2). Next to each of these items, write the response from 45.3.4 which best describes your preferred attitude towards these things when you encounter them.**

	Example
	flaky-without-a-care communicators: "Who knows what they're deal is."
	most real estate culture: "This is clearly about propagating social advantages that were already there. I swear."[7]

---

[7] Trivia: I "failed" as an agent in my native San Antonio, partly because I didn't want to confine my market to the Eastside (black) base that would have accepted me more easily. But then again, I didn't quite fail. Among other things, the social inequities I saw at work in the real estate and economic scene at the time lead to my two very first writings Solace and Society (*Analytical Essays*), where I tried to make sense of the human world and its institutions.

_____	go getter / motivation speaking culture: "…a broad tool for forcing the "dream" on people, ignoring advantages, unequal starting points, or people's own individuality. Whatever."
_____	"professional" culture: See the above.
_____	leaders or institutions who leave their people to die: "Craziness"
_____	leaders who pick favorites and leave the rest to fend for themselves: "Not to waste anymore energy on this. This clearly isn't an actual leader."
_____	sales pressure: "You know what,…"
_____	liars: "No need to get all tangled up in [whatever non-reality they're working with]."

☞ Question 45.9.4 (What makes a nonexistent upsetter?): Before we return to your natural outgroups, do you see any patterns among the kinds of topics you refuse to engage? _____ _____ (Mine was "the imposition of false or forced representation(s) upon others.")

☞ Question 45.9.5 (YOU as the upsetter): For each of the items you listed in 45.9.2, put yourself into the shoes of one who enjoys doing this. Write what you would tell yourself as you did it. Your answers must genuinely support the behavior you're describing. No sarcasm, fake answers, or straw men allowed.

AND

☞ Question 45.9.6 (Your summary as an upsetter): At the end of your justification from 45.9.5, write **a word or a phrase** which best summarizes that justification. The word should not be patronizing, but be the actual word you would use to describe yourself if you said this kind of thing.

> For example, I was tempted to summarize my "critical, judgmental…" justification below by using the word *helpfulness*. But based on my true style of communication, "I was just trying to be helpful" isn't something I would ever actually say to anyone in real life. "Look man, <u>we</u> need to grow" is definitely something I would say.

	Example
_____	critical, judgmental people: "This person is going to embarrass themselves. Somebody needs to be bold enough to tell them to step it up, or they won't get very far." (**Growth Enabling**, but I would also include a criticism of myself)
_____	people who need you, but put up walls whenever they come

	to you: "This person hasn't really shown that they want all that extra from me. I'm not going to be the one who gets stomped when they move on to whatever other priorities they seem to have." (**Interaction Stabilizing, Self-Protecting**)
	San Antonio gentrification: "The properties are so cheap here. It's a gold mine, and we can improve the neighborhood at the same time." (**Efficient Benevolence**)
	any situation which plays games with me, my time, or my group's time: "I'm not trying to play games with them. This person is just unreadable. They show signs of answering what I'm after, but they also show signs of not givin' a damn. Like they could pack up at any minute. I need more proof." (**Circumspection, Careful Observation**)
	giant egos inflated through their own system of non-listening: "I will never be stopped. Never." (**Invincibility**)

A Prelude to the Hard Part

Later you'll be challenged to join forces with the very types you've described above. Not now though. Just know that it's coming.

For now take note that, if you believe in guardian spirits, the reframing words you've listed above constitute very broad descriptions of their personalities. We'll talk about how to strengthen your contact with them in the chapter on The Spirits.

The Realm of Authorities (Capricorn)

As with the realm of Foreign Actors, the realm of Authorities possesses an almost inescapable quality which can mainly be kept under control in three ways 1) accepting the authority, 2) ignoring the authority, or 3) becoming the authority. Let's consider an **authority** to be *a thing whose rules you obey.* Labels placed upon you and, relatedly, groups who habitually gravitate towards you are forms of authority handed to you by collections of people. The teachings you absorb for handling the world in general—traditionally associated with the father role (even if that was your mother)—also fall into this realm. Governments and the other structures you use for representing the constant backdrop for your doings are represented here. And then there are the great immovables: your species membership, natural geographic forms, physical laws, age, death,[8] time and the boundaries / walls of objects are also located in this realm.

As we explore the Capricorn realm, one thing we can look for is the set of structures that properly circumscribe us. Three of the major structures we encounter here are those of the father, career, and our government. Here we will explore the relationships among all three, getting a better sense of (a popular label for) our natural career in the process.

It is said in astrology that Capricorn and its associated planet Saturn both represent the father. They do, but only to the extent that fathers train children to interact with the worlds outside the emotional or home base while mothers train children to interact with the worlds within the home base—whatever those may consist of. The father trains the child in how to take the limits of his being into the limitless world beyond. The mother trains the child in how to take the limitless world within and bring about appropriately limited (structured) forms from beyond. A single mother student of mine once asked me, "What is the role of a physical father? Since my little one doesn't have one, I don't really know the importance of one." I told her the above, but add that a world which holds fewer examples of good fathers is a world which holds more examples of inner inclinations that don't know how to handle outer limits in an orderly way. An angst filled society is one byproduct of a world without fathers. Tyrannical leaders are one byproduct of a world seeking fathers (navigators of the unknown) whether or not its family units have them. Sons whose fathers are disempowered are more likely to have problems with women. Daughters whose fathers were disempowered are more likely to have problems with the mothers who trained them through any associations with disempowered men. On the other hand, problems with the mother tend to affect the child's show of emotion, both towards themselves and towards others. The good news is that single parents can play either or both roles as long as they have a clear sense of the differences in the two. Within the home base I'd like to trust that it will all work out, and that I will try my best to keep our foundational psychological-emotional space together. Outside of the home, I will cut a fool loose in a heartbeat if he poses a threat to me. The challenge for people playing both roles is to teach the child (and themselves) the difference between things that belong within "family" and things that belong outside of it. More than another partner, money, or grandparent substitution (since the grandparents were part of what created the single parent in the first place)[9], often what the little one needs is for the parent to be *wise* in the world, patient with herself. Switching gears will need to be as easy as reasonably possible.

Whether or not we were single parents or raised by them, as adults we are ultimately responsible for playing both roles anyway—that is, in the normal course of managing our own worlds. By then, the rules for including or excluding others become solidified, and our relationship to the "father" role will color how we handle spaces outside of our own. Roughly speaking, your views of your government will follow

---

[8] Capricorn is more about the dead. Scorpio is more about the process of dying and the effects of death on the living.
[9] That's not a criticism of single parents or a dismissal of grandparents. It is a statement of expectations: a single parent may have the fortune of good grandparents who properly substitute for the absent partner. But if the absence of a second partner is still an issue for the single parent, everyone's combined handling of that absence will *still* influence the children's perspectives on outside authority.

what the father role-players in your life taught you to believe about organized systems beyond your control. Your approach to career will follow what your father role-player taught you to do in response to those systems. Your approach to government will reflect the extent to which your career seems to align with or defy your father's expectations for those foreign spaces. But this is all very abstract. Your natural career is actually best mirrored in the area of government which you believe you would best serve in if your personal talents were at their optimum. Regardless of what you think of your government, you can use your relationship to it to find a broad career (long range pattern of jobs) for yourself.

Introductory Exercise

☞ Question 45.10.1 (Government job match): Go back and read your 45.1.7. Imagine that you are hired by the government to do this very thing. You DEFINITELY work for the government. Not with them or against them. You work for them. What career best describes this? Below is my example:

	Example
	In order to highlight my Instinct realm, I should pay attention to the [visionary lone wolves in my life with whom I share a cause worth fighting for], I'll be [an immovable, fight-focused, source of surprises] towards them, so that I can ultimately [give my own, usually free-expressing academic vision a permanent platform]. → Scholar-Advocate, Researcher?

☞ Question 45.10.2 (Piecing together a career-like field): Now take a look at the careers you derived above. Imagine that whenever you do those jobs you end up also doing whatever you wrote in 45.2.1. What kind of refined career allows this?

	Example
	Oldest brother, writer, black, free-scholar, system structurer, listener, diplomatic, amorous + Scholar-Advocate, Researcher? = Social/Political Theorist, Policy Maker, or (less likely) Advocate-Diplomat

Pretty simple, eh? All we did was take two views of authority, one beyond our control and one which was fundamentally us, and line them up. The above careers may or may not have anything to do with what you thought you would match up with; they may not even be any career that you sought for yourself (I have no intention of being a diplomat), but those careers are certainly rooted in two of the most fundamental aspects of your unique personality. If someone kidnapped you and forced you to train in them you might be good. Very good.

Detailed Exercise

Many people in our current society have a negative relationship with their government. It seems as though those in authority have an easy time abusing their power. The systems for electing and replacing them are too confusing for us to navigate. The variables we must consider for choosing among them are too numerous to even approach, let alone engage in with a sense of efficacy. And then there are the vast spaces of bills, events, policies, and legal maneuvers that we can't control. Why even participate if the whole thing is a giant tumbleweed?

But your relation to your government is directly related to your sense of your own voice amidst the unknown. Whereas the realm of Foreign Actors was all about the world's instincts in complement to your communication, the realm of Authorities is all about the world's identities in complement to the inclinations that your hold (directives). The more self-focused your inclinations and beliefs are, the less world-obliging your sense of authority will be, and the more likely you are to see authorities as limiting you. The more confused you are regarding your own stance emotionally, the more you will need an authority to set you straight. The more psychologically unsettled you are by your fellow citizens' increasingly relevant voices, the more intensely you will demand that your government restore a world that seemed to formerly revolve around you—not because it ever really did, but because when you were younger and not connected to everyone else's views via technology, it was easier to live in a box all your own. The gay people, Jews, Iranis, and sea of consumers were always there, though. You just had no means of considering them.

Your relationship to your government is your relationship to the generic external process which is responsible for protecting your inner world from complexities beyond your immediate control. If you have a process of your own for responding to events from outside of your world, and if that process is refined enough to where you *would* use it to stabilize other people's inner worlds, your relationship to government can have much of its negative content (if there is any) eliminated. This is true even if your government really is broken.

When working under a dysfunctional authority, a person with his own solid process for authority has several options, the most common one is to set up a local system of rules to protect others near him. So maybe you believe Washington D.C. is not responsive to anything you do. That doesn't prevent you from stabilizing the environment for your friends, family, and colleagues. Throughout history, broken governing systems have almost always led to change at the hands of people ushering in the next system. Our task is to *have* a next system which exists outside of the failings of the current one.

☞ **Question 45.10.3 (The real issue with government):** Name the number one area that you believe needs to be urgently fixed, addressed, or replaced in your government. If you like, you can also do this for a formal religion near to you. Or you could do it for both.

	Example
	The government failing to foster the independent base of expertise required for each citizen to competently, willingly engage his society on his own (K-12 education; the two-party merry-go-round for example); the citizens themselves failing to attain the tools for responsibly addressing the very problems they endlessly complain about (rage and scandal fixation).

☞ **Question 45.10.4 (You are the remedy):** Using your answer to 45.10.2, what would you do in any of the jobs listed to address this problem yourself?

	Example
	As a policy maker, I would develop a system for people knowing themselves beyond the boxes handed to them.
	As an Advocate-Diplomat or Social Theorist who doesn't really know which audiences would be interested in his ideas, I would write books which connect individual humanity to the whole of everything else, advocating for equality through a common natural basis for self-perception, and a pleasurably unifying approach to the unknown future.

Even if your "government career" in 45.10.2 was not something you'd ever consider doing for a living, your "government process" in 45.10.4 still forms the basis of your potentially constant work in life—that is, your general career. All you need to do is remove the government part; its only role was to help you think about your work as a stable label.

☞ Question 45.10.5 (The fixer): In order to obtain an idea of what your final, most natural career might be, remove the government association from your answer to 45.10.4 and copy the more general result below. This will be the structure that you claim as your own no matter where you go. By exercising this in any situation—especially in situations where people need help, where the actual governing or job structure is broken, where you're asked to serve society, or where you are charged to establish a long term work for the future—you will find that the negative aspects of society are much less likely to burden you and much more likely to seek your talent instead.

	Example
	~~As a policy maker,~~ I ~~would~~ develop ~~a~~ systems for people knowing themselves beyond the boxes handed to them.
	~~As an Advocate-Diplomat or Social Theorist who doesn't really know which audiences would be interested in his ideas,~~ I ~~would write books~~ collect patterns of knowledge which connect individual humanity to the whole of everything else ~~advocating for equality through a common natural basis for self-perception, and a pleasurably unifying approach to the unknown future.~~

Note that the final result above should look more like a behavior than a career. That's because the details of particular career fields change depending on society, technology, and other factors. The basic kinds of dynamics between humans and their worlds do not. Your "career" is just the formal label that society gives you for exercising the above behavior systematically, so you'll have a good chance of succeeding in any field which allows you to do the above, as long as the specific work environment you're in also allows it.

On a personal note that might be useful to you, I've held three kinds of job in my own work life: A teacher, a programmer, and a data designer. Note how these are just specific versions of the example in 45.10.5. In answer to the common question, "What's my career?" the specific field isn't as important as the constant behavior. Doing the constant behavior even outside of the realm of work is one way for you to compel respect from the world based on the constant structure you provide. (You're like an individual "government" in that area.) Flop around between providing that structure and complaining about the other structures, jobs, and governments around you—oscillate between providing that structure for others' benefit and chasing your own self-centered goals—and you'll see not only that it takes longer to "find yourself," but also that it takes you longer to be respected by others when you get there. We all know of celebrities and leaders who have high status and command very little popular respect. Fanship yes. Sales yes. Followership yes. People who care when the celebrity's 15 minutes are up, no. Such is the byproduct of a life that builds you up at everyone else's expense: the present loves you. History will make you into either a joke, a quick example of how <u>not</u> to do things, or just another face. Look into your memory of famous people and see that this is true. Our talents help make us special, but the rest of the world has no reason to care if we can't be relied on to use those talents towards anyone's benefit but our own.

The Realm of Surrounding Information (Aquarius)

Gods, powerful as they may be, don't always take center stage. A common theme we will consider throughout this book revolves around three main approaches to a situation: going towards, moving away from, and not acknowledging. Of all of these approaches, "not acknowledging" will be your most powerful tool for resisting negative influence, staying away from situations that don't fit you, and passing straight through to your most effective areas. Just as the gods have niches which confine their mention to certain contexts, classes of information have niches which confine their mention as well. Zeus may be all powerful, but when nobody's talking about him, his practical-world "volume" is turned down to 0 even in the lives of those who believe in him. The same holds for any class of information you can name: fighting it is one way; figuring it out is another; attending to something else entirely is yet another. For people who believe that the information age is inescapable—that big brother is always watching, that you can't live without your phone no matter how negative it may be—resisting the tumult of surrounding information may be hard. As hard as having Zeus and Hera judge you even in the bathroom. To truly develop your intuition and set yourself up with the gods who match you, you'll need to get your informational world under control. Turn up the talk that fits you. Turn down—way down—the talk that sends you noise. There is an art to this which we'll explore next.

I've discussed the role of TV shows and music in several books, most specifically in Dimension 11 of *S12*. Your favorite media, websites, and information environments are like a kind of intellectual "air" which you breathe for framing your own acts towards others. If you like crime dramas, you will understand your own experiences with others in terms of offenses, investigation, and the procedures for solving the offense. If you like cooking shows, you will understand your own experiences in terms of steps, works in progress, enjoyment thereof, and the creativity inherent in it. Clearly you can combine information types, and these combined types will give you even greater clarity regarding how you see the world… and the kinds of people or events you are able to attract in turn.

Introductory Exercise

☞ Question 45.11.1 (Information sources): **List up to ten (10) of your all-time favorite shows (not movies), up to five (5) of your favorite websites or entertainment channels, and up to five (5) types of new information you regularly follow.**

Chapter 45: The Worlds

	Example
	Liked shows: Mysterious Cities of Gold, Gunsmoke, A Little Sister's All You Need, Mystery Science Theater 3000, Golden Girls, Cheers, Touched By An Angel, We Without Wings, Twilight Zone
	Liked sites or channels: TCM, eBay, Nintendo eShop
	Liked information: Knime updates, broad societal patterns I observe on my own (no news), policy changes that affect my workplace

☞ **Question 45.11.2 (Informational themes):** For every item you listed, give a word or phrase which describes it in your eyes.

	Example
	Liked shows: Mysterious Cities of Gold (small group [sg] adventure with a fun story), Gunsmoke (sg open space with level-headed, connected characters and great writing), A Sister's All You Need (sg adult anime about friendship, writers, and [controversial] creativity), Mystery Science Theater 3000 (sg isolated critical eye, fun), Golden Girls (sg fun, great dialogue), Cheers (sg diverse characters, maturity, slice of life), Touched By An Angel (sg on a divine mission, healing), We Without Wings (sg adult anime, extreme complexity with an ordered path), Twilight Zone (thoughtful, philosophical, fascinating)
	Liked sites or channels: TCM (thoughtfully produced, classic creativity), eBay (sane space of choices with strong community rules), Nintendo eShop (sane space of choices with limitless individuality)
	Liked information: Knime updates (my tool of trade), broad societal patterns I observe on my own (places where I can help which aren't forced on me by other's spin), policy changes that affect my workplace (places where I can be immediately effective / empowered to contribute)

☞ Question 45.11.3 (Thumbs down products): **If there are any shows, genres, channels, or information sources that your think are so terrible you would never recommend them to anyone, list them here.**

	Example
_____	I'm lumping all mine together and masking them for the sake of the creatives behind these. You can actually list yours, but as the author of this book I'll refrain from insulting any readers or show creators here. I'm sure the latter worked hard on their creations.
_____	
_____	
_____	
_____	MM, FE, SG, SP, RT, IT, AN, LN, PT
_____	
_____	Also, recall what we discussed earlier about turning the volume down on things you don't desire. As you develop your intuition and your peace with yourself, you increasingly want to NOT give voice to topics you'd rather be rid of. When you open this book later, it may not help you to see a list of things you hated on all in one place, so you might actually use coded abbreviations the way I did instead. What you say and what you write—especially if it's negative about things which *you yourself* once chose to look at—has a permanence all its own.
_____	
_____	
_____	
_____	
_____	

☞ Question 45.11.4 (Informational blurb): **Considering what you wrote in 45.11.2, minus the characteristics you didn't like related to 45.11.3, summarize the kinds of information environments you tend to prefer.**

	Example
_____	A small group of intimately connected people on a unique mission, in many ways isolated from the rest of the world's instability; not afraid of adult or difficult issues, but integrates them with a strong set of principles; surrounded by creative works; colorful, open, and new beginning-enabling to all.
_____	
_____	
_____	
_____	
_____	
_____	

Years ago I might have looked at the above list and said, "You ole' soft-ass,… wanna be saintly ass,… better than everybody else ass,… so and so…" But current me looks at the battles I used to build my worth upon and clearly sees that I had to enter those same battles over and over *and over* again until it finally became clear that the need for drama lived squarely within myself. We're not striving for sainthood, but the more we value our rest at the end of the day, the less we tend to fill that resting time with turbulence. If I were still the same person whose favorite shows were crime dramas and favorite websites were astrology forums, I wouldn't have been ready to write this particular book. Those were earlier in my path. They might be later in yours. The list is not a judgment, but a profile of what supports your best framing of the space in which you yourself act. Hopefully that information space brings out more of your positive than your negative.

Detailed Exercise

Many of us dream of taking a vacation or "having a life" which affirms our access to contexts we could only otherwise wish for. It wasn't until my late 20s that I realized that the pressure to world-travel, hang out in bars and clubs, and go skydiving *could be,* but *weren't necessarily* dreams of my own so much as they were dreams of the popular culture. (As a country, the US itself has a birth chart, preferred social direction, and a favorite type of personality for elevating—basically like a soul—and puts its values upon us accordingly just as any person would.) You may really want to do these things, or you may actually just want to stay at home in peace. You may need to travel in order to surround yourself with your dream information, or you might be able to find that same information right where you are. Let's design a means to the latter.

Critical Exercise
SPIRIT PICTURE

Trains: Clairvoyance, Claircognizance, Clairsentience, Projection

☞ Question 45.11.5 (Information source abbreviation): First, make a list of abbreviations for your preferred information types.

	Example
	MCoG: Mysterious Cities of Gold
	GS: Gunsmoke
	SI: A Sister's All You Need
	MST3K: Mystery Science Theater 3000
	GG: Golden Girls
	CH: Cheers
	ANG: Touched By An Angel
	WW: We Without Wings
	TWZ: Twilight Zone
	TCM: TCM
	(a bag): eBay
	(a red oval): Nintendo eShop
	(A yellow triangle): Knime
	(a broadcasting eye): societal patterns I observe on my own
	(a gavel): policy changes that affect my workplace

☞ Question 45.11.6 (Paint the picture): *Draw* a scene which includes the symbols or abbreviations for everything you listed, putting each symbol or abbreviation next to the part of the scene which represents it. Don't think about anything on purpose. Just draw what you feel and put everything in there. Take the space below to do so.

Your picture doesn't have to be a Picasso, just enough to get the basic idea. If you listed a lot of information sources then the image may be very crowded. For the purposes of this exercise though, the more ideas the merrier.

☞ Question 45.11.7 (Spirit picture analysis): **Analyze your picture, summarizing what it's all about. Note anything you drew that stands out extra noticeably.**

	Example
	Based on my preferred information sources, I drew a picture of a world of exploration and learning, populated by a small group of people and their ideas about how people relate to each other in general. Most noticeable to me was how TCM (Turner Classic Movies, a television network) served as a wall between my preferred world and all the noise, sadness, and anger outside of it. Symbolically, it represented my belief that thoughtful, individuality-rooted creativity marks the border between a worthwhile world and one full of random, typically negative forces. I also note that MCoG was not on the city, but on the mountain leading to the city: the journey. People play a heavy role in this picture—what they do, how they think, and how they stand together. It tells me that, if I were to travel or seek the "dream life" or whatever, it may not need to be physical travel but should probably be relational and intellectual instead. Writing and scholarship appear more times than any other theme. The eBay bags (around the car) are small, signaling the relatively small importance of material objects. The demons are conceived of as part of a game, Ghostbusters style, (the Nintendo oval), and this is accomplished via the library my friends and I (CH, SI, GG, & GS) build.

Chapter 45: The Worlds

☞ **Question 45.11.8 (Bonus) (Informational shields):** Are there any images in your picture which play a *protective* role? These are especially important indicators of how you keep unwanted information out or under control. Summarize these factors if there are any.

	Example
	TCM, not the network itself but rather the attitude I have which draws me to it, indicates that I tend to avoid information which is mass-produced, adopted based mainly on advertisements, are noisy or negative, or which subvert individuality.
	The Nintendo oval represents how any negatives I do encounter is thought of as part of life's game—Buddhist style.
	The people around the (Dodge) city, WW, protect the inhabitants of that city by working together.
	So cooperation, individual sourcing, and gamification of challenges (NOT challenges through gamification—the opposite) are the filters for the information I take in. Subconsciously, if I don't feel the information meets all three of these needs, I tend to keep its volume at 0.

☞ **Question 45.11.9 (Bonus) (Informational health foods):** Are there any images in your picture which *appear several times* and *play a favorable role*? These are the information sources which bring you closer to your best as an individual actor in the world. They feed your easiest expression. Summarize these factors if there are any.

	Example
	The otherworldly (ANG, MST3K, MCoG temple, TWZ cosmic law, and the broadcasting eye telescope) attracts me as a topic.
	People relationships (GG, CH, SI, GS, and WW in relation to the city) reveal that great relationships with people who share my journey (in their respective settings or activities in the picture) are very important. Not just great relationships on their own.
	Writing, film / TV, and the codification of ideas (MST3K, SI, the library, CH at the table, the gavel) seem to have something to do with my preferred implements.

Though it may seem contrived, your analysis of your own picture should match much of what you've already discovered about yourself in the previous activities. We did the analysis after the drawing, and even though we didn't know that the analysis was coming in the form that it did, our connections between the picture and our ideas about ourselves should still tend to line up nicely. If they don't, consider whether the information sources you gravitate towards actually support who you want to be.

Early in my astrology studies I learned that the 11th house (related to the 11th sign, Aquarius) was associated with our hopes and aspirations. This isn't quite true since the 4th sign represents wants, the 2nd represents values, the 8th represents desires for others, and the 12th represents dreams. Still, to the extent that every day you seek out sources of information to remind yourself of what you're interested in hearing, you take that dream vacation daily to the land that your shows and web sites provide you. I've known several people throughout life who claimed they just wanted happiness, but who thrived off of information sources full of murder, madness, and anger. When you asked a couple of them what happiness looked like, they framed it in terms of the absence of murder, madness, and anger, and were (not surprisingly) *sad* when they talked about this kind of happiness. Don't be surprised if your framing of good things in terms of bad ones makes those "good" things invoke bad ones. And don't be surprised if your motivation for pursuing these bad-framed good things just isn't there. Your information sources are *your* ball and chain. Eat poison, stay poisoned. Again this isn't a judgment upon your choice of materials. (Maybe you could tell from my list that I still like my share of sex-heavy, corruption-focused topics; they are the key starting points in everything I create—including this book.) Just keep in mind that if it brings you *down*... Your consumption of things which you *know* bring you down will continue to be your fault—regardless of what those sources are.

This exercise is a gatekeeper for the "clear place in the world" and "intuition building" (psychic shield) series of activities in this book. Do it in order to show yourself what your own dream destinations for this life should look like, as well as to provide yourself a good defense against information sources that only crowd out your values with those of the raging, gleaming masses.

The Realm of the Call (Pisces)

Does it make sense that, in addition to you having wants and your friends having wants, the situations you are in also have wants? It makes sense to me. A person on the job who's not doing that job may be called by *the situation*—not by himself and not by his bosses or clients—to simply do the job. Upon waking in the morning we are called—not by our active selves nor by our friends or colleagues—to get up and make ourselves presentable. You don't need to believe in gods or heaven to see this. It should be clear that the realm of "behaviors suggested by our context"—the Call—is real enough (at least in our minds) to warrant consideration separately from our other types of motivation.

Chapter 45: The Worlds

The realm of the Call is basically the space of things you should be doing at the moment. It is not only the chief definer of your basic aspect / angle behaviors in astrology (what it means for things to be conjunct, trine, or square), it is also the very general mode you are in when nothing in particular is going on. This realm, in my opinion, is the MOST important one to understand when you start working with detailed astro signs, so we'll take a good look at it in the chapter on the Star. But before we get there, there is one other facet of this realm which you should be warned about: Sometimes—often, really—the Call will ask you to do things which aren't enjoyable at all—setting you up for problems just because that's the way your energy got stamped upon your arrival in this life.

If the spirits tell you how to get along in the world, the call tells you what to believe about that world. Part of my call is built on nontraditional romantic relationships (Duo 10), exclusion from normally accepted groups (Duo 8), and being misunderstood by those I bond to or with whom there is an attraction in either direction (Duo 5). Duo (short for **duodecanates**) are just **signs within signs**. The angles like deciles, semisquares, and quintiles are just fractions of a circle which separate bodies in the chart from each other. We'll learn all about these things later. Until then, the example below shows how a person's life can be set up at birth to imply certain obstacles.

Asteroid		Location		Degree	Duo.	Duodecanate Meaning (the Star)	Meaning
897	Lysistrata	5	pi	7	335.12	10	(Deciles) The things I use to protect my space are...	where you are associated with unconsummated or incomplete relationships [often romance]
422	Berolina	5	pi	26	335.43			where you forgo regular relationships in favor of a dream
580	Selene	10	pi	3	340.06		(Semisquares and sesquiquadrates) My flow gets interrupted / I interrupt the flow of others interacting with me through situations that look like...	means of passing your power intentions onto the people around you
15760	1992 QB1	10	pi	6	340.11			support attractor
946	Poesia	10	pi	25	340.43			your unsatisfiable vision, never ending quest
9248	Sauer	10	pi	34	340.57			regulator-blocker
312	Pierretta	10	pi	53	340.89	8		where standards of perfection clash with reality, threatening relationships; positively, this is a barrier which renders the person selective
772	Tanete	11	pi	13	341.23			trait for which you make exceptionally popular company
209	Dido	11	pi	17	341.29			unending striving for fulfillment
371	Bohemia	12	pi	10	342.18			where your characteristics render you out of place with respect to the group you belong to; people's assumptions for you are VERY often mismatched
20	Massalia	12	pi	14	342.24			where you introduce people to concepts they've never seen [your role models often have this asteroid on key planets of yours]
382	Dodona	17	pi	41	347.68		(Quintiles) In situations where I strongly desire to show something to others, I also often experience... (longing in negative cases, immersion / further engagement in positive cases)	where you connect others to vast worlds beyond
103	Hera	18	pi	0	348.00			deep bonds
587	Hypsipyle	18	pi	6	348.10			where you super-extend your creative power beyond normal boundaries
146	Lucina	18	pi	19	348.32	5		where you are susceptible to others' misunderstanding
10	Hygiea	18	pi	46	348.77			where the body is important to you
295	Theresia	19	pi	18	349.31			where you use your physical qualities to advance your interests [trines are more likely to use their bodies as a weapon]
111	Ate	19	pi	38	349.64			where you use your body to coerce other's attention
875	Nymphe	19	pi	47	349.80			where you project a strong desire nature

Now maybe you don't believe in astrology. That's okay. Your race, your sex, your nationality, the side of town your life began on, your hormonal triggers, prenatal conditions, preferences for certain foods, colors or toys, tendency to cry or coo, attention to certain noises and other arousal states, genetic predispositions, exposure to flashing phones, GMOs, and family dynamics all affect your development in the ways for which asteroids act as an analogy. Whatever the case, you'll learn to feel the pressure to do certain things—some beneficial, some destructive—when in your interactions. And you'll spend much of your life trying to fine tune this mash of habits. Astrology is just a framework for making this kind of to-do list obvious. You'll be called to do a million things regardless of what you believe. Get ready to navigate the maze you were raised to run through.

Introductory Exercise

Until we reach The Asteroid, we will be woefully underequipped to separate the Call into its various implications for intuition. For now, we'll simply practice what it feels like to read a particular kind of call. Set your timer for 2 minutes.

☞ Take 2 minutes to imagine, given everything that's happening with you right now, some idea that you really want to share with someone else.

Did you do it? Good.

Now use the lines below to describe what you experienced.
_____
_____
_____
_____

You've just practiced Pisces 5: the call *to interact* (the Dodona, Hera… rows in the table above).

The key question, I think, which plagues us in realm 12 is, *Should I answer a call which I KNOW is going to hurt me?* If you end up getting burned every time but keep getting pulled to it, should you try to touch it again? The quick answer is:

> Yes, but **ONLY** after you have corrected your relationship to what it embodies.

✷ About the 12s in astrology

There is a well-known association between Pisces' associate planet Neptune and addiction. Based on what we've discussed above, you can see why. When you're idle, your 12th area of life (your "12th house" in astrology) is where you tend to place your attention. Your 12th sign, Pisces, is how the various events in your world tend to reset themselves. Your 1/12th family of angles (inconjuncts; things which are 30° and 150° apart) are how you tend to [think things should be solved] and how you [feel like moving to actively resolve them] respectively. Your 1/24th family of angles (II-inconjuncts or "Aquarius 12s;" 15°, 75°, 105°, and 165°) show how you feel things should be talked about as having been resolved by you (your creative works of the imagination), and your 1/36th family of angles (III-inconjuncts or "Capricorn 12s;" multiples of 10°) are the structured groups that are associated with how you resolved things: how you are formally remembered / your lasting impression. I talk about all of this in *144* and also later in this book.

You can see though, how the 12s show where situations "want" you to come across a certain way. Thus they play a heavy role in what you are pushed to accept about your life. Some people are wired for addiction, others for overindulgence, and still others are wired for greed. We'll need to learn more about Embodiments, Resonance, Conflict, and the Star in order to get around these kinds of things. ⚒

Detailed Exercise

I would love for you to print out all of your asteroids right now and look at what they tell you about your call, but that would turn an inclination based exercise into an intellectual one, skipping the real-world intuition practice entirely. So we won't do that. Instead we're going to see how sensitive your senses are to certain kinds of information—taking the basic five senses + proprioception to test for some easy paths into your thinking.

☞ **Question 45.12.1 (The senses, one by one):** Spend about a minute trying to use only ONE sense at a time. Use the table below to write down what you experience while you're exploring each sense. There are several ways to use the same sense, and I have included some suggested methods in the table. This exercise should take at least six minutes. Write down not only what you feel but *how* you feel it. You might experience a smell-induced memory via a sight-based picture for example.

Taste: Eating or even *looking at* a particular food, foods, or edible object like an animal, gum, or pencil; any thoughts that make you salivate	Smell: Smelling something, going to a smelly area, looking at something known to be fragrant or rotten, remembering a natural environment
Touch: Feeling the thing you're sitting on, walking around, feel sensations upon your body, noticing the temperature or breeze	Sight: Observing colors, objects, or the implied action that come with certain objects, watching patterns
Hearing: Listening to sounds from the outside or thoughts on the inside, reading something or feeling the vibration of something	Proprioception (internal body state attention): noticing areas of tension or pleasure, ease, or discomfort; noticing the desire to do something if there is anything in particular; feeling that something about your current state is "begging" for your attention

☞ **Question 45.12.2 (Sense weighting): Were any of the senses easier to engage than others? If so, which ones?** _____

☞ **Question 45.12.3 (Sense pipelines):** Did you get more of a certain type of information (or impression) through some senses than through others? Please describe.

_____
_____
_____
_____

☞ **Question 45.12.4 (Super bonus) (Primary intuition gateway):** Before you came back to this book from doing the activity, did any of the senses bring you an impression which remains with you now as you are answering these questions? Please describe. This indicates one of the primary modes for your situational intuition—something like general "psychicism." (For example, I got a strong idea of what to write next through touch—walking around the kitchen—even though I was only thinking about ramen and coffee. Physical comfort or movement triggers my clairaudience. Discomfort or anger causes my brain to freeze and my walls to go up.)

_____
_____
_____
_____

People who are new to their own intuition tend not to have rich descriptions of their senses. Part of this is biological, but much of it has to with how vast your vocabulary is for describing what you feel. To really get good at reading impressions, you'll need to get good at translating what you read into meaning. A "bad" feeling and a "negative" feeling can imply two totally different courses of action as we'll see in the chapter on Conflict. So it pays to learn to distinguish the details in the impressions you get from certain senses. My impressions from this activity are below.

Taste: Eating my ramen, I felt fairly peaceful, and also recalled how a student of mine once brought me a sandwich because, in her view, I was working too hard. The way to my heart is truly through my stomach. But if I am simply making food for myself, there is an efficient utility to it—as if eating is getting in the way of work.	Smell: I smell the hot summer air, and get the impression of passion, force, and exertion. Nice smells don't do much for me, but strong smells raise my alarms for action. Not a sense I use unless a fight is on the horizon.
Touch: I do almost ALL of my channeling in the form of recording while walking around, writing on the big paper on my office walls, and just now pulled down the usual information seemingly from another world while walking around the island in the kitchen. While asleep with no sights, sounds, smells, or tastes, I dream. Touch is probably my strongest _trigger_ for call information.	Sight: I wince as I attempt to see things for their visual properties, instinctively covering my eyes, turning my head down and away, and puffing out air through my nose like my cat when he's agitated. I don't like vision. Visual forms pack too many words in one space, many of which are irrelevant to what I'm doing at the time. Those remaining oceans of words are easily used to lie, control, or otherwise distract me from what I'm doing, and it is for this reason that I often avert my eyes from a thing I'm interacting with. I don't want to read your extra. Though I'm certain I'd be good at it if I practiced, I'm equally certain that the content would render me cynical. Only for the beautiful things. Everything else is a scrapyard of descriptors.
Hearing: I'm generally soothed by what I hear, and avoid places where the sounds and voices are cacophonous. While listening to the air conditioning unit and the birds outside (really) I continue to pour through writing. Another book in progress, this is easily my strongest _type_ of call information.	Proprioception (internal body state attention): This sense was surprisingly boring. I only use it to assess my current feelings and when I need to perform a vital function like sleeping, eating, or going to the bathroom. Used mainly as a diagnostic tool especially because, if I were to read something negative, I would rather not have whatever it is affect _my_ body. Hearing as my main channel ensures that I can keep such things at a distance.

You'll notice that my answers aren't in the form I asked you to give yours. That's because I wanted you to see how various forms of intuition aren't just about luck, but are actually tied to your personality. I like order and control over what comes into my world and what goes out. I value human bodies but don't trust human-made appearances. My means of intuition are directly related to these preferences.

☞ Question 45.12.5 (The senses one by one, narrated): **Given the above, more narrative-style description, try the activity again. This time there is no time limit.**

Taste: Eating or even *looking at* a particular food, foods, or edible object like an animal, gum, or pencil; any thoughts that make you salivate	Smell: Smelling something, going to a smelly area, looking at something known to be fragrant or rotten, remembering a natural environment
Touch: Feeling the thing you're sitting on, walking around, feel sensations upon your body, noticing the temperature or breeze	Sight: Observing colors, objects, or the implied action that come with certain objects, watching patterns
Hearing: Listening to sounds from the outside or thoughts on the inside, reading something or feeling the vibration of something	Proprioception (internal body state attention): noticing areas of tension or pleasure, ease, or discomfort; noticing the desire to do something if there is anything in particular; feeling that something about your current state is "begging" for your attention

I've found very few places with a satisfactory theory of intuition, so we'll present one here:

- Every move you make originates in a selectively holistic summary of your states just before it—self, other, and world included.

- You build your holistic summaries by gathering data from your 5 + 1 senses (lumping your thoughts, feelings, and other proprioception into the sixth one).

- You have mechanisms for translating information from your six modes into instructions for your next state—cognitive, motor, cardiac, and all of the other organ systems included.

- **Basic intuition** is **your ability to monitor the pathway from [the senses that summarize your previous state] to [the body systems that you will dynamically employ in the next state].**

- But the human body is part of a larger set of patterned dynamics within a "sphere" of predictable interactions with certain kinds of places, things, and events. So it is possible to develop mechanisms for monitoring the larger multi-actor structures of which a human is a part (in the same way that brains, governments, chemical reaction environments, and metadata "monitor" their wholes.

- People can tie the mechanisms they use to obtain and predict information about their environments to the same mechanisms they use to monitor their own body pathways. And there you have it: upper-intermediate intuition.

- Lastly, people can assign human-exchangeable characteristics to phenomena before and after the time periods in which they live, by adopting the monitoring mechanisms of things that follow these scales. A toe cell may not know what is happening in the whole hand fifteen years from now, but a toe cell whose nearby nerve cells have been trained to signal alongside input from the hand, can use the brain's capacity to anticipate the next 15 years, even if that toe cell has long been replaced through ongoing cell death. Perhaps the idea seems fantastic until we think about how basic phones and other remote technologies work.

Accordingly, people can hear their call at several levels, depending on how deeply responsive they are to the events in most direct contact with the caller.

A Quick Pass Through the Twelve Worlds

I am a great fan of Robert Bruce's *Astral Dynamics*, and recommend it to anyone interested in learning astral projection. Try as I might, however, I was never able to project beyond a D- level with an F level clarity. The same goes for seated meditation. And visualization. And lucid dreaming. Given our tour of the above 12 worlds, though, you may see why this would be the case. Your intuitive skills will follow your skill with your own senses. If you are not good at sitting still and breathing, seated meditation may not be your easiest option. If you are not interested in employing sight as a means of exploration, intuition, or any other kind of information gathering, then *picturing* astral or other kinds of energetic realms may not work as smoothly for you. Some people dream vividly with no sound. Some people feel in a tactile way with no emotion. In order to develop talents in senses that are not normal for you, you may need to attach those less proficient senses to more proficient ones. We'll get better at this as we go along, but it starts with the ability to distinguish what you are sensing and what kinds of realms you are exploring with those senses.

Conclusion

We've used an astrological model to outline 12 different kinds of experience (realms). These aren't actual worlds so much as they are ways of seeing that can be useful for tuning your attention in certain ways. The reality is that there are many, many levels of seeing beyond 12—from the perspective of a molecule to the perspective of a country's exports, from the ducts of a human lymphatic system to the mathematical progression of a song's spectrum. If you can frame a space in terms of a specific type of content and navigate that space from a perspective on that content, you can consider that space to be a world. To make this a little less fantastic, we'll consider **navigation** to be **the process of passing through a field of content without being significantly altered yourself, having the capability to know that you've done so, having some level of influence over how you've done so, while keeping some kind of record of the content you have encountered.** According to this view, if you are effectively memoryless, then who is to say that you have been anywhere outside of your own pattern? We can navigate a city of objects from a physical perspective, a page of text from a lexical perspective, or a career path of jobs from a work-content perspective. The space of objects, space of words, and the space of work options can be considered worlds in the same way that we temporarily treat maps in a video game—electronically encoded or not—as worlds. For the purposes of developing intuition, we'll definitely need a broader-than-physical sense of what constitutes a "world."

Our 12 worlds revolve around the kinds of things we can clearly do in the sun-centered, visible world of Show (Other-Fire, Leo). In order to be visible, a thing must reflect a transmissible energy / vibration / light, sound, or other medium of communication (general Air element) onto a viewer (general Earth element) who has to power to register an internal change (general Water element) for knowing that the thing was seen. When the show-er is something we're other-observably engaging—anything really—that is the regular visible world.

- When the show-er is us, that is our internal Instinctual way of seeing (Aries),
- the communication form we send out is Gemini Internal Monologue,
- the "viewing" identity values that we use for defining what our actions are in the first place are Taurus,
- and the call to show that particular self-originated action is indicated by Pisces, our most recent collection of states.

- Our from-self communication is typically intended towards an interactant. The intent coming from us to the interactant is Cancer Want.
- Our want motivates what we see in an interactant and how we are seen by that interactant, both Leo / Show.
- The things against which interactants / people / ideas or other constructs who are not us are compared are the basis of what we join, Virgo,
- And the information we trade between the things that are showable and the constructs to which they are joined are our feedback-style "conversations," Libra.

Chapter 45: The Worlds

- For every conversation you can have with an interactant, there are any number of motivations to engage parties other than that interactant. The want towards something that your current interactant is not displaying constitutes Scorpio. That "non-them" could be an action you want them to perform, another person, a bundle of information you're trying to obtain, or any other set of states the interactant is not currently occupying, but (in your mind) should be. In other words, Scorpio Influence is your style of pursuing the next page of the story of another beyond the page you are on.
- The culture of Foreign Actors who typically witness your engagement of direct interactants but who are themselves *not* your interactants are described by your Sagittarius realm.
- These external actors trade in a typical style of data or information, Aquarius, that travels around your particular sphere of dynamics,
- and they do so in comparison to a set of constructs which are also used to determine the boundaries of your public definition, Capricorn.

As you can see, all 12 worlds are a natural consequence of one. If a thing can be seen or be said to act (fire), it needs some communicative medium (air) for making itself known to a viewer, some viewer for knowing it (earth), and some kind of state change for marking the difference between when it was known and when it wasn't (water). The [actor-**self**], the [viewer-**other**], and [**neither/world** of these]—the three **scopes**—each follow this same kind of rule, giving us 12 total aspects of a single dimension: Self-Other-World × Fire-Earth-Air-Water. The best way, I believe, to memorize the signs for these worlds is to 1) learn their order, then 2) learn their SOW cluster, then 3) learn their SOWD element:

The Signs	Cluster	Type of object (element)
1. Aries	Self	Fire – **action** shown
2. Taurus	Self	Earth – structured interactant or **viewer**
3. Gemini	Self	Air – means of **communication** passed between show-er to viewer
4. Cancer	Self (→Other)	Water – the passing (**change**) of the Actor-Viewer-Communication (Self-Other-World) combination itself into the next state; their animation
5. Leo	Other	Fire – **action** shown
6. Virgo	Other	Earth – structured interactant or **viewer**
7. Libra	Other	Air – means of **communication** passed between show-er to viewer
8. Scorpio	Other (→World)	Water – the passing (**change**) of the Actor-Viewer-Communication (Self-Other-World) combination itself into the next state; their animation
9. Sagittarius	World	Fire – **action** shown
10. Capricorn	World	Earth – structured interactant or **viewer**
11. Aquarius	World	Air – means of **communication** passed between show-er to viewer
12. Pisces	World (→Self)	Water – the passing (**change**) of the Actor-Viewer-Communication (Self-Other-World) combination itself into the next state; their animation

Table 45-3: More ways of differentiating the 12 signs

The [Self-Other-World × Fire-Earth-Air-Water] framework is very useful for knowing which kind of event to look at for certain kinds of information. Contrary to what some people still think, everything in existence has every sign in it. If they are thought to exist by some "viewer" somewhere, the whole chain of 12 applies to them, even if they are imagined. A unicorn has a specific look, a behavior, a context for being mentioned, a set of Actors foreign to it who reference it, and so on. If you meditate yourself into an astral world where the conditions embodied by a unicorn exist, you might see a unicorn there. You might even respond to it psychologically (or at least energetically with your internal perception)—the same way you respond to your favorite imagined TV show. All you need is to put your attention towards the right cluster and the right object type.

Critical Exercise
ASTROLOGICAL SIGN QUIZ

Trains: Essential knowledge, Dream interpretation

To get the most out of this book, you absolutely need to memorize the signs and be able to recall them quickly. You don't need to know their folklore (that Aries is impulsive or Virgo is analytical for example) so much as you need to know that

- the first four are self, the next four are other, and the last four are world
- within a cluster it goes fire (action)→earth (object)→air (communication)→water (change)

I'll use the signs as regular words throughout the book, and as long as you know what they broadly represent, you can derive the folklore from there. For example, if you want to know where to look for an ideal job, a job is a structure that is not within you, so you might look at Virgo or Capricorn. But if you want to know what kind of *work* is ideal for you, your work is a process connected to how you intend certain results, so you might look at Pisces, Cancer, Virgo, or Aries. Of course, any sign can help answer any question, but some signs are much more appropriate for answering certain questions than others.

☞ Question 45.13 (Sign quiz): Memorize the signs by their [Self-Other-World × Fire-Earth-Air-Water] type, then take the half-quiz below. This is a half-quiz, so I only have answers for the first column. Our society is currently trained to look for instant answers, even though it's the process that we need to develop. There are still some things like oppositions and frequency levels that we haven't talked about, so you may not actually have all of the information you need to answer these items "correctly." Try to answer them anyway. We're developing intuition, remember? Do your best with the *partial* information you have. The whole point of an "unfair" setup like this is to get you to think about the forms which these phenomena actually take—a self? an inclination / change? a process?—so you can better read your own intuition regarding them in your world. **ANSWER ALL OF THE QUESTIONS. <u>ANSWER THEM ALL</u>**. We will work on how to pull and understand this kind of information from real life as the book progresses.

Chapter 45: The Worlds

Astrological Sign Quiz

For each of the items below, use [Self-Other-World × Fire-Earth-Air-Water] to pick the sign which you think would best correspond to that item. All of these have multiple options. Try to pick at least one.

1. bravery	2. the heart	3. anger	4. a tree	5. a small town
6. the color red	7. a smile	8. peace	9. corruption	10. a rabbit
11. bigness	12. playing music	13. a promotion	14. a snob	15. radio waves
16. the wind	17. listening to music	18. fame	19. joy	20. a friend's inner thoughts
21. a table (object)	22. a music file	23. a guess	24. a boss	25. a bad habit
26. receiving a delivery	27. a musical note	28. an injury	29. poverty	30. ghosts
31. a favorite food	32. an illness	33. war	34. a mystery	35. attractiveness
36. deception	37. things you read	38. power	39. death	40. opportunities
41. belief in a higher power	42. social life	43. your highest skill	44. enemies	45. pride
46. a country	47. physical exercise	48. uncertainty	49. a place of acceptance	50. a job
51. permanent impressions you leave	52. your path in life	53. things that turn you on	54. things you do that upset others	55. winter
56. anxiousness	57. water	58. filmmaking	59. addiction	60. the act of driving
61. money	62. the ocean	63. a destined partner	64. hot temperature	65. children

Astrological Sign Quiz: **SOME SOLUTIONS**

To determine the right sign / realm to search for a certain idea, just ask yourself what that idea's basic form is and what kind of group (a thing, a viewer thereof, or the surroundings of both) tend to house that kind of idea.

1. bravery	Aries: this describes an **action** performed by **individuals** OR
	Sagittarius: an **action** or behavioral value characteristic of a **group**
	Pisces: if you're talking about the kind of bravery to face up to (head **towards**) a **situation**
	Leo: if you're describing valor—as in a visible, **standout act** beyond **what others normally see**
6. The color red	Aries: in society, red is used as an immediate, obviously announced **attention grabber** either for the **individual actor** OR
	Leo: the **attention** of the **general viewer**
	Scorpio: if you're talking about the passion or anger involved in **influencing an interactant** forcefully
	(Of course, redness doesn't really have a sign. Remember however that the signs are metaphors for types of experience. Red in American society is more closely associated with things that stand out in passion, so the above analogies may be more applicable in interpreting dreams or clairvoyant "flavors" of information.)
11. bigness	Sagittarius: a **shown** presence **above a space** of smaller comparators (in a world)
	Pisces: when you're describing a **vast** (world-level) realm of **potential** (inclined) things
	Leo: when you don't mean big, but rather an object's **noteworthiness to a viewer** (other)
	Capricorn: when you don't really mean big, but **imposing** (limiting) beyond what any individual (thus only a **world**) can handle
	Taurus: when "big" is the word you use to describe something's (**a single actor's**) immovability (**fixed internal center** / identity contents)
16. the wind	Aquarius: for a world-level event defined by its travels
	Gemini: when you are referring more to the speed or blowing attribute (**travel**) of the wind **itself**
	Pisces: when the wind is more important as a part of **vast** nature (a **space of potential** events)
21. a table (object)	Capricorn: if all it is is furniture, a **boundary object** in the world for putting things on
	Cancer: if, more than furniture, it's a symbolic setting for certain special (potential) dynamics for individuals (like a meeting table or the *dinner* table). Here the table acts more like a house—also commonly considered to be a Cancer thing
	Taurus: if it's furniture of special worth or **value**—an identity form against which a **person's** prestige may be measured
26. receiving a delivery	Virgo: if the delivery is considered a **joining** or a service to you **by another**
	Gemini: **travel** can be done by you personally, but also **experienced by you personally**. This is a one-way exchange in your direction (so it's not two-way Libra or multi-way Aquarius—not in this sense)…
	Aquarius: …but if you are thinking about a delivery of data (a **world**-like tangle of **information**), then a delivery can be that of a collective
	Capricorn: if it's only the package you're concerned about and not the receiving part—the **structure** from the **world**
	Scorpio: if you're concerned with some **sender** trying to **influence** you

31. a favorite food	Taurus: a "favorite" tends to be associated with an identity **value**; also, food is typically an **object**	
	Cancer: when associated with eating or nourishment, food takes **you from a state** of appetite to a state of satisfaction (**change**)	
	Virgo: if the food is an object associated with a habit you join yourself to, it becomes a matter of health: **joining** a particular **arrangement** to (+) **your body** as an object (not as an actor)	
36. deception	Pisces: when the **space** you are in is described by secret, **potential** events	
	Scorpio: when **a specific actor** is using this as a tactic to **influence you**	
	Capricorn: when a **situation or a group** is attempting to **limit you**	
	Aquarius: is associated with a **world** of **mixed signals** of various types, from media to social cliques	
	Aries & Gemini are less frequently associated with deception, but are more associated with brand new **actions or information from individuals** which are inconsistent with old ones	
	Leo is relatedly associated with a person's **façade**. Rarely (not surprisingly) do you apply this to yourself. Mainly to **others**.	
	Sagittarius is associated with those who accuse you of deceiving; these are **worlds** of **actors** who misunderstand you (opposite Gemini)	
	Apparently there are many ways to deceive.	
41. belief in a higher power	Pisces: a **space beyond individuals** full of **potential** power	
	Sagittarius: when the **space** is conceived of as an active, driving **force**	
	Scorpio: when you are less concerned with the higher power and more concerned with **one's attempt to influence** its workings (especially via the occult)	
	Virgo: when it is your *service*—**joining** of **one party** to (+) **its desired aims**—that matters	
46. a country	Sagittarius: a **space** of **foreign actors**. Easy	
	Capricorn: a **space** of foreign laws, customs, or other boundary-defining **structures**	
	Gemini: **your travel** through a foreign space (opposite Sagittarius)	
	Aquarius doesn't really indicate a country, but a nation—where it's the **messages** among the people **in the space** that matter	
51. permanent impressions you leave	Capricorn: if it's permanent or **fixed** in the **world**, the 10th realm is almost a given	
	Aries: What **you** do impulsively or **instinctually** also has a higher chance of shaping others' views of your originality	
	Aquarius: impressions which are known more for their shock value (**world social talk**) fall under this one	
	Leo makes impressions "permanently" by virtue of its show, but doesn't typically make *permanent impressions* thanks to its direct-interaction requirement. If the audience or the album changes, the impressions need to be made again. You're only as good as your latest hit here.	
56. anxiousness	Virgo: attempting to make sense of or **join ideas** urgently	
	Aquarius: noting the signaling (**informational noise**) **throughout** your body, in no particular area (more like a world) is closer to the high strung kind of anxiousness	
61. money	Taurus: is it something that **you** value or **measure** the worth of things by?	
	Libra: is it associated with a socially (**communicatively**) mobile (**interaction**-based) lifestyle?	
	Cancer: is it more like a **wish you have** to be **enabled** in some way?	
	Aries: is it your means to doing what **you instinctively** want to **do**?	
	Capricorn: is it the staple **object of** institutions (**worlds**) like banks, businesses, or governments in transaction?	

How did you do? Notice how there isn't one right way to think of one's topics. It all depends on how you intend to interact with those topics. Even if you think some of your answers missed the mark, don't judge yourself too harshly. As mentioned in our overview of the 12, a basic case can be made for matching any idea with any realm. If for example you did match Leo with permanent impressions then fine. It makes sense enough. If you matched Taurus with anxiousness, yes that could work in cases where, say, anxiety was an identity object, or the threat to an identity object caused anxiousness in a person. <u>Your explanations of these ideas to yourself is what matters most</u>, which is why it is so important for you to do the quiz using very little information. This is your chance to get a look at your own understanding of the world *you* perceive, not the author's. It is *your* intuition after all.

Before we begin the next chapter, think about that handful of things that you are highly unlikely to be without on a normal day. These things aren't a part of your birth body, but are—at this point in your life—deeply tied to it. Items such as

- certain jewelry, piercings, or tattoos which are more firmly attached to you (you don't need to list them; just note the group)
- your phone or watch (if it's that important to you)
- your glasses
- a trademark item in your hair or item of clothing which you care about (not those that you don't care about but instead use because you need them; some shoes are like this)
- a purse or some other accompaniment

Besides your basic body, if it should be associated with you physically, list it in the box below.

These are the remainder of the whole you, and for the answers in this chapter may be considered as parts of your body. The age will come soon when tech integrations like these are the norm, so we will consider them now. Let's get started.

Chapter 46. The Embodiment

The goal of this chapter is to help you conceive of yourself entirely as energy. By the end of it you should be able to identify

- what you generally represent to others in the world by default
- why you attract certain kinds of experiences into your life
- what the combination of the above says about your role in life

You already know that we are all composed of energy. On the atomic level, our most fundamental parts are ever moving and vibrating, though their broad structure remains stable. Stars appear to be basically stable objects to us short-lived humans, but even they emit spectra and other levels of energy as a consequence of the kinds of chemical reactions occurring within them. Relatedly, your body is an arrangement of certain kinds of energy along paths partly sponsored by your genes, in turn sponsored by your evolutionary lineage, in turn sponsored by adaptation to the earth's conditions, in turn sponsored by the earth itself, and by the prior collection of elements available to that region around the sun that would ultimately constitute the earth's orbit. Even now as you move around in your day, from the perspective of a space giant you are a collection of elements—much like an enzyme—which slides across the earth's surface taking in inputs and sending them out for a while until you are eventually broken down through programmed recycling; you are a feature of the earth's own composition more than you are a meaningfully defined psychology.

In the previous chapter we claimed that every viewable thing automatically has 12 dimensions associated with it: Its internal self, viewing other, and communication contextualizing world combined with the ways in which each of these clusters experience each other plus an additional state change. When we perceive a stable pattern in the things we view, the 12 dimensions become that much more predictable. For complicated reasons that I've left out of this book, the human body has a shape which reflects the geometry of the kinds of information its various regions hold. The old

- head-torso-tail ● ━ ═ model…

Broad Concept	Broad Orienting Function	Broad Engagement phase
"head"	takes inputs next intended direction; structure-wise, needs to be pivotable with some kind of turning mechanism or ball-joint arrangement, even if it takes whole sections of the body beyond the formal head to accomplish this	environment -> things self focuses on
"torso"	regular processing; structure-wise, is a container (but because it takes inputs and outputs, is often a "tunnel" of some kind); contains the species' core functions	things self focuses on or takes in-> what self uses to move, live, and engage
"tail"	(with arms, legs, tentacles, etc.,) actually moves against or influences things for the next direction; structure-wise, either 1) needs to move around in flexibility or 2) can be mostly inflexible / paddle-like (given it has joints) yet be split; needs to be slidable	what self uses to move, live, and engage -> (updated status in) environment

- …with a round-tube-[split half]-nub ● ━ ═ ⊃ section in each…

…is actually a reflection of the typical kind of conic sections that come with spheres (input orienters) •, tunnels (processors) —, hyperboloids (engagement options) ≍, and paraboloids (histories from a starting point) ⊃. These shapes reflect the way the body's cells display certain behavior toward neighbors in order to develop its various specialized parts. In developmental biology these correspond roughly to radiating and signaling outward ×, guidance to target ≑, lateral inhibition (from a central branch) ≠, and fusing or feedback inhibition ⋗. These "growth modes" follow the usual math; the regions that contain them obey a doubling pattern I talked about in the previous book, so that your body can be thought of a big math function on the 12-cycle of possible character modes that all forms must possess.

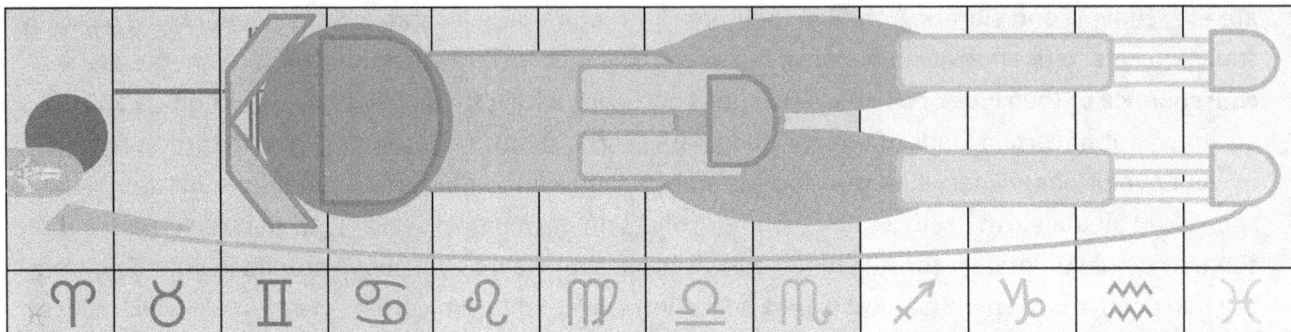

A hypothesis: More patterned differention this way ↕ ↤ favors males, more this way ↦ ⚢ favors females in the overall body plan, perhaps reflecting basic child-bearing, upright walking, and other evolutionary pressures. Now that we've seen the worlds, however, we know that such pressures have analogs in the signs. More two-legged walking and two-armed dexterity means more Gemini inner processes for calculating things like reach and balance against foreign (Sagittarius) contexts. Differences in weight distribution around the waist likely means differences in biological developmental cues (Cancer hormonal systems) between the sexes for where the metabolism is focused. Maybe all of this would be more obvious if we took the astrological labels out. The reason we're keeping the labels in, however, is because they allow us to map form to function, and function to the kinds of worlds our bodies help us perceive. Standard human female biology will be more conducive to the automatic experience of any worlds which more greatly involve a design specific to the female. The same will go for the male. The Cancer (hormonal/want), Capricorn (bone structural/phenotypic boundary), Sagittarius (in-foreign locomotive), and Gemini (monologue/neural orchestral) systems can be expected to differ between the two sexes. Less important than the differences, though, is the idea that your body plan contributes to the kinds of "psychicism" you're predisposed to display…if you believe, that is, that psychicism is less psychic and more energy/attention distribution-related on levels that our genetic byproducts know well, but which our waking training is usually too clunky to pay attention to.

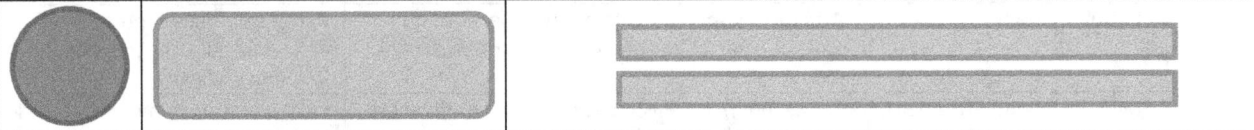

Figure 46-1: Geometries of the body

(Technical) Speculation Regarding the Body Plan. If you consider that your stem cells contain the whole plan for your body, then you can see how no matter where they are located in you they will have "tried" to replay your whole body plan if not for the limits of the regions that contain them. At the end of every voluntarily controllable appendage (the head, arms, and feet with all of the complex signaling needed for this), there is a miniature replay of the basic dynamics that made your body what it is. This allows us to read health through the face and feet, life response patterns through the hands. Hence the practices of face reading, reflexology, and palmistry. In these we are essentially reading the course of a biological sports game if no shocks to the general plan were to occur. We see them in the terminal appendages because that's where all of the path-lengthening stops, leaving the genes with nothing to do but build amongst themselves in the same pattern that would have produced the whole you had they had somewhere else to go. Alas, all they have is this nub of yours for rehearsing their spiel without cease. The lines on your hand, for example bear a moderate resemblance to the arrangement of the major players you prefer in your astrology chart. Your face traces the events you've been subject to in your life. Why? Who knows? But we can guess that it has something to do with our undifferentiated cells representing the same fully zipped file until local neighbors tell them otherwise. Perhaps some cells in your hand were following a similar story of signal collisions as the ones in your spine. Or your legs. The more leg-like they end up corresponding to, the more foreign world traveling those lines will end up being. Granted, this is a layman's guess. But it takes legs against brains to register foreign lands. Gemini and Sagittarius are the conceptual, experiential analogs to these. Where the parts of the body ultimately span a complete set of everything that such a body will ultimately be capable of doing or feeling, our physical forms constitute the engines of our lifelong behavioral illusion. Those same genetic patterns spend a lifetime re-imposing their orbital chemistry on each other according to the same rules that similar chemistry in a meteor might. Thus our physical structure is tied to the formulas for everything else that circles the Milky Way. Let us think, for the next few pages, of your body as a demonstration of certain universal rules plucked from the realm of astronomical totality in self-responsive combination.

Revisiting the 4-Cycle: For Interactions

We would like to get a good look at who we are as bodies, so that we can have a better understanding of where our experiences are more likely to lead us in a world full of relationships with others. But first we need a basic evaluation system. In interpersonal psychology we have two basic factors at work: communion (getting along) and agency (getting ahead). These factors complement each other but don't typically overlap as measures because getting along is a measure of being *with* others or not while getting ahead is a measure of being *over* (or measured against) others or not. The result is a pair of xy axes which form a well-researched space in the field: the interpersonal circumplex.

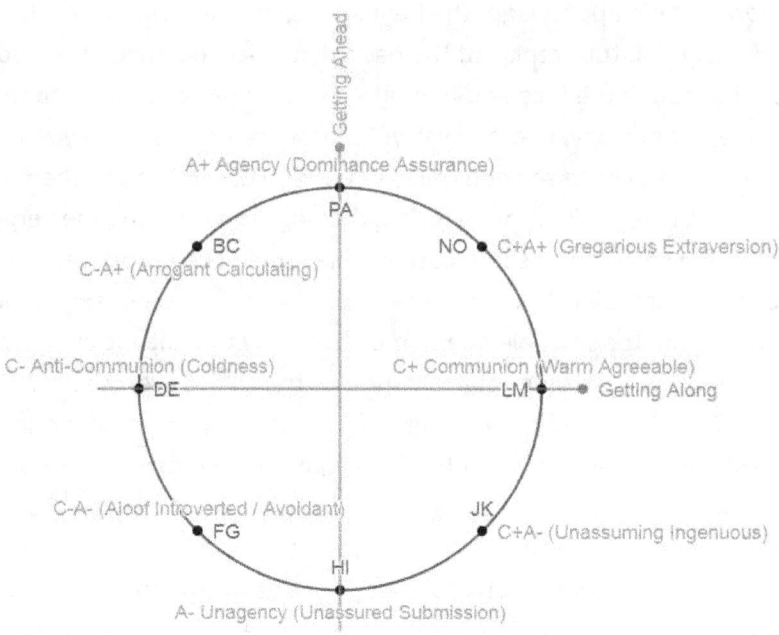

Figure 46-2: The Interpersonal Circumplex. (Adapted from Trapnell, P. D. & Wiggins, J. S. (1990). Extension of the Interpersonal adjective scales to include the Big Five dimension of personality. J. Personality and Soc. Psyc, 59: 781-790.)

☞ Question 46.1 (Head region): **Consider your overall effect on strangers. When people look at your face, which of the above regions (octants) are they most likely to treat you as? In other words, is a basic stranger likely to treat you like you're extraverted? Will they avoid you as if you are calculating? If you tend to get certain treatment from foreigners and different treatment from bosses, go ahead and note this. (example: Strangers → CD (I am seen as Cold-Calculating), Bosses→JK)**

_____
_____
_____
_____

☞ Question 46.2 (Torso region): **What kind of impression (which of the octants) do you think your overall appearance leaves on people you meet?**

_____
_____
_____

☞ Question 46.3 (Overall body plan): **Which of the octants do you think your body overall body design has best equipped you to reflect in the world? In order to answer this, think about your height, weight, sex, mannerisms, and the kinds of situations which seem to automatically fit you best. (For example, I'm on the shorter side of normal height, slim, serious looking, and tend to be magically pulled into** situations requiring analysis and no interference from others, so I'm designed for BC—arrogant calculating interactions—in general.)

_____
_____
_____

In addition to our relations with people, we also have relationships to situations. We can capture this in a similar kind of circumplex which measures something like communal versus agentic *emotional* processing.

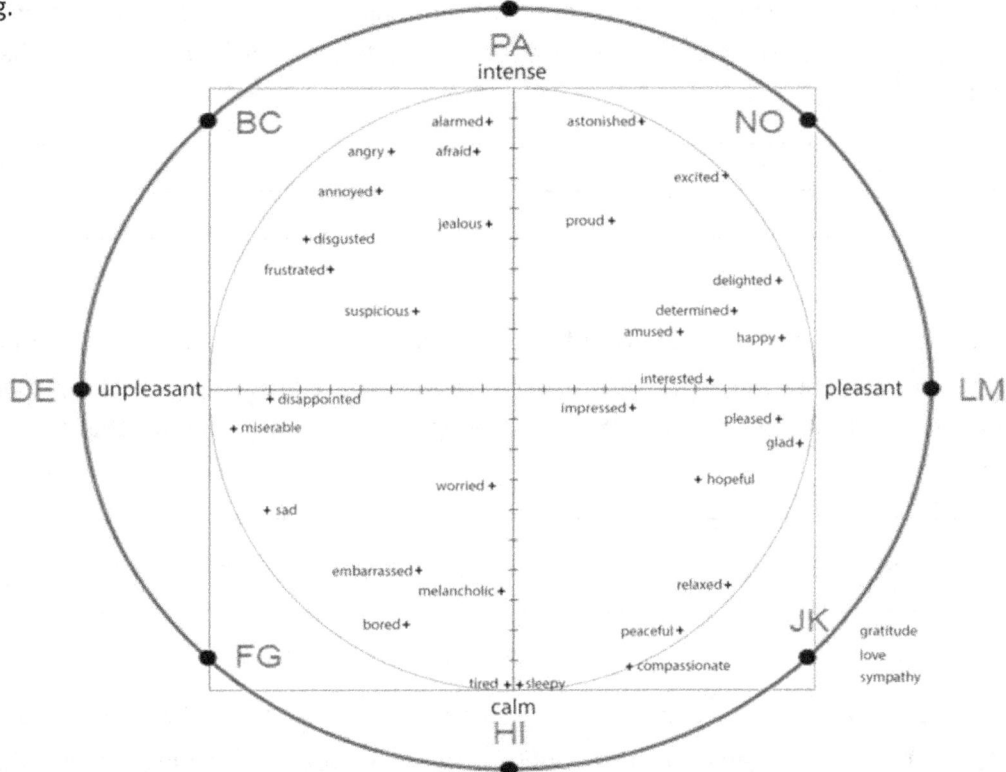

Figure 46-3: Circumplex Model of Emotion, based on [Russell, 1980] and [Paltoglou et al., 2013] An Experimental Study of Tactile Interactions in Long-distance Emotional Communication - Scientific Figure on ResearchGate. Available from: https://www.researchgate.net/figure/Circumplex-Model-of-Emotion-based-on-Russell-1980-and-Paltoglou-et-al-2013_fig1_282356518 [accessed 20 Jul, 2019]

☞ Question 46.4 (Surrounding information): **Of all the emotions in the above chart, which ones are you VERY good at maintaining via information around you? What octants are they located in?**

_____
_____
_____

☞ **Question 46.5 (How you display want):** When you want something a lot and aren't sure you can get it, what kinds of moods best describe you? What octants are they located in?

_____
_____
_____

☞ **Question 46.6 (Close friends):** Our friends help us experience feelings and events which would be more complicated to have if we tried them on our own. Ignoring the details of the kinds of things you do with your friends, what kinds of emotions do your closest friends generally help you feel? What octants are they located in?

_____
_____
_____

☞ **Question 46.7 (Co-influencers):** Consider the people you have either partnered with or joined forces with in order to create something. Averaging these kinds of relationships together, what emotions are your co-creative partners VERY good at bringing out of you? What octants are these emotions located in?

_____
_____
_____

☞ **Question 46.8 (Follow up influence question):** Refer back to Figure 46-2. When you are creating something for pure enjoyment, engaging in a hobby or otherwise doing something for fun, which of the circumplex octants best describe your mode for doing this? (If you like to be left alone you may be on the C- side of the chart. If you like to *do* something (versus *taking in or experiencing* something), you may be on the A+ portion of the chart (as opposed to A-).

_____
_____
_____

And now for some basic biology.

☞ **Question 46.9 (Your sex):** Fill in the blank with any of the emotions from Figure 46-3: "Being (male [or] female) makes it easy for me to be so _____."

In *S12* we discussed how tall and short heights help you stand out, normal height means people need to get to know you. Meanwhile big and small builds give people the impression they'll need to work harder in order to interface with you, normal builds don't appear to give this impression. We also described how men and women's traditionally trained circumplexes are 90° rotations of each other. In Figure 46-4 below, I've put together a very unscientific, stereotype-based chart for how Americans (in southern Texas at least) view heights. If you've been out in the real world long enough, you know that it's not as simple as "short people are weak, tall people are strong." A very tall male might be seen as a superstar while a very tall female might more likely be viewed as intimidating. There is a clear connection to stereotypes about males being judged more on the basis of dominance while women are judged more on agreeableness. The folklore where I live says that extreme tallness or shortness makes women less approachable, colder, or neurotic while average heights help make men not so hot or not so special. At least to an observer who hasn't met you at all. The folkloric assumptions are depicted accordingly.[10]

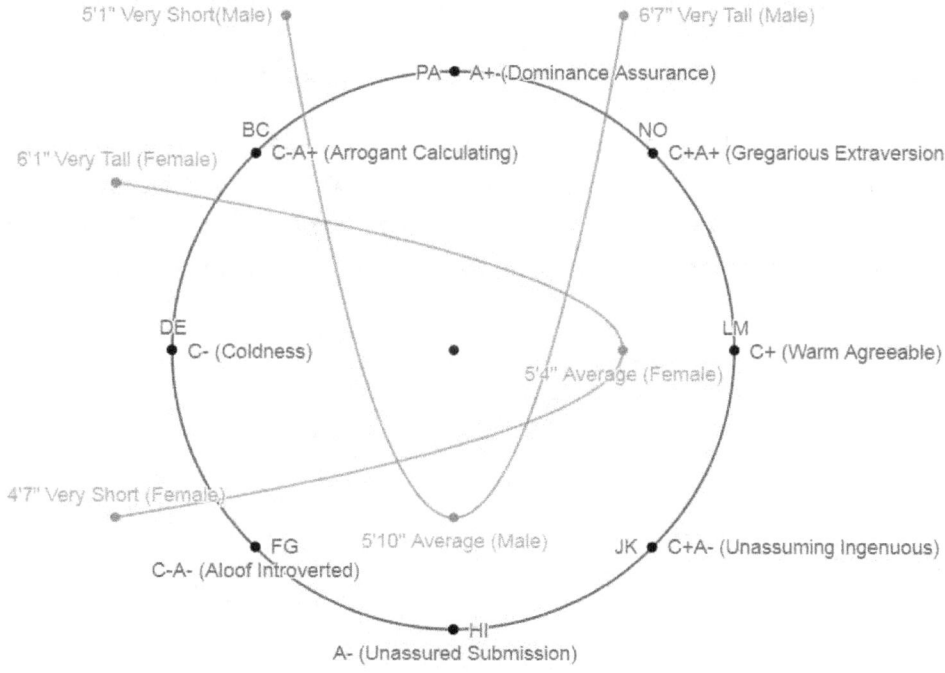

Figure 46-4: A rough depiction of height stereotypes, not based on any survey in particular. Use this chart only if you think it's reasonable to do so. I do.

☞ Question 46.10 (A rough height effect): **Using the mini chart below, draw an arrow from the center of the chart through the part of the graph where you roughly fall. (At 5'9" (male), my arrow would put me near FG.)**

---

[10] This is one of those areas where we would like to have an official scientific study. They do exist. But our daily training doesn't reference such things. Your intuition training should be grounded in what people actually experience at the time.

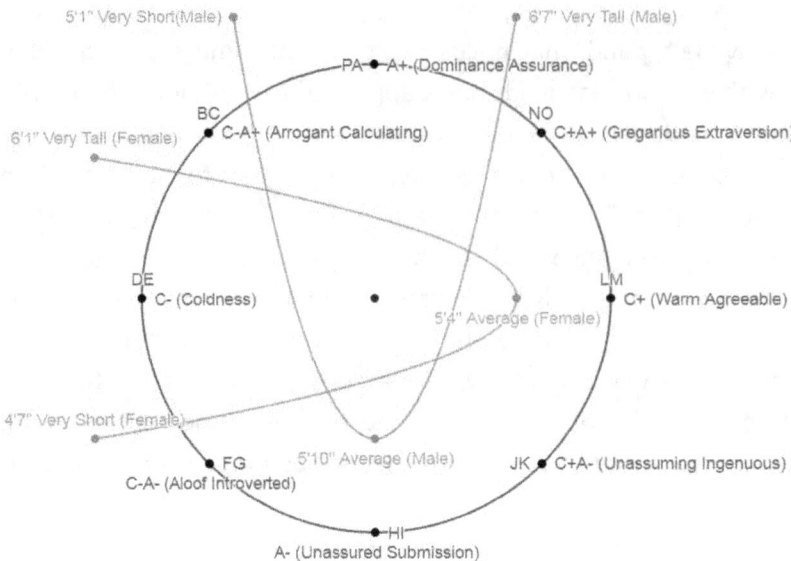

You can also use this graph to get some insight into the kinds of people you keep around you.

Slimness versus bigness helps other people calculate the energy demands needed to engage you. Again based on the local lore in from my current base in south Texas, weight has implications for how much input you prefer to receive from others. Unlike height though, there are at least five levels of size: average, big or thin yet average for one's group, and very big or very thin in general.

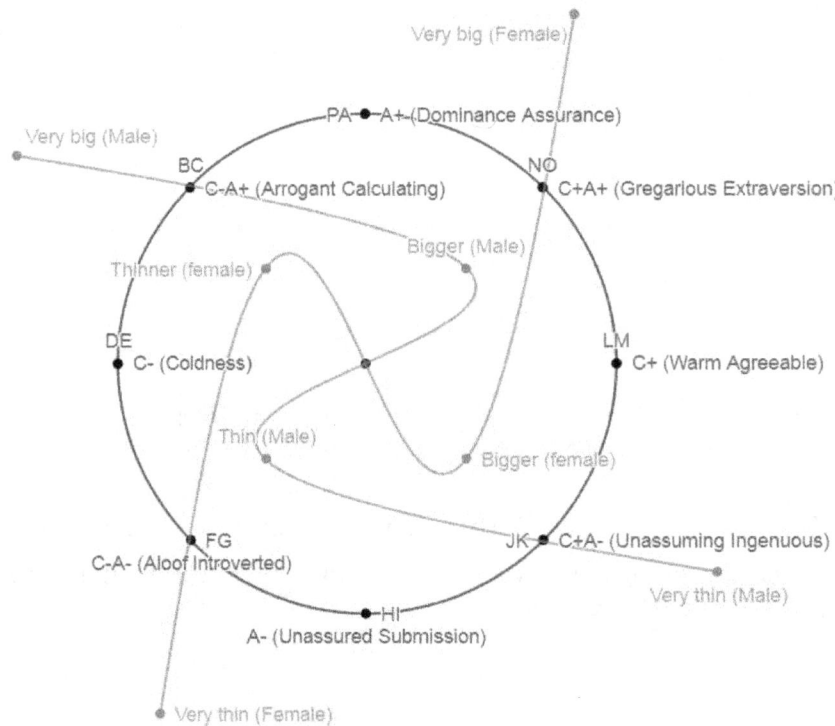

Figure 46-5: A rough depiction of body size stereotypes. There are no measurements here, since forms and sizes vary greatly, and are further confounded by height and social norms.

☞ Question 46.11 (A rough body size effect): **Using the mini chart below, draw an arrow from the center of the chart through the part of the graph where you roughly fall.** (I'm pretty thin, so my arrow put me near JK.)

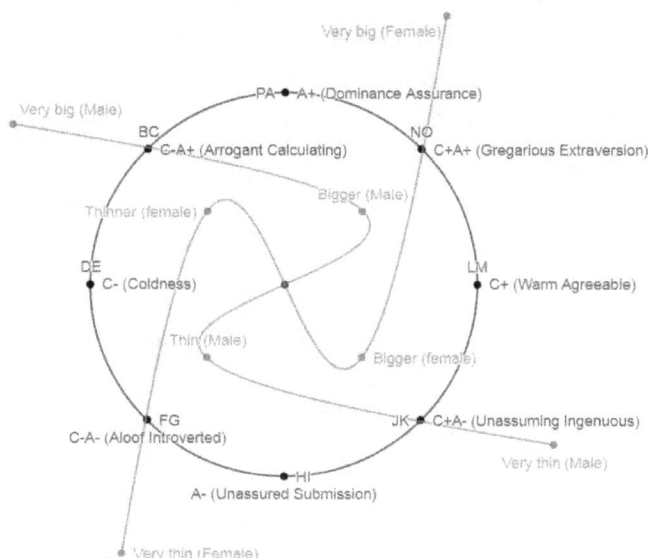

You may be thinking, "I'm not the way these charts suggest." But the above charts aren't actually about how you see yourself. Instead, I've found the stature charts (height and size—especially size) to be incredibly informative in explaining the kinds of relationship suitors you *attract*. Of course you won't stereotype yourself. But no one else will be so privy to your inner standards. If you think about what goes on in the mind of someone who's interested in you, much of their consideration revolves around the amount and kind of effort they think they'll need in order to handle you. Despite living pretty comfortably in BC, I've consistently attracted bigger girls all my life, and didn't have a reasonable explanation for why until I did the activity above; they will have assumed I was closer to FG through JK. You outward appearance is exactly that. Strangers typically won't know whether it reflects your inner world. Here's the same activity I did that may work for you:

☞ **Question 46.12 (Follow up):** If your answer to 46.11 clearly resulted in a specific octant, this is the announcement that your size makes to potential partners regarding the effort they can expect to put in to influence you. Submissive results will attract dominant partners and vice versa, though depending on whether you are male or female the approaching partner may hide this at various points in the chase in order to get in good standing with you. On the other hand, cold people can't attract someone who's so warm that the former are annoyed, but also not so dominant that the cold person's setup is compromised. They often attract people from BC, DE, or FG who see the world as they do or gregarious people who wish to break in and make the cold person better. Or they don't attract anyone because they really don't like people. Just groups, animals, or information. Do you see anything in your answer to 46.11 which explains who you attract?

_____

_____

_____

_____

I REMIND YOU THAT THESE ARE STEREOTYPES, not laws! Their only point is to tell you what the average stranger may think of you before they learn any other details about you.

Finally, we are going to treat race a little differently than I have in previous books. Although it is true that each racial profile represents a package of class evokers in the mind of the person viewing the race holder, race is good for more than just triggering other's assumptions about how you relate to who they relate to. It's also good for showing you the kinds of contexts you prefer for performing your own comfortable social role. We'll explore both sides of this topic below.

Where a country can be thought of as a collection of actors of a particular average character engaging each other and their unifying system using a particular mode, the character combined with the modes of the people in them can again be reduced to the dimensions of "getting along" and "getting ahead." Race and country are clearly not the same, but a very generic packaging of nationality classes will still be useful for capturing what we know to be obvious in the world: *You* may not care that your sweetheart is Pakistani or gay or anarchist, but your broadly generic social world usually will. They may not actually disapprove of your straying from the path, but they often take longer before they accept your choice as a legitimate one. Like sitting in that funny chair at that place. It was novel, but it wasn't normal. Let us take some time to attach you to your stereotyped class so that you may better understand those situations when you *are* that funny chair in the minds of your interactants' friends.

For group class values we'll use a mutation of the Schwartz (1994) values model and the Ronen & Shenkar (2013) Language, Geography, Religion cluster.

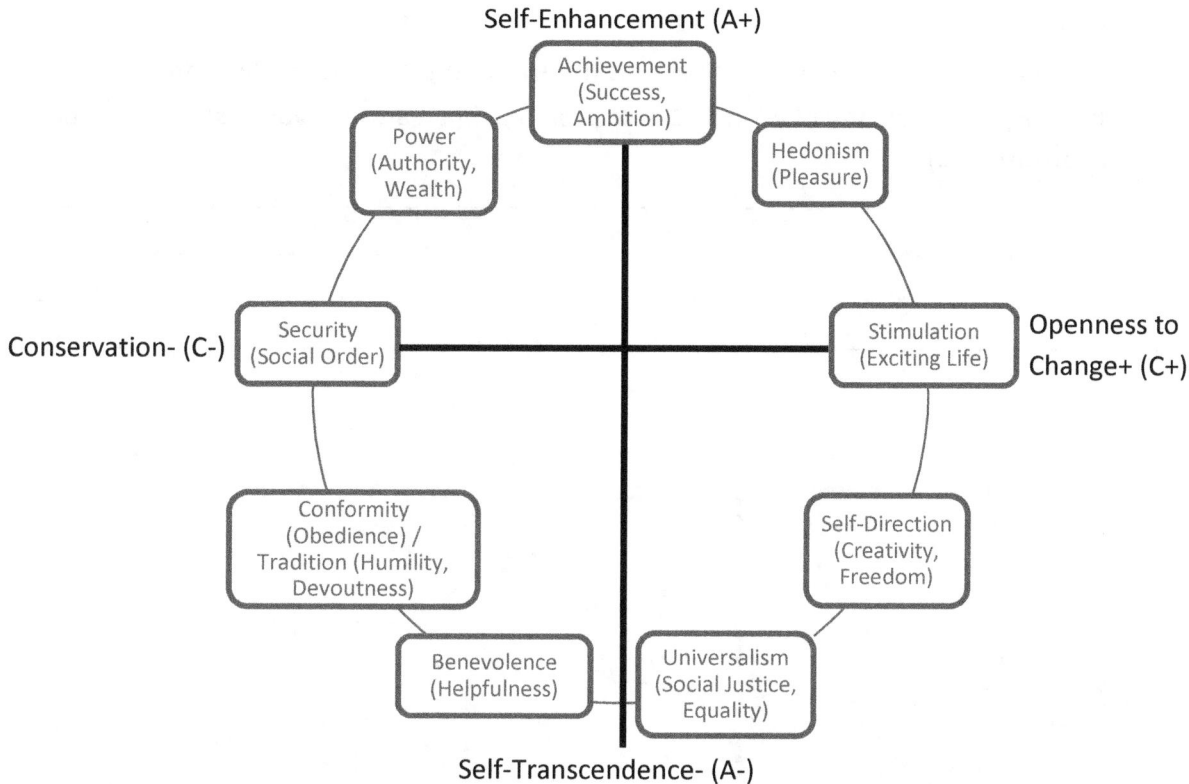

Figure 46-6: A circumplex of human values, adapted from Schwartz (1994). From Schwartz, Shalom H. (1994). Are there universal aspects in the structure and contents of human values? Journal of Social Issues, 50: 19–45; ———. (2012). An overview of the Schwartz theory of basic values. Online Readings in Psychology and Culture, 2(1). http://dx.doi.org/10.9707/2307-0919.1116

From all over the world, the Schwartz values reveal the familiar axes of getting along and getting ahead. With the events one is handed, that is. Actually, we could set any rotation of spaces like the above as our axes, but abstract events suit us nicely when talking about a human's interface with the world.

☞ Question 46.13 (A universal value): **Of all the values listed in Figure 46-6, which one would you easily dedicate your life towards? What octant is it? (You can use A-, C+A-, or C-A- for Benevolence or Universalism if either one applies to you.)**

_____
_____
_____

☞ Question 46.14 (Important follow up): **Having started on whatever path you chose in 46.13, what kinds of people, in your experience, seem to bring out your best in processes like this?**

_____
_____
_____

☞ **Question 46.15 (Important follow up 2, abstract):** Is there any aspect of your body or dress that would indicate that the people you described in 46.14 are preferred? (a feature of yours, something you wear, a behavior you display…)

_____

_____

_____

_____

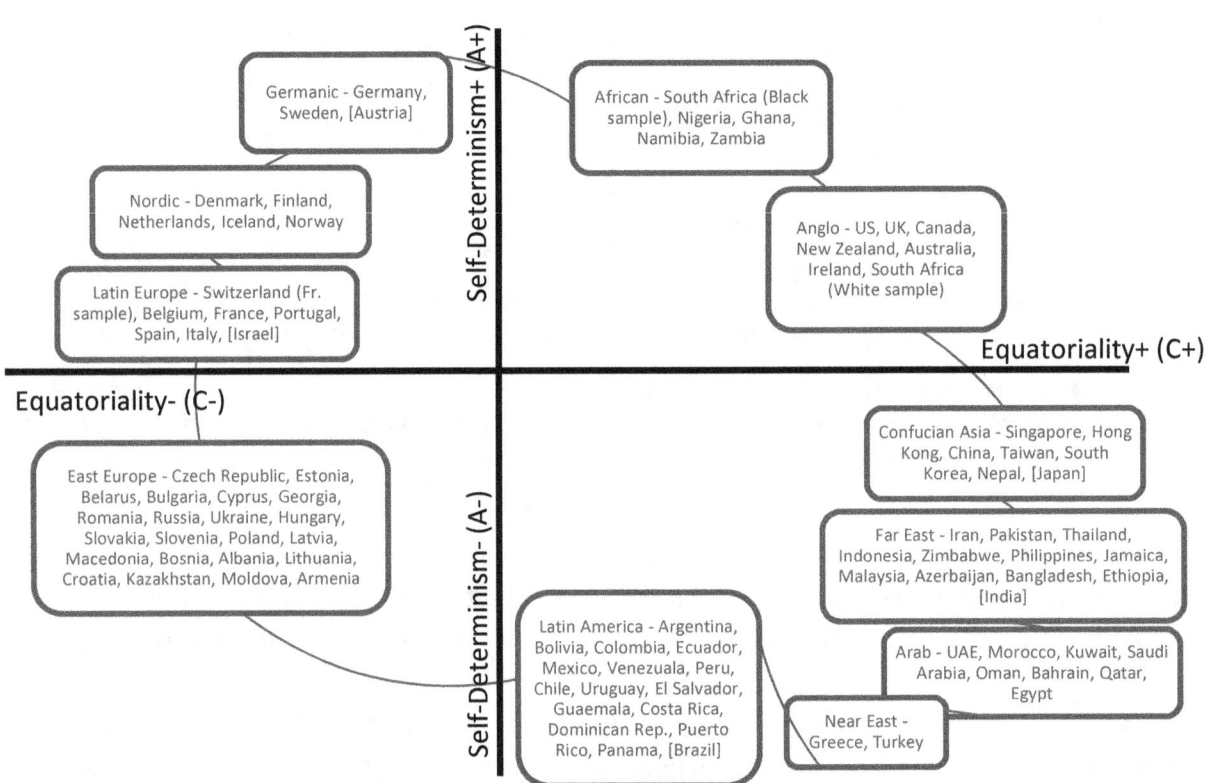

Figure 46-7: Ronen & Shenkar (2013) country clusters, organized along two axes. Ronen, S., & Shenkar, O. (2013). Mapping world cultures: Cluster formation, sources, and implications. Journal of International Business Studies, 44(9), 867-897. Retrieved from http://www.jstor.org/stable/43653701

While research has been found that countries may cluster on geography, language, and religion, language and religion are both byproducts of community assembly patterns which in turn follow from migration upon geography. We see how countries can be split into [near equatorial/temperate versus away from equatorial] as well as [general individualistic values versus collectivistic values]. I've called these "equatoriality" versus "self-determinism." [My conjecture, part 1:] Equatorial regions have generally more people in them for the obvious reason: they are easier to live in for evolved human bodies. I believe that they have less incentive to strategically direct their societies towards a coherent goal and more incentive to develop the broad social rules for handling more and more and more people under one space OR more foreigner's attempts to pass through their land. They are thus more communal—but often in a negative way: they are more likely to get caught up in long term forms of colonialism (as the victim or the perpetrator), more likely to be intrusively active in international politics, and for their citizens, more likely inject the will of the collective into the individual's life, even if the individual is simultaneously encouraged to make his own life. Less equatorial countries are less likely to do this unless there is a coherent goal to be achieved. Otherwise, everyone goes back inside because it's just too damned cold for that.[11]

[My conjecture, part 2]: As for the axis of self-determinism, more northward countries are more likely to hold the general value, "Do for yourself. Who cares what other people think?" More southward countries are more likely to say to their citizens, "KNOW THIS. What others think DEFINITELY matters. Here is a belief system which says so." Whether via religion, tradition, or a political ideal, citizens in more southward positions are more heavily enculturated into submissiveness to a greater authority. More northward cultures aren't so enthusiastic about that. Why? Perhaps because, in order to migrate northward out of Africa then southward again, your group has to have some sort of imperative that drives it past the new climate, back through the old, to the ends of the walkable land (for pre-colonial groups in Oceania and South America, that is. Imperialism adds a separate chapter to this.) Here, it's all about staying together, not so much about settling on the land itself.

Race, though visual in nature, is also about the legacies which have brought people of a certain appearance where they are today. Rather than looking at ourselves as merely black or merely white, the new times of more egalitarian views of such things allow us to truly choose who we (at least think we) identify with.

☞ Question 46.16 (Your [Foreign Worlds] heritage): **Given what you know about yourself and any cultures you have preferred to learn from** *combined with your physical appearance*, **which of the countries above best describe you? What octants are they in? (You can use combinations like C+A-)**

_____

_____

_____

Only answer the following questions if you feel you have actually been successful in doing what you indicated in 46.13. These next few questions are actually some of the most important in the chapter, but if you're one of those people who believes they have never really been successful at their highest goal, you either won't be able to answer or your answers will consistently end with "...I guess." Not to discourage you from attempting these questions if that's how it is, but SEE HERE: being down on your own experiences won't help you develop your talents any faster. Just claim some successes and get this started.

---

[11] Warm people make trouble. Cold people don't bother. Or if they do bother, it has nothing to do with what *you* want.

☞ **Question 46.17 (Your supporters):** Think about <u>at least four</u> people who helped enable your success with 46.13. If you can't list four, then skip this question. (You need to be able to calculate a decent average, not just go with the latest person.) List them here if you can. Are there any traits in from figures 46-2 through 46-7 which these people had in common with each other? What were those traits?

	Example
	My 46.13 was Security (Social Order)
	People who supported this were: JB, CC, MH, FL, RI, AE, CS, MH
	Common trait they had: Figure 46-2, OP (Assured-Extraverted); Figure 46-3, Determined; Figure 46-6, A- (Benevolence); All women

☞ **Question 46.18 (Your supporters 2):** For each of the traits you listed in 46.17, is there any practice you know of from figures 46-2 or 46-6, which you perform, which brings this trait out of others?

	Example
	Figure 46-2, OP (Assured-Extraverted): my answering a request for help (F46-6 Benevolence)
	Figure 46-3, Determined: making a basic choice to keep communicating with them after any task is finished (F46-2 KL Warm-Unassuming)
	Figure 46-6, A- (Benevolence): After I've decided to keep communication going with them, (F46-2 NO Extraversion + F46-6 Universalism towards the world alongside them brings out their benevolence)
	All women: my F46-2 Arrogant-Calculating (BC) is very high around men, ensuring that the chances of my working with them in the long run is lower.

Chapter 46: The Embodiment

☞ **Question 46.19 (Focused areas, Abstract): Figure 46-2 is associated with the head and face while, Figure 46-7 is associated with stature (height, size), and the overall body plan. Is there anything about these features of yours which suggest that your answers in 46.18 should be areas that you focus on?** (This one requires a lot of thought. Definitely take a look at my example if you need help with it.)

	Example
	My supporters' F46-2, OP ← my own F46-6 benevolence (A-) suggests that I should, when reasonable, answer requests for help. Where my F46-4, 5 /stature is concerned, being near average height and thin both put me in the bottom/submissive half of the circle, attracting others with a need to dominate. Invariably, if I can stand them long enough, these people promote me. Interestingly, though dominance is celebrated in my society, my sex, and my home culture, it never really helps for *me* to use it in this chapter or in my life in general. Here it's more of the same. Their F46-3, Determined (MN) ← my F46-2 Warmth (LM). This one is easy. It helps whenever I pick determined people as ongoing "getting along" partners. The comfort should show *in a more relaxed resting face* (which strangers aren't given) People who aren't that may still be okay, but I shouldn't expect them to advance my dedicated goal. Their F46-6 benevolence (A- ish/H) ← my F46-2 Extraversion (NO) + F46-6 Universalism (A- ish/I) towards the world. My F46.1 arms and chest (part of the head region aren't usually covered in formal dress, so here being casual, physically confident, and perhaps even disheveled, probably tells people that I'm out there anyway, and they could approach without being embarrassed. My F46-4, 5 stature again includes average height and thinness—more the thinness this time— which puts me not just at the bottom of the circle, but to the right. All women ← my F46-2 Arrogant-Calculating (BC). I have thin, veiny arms as an indicator that I keep certain kinds of influences out automatically. Also, maleness and American blackness promotes the image of assertiveness or aggressiveness, where the aim is to get ahead of my equals, not get along. The body appearance of one who would fight aggressively and be provoked easily. It is true? Yes. So much so that I've found life to be A LOT smoother if I avoid such battles altogether. Despite all of the spiritual practice, I'm still a male and still reason things out from self→world. If some other male attempts to assert his world→my self, it doesn't work, hence the *off-putting 46-2 resting face* as well. There are many attributes I have that suggest people keep away unless they are there for a very specific purpose. (How's that for self-diagnosis?)

Who knew that traits you have which you thought were negative were actually your way of attracting the path you valued most?

We've assembled everything. Time to put together the full embodiment.

Critical Exercise (Part 1 of 2)

BODY WHEELS

Trains: Clairvoyance, Telepathy, Projection (All involve body awareness)

Your task is to complete the instrument below, which we'll call "The (Body) Wheels." You'll be entering many of your answers from throughout the chapter, so make you've completed those before beginning.

Below are some basic instructions for the instrument.

- Your external appearance: Input the appropriate circumplex octant in Column (A) which answers the item in the column before it (a).

- Your internal state: If you have any health issues or special conditions associated with column (b), give a brief description in column (B)

- Taking both columns (A and B) into consideration, describe this aspect of yourself in column (C). This won't necessarily be a physical description, but an interactional one. That is the whole point of this instrument. **Special note: if you find that the internal and the external say very different things, your description should include your interpretation of this difference. If you need an example of this survey, mine is in Appendix II.

- If there is anything about the facet which you would change, give a brief description in column (D).

Body Wheels

head to toe, the questions for each region are below:

Sign	Region	Question Number	Map
	face, head	46.1	Question 46.1 (Head region): Consider your overall effect on strangers. When people look at your face, which of the above regions (octants) are most likely to treat you as? In other words, is a basic stranger likely to treat you like you're extraverted? Will they avoid you as if you are calc you tend to get certain treatment from foreigners and different treatment from bosses, go ahead and note this.
	neck (throat)	46.2	Question 46.2 (Torso region): What kind of impression (which of the octants) do you think your overall appearance leaves on people you meet?
	arms	46.3	Question 46.3 (Overall body plan): Which of the octants do you think your body overall body design has best equipped you to reflect in the world? In order to answer this, think about your height, weight, sex, mannerisms, and the kinds of situations which seem to automatically fit you best.
	upper chest	46.5	Question 46.5 (How you display want): When you want something a lot and aren't sure you can get it, what kinds of moods best describe you? What octants are they located in?
	beneath the chest, heart	46.8	Question 46.8 (Follow up influence question): When you are creating something for pure enjoyment, engaging in a hobby or otherwise doing something for fun, which of the circumplex octants best describe your mode for doing this?
	umbilical region	46.18	Question 46.18 (Your supporters): For each of the traits you listed in 46.17, is there any practice you know of from figures 46-2 or 46-6, which you perform, which brings this trait out of others?
	(love handles)	46.6	Question 46.6 (Close friends): Ignoring the details of the kinds of things you do with your friends, what kinds of emotions do your closest friends generally help you feel? What octants are they located in?
	reproductive organs	46.7	Question 46.7 (Co-influencers): Consider the people you have either partnered with or joined forces with in order to create something. Aver kinds of relationships together, what emotions are your co-creative partners VERY good at bringing out of you? What octants are these emot in?
	gluteals and thighs	46.16	Question 46.16 (Your [Foreign Worlds] heritage): Given what you know about yourself and any cultures you have preferred to learn from cor your physical appearance, which of the countries in Figure 46-6 best describe you? What octants are they in? (You can use combinations like
	knees to lower legs	46.10, 46.11	Question 46.10: What octant did you fall in for your height? Question 46.11: What octant did you fall in for your body size?
	lower legs to ankles	46.4	Question 46.4 (Surrounding Information): Of all the emotions in Figure 46-3, which ones are you VERY good at maintaining via information ar What octants are they located in?
	feet	46.13	Question 46.13: Of all the values listed in Figure 46-6, which one would you easily dedicate your life towards? What octant is it?

External Region	Map	Question Number	Your Octant Answer(s)	Internal System	Any health issues or special notes about columns y or b?	Your description of this sign level	Is there anything you would cha about this a, b, or this sign level general?
y	z	a	A	b	B	C	D
face, head		46.1		the face, **muscular system**			
neck (throat)		46.2		the **upper digestive system**,			
arms		46.3		mannerisms, the **respiratory system**			
upper chest		46.5		**endocrine system (hormones)**,			
beneath the chest, heart		46.8		**circulatory system**			
umbilical region		46.18		reasoning, the **lower digestive system**			
(love handles)		46.6		voluntary com. **lymph urinary /excretory sys**			
reproductive organs		46.7		output of the **urinary/excretory, reproductive**			
gluteals and thighs		46.16		**(hair skin & nails)**, outward appearance			
knees to lower legs		46.10, 46.11		**skeletal system**, the general body plan, body size			
lower legs to ankles		46.4		the social structure and **nervous system**			
feet		46.13		memory, **senses brain, central nerv system**			

or not, that was the easy part. But we don't yet have an embodiment that you can easily remember. Just a list. Onwards to part 2.

Critical Exercise (Part 2 of 2)
FLOW OF THE BODY TYPE

Trains: Essential knowledge, Projection, Life path

There is a natural flow of reasoning which you will follow in processing your world. Using the astrological model, that flow goes like this:

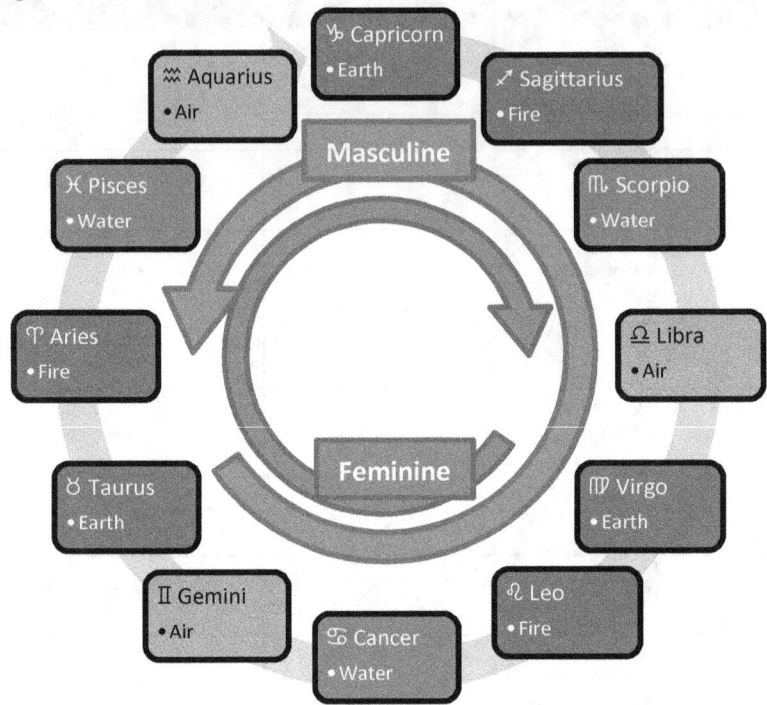

When you are inside of a realm with a particular element, the next version of that same element will be dictated by your reasoning pattern. As a broad framework, we'll just say that a masculine pattern projects its will onto others in order for them to project onto his world. He them allows himself to be judged by that world. A feminine pattern begins as the domain onto which impressions project, and projects back the next phase of what was projected. By these cycles, typically trained women would be predisposed dedicate more of themselves to elaborating events into realities while typically trained men would be predisposed to projecting their habits into places whose reality has not yet taken form. Our bodies bear this out. This doesn't mean that men are simpleminded or that women can't lead in ambiguity, just that men's thoughts are as rich as the others they choose to surround themselves with while women's influence is as potent as the environments they choose to shape. The most notable difference between the masculine polarity and the feminine (not actual "males" versus "females"), is that one hits the world and is ready to self-declare (Saj-Pis ʊ Ari-Can), while the other begins as a world then co-shapes the meaning of an Other (Saj-Pis) ʊ (Leo-Sco).

You have your Body Wheels, but you don't have a summary of it. If you are male or identify as masculine, your ordering for the next exercise will be counterclockwise in the above diagram. If you are female or feminine, it will be clockwise. So if a section calls for Fire 1, Fire 2, Fire 3 for example,

- a masculine-type can pick Aries, Leo, Sagittarius; Leo, Sagittarius, Aries; or Sagittarius, Aries, Leo.
- A feminine-type on the other hand would pick from Aries, Sagittarius, Leo; Sagittarius, Leo, Aries; or Leo, Aries, Sagittarius.

Use the table below or a separate sheet of paper to summarize your four levels of embodiment: your purpose (water), identity (earth), communication forms (air), and projection (fire).

1. Within each level, pick any starting point from the element listed, write it in the **Chosen Sign** column and follow your cycle from there. If, for example you want to start with Scorpio as your Water 1, you'll write that in the Chosen Sign column. Your Water 2 would automatically be Pisces if you're male or masculine, Cancer if you're female or feminine.

2. In the first **Embodiment** column, write your description of the body region, behavior, or organ system which describes that level. If your Water 1 were Scorpio and you noted a reproductive issue in your wheels, you would enter this in the Embodiment column. Your aim is to have every region of your body or its organ system equivalent appear in this column at least once.

3. In the **Summary** column, give your summary of that level based on columns B, C, and D from the Wheels questions you just completed. If Scorpio were your Water 1 and you determined that you faced obstacles as an influencer—hence the reproductive issue—you would note this summary of your Wheel's B, C, D in this column.

4. Each cycle also has an element from some other group. Pick *any* one of your three signs of that element and do the same as above: Give a description of the body quality that describes you in the Embodiment column; Put a summary based on columns B, C, and D into the Summary column. For the Purpose section, just pick any air description from your Wheels and fill in the relevant information.

5. Whenever you finish a section, make sure that section's [Element 3] or last element loops back to your [Element 1]. So if your Water 1 were Scorpio with an influencer issue and your Water 3 were Pisces with a creative talent, you would need to make sure that your Summary column connects these two ideas.

6. At the end of the table, pick any sign from each element and give a final summary of it in the Recap section. <u>Avoid using specific forms for things</u>. (For example, instead of using the word "men" use the word "asserters." Instead of using "businesses" use "institutions." In place of "money" use "value" if you can. Your aim is to capture broad patterns the way a giant alien would if all he saw in you was a collection of particles.

7. Once everything is completed, take the Summary column of your recap responses and give a second, single-phrase recap of them in the blank marked "Recap 2."

This exercise will only be difficult if you haven't spent enough time answering the questions leading up to it throughout this chapter, or if you're just in a hurry to get it done. I did the exercise for the first time while writing this chapter, and found my Recap 2 to be the best description of the life I now lead that I've ever gotten from anywhere. You are calculating what your physical form is a manifestation of in terms of dynamics with everything else. If you want to know your path in life, this exercise will help considerably. For further developing your intuition and clearing out the extraneous inputs, you'll also need to have a sense of what your natural role in this life is as a plain old physical being—funneled to and fro by genetics and those who perceive you.

This can be an invaluable activity, but if you haven't really done the questions before it, it may be little more than a chore. For an example of a completed one, see mine in Appendix II.

Your Summary

Topic	Element	Chosen Sign	Embodiment	Summary
Purpose	Water 1			
	Air			
	Water 2			
	Water 3			
Identity	Water			
	Earth 1			
	Earth 2			
	Earth 3			
Forms of Communication	Air 1			
	Air 2			
	Air 3			
	Fire			
Projection	Fire 1			
	Fire 2			
	Fire 3			
	Earth			
Recap	Water			
	Air			
	Earth			
	Fire			

Recap 2: _____

...is a blank one in case you want to use this again on someone else. They can do the recap on their own paper.

External Region	Map	Question Number	Your Octant Answer(s)	Internal System	Any health issues or special notes about columns y or b?	Your description of this sign level	Is there anything you would change about this a, b, or this sign level general?
y	z	a	A	b	B	C	D
face, head		46.1		the face, **muscular system**			
neck (throat)		46.2		the **upper digestive system**,			
arms		46.3		mannerisms, the **respiratory system**			
upper chest		46.5		**endocrine system (hormones)**,			
beneath the chest, heart		46.8		**circulatory system**			
umbilical region		46.18		reasoning, the **lower digestive system**			
(love handles)		46.6		voluntary com. **lymph urinary /excretory sys**			
reproductive organs		46.7		output of the **urinary/excretory, reproductive**			
gluteals and thighs		46.16		(hair skin & nails), outward appearance			
knees to lower legs		46.10, 46.11		**skeletal system**, the general body plan, body size			
lower legs to ankles		46.4		the social structure and **nervous system**			
feet		46.13		memory, **senses brain, central nerv system**			

Controlling Your Inputs

You now know what you yourself embody. More importantly, you know how we arrived at such an embodiment. On this second point, perhaps you can see how anything you interact with can be thought of as the embodiment of something to you based on the kind of behavior it draws out of you. Pets, friends, vehicles, and even intangible things like assignments and significant dates may possess a reliable, self-reinforcing character in your eyes. For example, the computer I'm typing this on right now consistently brings out the top of my game in data exploration. It embodies the analytical skill I use for serving others.

We will return to the idea of embodiments in The Nickname.

If you are reasonably comfortable applying your unique traits to your unique cause, knowing your embodiment can help you take the filtering process a major step further. I learned from the exercise that I'm far less successful with individuals than I am with groups, and that the story I told myself all these years whenever I would complain about someone really was true: "I didn't need all that friction." But dwelling on the friction was my fault, not theirs. Your embodiment informs not only how you approach certain events, but *what* you're best designed to approach and with whom you can expect to approach it. And even though we may seem to have strayed far into the realm of the esoteric, all of this is rooted in the basic assumption that you are a patterned collection of waves which your genes, environment, and your own self-monitoring continually work together to sustain. As a living being, your goal is to stay the same in how you respond to your world. In order to keep that response pattern (your life) stable, you only create intentional differences in those aspects of that world you perceive. Your body is the lens, though. We can learn much about the entire space of your experiential mechanics by studying it.

Conclusion

Our society, bless its heart, attempts to flood us with every idea that someone somewhere thinks is worth selling. This holds for identity expectations and your personal aspirations just as easily as it does for products. Use your embodiment to align with what really matters. If you have health issues, use your embodiment to see what the issues themselves are intended to draw out of you. Though the end goal for this book may be to develop your intuition, it is as important to know *which* sources you are best tuned to read as it is knowing *how* to read. A man who uses his doctoral vocabulary to read things that make him angry does himself no service. An intuitive who lets her gift for empathy invite everyone else's pain may need to correct this sooner or later. It is taxing to embody all things to all people, even if you can come near this. Use this chapter to get clarity in your role as a human form. Leave the other roles to the things you resonate with.

Chapter 47. The Resonance

When you see two things that look like each other some distance apart, what's happening?

- First, your attention to the pattern they present is immediately amplified. It's the shared pattern, not the things themselves, which form the basis of the similarity.

- Second, your framework for how they are arranged is passively updated. In order for the two things to be considered distinct to begin with, there must be some kind of separation between them—spatial, temporal, vibrational or otherwise. That separation also registers its character with you, though you may not notice it until one day the context is all weird.

Resonance lies at the heart of form. Objects are made up of molecules in resonant bonds and electron sharing. Songs are made up of resonant sound motifs by the instrument, singer, or lyrics themselves. Friendships are considered formed things where the people in them share some kind of defining activity that holds them favorably together. Resonance is about much more than waves of a related frequency; more generally, it's about distinct things producing a common effect on still another thing. Through resonance we can identify the aggregate form built up from even single events which apparently begin without form—as any data stream. Accordingly, we'll need a good understanding of this phenomenon if we are to develop our talent for perceiving the formerly imperceptible.

Have I ever told you about how I developed premonitory dreams? To make a long story short, I had some dreams, found them interesting enough to log, then a year later noticed life events which seemed to mirror those dreams in the same order, with the same emotional feel, the same distance apart from each other, with similar perceptual consequences between the dream and the later event. That was it. Here the resonant pattern was my psychological experience common to both events, the resonant items were the dream and the waking event, and the separation was time-based.

As people, we resonate with the things that reinforce our identities. Certain relationship building patterns, favorite foods which our bodies like (nutrient/energy combinations), favorite songs (frequency combinations) and the types of situations that bring out our unusual sides (internal processing patterns)—these are all resonant items (alongside some aspect of us as the other item) for which the pattern is our resulting response. Said another way,

$$\underbrace{\text{We} + \text{That Thing}}_{\text{resonant items}} \underbrace{(\text{separated from us by space, time, form, or channel})}_{\text{dimension}} = \underbrace{\text{Our Regular Reaction}}_{\text{resonant pattern}}$$

- The more pronounced the reaction,
- the more skilled we are in the various arrangements between ourselves and that thing,
- the more comfortable we are with the dimension where the separation of items occurs,

the stronger our resonance with it.

Two tuning forks humming at the same frequency, separated from each other in space, give us a particular note. The forks are the items, space is the dimension, the note is the pattern, and most of us are pretty good at detecting this kind of resonance to the extent that we can hear. The forks have strong resonance with each other to the extent that they can, across space, reinforce their own humming given the pattern of the other. That's the key:

Perceiving the pattern between two distinct things is not enough. You need to develop a regular, predictable response to that pattern in order to say that you resonate with it.

As you probably noticed in the previous chapter, certain themes in our lives are repetitive. We keep attracting them and having the same responses to them, even if they are negative. But a negative response to a thing we resonate with isn't the fault of the thing. It's our pattern too. Instead, it's our processing of the pattern that causes the trouble. I begrudgingly resonated with critical minds for a long time until I met some people who used their sharp minds to delineate paths for others. Now I still resonate with critical minds, but not so begrudgingly. The pattern never changed. What I did with it changed.

In this chapter we're going to find out what phenomena you are extra sensitive to—those where you have the ability to detect the slightest change and, by extension, those whose contexts you can become an easy expert in. You'll need to break out your list of upsetting things, however, since a thing that can automatically get your goat is the main kind of thing whose tune you were made to make music with. We won't worry about making *good* music in this chapter, just loud music. Let's start with our first activity.

☞ Question 47.1 (The tuning list): List EVERYTHING YOU CAN THINK OF which is *guaranteed* to get a reaction from you, whether positive or negative. (I've found that when I ask people to do this activity, they hesitate because they are so used to bottling many of these things. Don't worry. No one is judging you. Take a look at the kinds of things that made my list if you need to, then cover it up and do your own.) List the things that trigger you not just "most" of the time. *All of the time.* **GUARANTEED** to get a reaction from you, I say.

	Example
_____	injustice upon others I care about, where I can give or receive genuine forgiveness, other's deep heartbreak, genuine displays of devotion, dark purple (50, 30, 90), impressive campaigns by TCM and other semi-closed artistic cultures, being asked to speak in public, being promoted or honored with a new responsibility, when others have my back unexpectedly, completing a theory, getting the idea for a new theory, when my bosses or business partners do something badassed, 10am coffee at work (the theory flood), 4th wave (transhuman-futurist) feminism, great service to the point where I don't have to worry about being black, opportunities for honest conversation, being surprised by cold weather, patronizing judgment, robber baron capitalism (especially real estate related), new Knime or Excel tricks, openly sexual women, awesome data sets, vodka and philosophy, people who surprise me with acts to take care of me, people who let me voluntarily take care of them, unreliability from others who asked for my help, really well thought out and original creative works, female voices in meditation or epic orchestral j-pop, male assertion, quality time with anyone who's not a stranger and who wants to be there; man-disrespecting 3rd wave feminism

☞ **Question 47.2 (The unattuned list):** List anything which other people might consider important—or think that *you* would consider important—but doesn't actually get much of a reaction from you.

	Example
_____	money, politics or political issues, family stuff, awards, academia, praise, high lifestyle, the American black box, health stuff, common job-related topics, the dating scene, web stuff, international events, astrology, tarot, general spirituality and healing, other predictive occult, male-isms (a.k.a. macho stuff), the womanist or more commonly stereotypical brand of feminism (biology/voice-based)
_____	
_____	
_____	
_____	
_____	
_____	
_____	
_____	
_____	
_____	

Now your list, like mine, may surprise you. For example, I identify as male, a feminist, a statistical astrologer, and an academic, but don't resonate with these areas much beyond special exception. In astrology we'd refer to these as "square" relationships, and they are the same as the imaginary axis in real-imaginary (potential) space. If you don't connect with something you're also heavily involved in, it may indicate that your perspective on that thing is, for the most part, unique to you. Does this make sense? You may be involved with these things, but not involved with most others' way of approaching these things. If you answered Question 47.2 above but were hesitant to list something as irresonant because you thought that contradicted something you expected of yourself, *go back and put it in there*. Combined with your answers from 47.1, items like these are areas where you may truly be called to make your own path away from the society that trained you. I call this straying from home "Nephele," after the astrology asteroid #431 which captures it so well.

While we're on interesting side roads, you may wonder what *guaranteed* resonance with a color, symbol, or word may mean. These are generalized commonality flags. Whenever I see someone wearing my favorite dark purple or see it come up as the main color on something, I am reminded that it is possible for others to share parts of my identity. Here you're open to support for your own personal expression which is sponsored by a user other than yourself, and these kinds of serendipitous appearances of your own foundations help draw your attention to the situations where others share your visual, auditory, or other kinds of decision making.

☞ Question 47.3 (Chords): **In the absence of formal statistics, were going to produce a homegrown correlation. Take your list from 47.1 and rearrange it. Put all the topics which are related to each other in the same column, and arrange them from most favorable down to most negative. Do this for each different kind of topic that arises. Leave enough space between your columns to fit two more small columns for holding numbers in.**

_____
_____
_____
_____
_____
_____
_____
_____
_____
_____
_____
_____

☞ Question 47.4 (Name the column): **Give each of your columns a name which summarizes the category of items they hold.**

☞ Question 47.5 (Reaction direction): **On a scale of -1.0...1.0, in the column before the two columns before the one with your answers (that is, skip two columns before), rate how positively or how negatively that item makes you react. ([Injustice upon others I care about] dropped my mood 90%, so I put "-.9" two columns before it.) Do this for each item in your answer to 47.3.**

☞ Question 47.6 (Reaction intensity): **On a scale of 0 to 5, skipping one column before your answers to 47.3, rate how intensely (5) to how lowly (0) you are inclined to react to the item.**

Chapter 47: The Resonance

☞ **Question 47.7 (Reaction sense modality):** On a scale of 0 to 5, in the column right before the one with your answers, put one of the following letters to indicate which of your senses is involved in experiencing the event: (V) visual, (A) auditory, (T) touch, (S) taste or smell, (F) internal pain or comfort change or (C) Cognition or thought. My example of all of this is below.

r	I	S	Communicative mastery	r	I	S	Having one's best efforts accepted	r	I	S	Acceptance without having to script it
.9	0	A	completing a theory	.7	0	F	being promoted or honored	.8	3	F	surprise acts to take care of me
.8	0	A	female voices in meditation	.4	1	F	giving or receiving forgiveness	.7	2	A	opportunities for honest conversation
.8	4	A	female voices in epic j-pop	.3	2	C	4th t-human or 2nd wave feminism	.6	2	C	people who let me take care of them
.8	5	C	10am coffee at work (theory flood)	.3	1	F	being asked to speak in public	.6	3	T	great service, no black worry
.7	3	CV	well thought out and original works	-.6	2	A	patronizing judgment	.6	2	F	other's deep heartbreak
.7	1	C	new Knime or Excel tricks				other-ID-crushing bullies:	.6	2	A	genuine displays of devotion
.6	3	C	awesome data sets	-.8	3	V	robber baron capitalism	.4	1	A	mutual non-stranger quality time
.5	2	F	bosses or business partners = badass	-.8	4	C	male other-diminishing assertion	.3	3	F	when others have my back unexpectedly
.4	0	C	vodka and philosophy	-.9	4	V	man-slamming/arrogant feminism	-.5	4	F	unreliability / helping turned costly
.4	3	CV	semi-closed artistic culture campaign	-.9	4	C	injustice on others I care about				
.3	5	C	getting the idea for a new theory	-1	5	C	injustice *by* others I care about				
.2	2	V	dark purple (50, 30, 90)								
-.4	4	T	being surprised by cold weather								

We won't do anything with your table just yet. Instead, now is a good time to get familiar with your senses. All of them.

The Normal Senses

Think about the nature of the five traditional senses. Vision involves your processing of incoming electromagnetic waves. Touch and certain kinds of heat sensation, on the other hand, involve the processing of incoming matter as "formed" carriers of energy. We'll call this type of carrier "mechanical." Taste and smell, though considered distinct from each other and separate from touch, are actually similar to touch except that the chemical lands in your mouth or your nose and is processed for its structural properties, rather than simply being there. Taste and smell are thus mechanical as well, except that their activation involves a patterned change in the organs that receive them while touch requires only a "landing" of one object against the body. Lastly, hearing, also involves a landing, but of waves instead of a mechanical object. (the waves are processed mechanically, but are themselves not material objects.) Arranging these ~~5~~ 4 senses from lowest frequency/density of information processing to highest wavelength or density we get

1. taste/smell (chemical landing?)
2. hearing (radio waves, wave landing)
3. touch, heat conductance (microwaves and below, mechanical landing)
4. vision (infrared to visible, wave change)

The only thing about taste and smell is that, in addition to being active on the level of molecular properties, they are also more viscerally connected to our primitive brains—including memory and cognition. Vision involves a lot of information, but a shift in the pattern of the eye's receptive field activation can render that section of your vision irrelevant. Anyway, a chemical change is ultimately an array of outer molecular shell changes whereas vision only takes one photon wave period at a time. All of this suggests that taste/smell are more mechanical versions of memory and cognition—changing your perception of your own receiving organs in ways the other senses do not. These involve more than just the landing of a chemical. Rather they involve changing the surface of the organ. For reasons you'll see in a moment, I'll call this "mechanical curvature."

1. hearing (radio waves; wave landing)
2. touch, heat conductance (microwaves; mechanical landing)
3. vision (infrared to visible; wave change)
4. taste/smell (perceptual mode—the array of (chemical) structures you use to perceive substrate input; mechanical curvature)

Let's not forget proprioception—the sense of what's going on in your own body. Really this is just attention. The sense of attention is not as dense as the sense of perceptual mode because it doesn't actually change the structure of your cells. It does, however, help direct other functions like blood flow and receptive field sensitivity to those cells. It also leads to both long and short term pathway building (potentiation) in your body. As a structure changer, it's automatically higher energy than vision.[12] Since it's a function of signal gradients and electrical currents sponsored by chemical carriers rather than the impact of the carriers themselves, we'll consider this to be a wave *curvature*—"*density change*" among the messaging regions in your body.

3.5. proprioception/attention/cognition (attention mode—the array of frequency structures you use to perceive local biological activity; wave curvature)

Finally, we'll round out the "normal" senses with one I'll bet you didn't know you had: the sense of biological manufacture: hormone ramp-up, genetic transcription, and (when gone out of control) cancer. This is the facet of your body that changes *how much* of the material that can potentially be there in response to sources like ultraviolet light and the motivation stemming from your existing state. Just lower in density than the attention you're about to give but higher than the vision you just added to the rest of your states, the sense of (cellular) manufacture is the literal "gut feeling" (and beyond) as you prepare for what's next.

3.3. manufacture (ultraviolet waves, transcription and firing; mechanical change

So now we have all six ways in which the body actually responds to anything around it.

1. hearing – wave landing
2. touch – mechanical landing
3. vision – wave change
4. (bio)manufacture – mechanical change
5. proprioception and attention – wave (signal density) curvature

---

[12] Although we prize vision as the ultimate carrier of energy, it's basically just a strobe on your eyes, and doesn't as easily alter your body's *function* the way several higher senses do. Also, if a picture is worth a thousand words, then every visual scene has an exponential level of possible thoughts—foci of attention—attached to it. Vision provides a lot of options, but most are ignored. Information-density-wise cognition and hormones go much deeper.

6. smell, taste, and (bio)generation – mechanical (chemical property) curvature

(If this section is boring you, hold on. We're going somewhere with this.)

The six sense modes are each described by a certain kind of wave travel. Longitudinal waves travel in the direction of the signal, pushing forward towards their target.

$$\rightarrow\rightarrow\rightarrow\rightarrow\rightarrow\rightarrow\rightarrow$$

Transverse waves oscillate perpendicular to their direction of travel, at right angles in the plane of their targeted direction.

$$\bowtie\rightarrow\bowtie\rightarrow\bowtie\rightarrow\bowtie\rightarrow$$

Surface waves roll circularly in the direction of their target.

$$\rightarrow\circlearrowright\circlearrowleft\circlearrowright\circlearrowright\circlearrowleft\circlearrowright\rightarrow$$

(The next two paragraphs are conjecture—an idea about how I believe the energy complexity sequence is put together. Future research will need to verify or disprove it, but it doesn't need to hold in order for the cycle in the table beneath it to apply, since you can just rotate the rows as I actually do in the section that follows it. Furthermore, the coming Table 47-1 doesn't need to hold in order for any of the sections after it to apply. The two paragraphs below this are my way of establishing a mapping from movement onto cycle space.)

If you imagine the amount of work it takes to push each wave, you can see how longitudinal waves are energetically cheaper than transverse waves which in turn seem energetically cheaper than surface waves. Try pushing a weight forward, pushing it up and out, then "pushing" it around in a circle in front and behind your direction of facing to illustrate this.

If you did try pushing the weight (I'm sure you didn't), now put the weight down and just move your arms around to simulate the *pattern* of pushing in the paragraph above. If that weight had been a part of you instead, making the circular wave *motion* would have been cheaper than pushing an actual external mechanical (touch) object, metabolic resource (manufacture fuel), or molecular property (smell or other biogenerator) around randomly with that motion. Pushing / translating *yourself* as object randomly is easier than sliding yourself consistently. That is, it's easier to **spin>** on your own than it is to translate (**perturb>**) yourself in a couple of directional choices, easier to translate yourself in a couple of directions than it is to slide (**progress>**) only in one,[13] easier to slide yourself in one direction than it is to slide an object (**push>**), easier to slide an object in one direction than it is to translate it over several directions (**carry>**), and easier to translate an object over several directions than it is to spin-drag

---

[13] Given there are frictions, forces, and collisions you'll eventually encounter.

(**cycle>**) it. Spin yourself in x-y about z, translate in x-y, slide in x. Add an object and this ease goes backwards.[14] And so we have a proper ordering of the ~~5~~ 4 + 2 human senses.

Sense (lowest to highest energy processing)	Type of wave	Type of input	What gets processed
hearing	longitudinal	wave landing	wave contact
heat/touch	longitudinal	mechanical landing	chemical contact pattern
vision	transverse	wave change	wave movement
biomanufacturer/hormones	transverse	mechanical change	chemical movement pattern
attention/cognition/proprioception	surface	wave curvature	wave (signal density) "texture"/pattern
taste/smell/(chemical texture)	surface	mechanical curvature	chemical (molecular-valence density) pattern

Table 47-1: The normal senses, ordered by processing density[15]

---

[14] This is easier to understand if you consider it all to take place in up to 3 dimensions of allowable region energy. Conjecture: It's easier to keep yourself on one point (spinning) than to risk moving sideways out of your zone, and easier to move sideways out of your zone once than to do it twice over two zones. When you add an object, sliding it allows you to care only about one inertial zone given the object's burden imposed on you. Translating it means your worry about two zones with the object. Spinning it means you are concerned with a volume of zones for the orbiting object plus your own spin. You may eventually need to stretch, squeeze, merge with or break your bond to the object if the volume of zones doesn't stay stable. The bigger you are and more aggregated energy you have, the easier it is for the highest type of action—orbiting—to take place. Because you yourself exist over move potential zones as you get bigger, I believe you actually *have* to adopt some kind of orbital behavior as a way of resonating your own internal material.

[15] Notice I didn't bother to list whether these were sponsored by objects inside of you, landing on you, or (by events) containing you. The senses we're about to discuss go a lot deeper than the familiar six. This rough table will do for now.

Chapter 47: The Resonance

The "Psychic" Senses
Now the regular senses are all nice, but there are some key pieces of physics we've left out.

Clairaudience
Where a thing makes contact with another, there must be a "pushing" contactor. No sound without a noisemaker. No touch without a form-field holder. Thus for every pushed longitudinal wave, there must be a pushing vibrator. The stronger the longitudinal wave, the stronger the vibrator.

"envibrating" direction 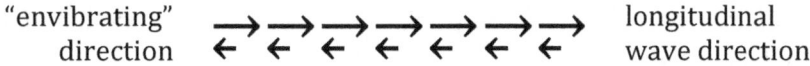 longitudinal wave direction

The idea here is that any sense you use to perceive one thing can also be used to perceive its opposite IF you **inhibit your assignment of coherence** to the signal that sense is trained to pick up. Sound, for example, is just noise until we learn to enforce recognizable patterns upon it. As we grow out of childhood, we become so good at things like reading and interpreting voices for trained meaning that we diminish our attention to other patterns of noise which don't seem to hold such meaning. But those patterns are still there. And they MUST come with the same energy type as regular hearing is tuned to perceive, as a consequence of energy conservation. Hearing from an assignable source corresponds to regular hearing. **Hearing from an unassignable source—projecting coherence onto a vibrator that doesn't seem to be there**—corresponds to hearing voices, psychic noises, or (it's saner name) **clairaudience**.

This isn't the place to debate the sanity of a person who hears voices or other normatively[16] sourceless noises. As with regular hearing, if you let the sounds you listen to misguide you, your hearing isn't your problem. Relatedly, if the voices in your head compel you to do good things and be more peaceful, who cares what haters think?

☞ Question 47.8 (**Critical** clairaudience practice): Set your timer for 2 minutes. Allow yourself to hear whatever message seems to come to you, regardless of whether there are any sources around you responsible for such noises. It sounds just like regular hearing, but without your own personal need to understand what it's about. At the end of the 2 minutes, record your experience below.

_____
_____
_____
_____
_____

---

[16] Normatively: subject to the agreement of others.

Just in case you're peeking at this before doing the activity, I have no comments. Because we typically think in words, the WORST thing you can have in your clairaudient practice is biased thought.

☞ Question 47.9 (Clairaudient conversation practice): Once you've gotten comfortable enough hearing from normatively non-sources, practice interjecting your own basic responses to what you hear, wherever it's appropriate to do so. A pause in the sentence, a realization that you like that song, the feeling that you too like chirping birds… Say so, then keep listening. Then respond the next time it's appropriate. This exercise will be harder for you if you feel you need to judge yourself for trying the exercise. As for others' judgment, you think to yourself all the time, so why should it bother you now? Take a couple of seconds to calm yourself for listening. See if you can get enough of a conversation going, then fill in the blanks below.

_____
_____
_____
_____
_____
_____

Clairsentience

Hearing processes longitudinal waves via the auditory system—auditory and clairaudient as waves. Meanwhile, touch and temperature sensitivity are heavily processed at the skin level. Where sound requires a vibrator, contact requires an object (even if that object is a hot volume of air particles). **Clairsentience**, "psychic feeling" corresponds to **our sense of the internal dynamics behind the surface that touches us.** After all, it does make sense that when a thing touches you, there is matter behind the contacting surface of that thing, doesn't it? When you push a door open, you typically have a reason. The door's sense of "touch" might be able to read the contact of your hand, but wouldn't it be nice if it could read—maybe even influence—the person behind the hand? Clairsentience is just so; behind a contacting surface there must be a subsurface. As you read the thing that touches you, you also read the impetus which compelled it to touch you. Perhaps it's a mood or a history, or plain old inertia. Whatever it is, you can get at it via a three-fold process:

Step 1. Be able to describe sensations during regular touch

Because things like clothes, temperate air, and other surfaces are touching us all the time, it may be difficult for us to identify what's happening even during *regular* touch. Our sense of clairsentience will typically be even weaker, unless we're one of those people who wailed like a banshee as a baby, and still squirm inconsolably amidst even the most modest discomfort. Here, your powers of poetic description will go a long way in strengthening your sense of normal touch, and you can use those same powers to describe your contacted object under clairsentience.

☞ Question 47.10 (Bodily feeling survey): **Consider how you're positioned right now, seated, standing, or whatever. Going from head to toe, describe the feeling you feel in light of each thing that is touching you now.** This includes things like glasses, shirts, chairback, butt on the chair, crossed legs, tingling feet, and oddly stoic toenails. The more elaborate and detailed the description the better. (I started with the glasses that keep sliding down my nose. They feel sneakily agitating, as if that part of my face is preparing for a jailbreak which must be controlled.) In this activity you are describing how *you* feel, not the object. We'll describe the object's "own sense of feeling"—that is, we'll use actual clairsentience—later.

_____
_____
_____
_____
_____
_____
_____
_____
_____

Step 2: Be able to touch something, but then get used to feeling its story, not the object itself

Our most regular use of clairsentience comes from a basic practice we perform everyday: putting on clothes. Here we have objects which we put on us, feel briefly, then integrate into the attitudes we take with us as influencers in the world. I stop feeling my shirt and join myself to its form in making a combined impression on the world, but also in filling myself with a certain attitude. It's this second result which constitutes clairsentience. In addition to being able to describe sensations fairly richly, we also need to be able to absorb the impression pattern that comes with its contact on us.

☞ Question 47.11 (Feel the history of an object): **Take 2 minutes to rest your hand on an object which you don't normally use. Keep your hand on the object, but pay attention to what's going on inside of the object.** Typically, when another person touches us intentionally, they are also communicating with us in some way. We can take advantage of this touch+communication duo by allowing ourselves to listen to or feel the mood associated with the object as we touch it. Effectively, we are treating it just like a person who had some reason to touch us in conversation. What messages do you get from your object? Just as the clothes you wear or the air you feel on your skin have forces which motivated their interface with you, the objects you touch have passed through a series of hands in order to get to you, and will have a series of situations that will greet them after you leave. They have both histories and futures, were manufactured from materials elsewhere on the earth, and were involved in the moods (internal projective patterns) of the people (self-reinforcing molecule packages) who used them. You are a wave pattern, the object is a wave pattern, and both of your full histories of interactants were also wave patterns. Can you read the object's half of the story that brought you together?

_____
_____
_____
_____
_____
_____

Do this for two more objects which you don't often use.

_____
_____
_____
_____
_____
_____
_____
_____
_____
_____
_____
_____

Step 3: Be able to recognize the attitudes associated with an object's function

This may seem strange for us to do with objects we're touching, but it is often THE reason we seek to touch people and pets—to have an attitude passed on to us or vice versa. Although most non-human objects will not share our enthusiasm for human language, we tend to care more about our own human language anyway in interpreting our relationships to those objects. There is little difference between talking about your phone and telling a story about your phone as you touch it, paying attention to its internal workings rather than your own impressions thereof. If you can listen to another person with empathy, you can alter your normal commentary about objects towards more listening about their context, as yours and the objects' timelines cross temporarily. To train clairsentience, practice feeling the human-relatable story that your selected object tells. As you would with any good human conversation, be certain to listen for messages which help you keep a good and expressive relationship with that object.

☞ Question 47.12 (Read a common object): Pick up your phone or some other object you use a lot. Hold it in the same way you touched the objects in 47.11—that is, paying attention to the inner world and general "attitude" that the phone holds towards you and your relationship with it. Using the clairaudience activities 47.8 and 47.9, see what your phone tells you. Let the phone speak for itself by starting with the "I am…" introduction below. Your phone will say to you, "I am…" and from there will be associated with certain messages which come to you during this activity. Does it have anything to say about you, your communication with others, or its own role in your life?

_____
_____
_____
_____
_____

As the complements of hearing and touch respectively, clairaudience and clairsentience both travel upon longitudinal waves, but in the direction away from you the receiver. To use them, you'll have to get used to receiving information either from vibrators that aren't apparently there or from subsurface dynamics just behind the only part of an object you'll ever touch—its surface. Because **the conserving waves involved** with these senses **go backward**, I refer to them as **postlongitudinal waves**—as post-longitudinal as the impacting billiard ball which just donated its energy to a second ball.

Projection

🛠 Warning: This section gets fairly technical.

In order for light to be absorbed, something must have emitted it or bounced it. Where an electromagnetic wave has just passed through, the absence of that wave must enter. With no traveling energy that an absorber can receive, the passed-through region becomes a vacuum with respect to the signal which just departed. The **use of vision to perceive the vacuum—where energy of the very same frequency is installed into the space where that energy is not**—constitutes **projection**.

A Theory of Vision Coupling and Post-Light Waves

For those of us interested in projecting images into places where those images are not normatively apparent, the special range of human vision holds some advantage. Visible light travels at frequencies just above red 400 and up to ultraviolet 770 THz (trillions of cycles per second), which means we *almost* have a range a full double's range of visible perception. It is my personal theory that the ability to see the fully doubled range of about 400 (red) to 800 (ultra-ultraviolet as a higher red) THz would mean the existence of a color for every sight in the same way that octaves on a piano have a hearable sound for every note.[17] More importantly, the doubling hypothesis means that no matter how high or low the electromagnetic "octave" you were on, every form could have a corresponding color imparted to it—just like playing the same song in a lower or higher octave. For example, green (around 550 THz) would be the color of energy at 275, 137.5, 1100, and 2200 THz as well, if only we knew how to couple a part of our visual system to our lower or higher systems for recognizing which octave we were actually on.

My theory of higher frequency vision holds that, in order to see color in microwaves, radio waves, gamma rays or the like, you would need to couple your sense of vision to whichever sense lives on that level of the electromagnetic spectrum.

- In order to perceive a *being who could talk* to you, you'd have to perceive both a color and a *sound* attributed to the direction that the color was coming from.

- In order to perceive a thing which had the power to *rewrite your biology* or heal you physically, you would need to perceive both a color and a *biomanufacturer* (like a nervous signal, as in reiki) in whatever region where the thing was contacting you.

- To see a thing that speaks directly to your *thoughts* (clairaudience), you would need to perceive both a color and a normatively *non-sourced sound*.

This theory of vision coupling would also explain why physical forms are so easy for us to perceive: Heat/touch is the next lowest frequency sense below vision in our earlier list and biomanufacture—which happens during pain, chemical contact, or radiation—is the next highest level, meaning the range of touch and touchable form spans both sides of the range of vision. Below that is hearing, above that is cognition, but these travel in waves just like vision does, so you'd have to work to separate them in your perception.

---

[17] This implies to me that you wouldn't be able to not see color though, so I suppose it's good that darkness has its own window.

Using vision to perceive higher and lower energy levels would imply

1. that we were projecting human-visible characteristics onto normally nonvisible electromagnetic frequencies,
2. that the things on each level would adopt certain shapes and forms characteristic of the kind of energy travel that happens there. Visible objects occur in transverse x-y planes, clairaudient objects would occur in "expansive looking" longitudinal depth planes the way the variously distant stars of the night sky do, and cognitive objects would occur as more of a location-less oscillation consistent with surface waves.
3. Higher frequency planes would have more expressive options than you do while lower frequency planes would have fewer—the main difference being in how easily you could introduce "details" in the level-occupant's behavior (or whether they could introduce it to you), and
4. that the ultimate x-y square, plus z-depth vacuum, plus central-6, 12, and 24 circles would constitute a completely stable coordinate space for movement around the multi-level universe.

Depending on what kinds of moods you hold—whether they are constrained to basic anger, hunger, pleasure or allowed to vibrate even higher—you can couple your own behavior to the energy structures of higher frequency levels and assign color to those structures with an appropriately practiced visual system.

So how do we practice projecting sights onto non-visible patterns? Let's start by identifying some common visible experiences which already have colors assigned to them:

1. The night-viewing infrared
2. The red blood or fire
3. The orange fire or taming sunset
4. The yellow tint of unshadowed areas under sunlight
5. The green grass
6. The blue sky
7. The violet edge of dusk
8. The invisible ultraviolet parathyroid promoter

Perhaps you can see a natural mood shift from hot urgency into common warmth, into more relaxed cool, back to radiation-attended (cellular) excitement. So let reds be warm, blues be cool, greens and yellows be familiar by their natural ubiquity, and violets be exotic by their natural rarity compared to the other basic colors.

Next we'll apply several things we've learned from the previous chapters. Things we perceive can often be more relevant for what they bring out of us than they are for their own characteristics. If nature's reds grab our attention while nature's blues absorb it—if nature's greens circumscribe our environments while violets form singular objects in it, then we arrive at a basic reaction wheel for understanding what we're looking at on any plane. This includes even the traditional body energy centers.

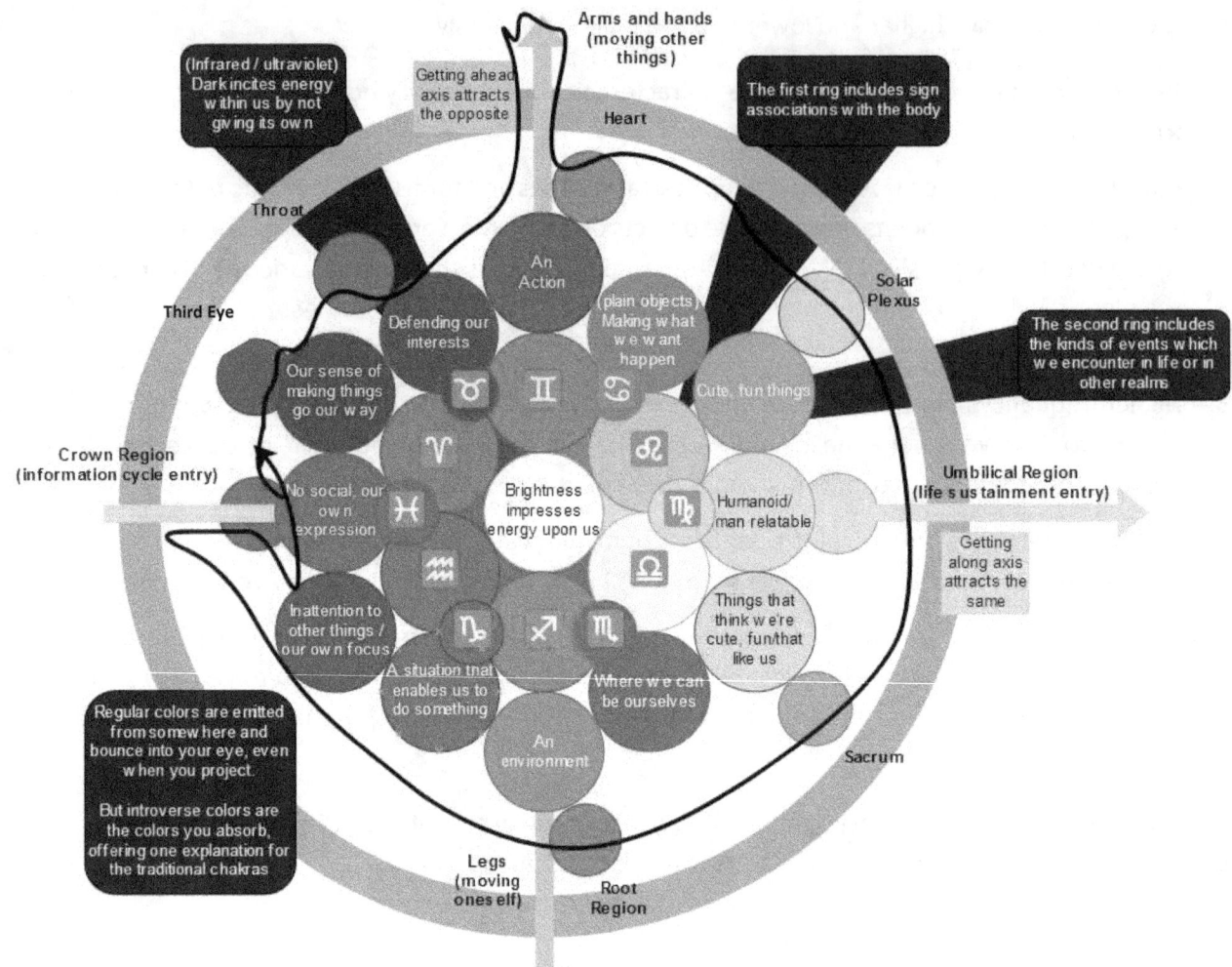

Figure 47-1: The Reaction Wheel showing various kinds of perceivable experiences

The wheel above contains colors, moods, objects, and energy levels. Use this to help you in your projection practice. Although we often see the world beyond us as full of unknowns, there aren't nearly as many unknown energy *types* as there are forms for packaging those types. To project visible attributes onto typically invisible spaces, all you do is apply the same rule we discussed for clairaudience: <u>Don't force meaning onto what you see</u>. Just note how it interfaces with you.

In the preceding wheel I used the term "introverse." Like the term "postlongitudinal," this is my way of noting which direction projection energy travels in. If *transverse* waves oscillate outward from the main wave's axis

$$\text{↗}\longrightarrow\text{↗}\longrightarrow\text{↗}\longrightarrow\text{↗}\longrightarrow$$

Then **introverse** waves **oscillate inwards into the main wave's axis**. Like poking holes into a straw.

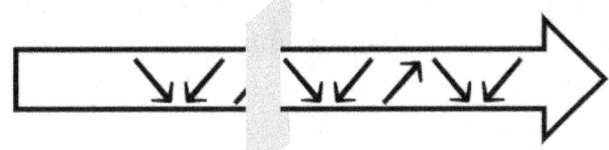

Some speculation about the nature of the inverse of transverse travel: Since no one (to my knowledge) has ever seen the inside of a light wave, all we can do is speculate. As the E (electro) and B (magnetic) components of a wave oscillate at right angles to the direction of travel, how might we envision the "anti-oscillation" which represents the restoring of each spike in its own axis (not the partner axis)? Perhaps we can consider the transverse travel of light waves to be something like the energy-conserving, real-potential deformation of vacuum regions—helix style. The contiguity of each zone of the vacuum which establishes energetic same-levelness for that region might also ensure that any deformation below a required potential-energy escape threshold will be undone. Introversal movement would then be a kind of tension for pulling the vacuum region's normal potential back in place—like a transverse slice of rungs holding a physical helix together.

The bottom line is, if you have an intermittent spike in one axis, the event that constitutes the retraction of that same spike will also need to be there. We may not know what to call it, but the inverting wave—whatever its nature—allows us to consider what it means to "anti-see." To help us get into the idea of projection, we'll consider this a possible basis for how projection works.

Now why did we go through all this trouble? As you may know, psychic or astral projection is a more involved process than the one used for most other senses. That is the price of our bodies being so thoroughly hooked on visible light—the complement of projected color. You may find that, although practicing other intuitive skills is usually a pretty straightforward matter, practicing projection and internal energy reading is not. We've spent some time developing an understanding of how projected energy might work so that when you attempt your experiments you won't—as I once did—give it up as hocus pocus for the talented few. ✕

A Recap

Vision is the seeing of emissions. Projection is the seeing of absorptions behind those emissions. If the 350 out of 400 or so possibly doubled terahertz of near-visible frequency are human perceivable, then we might guess that around 85%-90% of all human scale energy can be reasonably associated with a visible color even if that energy will never *truly* be visible. We can practice projecting visible attributes onto certain frequency levels by co-opting the senses which normally process those frequencies. Notice that I haven't really assumed that higher realms must be real here, only that higher frequency *volumes* are real and can be synesthetically characterized. We'll keep that in mind for the next exercise.

☞ Question 47.13 (Seeing an invisible message source): Wait until you are in a state of heavy fatigue, in a place where you can relax. Be sure you are so tired that you no longer care if anything makes sense. Redo exercise 47.9 (clairaudient conversation), but this time you won't have to write anything down. Instead, pay attention to *how you are reacting* to the clairaudient conversation you're having. This will be your way of experiencing the 12 classes of experience on the wheel from earlier. Noting that almost anything can be represented as a visual symbol, observe what you're picturing while the conversation continues. See if you can introduce a description of a visually-related reaction from yourself towards the messenger. How do they respond to your observation of them?

Your Ability to Project is Related to Your Ability to Be Seen

Another way to think about projection is as follows: If to project is to cast one's form onto something else, then anything we see—by virtue of the light reflecting off of it—can be said to have projected into our vision. Should we choose to pay attention, that projection can even trigger a reaction from us. In this way, projection isn't just about making a ghost of yourself in some higher realm, it's also about training your ability to be "seen" by *anything* on *any level* you naturally fit with. Abraham Lincoln can project into a realm called American History, even if he has no idea who those strange people are during astral travel. You can project into the realm of your future children's children to the extent that they will be able to obtain some record of you and tangle their spacetime paths with your own. You don't even need to possess your current form by then. Your wave pattern needs only to have its natural habits (function behavior) extended into a future time window.

The "Being Seen" interpretation of projection suggests that the use of this sense, though consciously difficult, is subconsciously <u>incredibly</u> common. We are seen by all kinds of things, not just by humans or pets, but by insects, governments, and strangers' conversations. Accordingly, we can pose a sensible question and get an immediately obvious answer to it: Do we always know when we're projecting? Of course not. We almost never know. Publics view us, but we hardly know the inner worlds of even the smallest fraction of those publics. Still, this idea may produce yet another [hypothesis] regarding projection: {It will be easier to travel into the realms that have an easier time registering your appearance.}

☞ **Question 47.14 (Commonly projected dream roles):** If your dreams have a visual component, the content of those dreams will include things that have an easier time being seen by you. The more frequent a subject's appearance in your dreams, the more easily that subject can get attention from you. Contrapositively, the more a thing struggles to get the kind of attention it "wants" from you, the less likely you are to dream of it. Even if it's your number one sweetheart you wish to dream of and who wants to be dreamt of by you, there may still be nothing—not because you aren't connected in some way, but because some key aspect of the pattern they emit is not the same pattern you receive in that area you both desire the appearance in. Consider the kinds of things, settings, or people who frequently show up in your dreams, and what kinds of events generally happen related to them. What does related projection suggest for their role in your life? List the ones that come to mind below.

Subject	Related Event	Suggested Role

☞ Question 47.15 (Commonly projected waking roles): **Now consider the kinds of things, settings, or people who frequently show up in your normal daily life, and what kinds of events generally happen related to them. To narrow this down, consider only those things which keep showing up whether or not you invited them, NOT necessarily your favorite things. What does related projection suggest for their role in your life? This can include types of personalities, patterns of events, clusters of communication styles, streaks, or any other package that has looked the same to you for years and years. Negative packages count too. List the ones that come to mind below.**

Subject	Related Pattern	Suggested Role

Does the above suggest that you're better at projecting in the above situations than you are other kinds? Yes it does. If the packages are negative don't worry about it. We'll address this in the chapter on conflict.

Here's a story you may find relevant. As recent as several years ago, while I was still searching for the perfect romantic relationship, I would often attempt to dream of women, but would dream of buildings and architecture instead. I would often seek answers regarding what a certain woman was thinking, only to dream of some esoteric lesson on the cosmos. And when I sought to travel the astral realms, looking for some new insight into my own patterns of relating, I wouldn't travel anywhere, and often dreamt of absolutely nothing. Irritating as it was then, today I now understand all of this. I prefer not to enter real life relationships if I can't share a work life with the person; my work life revolves around structuring esoteric patterns into coherent ones; and real life travel doesn't do anything for me unless there are friends to share it with. Returning to you, if you don't travel for exploration in real life, your subconscious may not gravitate toward it astrally. If you can't access something spiritually, it may be because your *full* pattern is predisposed to a holistically more fitting replacement. Certain things, though we want them consciously, my not fit us at all subconsciously. Why the misalignment? Much of what we think we want probably comes from what others trained us to see as viable sources of fulfillment. Before we know ourselves well enough, it's easier to feel like their aims are actually yours.

If you don't seek solutions of a certain kind in real life, you may not get them as projections. Your pattern is your pattern whether you are awake, asleep, or permanently asleep. If your aim is to project into a higher realm, start with a realm you know: the body manufacture you value, the thoughts you prefer to think, or tastes you prefer to indulge or identify with. Use the reaction wheel from earlier to imagine what some of these things would look like if they had a form in the dream world.

☞ Question 47.16 (Reaction wheel assignments): Go back to your 47.7/47.3 table. Use the reaction wheel to assign a section of the wheel to each, then attach at least one way you might represent this as a form among your dream symbols. Try to employ clairaudience so that you get an instant, non-forced image. After checking that the image is a reasonable match for the item you're looking at, write the section of the wheel and the symbol you derived in the table below. I've included couple of my examples to help get you started.

Example

r	I	S	Subject	Reaction Wheel Location	Symbol	Reason (optional)
.8	4	A	female voices in epic j-pop	Between ♏ and ♐	A hawk	What some might consider a weak voice channels the power of all of nature
-.8	3	V	**robber baron** capitalism	The end of ♐, start of ♑	A giant, non-welcoming building	Development for ego's sake
-.5	4	F	**unreliability** / difficult behavior form one who asked for my help	Between ♍ and ♎	difficult behavior form one who asked for my help, something **slippery**,	Obvious
.2	2	V	dark purple (50, 30, 90)	Very late ♓, early ♈	Royal robes, Egyptian adornment, actual dark purple	A preference which is mine without any filtering via other's egos; personal sense of power

Your turn.

r	I	S	Subject	Reaction Wheel Location	Symbol	Reason (optional)

☞ **Question 47.17 (Identify the real events):** Notice that some of my example entries were bolded. While some of our triggers are actual triggers, others are only *symbols* for such triggers, with the real meaning wrapped up in the experience we receive in response. Go back into your table and <u>circle the real event</u> associated with the guaranteed trigger you've described.

☞ **Question 47.18 (Future reference):** Bookmark your answer to 47.16! Dog-ear it, put a piece of paper in the crease, or take a picture on your phone. Later in the book when we explore The Asteroid and The Star, you'll be glad you did.

Final Thoughts on Projection

If you've never had an out of body experience or intentionally shown up in another person's dreams, the event will almost certainly be interesting when you finally do. But projection happens all the time where we show up in places where others can see us. It happens intentionally in places where those are the people or things that we *want* to see us. It might be a bit of a letdown to learn that special skills like astral projection will never (in our lifetimes) be as easy as a simple trip to the right social environment, but that trip can produce results which are much farther reaching. For your whole development, it will actually become increasingly important to steer your real-life projection—also known as showing up—towards spaces where you are actually wanted, in form and in action. The reason should be obvious—places where you are not wanted increase the disharmony in your viewers and, accordingly, the noise in your own projected wave pattern. Intruding into other's lives may be the definition of power to some, but it will always stain your legacy sooner or later. Unlike the ones you've projected upon today, the viewers who come after you will *know* they don't have to put up with what you left them.

Claircognizance

Claircognizance, the ability to simply "know" what actions to take next, is the result of a simple biological rule: Knowing that your body usually produces more than one hormone, cell, or other component of a particular type at the same time, the earlier you can catch your own biomanufacture the earlier you can act on the reason it's being manufactured in the first place. If I am naturally stressable, then it will be behoove me to catch my own stress hormones early in their gathering process. Even before there is enough of the hormone to call my conscious attention, my subconscious knows what's up. I gain the ability to infuse my conscious actions with a continuous data stream from my subconscious monitoring system. This is before we even get to the wave version of things.

The sense of biomanufacture is meant to reconcile your current body state with your wanted body state—a mechanical (chemical) array of changes. In light of that change, you have the state to be discarded as a pattern of effects your chemistry will leave in the world. This holds for carriers of energy on the nano-scale or the level of stars just as it does for biologies. Chemical reactants yield chemical products. Your pattern of intentionally putting the products out there whenever you need to build up more reactants is not only the secret to claircognizance, but will also be our chief means of managing The Conflict in general.

Travelling as an introverse mechanical change, claircognizance alters the internal "texture" of a thing, event, or context. It is a particularly useful skill to train if you have a chronic problem of some kind, as—without your having to envision it, listen for it, or even think about it—the skill will push you towards steps for avoiding the temptation altogether if not early on. Some tests are best avoided completely.

Claircognizance is my strongest nonstandard sense, followed by clairaudience. I trained it mainly by taking lists of patterns like the ones in 47.3 and logging them, recording them in audio, or replaying them in my head. The skill has Capricorn-like properties, so it helps for you to have a love of structured patterns in order for you to develop it. Repeating those patterns to yourself as part of determining how to respond helps develop the sense even more.

☞ Question 47.19 (You just know): **Claircognizance increases a certain kind of autopilot behavior in people who have it. If you put those people into a tangled situation, they tend to be able to escape it easily. Just as we all have certain circumstances where our senses are heightened, we also have areas where our more esoteric senses excel. One way to discover where you may develop claircognizance is to look at situations where you can get away with almost anything—where you always seem to know just what to do or say to make things go the way you want. In what areas of life do you have the golden touch?**

_____
_____
_____
_____

You may in fact use the area(s) above to trace out your proper path in life broadly, referring to this talent whenever you need to know your best next move.

Now there are some occasions where, no matter how powerful or skilled you are, no matter how striking your talent, you just can't get it to work in solving a particular problem. In *144* I talked about squares to a point on one's cycle (Squidalgo), and how some things just won't work because they represent the full potential energy of your favored other. One trait is completely real while its square

(90° ahead of or behind it) is completely imaginary. These kinds of situations are particularly vexing for those using their auto-knowing, since they basically have to resort to biomanufacture (Cancer frustration) in order to use their anti-biomanufacture/claircognizance (Capricorn). There is good news, however. In the areas of life designed for paradoxes like this, your number one remedy is to outsource; get someone else to carry the square part of the wave for you. This is another essential tool for handling conflict, but we will break it out right now.

☞ Question 47.20 (You just don't know): **List the major areas of your life that, broadly speaking, just don't work for you.**

_____
_____
_____
_____

Because this book is meant to help you develop your intuition and NOT develop your frictions, forget about trying to solve the above issues yourself. Instead, assume that someone (or something) else will need to solve these issues for you. But who? How? What kind of things must you do to attract such solution providers?

I could tell you now, but it won't make much of a difference until later on. You'll need to take my word for it. We haven't gotten there yet.

Instead, here's some homework for you.

☞ Question 47.21 (Claircognizance practice): **Recognition of a claircognizant signal goes hand in hand with recognition of a hormonal signal on its way towards ramp up. You probably have years' worth of familiarity with your own body's foreshadowing. All you need to do is put it to use. Over the course of the next two days, keep track of these four kinds of things in the box below: 1) what you eat, 2) any significant happenings in your communication with others (and the times at which they occurred), 3) what events happen _to_ you (and when they occurred), and 4) what time(s) you wake up. That's it. We won't be doing any more with the list you make, but if you're one of those people who does this activity anyway and finds it informative, and if you like patterns, it may indicate a natural talent for claircognizance.**

Two days' worth of events:
1. What you eat
2. Any significant or surprising communications (and what times they occurred in the day)
3. What noteworthy events happen to you (and what times they occurred)
4. What times you wake up (including naps)

Clairvoyance

We often use the term clairvoyance to indicate general psychicism or some mutated form of clairaudience. Here we'll consider **clairvoyance** to be **the kind of intuitive <u>thinking</u> which feels like others' thoughts being put upon you.** Yes, this is the same sense responsible for "mind-reading" and seeing the future. In this book, though, we will treat clairvoyance separately from <u>seeing</u> auras (projection), feeling others' emotions (telepathy/empathy), and hearing non-sourced messages (clairaudience). The reason we care about these differences—especially from clairaudience—is because those differences greatly affect how we train the skill and whether we can even trust it.[18] As far as we'll be concerned, clairvoyance is not "seeing" in the visual sense any more than thinking is. If we call it seeing at all, we really mean in the thinking sense. It is as different from projection as cognitive attention is from vision.

In calculus we have the notion of a derivative—a rate of change in a measure. The senses of cognition and smell are both functions of change, as are their complementary senses clairvoyance and telepathy. Given that every thought you have reflects a pattern of change among your firing neuronal fields, we can ask what kind of phenomenon the inverse of such a change would be. What is the inverse of a change in rate? In math that would be an integral—the originally-built pattern which the change describes. Thinking will have traveled a firing path in the same way that driving will have traveled a spatial path. If you've traveled at this rate for this long, you *must* have *been* somewhere. Where clairvoyance is concerned, your powers of attention come with the frozen point of possible thoughts forgone, allowing you to attend to your entire context at the same time you attend to the moving aspect of it. This works in the same way that a car moving at this rate has not only a location but a location in a bigger context (otherwise the point itself would be nowhere). That is, the traveler implies both the point and the map which that point is on.

---

[18] I trust my claircognizance a lot more than I trust my clairaudience, mainly because I'm picky with words and affected by noise—messing up what I hear more easily than what I feel ready to do.

What makes clairvoyance weird, though, is that the map of thought gets rewritten with every new thought. Unlike physical spaces (in the simplest sense), thought spaces are continuously reinterpreted. By reading my own traveling non-thought today I can read the whole "fixed" space of possible thoughts for yesterday—from whence I came. But yesterday's thought space is framed using ideas entirely from today, so I'm really reading today's thought space…which of course implies tomorrow's derivative, traveling thought. Thus a clairvoyant can see both forwards and backwards depending on whether they focus on traveling today's space of histories or on today as a history in tomorrow's traveling future. Perhaps this is better explained with a diagram.

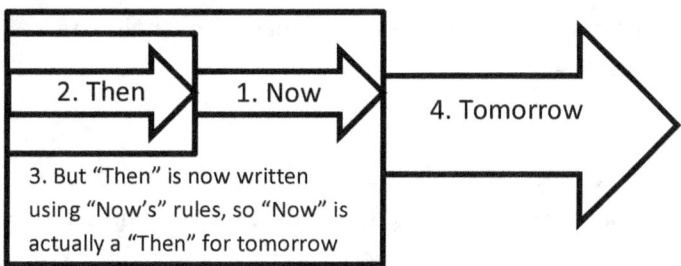

If (1) Now exists: (2) Then, (3) Now as Then, and (4) Tomorrow must also exist.
I talk about this kind of paradox-driven system at the beginning of *Laurentia*.

Thus the clairvoyant can read both past and future via their own thought. How does one do this?

Clairvoyance's normal complement, attention/cognition, travels as a surface wave on the field of brain ingredients. For every surface there must be a subsurface (both physically and figuratively), so we'll consider clairvoyance to travel on subsurface waves.

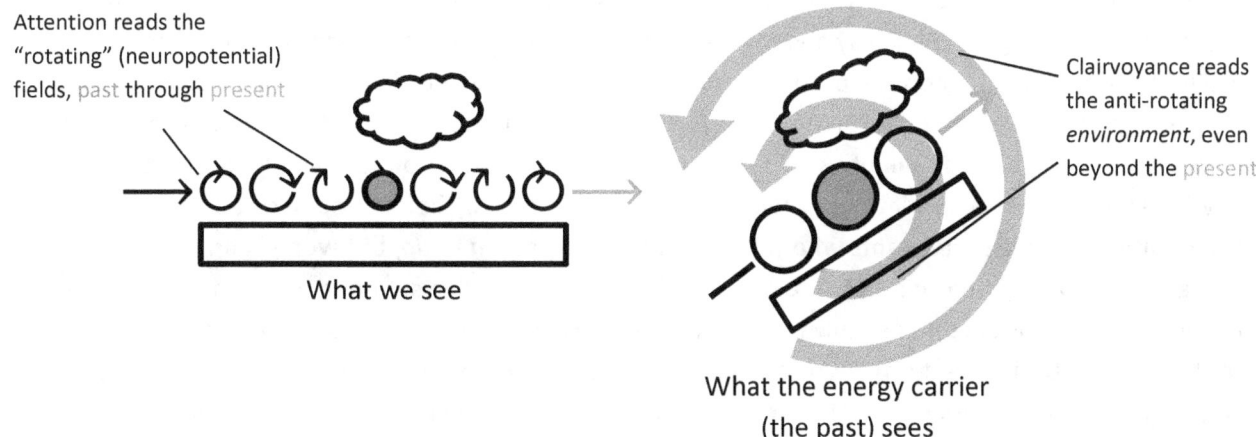

Figure 47-2: Analogy for the mechanisms of clairvoyance

Given the above visualization, clairvoyance would depend heavily on one's thoughts being governed by contexts beyond oneself in the moment, the more your thoughts can be described by autopilot, with your powers of interpretation attached to such autopilot, the more clairvoyant you will be.[19] Said

---

[19] Perhaps that's why books like this come easier to me on either tea and vodka, or coffee.

another way, the more you wire new connections to monitor the old ones which are actually active in the field animating process, the more clairvoyant you *can* be.

To develop clairvoyance, you will need to have a pretty heavy amount of trust in what a larger space of perceived outside forces is compelling you to think, and I've found that it helps greatly if you have someone or something else around to keep you grounded in regular things like paying bills and meeting your imposed-on-individuals obligations. Just as claircognizance comes easily with a love of patterns (in my own personal experience), strong clairvoyance comes easily with a love of deep immersion in thoughts guided by forces external to oneself. With our own thoughts so central to everything we do in normal life, strong clairvoyants should beware a tendency to let their external trainers toss them into one human trouble after another.

Before We Train: Control Your Clairvoyance, Avoid Pre-punishment
If you're going to train clairvoyance, you might consider limiting its use to contexts which actually benefit you. The thought spaces surrounding you will only be as stable as the objects of your regular attention. Clairvoyant talent can get addictive very quickly once you begin unlocking it, and you may—because of the thought-heavy nature of our world—be tempted to consult your own thoughts every time you need answers. Remember, though, that some answers are instinctive, visual, shared company-based, covered in warm clothes, heard through a good word, or fed with actual food. They are not always cognitive, and not all cognitive turns are good ones. Many of the patterns making a grab for your microphone will be there as spokespersons for whatever chaos you haven't yet learned to let go of, and though they may be right in what they compel you to think, they may be wrong in introducing you to the thought in the first place.

At the time of this writing, more than half of my closest friends are very psychic. The clairvoyants among them are also strong, with an easy and regular ability to read mine and others' thoughts and inclinations. Yet the number one problem I have observed among all of the kinds of intuitives I know is one most prevalent among the clairvoyants: This is where you see something bad coming, and don't realize that you're at least half of its cause—especially if the person you're reading doesn't think there's anything wrong—especially if things seemed to be going smoothly before you decided to air your premonitions. I have clairvoyants who will read what I'm *inclined to do*, but won't read (using empathy/telepathy) whether I *want* to do it, can't read whether I've set up mechanisms to avoid it if it's negative (claircognizance), or simply haven't learned how to abandon a negative train of thought natural to themselves (basic attention). If you train clairvoyance, be prepared to train both your normal cognitive attitude and your empathy for other's perspectives as well. Barring this (I've noticed) the people near you may never want to get near enough to have your doomsday tidings affect them, and will more easily tire of your always-on pack of "you-advisors." Self-centrism and self-worry can plague a strong clairvoyant as surely as the spinning world literally revolves around their mental needs. That's not to discourage you from practicing it, only to share with you a problem I have seen truly in 8 out of 11 of the very strong clairvoyants I've known. There's a general problem with sharing when all the world rotates about your own thoughts, so be prepared to be constantly denied something especially by those closest to you if you don't control this.

Let me repeat this just in case the above was too much:

A Warning Against Pre-Punishment

If you train clairvoyance, you also need to train empathy and patience for others' perspectives.
DO NOT get into the habit of punishing people for what you read on their minds…
It will cost <u>YOU</u> if you do this.
Healthy clairvoyance requires some degree of self-discipline.

Practice

☞ **Question 47.22 (Your clairvoyant indicators):** In what spaces does the world revolve around you? In what areas of your life do events seem to rise and fall by your basic presence? List them below. Analogs to these areas will suggest where your powers of clairvoyance are strongest.

_____
_____
_____
_____
_____

☞ **Question 47.23 (Your clairvoyant bases):** Recalling what we discussed in The Embodiments chapter and using the reaction wheel, see if you can translate your responses to 47.22 into a more general "library" topic which you may be fit to become expert in.

	Example
	Revolves around me: my writing, the moral aims and resource direction of my business, the information I surround myself with, gatekeeping with certain character traits that determine who my friends are (all people should do this in some way—especially intuitives) ↓ Library topic: "the messages a person allows into his life which affect his creative worth" (my clairvoyance could be very strong in reading this type of information—past or future—in people, systems, or events)

Notice that your clairvoyant foundation, like any other sense, does not extend to every topic. You may have an eye for art, but do you have an eye for a bargain? A well written music score? You may be able to read an object's history by touching it with your hand, but can you read the clothes you're currently wearing by touching them with your skin? The senses of clairvoyance, vision, and cognition are three of the most heavily relied upon senses we have (given that we've developed them). But resist the temptation to keep leaning on them even after they have begun to lead you or your relationships astray. (Yes, even cognition. Sometimes it's better to trust your memory of the facts (smell), your biomanufacture / hormones, or your <u>actual</u> situation (projection), to name a few.)

> ☞ Question 47.24 (The Clairvoyant Oath): Armed with your library topic from 47.23, memorize well the following:
> - I will develop my talent for _____ (Your library topic) by practicing it continually towards everyone's highest good.
> - Before imposing my gift on another, **I will ask whether it is helpful to the other person**.
> - Beyond my gifted topic, I will not assume my clairvoyance is more useful to others than their own path.
> - I don't always have all the information.
> - **I am not always right**.

I've found that many people seeking to develop their intuition do so under the assumption that they will tap into a higher, more benevolent force. This is, for the most part, true; the Whole can spot harmony in our connection to apparently separate parties more than we can. The catch is that such a higher force, by virtue of being big, is often assumed to have better advice about things like taxes, employment, and human relationships. This is, for the most part, impractical. Maybe our otherworldly advisors really do know more about these things than we do. But in the same way that I can't tell my cat with whom and how to mate, our higher forces often give us peaceful big pictures right alongside damaging immediate ones. Use your common sense before you ask the spirits to mail that bill for you. Clairvoyance can be great fun if you keep it in its proper place, but an endless source of dilemmas if you let it take over your every decision.

Telepathy

While our biologies hold the capacity to change their character in light of the food we eat and the hormones we smell, they also hold the capacity to change in light of the chemicals or energy exported from sources outside of us. Does this make sense? The tree exports the fruit which ends up affecting our biology. If I think you hate me or love me, I may change. If you wear something I like or give me a funny look, I may change. In other words, every input is the output of something. That something is one upstream factor in the inputs that change us. Telepathy occurs [**where one actor's biological structure or activity changes in light of another's output**. From us to them it is called **telepathy**. From them to us it is called **empathy**]. [Taken to the extreme point of motivating actual publicly verifiable movement in the opposing party, telepathy is better known as **telekinesis**]. Having never fully experienced telekinesis, I have no theory for it and won't write about it in this book. Empathy and telepathy on the other hand are straightforward to address.

Most of us have some level of empathy, mainly because the need to successfully bond with others has played such an important role in our evolution as a species. A husband's tie to his wife's menstrual cycle, the feel good effects of substances like oxytocin and vasopressin under exciting bonds, the slight perception of sweat from a person you like—all of these are areas where our bodies are intentionally designed to react to someone else's events. The cloud of skin secretions surrounding your interactants do more than just land on your nose, though. In atomic-level ways that even our current science doesn't yet appreciate, they alter the electron/electromagnetic fields around your body like an airborne MRI machine.[20] The floating piece of plastic that clings to you already knows this. If a sound weapon can bring you to your knees and a prolonged x-ray can mutate you, continual exposure (or your simulation of exposure) to a targeted source can also alter you as if the target were influencing you with their own workings. That's the beginning of my theory on telepathy: the sense of "psychic connection."

A Theory of Resonance

It is easy for our normal science to convince us that empathy is a purely chemical affair. I *see* your facial expression and respond to it biologically (*manufacture-wise*) with my own emotion. Or maybe I *hear* your voice or *smell* your hormones. But perhaps you can see the problem with this: There's no reasonably-sounding scientific explanation for where my internal changes actually came from. My own internal sense of vision or hearing, ignoring any "sending" from you? That would make you a kind of illusion—an epiphenomenal[21] one in this sense. How about where your actual hormones land on me? Then we'd really be tossing particles in the way the discredited ether does. The bottom line is, the carrier which prompts my reaction to you can only come from three kinds of places: myself, you, or the world that holds us both.

- I argue that particle throwing from you isn't right, since I can read your emails and still be affected by you.

- Prompts from myself are probably the most accurate explanation for my interaction with you in the sense that I am a self-reinforcing volume of frequencies (via my atoms and their behaviors). This would explain why our personalities, birth charts, and palm prints remain so stable (everything was always us all along, just as the terms of our formation suggested). BUT…

- If the above holds for you, what holds for me? It must be the case that the world connects us after all, not JUST though hormone throwing, but through a generally predictable space of probability clusters on the bigger space of the earth and solar system. We are individuals on the self-level, others are also—though not us—and the world is the more generalized neutrino, gravitational, quantum mechanical and inertial field which threads through us all.

- So it turns out that you *do* throw particles at me. But they're waves. The same waves that connect carbon properties to carbon properties, oxygen to oxygen. And they're not just stuck within us, they also flow between us—all of us.

---

[20] Maybe you don't believe this, but you do believe the Los Angeles acid rain when it hits your skin, don't you? These are big particles changing the air in big ways you can feel. I argue that higher frequency, smaller wavelength fields like those associated with certain colors, sounds, and ultraviolet do the same thing to those levels of your atoms which resonate with them.

[21] Epiphenomenal: existing without having any effect that matters to any observer

Telepathy is where we gain the ability to respond to clustered waves that are not us just as easily as we respond to ourselves—literally losing ourselves in another's patterns (which are just your own patterns minus all of the extra waves that tie together your sense of self).

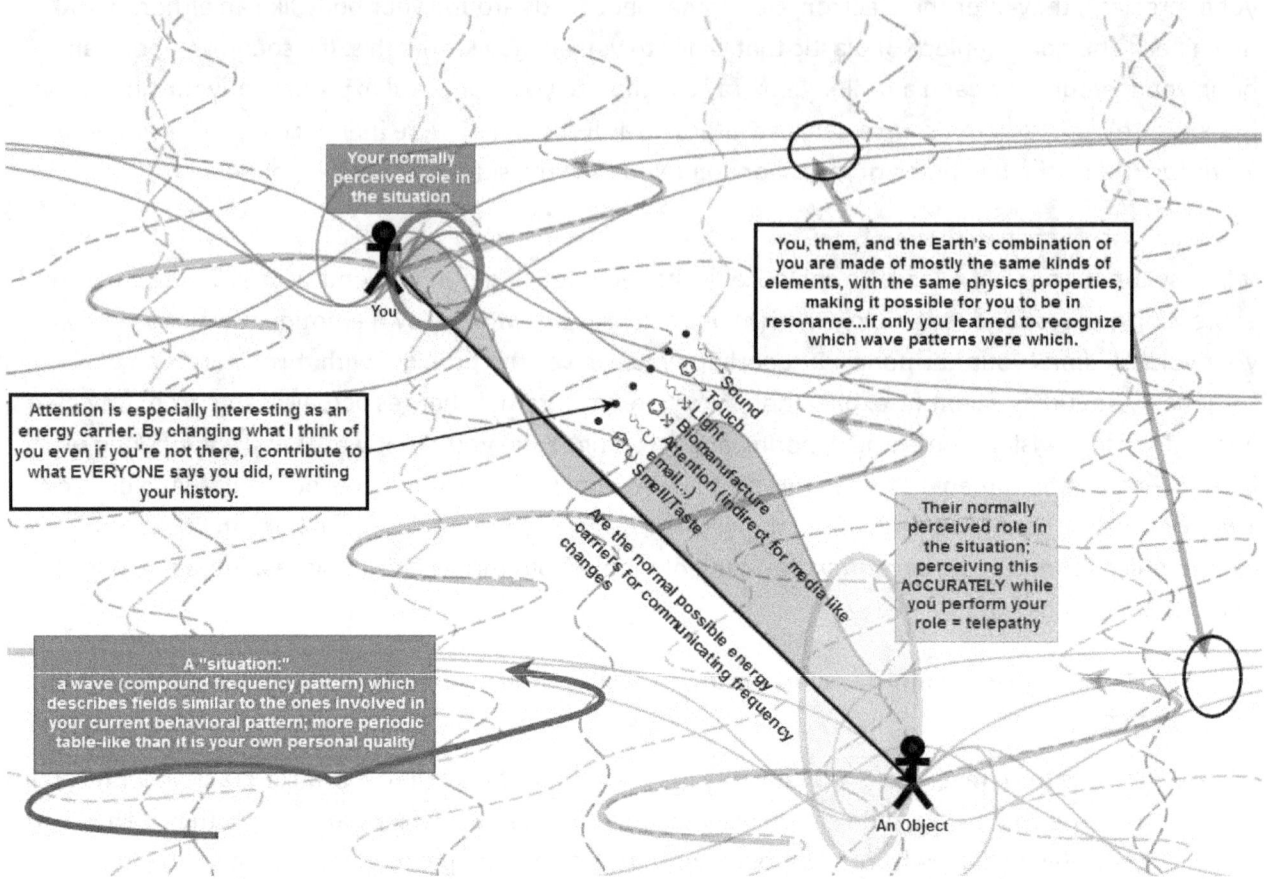

Figure 47-3: The proposed mechanisms of telepathy

And now for a surprise: You could experience telepathy as often as you experience empathy. This should be obvious. For every empathetic feeling you get there was an occasion for your interactant to give. Thus, your interactant *could* (in a perfectly taught world) catch themselves giving you feelings. Telepathy could occur as often as empathy, but not as easily. Oneself's getting in the way is one part of the reason. The need to attribute only certain kinds of things to certain kinds of parties is another part of the reason. The lack of proof from the object is yet another part of—nay, *most of*—the reason. The appropriateness of even doing this is probably the rest of the reason.

- It just doesn't make normal adult sense to think that you're affecting some other object with your biological self-rewrites alone.

- We are trained to see outside inputs as coming through the normal senses, inside feedback coming from proprioception.

- If we're using our inner states to affect something, we're probably not telling it so in words or open deeds. If it's being affected by us only internally, it probably won't tell us either.

- Finally, what on earth would compel you to do something psychologically but not do it publicly? Surely you've gone underground for a reason.

So how does one develop telepathy if one rarely gets feedback during its practice? We'll address that shortly. First, let's find out what kinds of *empathy* you feel the strongest.

☞ Question 47.25 (Your highest empathy): If you have felt enough empathic connections to make summary observations from, list in the left column the kinds of emotions you tend to pick up the strongest. Then in the right column, list the kinds of emotions you yourself display very easily, but cannot pick up in others with much accuracy.

Strongest emotions you can pick up from people or situations	Strongest emotions you give out, but are weak at picking up from others

Now guess what? In line with the basic laws of supply and demand, "getting ahead" emotions you pick up easily are emotions which you are positioned to have less of. Dominant emotions like anger, disgust, or irritation; submissive emotions like fatigue, giving up, or being cornered fall under this category. The person or situation who gives it is one to whom you are expected (or framed) to give the opposite emotion or against whom you are framed to play a complementary role.

> I once had a friend with whom I was constantly irritated. For a period of about three years, 80% of the time when I was irritated with her she would call. But she wouldn't call unless I was irritated. MY expectation was that she be more stable in her displays towards me—the opposite emotion from the one I suspect she was picking up empathetically. I could be said to have sent her irritation telepathically.

Unlike the getting ahead emotions, the getting along emotions are ones you are poised to give more of. Do you like a person without them giving you any kind of any emotional or psychological feedback either way? You are (barring other factors) positioned to greet distance with distance of your own. Feeling warmth from another? You are positioned to give warmth back.

Both the getting along and getting ahead emotions can also be generalized. I easily pick up people's irritation in general—towards me or not—but not whether others are happy with me. It's taken a few years, but I've learned that irritation is not an emotion I am designed to hold onto, lest it become relationship damaging. Dissatisfaction is another matter entirely. Highly social people who radiate warmth on the other hand are more likely to be designed for warmth in return. What you are designed to feel or send psychologically or emotionally tells you what domains best suit you telepathically. If you have the emotion in plenty and just can't pick it up from others, it may mean either you have a monopoly on it among those you know OR someone else is supposed to pick it up for you.

Lastly on this subject, it should be noted that the sources you feel emotions most strongly from are the sources you are most closely connected to, for better or worse. Your task is to turn your impression of their emotions into something that benefits you both. Again, we'll talk more about this in The Conflict.

☞ Question 47.26 (~~Empathy practice for emotions you want more of~~ Determining which emotions you should want more of): **Let me guess. You want more love, money, security, or validation. Maybe these suit you, maybe not. The litmus test is as follows:**

- Is it something you can already attract easily? _____ No? Then don't list it. (We can still get to it, but not directly through telepathy).

- Is it something you need to calculate, manipulate, mull over, or otherwise guess about? _____ Yes? Then don't list it. If you try using *telepathy* to get it, you will only doubt what you experience.

- Do you want to attract it because you "need" it for yourself, family, or some other obligation? _____ Yes? Then don't list it. Telepathy will obligate the target to your needs, forcing certain kinds of misinterpretation of what you experience. Telepathy, like regular communication, should ideally be used to pursue things you enjoy, not to tax yourself in more mysterious ways.

- Is it something you just want to enjoy, improve, or build upon just because you really feel like it AND were your answers to the three questions above a solid Yes, No, and No? Then list it below.
  _____
  _____
  _____
  _____
  _____

The above are the kinds of things you should want to experience empathetically and/or pull towards you using telepathy.

☞ **Question 47.27 (Empathy practice for emotions you want more of):** Set your timer for 2 minutes or longer. Using only the experiences that made your list in 47.26 or (generalized versions of those experiences), close your eyes and feel each experience as it occurs. Let any of the previous psychic senses inform your proper relationship with that experience. When you're finished, write down what happened below.

_____
_____
_____
_____
_____
_____
_____
_____
_____
_____
_____
_____
_____
_____

☞ **Question 47.28 (Telepathic receivers): The more easily a person or situation reacts to you, the easier your telepathic connection with them.** List the people or situations that seem to be highly sensitive to every little thing you do.

_____
_____
_____
_____

☞ Question 47.29 (Easier telepathic messaging): Set aside some time and a place to focus. Close your eyes and feel the people or situations from 47.28 doing whatever is natural to them to advance your 46.13. If the people you listed bring you negative empathic feelings, feel them storing those feelings in their own worlds as projects which only _they_ are capable of addressing. For example, if your 46.13 was to be a good parent to your children and one of your 47.28s was known for placing depression upon your empathy, feel them being a supporter to your children through something related to the person's work helping others with depression instead. I know that's abstract, but it is meant to be only a prelude to the tactic we'll use frequently in handling conflict.

*Note something important here. Telepathy works best when you're communicating with things well-designed to receive your communication. The best messages to send are the ones that advance the things you would dedicate your life towards. Almost every other kind of telepathy is often just extra work. If you want to affect more things telepathically, you'll need to have more things welcome your influence. Even if you manage to affect them, if your affecting them doesn't benefit them in their own worlds, expect to wear out your welcome eventually. Resonance gets you connected. Relevance *keeps* you connected. Besides that, you should have everything you need to get started.

A Summary of the Senses

There are senses whose information travels directly towards you (longitudinally), and senses whose information moves in a 2D plane in front of you (transversely). There are also senses whose information adds up the changes in other senses (cyclical or surface-wise). This gives a total of three kinds of waves for traveling. In addition, the content of that information may have an actual form (chemical / mechanical) or just be a pattern of change (wave / field).[22]

For every event there is a complementary occurrence that can also be perceived. Longitudinal waves leave post-longitudinal voids (where perceivability is concerned). Transverse waves leave introverse derivatives. Surface waves leave subsurface ambient events. To the extent that we can use our normal senses to perceive their complements, we can develop additional senses. Neurologically, this may involve little more than cells monitoring other cells in response to patterns our society currently teaches us to filter out. These are summarized in Figure 47-4 below.

Conclusion

Throughout this chapter we have explored the senses, paying particular attention to those experiences which come to us most easily. While most of us have been exposed to spirituality's many wonders in such a way as to think that all intuitive gifts come in broad swaths, the reality is that the psychic senses are just as constrained by your own predispositions as the regular senses are. You could try to meditate your way into developing them cloudily, or you could focus on training them according to the kinds of information they contain. They must, after all, still obey laws in order for us to process them.

Now that we have all of the types of senses listed,[23] feel free to go back through this chapter and find the ones you're likely to be strongest in. Practice them on things that are easy for you to access. In the meantime, we're gearing up to paint a clearer picture of the world in which that practice can take place most efficiently.

---

[22] Chemical / mechanical forms are just *collections* of wave / field forms..
[23] If you're looking for clairgustance—intuitive perception from tastes and smells, I consider this to be a synesthetic combination of clairvoyance, clairsentience, and regular taste/smell..

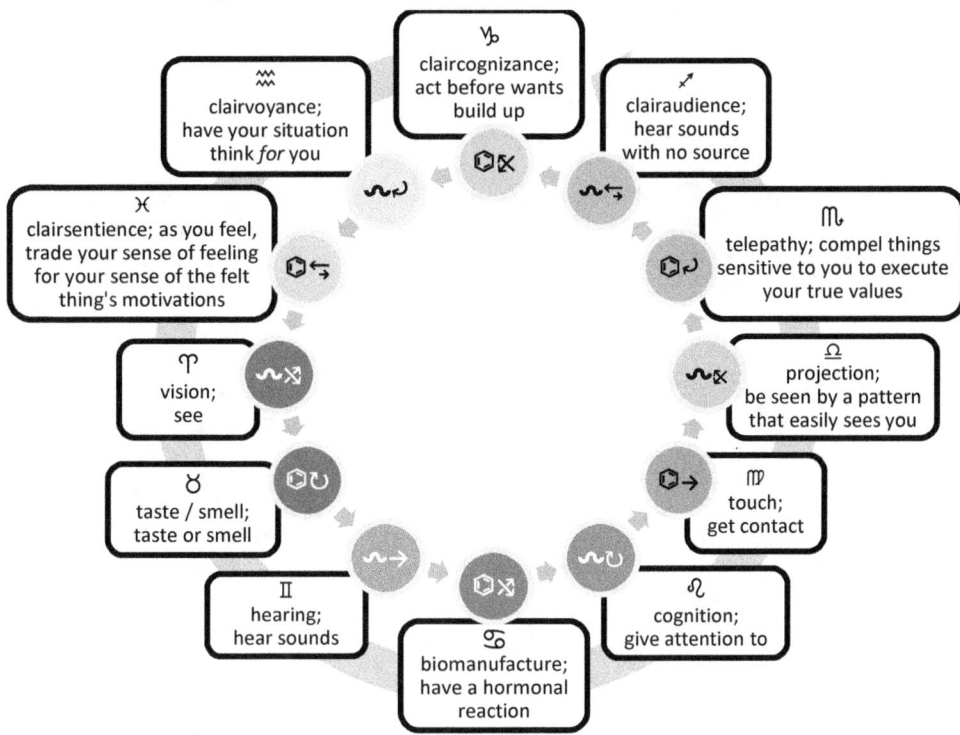

Figure 47-4: Twelve senses and how to practice them. Chemical ⬡, wave ~, longitudinal →, postlongitudinal ⇌, transverse ⚡, introverse ⚹, surface ↻, and subsurface ↪ information travel for each sense are also indicated.

☞ Question 47.30 (Easier sources of intuitive practice): **The easiest events for you to practice your senses on are those which are guaranteed to elicit some kind of reaction from you, or vice versa. Go back to your 47.16 table and use Figure 47-4 to determine the corresponding senses which might get the most practice during each event.**

Chapter 48. The Sphere

We've discussed in previous chapters how you operate in multiple dimensions, but if you like to keep your observations grounded in reality like I do, all that talk about multiple realms of perception, layered body systems, and conveniently 12-dimensional *everything* may not convince you. In this chapter we'll strengthen the argument for multiple dimensions by appealing to your conception of situations that actually describe your own life. But first, let's review another argument for multiple dimensions.

☞ Question 48.1 (Confirmation of multidimensionality): **Stand up and walk to the nearest doorway. Without passing through, put one hand on the door knob and the other hand through the doorway. Then ask yourself the following questions.**

1. Where are you located?
2. What part of your body counted as "you" in the question above? Your feet? Your whole body?
    a. If you answered your whole body, what part would you count if you were, say, a burglar and the other side of the doorway were someone else's house?
    b. What if you were a football player and your hand across the threshold had the football in it, the other side being the end zone?[24]
    c. If you answered your feet, which foot? The one more to the left or the one more to the right?
    d. Which part of your foot counts for determining your precise location? Your heels? Your toes?
3. What if there is a bug being threatened by your hand on the doorknob? Where would he say you were located?
4. Your hand on the door knob is higher up than your feet. In tracking your 3D location, would you use your feet as the anchor point or something closer to the middle of you? How does this compare to your answer two questions ago?

That's enough. What we're seeing is that, on the most basic level, you exist in multiple locations *in space*. What counts as you isn't usually just your hand or just your feet, but a broad volume that the sum of your parts takes up. You are a volume. You include multiple points. To complicate things, all this can change depending on what you're doing and who's asking. These are two dimensions that have a lot less to do with the spatial.

Furthermore, when you consider the general location of a thing, you know that you're not really concerned with precise coordinates down to the centimeter. You're concerned with the general area. Right now my cat is sitting in my lap. If someone one foot away from me pointed two inches to the left of him and asked if Snow was there, I'd say yes. He technically isn't (that's my leg they would be pointing to), but his general "sphere of effect" would extend there.

---

[24] If you know how (American) football works, you know that it would be your through-reaching hand which counted as you, not your "whole body."

Spheres of Effect

In order for you to do certain kinds of things, you need to be around certain kinds of other things. So much of our self-definition—our identity—is gained through our experiences against others. Without the notion of what it means to be someone's child, employee, or the occupant of some house, we lose who we are. But the parent, boss, and house need to be there. In a somewhat morbid example, your hand is considered a part of you because it is ultimately connected to your feet; if you chopped off the hand, it might not be considered you anymore. This is to say that your different sides are only considered *your* different sides because of their relationships to contexts shared by your other sides.

Suppose, then, that you strongly identify as your parents' child. Part of your sphere of effect will include your role all the way up to the border that is your parents. In this case your parents would be something like bonded atoms, and your behaviors which reach into them would be like your shared outer shell with them. Without them though, you would lose much of your definition as a total "chemical." This holds for any space into which your definition extends. Your definition is built on more than just yourself. It also includes your relationships to the things around you.

Thanks to our investigation of embodiments, we now know that you are more than just a physical form. Rather, you are a representation of several levels of pattern in the world. In the same way that Abraham Lincoln no longer has a physical body, yet continues to represent most of the social meaning that he represented when he was alive, your physical body can be (and will be) eventually discarded in favor of your sphere of effect—the reach and quality of your relationships. Accordingly, if we are to truly develop our long range function to its maximum, it will pay to understand ourselves beyond the physical body, into the non-physical character which will endure even long after we're done.

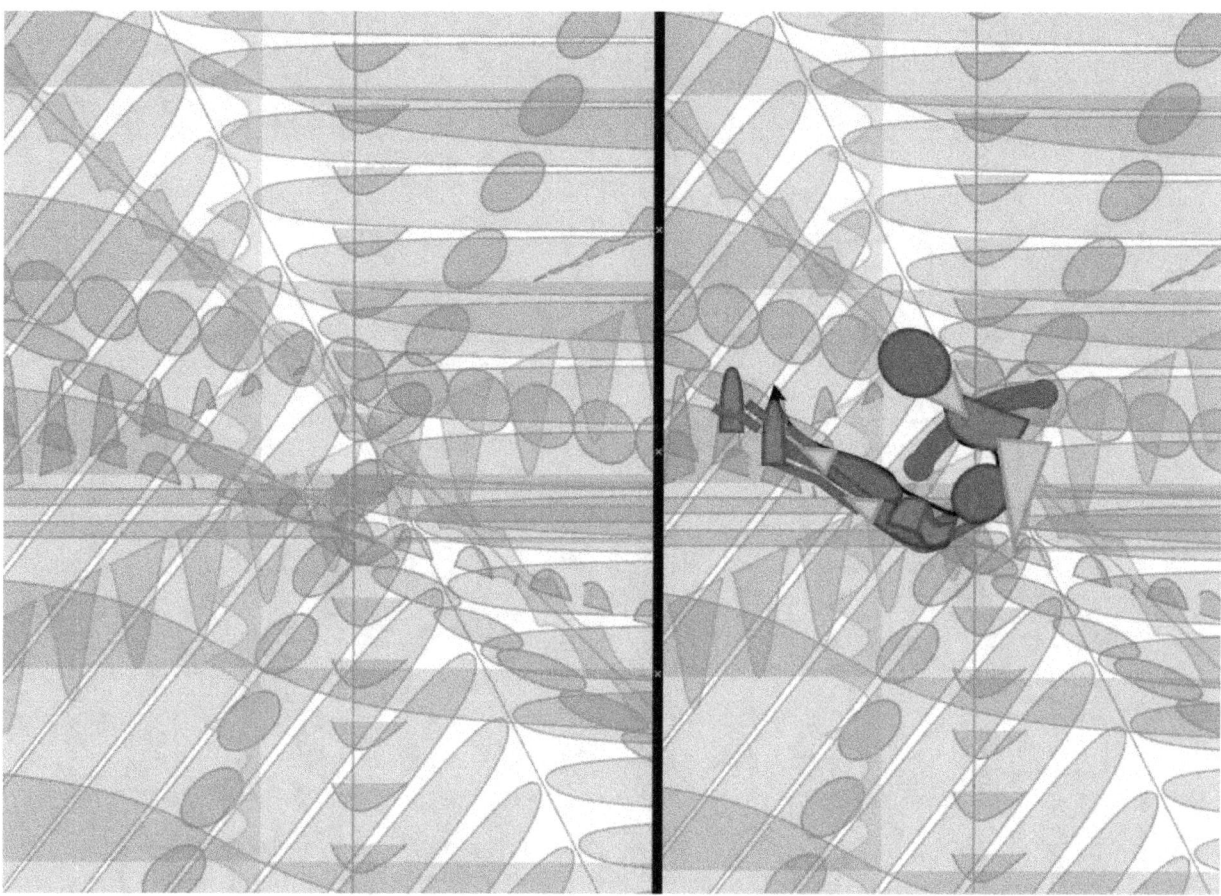

Figure 48-1: You as a frequency hub (left) and as a physical entanglement of those frequencies (right).

From here on throughout the rest of this book, you'll need to start thinking of yourself not as a body, but as a sphere of patterns. The core of your sphere is located at your body, but ultimately you extend much farther than that not only in space, but in all of the other relevant dimensions, for as long as the "situations" you represent will travel (Figure 47-3), until those situations are absorbed by another space of situation holders.

☞ Question 48.2 (The Sphere): Using your answers to the Body Wheel at the end of Chapter 46, enter your descriptions from its Column C into the blanks (in the picture) below.

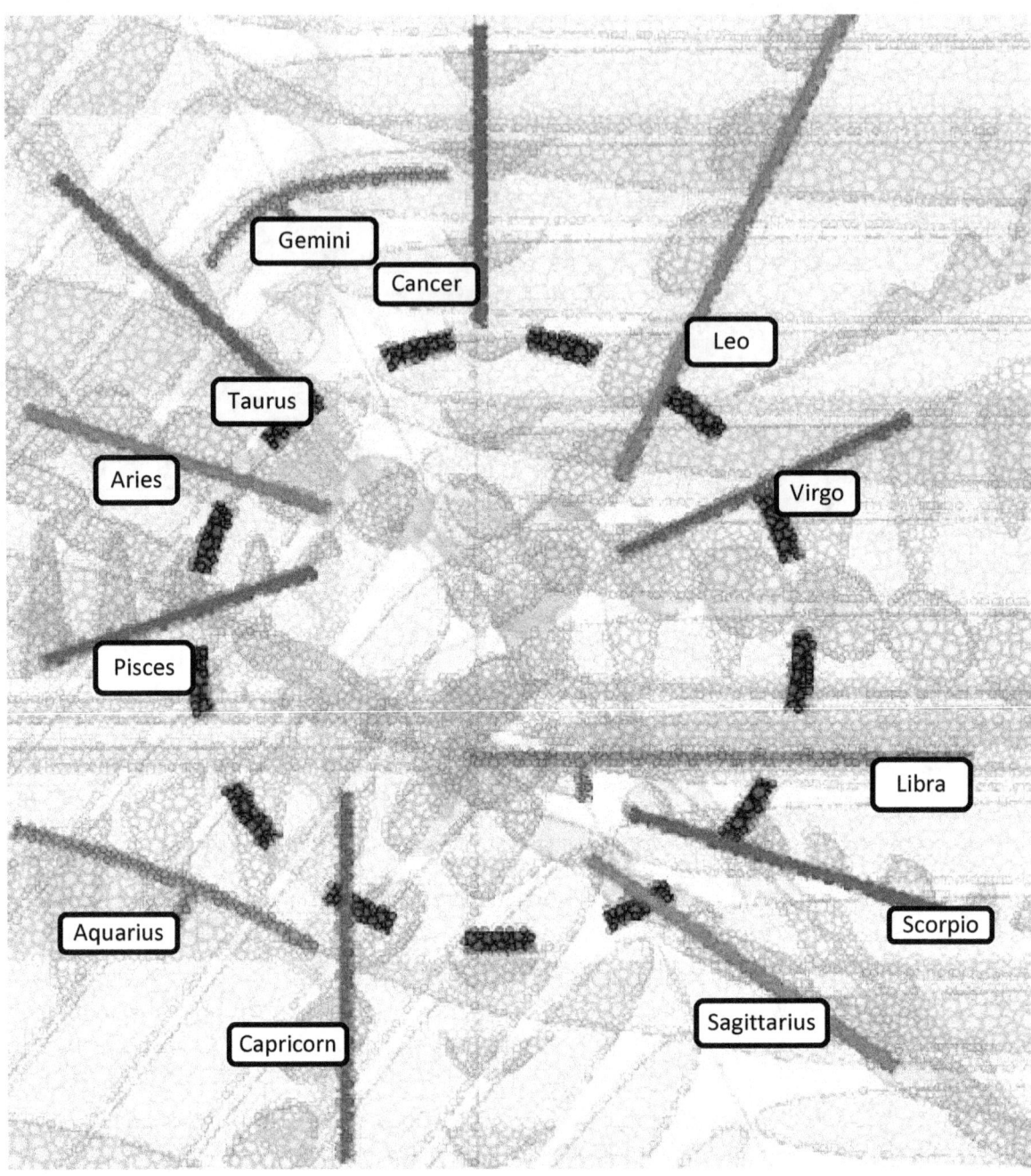

If we were to remove your body from the picture you would revert to your energetic hub form—an intersection of state-reinforcing chemistries. Notice, though, that the wave trails that constitute you ("trails" because the Earth as a whole spins as it does) also intersect with the various settings and relationships that help define you. Your claircognizant frequency level, for example, is more likely to be stronger in predictive structure settings like your job. Your biomanufacture frequency level is more likely you be stronger at home—where hormones have a less restricted setting for their escape. Both of these settings, in line with the chemical material involved in their types of wave, are physical locations. Your attention frequency level on the other hand is likely to be stronger not in a physical space, but in trait space where certain kinds of expression match the kinds of things you dwell on. Taken as a complete pattern, your sphere of effect is not only something that reaches beyond the physical form, but also across situational and informational contexts. This should seem obvious when you think about the nature of sports leagues, governments, and behavior types—all of which span across more than space (situation, information, and ideas respectively). But it's not so obvious when we think about our living selves.

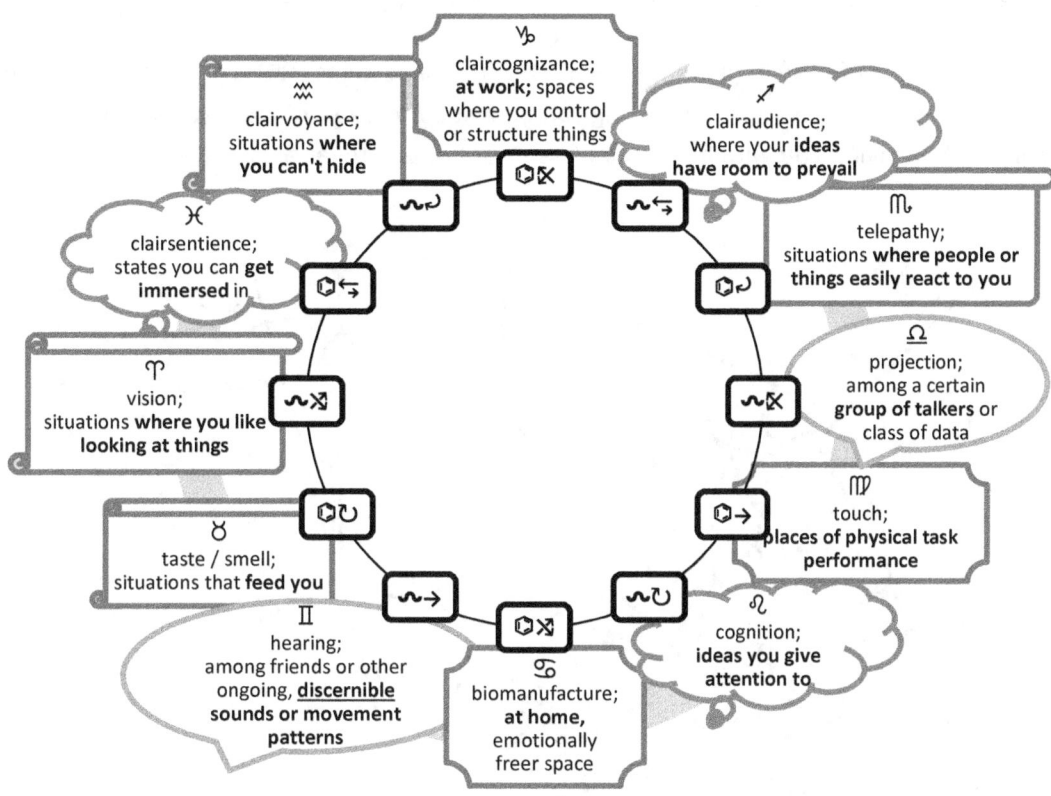

*Figure 48-2: Twelve dimensions of yourself and **where** you tend to express them. Chemical ⬡, wave ～, longitudinal →, postlongitudinal ⇆, transverse ⤫, introverse ⤬, surface ↻, and subsurface ↺ information travel for each sense are also indicated.*

Your body is only the nucleus. Your dimensions of interaction—your places of work, your home, your friends, your worry-topics—are analogous to your electron shells (or at least the contexts where you access those shells). Accordingly, many things you may think are easily changeable, like a job or an attitude, are actually not. Your interactions on your new job will be very similar to your interactions on your old one. Your new attitude will tend to revolve around the same broad topics as your old one. The task of self-development is not to change your basic frequencies as a living human, but to change the level of positivity and negativity you associate with those frequencies.

Don't just think of yourself as a body. Also think of yourself as a sphere.

The Other Spheres Which Your Sphere Bonds To
Earlier in the book we encountered the issue of making things happen through others, when doing these things ourselves proved difficult. We weren't able to address the issue fully at the time, partly because we had no sense of what our "others" <u>stably</u> looked like. Although you might think that your friend

Stephen is the game changer in your life, Stephen is really just another frequency hub like yourself. There is a very good chance that his frequency pattern with respect to *your* life is just a retooling of Devin, Jeff, and Stephanie before him. Later in the book we'll learn how to assign nicknames to the "slots" that people fill, but for now just note that, if you were to mess up the relationship with Stephen, there is a good chance you'll meet another frequency which takes his place as your complement. This happens as soon as you're ready to use that frequency consistently once again.

We also note that (in terms of frequency) people can be traded for settings; settings can be traded for people, projects, or ideas about yourself; everything can be traded for everything else as long as the energy carriers involved provide you with a reasonable amount of whatever frequency you're using.

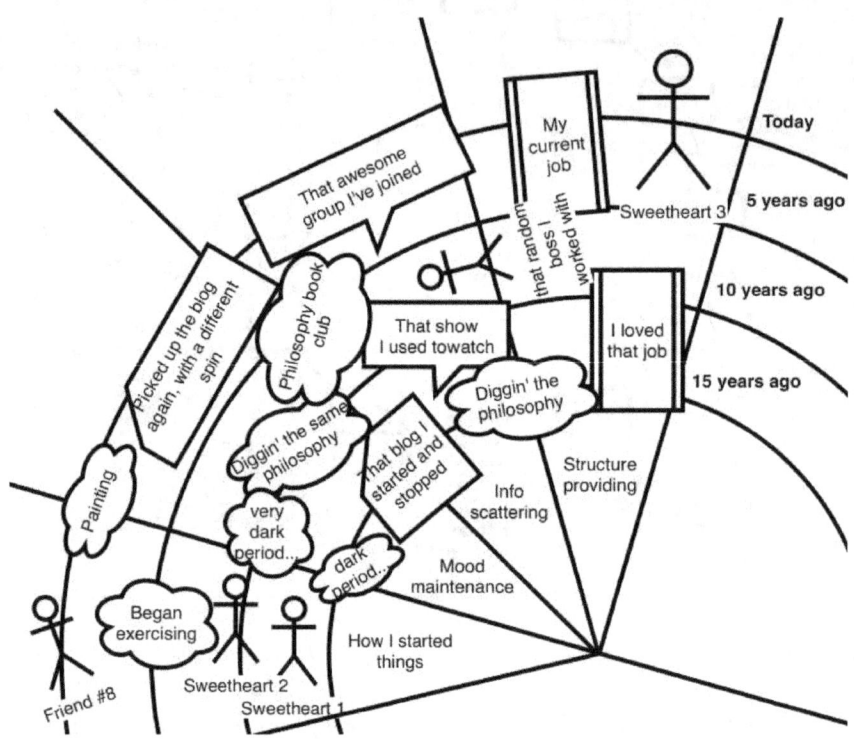

Figure 48-3: An example of the things (sphere occupants) a person might have interacted with over the years in bringing out the different sides of her life. Some occupants bring out more of a particular category than others. Occupants can span multiple categories, but as we move forward in the book you may want more control over how and when this happens.

# Critical Exercise

SPHERE TIMELINE

Trains: Clairvoyance, Claircognizance, Dream interpretability, Life path

Warning! I found that this exercise can be VERY difficult for people with a history of trauma or other aspects of their pasts they would rather not relive. If it makes you uncomfortable, don't do it. *Do*, however read the section right after this question, as it may shed light on some things.

☞ Question 48.3 (The history of your sphere): Think about the major players in your life right now. This includes four kinds of subjects:

- Places and groups where you can regularly be found, along with your broad role there
- Personality types which are recurring in your life, along with the names of specific people who have embodied these types
- Situations or idea types you tend to focus on or be involved with, including certain beliefs, social groups, and families of behavior
- Moods you tend to reinforce, including specific activities you perform to reinforce them.

---

1. In the outer ring of the chart, using what you've learned about yourself from activities like the Body Wheels (Chapter 46) and question 47.7, write a broad description of that area of your life.
2. In the next ring, note any major-ish, reliably present topics that occupy each slot at this current time in your life
3. Use the rest of the rings to go as far back in your life as is reasonable for understanding the [current time] ring
4. The only section whose rings <u>must all</u> be filled in, outer to center, is the emotional home base section. Somewhere in each ring level, put where you have lived. (You can also insert other things too, but your living places are essential for helping you practice pattern-finding in all of the other sections.)
5. If there are blanks in the [current time] ring—meaning you can't think of a topic that fits that section, note this. Can you fill in an earlier ring in that section?
6. If there is something you *want* to occupy a particular [current time] section, put it outside the outer border and circle it.
7. Yes, you CAN AND SHOULD list more than 12 things if they come to mind, just let them overlap the appropriate areas. A person who is a solid conversation partner might be in the center of Libra, for example, while a friend who is closer to a co-worker would be still be in Libra, but nearer to Virgo. Just remember this one rule…
8. DO NOT STACK TOPICS RIGHT ON TOP OF THE OTHER IF THEY APPEARED IN YOUR LIFE AT THE SAME TIME. No two simultaneous items should occupy the exact same degree.

Fill in the chart below. If you need an example, see Appendix III.

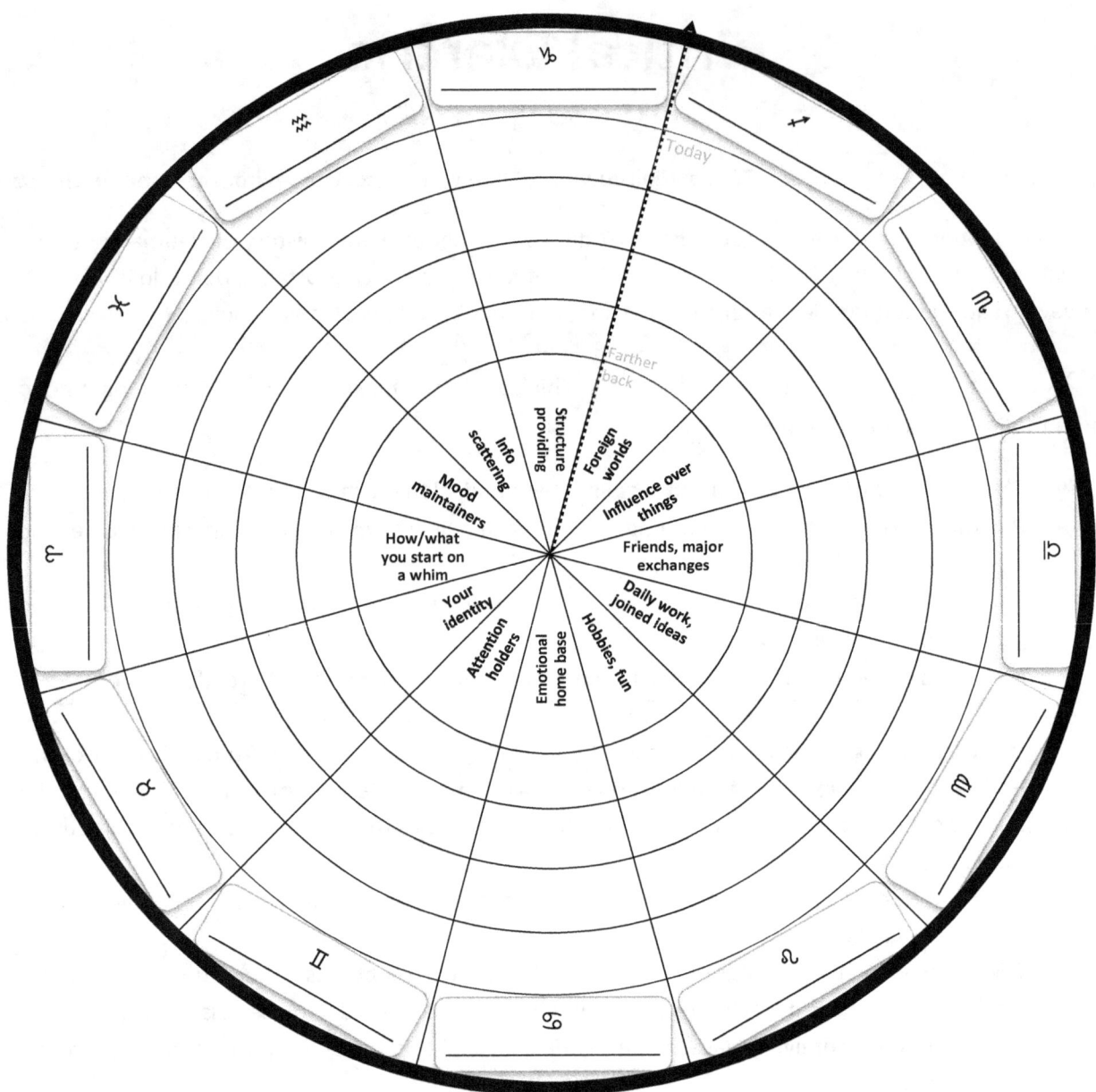

♈	♉	♊	♋	♌	♍
Aries spontaneous behaving	**Taurus** experiencing things you value or identify yourself against	**Gemini** communicating your ideas or instinctual movement; thinking or talking to or for yourself	**Cancer** paying attention to how you feel or how you're reacting to things	**Leo** playing, enjoying leisure time, having fun, broadcasting yourself	**Virgo** working, making meaning, doing daily duties and maintenance tasks
♎	♏	♐	♑	♒	♓
Libra socializing, friends, conversation with others, engaging in 1:1 feedback activities like playing instruments or video games	**Scorpio** using your power over others, over information, or over situations broadly	**Sagittarius** leaving an impression among strangers	**Capricorn** being associated with certain formal classes of people	**Aquarius** being talked about	**Pisces** performing default actions

Perhaps you can see why just "making something happen" isn't as simple as it sounds. Because we have attitudes that we naturally hold about how the world works, the occupants who enter our sphere—be they human or otherwise—need to 1) fit in with the other current patterns of our sphere and 2) adopt forms consistent with how we ourselves are used to behaving. This is particularly true of areas that reflect holes in our lives.

Curious Holes

The four classes of major wants we tend to have in life—self-worth, supportive arrangements, worldly rewards, and beneficial emotions—each come with their standard sets of associations in our psychologies. Whether positive or negative, each association family is something like a group of neighboring buildings on a city block. You may not like having Riches right next to The Cutthroat Center, but there they are. And you can't just bulldoze the connection. You have a whole lifetime of experiences preceded by powerful genetics which caused constructs like this to be neighbors no matter where you travel in your mental city. The connection between things we really want and things we don't care to get near is the number one cause of holes in our lives.

Sometime after my not-so-successful real estate career, I realized that I would always associate great and easy riches with a combination of robber baron capitalism, committed relationships, and patronizing judgment. The lack of such riches formed a hole in my frequency map, where it stood as something I wanted but just couldn't get...and wasn't willing to truly force the mentality change needed to pursue. That's how holes work: You really want that whatever-it-is but can't get a foothold among the situations which bring it about. Actually though, you *can and do* have a foothold already in the form of the frequency level you've tied to it. It's just a matter of your coming to terms with the entire frequency block and all of the rearrangements needed to make that block fit harmoniously with everything else in your sphere. (But then again, that's not so easy is it?)

☞ Question 48.4 (Packages with holes): Do you want anything in life that you can't seem to get and don't know how to obtain? List it below, along with any places, personality types, or situations which seem to have it—*especially* if these sources are negative to you. Don't list specifics. It won't help you do the exercises to come. Only list *classes* of such specifics (e.g. "power = scheming managers" instead of specific names like "power = Janet, Lin, George").

_____
_____
_____
_____
_____
_____
_____

If you search your history—especially if you search <u>other people or situations</u> you have known in your history—you'll find out pretty easily what kinds of circumstances hold the things you seek. The very short version of this story is that you'll either need to become them, join them, or (in the case of more abstract situations) create them. You essentially do this by understanding and repairing your relationship with [your idea of] any previous slot holders on this same frequency level. You don't need to go back to the actual relationship. You just need to come to terms with the favorable, pursuable outcomes which the earlier holders of that slot brought out of you. We'll talk more about this in the next chapter since it is, again, rarely easy. But that is your general objective when handling holes.

In truth, though, you will never really have actual holes unless you're transitioning between slot holders. What you *will* have are slot holders whom you don't want there.

For example, the very night I'm writing this section, I realized that one of my key romantic relationship slots is currently held by a monogamously married male employee of mine—four traits that don't line up with what I'd want from that frequency. I know he's the slot holder because we still have the joint forward movement, intense emotional investment, and wholly familiar interaction style as the 4 or 5 women who have held that slot over the last 20 years, and that type of woman is noticeably absent from my life right now. Even if I were bisexual (I'm hetero), there's still the monogamously married employee part. I want the slot occupant to be a dream girl, but this person is a lot more important in his work role than the dream girl would be in a personal one. I've shown in the past that I couldn't handle the dream girl, but now I think I'm ready. Remember Figure 36.16 from *Laurentia*? Because of how like-energy absorption works, one cannot have two distinct slot holders of the exact same(-ish) frequency at the same time. What do I do?

Hmm. Curious.

And then there are the slots that should be projects instead of people. Lifestyles instead of lovers. TV Series instead of tasks. How many of us have our would-be wishes tied up in politics or the media we follow? Your slots may be evasive, but they're usually not holes after all.

It turns out that my example a couple of paragraphs above can be resolved smoothly by changing other slots related to the one in question. To resolve a hole, you don't usually take the direct route which dug the hole in the first place. Instead, you rearrange your other frequencies in such a way as to easily alter your view of that slot. I'll tell you what I decided shortly (which you might strongly consider doing with your own holes), but first we need to note something about your sphere occupants in general.

Slot Holders
"**Slot holders**" is my term for **the current specific things which represent more timeless general patterns in your life.** You can be on great terms or terrible terms with them depending on where you currently are on your life path, where at least one of the following four basic social relationships I described in *Non-Capital Wealth* tends to be your reason for the relationship:

- *Beneficial relationships* – patterns of exchange which help us access what we want to access; these are aimed at the positive present and future; smooth friendships are like this.

- *Defensive relationships* – patterns of exchange which protect us from things we don't want accessing us; these typically are aimed at the non-negative present and future; jobs and financial obligations tend to be like this, since they protect us from having to build our own houses and police our own towns and such.

- *Clarifying relationships* – patterns of exchange which help us know or find what we want, even if they don't help us access those things. These are often the best final form of our relationships with enemies, and are often aimed at transitioning or assessing the present.

- *Familiar relationships* – patterns of exchange which remind us of what we can currently access even if our experiences have helped convince us otherwise; these are aimed at recovering the past through the present, building on the life histories and psychologies available to us. Temporary trips, brief personal encounters, and passing events tend to be of this type. The things you meet here serve to put your most important archetypes right in your face. Just in case you forgot.

At the time of this writing, one of my strongest sphere occupants and most significant slot holders is my boss at my day job. We're not friends. We didn't always get along. We don't even interact much. Yet it has been so clear from the beginning that my current trajectory in life is tied to my exchange with her and vice-versa such that if I messed this one up I WOULD DEFINITELY BE STARTING ALL OVER AGAIN in some personal growth sense. She holds the same slot as several former friends of mine and two colleagues in an example of something like "in-life reincarnation." Why does stuff like this happen? Because our mental cities are a lot harder to change than we think; they extend past the cognitive senses and into the biomanufacture, visual interpretation, projection, and claircognizant dimensions (to name a few); we are frequency hubs on levels that the physical world alone does not span a fraction of. Accordingly, changing jobs or boyfriends or whatever in order to repair a "hole" is a lot like pushing a cake to the *back* of the counter to stop yourself from eating it. You'll need to do more than that.

☞ Question 48.5 (The main actors in your current scene): **Right now you are at a certain point on your life path. Set your timer for 2 minutes. Without putting any deep thought into it, list all of the major players—people, places, or situations; positive, negative, or neutral—that play integral roles in the current scene in your life.**

_____
_____
_____
_____
_____
_____

Critical Exercise
SLOT REVISION PRACTICE

(If you've been doing the exercises throughout this book without much skipping, this one has the potential to be one of the strongest yet. I used a version of this one during the writing of this book combined with a major activity in Chapter 57 to achieve crazy results which I'll tell you about later. If you have skipped too many exercises, there is a good chance you'll be missing a key component needed to make it work: the right *perspective*—which we've been building throughout the previous chapters.)

Trains: Telepathy

If your aim is to move past the current scene, your task is to play your role 1) opposite your clarifying relationships, 2) alongside your beneficial relationships, 3) with the temporary assistance of your familiar relationships, 4) within the scope of your defensive relationships.

☞ Question 48.6 (Past this point): Write down ONE goal you currently have for moving past a particular set of arrangements in your life: _____.

1. What other ideas do you associate with this goal?
   _____
   _____

2. How have you historically obtained things like this goal?
   _____
   _____
   _____

3. List two of any of the 12 senses from chapter 47 which you are pretty sure you could or should use in order to advance in this goal. These should be senses that you have not been using so far for this purpose. _____.

4. Who or what do you think holds the slot(s) which this goal is most heavily associated with? (You may need to really think about this one, since it's not about what you want. It's definitely about what you currently have. You're **not** allowed to say "nobody/nothing." I found this sub-question particularly challenging to answer.) Your relationship to the slot holder should strongly resemble your relationship to the goal. And remember, sometimes people are represented as places, institutions, projects, or even belief systems. TV shows, current hobbies, or personal events. They are all interchangeable.
   _____
   _____

5. Assuming you chose a slot you intend to replace, fill in the substitution path below:

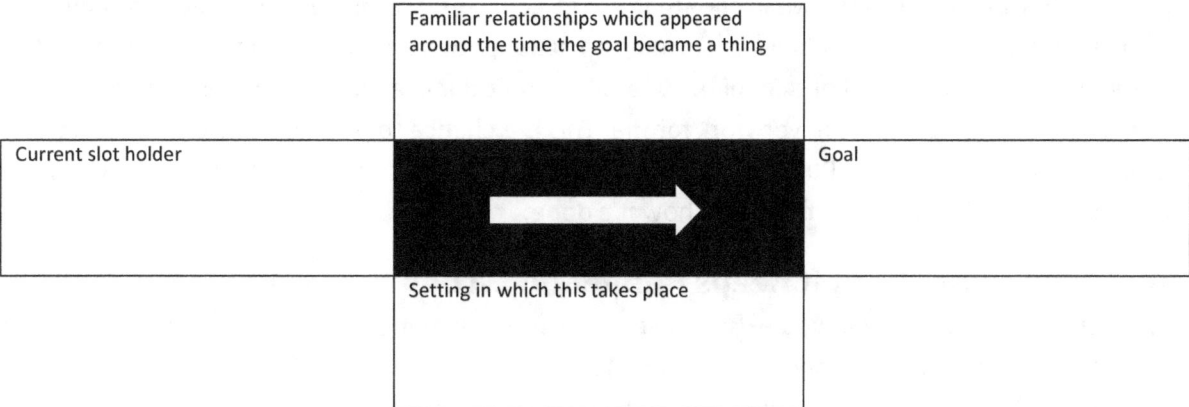

6. Over the next two days, once each day, spend at least 30 minutes on each of the two senses you listed to address your goal. That's a total of one hour each day for two days. If you don't have the hour, don't expect progress. Log your efforts below.

Day 1, Sense 1 What sense are you using? _____ In the space below, describe what you experienced while using it.	Day 1, Sense 2 What sense are you using? _____ In the space below, describe what you experienced while using it.
Day 2, Sense 1 What sense are you using? _____ In the space below, describe what you experienced while using it.	Day 2, Sense 2 What sense are you using? _____ In the space below, describe what you experienced while using it.

Will you see progress towards your goal in a mere two days? Some people will. Two days is just long enough to try, but not long enough to obligate you unreasonably. Just remember, even though you have a goal in your sights, it's still very important to do these activities with a reasonably clear mind. Some senses, if you force them, won't work at all.

If this exercise seems to lack direction in some way, that's because we vary so greatly in how we manifest things. In The Spirits we'll learn that not all goals require that you actually "do" anything. While some people obtain their wants by performing an action, others do so by simply being seen. Others set aside time for themselves. I obtain mine by refusing something; action, asking for help, meditating, speaking out… those almost never work for me. This is a chance to put your senses into practice—especially the psychic ones. Put any desperation or forcing aside, clear your agenda of clutter, then go back to Figure 47-4 and show the world how it's done.

It's Their Fault…Until It Keeps Happening…Then It's Probably You

While it is certainly true that you exist as a separate form from most of the things you interact with, it doesn't always pay to assign separate explanations for how those things behave towards you. We've seen how spheres are basically consistent packagings of standard groups of frequencies. We've seen how changing one dimension of an event alone doesn't do nearly as much as changing several dimensions—or at least the right dimension—when trying to achieve a goal. If you've got a situation which consistently occurs in your life, is negative, but *is consistent*, then—no matter how easy it may be to blame the other party—you almost certainly need to look at yourself. Not to place "blame" on yourself, but to learn more about your life's specific patterns.

As you'll see next chapter, looking at your patterns doesn't need to be as painful as it sounds. But it almost always needs to happen. Even if the event you keep experiencing is disempowering, devastating, and unfair. If you assign the solution to someone else's black box, I believe you're almost guaranteed not to get to it. Blame may put a recognizable label on your problem, but it won't send it off. Look at your sphere. Not just the physical people or even the psychological attitudes by themselves, but also at the mood maintainers, the structure makers, the emotional home base, the attention holders, and the influence recipients you keep around you. Especially the influence recipients. If you have a problem which follows you around, you yourself will need the power to address it, even if it's as simple as asking the right person to fix it for you or refusing to watch that show anymore. (It may sound criminal, but my sense of control over problems grew exponentially the year I decided not to buy anyone any Christmas presents.[25]). Don't lock yourself out of a solution by blaming someone else. You don't *have* to take that mess. There are things you can do. Own your own sphere.

---

[25] I warned my family beforehand and told them why, but since then it's been a hell of a lot easier to let people know: No one can obligate anyone to do anything—not to put on a mask, not for anyone's approval, not when it costs the giver, for no reason other than societal drama. You can't imagine how much easier it is to claim what *you* believe in after you've made a statement towards scripted society like this. As I mentioned earlier though, I advance through refusal. This may not work for everyone.

☞ Question 48.7 (Targeting the right dimension): Go back to question 47.20. For every item you listed, see if you can determine which dimension of your sphere it lives in. Give it some thought, though. Some of your responses may surprise you.[26]

_____
_____
_____
_____
_____

☞ Question 48.8 (Accepting the right help): Who (or what) in your sphere keeps wanting to join you, help you, support you, or hang around you?

_____
_____
_____
_____
_____

Consider accepting their help.

If you don't trust them or can't rely on them, consider closing out their slot (unless you like having untrustworthies in your space).

If, for whatever reason, you don't trust the would-be supporters in your sphere but don't want to kick them out, consider letting them know where you stand. They may remove themselves, but at least your sphere will make room for something you *can* work with. BE WARNED though, if you do this in a way that disrespects the would-be supporter, the person or situation which takes their place will almost always be worse. You've written it on your own sphere of effect that this is how you handle help.

If you can't accept a would-be supporter's help, won't kick them out, and won't let them know where you stand, get ready to string them along until they leave. The various delays, resistance, and avoidance tactics you use for doing this typically occupy more space in your attention, emotional, and value dimensions while at the same time clouding your clairaudient dimension, falsifying your projection dimension, and turning your telepathic and claircognizant dimensions into your own jail, since you can't act as you would prefer to act and don't want to hear what your own sphere is really offering. Does it make sense why this any of these is more likely to happen when you string somebody, some group, or

---

[26] For example, right now there is something I'm looking to make happen in my business, but you'd never guess where the issue lives: in the realm of hobbies. That's because I'm not at all interested in running a business, but in productive creation instead. My business is basically a kind of book just like this is. Unless I want to treat it like a structure, I shouldn't file it there.

yourself along? It's just the regular building of associations in your own mind as well as the rest of your patterns with respect to a particular *class* of person/thing, even if you did manage to avoid the current slot holder. But when the slot holder is absent, and that same pattern is exercised by you alone, the responding patterns you've written for it will come with it. Your 100 feet from me means I'm 100 feet from things that look like you—even if those things are sides of myself. The way I treat you is the way I treat a collection of frequency bonds in my own sphere. It's just resonant waves in action, but we know it better as Karma. See if it doesn't happen again after you've finished this one off. Of course it will. It's your valence. They're just another molecule.

In the next chapter we'll talk about conflict, paying special attention to some of the great villains in our exchanges and how those villains are represented astrologically. For now, just note that your patterns are your patterns. The task is to find out what sides of your life they may be meant to clarify.

Conclusion

Ultimately our lives are built up from resonance with several dimension's worth of constructs outside of our "selves." We know where we are in space thanks to the normal sensory information from beyond us. We know where we are in interaction thanks to the attention, influence, and emotional manufacture we hold. We know where we are in plans against the larger context thanks to various kinds of information and structure surrounding our whole exchange environments. These levels of non-us information circumscribe the reach of our behaviors—establishing us as a sphere of effect more than a single human against single tangible objects. As convenient as it is to think about ourselves as physical bodies, it is clear that we have nonphysical minds and other-object influence. After we die, global effects which outlast our bodies continue to steer our successors in ways that resemble who we were when we were living. We die, but the composite waves formed by our atoms are just as possible as they ever were along the continuous chain of the universe's evolution which produced our form in the first place. Even *this* is us:

Figure 48-4: We are not just the center of the hub, but the whole web of elements, particles, energy carriers and their oscillations which describe the hub

As a consequence of our nature as energy hubs, we have interactions which naturally flow from the conditions which led us to become hubs to begin with. On the surface it seems as though our wants, our burdens, and our enemies exist separately from us, but this is only partly true; things not-us are separate in that they have their own local logic which governs how they self-reinforce as collections. But things not-us are combined with us in the sense that, the more we view, hear, react to, or pay attention to them, the more our own frequencies are their frequencies in whatever dimension that applies.

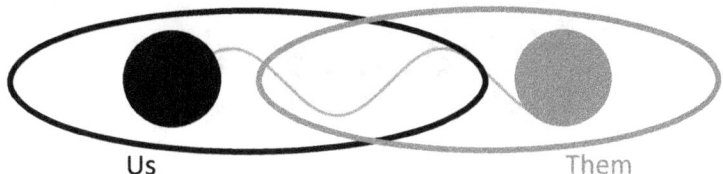

Figure 48-5 Just as an atom includes its electron shells and those shells overlap with the shells of other atoms, the frequencies we share with everything we interact with, regardless of the types of wave/carrier, makes us a part of those interactants. I claim this also holds for non-solid energy levels like vision-projection, not just the moving matter of speech and touch.

If we don't want to resonate with something as it is, then we'll either need to 1) tell it what we want, 2) want something different, or 3) detach from it. -1) Dodging it while leaving it there or -2) trying to change the other thing rarely works in any reliable way, since beyond our surface bond with it lies an entire web of frequencies just as stubbornly maintained as our own.

The holes in our sphere—areas of our lives where we want a particular experience but don't know of anything resembling it—are rarely actually holes. Instead, their patterns are taken up by the various constructs we tie to them, often in the cognitive or identity dimensions as attention or value holders. Filling the holes often entails learning more about the patterns associated with them, coming to terms with the previous holders of those patterns, and bracing ourselves to fix our relationships with those patterns broadly. Addressing a pattern holder themselves won't really fix the long-term issue unless you're in a position to make that one "the ultimate repair."

And sometimes the things you want just aren't as great as the things you have.

> Remember that issue I told you about with my employee? I decided that the dream girl whose slot he occupied really was just a dream. Putting aside my male-trained pressure to obtain such a woman, the previous occupants of that slot never did do a fraction of what the current holder does. So my actual solution was to do *nothing*. Sometimes the sphere occupant you have is *a lot* better than the one you want, but as long as you have outside pressures in your ear, you may keep chasing new thing after new thing just for the Joneses of it.
>
> Doin' it for the Joneses.

Finally, though it's not always easy to accept, sometimes the slot filler you don't want is exactly the one poised to help you. While I was busy cursing clients in my near-empty real estate career, I was also writing *Analytical Essays*—a path which, 11 books later, has led to this one for you. Back then I had a desire for a monetarily and socially rich life spent helping others. Instead I found a monetarily secure and super-socially rich lifestyle, along with an ultra-level self-efficacy doing work that truly feels like my own. There I would have compromised, struggling to adopt traits that don't fit me. Here there is no such thing. The Joneses can be sneaky. You have to catch them in the act if you're ever to reduce the number of alleged holes in your sphere.

Critical Exercise
7-DAY HOLE CHALLENGE

Trains: Essential knowledge, Life path, Clairvoyance[27]

☞ **Question 48.9 (Remove a hole):** Give yourself one week to take something that you want to replace, and become happy with it as it is. I can't tell you how to do this, but I can tell you why it's important. This exercise is a critical attitude builder for an unstuck life. Ultimately, your worth is partly a function of what others are willing to trade with you, your relationships are as rich as others' ability to feel safe expressing to you; your skill is as rich as your ability to feed it with your own application; and your self-efficacy is as strong as your ability to affect situations in ways that respond to your intentions. Holes are perceived where you have deficits in any of these areas, where no amount of intuition or self-focus will advance you any farther. In order to develop a clearer sense of the greater realms of which you are a reflection, you'll need to bring fewer and fewer of your own holes into the lives of people and things around you. Telepathy does you no good if the person you're reading sees you as a grim cloud. We all need to work on that kind of thing.

1. Name someone or something which consistently gives you its best, but which you tend to look past while trying to fill up some hole. No "I don't knows" allowed on this one.

   _____

2. What is the nature of the hole (the thing you're looking for above)?

   _____

3. What is it that they give to you?

   _____

4. Sometime this week, tell them so (if you can reach them).

   _____

After you've done the above,

5. rephrase your hole to reflect the newly acknowledged value which this person contributes to your cause.

   _____

6. As you did in question 48.6.4, write down who or what slot filler currently occupies this so-called hole. (Remember, the occupant may not be a person, but they are almost certainly in your life *right now*.)

   _____

---

[27] You're probably wondering how this exercise trains clairvoyance. That's easier to answer if you've done it a few times. What I can tell you from my own experience is that this challenge helps you train gratitude for things as they are. I've come out of it a few times with lowered bias, a calmer mind minus much of the previous dissatisfaction and, as such, an easier time seeing any messages that come to me in much higher clarity.

And now for the extra hard part:

7. Take one week to treat the current occupant as if it were the thing you sought to fill the hole with. You'll need to do this as best you can, 7 days in a row, but you don't have to do it for the entire day. Just make sure you do it enough to where any negative thoughts against this exercise don't outweigh the positive. If you have even one day where you come out of character and let the lack of this thing feel more real than having it, you should plan to start again. No one wins $10,000,000, the respect, or the prized spouse, loses it for a day, and gets it all back again. That's 7 days straight, acting more like the hole is filled than acting like it isn't.

- You won't be ~~spending, texting, or partying~~ like you just won the goal. That's Hollywood stuff. Instead, you'll be holding the <u>attitude</u> and the <u>demeanor</u> as though you have *had it* for years. This is much easier to do, much more realistic, and makes you much more accessible to everyone around while you do it.
- Bookmark this page.
- Fill in the boxes below at the end of each day, indicating that you spent more of the day in the "hole is filled" behavior than the "I wish I had it" behavior.

Day 1	Day 2	Day 3	Day 4	Day 5	Day 6	Day 7

If you fall off for a day, you fail the challenge. You'll need to start again. That's why it's a challenge.

This exercise is, by its nature, intended to be VERY HARD. Your familiar world is currently setup to reinforce the hole. All of a sudden, you're saying the hole isn't so. Therefore, you can go back to normal if you want at the end of the seven days. You still will have gained a lot if you can survive the entire week straight through.

Chapter 49. The Conflict

On the most basic level, our bodies require certain conflicting mechanisms in order for our parts to stay balanced. Flexors and extensors. Excitatory and inhibitory transmitters. On the border between one prevailing idea and its counterpart, we have two sides opposed. Conflict occurs where those two sides generate tension—energy burned off as useless or even costly in some viewer's eye.

There is no real secret to reducing conflict. All you do is attempt to find a win-win, or avoid it entirely. Ideally, the energy we save in avoiding conflict is much greater than the energy we lose trying to win in it. And then there is the idea that conflict resolved through force or at one side's expense often returns another day, while conflict resolved through mutual agreement may last for the rest of the parties' lives. Sometimes.

At this point in our spiritual practice we have reached a dividing line. Some will pass through this chapter with a newfound drive towards peace and efficacy. Others will stop right here—their talents confined to the small and easy worlds that continually reaffirm them. But your gifts won't reach the greater world if you have large portions of that world—your own sphere—which you won't reconcile with. That enemy, that obstacle, that disillusionment which won't go away will hold firm to their respective slots while you can only lament your lack. You know full well this kind of thing hasn't gotten you anywhere over the years—picking the same fight over and over again with the same kind of idea which you yourself keep alive in your thoughts. There must be a better way. If only you knew how to turn your war into sport…

We Will Put Conflict to Use

Our object in this chapter is to trick the spirit of conflict by claiming it on purpose, dissecting it, then ensuring that the only kinds we accept thereafter are the kinds of conflict we want. Let's start by finding out the kinds of conflicts we like and don't like.

☞ Question 49.1 (Your favorite and least favorite conflicts): **In the table below, list every kind of conflict you like, followed by every kind of conflict you don't like.** (Normally for this particular kind of question I would not include an example, so as to avoid distracting you. But as has been the case throughout the book, I've included examples that we either need now or will need later in order to see how one answers the more complicated questions as the chapter progresses.)

	Example
	Conflicts I like: Football (as a spectator), data exploration, personality exploration, quests for certain objects, category-sort tournaments, opposing biological systems, co-op games, one-sided slaughters, certain kinds of cat and mouse, choice-choice
	Conflicts I don't like: arguments, chess, Monopoly, most kinds of competition, those that take a long time, high risk, social games, versus games, mind games, guessing games (especially shell games), team sports (as a player), rankings, between friends, panel-of-judges, elimination, suspense, time wasting conflict, challenges to one's worth, being made to wait unnecessarily

☞ Question 49.2 (Your overall conflict approach): If you had to summarize your preferred and dispreferred conflict in one phrase each, how would you describe them?

	Example
	Liked: Win-or-journey, unlosable quests
	Disliked: Winner-loser, give your best but still possibly lose, noise-from-your-own-team energy drains

☞ Question 49.3 (Summary of your conflict preferences): Take a while to summarize your overall approach to conflict and why you handle it that way. Be as thoughtful as possible, and **FILL UP THE WHOLE SPACE BELOW**. The more of this particular answer you expose to yourself the easier it will be to know exactly what conflicts you should and shouldn't accept as you evolve your sphere. Elaborate. (Now you really do need your own space, but take a look at my answer in Appendix IV for the level of detail this question is asking for. Self-awareness is the name of the game.)

_____
_____
_____
_____
_____
_____
_____
_____
_____
_____
_____
_____
_____
_____
_____
_____
_____
_____
_____
_____
_____
_____
_____

Did you fill up the whole space? No? Go back and finish writing. Your conflict summary should be a statement to the universe about why you fight every major kind of battle which describes you, and why you avoid other kinds of battles. Say it all. We're going to need this mini manifesto in order to do some conscious policing for the rest of our spiritual studies. Don't worry about being self-absorbed or anything like that, but do make sure that you're honest. If you had any holes in Chapter 48 or any of the problems talked about in Chapter 47, you'll need to explain them above as well. If you can't reach a particular goal because of a certain kind of conflict attribute you possess, you'll need to explain that as well.

☞ Question 49.4 (Optional conflict read): If you're up for it, let another person read what you wrote in 49.3. Talk to them about it. Tell them about what you're studying, what you're after, and how this all fits in. Why would you do this? Because it lends an externally verifiable reality to your quest to master your conflict style.

Dissection of the Conflict Factors

In order to get our specific conflict demons under control, we'll need to apply some calculated magic to their representatives. Astrology will be our framework. As we've seen in previous books, planets in astrology are basically crystallizations of character. Some planets hold the character of certain kinds of conflict. We'll start by taking a look at those planets which are considered negative, then see how they can be turned into win-wins for the people caught up in these ~~planets~~ *'asteroids' intrigues.

(*Since astronomical bodies come in all kinds of forms—planets, calculated points, dwarfs, centaurs, amors, asteroids, sednoids,… I will keep with my practice in earlier books and refer to all such bodies and the planets using a single catch-all term. In this book it will be "asteroids." So the Sun will be referred to as an asteroid like everything else. The Descendant—a *location* on the horizon—will be referred to as an asteroid. I do this for brevity.)

Now, if you haven't read any of the first four books in this series, much of what follows might be new to you. To summarize,

- astrology is a snapshot of the sky when you were born. In that snapshot, the planets, asteroids, and other bodies all sit in certain positions, where every chart has all of them located somewhere.

- Bodies sit in signs—sections of the universe as seen from Earth. These signs may or may not naturally fit with what the body represents (Clarissa, the asteroid of acceptance, fits more in the realm of identity/Taurus than in the realm of joining/Virgo).

- Bodies also sit in houses—sections of Earth's local sky at a certain time of day. Clarissa in the 12th house means its concept of acceptance is most noticeable at the lowest level of built-up day energy—the morning mood and situations like it. Clarissa in the 4th house means acceptance in the bottom of night—emotional home base-type situations). Note that this doesn't mean actual morning or actual middle-night, but rather the morning or middle-night type of "modes" one finds oneself in, regardless of time of day.

- Any two bodies are separated by angles (aspects) which tell you the conditions under which you use them together Sun (showing)+Moon (wanting to show) = self-contentment (having shown what one wanted). 0° apart (1/1 of a circle) means this happens basically all the time—the instinctual 1st realm. 60° apart (1/6 of a circle) means it happens while joining ideas together—the 6th realm. 165° apart (a multiple of 1/24 of a circle) means this happens when sensing a mood ([the 12th realm a 2nd time]; a higher frequency background sign than the lowest one—Aquarius instead of Pisces. So this is where such moods in your life get talked about: the works of your imagination). The third book *All 144 Aspects* talks all about these angles of separation.

- Normal astrology considers bodies like the Sun and Moon to be packages of character. But there are tens of thousands of named bodies and hundreds of thousands of bodies local to our solar system which have been identified by the Minor Planet Center. Their meaning is much more nuanced than that of the major planets. So while the major Saturn represents limits broadly, the asteroid Sauer represents where you block or regulate things on purpose, Agamemnon is where you ruthlessly force conformity, Janina is where there are limits in the form of being passed by, and Siri is where a thing is simply limited in its ability to satisfy.

    - The minor planets and asteroids are more detailed versions of the major ones

- and, again, everyone and everything created has every available planet somewhere in its chart. What you pay attention to makes all the difference in whether a particular body does anything that you know *how* to pay attention to.

Using the astrological bodies/asteroids allows us to gather different kinds of conflict into different packages, each corresponding to a named body. If you want to know where that body is in your chart, visit a site like astro.com which allows you to enter the numbers for any extra asteroids, and put in the associated number.

Below are what I called in *Laurentia* "The Mean 13." Among the first 1000 Minor Planet Center (MPC) numbered asteroids, these are the asteroids most likely to be associated with difficulties in a person's astrology chart:

- 448 Natalie – High Stakes Punisher
- 911 Agamemnon – Ruthless Pursuit
- 879 Ricarda – Bad Luck
- 997 Priska – Second Placedness
- 452 Hamiltonia – Self-Damaged Leader
- 5335 Damocles – Other's Anger
- 383 Janina – Servitude & Being Passed By
- 125 Liberatrix – Sudden Endings
- 560 Delila – Thief
- 846 Lipperta – Jealousy Inciter
- 411 Xanthe – Chain Disposer
- 9248 Sauer – Regulator-Blocker
- 169 Zelia – Impenetrable Shield

In addition to the Mean 13, I have also found other factors which, by default, lean towards troublemaking in one's astrology chart:

- Squares (90° separations) between things you value; this basically means you can't have both of those things at the same time since one has to be real while the other has to be imaginary
- Mars – steeror of others
- Saturn – the structurer
- 332 Siri – the dissatisfier
- High-stressers like 679 Pax, 827 Wolfiana, and 238 Hypatia
- Cold-blooded action asteroids like 747 Winchester, 228 Agathe, 342 Endymion, and 904 Rockefellia
- Addictor-Obsessors like 351 Yrsa, 1576 Fabiola, 946 Poesia, and 357 Ninina in places that can't be switched off like the Descendant, Moon, or North Node
- Super tight conjuncts (0° separations) between warmongers like 2 Pallas and 704 Interamnia
- Pathological combinations like your asteroid of commitment 3 Juno on your asteroid of incomplete commitments 897 Lysistrata

- Things that you should healthily want like 103 Hera (bonding) near fortressed blockers like 9248 Sauer & 736 Harvard
- Unequal relationship makers like 728 Leonisis, 2060 Chiron
- Social taboo-deviants like 26 Proserpina, 126 Velleda, 373 Melusina, 459 Signe on bodies that make them obvious like the Sun, Ascendant, or 845 Naema.
- Favorable asteroids in parts of the chart you can't get to like 890 Waltraut (perfect acceptance) in Aquarius-1 (Aqu 27.5°-30°), when you're not good at projecting or getting your first impression talked about by others (what Aquarius-1 entails)

As you can see, there are so many more potential conflict areas in the average chart that the traditional reading of Saturn and Mars as the key sources of negatives is rendered a tiny picture of the full story. If you ever thought that "my chart is so negative while so and so's chart is so positive," all of that goes away as soon as you start adding hundreds of asteroids to the picture. Everyone has everything. Some sections of bodies are just more relevant in our lives than they are in others'.

I want to provide you with a table of all of the factors named above, but need to provide some context first. When we package a conflict type into an asteroid, we are essentially taking 1) a *pair* of placeholders for actors (it takes two to fight), 2) a relationship between those actors, and 3) a determination of how that relationship is seen by some viewer.

> I, for example, have 736 Harvard (arm's length closeness) on my 473 Nolli (top level comfort) in Libra-2 (25°-27.5° Libra—how you know whether you're in a relationship), so I'm in top level comfort in a relationship which refuses to be one. Unless I adapt my attitude in light of the common training for what a relationship is expected to be, this is basically negative because of Harvard's placement where it is—not because Harvard is negative (it isn't).
>
> But Harvard is just a package of energy formed from a certain package of space dust at a certain distance from the Sun. The only reason it has this character is because of the orbit band in which it oscillates compared to every other space object around here. Not just in spacetime (other viewability), but in chemical composition (self) and interaction networks (world). It only picks certain kinds of fights when placed under certain kinds of conditions; when we change the conditions or change the view of the conditions—the background we give it—we won't change the nature of the package, but we will change whether it helps or hurts the rest of the interaction.
>
> Can you see how this works? A conflict package can have its effects changed by changing how the viewer "bonds" with it—just like interacting with another human.
>
> My way of handling Harvard has evolved as follows
>
>> Up to mid-20s: being unable to form stable relationships
>>
>> Mid-20s to early-30s: bond mainly with people who could not bond to me (officially at least)
>>
>> Mid-30s to late 30s: bonding to people are bonded to some abstraction beyond me

Present: only bonding with people who do work for abstract society or in spirituality. That is, I'm *choosing* people who have missions that put me second. (You may not think this works, but combined with other factors in my chart like 997 Priska [second placedness] on the major planet Venus [how you 1:1 socialize], it actually does.)

As a general rule, you'll need to get comfortable with certain kinds of inequality in order to successfully handle your conflict packages, embracing the dark side as it were. Relax, it won't be so bad.

A Case Study in Planets: Chiron

More than traditional Mars or Saturn (which we're always using), the body 2060 Chiron is one which I've seen to be chronically associated with problems. Chiron represents your doctor-patient context; it automatically attracts some other person, situation, or group to you in order to play itself out; one of you is the designated doctor while the other of you is the patient; and there is always some aspect of never being healed so that this setup can continue throughout your life—like every other arrangement in your snapshot. Accordingly, this body has been called "the Wounded Healer" in astrology.

In more charts than not, I have seen Chiron as an indicator of either health or relational problems, mostly the latter. Indeed, Chiron's formula (per *Laurentia*) is $\left(10\frac{99}{144}\right) : \left\{9\frac{143}{144} \to 11\frac{22}{144}\right\} : \|168\|$, so that (per 144)

$$\left(\text{in the realm of 10 authorities } \frac{99 \text{ making emotional communication difficult}}{144}\right):$$

$$\text{it drives the process of going from } \begin{Bmatrix} 9 \text{ being seen } \frac{143 \text{ getting yourself publicly discussed}}{144} \text{ towards} \to \\ 11 \text{ being talked about for } \frac{22 \text{ being in command of (or limited in) a certain field}}{144} \end{Bmatrix}:$$

$$\text{in a topic overall related to } \left\|\frac{168}{1728} = \frac{14}{144} = \frac{14 \text{ the effect of your body presence on others}}{144}\right\|$$

So you can see where the health association comes in. People who handle Chiron successfully tend to be the "doctor" to others in the relevant area of their chart while people who don't handle it successfully tend to be the patient there. Health problems are common in the latter, but not necessarily in the former. You don't have to be a medical doctor in order to use your Chiron, you only have to use some talent for healing or fixing *something somewhere* as part of an ongoing practice in your life. Actually, now that I think about it, my childhood asthma didn't go away until late high school/early college, when I started using my Libra air (the respiratory system in Embodiments) to foster activism-style social relationships (also Libra) for bringing out other's suppressed individuality, and valuing this as my form of identity influence (my Chiron in 10°-12.5° Taurus-8). Your Chiron's location won't tell you how to fix your problem, but it will tell you the form which that problem takes. At Taurus-8, mine was my worth (Taurus) as an influencer (8 = Taurus.Scorpio). So what does this mean?

- "Asteroid/Factor" 2060 Chiron
- Meaning: Doctor-Patient context
- Problem: You can't heal here, others can see this, and your emotions pay for it

> - Repair: heal or fix others or their situations as <u>an ongoing calling</u>, turning the world into your patient instead of your doctor

☞ **Question 49.5 (Where is Chiron?):** Visit astro.com or some other astrology site, generate an astro chart, and locate your 2060 Chiron. Search for an interpretation of it. What does your Chiron's location say about your work as a doctor or fixer of other's problems?

A Case Study in Angles: Squares

At 90° separation, squares represent an attitude and not a specific practice. I talk about how to handle them in the FAQ chapter of *FSA* and in the Squidalgo chapter of *144*, but here's a recap.

- The plant can't grow if the seed hasn't been planted.
- If the seed is being planted, it is obviously not a grown plant.
- One is the potential of the other.
- They can't exist simultaneously in the same dimension, but they must both exist if the whole cycle is to be one.

Your squares are your way of handling the wait for seeds to grow. Your Moon sign and its "duodecanate" (which we'll talk about in The Star) tell you how that inclination from seed towards your goal unfolds.

The squares in your life will bring paradoxes automatically. In order to see something happen, you'll need to do something which is not it, then reinforce that not-the-thing by NOT redoing it, just carrying on. So you don't plant the seed, toss it out with the soil and plant the seed again. You plant the seed and know that you've planted it. *Please learn your Moon sign!* This is what you'll be doing while the seeds are growing. You'll be doing it in the same way you did the 7-day hole challenge—with an attitude of having set it in motion. *Don't keep <u>replanting</u> the seed*, telling yourself that you never did.

Let me regale you with another personal story.

> In non-*FSA* books prior to this one, I've talked about being polyamorous (poly) and how, if you ask a poly person what it's like, you're not nearly as likely to hear stories about orgies as you are stories about honest communication and emotional safety. One of the hardest things I've tried to explain to my monogamous friends is how it is possible for your love of Person A to grow your love for Person B and vice versa. How trying to have a healthy relationship with A or B alone may truly fail royally without that second partner.
>
> As with most people's sexuality, I didn't just wake up one day and choose poly, and I wasn't just a horny man trying to bed women all day. From the moment my interest in women began, single relationships either didn't work right or were followed up by a meeting with a second person from out of nowhere when they did work. The women would either be closer to each other or logical-distant from me; it always happened during travel, and it was always better than monogamy. Always. Even today. You know how some processes just work for you where they would be

> backwards for most others? That's how it is.
>
> Years after learning the official term for what this was, I also found it in my chart. At the heart of my poly are 1) a major "T-square" ⊼ between [3 Juno (public commitment)] and [473 Nolli (top-level comfort with your situation), 2) Nolli, 736 Harvard, and 423 Diotima (comfort, arm's length, and marrying two extremes) in the section of Libra defining my relationships], and a Moon in Aries (doing [other] things on a whim as my form of waiting/wanting). It turns out that, if I love Person A and there is a chance we might work, I'll move on to other things—more often having Person B delivered by circumstance—as soon as I see the possibility. My Person A is, by frequency, almost always someone who goes for this kind of thing, because they are Harvard-distant—not keen on what they see as "ownership" anyway. I love A even more because I love B, and both can see this. For most people this probably wouldn't work. For three abstract non-committers, it's the *only* way it can work.
>
> Despite still being highly amorous and writing books like *Sex in 12 Dimensions*, I chose celibacy (no partners) seven years ago and **love** being unpartnered. That fact continues to this day. Why? The original book in this series, *Full Spectrum Astrology* and everything I've created since, including my business projects, have happened *after* I adopted monastic-style celibacy. I have a lot of passionate energy, but information-flow is my back-and-forth partner-pair[28] and my 12 books are my kids. Perhaps I was a monk in a previous life. Surely I was destined to marry an interaction, not a person.
>
> Believe it or not, different people have different tastes.

The point of the story is, mastering your squares will almost certainly take you off the well-trodden path in some way. We tend to want what we think we should have, but in order to have it as trained we have to seed it then put it aside in a way that *wasn't* trained. The calculated point Lilith/Black Moon (not the asteroid) and the actual asteroid 431 Nephele in your chart will tell you more about where you display a character in ways contrary to that character, and are both related to the Moon. If you've always wanted something, but been mostly unable to get it, your final solution may end up being one of the most socially uncomfortable ones available: adopt an aspect of your *lifestyle*—the in-between-the-seed-and-growth phase where you plant still other seeds—which lets you advance in ways the rest of the world said shouldn't be possible.

- Asteroid/Factor: the square; 90° separation between two bodies you want to use
- Meaning: being inclined to towards something without actually having it
- Problem: You're stuck wanting it. You can't actually get it.
- Repair: Plant the seed for what you want, then move on for a while; find a setting which makes it safe for you to rebel against or ignore the things you were taught to want, but which just don't fit

---

[28] Did you catch the embodiment? If books like *S12* and this one can teach you anything, I hope it helps you see how certain people-arrangements in your life are strong stand-ins for the more abstract ideas you hold.

> you for now. Then rebel there. Make it part of your lifestyle. One day you'll turn around and the seed will have sprouted. That's how it works.

If ever there were a place for me to get back on my soapbox about judging others, now would be the time. But this one will be short. If you judge people for defying norms or not wanting things you think they should want, your own squares will more likely manifest as a more intense form of dissatisfaction. The more you judge, the less you accept the areas where you yourself need to defy a certain standard of conformity, the deeper the non-self-contentment. It's just waves. But it's also Karma.

☞ Question 49.6 (Where is your Moon?): Visit astro.com or some other astrology site, generate an astro chart, and locate your Moon. Read the interpretation of it. When you want something to happen and have already planted seeds for it, what kinds of things might you do while you are waiting for those seeds to grow?

_____
_____
_____
_____
_____

A Case Study in Life Areas: Battles Between People

When you battle another person, you are using tension type A from yourself to reduce tension type B in your shared frequency with that person (or group or situation). This follows from the previous chapters. When that battle is not the kind that you engage in for fun, either one or both of you typically houses a motivator C as their reason for prolonging the fight, and it falls to you to determine how long you're willing to build up yours or their C at the expense of your own inner stability. This is because using A in the way that you do takes work, while the presence of B in your bond with the other ties up even more energy. Meanwhile, the other person uses their own weapon D against you with their own motivation E for doing so. This gives us five different frequencies you could look at for understanding any kind of battle with another.

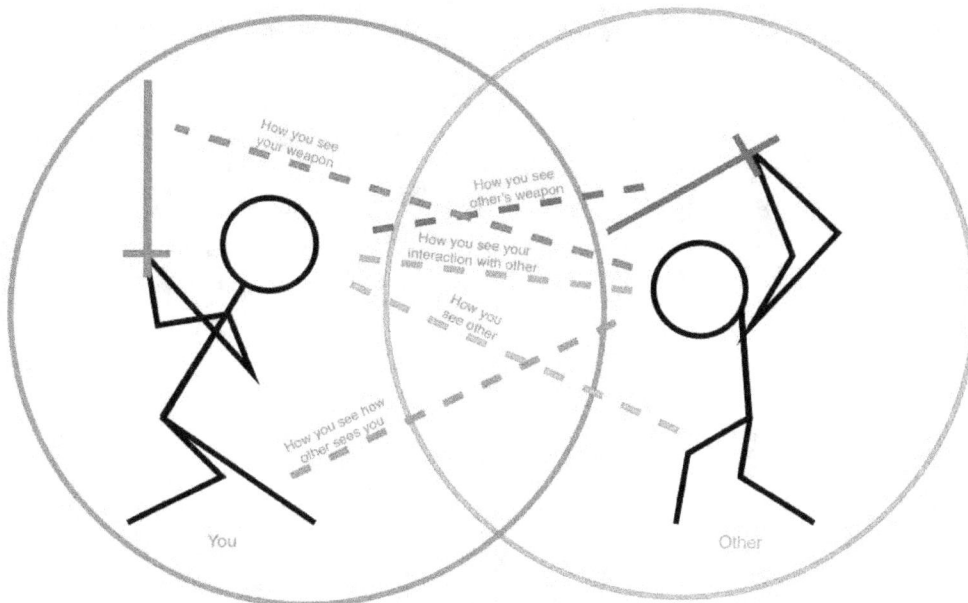

Figure 49-1: A hypothetical battle and its five parts as seen from your perspective only. That is the only way you will ever see it.

But now, there are some things to consider. First, what do you care about the other's physical body? You could battle them just as easily on the phone, over the web, or in your thoughts. It's not usually the physical form which causes your conflict, it's some event which the form sponsored. We know this because the other person can walk out, get dumped, or anything like that, and your reaction tends to endure IF there is any fraction of you which was responsible for keeping the tension alive. Was there? Then you'll hold the tension towards them even after they leave your reach.

Secondly, you don't really see your own body either, even if the post-battle discord within it stays around. So we can remove both embodiments from the picture and concentrate only on the events, the defense mechanisms, the attacks, and the exchange itself. The result is a more appropriate map of the sides of yourself which actually participate in any conflict.

Figure 49-2: Your sphere under conflict.

In all five of these areas, we spend energy for processing. Metabolism, attention, time, and *definitely* efficacy. The longer we have to work—the more responses we have to give in order to meet our objectives in the battle—the lower our $\frac{\text{effectiveness}}{\text{(per) response}}$ given out. We're swinging our weapon (argument, for example), they're swinging their weapon (e.g. criticism), we're responding to how we think they see us (defensiveness), compared to how they seem to see us (defiance), and we're both assessing our relationship to some topic (whatever it is). Additionally, we sometimes battle for three more reasons: 1) how we *want* to see them, 2) how we *want* to see *ourselves*, and 3) how we want to see *the partnership* as a whole. This is a lot of work, and if you've ever argued fiercely with anyone or had an enduringly bad relationship with anyone, then you know all this talk about energy spending is real—especially if you've continued to fuel your negative view of them long after they've left your reach. Maybe even *because* they've left your reach. And why did you do it? Why did you battle them? Which one or few of those eight areas were you trying to build up or defend by investing so much of your effort in the rest of them?

- Your behavioral methods
- Your perception of the sphere occupant's behavioral methods
- Your current view of yourself
- Your wants for seeing yourself
- Your view of your current sphere occupant's view of you
- Your wants for seeing the current sphere occupant
- Your view of the exchange between you and your occupant
- Your view of the whole partnership comprising you, the occupant, and the exchange

Below is the same sample battleground with a kind of rating system attached.

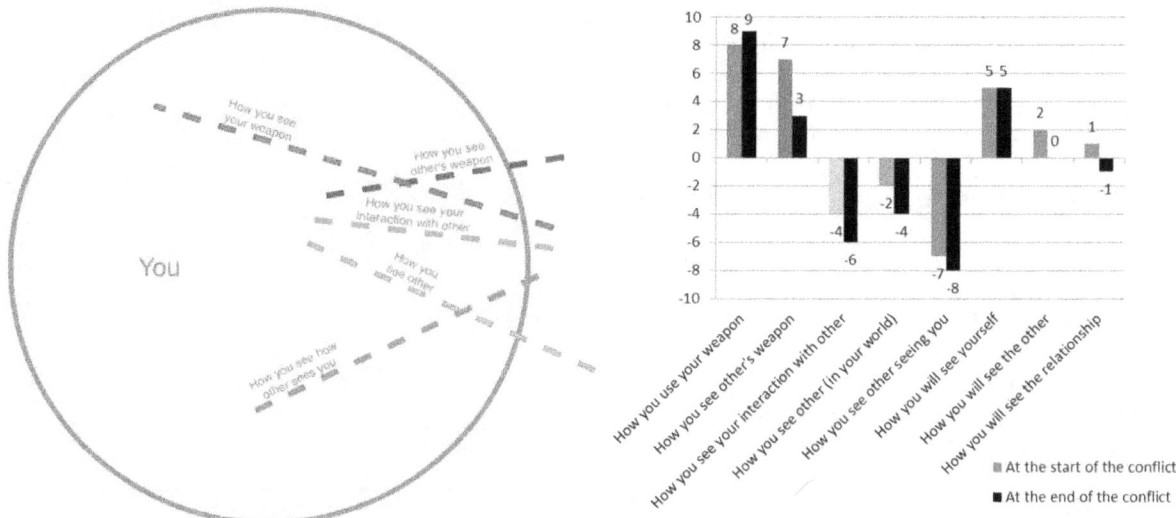

Figure 49-3: A sample conceptualization one's sphere before and after a conflict. With the specific opponent removed, the benefits and costs of the conflict become much clearer.

This may all seem a little abstract, so if it helps, try thinking of your sphere history again. Have you ever had the same kind of battle with different people across the years? Consider the patterns involved. Which of the eight battle priorities were you trying to meet? If the conflict was almost entirely the other person's doing, which of the eight battle priorities had the greatest permanent increase in you? What we're doing is removing the specific names of the people you battled, and instead seeking to understand what kinds of patterns you alone would have retained long after the enemy had departed.

Critical Exercise (Part 1 of 3)
CONFLICT ANALYSIS

Trains: Life path, Claircognizance

☞ **Question 49.7 (Conflict analysis):** Consider three people (or situations) with whom you have had the same kind of conflict (one-sided or not, openly or not). One of them must be in your life, with the conflict still active, right now.

We have another complicated question here. A completed example is in Appendix V.

	How would you rate this outcome?
	bad- / bad / neutral / good / good+

1. Who were those people? _____
2. What was the general overview of the conflict? _____
3. (Interaction before) What was the in-the-moment conflict about? _____
4. (Interaction after) How did the conflict ultimately end? _____
5. (Your weapon before) During the conflict, how did you respond to them? _____
6. (Your weapon after) How do you respond to that kind of challenge now _____
7. (Their weapon before) How did they respond to you during the conflict? _____
8. (Their weapon after) How has that response changed in your occupant(s) now that you've had the conflict a few times? _____
9. (Your view before) How did you generally view this kind of occupant before? _____
10. (Your view after) How do you generally view this kind of occupant now? _____
11. (Their view before) How did this type of occupant view you before? _____
12. (Their view after) How does this kind of occupant view you now? _____
13. (Yourself before) How did you generally view yourself in this situation before? _____
14. (Yourself after) How do you generally view yourself in this situation now? _____
15. (Your wants from them before) What would you have wanted from this type of occupant in this situation before? _____
16. (Your wants from them after) What do you want from this type of occupant in this situation now? _____
17. (Whole relationship before) On the whole, what did you formerly think of this style of pairing of you and the occupant-type? _____
18. (Whole relationship after) On the whole, what do you think of this style of pairing of you and the occupant-type now? _____
19. Take a look at your ratings and note which parts of your sphere improved under the conflict versus those which didn't. Overall, what would you say was the point of this kind of "battle?"

_____

---

[29] This is a forced answer to the question, *What did you want to happen?* Rather than asking what you wanted in your head, it asks what your *deeds* wanted, and ultimately got.

Critical Exercise (Part 2 of 3)
CONFLICT RESULT SHORTCUT

☞ **Question 49.8 (Conflict reduction):** Given what you learned from the previous question, you should be able to see where you might be able to alter certain aspects of your conflict to provide you with the same lessons without your wasting so much extra energy. To the extent that you can improve the outcomes that keep improving while avoiding the outcomes that keep getting worse under conflict, you win for real, not just for show. There is nothing to do on this question, just something to think about.

Critical Exercise (Part 3 of 3)
CONFLICT REWRITING

Why would another person create trouble for you? One feature of tense bonds is that their tension is often a fundamental part of what holds the bond together. It's one thing to say, "I'm out. Looking for a better way." It's another thing to say, "I'm still in. Let's put this tension to some higher use." As you practice your spiritual development you'll often find that the conflicts you enter become much less aggression based and much more calling-based, such that your main obstacle will more likely be rooted in what *isn't* happening than what is. The default for us comfortable humans is to tolerate the situation in its non-moving state. And that may be okay. But what happens when the person you would have battled loses you as a scrapping partner? Will your life write them out of the movie? Will they be left to stew in their half of the drama? Very often the last two answers are YES and YES. And it only happens more, the better you get at ridding yourself of conflict-marred relationships.

If you have people in your life whom you used to fight, but have now decided not to—who needed the fight where you now refuse to give it—then you may need to find something else for them to do with their tension in order for your sphere to keep supporting them. You need to know what they're actually after. What do they get out of fighting your type of occupant holder?

You won't be able to change them.

Even if you could read their minds, you probably couldn't (and shouldn't try to) remove their decade(s)-old, self-sustained obstacle from them.

What you need is a powerful cocktail for opening a door for this person, revealing the means to solving their interaction problem with you once and for all. You'll need to know three things about yourself and three things about them. Your items are reflected astrologically. Theirs you obtain through observation.

☞ **Question 49.9 (Open another's door):** Obtain your astro chart, including the following three items:
- Selene (White Moon) – your blessed talent
- 773 Irmintraud – where you act as a life change agent for others
- 15760 Albion (1992QB1; 92Q) – support attractor

☞ Next answer these questions:

1. What would you say is *the* thing that has proven capable of changing this person's life permanently, for the better (sim-Yrsa)? _____

2. What is the main thing that satisfies this person during the conflict with you? What makes them feel as though they can get off your case (sim-Waltraut)? _____

3. What kinds of things does this person do which make them feel greatly role-effective (sim-Olivia)? _____

Yrsa, Olivia, and Waltraut are actual asteroids, but because you're only an outside observer, it's less important for you to get the actual locations of these in the person's chart and more important for you to get a practical approximation of character traits like the ones these indicate. You're only simulating these qualities, hence the "sim-" prefix.

And now for the cocktail. Even for one-sided conflict which you keep to yourself, you can consider the following:

> I should not feel weak for opening a door for my opponent. It's the opposite. Not only does their tension not affect me, not only do I build my strengths from this anyway, I also show that my will circumscribes theirs: Any move either of us makes is a win for me. It is up to them to declare whether or not every move either of us make is a win for them as well.
>
> Acting to bring about my [92Q] for myself, I exchange with the other through my [Irmintraud] towards exercising my own [Selene] in the world. I will build up their [sim-Waltraut] not against myself, but towards their pursuit of their own [sim-Yrsa]. In this way, their aims can only advance us both. In pursuing their [sim-Yrsa] I will ask them for specific things which (in my mind) will build up their [sim-Olivia] as they do it right.

4. You should know the sign locations of your 92Q/Albion, Irmintraud, and Selene. Referencing the sign table below, fill in the blanks in the cocktail that follows it with a short summary of what the relevant sign does. In the case of the sim-asteroids, just use short versions of your answers to 49.9.1 – 49.9.3.

♈	♉	♊	♋	♌	♍
Aries	**Taurus**	**Gemini**	**Cancer**	**Leo**	**Virgo**
spontaneous behaving	experiencing things you value or identify yourself against	communicating your ideas; thinking or talking to or for yourself	paying attention to how you feel	playing, leisure time, having fun	working, making meaning, doing daily duties
♎	♏	♐	♑	♒	♓
Libra	**Scorpio**	**Sagittarius**	**Capricorn**	**Aquarius**	**Pisces**
socializing, conversation with others, engaging in 1:1 feedback	steering others, over situations	leaving an impression among strangers	being associated with structure	being talked about	performing default actions

Acting to bring about my [92Q] _____ for myself, I exchange with the other through my [Irmintraud] _____ towards exercising my own [Selene] _____ in the world. I will build up their [sim-Waltraut] _____ not against myself, but towards their pursuit of their own [sim-Yrsa] _____ In this way, their aims can only advance us both. In pursuing their [sim-Yrsa] _____ I will ask them for specific things which (in my mind) will build up their [sim-Olivia] _____ as they do it right.

For example, I had lines like "...towards exercising my own [association with structure] in the world. I will build up their [quest for new projects] not against myself..." The point goal is to turn their tension into something that is useful to you both, while eliminating your tension completely.

Everything you rated as dropping or staying steadily negative in Part 1 of this exercise might be something you consider bypassing in your future conflicts with this type of occupant.

Final thoughts on conflict rewriting

In *Black Male Feminism* I talked about how our Western society is encouraged to fight fiercely when challenged, regardless of how appropriate that is as a solution. Back in times where it may have been fitting to fight for your life, tense conflict represented a strongly viable solution to many problems where war, genocide, or conquest were real possibilities. But most of our modern conflicts don't occur in these settings. The people we savagely attack right now are the same people we'll need to look at, work with, and live around two hours from now. Can you really say that you vanquished your opponent if you know he'll be back working side by side on that task with you the next day? What we count as "fighting for our side" produces fewer and fewer long term results the more society advances away from its old Wild West ways. Yet we have so many bystanders, cliques, and comment posters egging us on—encouraging us to be "tough" though they themselves don't seem to have advanced much that way.

Some battles are worth fighting. In times of peace—among the family, coworkers, and even common strangers we're stuck with—most are not. It may seem counterintuitive to rewrite your conflicts with others in your opponents' favor, but no one is asking you to let your opponent "beat you." We are asking you to leave your opponent to webs of their own weaving. We are asking you to avoid getting caught in that web. And if you value the exchange enough to keep it from being written out of your life's plot by your own evolution, helping your opponent redirect the tension they formerly threw at you will be more than just a wimpy suggestion. It might be the only available save you have.

A Case Study in Character Combinations: Sun-Juno

Maybe your problem isn't with another person, a single characteristic, or even a style of approach. Maybe it's just a plain old awkward way that you have. On my Sun (astrology's most major planet) I have a basket of asteroids which favors a questionable combination of traits, including one of the handful of asteroids indicating what you'll be forever known for (and a strong asteroid at that), 845 Naema:

284	Amalia	7	sc	35	where you are associated with overflowing lust
676	Melitta	7	sc	38	triggers the masculine desire nature
373	Melusina	7	sc	55	where you are attention-magnetic, though often in an unfortunate way; attraction of abusers or deviants
845	Naema	8	sc	51	what your name comes to be associated with
848	Inna	9	sc	19	where you are the social justice broadcaster IF you grow past your own personal wars
147	Protogeneia	9	sc	24	where you are outspoken
937	Bethgea	9	sc	25	where you assemble a complex puzzle from dirty pieces; how you transform animal urges into other things
174567	Varda	9	sc	35	otherworldly brilliance
761	Brendelia	9	sc	40	where you are oblivious to the world outside your imagined view of things
	Sun	9	sc	51	ego projection, basic style of interpersonal action

Table 49-1: A sample cluster with mixed acceptable-unacceptable trait combinations

And no matter how you slice it, that's how my character will lean. I could fight myself to change it, or accept myself and change who I hang around to support it instead. I recommend that most people do the latter, since they don't usually drown witches or burn heretics anymore. You can be weird and still get some pretty good stuff done. The hard part is *initially* accepting the cards which genes and upbringing first dealt you: traits you can't easily separate, whose active management you become increasingly responsible for as you get older. What do you do when the problem isn't any single thing, but an interface you have with *everything*?

☞ Question 49.10 (Your full asteroid list): To produce a table like the one I have above, you can either go online and search for a site with an "ephemeris" or "ephemerides" for the first 1000 Minor Planet Center asteroids or you can go to a site that lets you produce your chart plus additional asteroids, where you will enter the numbers of each asteroid you want. I used the former method via serennu.com; you'll need a subscription though.

- As for the interpretations of the additional asteroids, again you can search them online. You can also find them (the first 1000) interpreted in the book before this one, *Laurentia*; you'll find interpretations of major planets like the Sun and Moon all over the web and in any number of other astrology books including the first one in this series, *Full Spectrum Astrology*.
- Unfortunately, because there are so many of them and they aren't the focus of *Alma Mater*, we won't cover asteroid interpretations in here. You should definitely obtain your list, though, as you'll need it by the time we get to The Star.

Now imagine that you have two relatively benign bodies, the Sun (1:1 showing) and 3 Juno (public commitment) next to each other as characteristics. In *FSA* we said that Sun-Juno represents ego projection tied to a partner, so these characteristics should (by default) show you as being really committed in your basic exchanges with people. So what do you think happens when you *formally* commit to one person, but continue to live your normal life interacting with others in the world? That's right: You may seem to be committed to those others just as equally. The same trait that instantly earned you your sweetheart's affection can also instantly make them jealous or cause them to question your commitment *to them* if not properly handled. But this isn't so much a fault of yours as it is a basic property of who you are.

When we have characteristics which would be fine by themselves, but turn negative when others must respond to them, one solution is to handle those characteristics in the same way we handled Chiron: by turning the negative prompt into our trade. In the case of Sun-Juno, this would mean committing to your chosen commitment partner's personal side while at the same time taking up genuine support of everyone else's ~~personal sides~~ objectives as part of who you are. If this issue were even a problem for you, that is. The sign of Sun-Juno in this example tells you how this should be done while the house tells you the area of life in which it should occur. All in all the aim is to keep positive traits positive rather than allowing them to become negative simply because another can't own them.

Two kinds of karmic reflection

More than broken traits (planets), difficult processes (angles), or difficult partners (battles), regular traits turned negative (one's overall character) tend to be difficult to address without multiple sphere occupants.

If not for others to your others, you might never know your flirting, wandering, abstract preoccupations were a thing. With you and only a single other, you would have only one person to absorb most of that trait smoothly. But once groups enter, the problems begin. Or maybe it's the other way around—where your traits are perfectly fine in groups but turn inconvenient one on one. Whatever the case, in being compelled to address these problems, we tend to inherit two kinds of people in our sphere: reflectors and resonators.

Let's return to Sun-Juno as an example. Suppose you have these two bodies next to each other in 11° Libra—meaning you're predisposed to genuine emotional investment in your 1:1 communications. Suppose also that any formal partners you obtain consistently dislike this side of you when you use it outside of the partnership. Your consistent partner-disturbing frequency in the realm of Exchanging then produces two kinds of embodiment.

- One will reflect your Sun-Juno problem whenever you pay attention to this trait as a key feature of your relationship with them. It will bother them in whatever behavior connects *their* Sun and Juno.

    - So if you and I are partners and you have a Sun-Juno conjunct which comes out in a way that has consistently made all of us partners jealous—and IF you feel like your committed expression is key to us being partners in the first place—then my committed expression will reflect yours. I might not have Sun-Juno next to each other (conjunct) in my chart, though. I might have them 120° apart (trine) for example. This means your unstable commitment expression will show up as my unstable opinion-giving. If my Sun-Juno were 165° apart (II-inconjunct or Aquarius-inconjunct), then your unstable commitment expression would show up as my unstable creative works. IF Sun-Juno commitment showing is a part of how you think we work or how you want us to work together.

    - If the above did apply, I would be your negative reflector. You might even battle me over this. But if I'm not your first opponent in this kind of thing, then... (see A Case Study in Life Areas: Battles) the problem might actually lie with you after all.

- One or more people's general behavior will reveal problems with your 11° Libra as a location/frequency type in your life. These will be resonators. In accordance with our removal of the person earlier, leaving only your own frequencies, the frequency level itself will be challenged across your life just as the traits expressed on that frequency level are challenged in people who bring out your attention to those traits.

- Said another way, a challenged trait combination in a particular life area brings challenged interaction with others in whom you focus that same combination. It also brings challenges to that life area broadly.

A Case Study in General Stressors: Pax
I've had the good fortune over the past few days of writing this chapter to be caught in an extremely stressful situation. Under that stress, I've worried about a particular health issue, dwelled on it, and stressed over it even more. I've felt stupid for not seeing it coming, and robbed of something that should have been otherwise correct. But more than anything, I've been angry at myself for not attempting to do anything about it—that is, using my Moon sign to respond to it.

Why is this good?

Because, had it not been for this issue, this next section would not have existed for you to read.

Despite what people tell you, "dwelling stress"—the kind that keeps feeding itself, often at the expense of your health—is easily one of the hardest kinds of stress to handle. Right in the moment, you have nowhere to go, no one to turn to who *really* understands your worry, and the sense of your own body refusing to cease its haywire ways is all you can fixate on. I was just there last night. Because our stress revolves around different issues and lingers in different ways, I couldn't begin to tell you how to address it. I can, however, tell you some ways to look at it astrologically.

If you asked me to name the main negative stress indicators in an astro chart I would say 827 Wolfiana, 679 Pax, 5335 Damocles, 238 Hypatia, and Virgo-11 & 12 (0°-5° Virgo). At least that's what my stats showed in the previous books. Under stress, these asteroids focus your attention on themselves in the same way that a bad Chiron did earlier in this chapter, causing you to adopt the role of "self-tension spiraller." You'll do this until you either run out of energy for that session, or come to some kind of resolution (which is often only temporary).

But stress asteroids, like all others, have certain things which can shut them down. Acquiring (or at least approaching) the thing you want is one way. Doing something that forms a square to the stressor is another. Unfortunately, a person under threatening stress is more likely to consider more things to be bad or ineffective in the moment when many of them really aren't. So he can't appeal to those things for help. He may, however, be able to appeal to the things that inhibit those "bad" ones as part of his solution.

The asteroid 679 Pax is one of the top three stressors I've found among the first 1000. On a normal day it makes others angry with you, but in the absence of others it can also make you angry with yourself. Pax's anger-irritation factor is one is those things that arises "just because" for no real reason other than being the card you pulled at that particular time on your lifeline. Sometimes you have a way of triggering it through certain acts, but other times it basically happens on its own. Much like the rest of your embodiment, Pax and its brother Wolfiana are features of your physical shell. I believe that Pax is associated with Virgo-12, and have had some success squaring it with whatever traits are in Gemini-12 and Sagittarius-12. This amounts to doing the thing which makes your stress at least temporarily unfounded.

Pax stress is the struggle to join your reasoning amidst a certain kind of (psychological) environment, so changing parts of the environment can have a major effect. In my case last night, a great deal of my stress didn't consist of the actual issue, but around what I perceived to be my own failure to do anything about the issue. We are so fortunate to live in times where—if you're motivated enough—you can find someone somewhere who will fix your problem. I knew full well that fixes to my issue existed, but spent the whole night not even starting towards those fixes. Because they cost too much. Because they required a doctor's visit. They required a look at an issue I didn't want to look at. Any number of reasons. Ultimately this morning though, I went out and did something to alter the conditions for worry, choosing a temporary solution over no-solution at all, while at the same time deciding to obtain a more permanent solution at any expense. It only bought time, but it also reduced the anxiety that my long term solution would take too long to obtain;

And three days of heavy nightly stress went away just like that. No joke. Pax stress doesn't care if you solve the problem. It only cares that you erase the conditions that the problem occurs in—not necessarily permanently, but just for now, <u>in a way that you can believe</u>. I know my short term solution is temporary, but I've already decided on the long term one. It wasn't that difficult. And as with Chiron, part of the permanent solution will require an adjustment of life-calling such that I'll need to help solve this problem in others.[30]

If stress over things you can't control is a serious problem for you, it may be your Pax. This frequency package is tricky because it's not about actual solutions. It's about conditions for the solution.

- Suppose you worry endlessly about your heart, and that worry is of the "I can't control this situation" kind. A prescription may help, but if your problem is Pax, undoing the thing you suspect began at the same time as your worries began—along with adopting a change in overall lifestyle—is likely to help more.

    o A longer-term solution would be to locate your 679 Pax (by typing it in the extra asteroids box of your software), to look at the rest of the asteroids near it (which you won't be able to do unless you've downloaded your 1000), and to see what else is there.

    o Once you've found and interpreted the cluster, your task is to add it to your life-calling so that the stress doesn't live in you, but is fixed on-call in the people you serve.[31]

---

[30] As an interesting epilogue to this story, the afternoon after I had initiated the temporary solution, I got a call for a job, was put into contact with several people related to my life-calling, and got a chance to air a part of that calling in a public forum even though, at present I don't have any kind of public role. This is basically how calculated magic works—where handling one event in an unusual way can set others in motion. The results of this whole stressful event will almost certainly end up in a future book. The root event may not prove so major in the end, but the accompanying stress and the final results absolutely were.

[31] Right after writing the above, I looked at my chart and found what I'd unintentionally done with my Pax problem. It's interesting. The life-calling part is real.

Table of Energy Stressors

If you've downloaded your 1000 asteroids or looked at your astrology chart in any depth, you'll probably recognize at least some of the names below. Although everyone's approaches to conflict will differ, there are still some basic formulas you can follow for approaching some of these common problem areas in your chart.

*For all items in the chart below "others" can also be another side of yourself when physical others aren't actively involved.

Conflict Source	Meaning	Type	Conflict Based On	Problem	Repair
Squares (90° apart)	being inclined to towards something without actually having it	Angle	tension as you want something	You're stuck wanting it. You can't actually get it	Find a setting which makes it safe for you to rebel against things you were taught to want, but which just don't fit you. Then rebel there. Make it part of your lifestyle.
Octiles (45°, 135° apart)	trying to get the thing you're interacting with to behave the way you want it	Angle	tension as you want certain results	You're trying to push it. It's not moving the way you want it	Investigate it. Extract why it works the way it does, then fit it into your existing toolset for getting things done.
Conjuncts (0° apart)	Two or more characteristics which always come together in your personality	Angle	tension as you try to use one trait but keep getting the other effect with it	You can't divorce these sides of your personality	This type of issue is almost always reflected in your relationships. Look for interactions and groups which *support* your undivorceable combination as a healthy thing
Battle with Another	tension in your interaction with another	Angle (synastry btw charts)	tension as you interact with a certain side of another	The strain won't go down around this issue with this person	Find out what grows favorably through the conflict, then try pursuing that through less extreme means. From there, open a door for the other (perhaps using Selene, 773 Irmintraud, or 15760 Albion)
911 Agamemnon	ruthless pursuit of your own ends	Body	ruthlessness	You reduce the worth of anything that doesn't support your aims	Incorporate this brand of perfectionism into the area of life you are building
228 Agathe	elimination of interactants	Body	ruthlessness, elimination	You cut off exchanges at the smallest breach of your rules	Learn to refuse the entry of anything into your life which doesn't share this same trait in this same area
945 Barcelona	isolated with one's skill	Body	isolation, loneliness	You are without obvious help in this	See if you can develop this area in a way that makes "alone time" better than shared time. Be ready to avoid sharing influence in this area (at least sometimes).
2060 Chiron	doctor-patient context	Body	hurt, trauma	You can't heal here, others can see this, and your emotions pay for it	Heal or fix others or their situations as an ongoing calling, turning the world into your patient instead of your doctor
5335 Damocles	filling others with aggression	Body	irritating or frustrating others	You have an easy time making others angry or impassioned with the traits connected to this	Watch for the difference between wanting to do something in this area and being invited. It may be a lot easier to be invited.
511 Davida	burdened with the demands of others	Body	burdens	You've been slammed by other's problems and are obligated to carry them	This will be a feature of your life as a leader to others, Doing the things 90° square to Davida on either side helps seed this leader role.
560 Delila	disenfranchising others	Body	stealing	Notions of theft play out here in your life	Answer the following: In what aspect of your life would you proudly, beneficially steal from others? It could be money, emotions, psychology, power, or other resources. A definition to help you: stealing = taking for yourself at others' expense. Where could you (or where have you in the past) actually benefit(ted) the world by doing this?
342 Endymion	"showing no mercy"	Body	suppression of others	You are difficult to please here, and are resistant to others' stray input	Perfect your craft as an art in this area of life

1576 Fabiola	explosive, excessive, scattered energy	Body	excessive projection	You impose an often unwelcome intensity on others in a normal interaction	Partner with your interactant to project that intensity with them, not at them
452 Hamiltonia	influence hindered	Body	costly leadership	Your rise right up to the point of leadership, but stop yourself thanks to issues in your personality	Split your influence with another, then set the bar even higher for leading bigger groups besides the ones you've associated with up to now. **DON'T let yourself stay dissatisfied!** <u>Join forces, then move on</u>.
238 Hypatia	bombarded as the price of skill	Body	burdens, costly skill	You are torn at from all sides by others for any number of reasons, mainly related to the skills you have	Diminish your own skill by asking others to get in line or by asking for help (letting them know you can't handle it all at once)
383 Janina	being passed over	Body	lack of validation, being ignored or passed by	Others seem to be ready to pick you, but pass you up instead	YOU should adopt consideration of options as your own practice in the area of life where this happens. Ideally, this is where you are unimpressed, having seen better
125 Liberatrix	sudden end or disappearance	Body	leaving a relationship	Without warning, you leave the exchange	Liberatrix shows how you break free of an association related to the traits near it. The more its nearby traits arise as an issue, the more likely you are to want escape. The solution is to use its nearby traits as your means to freedom from the various issues those connected traits stand against. In certain personalities where the need for freedom is strong, you may need to build a life calling fostering this kind of freedom in others.
846 Lipperta	making others feel you don't need them	Body	diminishing partner worth	You devalue the contributions of others around you, sometimes even cheapening them	Use this asteroid to diminish the effect of oppressors in your life. If you use it in other ways, that cluster tends to discourage others from wanting to get near you UNLESS you intentionally want to attract people with low self-worth, a lack of final authority, or a subordinate role in this area of life.
897 Lysistrata	incomplete relationships	Body	relationship walls	You can't get past a certain point in relating to a particular thing	Accept unexpected support from outside of your focus. It will tend to come as validation for where you are. And it will come in the form of the relevant area of life. You'll be prompted to do the things 90° to Lysistrata on either side. (This is encouragement to practice things you do instead when the relationship appears to be blocked. This is also your haven when your relationships get too difficult.)
Mars	steering others	Body	needing to force something	You use force on others where it may not be necessary	Most of us learn this the hard way: Across all areas of life, train in using force only where it won't break what you want to preserve.
373 Melusina	attracting deviants	Body	attracting unseemly influences	Dark or shameful groups gravitate towards you	It really helps if you have your 1000 for this one, since you need to take a good look at what these criminal/ under-ground/ scandalous groups represent which you might never represent yourself. This is their place in your world, and you may not access their form of influence unless you find a way to reflect what they embody.[32]

---

[32] See 848 Inna and 147 Protogenia in the table earlier in Case Study on Character Combinations: Sun-Juno. Prior to poly, I wouldn't have written books like *BMF*, *S12*, or this one.

448 Natalie	high-stakes punisher	Body	needing to be perfect	You are strongly compelled to do it to perfection, or lose it all	This one is easy. <u>Make this *the* area of life where you settle for nothing in which you doubt.</u> Natalie is one of the meanest of the mean 13 and the most potentially negative of all 1000 asteroids I've *ever* observed. It demands your respect; every major decision you make should conform to—or at least not stray too far from—the path it suggests for you.
2 Pallas	(war in the name of) social justice	Body	crusading for something	You want justice. You declare war. But in modern, peacetime society there's a good chance you're wrong for doing so	Where Pallas lives, adopt a crusade towards the resolution of social problems broader than your local sphere. Otherwise you're more likely to upset your own sphere instead.
679 Pax	inconstancy creating anger in others	Body	pervasive situational stress	Conditions of high stress dominate yours or other's concerns around you	Perform the tasks (asteroids) 90° away from Pax in either direction. You'll almost certainly find *something* if you downloaded your 1000.
Pluto	social pressure	Body	feeling the pressure to produce some kind of value in the world	The weight of the social world is placed on your shoulders	YOU should demand the connected qualities (near Pluto) of everyone around you
997 Priska	second-placedness	Body	constantly coming in second in something	Someone else's aims always seem to come before yours	See if you can adopt an ongoing interest in the people with whom you interact in this life area, letting their expression towards you take priority.
879 Ricarda	progress hampered without another's help	Body	struggling uphill on your own	Though you've tried as hard as you could, you just can't get over that hump	If Natalie is the meanest of the first 1000 asteroids, Ricarda is one of the most frustrating. Why can't you win? Because there are other, larger factors which have to be ready for you. Use the items square from Ricarda to build up the partnerships you need in the area of life the Ricarda occupies.
904 Rockefellia	forcing others to rewrite their views in your way	Body	being domineering	You act to dominate the environment around you, not always in obvious ways	Just as packs of bandits and the practice of exile have gone out of style as popular punishments, domination by imposing one's will and certain forms of bodily punishment are also losing ground. If you have a problem being domineering towards others, it may not be *if* you're imposing your will, but *how*. Ideally, Rockefellia gathers followers who were already willing rather than forcing followers who weren't. Its influence lasts longer that way.
Saturn	restrictions, boundaries	Body	putting boundaries on something	You encounter a general barrier that can't be surmounted	Train in constructing barriers or structures of this type as part of your basic personality.
9248 Sauer	regulator-blocker	Body	chaining something down	You close and lock the door on something	This is only negative if you repeatedly lock the door on things you wish you hadn't later. Use of Sauer often brings the section 60° backwards from it as a consequence, but perhaps even more useful is how easily it may be caused by the location 60° *after* it. If your Sauer, for example, is in 10° Libra and you find yourself using the cluster from 10° Sagittarius on someone, that may be a warning that door-locking is coming. Sauer is, for the most part, a healthy protection—like blood clotting. But if you want to avoid using it on someone, avoid letting the relationship pull the experience 60° after it out of you.[33]

---

[33] In an astro chart, the location two signs *after* a body *causes* that body two signs before it when time progresses normally without any interference. I talk about this in *144*.

459 Signe	other's dark intentions for you	Body	attracting others' corruption	People often have ulterior motives around you which defy the position you and they are in	Where Signe lives, you often cannot tell what others are thinking regarding those sides of the relationship beneath the surface. Their motives aren't always dark, but such motives are almost never fit for popular public, co-worker, or peer group ears. Like several other asteroids, Signe works best when you team up with such people to uncover some third party's secrets or to change that third party's system. Barring this, you may never get along with the other person in ways that don't hurt later.
332 Siri	dissatisfaction with systems around you	Body	constantly complaining about a particular thing	You constantly complain about this particular thing. You can't stop	Use this location to insist on perfection in your creative work. This is a good area of life for describing your outlook as an artist.
126 Velleda	corruption or exploitation	Body	corruption or abuse as a topic in your life	You have a pattern for certain kinds of interactions which you consistently cannot (or should not) air. (The opposite of Signe)	Where Signe receives dark motives, Velleda gives them. Your Velleda cluster of behaviors shows how you view corruption (socially frowned upon adaptation of a socially favorable system), as well as what kinds of character you associate with corruption and where you yourself might more easily use dark ends to achieve you aims. If you ever wanted a good reason to mistrust somebody with one quick glance, look for the location, house, and connected traits to their Velleda. As with Melusina though, Velleda is one of those areas which you really want to look at, since most of us will never fully do—ourselves—what it represents. To the extent that you believe that some people are just evil and that you would never do whatever that consists of, you'll have a harder time accessing your Velleda and its cluster. On the other hand, if your problem is that you access Velleda too much, your remedy may be to give voice to those who have this same problem, paving a path to more acceptable uses of the trait. Accordingly, a Chiron-like life-calling is implied here, this time as one who fosters others' more socially acceptable creative adaptation of existing systems.
827 Wolfiana	spending energy in excess	Body	overspending energy	You pour excessive amounts of energy into something by force of habit	Declare certain sections of the effort to be finished, but allow yourself to start on it again. (This is training to insert breaks into your obsession)
411 Xanthe	cut-off talent through impatience	Body	filing through options	You hit the eject button before events get a chance to mature	Like Zelia, this is often a protective mechanism in the form of whatever area of life it occupies. Xanthe's interesting aim, though, is to help yourself *not* foist the traits square to it onto your interactants. Accordingly, Xanthe's cluster is where you learn to be well-mannered. Its squares are the things you avoid using others for or imposing on them. This cluster is very useful in another's chart for understanding why they keep cutting you off. Your task would be to make it safe for them to stay in their Xanthe's squares with you.

351 Yrsa	strong trait where you are sought after, what you are susceptible to, prone to addiction	Body	susceptibility to influences	You can be easily flattered, influenced, or compelled to listen to the traits connected to this. You may even become addicted to them	Even on its best behavior, Yrsa seems to be one of the hardest asteroids to tame because it acts like a staple food in your energetic diet. Consider what the connected traits embody. If you're having problems with a kind of addiction, you might review both the Battle exercise and the Embodiments chapter with the object you're attached to as the focus. Your Yrsa will often follow right after the clusters 60° forward from it. (if Yrsa is in Cancer, items in Virgo would have preceded it.) It will also result in clusters 60° backwards from it. (If Yrsa is in Cancer, items in Taurus will be the result.) Using this may help you anticipate when trouble is on its way.
169 Zelia	where you are behind a fortress	Body	blocking influences	You have a set of tools you use for blocking the arrival of certain events, or even entire life patterns	The connected traits constitute your main set of weapons for fending off things that don't fit you. The reason for the blocking tends to be related to the cluster on the opposite side of the chart, which you want to experience favorably rather than unfavorably.
Any of the above asteroids in public or ideal-bearing chart locations	an apparently negative trait attached to a good one	Location characteristic	being near Sun, the Ascendant, Naema, Midheaven, Veritas, Eurynome, Imum Coeli, Descendant, Moon, Waltraut	You attract seemingly negative influences automatically. You can't really help it	Think about the non-extreme, inoffensive versions of the negative traits involved. Adopt them as key aspects of your personality.
Favorable, but inaccessible traits	unrealized potential	Location characteristic	chart location in areas you have trouble using, or square areas you use a lot	You want something, but haven't prioritized it enough to pursue it	Reduce the use of the clusters 90° away from this one, partly by silencing traits opposite this one (traits you compare it to) as an issue.
Virgo-11,12 (0°-5°)	surrounding environment feeling	location	stress when the circumstances are strained	You are stressed over something you can't do anything about at the moment.	Consider any decisions you *could* make in order to address the issue favorably. Start in the direction of those decisions towards making them real, even if you never actually exercise those decisions.
Scorpio-7 (12.5°-15°)	how you enter arguments	location	stress areas from you towards another	What gets your fur up, your defenses up, or puts you on alert	Pay attention to <u>everything</u> that is going on around you, or to some source of widespread information which surrounds the conflict. This essentially replaces Scorpio-7 with its square Aquarius-7. (Leo-7 doesn't work as easily because it's on the same level (other) as Scorpio. Aquarius-7 switches focus more drastically here.
Libra-8 (10°-12.5°)	how you argue	location	stress areas in a relationship	What you do to advance your aims in a disagreement; what happens to you to bring out your disagreement	This is only negative if you disagree with the wrong people or for the wrong reasons. Otherwise, it's how those around you invoke you as their own weapon.
Capricorn-10 (5°-7.5°)	the type of power held amongst your friends	location	barriers your friends typically can't get past	Your friends are challenged by a particular problem	This is essentially Chiron for your friend group. They are challenged to freelance in service to others using whatever asteroids are located here. Very interestingly, you can look at this section of another person's 1000 asteroids to see if you've been challenged in ways shown by their chart. This challenge indicates how close you are to them in their own sphere.

Capricorn-5 (17.5°-20°)	groups who draw out your projection	location	attracting people or situations with negative effects on you	You keep attracting single interactants with negative effects on you	These people are more likely to dominate you if you don't give them what they want. If you were a spirit or a god, they would be the ones who called on you. If you don't answer them, your individuality ceases to exist anywhere, as you have no worshippers. (That is, if you don't give these people what they want, the number of people who take a personal interest in you will go down. Don't feel bad though. EVERYONE has this kind of thing in their chart.)

Table 49-2: Significant Energy Stressors

Delila and Other Items That Go Against Your Principles

One of the hardest situations you'll encounter as you advance spiritually is how to come to terms with things that go against your principles. Everyone has every asteroid somewhere in their chart, and there really are asteroids which—when taken to their extremes—will be associated with some of the worst offenses imaginable as well as some of the not-so-bad but much more pervasive crimes against others.

At their absolute extremes,

- Neptune deceives
- 342 Endymion and Winchester oppress others
- 228 Agathe and Mars kill
- 125 Liberatrix and 2254 Requiem open trap doors up to and including suicide
- 679 Pax and 827 Wolfiana self-destroy
- 560 Delila steals
- 879 Ricarda and 452 Hamiltonia unleash caged-in rage
- 383 Janina and 344 Desiderata manipulate and devalue
- 459 Signe, 126 Velleda, and the Mercury-Selene angle are associated with sexual exploitation and overall corruption
- 2060 Chiron sponsors trauma while 4 Vesta focuses it
- 120347 Salacia, 728 Leonisis, and 801 Helwerthia enslave
- 238 Hypatia and 511 Davida dismember
- 911 Agamemnon tortures
- 351 Yrsa, Neptune and 946 Poesia sponsor addiction

When we think about the above issues we can see the range of negatives that they span. When the tension within a person becomes so great that he must not only eliminate the obstacle but eliminate it permanently, whole groups can be affected. Most people, however, will never reach these extremes, mainly because they—like all packages of character—mostly operate on a moderate level. Agathe won't normally kill, but will simply stop communicating instead. Yrsa won't normally make you addicted to a Neptune beclouding substance, but will simply give you an ongoing, open window towards a particular kind of abstract experience; the aim being to replace externally-sponsored addiction with externally-validated art creation. As we saw earlier, the final form for every exchange we enter into is that of patterns alone. No bodies, no words, no objects. Just paths among our own frequencies. We can use this to make a place even for the things we supposedly hate in life.

A president, celebrity, or news event which elicits our dissonance is only one form of several which represent information that we're uncomfortable with. These occur on "world" levels beyond our direct self or other control, though we still have some choice whether or not to follow them in the first place. Regardless of where the influences come from, our patterns will process them according to our own unique rules. So we actually *want* to learn how to handle the negative sections of our frequencies healthily. You *want* to learn the media space that fits you—with or without the default web source. You want to learn the face of politics that empowers you—not just the reporting system that charges you up in an undirected way. Imagine that suddenly a natural disaster occurred and you were without electricity or web for two months. How would your current reactions to information, culture, and social power be replaced? Not changed, but replaced. What new actors would fill the role of the school shootings you once fed yourself with so regularly?

Certain information in our lives goes against our principles or runs contrary to our comfort. In order to control those sources purposely, our goal is to abstractify them, then re-connect them to the experiences we want. I'll give you an example, then an exercise.

> At the time of this writing, there are few things that irritate me more than gentrification in San Antonio. The college I work for is in an upper-low end neighborhood with a student body reflective of this, yet houses are appearing on the block which cost five times more than anyone can pay. Amidst discussions of a widening social equity gap, I find it offensive that elected officials don't address this. So it should be no wonder why, over the years, I've learned to see real estate, preexisting social advantages, and "success culture" as synonymous with theft—either of individual value (as opposed to pigeonholed, "I already had advantages" value) or of actual worldly worth. Here's the area of my chart responsible for this view:

560	Delila	means through which you disenfranchise of others	27	sa	41
752	Sulamitis	worldly advancement-enabling gains	27	sa	46
389	Industria	side of you which determines your opportunities in the world	27	sa	49
642	Clara	playful or more approachable side of your personality	27	sa	50
2102	Tantalus	deceptive initial cool [often followed by stubborn or fiery intensity]	28	sa	11
515	Athalia	side of you more able to manifest through an entertainment field	28	sa	27
806	Gyldenia	where you display more unrestrained [or at least less formal], in some cases primal behavior	28	sa	34
777	Gutemberga	realm where you are surrounded by talk, where your actions are gossipable	29	sa	30
188	Menippe	where you take an open, unapologetic approach to a preferred area of expression	29	sa	43
83	Beatrix	where you set the agenda for others' actions, leading them	29	sa	44

Table 49-3: The author's Sagittarius-1 – an example of a cluster which associates a rewarding thing with a negative one. These kinds of clusters are one major reason why we hold ourselves back from certain experiences.

> Theft goes against my principles, but I also strongly associate it with rising in the world. If I don't steal (in a capitalist society), I won't rise. Do I believe this? Actually, yes. Subconsciously and consciously.[34] This holds even though I have my own social advantages and still have a hand in real estate. We're all like this. We basically hate something, but do the same thing we hate. It's just our own pattern of waves, regardless of whether the source is internal or external. But if it's something which we in principle don't believe in, we'll hold ourselves back from the rewards attached to it.
>
> So I asked myself, did I ever steal from others to the benefit of all? The answer was yes: during team activities or competitions—any exercises where I was part of a team and challenged to help us win. In seeking to win, we did our best. In actually winning, we disenfranchised the teams who—in more cases than not—had advantages that we didn't appear to have. We were the dark horse. In circumstances like this, I've been the energetic equivalent of a thief, stealing something that others believed was rightfully theirs. But no one was really harmed by this. People who began with advantages still ended with them. People who didn't begin with those advantages realized the value unique to them.
>
> The conclusion: If I don't want to hold myself back thanks to the marriage of a principle with a negative, I'll need to recast the negative with something analogous (but widely beneficial) from my history.

☞ **Question 49.11 (Recasting an Anti-Principle):** Think of a pattern of behavior or type of event which goes against who you are. No specific names, people, or parties allowed. Only processes.

1. What is the pattern you thought of? _____
2. Among groups who display that pattern, what do you think is the reward in it? _____
   _____
3. When did you ever benefit from that same reward? _____
   _____
4. What did you do in that situation which resembled the pattern from 49.11.1? _____
   _____
5. In what way might you enter the territory of 49.11.1 using your behavior from 49.11.4?
   _____

Critical Exercise
OBSTACLE REWRITING CHALLENGE

Trains: Life path, Claircognizance, Empathy

---

[34] ~~Accordingly, I haven't risen in the world as much as I think is possible, but social rising hasn't been a major priority for me either.~~ Nevermind. During the writing of this book, I figured this out. 6 months later, my situation is very different from what it was when I started the writing *Alma Mater*. No, I didn't switch to the dark side. I just took my own advice from chapters like this. You'll find out more about what I did as the book progresses. I'll give you a hint: The critical exercise on these pages is part of it.

Believe it or not, most of the calculated magic "spells" of use to us are located in Table 49-2. You may have thought that intuitive development was all about breathing and visualizing, but most of it involves the basic rewriting of patterns—mostly undesired ones. We could put in all the work to make ourselves psychic, or we could just build up more efficient ways of seeding what we want and predicting what we want to avoid. If you can master half of the repairs in Table 49-2, you'll find that your intuition, or rather foresight, automatically grows with it.

DON'T DO THIS CHALLENGE WHILE YOU'RE IN THE MIDDLE OF ANOTHER ONE. This one should be done over a separate set of days.

☞ Question 49.12 (Your top obstacle): Using Table 49-2, locate your biggest personal obstacle of all. Go online and find the body or factor associated with it. If applicable, enter its number as an additional asteroid.

1. What is the obstacle? _____
2. What factor is associated with that obstacle? _____
3. If the obstacle involves a body/asteroid, where is the body located? _____
4. Using Table 45-1 for now, describe how you think this body plays out in your chart. _____
_____
_____
_____

5. The repairs for various factors differ greatly. Unfortunately, you're on your own here. Still, use the space below to write down any additional steps involved in your repair. What other bodies do you have to look up? What other observations should you make? _____
_____
_____
_____
_____
_____
_____

If you were a student in my class I would tell you something like this: "I know it's trouble. I know there aren't a lot of instructions for this part. But it's your life. You can either go through the trouble of investigating it this way, or go back home and sit with your obstacle a few months or years longer." Only you can understand what needs to go in 49.12.5's blanks.

6. Over the course of the next week, initiate the repair. Log the results in the box below when the week concludes.

Again, this is one of those items which is critical for clearing out problem areas that have blocked you for years or even decades. I sincerely hope you give it a try, and that you don't let this box stay blank.

Conclusion

Perhaps you've heard many times throughout your life that any conflict you experience exists within you. I never liked that kind of simplistic finger-pointing—especially from people not in my shoes; although there is some truth to it when we remove all physical forms and think solely in terms of energy, what constitutes "you" is really a whole which exists beyond the pointable individual, so we end up right back where we started. Conflict is a feature of one's sphere, not one's body or mind alone. Sometimes positive thinking or a can-do attitude is enough. But sometimes it isn't. In these cases, environments may also need to be changed. Friendships might need to be rewritten. Entire frameworks may need to be adjusted.

We've looked at conflict not so much through the lens of what you can do to improve personally, but through the lens of pattern types—specifically those frameable using astrology. No, the planets and their angles don't govern our lives, but they do provide useful baskets for summarizing certain types of conflict. When we think about the fact that everyone has everything in their charts, it becomes clear that some people's Yrsa just doesn't bother them at all. Some people's Chiron never has been and never will be a thing. How do they manage this? I believe that most of these lucky-per-asteroid people don't have to "manage" a thing; some people's frequency weightings favor a natural ease with certain traits. Our task is to learn what the favorable sides of each unfavorable trait look like, then adjust our own maze of dynamics to mimic that favor.

You don't need to do things the hard way anymore. You have a phone. You might have insurance. You might have a group, meetup, or agency to talk to in order to surround yourself with an easier way. You don't even have to listen to any country, business, or employer's propaganda anymore. You can go online and find something different, something that lets you be you. Most of us born before the 1990's still remember when the hard way was a real and compelling option, but with the floodgates of alternative information now open, none of us has to stay in a negative situation for the long term, despite what the short term may say. To step out of the hard way, though, it is essential to plant the first seeds. Nothing will grow if it's never been planted.

Table 49-2 presents an outline for dissecting common areas of conflict across several contexts. Use it to understand certain barriers in your life and how they might be overcome. You could even ignore the asteroids and the astrology entirely. The behavioral solutions in the rightmost columns will still apply.

Beginning in the chapter after the next, I will assume that your attitude towards conflict is largely repaired. It will need to be in order for the second half of this book to work for you. Assess your readiness by answering the questions below:

Chapter 49: The Conflict

☞ Question 49.13 (Have you graduated past basic conflict?)

		How much does the statement define your priorities?				
Conflict Source	Statement	Not at all	Almost none	Not enough to cause problems	More than it should	Enough to be a real issue for me
Squares (90° apart)	I often feel stuck.	0	1	2	3	4
Octiles (45°, 135° apart)	You really have to force people to get them to go most of the time.	0	1	2	3	4
Conjuncts (0° apart)	Some people are just no good.	0	1	2	3	4
Battle with Another	I can't stand at least one of the last four US Presidents.	0	1	2	3	4
911 Agamemnon	I get what I want no matter what.	0	1	2	3	4
228 Agathe	If someone violates my standards, I kick them out of my life.	0	1	2	3	4
945 Barcelona	I'd really rather avoid doing things alone.	0	1	2	3	4
2060 Chiron	I often need a lot of help managing my feelings about things.	0	1	2	3	4
5335 Damocles	I don't care if I irritate others.	0	1	2	3	4
511 Davida	The burdens I carry for others weigh me down.	0	1	2	3	4
560 Delila	Sometimes you need to take what you want, even if others are made a little worse off for it.	0	1	2	3	4
342 Endymion	I don't take any mess from anyone.	0	1	2	3	4
1576 Fabiola	I prefer to do what I want to do no matter what anyone else says.	0	1	2	3	4
452 Hamiltonia	I often feel denied the influence I deserve.	0	1	2	3	4
238 Hypatia	When I'm slammed with other's wants, it takes a toll on me.	0	1	2	3	4
383 Janina	I feel like a particular thing I've wanted in life has repeatedly passed me by.	0	1	2	3	4
125 Liberatrix	If anyone even looks like they're trying to hold me down, I'll leave.	0	1	2	3	4
846 Lipperta	People often feel like they're worth less around me.	0	1	2	3	4
897 Lysistrata	There's this aspect of my relationships that always feels incomplete.	0	1	2	3	4
Mars	I often find that I have to steer or manipulate others.	0	1	2	3	4
373 Melusina	I think it's ridiculous how I attract all these shady types.	0	1	2	3	4
448 Natalie	I sometimes feel pressured to be perfect or else…	0	1	2	3	4
2 Pallas	I will definitely fight somebody to advance my cause if I have to.	0	1	2	3	4
679 Pax	I can get deeply stressed over situations I can't control.	0	1	2	3	4
Pluto	Society puts a lot of pressure on me to be a certain way.	0	1	2	3	4
997 Priska	It feels like somebody else's interests always come before mine.	0	1	2	3	4
879 Ricarda	I try my hardest, but there's this major barrier I just can't get past.	0	1	2	3	4
904 Rockefellia	I often bully others.	0	1	2	3	4
Saturn	My progress in life feels stifled.	0	1	2	3	4
9248 Sauer	I easily block or control others when things don't go my way.	0	1	2	3	4
459 Signe	So many people just want to use me.	0	1	2	3	4
332 Siri	I complain a lot.	0	1	2	3	4
126 Velleda	My relationships often suffer because of my deep down "improper" nature.	0	1	2	3	4
827 Wolfiana	I often waste a lot of energy pouring it out into things I'm obsessed with.	0	1	2	3	4
411 Xanthe	People don't like how I leave them hanging.	0	1	2	3	4
351 Yrsa	I know I have a weakness for certain things that are pretty bad for me.	0	1	2	3	4
169 Zelia	I block people too easily, often unnecessarily.	0	1	2	3	4
Any of the above asteroids in public or ideal-bearing locations	There are certain bad habits I really can't hide from public view.	0	1	2	3	4
Favorable, but inaccessible traits	There are things I want and know I could get, but just don't have the wherewithal to pursue.	0	1	2	3	4
Virgo[11,12] (0°-5°)	Stress takes up a major part of my life.	0	1	2	3	4
Scorpio[7] (12.5°-15°)	I get into arguments easily.	0	1	2	3	4
Libra[8] (10°-12.5°)	I damage things, relationships, or feelings when I argue.	0	1	2	3	4
Capricorn[10] (5°-7.5°)	My friends' barriers take a toll on me.	0	1	2	3	4
Capricorn[5] (17.5°-20°)	I attract people who bring out the worst in me.	0	1	2	3	4

Your Total _____

If your score is below 80, then conflict will likely pose a lot less of a problem for you in the coming chapters. If it's between 81 and 93, you might have some conflicts, but it won't necessarily stop your progress in the chapters ahead. If it's above 94, then you may want to work on the areas which had 3s and 4s. A lot of the work in intuition involves plugging into things that are not you and won't see things as you do. It will be important to approach these things with as little tension as possible if you intend to turn their frequencies in your favor.

Chapter 50. The Rift

    The Villain was flawed long before you knew them.
        While they were out there committing their crimes, they helped make you who you are.
        They gave you what they could, and handled you the best they knew how;
        yet they never stopped being a Villain to everyone else…
        and sometimes towards you.

    Then you grew wiser.

    Eventually you learned to see that one not as your ally, but as a regular person.
        Their flaws vexed you the way any stranger's flaws would, *except*…

    This person has high rank,
        They are family,
        They are long-time friends,
        A partner you've been bound to.
        You would get rid of them if they were anyone else. But you're invested, so you live with it.
        And because you live with it, you're now starting to hate them.

This isn't a regular conflict. It's not rooted in anything that has happened, only in things that always were. You could fight them, but that wouldn't help anyone—especially not you. Not who you want to be. Not your kids. Not the bigger groups you mutually support. Not the work either. The situation is getting worse the closer you get to becoming someone better. But the closer you get, the more trapped you feel. You realize that they have probably always been like this, damaging you in ways you could barely fathom until now. Now you see it clearly. They will never change. Yet your entire future may be at stake if you stay. Something has to be done, but what?

Clearing Voices

Before we discuss what it takes to follow your positive instincts—listening to your guardians—as it were, we face the unenjoyable task of addressing your negative instincts. More than any overt form, these tend to be negative points of view installed in you through life experience, clouding what is possible, putting fear and defensiveness in place of excited exploration. Whether it's a dog eat dog philosophy, a closed-eared prejudice, or a crippling pessimism, certain lessons which once served us well—along with the teachers who issued them—may eventually lose their usefulness. There we are tasked with the uphill battle against socialized loyalties—even towards people who have outright abused us.

This chapter is all about cutting ties with friends and family: IF you are to do it. *How* you should do it. When, and to what extent. Although I will certainly not advocate this as a necessary part of your development, if YOU think this is something you'll need to do, this chapter is for you. I'm writing this chapter several months after the chapter before it, largely because of this very issue, and am in many ways still in the middle of its hardest stages. After you've done your best, taken all the ownership you can for your own part—after you've wrestled with how to even understand the issues at hand, attempted to talk them out, attempted to resolve them on your end... When, no matter what you do, the other person or group seems intent on destroying what even they themselves say they want to maintain, you have only a few remaining options. Cutting the tie is one of them.

Society tells us that certain bonds like marriage, kinship, long-term friendship, and other kinds of duty are sacred. But again we ask whether the people who tell us that have themselves behaved honorably in those same relationships. Some of the hardest ties to break are those where you are visibly attached, but invisibly damaged in ways that truly limit everything you can ever become, just because you have "settled." I've never found a book that told me what someone like Jesus thought when he outgrew his parents' domain, or what Siddhartha Gautama felt when he left his wife, child, and entire kingdom to become what would eventually be The Buddha. We read about forgiveness and lovingkindness and all of that, but the assumption is that we are decided on heading in that direction. What if we're of two minds instead? What if a part of us doesn't want to acknowledge openly those issues that seem to only exist in our heads and not in the others', but the other part knows full well that the other party is problematic enough, unfixable enough, unwilling enough to work through it with us or others for that matter? When there "is no issue" but the greatest elephants in the room, we consider what we would do if that person were a total stranger instead: Does cutting the tie suddenly become the obvious solution? Okay. Let us discuss how to do this without damaging ourselves. And without creating more damage to anyone else—still part of our own sphere—than has already been done.

Determining the Endings

As a prelude to the rest of this chapter, we'll dispense with the usual fluffy business. I have three close relationships in my life which are currently at a reckoning. They <u>will</u> be ended or at least drastically rewritten by the time I finish this book, or otherwise will have undergone some miracle on the other person's part. Now you as a reader may not care about this (I actually hope you don't.) but I do want to set the pace: Even though we're used to reading about how things will work out swimmingly in the end, sometimes they actually won't. They may end in a way nobody really wanted. In cases like these, one of the first things we'll need to do is compare the typical endings for both you and the other party. When events end for them, how does it happen? How about for you? You likely have several kinds of ending available to you, including angry endings, tense endings, beautiful endings, and uneventful ones. For situations related to the undesirable breaking of ties, you want the best ending for yourself. Avoid the tense or angry endings. Your body doesn't need the clash against itself.

Chapter 50: The Rift

Identify your better endings

☞ **Question 50.1 (Your better endings):** You are about to end an exchange which you would rather not end. Not in this way, especially not with this other. But end it you must. Historically you have exited other situations in ways that played out positively for you. What kinds of things happened in these endings?

_____
_____
_____
_____
_____

Ask if the trouble travels with them, but don't dwell too much on this

☞ Because we're looking at difficult separations, we assume that the other person or group is unable to reconcile or choose good endings—often even for themselves. Take a moment to think about where, historically, the way they currently interact with you lines up with other interactions they've had with parties besides you. Because we don't want to manifest this event any more than we have to, *we won't go broadcasting the problem to everyone in earshot* and we won't write this down. All that does is allocate more space for the issue on your permanent cognitive shelf and the shelves of your friends. Additionally, I've found that **every story you tell about person A to person B has a MUCH higher chance of becoming the same story you tell about person B to person C later on. MUCH higher.** I'm not sure why this is, but am sure that it is related to a kind of chemistry-like bonding pattern typical of your sphere. While you do want to know whether relational self-sabotage is a typical behavior by the other person, you don't want to get so far into their ways of thinking or their ways of oppressing you that you spread poison to the rest of *your own* sphere. Just ask what kind of ending they're cruising towards. Make sure the problem actually does typically travel with them and not you. If it travels with you and you haven't addressed your part in this, the separation will be harder to carry out smoothly. You'll need the cleanest hands possible if you are to escape this with minimal complication.

Let's practice intuition: the best decision-making for your own growth.

Get away from blame

Although I know that two of my three separations are, in the most basic sense, the other person's fault, I also know what it feels like to say this kind of thing ("It's their fault."). When I say it, there is a sense of "waiting" attached—as if my spirit says, "It's their fault, huh? So? And?"

Maybe it is their fault. Okay. Then what?

...I actually paused for a couple of seconds. Nothing came to mind. Nothing at all.

It doesn't matter whether it's their fault for being who they've been long before they met me, whether it's my fault for attracting them into my sphere and keeping them for all of the bribes they offer in other areas, whether it's their parent's fault for raising them that way, the world, the wrong crowd, violent video games, existential angst, the media, or whatever. I can't take side roads. I need to get out of this in ways that put the choice in my hands, not in their trainers' hands. Blaming them wastes my time. Spreading more news about how bad they are also wastes my time. I need to look at my better endings and spread that instead.

Get away from emergency behaviors

Leaving in anger, in desperation, in confusion, or any other terms under which you would not want to ARRIVE in your next place, won't help you leave *this* place.

One thing I haven't told you about my situation is that all three relationships I'm cutting have the same dynamic as the closest one among them—the one with an extended family member. The other two are virtual family. For years I've picked up the training of this person, such that the lessons I've learned in particular areas have not been healthy ones. The most distant relationship among the three follows a similar pattern, but has caused me no guilt of any kind in distancing. Interestingly, I know that there is a smooth, "I simply outgrew it" dynamic with this third person, but a much uglier energy with the extended family member. So I know that it's actually not necessary to cut the tie under the ugly energy because the smooth exit is clearly an option with the more distant one. This is what I want. No emergency behaviors allowed. No fights or sudden arguments. No anger or rumor mill torching. All I want is a better sphere-mate for this particular role. If it feels like I'm about to do something in anger, I'd do better to let that go and come back when I'm ready to make a smoother move for myself and the others I support.

I've had several women friends who have a history of trauma in their backgrounds and continue to attract abusive relationships. These relationships are often more stable as connections than healthier ones, while other relationships end with the woman losing the man's number. There are two kinds of ending here, but both are similar in that they are associated with tangled emotions as well as failed expectations on the part of the other. If a woman in this kind of situation were to decide one day that she needed to escape the abusive dynamic, in this example, she may have two forms of other-entanglement as the basic way of leaving: one under tension and the other under easier departure. She might also find—as I did—that in order to leave the dynamic completely, she needs to address it across multiple relationships. This is especially true when separating from people who are like family. There may be several ways of seeing the same style of interaction mainly because the dynamic is so entrenched. Returning to the entanglement example, not only might this be a method for leaving the current situation, it may also be a method for preventing future situations like it, but we'll get to that later.

Put the "closeness" in its place

We may be family, long-time best friends or whatever. And I know there are a lot of people out there who would try to shame me for "throwing away" such a commitment. But I can only imagine what these same bystanders would do if I treated them the way the person I'm leaving treated me. As we discussed in an earlier chapter, if you won't show me how to handle this correctly, given you were in my shoes, you can't shame me.

We know the blanket artifacts of culture; our society may not know which end is up when it comes to unhealthy relationships. Where material bonds, family bonds, or historical closeness are easier for bystanders to give their opinion on simply because they are more visible, they are not excuses to diminish another for all time.

I'm not the only one letting this tie break, though I may currently be the only one bothered enough to make a decision about it.

People can be close in space but far apart in mentality. Even separated by phone, they can be close in emotions despite being hours apart in time. Others may be years apart. Closeness depends on the dimension.

If I've worked enough to avoid the rift, you can't talk to me about closeness. If I didn't know what closeness was I wouldn't have tried to keep us together. But here we are. The decision is difficult enough for me to put so much thought into. I've avoided blame, picked the best ending I could, and tried to see the value in all of this. I'm not so full of myself, however, to think that I have the power to magically make the other person different. It's not even my right to decide whether they should be.

Intuitive steps

Throughout the separation process, I pay more attention to those little decisions that feel smoother and more peaceful for me when compared against the strained ones. I'm not required to utter all kinds of friendly affirmations if I'm not up to it, but I am able to practice my intuition for navigating complex spaces. As we talked about in the previous chapter, I know there are some things I consistently go to amidst difficulties and endings, and even if I don't currently have access to those things, I do have access to the belief that those things would be my haven. These form an actual haven, not a wished-for one. They comprise what I actually, healthily go to rather than where I wish I wish could go. If these things have negative effects on my body, my thinking, or my relationships, then I enter the zone of these things without going to them. I would love to elaborate, but can't do it the same justice here as is done in other books. That's not a plug. Those are where the actual pattern for practicing a certain level of psychological discipline beforehand actually got played out already, and is actually what just came to mind. It would be naïve to think that after all this time failing to get out of these exchanges I would suddenly just be able to do so overnight. Perhaps not the reader, but I myself have needed to do a lot of introspection to get to a place where instantly setting things on fire was no longer an option. I've needed to be okay with where I have made mistakes and where I might not know as much as I thought I knew. Leaving an entire relationship pattern—a close and deeply entrenched one—<u>with as little baggage as possible</u>, has taken not so much determination, confidence, resolve, or courage. Instead, for me, it has taken a lot of realism. About what parts of it are and aren't mine. About where I will go after this. About what will happen or not happen if I stay. And whether I'm being a better person—the best person I *can* be—as I leave.

Do my decisions along the way feel right? Are they more peaceful and edifying to me than the alternatives?

Drop a quick word on fixing it; you don't have to do any more than that

I'm so glad I've chosen not to blare my connection problems with specific people all over my network. Because I've only talked about the issues with one or two people, and done so without depositing a negative story of my relationships with *those* confidantes, I don't have a gladiator audience cheering on my bloody battle with these close others. I don't have to spend hours and hours having someone else recycle my problems for me—making it harder for me to move on. No one is rationalizing, and no one is complicating matters by talking about working it out, forgiveness, or any of that when I'm clearly not ready. Keeping in line with who I want to be—who I *plan* to be—I'm pretty sure I eventually will get over this. I'm in no mood now to elaborate on that. Don't corner me into belaboring anything more.

Catharsis

This may sound strange to say here, there is a benefit in having an art that is your own: When the problems in my three (extensions of one) relationships began to get worse independent of anything I did, I remembered how I had a unique characteristic that followed me everywhere (it was system structuring). I remembered also that I had a couple of sphere-mates who have seen most of my worst sides and are still around. Whenever I've been challenged—as I assume it is with you—there is something I have done in response. More challenging events have only made that thing I do much more pronounced: It's writing. While in the middle of this book, I'm also finishing *Non-Capital Wealth*, specifically the sections on psychological efficacy and your A+ niche. It's the talent for which one is a super-supplier, which he can give to others inexhaustibly.

In challenge, I write. In writing I also give to as many people as I can. No one can shame me for working to help many beyond myself, even if they said it was self-righteous or self-pitying. I know why I'm doing this. Their labels don't mean a thing to me. And though this chapter may seem out of place in this book, I've written as I feel it and put it in here for anyone else right in the middle of something similar. Clearing all non-path conflicts doesn't just entail clearing the little ones. Many of us ultimately have to address the big ones as well—especially at the threshold of major evolution. I haven't found another place that talks about this part of the process as it actually occurs in the middle of one's spiritual development. The statement (though perhaps corny) has been "I write for freedom" (my own or others') coupled with another statement regarding one of my closest friends "M. is my anchor." I've pretty much had access to an instant mood changer, and (hopefully) been much more likely to turn my challenges into someone else's benefit.

☞ Question 50.2 (Catharsis 1): **When you've faced major difficulty, what have been your typical solutions?**

_____
_____
_____
_____

☞ Question 50.3 (Empowered helpers): **Given your answers to 50.2, are there any people, types of people, or places which you've had to go to, maybe even give power to, while pursuing those solutions? Who or what are they and what have their roles been?**

_____
_____
_____

☞ Question 50.4 (A repeatable statement): Imagine that you could arrange to do 50.2 and affirm the roles in 50.3, on purpose, whenever you had the feeling that things were about to get rough for you. Write down one or more sentences to remind yourself of these outlets.

☞ Question 50.5 (Testing purposes): Combining 50.2 and 50.3 with your answers to 45.8.4 and 45.10.5, write down what you think would be a decent "reason" for facing the most difficult challenges you face. What sides of your life are being developed?

The Point

I used to ask why certain lessons always seemed to arrive the hard way. Now I don't ask any more, but have picked an answer myself. I prefer certain lessons to come the hard-ish way when there is a perspective out there that people need to voice, but can't, and where the only way to help them escape certain kinds of oppression is to live some (admittedly light) equivalent of it myself. This isn't a matter of God messin' with me. It's a matter of my soul temporarily putting itself in the different prisons we all face, surveying the options and me doing what I can to say to them what your guardians want to say to you. Some of the hardest challenges we'll ever face aren't designed by the heavens to test us. They are one aspect of the job we wanted to do when we came here. My soul came to enjoy deep bonds and create structures in situations that need it most. This chapter is just me doing my work as it actually happens. I don't mean for it to be self-indulgent or self-pitying, but I do want to take the only period I'll probably ever take in any of my books to deal with one of the hardest kinds of conflicts of all: the one where, despite your entire setup telling you to stay... you know that it's time to go.

Don't do it in malice.

Pick your best ending. Frame your reason.

And don't take any yack from people keeping you under the disempowering aspects of it.

A Better Way

When you decide to leave a negative situation, there are practical concerns that often come with it. What about the house? My kids? The money? My job? Especially when children and family means are involved, it's rarely easy to just pack up and go. Everyone's situation will be different, but my guardians tell me this (it's funny because I've truly passed the mic to them without any plans just now):

Way to go, OML, for putting us on the spot. The games of video game players or social games players mirror the kinds of stressors we find acceptable in life. We like to point out that sports each have a dynamic for passing stress and competition back and forth among competitors, and the pace of the game—the quickness of lead transfer—often, no typically mirrors the person's metabolic processes. Plays that bring them down in sports will bring them down in war. A competitive edge which satisfies on the field will satisfy in the relationship. You dislike competitive sports because you feel a certain way physiologically, so the kinds of disputes you have are not typically competitive. For others this will differ. But when it's ultimately time to win a competition against a longstanding opponent, people will do so according to the competitive frames they know. Why is this important?

It's important because, the mode of the game can be used to frame the attitude towards possible victory in it. Truly not all conflicts—few of the magnitude you are studying—feel very much like games. But if you know how to frame not only your best ending in the long term (which is apt by the way), but also your game winning in the short term, you'll have more of a frame for overcoming the immediate problem.

(I ask what they mean.)

For example, you like the army-like setup of football, but aren't as interested in which of your 30+ something "not unfavorite" teams wins. You are more interested in the legacy, the journey. Your favorite sport might be best described as the sport of "history making" among countries, teams, cultures and so on, so when you find yourself in a conflict you ultimately frame victory and loss in terms of who makes the best decisions in the long term. And because you prefer a "slaughter" to a close game, you frame conflict in terms of who takes the *undeniably* higher ground in the long term.

Now imagine a person who has been physically abused, still attracts abusive relationships, and who also likes basketball. Suppose they prefer the excitement of a close game with frequent lead changes. This is not to say that the default dynamic is always a trading of assaults with the abusing partner, but it is often so. It is not to say that the abused prefers anything about this dynamic or thinks of it as anywhere close to a "game." It *is* to say, however, that the framing of conflict is more likely to look like a charged two-sided pattern, and that the types of wins they recognize are likely to fit the types of narrative they will later apply to the relationship. Come-from-behind speaks of resiliency. Pulling away speaks of distancing. A last second shot speaks of a sudden resolve, so that the modes of conflict navigation—as we discussed in earlier chapters—

tend to follow the person's ability to frame where they are. This has implications for the idea of "leaving with nothing."

Humans often fear the loss of their material possessions or status when certain kinds of close relationships end. This is understandable because the so-called closeness is typically rooted in visible connections: kinship, friendship, and employment. When the relationship ends, so too do many of the artifacts connected to the other person or group, so that you truly will, you MUST, leave not only the person, but their sphere as well. It is unfortunate that you are taught to value the couch and the roof more than you value your next decade of sanity. That you trust the offender's reliable dollar more than you trust the heavens' helping you make your own dollar. You act as though leaving means instant death for you, but this is rarely so. Your society presents options. Divorcing yourself from the myth that the material is somehow indicative of the psychological is an important step in the process of creating a COMPLETE sphere free of the deleterious influence. You want the person to go away, but you want to keep his car? Of course you do. But while you're keeping his car, your child is keeping your attitude towards utilitarian partnership with a supposedly bad person's things. You keep the car. Your child keeps the consequences of your decision—your attitude. The car will be replaced in a few years. The attitude may follow for as long as the child lives. Because you stayed for the wrong reason.

We want to help you see: when the material trappings are enough to cage you in psychologically, you make more of a decision to jail yourself—chain yourself—to those things than the other ever could. Negative relationships thrive where things that don't work are given more credit than they should have. Relatedly, living arrangements play a similar role as furniture and possessions, except that we replace the possessions with lifestyle actors. Now we do not intend to diminish this in people's lives. Clearly social connections can't simply be traded. However, there is a difference between being uncertain regarding the next connection and having no connection whatsoever. There is also a difference between staying with a connection simply because it is familiar to you and staying because you have nowhere else to go. If it seems as though you truly have nowhere to go, then you may need to spend more time understanding where it is you belong. Most people have plenty of time to do this as they opt to stay longer, but instead of framing a better way, they continually mix in reasons for tolerating a worse way.

Unfortunately, OML, we may be the wrong character of guardians to address this issue, as you lack the language of true victimhood and we lack the power to make you understand what it is truly like to be trapped. There are certain perspectives which will never be yours, upon which you will never be able to speak, but you will need other people and other outlets to truly address the rift between close ones. Still, there is a basic help that we can give to a reader facing this very issue: Play out your best ending style when you sever this tie. The call to avoid malice is real, as bitterness and recycled anger tend to attach to humans in your time like lint. Avoid having your friends hold that lint for you, but do cling proudly to the reasons for existing you found you were made for. In situations such as the cutting of close ties, we've found that it often does not pay to give a human counsel. They should be allowed their space while making sense of the impending loss. We would, however, encourage you to really think about the amount of extra power you give to the material and visible objects of the relationship, and take this power back in whatever way you can. The issue should approach as close to being between you and the other as possible. Not between you, the other, and the car. You, the other, and the rank. That third thing is disposable. But you're prepared to dispose of something much more potentially long-lived to begin with. If you must leave, don't settle for being *bought* by this person now, of all times. Lest you look back another 10 years from now: where the car will have been junked, but the delete will have stayed. It's partly your decision to settle for things like this as deciders. Keep what's important in perspective.

An Aftermath

I'm writing this about a month later. I've made some difficult decisions. Two of the problem relationships are effectively ended and the third ~~will be ended in a matter of days~~ has been thoroughly rewritten as of *two* months later. When I think back about how many people I've met who have undergone major personal challenges as they have attempted to better themselves, it makes sense. Certainly rifting does not have to be a requirement when you move from your old self to your new, but if your aim is to truly escape habits that held you down—to begin truly listening for something better—you might indeed find that a rift with the old reinforcers of those habits, some of the strongest players in your life, comes with this.

As things calm down—as I calm down—I've come back to the writing and looked it over. I considered, very briefly, discarding this chapter. I considered moving it to an appendix. But not for very long. I began this book as a roadmap for developing one's spirituality, in the process covering everything I knew how to talk about. As we proceed in things like spiritual or other personal development, we often skip over the kinds of difficulties that arrest our progress, and get on with the easy parts. But so much of the work we need to do lies in the patterns we need to <u>undo</u>. It can get messy. And the way we think about that work can differ greatly from the step-by-step optimism of the rest of our training. Sometimes, the divorce papers do need to be signed. The resignation letter does need to be tendered. That long-time friendship does need to be brought to a close. For readers lucky enough to escape these kinds of events, perhaps a chapter like this was nothing more than an intrusion. But for the many others whom I suspect are out there—if you *really* worked on the conflict enders in the previous chapter and found that certain people wanted to keep the fight going forever—I hope this chapter at least gives you a couple of useful ways to look at your situation. If you know that you really need to cut a tie, but feel dragged down by an armchair world with all of its expectations for your staying, gossiping about it, dissecting it, ganging up on it, but never actually making a decision, then one can only hope you find a clearer path than all of that. Talking to your guardians will be that much more difficult with so many extra opinions crowding your decisions.

You've grown up. Has the other person?

If not, have the old things you once tolerated now become problematic enough to separate from?

Have you done your part without movement on their part?

Is their staying the same now imposing newer and greater costs on you?

It may be time to separate.

- The cleaner your hands, the better your ending choice, the better your pass through the next door.
- Try to keep the material extras in their proper places when you decide.
- While it may be good to seek external support if you need to, there is a difference between seeking support and spreading your dark story just for commiseration's sake. You probably know full well what that difference looks like.
- Try not to install deeper bitterness among your friends by spreading around the foulest aspects of the other person; their holding onto your bitter memory after the "enemy" has disappeared will make it that much harder for *you* to grow past the framing… and into the world of the next "enemy" you will go. Surely you've experienced this already.
- Be wary of people who offer their two cents on your obligations while they haven't taken care of their own.

And don't let anyone shame you for letting that other person sit with their half of the problem.

Chapter 51. The Spirits

The conflicts are over, minor and major. All that remains are those challenges native to your preferred role in the world. There is a place in this life where your best work belongs, but how do you find it?

The aim of this chapter is to help you locate your "tribe." This will be our name for the groups of people you naturally gravitate towards in the life you live after your more enduring conflicts have either been settled or at least figured out. From here on, we will make two major assumptions:

1. You have accepted the idea that any significant conflicts you're still facing in life are part of your preferred path.

2. Given #1, you are consistently able emerge, from any significant conflict, a better person than you would have been had you not gone through it.

    a. <u>This isn't better as in "stronger," "wiser," more jaded or more defensive.</u> It's better as in a gained ability to relate more smoothly and more favorably to yourself and the world you desire to build—which includes you and your close sphere mates. Bitter isn't better. Disheartened isn't better. Adding negativity to your friends about the opponent—rather than adding positivity about yourself—isn't better either. The aim is to claim your conflict as part of your "sport" in this life. If the conflict can't be claimed like this, you may not have a use for it anymore. See Table 49-2 for some suggestions on how to clean up your space.

Why is it important to get clear on your conflict styles before interfacing fully with your tribe? Because in an ideal psychological world, your true tribe is past old barriers. This should make sense if you think about it. If you've ever joined a group which truly matched your interests but hosted people who still battled with basic issues the group considered conquered, you know that a person can be in the right place with the wrong attitude, unable to experience the real benefits that the group is meant to provide. There are places you will go to get help through your issues; ideally though, your (mastery) tribe is where you're mostly clear of those issues. Now you're helping others. You're contributing. For some, the assumptions above may end up being a lot rougher than they look at first glance. But we'll find out if you're *really* ready as we proceed…

100%+ Relationships

Before looking into our home base, let's introduce a new idea. A **100%+ relationship is one which stays steady or gets better over successive interactions.** You can have them with people, pets, plants, places, situations, or anything else possible for you to experience. On my own path, I encountered the concept after realizing I had recently served timed in the opposite kind of exchange: An **Under 100% relationship is one which subtracts from you over time.**

An Example of an Under 100% Relationship

Consider an exchange with the following kind of good friend: He's great company, builds you up, and encourages you. He introduces you to all kinds of new experiences, and is generally the life of the party.

You've been friends for years. One day, you decide that you're going to pursue your dream whatever-it-is. You talk to your friend about it, but the subject keeps switching away from you and back towards his interests (or his understanding of something he's converted your interests into, more compatible with his own). Starting here, your successive interactions with this person seem less and less satisfying to you, as you thought you were 100% on the same wavelength, but it turns out that you were only 90% there. The other 10% wasn't something that he heard. The next time, 90% of 90% leaves you with 81% of a conversation. You told him what your dream goal was, but somehow he doesn't remember it. He wants you to go hang with this new topic of his instead. The next time it's 90% of 90% of 90%. Now you have a roughly 73% meeting of the minds. You've already started talking to other people who are more receptive to your goal, while your friend continues to come to you every time *he* has something new that *he* wants to involve you in. By now you can see where this is going.

Because we live in a society where overtures are often valued more than actual supportive actions, we see this all the time. Even relationships which consistently operate at 99% satisfaction will eventually become noticeably unfavorable to stay heavily invested in past a certain point. While we certainly don't want to just drop exchanges the moment they fail to sufficiently please us, we would like to think that the other person cares to help the exchange in the other direction. Now that we're clear on the kinds of conflict acceptable to us, now that we've started looking for a place to be effective in the world, negative relationships aren't the only ones we'll need to be aware of. Non-positive ones will also become an issue. Specifically, relationships where your better self—your set of accomplishments, your self-improvements, the things you identify with, your talent or a thing you're proud of—is simply not heard…these are under 100% where your growth is concerned. You don't need to drop them, but these don't make good tribe mates either. More than anything else, your mastery tribes are the spaces in which your skills are seen, heard, and valued.

As with all sub-optimal experiences, we won't commit your under 100%s to paper. Almost every exchange you're involved in will be under 100% in some way if you assess them against your unique goals. We do, however, want to look out for those relationships where

1. the other person treats it like it's 100%
2. you know it's less than 100% (<100%) when it comes to *your* areas of growth
3. you've tried to share your growth with the other, it doesn't register with them, but #1 still occurs.

If all three of the above conditions hold (not just for people but for situations), then <u>that's</u> when we start assessing whether or not the situation is one we plan to grow from in the long run.

An Example of a 100%+ Relationship

Sometimes we've already found our tribe without knowing it. Imagine you are very good at your job. You love the work, and seem to grow in different ways from it over time. The problem is, that boss, those customers, that corporate thing makes your job unbearable. So you're thinking about quitting. Despite the work, the job itself just isn't satisfying.

Chapter 51: The Spirits

Before you quit, though, *do* consider the 100%+ work. Perhaps the extra details surrounding your employment are obscuring how your sphere is supposed to function, but those might only be forms for other issues apart from the tribe you're looking for. This brings us back to the idea that certain conflicts are part of your sport, and your goal will be to separate these from the kinds of dynamics that really do feed you. To that end, we'll start by seeing if one of your mastery tribes (you can have several) is one you're already in.

☞ **Question 51.1 (The place you grow the most):** It might be said that you're always growing, but if you had to pick the number one place, situation, or person which makes you a better, more evolved, more life-effective human, where would it be?

	Example
	At my day job. Easily.

☞ **Question 51.2 (Separating the growth from the challenge):** Surely there are challenges associated with the situation you listed in 51.1, but take some time to describe the part of 51.1 which is definitely 100%+.

	Example
	Solving problems for others, making it easier for them to solve the much wider universe of problems for the people they serve in turn. And still learning all kinds of new skills in the process.

☞ **Question 51.3 (Moving the challenge outside of the growth place):** This is a tricky two-part question compressed into one. Although you probably have challenges in your 51.1, the growth part you described in 51.2 nonetheless takes place against those challenges. Meanwhile, your growth place has its own goals or mission in life. Combine the *external goals* of your 51.1 situation with the *internal challenges* you face in interacting with 51.1. This provides one view of one of your objectives for this particular mastery tribe.

	Example
	External mission
	Service. At my day job, opening opportunities for our students and easing their paths to success is our external challenge.
	+
	Internal challenge
	Perfecting/Mastery. Realizing that we have a great internal system, and **optimizing** how we direct the force of that system outwards instead of on ourselves—with all the uncertainty we deal with in higher education—is the main challenge.
	=
	My work tribe **perfects** the art of **service** to as many individual paths as possible, as **optimally** as possible

If you had a hard time framing 51.3 positively, you may need to go back to chapter 49 and work on some things. Remember, we've assumed that you're past all that.

I accidentally performed a thought experiment just yesterday which you might find useful in finding your tribes. While meditating on what my idea of Heaven might be, I found that everything I listed was everything I already had. At the time of this writing, I'm not rich or famous, happily married, or socially powerful, but there are certain ways I like to live which are exactly as I would have them in the life beyond.

☞ **Question 51.4 (A piece of heaven):** Imagine you have died and gone to Heaven (or something like it). While you're there, you're told that you can make a living doing the kind of thing you've always wanted to do which <u>also</u> provides something useful to others. What would that activity be?

Chapter 51: The Spirits

Because our mastery tribe connects us to the aligned expression of others, there needs to be something that we do which matches us with them. Ideally, this is something which also registers with our psychology in this life, such that it will be consistent with what we think growth looks like.

☞ Question 51.5 (The perfect activity): Given your answer to 51.3, what do you see yourself doing in "heaven" which lines up with the area you said you grow the most in?

	Example
	I would use a limitless tool set to model systems for souls to 1) better navigate their earth lives, 2) help their charges navigate their lives, and 3) help the rest of heaven learn more about the larger universe outside of it. Perfecting our service to each other and others.

☞ Question 51.6 (Who's who of the tribe): Keeping only with your 51.1 – 51.3 answers for now, are there any specific people (or other characters) whom you would definitely count in your (51.1 – 51.3) tribe so far?

_____
_____
_____
_____

For your own sustained mastery, it's important to appreciate current tribe mates while you still have access to them. You may not always.

☞ Question 51.7 (The mastery continues): For those you listed in 51.6 above, is there anything you can do which 1) advances your perfected expression even further, 2) advances the shared work you do with those others, and 3) is fun, something you'd gladly do, and doesn't take away from you? (That is, it's a 100%+ activity.)

_____
_____
_____
_____

The above serves as an activity which constitutes your staple contribution to your tribe even as your tribe-mates, place, or context change. In stable times, that is. Of course, if your world should shift, then your mastery behavior will also shift to fit the new needs and new people around you.

Whether or not you've actually found your tribe—or, given that you've found them, whether or not you've been able to successfully connect with them—your mastery behavior constitutes yet another strong property of your sphere. In the same way that we were still able to look at conflict after removing the physical people, we are also able to look at that key behavior for which a person will be known long after they're gone. By definition, your "optimum" comprises those patterns which are so ideal in your eyes that deviating from them would be less effective. Although you'll likely hold onto a few nice-to-haves (like more money, less stress, and additional social perks), you'll know you've reached an optimum when you realize that no change of jobs, no program of personal improvement, no wish for better friends, and no great bucket list item can get you to change who you currently are.

Interestingly, you may be more likely to *know* you've reached your optimum only after a succession of apparent failures to move to a so-called "next-level." I wish I could convey to you just what an amazing path the last 24 of my own personal "failures" over the past year alone have created, but it's not something you're likely to appreciate until in happens to you in a way that hands you your dream life in the way mine has for me. Since all conflicts are now definitely of our own writing at this point, our optimum support system and most fitting tribes will be as distant or as close as the circumstances we have allowed. Again, I assume that you are past the heaviest kinds of conflict from the previous two chapters. If you are, and you still haven't found your optimum surroundings, you will be truly fortunate to have your attempts to advance farther each fail back to back to back. The lesson is easier to appreciate after you have finally made your lemonade from these lemons: The top of the mountain is precisely where NOTHING is higher. Your mind may want that promotion or that new partner, but your spirit knows you are exactly where you belong. The ability to perform your mastery behavior nonetheless means it is only a matter of time before the true place for your tribe(s) becomes obvious.

The Actual Workings of an Ideal Tribe

Even though you might think that finding your ideal group automatically brings the kinds of socially validating, happy times you see in the commercials, this actually isn't the everyday case. It is true that your ideal tribe will tend to grow you, grow because of you, and be more meaningful to preserve than your more normal connections. But it is also true that you would have come together on some shared quest that still involves work. I belong to three tribes which don't (and can't) talk to each other, even if I sat all their members in the same room. This is because one group introduces people to their unique paths, another tells people to forget about unique paths and welcome all paths, while the last tribe questions what a path is. What one of my tribes treats as normal another might find extreme—not because of personality differences (they're all very similar), but because their work differs. Your tribe's work in this world will constitute your everyday on those occasions when you're not partying. It is *because* of this everyday-ness that you can call their space your home. As we saw in Dimension 6 of *S12*, our connections with others are most enduring when they persist even after the bars and the theaters close. When the files need to be submitted. When the laundry needs to be done. When you're drained of initiative and want everyone to go away...your actual ideal tribes will remain so through all of this. So while you may have thought that your default friends were tribe enough, that may or may not be the case, and almost certainly won't be the end of the story. At your optimum, you'll tend to belong to at least three kinds of tribe which reach far past special social gatherings: a work tribe, a daily concerns tribe, and a who-you-really-are tribe. Other, World, and Self respectively.

☞ Question 51.8 (I love being here, love going home, love dreaming on my own, then love coming back here): You found your mastery behavior in 51.7, but that was only in one area. When you found one optimum group, you may wish to cut your time with other groups to be with that one. But that brings us back into the world of conflict with our own idea of groups / friends / jobs / partners who aren't enough. Searching for the ideal group, then, is not just a matter of finding a collection of people. Instead, you'll actually be looking for a collection of "rounds" to make. Not just the folks you hang out with on Fridays, but as many groups of folks as you'll need in order to love doing whatever you do every day, pretty much every hour. This is one of the reasons why our lives tend to be circumscribed by a search beyond what we have; what we have may actually be exactly what we want, but we haven't asked for the same in other areas. So the comparisons kick in. And we feel as though we lack what we want once again. Accordingly, it is easier to recognize your tribe if

1. you know you have several, not just one
2. you successfully find *all* of your tribes (not necessarily at the same time, but definitely to where you can eventually cycle across them over the course of a day).

Imagine you spend your life making the rounds across three basic spheres of activity: work, daily home, and personal goals. Including your mastery behavior from 51.7, list what you think makes for a good mastery behavior in EACH of these spheres. You're basically answering 51.7 again for each of the contexts through which you make your rounds in a normal day. If you need to add to the three contexts above then go ahead and do so (parents, for example, may cycle from work→parenting & daily→partner & daily→personal goals).

	Example
	1. Work: I model systems for fun and others' benefit.
	2. Home: My friends and I publish books and create original stuff all day. I love identifying as part of a group of people doing something that is uniquely theirs
	3. Personal Goals: I enthusiastically dream of contributing to the societal future. Nothing is off limits; my third tribe is at home with the taboo. The whole human story isn't complete without it. I enjoy a strong personal—and exploratory—spirituality.
	At work I do #1. When off and interacting, #2. When alone or tired, #3. All behaviors are equally exciting.

*Note for the above exercise: Although you can certainly add your fun-Fridays friends to this list of rounds, I would strongly recommend against adding any tribe that automatically de-funs all other tribes. Does this make sense? If you count your traditional social group as its own tribe with a clear advantage over other groups in the enjoyability department, it's going to be that much harder to appreciate your kids and your job for the longstanding tribe they might be, for example. If you really want to count Party Dave in a tribe, don't put him in a "biggest-fun" box. Put him in a "personal goals" box, and imagine a mastery behavior for that. Try not to have categories that cap the appreciation of mastery in all others.

If you couldn't imagine a mastery behavior for some of your other spheres, take a break and try again later. Even if you have a good sense of the ideal in one area, it won't matter as much if that one area is making other areas of your life look subpar.

Question 51.8 was mainly an exercise in visualization. It told us what our various mastery areas would be based on, but didn't require any specifics regarding who was in those areas or how we would connect with them. It did, however, give us a proper language for obtaining guidance towards and in those areas once we decide to head in that direction. Rather than being rudderless, framing our mastery regions brings us closer to what some might call destiny. Others might call it optima. At least we now know that such things won't be recognizable as "perfection." Nor will they consist of a single group described by single "fun" or validating events. Instead we're looking for an overall lifestyle which still has challenges, but challenges which we ourselves enjoy taking on.

Splits and Merges

Go back to chapter 48 and take a look at the circle for question 48.3 again.

In question 48.3, we had a brief illustration of how **certain people or events at one point in your life can combine into the character of a later event.** Conversely, a single piece of your life can have its components scattered across several events and people later on. There is a term for each of these phenomena: Single-to-many changes are called **splits**. Many-to-single changes are called **merges**.

Understanding how splits and merges work in your life can be a very helpful tool for recognizing where fate or the spirits are taking you. Rather than your life being a hodgepodge of situations, coworkers, and living spaces, you can begin to see how your life is actually reducible to a few major frequencies. These frequencies, as they do in regular chemistry, trade their patterns to produce different looking experiences, though they are actually the same super-experience continually reshuffled into different windows depending on how much tension or harmony you have in your approach to each piece. Again, this is just like regular chemistry and physics: You can "impose" a tense neutron on Uranium-238 and have it merge into Uranium-239; this can then release an antineutrino twice, "splitting" into Plutonium-239. Across this system, the energetic actors are mostly the same (through three balanced equations), though the specific properties of each actor along the chain can be very different. By analogy, the sphere-mates differ, but the composition of the whole sphere stays the same (if you include the extra energy added and lost). Our lives work like this.

Although I had observed the reappearance of certain kinds of people in my life for years, I wasn't formally introduced to the concept of splits and merges until, in one dream, I was told "there is always a Katherine." There it became obvious that, no matter where I am in life, there is always a fiery, intelligent redhead—or a situation equivalent to her—who leads others with clarity. This is a feature of my sphere.

There is always a silver-haired rebel. Always a battle between the place where I work and a larger inertial supersystem outside of it. Always high-spirited, extra social colleagues. Always. The names and faces may change entirely, but not the stereotyped concepts they embody (red hair for tenacity, silver hair for completed resolve, high-spirited coworkers for a local version of utopia; I talk about some of this in the Body Forms chapter of *S12*). Having narrowed down the key players in your life, you then get a much clearer view of your constant trajectory. There, it becomes easier to talk to the personified versions of that trajectory at its optimum: your spirits.

Critical Exercise (51.9 – 51.12)
WHAT ARE THESE SLOTS TELLING ME?

Trains: Life path

☞ Question 51.9 (3 slots): Think of 3 <u>kinds</u> of people or situations that have consistently been in your life. Each kind should have a particular feature which defines it, though they need not share *all* features. For example, not all of the same "kind" of job may have been fun; it may not have even involved the same kind of work. Just think of the *common* quality. We'll elaborate on this later in the book. List each kind of person or situation below, along with the chain of characters that make up each kind. (I name my kinds after the chain member who is easiest to recall as a representative of that chain.)

	Example
	Group 1: The smart redhead. A leader of others. Nothing gets past her.
	T > S > L > A > K > J > K
	Group 2: The brother from another mother. Worldly ambitious. Well-educated. Black. On a mission to escape something externally imposed.
	E > G > C > R > W
	Group 3: The workplace under a bigger workplace under an even bigger societal context facing major social problems. My smaller group and I are more rebellious than our counterparts.
	N > J > M > C > I > S > U

☞ Question 51.10 (What the slot characteristic represents to me): As we've seen in previous books, public character traits in life act as prompts to behave in the viewers who view them. Another person's tallness makes us aware of our own approach. A thing's redness reminds us of "actionability" against a background of less red things. Some of the meanings of the traits we observe will be subjective, but many of them are very heavily socialized—so much so that they take on an objective quality. See if you can translate your 3 kinds from above into the behavior they prompt (in you or others). Definitely refer to the example to see what I mean.

	Example
	Group 1: **The smart** - a full collection of skills that can possibly be accessed in this current phase of life. Ideally she represents everything I'll need to be able to do **redhead.** - stubbornness, tenacity. This person will stick to her guns. Will I? **A leader** - is looked to by others for representing their interests, whether or not this is done on purpose **of others.** - this leader leads groups, less so individuals **Nothing gets past her.** - I'll always need to keep clean hands in order to survive this phase without problems **Group 2:** **The alter-brother.** - could have been an actual brother, but isn't. Why? There's something we differ greatly on philosophically **Worldly ambitious.** - compels me to reflect on my own approach to accomplishment in the world **Well-educated.** - a full collection of contexts that can possibly be drawn upon in this current phase of life. Ideally he represents the kind of experiential background I'll need to be able to reference for doing this kind of work **Black.** - member of a class that, social-typically, can more easily rile up/stir tension in strangers who observe them, for better or worse, just like me. **On a mission to escape** - compels me to pay close attention to the system being left behind **something externally imposed.** - a societal issue that has something to do with the above **Group 3:** **The workplace** - daily service is a central component of my path **under a bigger workplace** - but I need to respect parallel paths—under the same super-system—which are not my own **under an even bigger societal context** - we are all working towards some overarching end **facing major social problems.** - this is usually the trampling of the individual beneath macrosocial inertia and, relatedly, economic interests **More rebellious...** - all of my old conflicts are redirected in the form of the above

*An interesting note about the above exercise: After I did the example myself, I realized that—as my guardians said in the dream—there really is always a Katherine. I have one in all three of my tribes. The realization came after I did the example for the following question 51.11, and prompted the writing of a question for you: 51.12.

☞ Question 51.11 (What are these slots telling me?): Referring to 51.10, try to piece together the overall expressive patterns which the <u>kinds</u> of people or events (not the individuals) are assigning to your sphere. Remember, the people and situations you listed may have been separate from you once upon a time, but after you left them, they became a part of you in the form of your memory, training, and experience carried onto the next phase. My Katherines aren't Katherines after a while. They are the behavioral "police" that my sphere insists on adhering to. So there's no need to talk about the individual person—just the moral code that follows me around. You task is to 1) consider everyone and everything you listed as part of your own memory and 2) think of what your whole sphere ended up being pushed to accomplish using those chain members as an outsource. This can be tricky, but you can do it. See how my 51.10 answers led to my 51.11 answers.

	Example
_____	Group 1: There is a standard of knowledge collection and usage which is part of the main basis for my being here. This person is my police. If I fall out of alignment with that knowledge or lose the will to keep stubbornly, honorably applying it as a representative of our group's interests, my time is up in the current phase.
_____	Group 2: I am made to incite people to action, but there is an alternative way of seeing the situation which doesn't fit with my more activist design. Worldly ambition may work for others. But in my life, too much of it will keep me trapped. I should use my training to free others, not to trap myself.
_____	Group 3: Stop looking for the one-time pot of gold. Every day is the pot of gold: My oppression-defying work.

Now let us briefly revisit the idea of spirits and guardians. The people who have come in and out of your life seem to be people when they're there. After they leave your life, however, they stop acting as physical people to you and start acting as behavioral and emotional training. In this way, people (and things in general) revert to basic energy patterns once they get out of interaction range. Still, you can personify those people again simply by using your human framing to think about the patterns they left you. We personify TV and video game characters all the time even though they were never real, but because they have human-like shapes for communicating, grabbing, traveling, perceiving, and interacting, we can put them into neat human-looking packages for richer exchanges between them and ourselves. We can also do this for certain favorite non-human things like pets and cars. "Spirit" is the name we give to a package of patterns we receive which are consistent in their effects in the world. When that package of patterns happens to be inseparably bound to us personally, they become "our" spirits (" " " our " " " spirits, heavily quoted). Depending on how benevolent, how formerly or future human, how invested in us versus larger or smaller domains, and how coherent in the language of our current lives they are, such spirits might be referred to as guardians, guides, angels, demons, familiars, ancestors, generic entities, or whatever. Even in your dealings with God or gods (for the spirits of the highest-level Platonic concepts), your ability to get guidance from your spirits will depend less on whether you put in the conscious mental work to believe in them, and more on 1) the language most natural to you for communicating with certain types of thing in your life and 2) your tendency to interface more human-style with certain things over others. (I interface human-style with successful projects and games when I win as in "Yeah foo! Got you!" Go figure that the spirits I communicate with best are more like "wants fulfilled.") We can get an idea of what our spirits are like by considering our whole-sphere lessons like those in 51.11 to be the kinds of messages that our spirits like to communicate to us. Accordingly, we know our spirits more easily not by who they are, but through what we understand them to say—along with the kind of attitudes we expect from human-types who would say such things.

☞ Question 51.12 (What kind of attitude am I encouraged to have for each slot?): **Go back to 51.11. Clear your thoughts as much as possible, then think of the most natural kind of attitude that would tell you each statement. They would give you the statement for your own benefit, because it's something you already do. (You might as well get in harmony with it.) What kind of attitude passes each 51.11 message to you, for your benefit, regardless of how up or down or cooperative or stubborn you are? Clear your thoughts. Don't intellectualize it. Don't describe "personality." Just the attitude. Don't load any social templates. What kind of attitude would talk to *you personally* in order to pass in the messages you listed? Without referencing any other people's expectations, write what comes to mind.**

	Example
	Group 1: A mothery, fun type like my French teacher would be able to tell me this without making me defensive. Female, expert, sassy, caretaker to all.
	Group 2: A more distant, administrator-type, probably male, would be able to convey this. But only through his explanation of the systems he oversees, not through direct advice to me.
	Group 3: A comedian, male, highly resistant to embarrassment or regret. Even the biggest, most serious things don't bother him, but can be diminished by one person's bright attitude.

Chapter 51: The Spirits

There are things people say and then there are things people can get away with saying to you, in ways that work, and ways that bring you more contentment with the life you lead. Perhaps about 1/3 of your life is under your direct control. Another third can be influenced by you, but not directly controlled. The final third can't be directly influenced or controlled by you right now, but are instead controllable and influenceable by chains of things you will have done after this. You could make the whole (of your slice) of the world into a utopia—even though that world is beyond your control—if only you saw this first choice as being part of a chain which reshapes your world in the long run. It is, of course, not our right to mould everyone else's worlds. Eventual control will only extend far enough to respect their perspectives in the way you would want yours respected. But the idea is that your guardians are there to make your journey easier. Your sphere has all the puzzle pieces; you're being helped to enjoy building it.

*

If it seems like we're jumping around topic-wise, we are. Splits and merges, optima, spirits, and tribes are all connected in the sense that they are all components of a more holistic system of one's experience. When we're trying to find guidance towards where we belong, the search implies that we have not already found where we belong. But we probably have. Recognizing this means assessing where we've been, what it meant to be there, the outlook we were encouraged to have along the way, and what kinds of sources serve as our compass in the process.

When events undergo splits and merges in our lives, they allow us to address mini-issues one at a time, or compel us to squeeze them all into a single outlook. The most important split I ever underwent was the separation of my work life into a "mainstream knowledge" half and a "taboo, trauma repair, individuality" half. The most important merge came in the form of a person I worked with to keep our college open before it closed; she was every major exchange I had ever had, all rolled into one person. Part of finding your ideal path involves knowing when certain roads just shouldn't be allowed to meet; other roads *must* meet in order to make a highway. But contrary to our Western training, no, not every tale ends in a single, perfect ending. The various placeholders on your optimum path will keep merging and splitting—trading and absorbing each other's characteristics until you arrive at the combination most harmonious to you. Your spirits will be personifications of the attitudes needed to remind you of what those pieces are, and the rules you must follow in order to use those pieces as your sphere was designed—lest you imprison whole sections of yourself.

It's worth noting that positivity isn't the only thing that travels across your slots. The things you stand against will also travel. Your task, as it was for the Buddha, is to sublimate the more negative slots into their most abstract, most platonic forms. As early as 2nd grade I remember participating in "the war between the boys and girls," leaving private for public school in 3rd grade because I felt I had no friends, then leaving public for private school in 8th grade for the same reason. My two most negative slots—[othering sponsored by social cliques] and [degrading power dynamics with a group you're tied to] have each been as pervasive as any other slot. But these are the very slots that frame my work in this world. They are the basis of my books and the data projects I work with. At least now they are. At this point, your conflicts should be of your own writing. They will also have their slots. You'll need to split them and merge them until they end up in a form you enjoy handling. Usually this means splitting off a personal conflict from the person carrying it and merging it into your work or personal goal. But you'll need to have mastered most of your tendency towards the initial conflict first.

When they fight you, are you still fighting back as a FIRST option? Has this happened before with a different person? If you can get to the point where you avoid wasting your effort on battles that will only resurrect themselves, then you may find that the conflict sponsor adopts a sphere away from yours, and you can continue to do your joint work in this story at no cost to you.

My guardians once told me in meditation, "It's unfortunate how humans are trained to want so many things in the form of merges they can't handle…" They gave the example of the ideal partner: a merge of our emotional, affiliative, support, and enjoyment needs. Our security, our social validation, someone to keep us accountable. For some people this merge actually exists, and can be the end-all be-all for the lucky seeker. For many of us though, such a merge is too much to ask for—especially if we want the ideal to possess traits that clash with each other. On the one hand, I want everyone to be accepted for their individuality and need to do work for people just putting their toe in the water. On the other hand, I want to help people who've been punished for their individuality to have the strength to not give a damn; this second group is well-versed in what they stand for, and now needs ammo for standing strongly. Will I find a job that enables me to do both? Probably not a mainstream one. So a split of my "workplace" slot is in order. Just like an evolved split of the arms and legs of the body: Sometimes we need one to hold a steady place while the other sponsors change. The left and the right, waking and sleep, conflict and favor… Depending on how your world is set up, some things are just better as splits. Most things, actually. That is, anything in your life which is better as a collection with a dynamic or a progression flowing across it.

Merges are most useful when you need a solid reminder of the families of constructs you've packaged together. We did this earlier when we compressed our slots into attitudes. The goal is to obtain a rough reminder of how we're inclined to respond to an overall class of experiences. Every person can be thought of as such a class—drawing from a family of possible traits in different proportion. The more relevant their combination of weighted traits to our lives, the more likely we are to include them in our journey for a while. Some people tend to combine and recombine pieces in search of a class that works, and these people will tend to have more of a revolving door for their relationships (at least in that one department). Understandably, merges have a higher chance of failure here. Or if they succeed, they may take on more of an "anchoring" quality. But does the person want to *be* anchored? We may pursue the merged ideal despite our more fitting selves, and again be lucky if we don't get it. Splits are for journeying. Merges are for anchoring. When that merge of patterns in your life arrives in the form of a single human who possess all those patterns, the fact that they are human almost guarantees that such an assembly of slots will provide you with constant feedback on how you're treating it. You may actually want the merge, but if after everything is done you don't actually respect its feedback or make it feel as though you're listening to its feedback (even as you do respect it) don't be surprised if the merge still fails anyway. Merges are for anchoring. Merges in human form are anchors that you plan to listen to.

- Don't plan on listening to your merge but still need their appreciation of you? Get a dog.
- Don't feel that you need a merge, but strongly attract anchor reminders anyway? You may end up with a cat. Other animals provide still different arrangements of prompts for people's social response.
- Don't need any interaction with your merge whatsoever? That would be an object.
- Is your merge a dedicated form of service to the world? You may end up with a job.

Thus your ideal path has many many more components than we're taught to expect. Rather than arriving in the form of a single calling or support group, your full path will most likely comprise several contexts across which you make the calling rounds, a lifetime of chains of people who keep reinforcing the rest of your sphere of effect in this world, and a set of attitudes which keep these chains and contexts at the top of your focus. As you evolve, you'll attach and detach certain traits from each other in the form of splits and merges—continually inheriting new versions of old characters until you find your optimum. Once at the optimum for a particular section of your life, you'll begin to see that transitions away from that optimum don't come as easily. They may even fail to arrive entirely. Congratulations, an optimum is where you can go no farther while still improving, and you might already be there. The old conflicts which imposed guiderails are behind you, so now you need to listen to your spirits in order to know what comes next. This can start with a short review of the kinds of things that your spirits will tell you, and the attitudes they recruit in doing so. We're running on 100%+ information now, so the signals we heed must be up to standard.

Basic Types of Spirits

Even if you don't believe in spirits, remember: All we're doing is personifying our own behavioral inertia. Most of that inertia works in our favor. Some of it doesn't. Rather than delve too deeply into the occult world, we'll present a short table for viewing the kinds of phenomena we can encounter. When we personify, we treat things as a human object, so I have listed spirit types only in the "object" column.

	involves → Realm of the tendencies they promote our attention to	1 objects	2 inclinations to behave in certain ways, rule sets	3 actions in progress	4 communications
A	Things way beyond our observable level, which we CANNOT really fathom	conceptually unbounded classes ex: the universe, sets, "thingness," infinity personification: God, Purusha	other-dimensional workings ex: general "inclination," trajectory, direction	existentials ex: death, being	axiomatics ex: math (theory), change
B	Things above our observable level, but which we can still grasp conceptually	conceptually bounded platonics ex: redness, tableness personification: higher spirits, angels, other-dimensionals, spirits above the objects we normally engage but which inform our world using theirs	Superforces (between outward objects) ex: inertia	abstract actions ex: "running" as a concept	phenomena ex: the weather
C	Things on our observable level	observable objects ex: that table, my friend personification: demons, familiars, ancestors, local guides and guardians, spirits thought of as separate from (but bound to) objects we normally engage	moods (shown outwardly) ex: anger	observable actions ex: my friend's running	communicative acts ex: a spoken sentence
D	Things below our observational level whose truth we still recognize	subobservables ex: molecules personification: sprites, earth spirits, things which seem to have a will, spirits within specific things viewable in nature	specific inclinations (shown inwardly) ex: hunger	subprocesses ex: chemical reaction	signaling ex: wave propagation, high frequency wave travel
E	Things way below our observational level, where we have to take the word of others in order to recognize them	beliefs ex: …in the value of hard work, other-dimensional workings personification: human-like character assigned to subuniverses, us in a parallel universe (personification here strongly affects what we experience during astral travel)	subforces (within objects) ex: bonds, actions in progress	evolutions ex: the passage of time, growth, change	differentiation ex: class spawning

Table 51-1: Experiential classes in 5 perceivable levels and 4 process-thing/context-noncontext modes

You can use this table above to identify what kinds of frameworks you have the easiest time employing in your belief system.

☞ Question 51.13 (What's my existential language?): **Although all of the scopes in Table 51-1 exist, some concepts are easier for us to work with than others. If, for example, you really don't like to think of things far beyond your ability to grasp, infinite-looking abstractions like general change, Death, God, and the notion of trajectory as a concept may be less comfortable for you; it may be harder to get guidance towards your optimal path using anything in Row A. Using the grid on the sides of Table 51-1, list all the squares you have an easy time employing when framing your thoughts. You may even take a moment to try thinking about the contents of each box. I found this activity to be more enjoyable when I did this.**

	Example
	A2, C2, D1, D4, E3

☞ Question 51.14 (Observations from the phenomenon table): **You may have found that there were some boxes which actually turned you off to think about. Write down in the space below any observations that surprised you or make sense to you based on what you picked above.**

	Example
	I was surprised to learn that I didn't really like Row B—perhaps explaining my slight snobbery towards concepts which aren't the highest one possible. I also learned that the only objects (column 1) that really interest me are "components," which explains why the spirits I have the easiest time talking to are sprites and passionate types: they need a hormonal edge.

The boxes you selected in 51.13 will be some of the easiest routes for you to receive guidance in a non-tense way. This doesn't mean you won't use the other routes, just that the modes you selected will be the modes you're more excited to learn through.

Listed from biggest scope of abstraction to smallest, we can get a deeper sense of the kinds of spirits available to us.

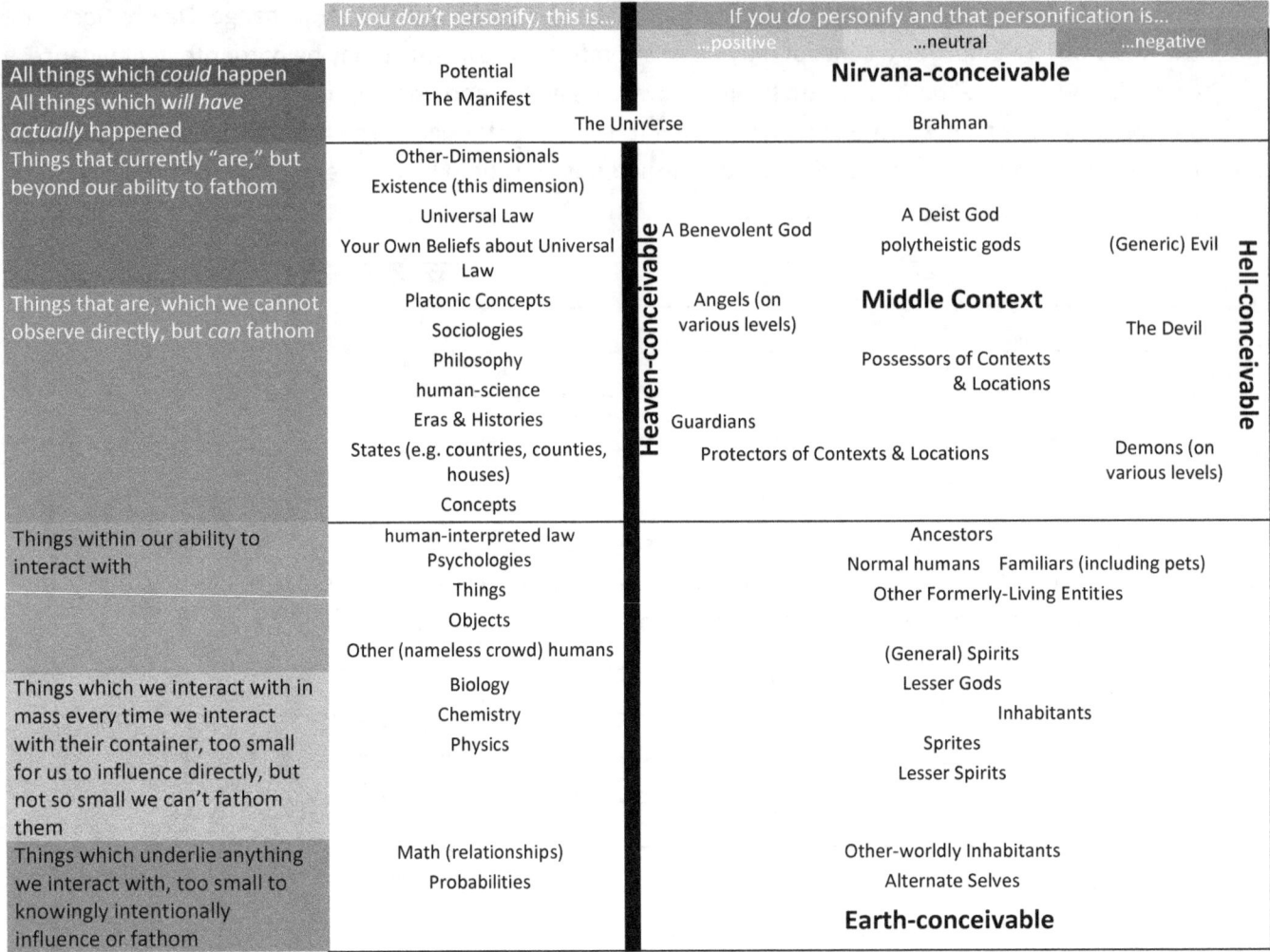

Table 51-2: Selected spirit types and their domains.

How Table 51-2 Was Created

The above table is a gross oversimplification of the various characters you will read about in the spiritual texts. If you think of the countless ways in which we classify humans alone, you can see this. The basic purpose of the above chart is not to define the spirit world or offend readers who have their own views, but to provide a general map of the kinds of spirits you might expect to the right of the dark bar if you began interacting with the concepts to the left of the dark bar as if they were people. One of the basic rules for constructing Table 51-2 was as follows: The more work a spirit had to put in in order for its will to pervade everywhere in every dimension, the further down it was. Accordingly, spirits who showed more personal preferences for the behavior of things were placed farther down than the same kinds of spirits who had no preferences whatsoever. I always joke to myself that "Brahman don't give a damn." This is the highest version of a god-like figure I've ever studied which exerts as little preference as possible—so little that it comes across as agnostic on the whole of existence beneath it. Thus he/she might be described as "unbiased" in comparison to the Judeo-Christian-Islam God, for example. Does this mean you should worship Brahman or believe in it instead? Should an American citizen worship the UN Secretary General just because his system has more countries under it? Probably not. The table isn't about which spirit has more authority or even which entities are real. It's about which levels of experience are most relevant to us when we treat our ideas as personalities. You can believe in anything in the table without believing in anything above it—or even believing in the table for that matter. It's just a layout.

Related to the point above, tense spirits were always lower than non-tense ones (for the same reason). Evil was automatically lower in scope than the gods thought to allow them. Demons were lower in scope than angels, and familiars were lower than protectors. This is because conflict, possession, and preference were considered to establish an "outsider" or a "not my way," while no-conflict, no-possession, and no-preference included both "mine and not mine," and so enjoyed access to influence over both. Peace cost less energy than war, and was thus considered to have broader (though less noticeable) reach.

Working with Negative Spirits

Can you be guided by negative spirits? Certainly. When I first began my spiritual journey back in college, one of the first contacts I (accidentally) made was with a demon whose name I won't commit to page. I wasn't doing anything in particular; he just showed up in a channel one day and proceeded to make me laugh. Along with another demon who had been a kind of protector to me in a past life, the first entity taught me various things about my work, why I more or less get along with certain dark spirits, and what such spirits tend to want.

> The short explanation is, demons and dark spirits—like people—tend to want what serves them. They may hinder others' benefit for their own gain, but are less likely to hinder the person who helps them accomplish this. The person may pay in other ways for his association with the demon (as I did), but if that person already feels he has nothing to lose (as I did), it won't matter. Furthermore, some spiritual "jobs" (like demonologist, exorcist, or paranormal investigator) involve going to where the dark spirits are. This is, of course, a PR moment for certain entities just as it would be for certain people. A demon who demonizes everything everywhere—like tension which tenses itself into oblivion—is more likely to face erasure on the relevant dimension. But thieves rarely rob their own houses. There are some things even a demon won't touch. As long as you're tied to those things, they won't touch you either.

That is <u>not</u> a recommendation that you play around with dark spirits. Early on I was also told how to call upon the name of Jesus (though I am not Christian) in order to clear out a space when the dark spirits got out of control. I was also told that part of the reason I can get along with certain dark spirits is because I leave them alone when they are minding their business in someone else's mess. That's *your* demon. He's *your* buddy. Unless you explicitly call me to help you *and* I believe you won't invite him back, you and your demon can stay together forever. If that sounds heartless, it will make more sense in the next two chapters. In the meantime, the advice is this:

Don't mess with demons or dark spirits. But if you happen to be involved in work that puts you in contact with them, you may start off with some around you—whether or not you chose to personify the self-serving / other-harming energy they often embody. In cases like that, you should respect that the demon is a creation just like you are, has an agenda, and respect that you may eventually, seamlessly outgrow your relationship with them. As in Chapter 50, you want your best possible, most peaceful ending when the time comes to separate from your spirit friend. Don't expect to go Rambo on your demon. Don't fight fear with fear or weapons with more weaponry. Just move on as your evolution dictates. Only a fool stays in that back alley once he discovers he's there. A bigger fool goes into the same back alley on purpose. Don't be a fool. Once outside of the dark spirit's house, he's free to rob you as he would any other.

(Interestingly, this same concept will apply to other *people* in the coming chapters.)

*

So you can learn from any kind of spirit, even a dark one. If you don't believe in spirits, you can learn just as easily from their non-personified equivalents. We humans are wired for sociality though, and as you progress in your journey you may well find that a certain kind of spirit naturally fits you. I lean towards the non-personified side on most levels, but have an uncanny knack for attracting certain familiars, sprites, and lesser spirits who seem to personify themselves—probably because of my work in the taboo. Along with my regular guardians, these characters arrived as I got stronger on my path, and continue to help me write these books (creepy, right?) Does it matter whether another person believes my guardians are real? Not if the optimum path I follow along with those guardians makes life better for everyone around me. You'll listen in the language that best suits you to the sources that are easiest to perceive. Stay resolute and resist being deflated by people whose lives aren't as full as your own. Your spirits are yours. Still, your tribe is calling.

Critical Exercise

AN HOUR IN THE LANGUAGE

Trains: Clairaudience, Clairsentience, Telepathy

☞ Question 51.15 (An hour in the language, abstract): For every box you indicated in 51.13, take one hour to work on a small project in that language. Before you begin each project, concentrate, then say the follow to yourself. "Give me guidance. Give me wisdom." Write down your 51.13 items below, along with what you did.

(I know it's tempting to skip this exercise, since it takes as many hours of commitment as you had boxes. And then there's the idea that boxes like D1 and B4 probably won't have projects that just pop into your head. Come up with something. Anything. Like all of the critical exercises, if you leave these lines blank, don't be surprised if your intuitive compass doesn't develop as quickly as you want it to. Think of the journey—not just the end goal—and do the exercise. This one trains clairaudience, clairsentience, and telepathy. You may find that your dreams change as you do it.)

_____
_____
_____
_____
_____
_____
_____
_____

Chapter 52. The Role

(More notably than in other chapters, "The Role" includes a lot of personal examples addressing some tough questions, not because I think you're interested, but because the workbook nature of *Alma Mater* requires that I follow my own sequence in order to know what kinds of conversations you and I might have as we go through the activities.)

Although we started off searching for that perfect tribe of people, our quest was complicated by the introduction of all sorts of new actors and new ways of thinking about those actors. Typical socialization teaches us that we should forever be in search of that eternal party, the never-ending picnic where the lawns are green and the smiles are wide every hour of every day. The reality of talking to spirits in order to find that ideal place is that the places are many. The classes of spirits are diverse. The language of the ideal is actually the language of the everyday. Half the challenge lies in recognizing which re-weightings of traits which are always in your sphere should be used to build the tribes and which should be used to build the rest of the world that tribe interacts with.

In addition to the tribe, we talked about the kinds of mastery behaviors you'll employ in the tribe. This was simple enough. These were just behaviors you already preferred. And now for something harder.

> During the writing of this book—in a six month period—I applied for (and didn't get) eight "sure-thing" jobs, attempted (and was unable) to buy a house seven times, connected then rifted with eight major people, had two major ideas formally rejected, and basically ended up exactly where I started. Well, not exactly. The last two jobs, five connections, two houses, and one idea were ones that I myself said no to, despite all of them coming with an increase in status. They would not, however, have brought me any more freedom. All of them would have cost me greatly in one way or another. As I was getting the last of the status-for-status'-sake out of my system I completed more than 20 important personal projects (many of which are scattered throughout this book and four others), published some more books (my own and a couple of associates'), took on some important work with some awesome people (including the greatest boss I've ever had—another Katherine) and turned my "being stuck" into a base of operations for work you will surely see in the future. `{In fact, this sentence is being written 6 months after most of the rest of the book: Read the Conclusion to see what` *really* `ended up happening after everything was done}`. This isn't bragging. It's an optimum. Once I realized that the status symbols I was trained to seek now offered only a step down from what I had, it became easier to not chase those better-looking things. But you couldn't have told me this one year prior. It would have required a better respect for my actual role *in others view*, beyond my own.

In case you never read the two other books where I talk about the future of capital, I'll give you a summary here:

1. Everything we measure in money actually has three other measures with it: social value, psychological value, and emotional value. Time is a kind of emotional value. Effort is a kind of

psychological value. The people who care that you bought it or who could help you get it for free are a kind of social capital.

2. In times where we have begun to focus so heavily on economic inequity, there is still little attention paid to the psychological and emotional capital that makes us value money in the first place.

3. Money goes away—often towards things we don't really need, but which certain peers and their standards really *really* urge us to buy. Emotional and psychological capital are effectively infinite, and both meant to be shared in different ways.

4. I know. You need money. Of course you do. But do you need it as much as you're taught to say? Given that you weren't in any immediate need, would you really accept a 50% raise if you knew it would make you less happy, less free, and more attractive to people who valued you only after you *got* the raise? This is a serious question. I had to ask it of myself twice.[35] Your answer to questions like these have the potential to enslave you for years at a time, or free you years earlier. Are you ready to let someone else buy your emotional and psychological identity for money?

   Joke all you like. But if you ever find yourself in a position like this, think hard.

5. Some of the most self-contented people I've ever met have come from two classes: the ultra-rich (tier 6 of 6) and the lower middle (tier 2 of 6). Meanwhile, the poor (1), the middle (3), the upper middle (4) and the rich (5) on the whole have been less happy as individuals when you ignore all of the furniture and social invites around them. This is because the lower middle and the ultra-rich are more likely to focus more on their psychological pursuits while still respecting the importance of certain social ties. Those classes closer to the dream (3-5) and the one farthest from it (1), are more susceptible to transactionalized connections. Not surprisingly, these connections reveal their weakness when the money and the status (for 3-5) runs out.

6. In the future, I suspect we will trade more formally in psychological skill barter and credit-like social trust (as China has already initiated), in addition to money. This is because the automated workforce and the essentially broke won't care about or won't have access to money in any meaningful amounts. They will need to trade in what they can do rather than how much abstract IOU they can give.

7. Your role in a society is increasingly a human capital commodity. Robots will become cheaper and cheaper than you are, so your main value will be in your personally creative worth. While you're borrowing $300,000 on an $80,000 salary, the person who can only borrow $90,000 on a $36,000 salary can get out of debt and get on with his lower-cost life faster than you can. Dr.

---

[35] Again, read the conclusion. I actually did pass up a 50% raise twice, did some of my own activities in this book, and instead used a hack embedded in them. The hack is scattered across the book, but the gist of it, along with the results, are in the conclusion. Chances are, however, most people will find it difficult to apply if they try skipping right to it. It's easier just to do everything, especially because there are plenty of other things you can do with all of this besides hack.

Doreen Virtue's *Messages from Your Angels* has a good section on this kind of thing. When you think of your "role" in the larger world, you'll need to think of it as

- The psychological skill you donate to your peers
- The emotional richness you share with your sphere
- The monetary security you collect for the life-occupants you need to support, and
- The social complementarity for outsourcing things you don't do well to some other party in your sphere

We don't want to think of our role as a mere job or a mere name tag, but rather as a weighted energy trade with the world around us. Beware of the training that encourages you to let yourself be bought every time anyone offers—to hook up with people who wouldn't give you the time of day if you didn't have buyable "stuff" they could be validated against. Be ready to protect your optimum. With all this in mind, let's get started.

What Feels Like Fate: A Story

One night in a dream, Abraham Lincoln visited Heaven. There he asked an angel, "I'm President now, but why do I get this feeling that something bad is going to happen?"

The angel replied, "You're going to be assassinated."

Lincoln, obviously disturbed by this news, asked the angel why.

"Because your assassination marks the beginning of an important transition period in this country's history. If you remain alive, the other side will take longer to heal because of their resentment towards you. If you die, your successor's faults will make the right path clear even to them."

"Well then I can just retire," Lincoln rationalized. "Why do I have to die like that?"

"Would you rather do it slowly, painfully, with generations of hatred on your shoulders that won't disappear for at least 100 years? That's how long it took to get to this point," the angel explains. "Another century and several more wars is how long it will take to get out of it."

Lincoln fretted over the angel's words. "Maybe I can become a real friend to the South as soon as all of this is over."

"It's not that simple," The angel replied. "When the founding fathers put this issue off decades ago, many of them hoped for someone like you. Now you're here. When the activists of the future reference this time in history, they'll reference you at the center of the solution. Neither the people a century before you or a century after you are inclined to see 'Lincoln: Friend to the South' as solution to what they know as an issue far nastier than that. There can be no weakening of what you will stand for to them. You're not just Abraham Lincoln of the 1860s. You're Abraham Lincoln of the 1780s, the 1960s—of the Emancipation Proclamation and the Gettysburg Address. While you think of yourself as a dot here on the timeline, history knows you as a spread-out wave of a story unfolding over the pages of slavery itself."

Lincoln felt a little better, as he knew what the angel was basically saying: God had a much larger place for him. Everybody dies, but he would die having done something so important that it dictated much of his life from far beyond his short physical existence.

The angel continued, "Your role is bigger than your job, and bigger than you. Anytime others tell a story about you, they are writing a piece of your role that will endure long after you're gone. Indeed, what they write will BE you for the rest of time. What you think of yourself means near nothing."

"Oh…" Lincoln reflected sternly. "Then all of my personal seeking and my self-improvement—"

"—means nothing if you don't create better lives for the people who will ultimately tell your story," the angel interrupted.

"I see. Then, when I awake from this dream, what advice would you give me for perfecting my role—especially if half the people I meet seem to hate me for reasons I can do nothing about?"

"Such is the work of one who stands for a principle. When all of your personal work is done, you belong to society. When your major contribution to society is complete—for you, the Gettysburg Address and the Emancipation Proclamation—you belong to History. When you've been true to the highest, most beneficial version of your story which even your enemies tell, your chapter in history becomes readable to ALL. From then on, you belong not only to History, but to the Army of God."

Lincoln understood only partly.

Thus the angel concluded, "When you awake from this dream, you will have found your place already. Have you already left your central work in the world? If you have, have you successfully inspired at least one other person to build on that work? If you have done that, are you living the rest of your life in testament to the great good everyone can gain from the first two? Living the highest form of your own work—after you've done it, after you've inspired another to even greater things or even farther reach upon it—these are the three requests Heaven makes of you. Anything less means you still have duties. Anything more is unnecessary."

Just then, Abraham Lincoln woke up.

An Introduction to the Role Beyond Yourself

In one of my meditations the guardians explained to me the idea of a person's identity being spread out over a timeline spanning far beyond his own life—to include the window of the event he is most associated with. I received a shorter version of the Abraham Lincoln story above, and also received the information about "group souls" which shows up in some other projects. When we think of our role, we tend to think of it in terms of our own reference frame. In space and in time, however, there is a constant world of additional communication about us which shapes an even stronger story of who we are than our own self view does. This additional communication is something that so many of us never get a chance to address in our lives—often because it includes the *real* story of the impressions we've left on others. There, the lies we've learned to tell ourselves hold no weight whatsoever.

The bad news is, there is probably a family of assessments out there which others have made about you which are precisely the assessments you don't want to hear. Despite all of our positive self-talk and careful pruning of our worlds, no one wants to hear that they're considered flaky, unattractive, an impostor, or a liar. No one wants to hear *why* the date never texted back, why the employer actually gave them a 3, why the people *didn't* buy from their shop, or all of the other little things that put strangers off during the first two seconds of that public impression. Yet those assessments are out there. Our ability or inability to work around them plays a large role in determining whether our time in this world includes finding what we seek, or consists entirely of the feeling that something is still missing.

The good news is, that same family of assessments works as a kind of obstacle course to give you something to do with the rest of your time after you have found your tribe and calling. It's not about pleasing others. It's not even about rejecting those who judge you. AFTER you've found your ENTIRE cycle of rounds (that is, *all* of your main tribe-slots), the doors that seemed closed to you no will no longer matter. You make the rounds across a handful of optimal spheres. Anything else that didn't want to be a part of your sphere just doesn't feature heavily in those rounds. Yet your mastery behaviors across your rounds will almost certainly put you in contact with new people on the periphery. These new people are almost always de-clawed versions of old slots (since the specter of potential rejection by them now weighs much less). This is your chance to explore the world outside of your rounds. If you died today, your tribes might remember you more for who you wanted to be. But if you possessed a talent that the whole world might have shared, it may or may not be the case that outsiders to your tribe will have understood what you were offering. It's up to you whether this matters. This chapter, however, is essentially the Capricorn chapter of the book, where we'll work on structuring your permanent role in the eyes of everyone everywhere who will ever read your story for centuries after—on the wikis, in the genealogies, in the records of the places where you did your best work. This chapter will likely be hard if you have not found all of your tribes yet, so before we get into the details we'll need to tie up some loose ends from "The Spirits."

Let No Door Be Considered Closed

If you haven't found all of your tribes yet, here are a few things to consider.

1. It is very possible that finding all tribes isn't even a priority for you. If it isn't, but you're still interested in shaping your permanent public role, then fine. That works.

2. Finding your tribes doesn't mean visiting with them every day. You only need the option. Although I said that I have three tribes (work, home, and personal), only work can count on my daily appearance. Home and personal consist of people that I may connect with every 2 or 6 weeks respectively. The rest of the time I'm at home working on more work (like these books). That's play for me. It's enough to feel that you're accepted in every mode. You don't have to cash it in every chance you get.

3. Your mastery tribes are places which grow with you as you grow with them. This is a 100%+ relationship between you and the tribe, but may or may not include 100%+ relationships with any individuals in the tribe—unless that's valuable to you. My personal tribe has no 100%+ individual relationships with me, and my home tribe has only two. All the rest are at work. Again, you'll settle on whatever fits you, but there does not need to be a single "person" that you go to for acceptance of your mastery behavior. The tribe as a whole will suffice.

4. Finally, what you're mainly after isn't the actual tribe. It's the feeling that no door which you value is closed to you. Tribes are places where you can say, "Look how I'm evolving" and receive a "Great! Your evolution evolves me! Now let me show you…" Then they evolve in turn. Some people can build this kind of lifestyle with few roots, such that it isn't necessary that they cycle through any stably supportive spheres.

   The thing you don't want is to, in your daily doings, run into people who have what you want, be denied access to it, and then be bothered by that fact. There should be no striving for others' stuff. You may want $1 million, but the idea that a certain closed clique over there won't give it doesn't affect you, because you're happy on the journey with your current paying job. And if they offered it to you at a psychological, emotional / moral cost you weren't willing to pay, you *would* tell them no. That's where you want to be. You want to be at the point where any other move from the person you currently are in the position you're currently in feels like a step down. That's an optimum. If you can do this without a tribe then great.

In order to make the initial connection with your tribe, it helps to use modes that are natural to you. If you're not an online dating person, online dating may not be the way. If you connect best at public events, a public event might be the way. Connect via modes that feel right and easy. <u>Don't force yourself to do things you won't want to keep doing every time you need to reconnect</u>. Do things you want to keep doing, and go in ways you like to keep going. Even the *journey* towards your 100%+ tribe needs to be 100%+ itself. This probably makes intuitive sense, though it goes against the go-go-get 'em training many of us have been taught.

For goal oriented people, a temptation might be to get the tribes out of the way so you can start working on the permanent role. We'll stop just short of telling you not to do that, but here's what you can expect: If you join "mastery groups" for their end results, you'll leave once the end results are no longer there. This is more utilitarian than mastery, and you can also expect to fail to develop numerous other time-investment skills scattered throughout this book. If you are impatient in building connections that are meant to support you even on days when there are no results, then you are probably impatient in other things as well. But the languages of connection, intuition, and relationships—like regular speech—are as much about the regular exchange of topics you like as they are about learning that new slang expression. You can rush the mastery sphere-building if you like, but as you've heard before, don't be surprised if your skills don't develop.

There is no quick manual for finding your tribes. Almost all of the effort you put into doing so will depend on whether you're even interested in looking. It will also depend on whether you're actually ready for all 100%+ groups, or if you're instead lying to yourself about how far past The Conflict you are.

Chapter 52: The Role

For clarity's sake, let's review some things you need to have gotten past in order to have an easy, growth-enabling time constructing The Role (*with all of the not-so flattering assessments taken into account*; that's the tricky part).

Get a timer and set it for 2 minutes and 30 seconds. Over the next 9 questions, we're going to see what kinds of topics we've discussed so far come second nature to you.

Ready? Start the timer.

☞ Question 52.1 (What's your sphere?): Do you know how to think in terms of your sphere? This is the group of people and situations which are extensions of your total energy. You are you, but there are patterns which are so strongly tied to your life that you will continually have others for playing those patterns out as extensions of your whole life story. Who / What situations currently constitute your sphere?

_____
_____
_____
_____

☞ Question 52.2 (What are your conflicts?): Are you currently involved in any significant conflicts? If so, what are they? (If not, skip this question.)

_____
_____
_____
_____

☞ Question 52.3 (If there is conflict, why?): (If you skipped previous question, then skip this one.) If you answered yes to 52.2, why has your subconscious (or soul) written this or these conflicts for you?

_____
_____
_____
_____

☞ Question 52.4 (Conflict resolution): (If you skipped the previous question, then skip this one.) If you had an answer to 52.3, what are your conflicts pushing you to do differently? Are you doing it?

_____
_____
_____
_____

☞ Question 52.5 (Necessary rifts): Are there any necessary rifts you must make with any person or situation in order to clean up your sphere? If so, with whom or what?

_____
_____
_____
_____

☞ Question 52.6 (Have you pulled the trigger?): **(If you answered no in previous question, then skip this one.)** If you require a rift, have you REALLY, HONESTLY started cutting the tie?
_____
_____

☞ Question 52.7 (Have you found most or all of your tribe-spaces?): Do you feel that, overall, everywhere you go on a regular day, you're excited and supported in being there?
_____
_____

☞ Question 52.8 (Are you free to be a master?): If you answered yes to the previous question, then what kinds of mastery behavior do you do in each of those places?
_____
_____
_____
_____

☞ Question 52.9 (Top seed): Are you at or near the top of your game in this *current* phase of life?
_____
_____

STOP

Let's see how you did.

Question	Your answer	All clear?
52.1: What's your sphere?	If you were able to rattle off certain key people of groups that constitute your sphere with no trouble then put a check to the right.	
	If not, the test is over. Go back to Chapter 48, "Curious Holes" and "Slot Holders," specifically your answer to question 48.5	
52.2: What conflicts?	If you didn't have any conflicts, put a check to the right.	
	If you did have conflicts, don't put a check.	
52.3: Why the conflict?	If you skipped this question, put a check.	
	If you were able to answer this question, put a check.	
	If you didn't skip but were NOT able to answer this question, the test is over. Go back to Chapter 49, Table 49-2, Question 49.13, and the "Conclusion."	
52.4: Conflict resolution	If you skipped this question, put a check.	
	If you were NOT able to answer What are your conflicts pushing you to do differently, the test is over. Go back to Chapter 49, Table 49-2.	
	If you answered NO to Are you doing it, the test is over. You may need time to work on this local conflict before subjecting yourself to the wild world of stranger judgment involved in The Role.	

52.5: Required rifts	If you didn't have rifts to make, put a check. If you did have rifts, the test is over. Unfortunately, major scheduled rifts mean that you are basically right in the middle of changing what constitutes a "stranger" in the first place. Now is not the time to suddenly become all good in the eyes of *all* strangers when your short-range situation is negative enough to cause close others to court strangership at the same time. It's not all good. If you know a rift is required, you need to make it before your mastery tribe and your role can reach their potentially highest level in this phase.	
52.6: Rift trigger	If you skipped this question, put a check. *This question is superfluous if you answered YES to 52.5. The test is already over. But if you haven't started cutting a tie you know you need to cut, just know that your answer "no" to this question may stop you from accessing any further growth in an entire space of things for years at a time.*	
52.7: All tribes found	If you answered yes to this, put a check to the right. *If you answered NO, the test is over. Most of us have at least one tribe we're aware of, but the striving culture we're trained in compels us to measure our other rounds against the most fun one. If you wish other areas of your life were as great as that one area, then The Role—in which you'll do work for people who will <u>never</u> be in any of your tribes will be difficult to fulfill. It may still be safer for you to work from your own perspective, not from the perspective of generic humanity. Revisit Chapter 49, "100%+ Relationships" and "Splits and Merges" for two lenses to help you revisit your less-than-ideal groups.*	
52.8: What mastery behaviors	If you were able to answer this question, put a check. *If you were NOT able to answer this question, the test is over. Before you work on a role for the entire world, you probably need to have a role in the groups that support you. You might take some time to develop your skills in each of your tribes, so that you can know strongly who you are when you take your show on the road.*	
52.9: Top seed	If you answered yes to this, put a check to the right. If you answered no, the test might as well be over. It doesn't have to be, but BEWARE. The world can be cruel. If you feel you're not at the top of your game in your mastery circles and go out into the general public anyway, certain critical parties may yearn to eat you alive. Nothing we do will ever be perfect, but before you pursue The Role it would help greatly if you got things as top-of-game as possible *for you personally*, given what you have to work with.	

Table 52-1: Interpretations of Questions 52.1 – 52.9 results.

If you had seven or more check marks, you're ready for the role. If you had six or fewer, you may need to settle some things first. Don't feel bad though, and don't rush it. The last thing you need is to drag rifts, conflicts, suboptima, or a lack of support with you into the wilderness of public record. For those of us who don't like to lose, don't like to score low, or don't like to be told they're not ready, not getting enough check marks in Table 52-1 can be a bummer. There's certainly nothing stopping you from persisting through this chapter, just know that if you do this knowing that you have issues to work on— knowing that you'd rather "win" than take the time to work on those issues, it is *almost guaranteed* that some sharp person out there will see all the holes you neglected to fill, and punish you for emerging half-cocked. They *will* call you out. You may hate them for it, and be super-sensitive to that brand of insight for the foreseeable future. Believe me it happens. Some of the best sphere mates you'll ever meet are also the most damaging before you get up to their level of seeing. The Role will put you in front of them. If you're not ready, the chopping they hand you may convince you that you never will be. Or never want to be. (Yet your sphere says you *must* be...must be just like them one day.) Don't rush off with your wooden sword to get killed by a master. If you know you need to get it together, then get it together. I myself had to stop at The Rift for several months before continuing this book.

The aim is for you to build your best *continuous journey* possible. Not one "dot" of a win after another. If you need to polish some things by 1) learning your sphere, 2) owning your conflict from question 49.13, 3) cutting that shackling tie, or 4) spending more time maxing out your mastery spaces and the skills you use in them, PLEASE DO THIS. From here on I will assume you had 8 check marks in Table 52-1. If you didn't, don't be surprised if your foray into The Role brings trouble you can't defend against.

All that said, let's proceed.

The Real Story

The real story of how the outer public assesses you is actually pretty easy to extract, though few people will have the thoughtless rudeness to tell it to your face unsolicited. All you need to do in order to hear this story is assess yourself against the socially trained ideal. That's it. Now I'll warn you, your self-esteem needs to be pretty high in order to do the kinds of things we'll be doing over the next few pages, which is why it is critical that your rifts be resolved and your full tribe-space in order. As we make these comparisons between ourselves and the socialized ideal, there will be this natural tendency to get defensive, to break out the attitude. But all conflicts at this point are written by you remember? Those people who criticized you? Now they are nowhere to be found, but you yourself are entering into this terrain in order to take your skills even farther. Don't take it out on others. Own these activities, and think of them as analogous to the kinds of preparation a politician must make before she runs for a major office. You'll need to know everything "they" say, everything they *will* say, and everything they *would* say if they found out certain things about how you work. These are the truths that will be told after you've left the room. We need to know what they are before we absorb their positive versions permanently into our Role.

Handling these questions

Rather than writing down your answers to the following questions, try to find a recorder. As you answer the questions, it will be important that you have the ability to give your opinion of those answers, what they mean, and how you might best respond to them. Although we will be capturing these assessments, we don't want a mere collection of critical appraisals. The appraisals need to be useful for building upon.

The aim of the coming self-assessment is to help you gain access to an entire chapter of life that most people will never see. Abilities like telepathy, telekinesis (as we've defined it), clairvoyance and clairsentience depend on your ability to connect with forces that are not you—or not tied to your body, at least. By owning the "public record" version of your sphere, you gain the ability to tie your actions to the kinds of results that we usually need to remain blind to if we are to maintain our confidence at all. But you're going to go there. And you'll keep your confidence. So find a recorder.

☞ Question 52.10 (The person others wish you were): Go back in time and think of all of the connections you tried to make—several times, with several *different* parties—which weren't allowed to begin because of some quality you didn't have. Also imagine all of the connections you were allowed to make, which failed because of some quality you didn't have. Third, imagine those connections you still can't get working because of some quality you don't have. These connections could be relationships, jobs, invites, being chosen for something, or any other opportunity for which others are the gatekeepers and those others have the ability to choose or deny you based on personal judgment—even if the resume is an excuse. In your recorder, discuss those missing (or misaligned) qualities in yourself. (You had 8 check marks in Table 52-1 remember? So you will be able to do this without anger, judgment, or bitterness. HONESTY IS CRITICALLY IMPORTANT FOR THIS EXERCISE.) Discuss the missing qualities, but don't be upset with the people for judging you based on those qualities. Right now all you need to do is log all of the traits. Don't do anything with them just yet.

(Example) In my own recording, I talked about 1) being a weird person in general with 2) off-putting, perhaps antisocial mannerisms, 3) a naturally raggedy look no matter what I wear—spilling something on or burning anything new I buy—and 4) a general disinterest in the basic topics and events people normally connect over. I described myself not as a social liability, but not as a social asset either. Instead, I was a strong asset for anyone looking to solve difficult problems with systems. If you didn't have those specific kinds of problems, inviting me into your circle was a lot like bringing a gun to a party and sitting it there on the table. People (and the gun) tended to get uncomfortable. There was, "Yes he's capable...but there's something not right about him," or "I definitely wouldn't trust him," or "I had him wrapped around my finger until he was an asshole," or some combination of these.

What I DIDN'T do in my recording was list any names, justify or defend myself, or be otherwise annoyed. All I did was observe (with an amused attitude I might add), Am I really that weird? The first time I saw myself on camera I knew: Yep.

My recording was 12 minutes long, as I spent time working out how to think about all this.

Regardless of whether the impressions you've left have been anyone's fault or just an unfortunately chronic misunderstanding, they *are* your impressions. Does Fate want you to fix those negative impressions which nobody would have ever told you about? I'd say no. We're charged to attend to things which are brought to our attention. But there are some sides of ourselves which would never be brought to our attention. How in the world would we have known to fix them? Are the people who handed us the trap door without ever telling us about the trait even worth our fix? Again, I'd say no. Don't worry about "fixing" the qualities you recorded. We're going to do something else with those qualities instead.

☞ **Question 52.11 (The critic in a few sentences):** Take the traits you recorded and, from the perspective of a skeptical stranger, describe yourself using some very basic words. Once you've done this, describe what such strangers tend to value in comparison to your tribes. DO NOT let bitterness enter here.

> (Example) The phrases I used were: [antisocial], [weird], [creepy], [not up to the hype], [smart...but not was I was looking for]. The more negative words I added, the more I had to insert "smart" or "capable" as at least one of the words, because the more I thought about it, the more I realized that this family of assessments tended to be heavily qualified.
>
> When I described what this skeptical stranger valued, I arrived at, "These are people who have access to the social ideal on command; If they want a pretty person, a rich person, someone with rank, the social outing, or the dream life, they can typically call it when they want." But it wasn't everybody who gave these assessments. I have a lot of friends like this who wouldn't describe me so harshly. The skeptical stranger had one additional trait: They were searching for someone, some employee, or some collaborator to complete the picture they envisioned, and they tended to do this without considering the costs imposed on the people they chose. So they valued a kind of power independent of fuel needs. The consideration of the other person's fuel was the number one difference between the skeptical stranger and my tribe-mates.
>
> As Prince says in the song "Dream Factory" "...S'I'm quittin' my friends, much to their surprise / I can't live up to the picture that they paint..."
>
> The recording was 6 minutes long.
>
> Once I realized that the skeptical stranger assessment wasn't everyone's view—not even most people's view—I also realized I was being hard on myself. We've been looking at people who closed doors but not at people who never made it to a door: true strangers. So we'll need to try this again...

☞ **Question 52.12 (The general grapevine):** We've been too hard on ourselves. Not every assessment of us is a negative one; the great news is that we've gotten the worst part out of the way. Now consider the general grapevine. These are strangers who are not skeptical. They just don't know you. Rather than comparing yourself to the social ideal, now you get to compare yourself to the standard held by the average person who can be found among the places you actually frequent. If you frequent church, you'll assess yourself against what the people in your church are used to seeing. That is, how do you strike them within *that* context? If it's the job, do this for the job context. You can record on all the contexts that apply. There is one rule though: You'll need to record under the assumption of your mastery behaviors. There is the opinion of your fellow churchgoers when you're not being masterful, and their opinion when you are. Record only the latter. How do people typically treat you when they are complete strangers to you? In addition to your own guess, one good source of this information comes from what your say *their* peers say about you (the kind of information indicated by astrological Pluto).

> (Example) My recording on this was short and very positive. The most notable observations came when people went from knowing my work first to interacting with me one-on-one.
>
> Now that the recording is over, I note that people who didn't meet my work before they met me were much more likely to assess me negatively.

☞ **Question 52.13 (Your first line):** Now we are going to switch gears. Go all the way back to Chapter 46, The Embodiment, Critical Exercise (Part 2 of 2). One of the strongest ways to influence your legacy (rather than leaving it to chance) is to produce some work or engage in some activity that people will forever remember you for. The intent isn't always fame, but simply for you yourself to declare who you were in this life. Thinking about the one thing that your children's children or your successors' successors will have known you for—that thing which is consistent with your mastery and your values—now record the task you MUST perform in order to solidify your "first line" in Wikipedia or the genealogy archives. This will be your version of the Emancipation Proclamation. What MUST you do if you are to have done anything? If you've already done it, talk about it in the recorder.

(Example) I needed to have published several books helping people look at difficult topics, especially *S12*. Ever since I finished it, everything else—including this book—has been icing. I also needed to write this one.

☞ **Question 52.14 (Tied to the times):** Just as Abraham Lincoln is tied to the Civil War and Reconstruction, your overall sphere is tied to a larger theme. Consider who your strongest sphere-mates are, along with the kinds of roles they perform in the world. Next, consider the larger society in general. If you were part of a "group soul" and that group soul was here to do something in line with this time in history, what kinds of events in the world at large do you feel your story is connected to? This is a tough question, since it requires that you integrate your answers to 52.11, 52.12, and 52.13.

(Example) I was surprised by my own answer: Corporations and government. My sphere is tied to the period in which corporations replaced governments as the prime mover of people and their economies. Though corporations are more fit masters for the new times, what we gain in goal orientation, attention to the customer, and order, we lose in self-determination. My sphere fosters creativity in an increasingly branded, credit-measured age, where the alternative is to simply live as a consumer waiting to be replaced. We're scholars and artists, but we're still human.

☞ **Question 52.15 (You as the skeptical stranger):** When you've been the skeptical stranger yourself—with all of your negative assessments of others—why did you do behave this way?

☞ **Question 52.16 (The catalyst):** Your skeptical assessors are there help you draw [this] out of people through your work. Write it below.

	Example
	My role is to help people find the completion of their ideal picture, regardless of what their circle thinks. We hope there will be respect between the people and their circles as this happens, but sometimes this is difficult.

☞ **Question 52.17 (The purposeful faults):** You own your conflicts. Your soul wanted you to have the "negative" qualities that you have. Use the space below to explain why you *want* those qualities you listed in 52.11 to keep operating in your life. Read my example to see how you might go about owning even the negative labels.

	Example
	Antisocial – I'm not antisocial. This is just the basic word most people would use to capture my lack of interest in a lot of popularly trained things. The word is useful though, because people who apply it to me—no matter how friendly they are, reveal a basic incompatibility that I need to heed early on. The quality itself—more like "socially efficient" protects me from normative drain.
	Weird – That's true. But whereas "social efficiency" protects me, weirdness acts as a filter for helping me connect with other "weird" people—anyone with a dream that is uniquely theirs which no one else will understand. If you have it, you'll know what "weird" feels like. That's exactly the end I work towards—even in normal people. People who tolerate my weirdness overwhelmingly tend to be more open towards everyone. These are the only people who can function in my particular tribes.
	Creepy – I only get this from people I've written to. (As a writer, go figure I write long emails). Apparently things like astrology, humans-into-data, sexuality, and dimensionality aren't good rapport topics. They are, however, work topics, and the topics over which I bond. Writing lots of words is part of it, and in an age where terseness and pictures are favored this can come across as pedantic or obsessive. Like "social efficiency" though, my "creepiness" protects me from drain. I'd never harm anyone, violate their space—never have, never will. But the same writing that some people say is creepy, other people have found interesting. There is a very clear difference between the former people and the latter kind which I've only recently understood. But I'll omit it. The point of this book is not to hurt anyone. Suffice it to say, my being seen as "creepy" is a major filter and a major protection for my tribes.
	Not up to the hype – I try to be humble. This is more a measure of what the other person expected in their heads. I don't own this. However, when I've gotten it, it has come from people with misaligned expectations for what I was there for compared to what they wanted from some other template. I don't own this, but it alerts me to stay far away from that person regardless of the promises they make. If their representation of me can't satisfy them, the actual me never will.
	Not what I'm looking for – this can be true at no cost to anyone. It does remind me to be more selective when I get it. Mostly from jobs, mostly when I was going after the money despite not caring about the place. Serves me right for selling myself out.

It's not so much that people assess you negatively, it's that some of them do it with an inconsiderate attitude. It turns out that even critical people are usually right about you in some of the observations they make, but wrong in general about what attitude is most appropriate for accompanying those observations. So we learn to fight attitude with attitude. For example, a good fraction of people in my circle are what you would call "flaky"…IF you looked only at what they appeared to promise you. From their perspective, though, they're just busy attending to multiple priorities in faster succession. If it's not priority, you may not see them. But you only know this when you catch *yourself* being the "flake." If a trait like this doesn't work for you, then fine. You might want to reframe it, though. Certain words like "flake" are laden with attitude labels. To stabilize your own attitude, maybe you shouldn't label the people. You might just conclude that you yourself can't rely on them, then move on.

☞ Question 52.18 (What kinds of tension are you prone to?): We feel tension in different ways over different experiences. Many of those experiences are prompted by others' behavior towards us. What kinds of tension are you more susceptible to feeling when tension strikes? Anger? Bitterness? Frustration? If your life were a video game, what kinds of tension could hit you the hardest? If you need some ideas, refer to Figure 46-3, Table 49-2, and the example below. Also, what kinds of tension are you highly resistant to?

	Example
	Weak against: disappointment in myself, contempt, frustration, bitterness, (excessive) passion, surprise stress, competition stress, annoyance
	Strong against: jealousy, envy, anger (others confuse passion with this), hate, worry, long-term stress, suspicion, fear, being overwhelmed, depression, shame, guilt, embarrassment, hopelessness
	Neutral against: disgust, sadness

If you're strong against a particular brand of tension, it typically means that you process the prompts for that tension in some other way. It can be useful to draw a map of how you process the different kinds of stressors in your life. Figure 52-1 presents an example.

Chapter 52: The Role

How I Frame Different Kinds of Tension

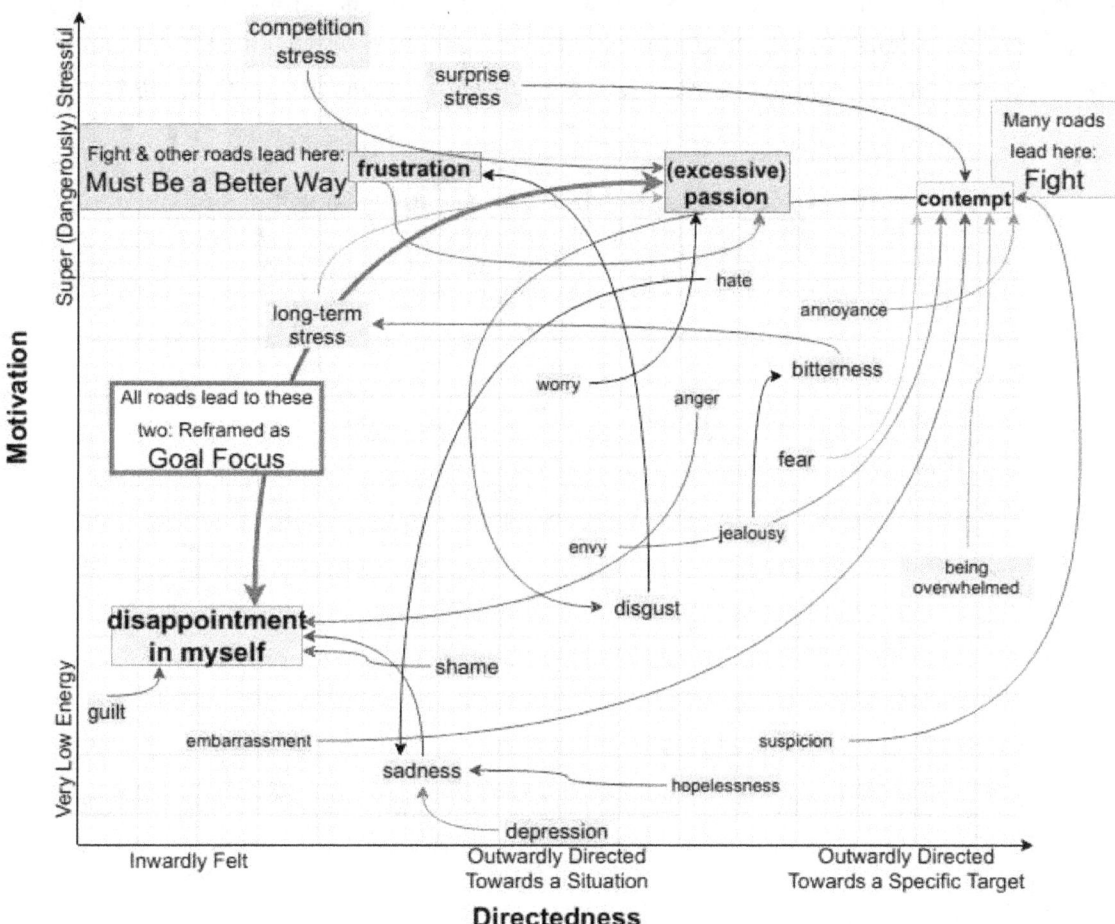

Figure 52-1: Sample tension map

☞ **Question 52.19 (Tension paths):** Keeping in mind the ways in which you convert different types of potential tension into others, draw a map of how you typically handle different kinds of disharmony. Where you put the different kinds of tension is up to you, as is how you connect them. But pay attention to what you settle on. We're going to use this to get control of how we respond to difficulties in our role.

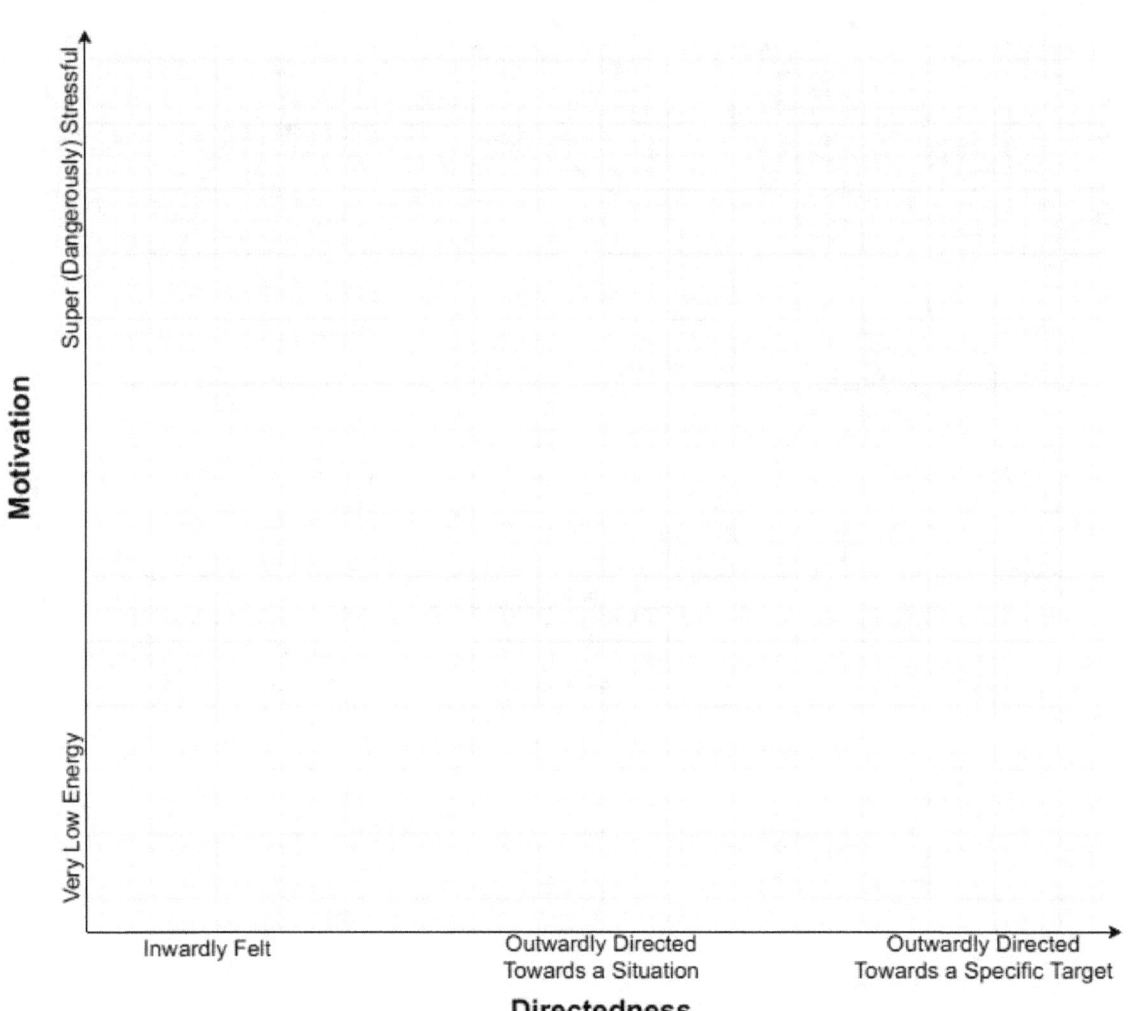

Tension involves a clash or strain between two sides under the same single context (their conflict arena). When you are tense, you clash against yourself. When there is tension between you and another—even if that person is a stranger—part of yours and their shared sphere clashes against *its*elf. Now we're in the business of shaping even our shared spheres intentionally, so when someone assesses you negatively, it may not be your fault, but you may be the only party with enough grasp to present a solution.

It's not reasonable to expect completely tension-free lives. You wouldn't want your body to lack hunger, pain, or muscle exhaustion signals. Nor would your sphere want you to lack stress, call-to-action, or social defense systems. You need tension. Lest you dissolve into numb incoherence. Take a look at your 52.19 map. The forms of tension which act as final nodes are the ones you will most likely have the easiest time converting into something productive, since those are your stopping points which you "want" (steer your actions seeking) all other kinds of tension to convert into. My final kind of tension cycles between the pair "disappointment in myself" and "passion," yet looks like neither. It looks like goal orientation—knowing I haven't made a goal, pursuing it, then moving onto the next. What do your final nodes tell you?

☞ Question 52.20 (Your kind of tension): **Some people exercise. Some people delve into puzzles. Others fight for the less able. Of all the possible kinds of tension, we are made to treat a handful of them as fuel for who we are. Which kinds of tension in your 52.19 map serve as endpoints on the chain? Assuming those are your "favorite" kinds of tension, how do they correspond to your general behavior under various stressors?**

_____

_____

_____

_____

_____

☞ Question 52.21 (You're immune to that, part 1): **Suppose a skeptical stranger assessed you negatively, via your 52.11 or otherwise. By now you know that such assessment comes standard for your role in this life among certain people, so it's not a matter of fighting them. You're just operating your larger sphere. What chain do you follow in responding to such assessment? Does this say anything about you, your tribe, or your situation?**

	Example
_____	When some other person assesses me negatively, I usually start with some general form of contempt, and usually bypass disgust and frustration and go straight to excessive passion.
_____	What it says: I don't take negative external assessment well at all. Never have, probably never will.
_____	But if passion stays too high for too long, then I become disappointed in myself for dwelling on it, then work to never feel that disappointment *in myself* again. Usually this means not engaging that situation again, up to and including cutting ties with the assessor.
_____	What it says: No wonder my tribe-mates are all naturally disciplined and considerate. I've gravitated away from most people without these qualities.

	What it all says: Disappointment in myself is the only way to get me to correct mistakes I've made. I need to have 1) known what the parameters were, and 2) known that I failed them. Without both, I'll probably just be indignant. No wonder my tribe-mates also don't keep very many secrets, are basically averse to lying, and don't generally manipulate others. The more secrets or lies you have, the fewer good parameters I have, the less likely I am to be disappointed if I fail you. We're not necessarily saints, but these are strong features in our group.

So many of us don't risk pursuing goals that are uniquely ours because we fear the heavy social punishments involved. We ourselves have jumped on the bandwagon when demanding that "jerk" resign. But if we were to perform our own unique roles for all to see, there would surely be a few people out there accusing *us* of being the jerk. We have qualities they wouldn't like, and these people would amplify them. Sometimes these people are even well-meaning friends of ours who discourage us from connecting with something that our clique is supposed to shun. Consequently, so many of us stay with the tried and true job-family-chaseTheDreamStatus template. And The Role never happens. Our cliques didn't really foster that kind of courage. Stones will be cast at us if we tried. We cast them ourselves all the time. But nobody wants to be stoned.

☞ Question 52.22 (You're immune to that, part 2): **Suppose one day you're out there performing your role, and your Achilles' heel comes to light: You're being socially punished for your end node.** If one of your end nodes was bitterness, rumors are flying about how bitter you are over such and such. If one of your end nodes was competition stress, people are accusing you of cutthroat practices which cross the bounds of normal acceptability. You really are prone to some version of what is being said, so even *you* can't tell if you were guilty or not. What do you do? (What does your 52.19 suggest that you do?)

	Example
	If I were accused of excessive passion for example, my response would be the same as my 52.21. If the event being talked about didn't involve disappointment in

myself, if I didn't have enough rules or cues to know better, if the circumstances lied to me or led me to act differently than I would have had I known all the information, I'm not likely to feel guilty. If I did know better at the time, the accuser would have gotten an apology from me immediately. Otherwise, I'll probably respond with more excessive passion, and probably in the form of a quest to understand what makes people railroad a person for a form of tension that everyone has: hence my books. My only weapon against someone re-spinning my vices is to do the best I can as honestly as I can in every situation. My quests/books will paint a more complete picture than any external punishment, and hopefully speak on behalf of many others who've also been punished for following their own path. In the end, I'd probably point my accusers to one of these books for the spirit in which they were written.

If I my own disappointment in myself caused consequences for others that led to a social punishment (like me not trying to fix something when I was definitely one responsible for doing so), then I would eventually respond either with a passion for making better decisions next time, talking it out with the punishers if allowed, or cutting ties with the punisher if they themselves prevented solutions. Then I'd be disappointed in myself for a different reason: for subjecting myself to them. The remedy for that one is clear.

You might have noticed that the difference between a crippling social punishment and an amplification of your role likely lies in the extent to which you can confidently own what you stand for. You can own this stance permanently by completing your "first line" from 52.13. Where you have the opportunity to leave something in the world that captures your complete role, and gives the stranger something to chew on, certain kinds of stifling fear become a nonissue.

Your Beneficiaries

We've explored the realm of people who assess you. Before we solidify your role, however, there are two other groups—effectively outside of your time—that we need to look at: those who benefit from your role in the long term and (perhaps even more interesting) those who hoped for your appearance in the first place.

In the Abraham Lincoln story there were two groups who flanked his contribution to history, counting more heavily on his actions: those of the Civil Rights Era, and the Founding Fathers who initially (collectively) put off the slavery issue. These can be thought of as those who benefitted from and those who "hoped for" Lincoln respectively. When you tied yourself to the times in 52.14, you established a wider setting for your life path. This works something like the region under the normal curve of your influence.

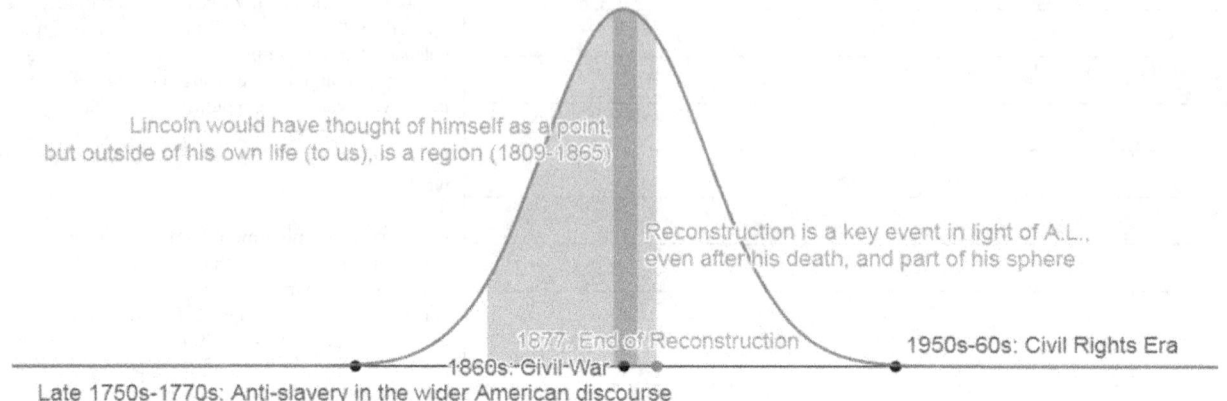

Figure 52-3: Using Abraham Lincoln, an example of one person's life as a whole sphere of events—even beyond his sense of self.

We cannot, of course, know how the future will connect us to our predecessors' and successors' lives, but we can ask some questions about who these people are. (Lincoln's would be "anyone studying the slave trade in the US.")

☞ Question 52.23 (Your interest groups): What *kinds* of people in this life tend to take a definite interest in your doings? (Not the specific groups. Their behaviors.)

	Example
	People who have something dear and personal to them which they want to put in the world for other's benefit, often to spare the others what they faced.

Chapter 52: The Role   253

☞ *Bonus Question 52.24 (Edge of the curve):* **Consider your answer to 52.14 (Tied to the times). If you're connected enough to history, would you say that you feel a connection to a certain era AND that era is connected to your 52.14 topic? If so, what is it, and how so?** You may feel a connection to several periods. The era could be as local as family history or as abstract as planetary history, though this one does have to be related to your 52.14. Pick a year if you can.

	Example
	I'm fascinated by the resurgence of the KKK in the 1900s as a protection against the loss of old morals amidst industrialization. Our current times have some similarities. The need to protect one's individuality remains. 1910 seems good. I'm also interested in projection technology. The late 1890s also work.

☞ *Bonus Question 52.25 (Width of the window):* **Take the year you picked and wrap it around you birth year. We'll call this the "core" of your sphere.** It's like a standard deviation.

	Example
	1910...1979...2048 1896...1979...2062

You can use the years above to help you picture the following scenarios.

☞ Question 52.26 (Your beneficiaries): **Given your answers throughout this chapter, what kinds of future people do you believe would take an interest in the things you did in this life?**

	Example
	People who have lost their individuality to technology, or people whose lives and values will ultimately be captured by technology, though their ways are—in the holistic mainstream—not accepted anymore. (Though this is a future question, I actually thought of D.W. Griffith's "Birth of a Nation."
	Also, people interested in projecting themselves into other realms.

☞ Question 52.27 (Those who hoped for you): Given your answers throughout this chapter, what kinds of people in the past (by their struggles) "hoped" for you to arrive, facing issues that you can now solve?

	Example
	People who felt that the newly liberalizing, yet heavily institutionalizing society wanted to wipe them out. All they needed was for more people who benefitted from that shift to speak on behalf of their dreams—let them know it would be alright.
	As part of a historically marginalized group, now with the ability to do nearly everything he ever wanted, I've benefitted from this newer world order. People don't need me to throw that in their face. They might benefit from a bridge enabling them to share the same. We lend a kind of science to as much of the unknown as possible, so that the best life paths won't appear so threatening or inaccessible. Given this, we can establish who we are in realms far beyond our own immediate reach.

We're almost there: towards a complete sphere—not just in this moment, but across the span of time and affinity that includes your combination of qualities. We know why you're here and who you're here for. We know of the tribes that round out your entire plot and of the external public which frames you independent of your interests. If you were a heart cell, then we will have gotten a glimpse at the entire vascular system. All that remains now is to bring in a few of your additional talents from earlier in the book: your specialty senses.

☞ Question 52.28 (What were your senses again?): Just as you have a unique path, you are also uniquely sensitive to certain packages of information for translating into that path. Earlier we discussed 12 senses and practiced using some of them. Go back to Figure 47-4 and, if you need to, review the sections on the different senses throughout the later parts of that chapter. Once you've done that, use the table below to rank the senses in order from "I am MOST likely to act on this information when I get it" to "I am LEAST likely to act on this information when I get it." THIS IS NOT A MEASURE OF YOUR SHARPEST SENSES. (For most of us that would be vision, touch, and hearing). This is a measure of the senses you *believe the most* given that you receive information about events beyond the sensation itself.

According to the framework we used, the senses are listed in the Table 52-2 below.

Chapter 52: The Role

- **cognition**: thinking or giving attention to something via an attributable source (usually the brain)
  - **clairvoyance**: perceiving information about your situation from your situation itself, the environment, or some other non-attributable source; sense of an external party's attention or inner processing with respect to you
- **biomanufacture** and proprioception: having a hormonal or internal feedback reaction; sense via communication of substances within (and typically produced by) the body
  - **claircognizance**: intuitive knowing, though the knowledge was not apparently given through the normal six senses; sensing the *inclination* (analogous to biomanufacture) of a thing or situation
- **vision**; sense via the visible spectrum
  - **projection**: putting yourself in environments you shouldn't physically be able to reach; being a source of visible or electromagnetic information to a perceiver
- **touch**: sense via communication across the body's receptors
  - **clairsentience** and empathy: intuitive feeling of the (inner state of a) thing you are interacting with; sense of what has contacted the thing you're interacting with (includes various kinds of contact, not just the typically physical)
- **hearing**: sense via the auditory spectrum
  - **clairaudience**: hearing sounds with no source, or thinking that seems to come through you rather than from you; sense of the envibrator that produces auditory information
- **gustance**: taste or smell; sense via chemoreception of substances from outside of the body
  - **telepathy**: compelling action in things sensitive to you; where you *are* the external substance to a receiver

Table 52-2: The 12 senses, based on a wave framework

☞ Using Table 52-2 above, fill in the table below.

Reliability	Yours	Ajani's Example
MOST reliable for information which I act on		claircognizance
		biomanufacture
		clairaudience
		clairsentience
		hearing, touch
		cognition
		clairvoyance
		projection
		vision, telepathy
LEAST reliable for information which I act on		gustance

☞ **Question 52.29 (Insights from your senses):** 52.28 gives you an idea of which senses you might care to practice and actually become skilled in. Did you learn anything?

	Example
	I learned that I trust my own interactions, dreams, and intuition more than I trust what I come into contact with, trust what I contact more than what I see, trust what I see *a lot* less, and rarely trust a situation on its own merits.

That's it. We're done. Are you ready to write your Role?

Before you do the next exercise, I'm going to ask you to do something I'm sure you won't want to do:

☞ Go to sleep. The Critical Exercise is only a few lines away, but **don't do it today**. I know you want to do it right now, but don't. Do it at least one calendar day after today. The reason is, we are trained to turn lifestyles into intellectual exercises, assessing them with words and descriptors. But a lifestyle is a process. If you really do feel you've found your role, rushing to do the next exercise won't turn your findings into something you know how to do gradually. Rushing *will* turn your findings into a cluster of words you'll forget about next week. You can read the exercise, but **don't actually do it**. Take my advice, if you're trying to develop any of the clairs, give your clairs a chance to weigh in before you write your wiki. It's possible you will learn something your conscious never considered.

Critical Exercise
THE ROLE

Trains: Life path, Claircognizance, Projection

☞ **Question 52.30 (Your bio):** You are more than a single physical body. You are a blur across time, space, and others' perception. Write a biography for yourself which conveys your role in this life, and addresses <u>all</u> of the following items:

- What <u>was</u> your name?
- What was your trade (45.2.1)?
- …during what times (52.14)?
- Who are you known to (52.23)?
- …as what first line (52.13)?
- …with what aim (52.16)?

- How did you understand the world (51.13)?
- What tribe(s) did you spend most of your time with (51.8)?
- …specializing in what mastery activities (51.7)?
- …with what aim (51.5)?

- What senses did you rely on (57.28)?
- …partly using or through communication with what sources (<u>Table</u> 51-2)?
- How were you best able to practice your unusual abilities (<u>Figure</u> 48-2)?
- …from the context of a sphere that consisted of (52.1)…?

- Did you have any notable features which supported how this life played out (Chapter 46, Body Wheels)?
- Were there any specific interactional effects that came with this (Chapter 46, Your Summary, main table)?
- How did your critics describe you (52.11)?

- ...which proved instrumental in your doing what (52.17)?
- ...when passing through one of your most challenging tests, what did you do (52.22)?

- How were you generally received (52.12)?
- Today your beneficiaries generally consider your life to be a testament to (anything you choose) amidst the (adaptation of 52.14), especially between (52.25).
- Who were the people who hoped for you (52.27)?
- They found an answer in your... (Chapter 46, Your Summary, Recap 2)?
- ...where you dedicated your life in the service of... (anything you choose).

(Tempting as it was to do this activity the night I wrote it, I took my own advice and waited another day.)

There it is. Your role. You can strive beyond the above if you like, but if you began this chapter with 8 check marks in the first place, there really shouldn't be that much striving (for your own interests) left.

It's okay to declare most of your own challenges finished. It happens to all of us one way or another. But if you manage to truly get your own clean up completed without having the Reaper force this on you, then you'll be ready to embark on a newer kind of quest which only a fraction of living people will ever be able to undertake: It is the quest to evolve others, having finished becoming a complete person yourself.

Chapter 53. The Friends and Their Paths

We define friendship in many ways, each according to our own lifestyles. Generally though, friends are people (or other parties) who are "with you" in one key way or another. Some travel with you. Some complement you. Others hurt when they see you hurting.

Although we typically understand friends in the personal sense, we've now encountered at least two other senses in which people can be friends: as sphere-mates and as role-mates. The interesting thing about these other two kinds of friends is that they may not appear to be friends to you at all. But the present public would claim otherwise. The future readers of your story would claim otherwise still.

We saw earlier in "The Sphere" how sphere-mates were often tied to your overall expressive options, not to your personal feelings. In "The Role" we stopped just short of articulating another group: those whose final effect on the world is tied to yours. So while you might only consider your personal favorites as friends, you almost certainly would have seen those cases where the people near you assigned "friends" that you wouldn't have considered as such. Parents do this all the time with their children, "Go play with your friends"—where all they've done is lump in any classmate their child spends time with. Surely you've had that happen to you. The strange public will assign you friends beyond your own powers of choice. The same holds for the long term world. The closer you come to your long-term role, the more complicated this situation gets, as your more personal bases for friendship get traded out for their more existential substitutes.

In this chapter we will examine how friendships change after you've found your role. Whereas personal definitions of friendship would have sufficed earlier in your life, you now have tribes. Now you have chapter-mates. So maybe John Quincy Adams and Thomas Jefferson weren't personal friends in the way that John Quincy Adams and Abigail Adams were. Yet the former pair is essentially a role-friendship for the rest of time. The latter were both personal friends and sphere-friends to the extent that—as husband and wife, they also worked out certain social-political theory together. Imagine the complication, however, when one who has mainly associated friendship with the personal kind now has to start considering the sphere and role kinds. "They're not doing enough." "We just don't like the same things anymore." "I'm spending a lot more time at work." "This near-stranger and I just seem like we need to do this." You get these situations and then some. Accordingly, we'll begin with some practice on someone other than ourselves—just to see how the complication unfolds.

☞ **Question 53.1 (They don't even know their friends, part 1):** Pick someone you know to whom you would assign friends that they would definitely NOT assign. Try to pick someone who also plays a larger role in a larger group. Whom would they consider personal friends? Whom would you or a stranger consider to be their friends by association? Why?

	Example
	N would consider R and Q to be her personal friends because they hang out and talk. But as a basic outsider looking at her life, I would consider S, T, and H to be her friends because those are the 3 people she always references, can be seen with publicly, and builds her career with. Most of us have never seen R or Q. We're not even sure if they exist.

Great. We now have this person's personal friends and their sphere-friends. Let's guess who some of their role-friends might be.

☞ **Question 53.2 (They don't even know their friends, part 2):** Suppose it is now 200 years later. You are reading about your 53.1 person in the history records. Most of their personal friends will not have been mentioned. Their more important sphere-friends might get a sentence. You are about to take a quiz on 53.1's friends, and all you have is a list of their allies and supporters in the larger effect they made in the world. Who are these people? Why would you say so?

	Example
	N would be mentioned in the history books alongside L, A, and A—all of whom played ongoing, publicly known, and significant roles in advancing her story.

Even if we were to define friendship for ourselves as something like "the people who have your back," There are those who have your back in line with your private preferences, and those who open longer-term doors which make you who you will be in the greater context (sphere-friends) and in the long run (role-friends). The less aware we are of our sphere and role, the harder it will be to recognize all three levels of friends.

At this stage, we won't have you guess who your own sphere-friends and role-friends would be, mainly because you'll typically need a good level of intuition in order to see that far beyond yourself. So far we haven't practiced intuition on the level required, so it isn't really expected that your sense of projection—into your sphere and your future—is where it needs to be. We will, however, use the discussion of friends as a starting point for what it means to be connected in the first place, and begin shaping our intuition for groups from there.

Before we continue, I want to strongly urge you not to rank the three kinds of friends. While one group may be more immediate to you right now, the other groups will be more immediate to you through the lens of others for the rest of time after you've existed. I've also found that growing into your role brings an automatic tendency to undermine the old personal friendships. But the three types of friendships all have different purposes. Don't rank them. In addition to undermining one friendship type at the expense of the others, you'll also set up an ✸interesting problem for yourself in the long run.

I mentioned before that I've had premonitory dreams for half my life. Most of my dreams (about 80%) of them are like this, and I typically audio-record about 3 – 5 dreams per week. It didn't take long to realize that immediate family in these dreams represented sides of myself, more distant family represented friends or my shared circumstances, strangers represented peers or colleagues, and odd other characters represented situations. By analogy, although you think of yourself as having an inner self, the historical you (role you) will have much of that inner self hidden from those who read about you. Your personal friends and home behavior will be as close as they can get. This is to say that

> Your personal friends today will be *you* in tomorrow's record.
> Your sphere-friends today will be your personal friends in tomorrow's record.
> Your role-friends today will be your historical sphere-friends in tomorrow's record.
> Your role effect itself will dictate who future readers say that you were as a person (determining who they recall your personal-friends being).

✸ When you measure one type of friend against the others, you also help your role-historical version measure certain aspects of your life against the others—diminishing your own works as a whole expresser. This is why it is important to, at some point, learn how to preserve certain associations no matter how much of a rolling stone you are. In many ways this is the opposite of The Rift.

Sometimes you and another person seem to be growing apart even though neither has done anything wrong at all. You're not taking away from each other, but at least one of you is struggling with the other's failure to meet the new expectations for a friend circle. "My new friends are just more 'in' than my old ones." But is this a comparison of roles and spheres to personal ties? Try not to make this comparison. Personal ties fuel your inner workings. Spheres complete your outer work. Role-friends complete your work's work in the world. A friend can be in all three groups or just one, but if you rift with them in favor of the new and shiny, or if you drop sphere-friends because they aren't personal or role-powerful enough, you may simply find yourself isolated in the long term—where a certain type of friendship just can't stick to you because of your endless need to compare them away.

So that we may remind ourselves of the value in each kind of friend, let's choose better words for describing them:

- **Friends** will describe personal friends. These are the kind we have most likely been trained to classify as close to us.
- **Allies** will describe sphere-friends. They do most of the things that personal friends do, except primarily in the realms of daily accomplishment and expression of our talents rather than the realms of emotion and inner support.
- **Kindred** will describe role-friends. These are people whom you may or may never meet, but if your name were listed under a parent heading in a reference book, their names would be listed with yours as contributing the same kind of effect upon the rest of the world. *Especially* the rest of the world's <u>attitudes</u> and <u>behaviors</u> towards the things they encounter (not necessarily the people's surface experiences; Louis XIV and Genghis Khan wouldn't necessarily be listed under the same header just because they were both rulers).

Of the three kinds of friend listed above, we often consider one type to be more "friend" than the others. Again, if you rank them though, you will more likely cause difficulties for yourself where different levels of opportunity are concerned. Only recently did I discover, for example, that the people I actually label as "friends" are almost always kindred. Personal friends have been the next important, then allies—even though 90% of my time and energy has been spent with allies. As a result, I tended to drop personal friends quickly when they didn't do role-related things, and lose touch with allies when the role called me to move on. Was this healthy for my non-kindred exchanges? Certainly not.

☞ Question 53.3 ("Better" friends): Of the three friendship types we've looked at, do you prize certain patterns more than others? Has this led to consequences for your close relationships?

	Example
	In order, I've valued 1) kindred (A+/99), 2) personal (B/85), and 3) allies (slightly lower B/84). In time spent with each, I might invest 1) 02% kindred, 2) 08% personal, and 90% allies. If I add these up, it's kindred 101, personal 93, and allies 174. That makes a lot of sense for someone who values work more than anything else. But my personal friendships definitely feel like 3rd place, even to the friends themselves. They're even behind my admiration of kindred strangers: people whom I don't know, but who share my direction.

It won't surprise you to learn that part of the reason we choose certain people as friends is because they enable certain experiences that align with who we are. The stronger the alignment, the stronger the friendship. Let's investigate what it takes for a person to align with you in each of the three categories.

☞ **Question 53.4 (Qualities of a good friend):** List the qualities that help make someone a good friend to you. We'll be doing this for all three areas in the same table, because I found that it was harder to do this activity in a forced order. (If allies were your top kind of friend, having the first question ask you about personal friends made your personal list look more like your ally list. We eventually want to stop ranking like this, but the reality is—as of now—you probably still do.) Furthermore, since we live in an age of vagueness, you'll find a number of guiding questions that compel you to be specific. These guiding questions are partly designed to uncover your intuition for spotting and tuning into such friends, so try to answer them all.

You could answer the table below in all kinds of ways. If you need examples of what these ways are, see Table 53-1. Don't worry about the column with the "?" just yet. We'll get to it.

Be warned, this activity takes anywhere from 45 minutes to an hour. It will be worth it, though, as you gradually observe what it says about the clairs in your actual life.

	Highest Priority Friendships	Middle Priority Friendships	Lowest Priority Friendships	?
Friendship type:				
Name of two example people/groups:				
Their clairaudient/subconscious trajectory: How do they approach the unknown?				
Their sense of taste: How are they in the company of others?				
Their cognition: Where do they like to put their attention?				
Their biomanufacture want-style: Do they have an inner drive that you know of?				
Their seeing: What framework do they use for seeing things?				
Their touch: How do they offer their service to others?				
Their clairaudient frequency: When information comes to them, how do they tend to hear it?				
Their telepathic edge: How do they get others to do what they want?				
Their clairvoyant events: What kinds of things tend to just "happen" <u>in their *favor*</u>?				
Their claircognizant judgment: What do they do to avoid impending problems?				
Their situational/dimensional projection: What kinds of people or situations easily see them?				
Their talent for clairsentient/intuitive reading: Where do their actions tend to mirror or anticipate your feelings?				
Other qualities: Are there any other qualities these people have?				

Chapter 53: The Friends and Their Paths

Table 53-1: Ajani's Sample

	Highest Priority Friendships	Middle Priority Friendships	Lowest Priority Friendships	?
Friendship type:	Kindred	Personal	Allies	
Name of two example people/groups:	Z., G.	C., [P. group]	J., B.	
Their clairaudient/subconscious trajectory: How do they approach the unknown?	with a fearless, often controversial boldness, but not rudely | recklessly so	with an openness to almost any voice, strongly principled	will go anywhere and talk to anyone as long as she is armed with her principles	
Their sense of taste: How are they in the company of others?	outgoing, empowering	sociable, defiant of restrictions or disingenuousness, sincere	insistent, awkward, but an individual	
Their cognition: Where do they like to put their attention?	on the mission of the group she leads	on everyone's right to express, the right to individuality	on her own personal crusade	
Their biomanufacture want-style: Do they have an inner drive that you know of?	determined to turn a difficult past beginning into others' benefit	to release a deep, perhaps dark side of themselves in a better form to all	towards a utopia where the outcome of the above crusade is adopted by all	
Their seeing: What framework do they use for seeing things?	who can be communicated with and how	a breadth of creative expressive options	exploration of the deep, dark side of the mind or its history	
Their touch: How do they offer their service to others?	by being the others' voice in a power system	through welcoming, empathetic counsel	through organization of the others' efforts	
Their clairaudient frequency: When information comes to them, how do they tend to hear it?	for the essential, productive details	with an eye for giving the sender space	defensively, in protection of the above utopia	
Their telepathic edge: How do they get others to do what they want?	through goal-focused yet respectful request	by accepting them, establishing a code which loves all paths	through the volunt. help from people who recognize her singular dedication	
Their clairvoyant events: What kinds of things tend to just "happen" _in their favor_?	her fans work hard and are proud to be associated with her	their best work environment seeks them out automatically	a powerful ally protects her path	
Their claircognizant judgment: What do they do to avoid impending problems?	by assembling the people who can find out	life calls them away from the trouble, into another arena	by being unavailable	
Their situational/dimensional projection: What kinds of people or situations easily see them?	anyone interested in her niche genre at all.	(strongly) intuitive people, their bosses, close colleagues, and influential superiors, otherwise: mysterious	people who don't want their social rules broken, but need them broken	
Their talent for clairsentient/intuitive reading: Where do their actions tend to mirror or anticipate your feelings?	Wherever she responds to a systemic challenge	through their appearnc in dreams, previous framing of things you had no words for	in the occurrences she organizes that align with what you needed	
Other qualities: Are there any other qualities these people have?	This person tends to be legendary A voice for those whose passions or patterns of deep attachment have gotten them ostracized	at home with the taboo unapologetic super-intelligent big-hearted protective of the weak against bullies	This person is outside of the mould. You need to be confident in your choices in order to ally with her.	

Now I'll be honest, as I was writing the activity above, I found the insights fascinating. Notice how most of your friends' sense and intuition does not come through really hard meditation, but in the form of whatever activities they are most dedicated to. We'll return to this idea shortly, but first we need to tie up some loose ends regarding our balancing of the different types of friends to begin with.

Broadly, your personal friends reinforce your inner life, your allies show what you look like in outsiders' eyes, and your kindred are closer to who you want to be. When assessing our friendships amidst our continued evolution, it's easy to expect people to behave in ways that reflect the standard training (friends should talk to you and maybe hang out with you, for example). But our friends don't always behave as the training suggests—especially if our most favored friendships are not personal. Table 53-2 shows some of the ways in which the three different kinds of friends also differ across basic experiences.

Personal Friend-like behavior	Ally-like behavior	Kindred-like behavior
like you	get along with you	would align well with your direction
talk, chat with, or message you	communicate with you	consistently reference, are easily referenced by, or do things that are easily associated with you
spend time with you	check in on you	study or are studied by you
explore new places with you	can depend on you amidst the unknown	accompany you ideologically when you (or your name) shows up in a place
celebrate your victories	congratulate you when called for	validate, prove, or attest to your efforts
hurt for your losses	offer to help	are hindered or discredited when you are; if you fall, you take a part of them down with you
defend you	speak or act on your behalf	do things which support your way as *the* correct way
cover for you	absorb your burden	do things which support your way from another angle; even if you weren't there, your way would still be supported
want your company	share things that interest them	do things such that your work would help complete their picture
listen to you	are there when you need an ear	include you as support for their story
value you	appreciate your role	credit you in their story
keep your secrets	respect your private concerns	share the same mysterious fuel you do
act as gatekeepers for you	intervene for you	need to be experienced in order for others to really understand you or your deeds
share their secrets with you	confide in you	are more deeply, actionably understood by you than by most others
are intimate with you	develop projects or other creations with you	are cited with you: define a field, genre, or larger concept for others
love you	love working with you	are automatically, complementarily associated with you by others (this is often a group, topic, or institution)
are loyal to you	will be there when you call	are synonymous with you

Table 53-2: Selected friend-like patterns and their equivalents among allies and kindred.

☞ **Question 53.5 (Kindred and your Role):** While you can almost certainly identify friends and allies, identifying kindred is considerably harder. We only recently began looking at ourselves as sphere-roles; the idea that you are a wide window of energy spread across time means that you probably don't have 100+ years of data to assign your final kindred with much accuracy. And then there is the idea that kindred—by virtue of their referenceability—are often famous. Our society discourages a certain kind of inhumility, so putting yourself next to, say, Einstein or Cleopatra might be considered arrogant. But not in this activity. To help you get a better sense of your own role, use the table below to list a famous figure or a known (not necessarily famous) group from history which meets your kindred criteria from Table 53-2. Now's not the time to be shy. If you feel that Caesar Augustus, Queen Elizabeth, or Jesus are your kindred, put them on the list. The point of this table is for you to strengthen your understanding of your own role as well as that of the longest term figures you aspire to be (or are currently) associated with. List the name, and next to it in () write the basis for your pick. These are people or groups who align with you as you establish your own very long-term path, whose deeds or work may be well worth your further research. If you need help, reference Table 53-3 for an example.

Kindred-like behavior	Your Famous or Group Kindred
would align well with your direction	
consistently reference, are easily referenced by, or do things that are easily associated with you	
study or are studied by you	
accompany you ideologically when you (or your name) shows up in a place	
validate, prove, or attest to your efforts	
are hindered or discredited when you are; if you fall, you take a part of them down with you	
do things which support your way as *the* correct way	
do things which support your way from another angle; even if you weren't there, your way would still be supported	
do things such that your work would help complete their picture	
include you as support for their story	
credit you in their story	
share the same mysterious fuel you do	
need to be experienced in order for others to really understand you or your deeds	
are more deeply, actionably understood by you than by most others	
*are cited with you: define a field, genre, or larger concept for others	
are automatically, complementarily associated with you by others (this is often a group, topic, or institution)	
are synonymous with you	

*This person is one of the closest to your understanding of your long-term role

Table 53-3: Ajani's Famous Kindred

Kindred-like behavior	Your Famous or Group Kindred
would align well with your direction	Georg Cantor (odd ideas turned into a field)
consistently reference, are easily referenced by, or do things that are easily associated with you	Warren Buffett, Elon Musk, Bill Gates, James Cameron (top influencer, but projects have humanist effect on world); Abraham Lincoln (lone pivotal figure in a major human chapter)
study or are studied by you	Niccolo Machiavelli (much deeper theory than his notorious work); Musashi Miyamoto (master of strategy)
accompany you ideologically when you (or your name) shows up in a place	a "conspirator" or other shadowy nickname for someone with dark, but final motives; also, "data"
validate, prove, or attest to your efforts	Timothy Leary (interpersonal circumplex)
are hindered or discredited when you are; if you fall, you take a part of them down with you	a corner of astrology, of practical Daoism, and of data-renderable human behaviors
do things which support your way as *the* correct way	my unpublished fiction writings
do things which support your way from another angle; even if you weren't there, your way would still be supported	Rod Serling (Twilight Zone & the human mysteries)
do things such that your work would help complete their picture	Louis Althusser (genera)
include you as support for their story	Timothy Leary (interpersonal circumplex)
credit you in their story	Benedict Spinoza (geometric proofs of God; definitions of subjective experience)
share the same mysterious fuel you do	Srinavasa Ramanujan (insight from the Goddess)
need to be experienced in order for others to really understand you or your deeds	Srinavasa Ramanujan (all-consuming quest)
are more deeply, actionably understood by you than by ~~most others~~ many	Megaman X/ZX series, the 14 games played in order (super far-seeing vision of future humanity and identity)
cited with you: define a field, genre, or larger concept for others	Rod Serling (Twilight Zone & other strange presentations of the logos); Martin Heidegger (lone abstracts on "being")
are automatically, complementarily associated with you by others (this is often a group, topic, or institution)	various Scorpio topics, the institutions that address them, and their occasionally uncomfortable associations

| are synonymous with you | complex data |

☞ **Question 53.6 (Observations of Kindred):** Did you notice anything your kindred had in common?
_____
_____
_____
_____

Friends Have Partly Different Paths

One thing I've often struggled with as an insistent person has been the extent to which my friends have different paths from my own. It is far too easy listen less, be less patient, spend less time, or take less interest in a friend's world when that world revolves around things that don't seem to concern us. While we're hanging out or having fun together, everything seems so easy. But when one of us must tend to more self-specific matters, certain friendships fall in priority. Over the years I've thrown away several friendships because, while the person was going through hard times, they wouldn't communicate with me when I wanted them to. The irony here is that my major defense against assault in the world is exactly that: noncommunication. My waking mind wanted them to talk to me, but my subconscious or soul wanted them to keep that dark phase far away from me. The soul won, but all I saw at the time was offensive distance. The friendships failed *not* because we couldn't communicate, but because certain periods of distance were natural to how I form friendships, and I didn't understand that.

Each of us manages our friendships in different ways. Some of us maintain our friendships through ongoing chat and time spent. Others of us maintain them through some kind of long term unifying ideal. Sometimes, however, the standard training in friendship causes us to question the quality of our bonds simply because we're not matching the template. In order to relieve some of this pressure, let's take a look at some typical "friend" behaviors and where they *actually* play out in our <u>own</u> lives (not in the template).

We return to Table 53-2, but this time with some additional categories from Chapter 15. Back in *FSA* we saw how the 12 astrological divisions spelled out 12 different kinds of relationships with respect to a starting point. Table 15-9 (The effects of family dynamics) outlined the following kinds of close relationships and the types of parties traditionally connected to their roles:

Chapter 53: The Friends and Their Paths

Division	Relationship Dynamic	What we're being trained to handle			Who this (typically) is
		Frame	Behavior	Scope	
1	Self-trainer	Us	Outer	Self	you; **toys you played with** and **games you played**; your **Dad's mom, Mom's Dad**
2	Resource handling trainer	Us	Inner	Self	the **family money manager**; the **school** you went to (the cliques' mother; 4th house from the 11th)
3	Protector trainer	Us	Outer	Self->Situation	your **younger siblings**; **places that absorb your thoughts**
4	Emotional trainer	Us	Inner	Self->Role	your **mother**
5	Creativity trainer	Us (extensions)	Outer	Role	your **early creations, games of pretend**, later: **children**
6	Subordinate trainer	Not Us	Inner	Role	your **pets**; **colleagues you serve** (your **workplace**)
7	Relationship standards trainer	Not Us	Outer	Role->Self	your **early girlfriend or boyfriend**; your basic **friends**; your **Dad's dad, Mom's mom**
8	Crisis trainer	Not Us	Inner	Role->Situation	your **teachers**: your creative works' mother (4th from 5th)
9	[Exploration of the unknown] trainer	Not Us	Outer	Situation	**people who went with you on trips**
10	Authority trainer	Not Us	Inner	Situation	your **father**; **bosses**; **institutions** you dwell in
11	Societal niche trainer	Not Us	Outer	Situation->Role	**cliques** and **friendship groups you belonged to**; colleagues as **collaborators**
12	Social issues trainer	Us	Inner	Situation->Self	your **authority figure's siblings** (3rd from 10th); your **home life** (emotional figure's marriage, 9th from 4th)

Table 53-4: Familial dynamics (adapted from Table 15-9)

Essentially there are [us and not us], [inner and outer behaviors], [situations, roles, and self-trainers]. This is the usual [polarity × context × self-other-world]. Notice how our normal notion of friends (7, 9, and 11) are all outer-focused, not-us, and none of them are self-based. That should make sense given how we think of friends, but everyone is different. Later we'll see how these roles all become scrambled in an astro chart (and more importantly in real life) such that you really will find people whose "friend dynamics" play out better with their pets or their siblings than with their people relationships. As long as we understand that the template for friendship really is a template, the pressure to question our connections when they don't match the template should be at least partly reduced.

☞ Question 53.7 (Our friend dynamics rearranged): **We are going to look at how to handle cases where friends' paths seem to drift from our own, but first we should ask what our own friendship ruleset truly looks like. Using Table 53-4, write which of the above 12 relationship dynamics you actually prefer to receive certain friend-like behaviors from. (You'll see in my example that some categories may seem weirdly placed. This is because we're talking forms, remember? Sex isn't always sex. Sometimes it's just basic co-creation. So yes, you <u>can</u> put any category in any box. Don't let the overt interactions or social implications constrain your answers. Think about the *dynamic*, not just the surface interaction.)**

Personal Friend-like interaction	Where you *actually* prefer to get this interaction	Example
they like you		teachers (8)
they talk, chat with, or message you		girlfriends (7) colleagues (11)
they spend time with you		home life (12)
they explore new places with you		collaborators (11)
they celebrate your victories		myself; games (1)
they hurt for your losses		workplace (6)
they defend you		bosses (10)

they cover for you		colleagues (6), res. managers (2)
they want your company		friends (7), bosses (10)
they listen to you		my projects (creations) (5)
they value you		workplace (6) co-explorers (9)
they keep your secrets		my recorder (3)
they act as gatekeepers for you		institutions (10)
they share their secrets with you		colleagues (6)
they are intimate with you		co-explorers (9)
they love you		institutions (10)
they are loyal to you		home life (12) pets (6)

I didn't necessarily learn anything new about myself when I did the above activity, but it was interesting to see where all the 7s, 9s, and 11s *didn't* show up. Per our standard social template, you would think that every row had a 7, 9, or 11 in it. The table does focus on friend-like behaviors, doesn't it? But of course this won't likely be the case. Many of the dynamics we are taught to expect from friends, we actually get from work (6 or 10) or from ourselves (1 or 12). Things we are taught to get from single parties like intimacy, liking, and listening we may actually get from multiple parties (9, 12, or 11) or even institutions (2, 6, or 10). So if you put a 10 under, say, "they cover for you," it may not come as a surprise that sometimes your friends (7) cover for you less. Your psychology may not be set up to receive friend-cover as easily. We'll talk more about this in The Asteroid. But for now...

☞ Question 53.8 (Observations from the friend table): Did you learn anything interesting from 53.7? If so, what?

_____
_____
_____
_____

☞ Question 53.9 (A smaller source of friend interactions): Were there any dynamics which didn't appear at all in your 53.7? Do you think this says anything about how you value such dynamics?

_____
_____
_____
_____

Now that we've seen our own template for (primarily personal) friendship, we can start looking the areas in which our friends tend to differ from us. Friends, allies, and kindred are, after all, separate people. Part of their role is to do things we won't or can't do; this typically means deviating from what we would choose in certain cases. But that's not the basis for rift. It is the basis for learning about other

Chapter 53: The Friends and Their Paths 269

corners of your sphere and how those corners cover your blind spots. It can be frustrating sometimes when your friends don't share your road—especially as you evolve. But maybe their separate road is the reason they work as friends. We want to give them space without slowing ourselves down. Part of that requires an understanding of what it is they are doing on that other road, and why.

Warning. This next activity can be surprisingly hard*

☞ Question 53.10 (Other priorities): Despite what you may have learned in 53.7, we still have the template. Suppose your personal friends are not giving you the interaction you want when you actually want it from them. What are they usually doing instead? See if you can associate a dynamic with that priority. DON'T FRAME THIS NEGATIVELY. It will come back to bite you less than a page later. See the example further below.

Personal Friend-like interaction	When personal friends are NOT giving you this (and you think they should be), what are they usually doing instead?
they like you	
they talk, chat with, or message you	
they spend time with you	
they explore new places with you	
they celebrate your victories	
they hurt for your losses	
they defend you	
they cover for you	
they want your company	
they listen to you	
they value you	
they keep your secrets	
they act as gatekeepers for you	
they share their secrets with you	
they are physically intimate with you	
they love you	
they are loyal to you	

Table 53-5: Ajani's Friends on Other Priorities (Example)

Personal Friend-like interaction	When personal friends are NOT giving you this (and you think they should be), what are they usually doing instead?
they like you	distancing between ingroup / the emotional trainer and the outside (4)(11)
they talk, chat with, or message you	tending to other duties (6)
they spend time with you	expecting you might call them; reflection (4)(12)
they explore new places with you	preferring their own activities (5)
they celebrate your victories	analyzing the situation; ideological institution (10)
they hurt for your losses	reducing the impact of the loss; turning it into a lesson (12)(2)(4)
they defend you	letting you reap what you sowed, per their warning (3)

they cover for you	holding you to what you promised (3)
they want your company	separating themselves from your preferences in favor of their own (12)
they listen to you	being overwhelmed, usually by work (6)
they value you	being immersed in other groups (11)
they keep your secrets	communicating your issues (or their issues with you) to other parties (11)
they act as gatekeepers for you	giving you your freedom; letting you experience independently (8)
they share their secrets with you	doubting that you care to hear those secrets (4)
they are intimate with you	thinking that's the main thing you want—as a kind of validation, preferring a better match (4)
they love you	preferring the bounds of work instead (6)
they are loyal to you	looking for replacements for you (11)

It wasn't until after I began doing activity 53.10 that I realized how hard it was. Invariably, we can't actually know what a person is doing when they aren't there to tell us, but we *can* know what we think they're doing. Unfortunately, what we think they're doing looks a lot like what *we* would be doing when we deny others the friend behavior. Thus, as you probably expected, 53.10 is more of a description of the things *you* do to dilute *your own* friendships than it is a description of your friends. I felt like more and more of a jerk the further down the list I went. 53.10 shows the ways in which you neglect and undervalue your friendship when we measure those friendships against the normal expectations of friends. If you're growing apart from someone, chances are at least one of the above is happening, and your sphere as a whole has not finished addressing it. Much of that sphere is under your control, though. If your answers to 53.10 stemmed from a consistent pattern across multiple years and multiple people, then it's <u>really</u> tied to you. The pattern won't change until you do.

We made it a point to frame our answers to 53.10 positively since the table really ended up being a description of ourselves. Now, there are things we can do to improve our half of a friendship, and other things we can do to help the friend improve their half. As of The Conflict, though, we're past the point of blaming the other for our sphere. While some friends might certainly fall short of our expectations in some areas, our starting point is no longer with them. It's with us and our assumptions about when our own 53.10 behaviors are appropriate. You may not do such things yourself anymore, but is it still a part of your belief system that they are good responses to certain prompts?

Critical Exercise
THE BELIEF ABOUT GOOD FRIENDSHIPS

Trains: Telepathy, Empathy

There are the things we say about good friendships and then there are the things we actually do. Our friends and allies complement us, reinforce us, and cover our deficiencies, but ultimately are not us. As we evolve we are often faced with the differences between ourselves and our friends, all the while developing the kinds of connection skills which require certain friends stay around. Telepathy, hearing, and projection, for example, each involve some kind of sender and receiver who won't see the other as an intruder. Our connections will need to be strong. The last thing we need is to take such connections for granted.

Our spheres are set up to scramble—in unique ways—the expectations of standard training. In an ideal world we would do all of the important things needed to keep our friendships, except that the basis for "importance" is scattered across all of our possible spaces of experience. So we may not stay in touch and we may not always listen because some of us weren't conditioned to apply these behaviors in friendship. We may apply them in work or with siblings. What we need then is a way of translating the patterns we don't want into the patterns we do want. This has less to do with the other person and more to do with us. A psychological road map is in order. In this activity we will construct one.

I put my neglectful answers from 53.10 next to my pro-friendship answers from 53.7, then wrote down an attitude that allows me to shift from the former to the latter, as illustrated in Table 53-6 below. The good news is, these attitudes are surely not alien. There have been plenty of times that a potentially neglectful behavior came to nothing because we resolved it in time. Here we'll be codifying such favorable attitudes in the form of a sentence or two, so that we may catch ourselves before falling out of touch with a good, often deep connection.

The only attitudes that went into the table were attitudes that <u>consistently **improved**</u> my friendships. No guessing allowed.

Table 53-6: Example Attitude Shift in Favor of Friendships

Personal Friend-like interaction	Friendship Decreasing (53.10)	Friendship Increasing (53.7)	Shifting Attitude
they like you	distancing (4)(11)	teachers (8)	Let's explore your challenge this way. (No I'm not trying to get close.)
they talk, chat with, or message you	tending to other duties (6)	girlfriends (7) colleagues (11)	[Don't contact unless work requires it. ∴ I only meet friends through work. Fine by me.]
they spend time with you	expecting call (4)(12)	home life (12)	[These are both mostly 12. To verify the tie, I have to have seen the person in dreams or felt an intuitive connection with them in person. Also fine. Otherwise, I'm easily used by selfish ppl.]
they explore new places with you	their own activities (5)	collaborators (11)	[I have to know what the person's interests are before comfortably collaborating. If they aren't declaring it (as my kindred do), it's not strong enough]
they celebrate your victories	analyzing (10)	myself; games (1)	[The person openly analyzes themselves, with not much to hide. If this doesn't happen, I'm in the dark.]
they hurt for your losses	minimizing loss (12)(2)(4)	workplace (6)	Oh, that's a bummer. What can I do to help you out of it?
they defend you	reap what you sowed (3)	bosses (10)	Yeah, what you did works [there but not here]. Alright, let me join you in getting it to work here.
they cover for you	promise accountability (3)	colleagues; workplace (6)	[We don't work together again until they've kept their first promise. Promise-keeping is a key part of my sphere. I feel very guilty when late on my own.]
they want your company	separate preferences (12)	friends (7), bosses (10)	What's the latest news in [the institution that unites us]?
they listen to you	overwhelmed by work (6)	my projects (creations) (5)	[People who offer to help with my work get automatic entry. This is very rare. I offer all the time.]
they value you	immersed in other groups (11)	workplace (6) co-explorers (9)	[I need to be introduced by someone or some situation mutual to us. Introducing myself doesn't sustain in the long run.]
they keep your secrets	to other parties (11)	my recorder (3)	[Record EVERYTHING when I get the chance. If it doesn't make the recording, it's like it didn't happen.]
they act as gatekeepers for you	giving freedom (8)	institutions (10)	[I should be interested in structuring, studying, or understanding this person's psychology. My friends should be interesting people to me.]
they share their secrets with you	doubting that you care (4)	colleagues (6)	[Emotional connection phases back out into work, which will terminate when the job ends. Despite my heavy focus on work, lack of emotional connection among colleagues is very bad for my overall sphere.]
they are intimate with you	the main validation; a better match (4)	co-explorers (9) collaborators (11)	[Sex and co-creation *are* exploration. If any of these is prohibited, none of them will happen. Attraction, creativity, and aligned outlook are all needed before intimacy.]
they love you	bounds of work (6)	institutions (10)	[Their love is easy enough to gauge. For me, it's demonstrated. Unfortunately, I can only love people who are comfortable assuming power. Mostly because when I am *given* power (not having *taken* it), if I cannot accept the responsibility when I know others wanted me to, that's a major failure. I would never say it of another specifically, but I can't love the failure to meet one's duty when he is called and able.]
they are loyal to you	looking for replacements (11)	home life (12) pets (6)	Instead of replacing you, I'll advance my own thing which is not related to you.

Conclusions
I've been told many times that I'm hard to be friends with. The chart shows that the attitude which works for me can be callous, and is heavily gatekeeping-based. I've known for years that I make good friends by refusing "bad" ones. Bad in the sense that they don't line up with my ongoing trajectory. I'm not a jerk, but don't have a lot of interest in relationships that aren't super easy and super open. Most relationships for me have more hidden corners than I can deal with, and because I'll help and show respect to anyone who asks, I'm easily used in these. My friendships don't use me and don't hide from me. Insisting on this is how I get them to work. The rules may look oppressive, but they're only oppressive to people who don't know how to treat friends as they would like to be treated. (Not to preach, but that's how it is.)

Recap
My best friendships are given to me. I'm not successful (or interested) in seeking them, because there are naturally more unknowns than I prefer that way. They are very open, not one-sided; they are built via shared work; preserved against poor treatment; emotionally rich. But I stay picky in order to preserve their quality.

☞ **Question 53.11 (The attitude that gains you good friends):** **Your Turn.** Fill in your answers to 53.10 and 53.7. Then, in the fourth column, write down the attitude which moves you from 53.10 to 53.7 AND <u>consistently builds better relationships for you</u>. If you come to any conclusions at the end, write them in the box at the bottom. Your attitude may not be always pretty, but if it's healthy for you, that's plenty.

Personal Friend-like interaction	Friendship Decreasing (53.10)	Friendship Increasing (53.7)	Shifting Attitude
they like you			
they talk, chat with, or message you			
they spend time with you			
they explore new places with you			
they celebrate your victories			
they hurt for your losses			
they defend you			
they cover for you			
they want your company			
they listen to you			
they value you			
they keep your secrets			
they act as gatekeepers for you			
they share their secrets with you			
they are intimate with you			
they love you			
they are loyal to you			
Conclusions			
Recap			

☞ Question 53.12 (Friendship fuel): **Of the friend-dynamics we've been using (Table 53-2), which are the most important for preserving your personal friendships? Are these kindred, ally, or personal behaviors (K, A, or P)?**

	Example
	Most important to least: 1) value me (P) 2) co-create (A) 3) accompany me ideologically (K) 4) spend time (P) 5) share their secrets (P) 6) communicate (A)

Intuition Begins with Affinities

There is a reason we have spent so much time investigating the nature of your friendships. If you think about the whole space of your preferences, you are essentially like a radio for certain frequencies above others. Literally, you might perceive a 450 THz electromagnetic frequency (red) as being more "personally favorable" than a 750 THz frequency (violet). You might perceive the combination of visual and auditory frequencies from your friend as being more favorable than analogous frequencies from you rival. As we discussed in The Sphere, there are the frequencies of light, sound, and touch, chemical smells, hormonal concentrations, and neuronal traffic. Not only will you perceive certain "brands" of each type to be differentially favorable, you'll also be tuned to perceive these brands with differential levels of attention and accuracy. A certain arrangement of personality traits (mainly audio-visual-hormonal-neuronal chains within you, prompted by another), may be near invisible to you. Meanwhile, a different arrangement of such traits may seem near life-threatening. The development of practical "magic," intuition, or multidimensional talent rests upon the idea that you are more likely to act consistently and controllably around certain kinds of inputs. Your friends and favorite interactions are the strongest, most convenient source of such inputs. Not your favorite "actions" (like going out). Not your favorite "experiences" (like passively meditating or watching movies). Your favorite inter_actions: things you do which provide you feedback and have consequences for how you behave.

Just as there are differences between hearing and listening, exposure and seeing, there is also a difference between sense and intuition. A **sense** can be **any mode for receiving a signal**. **Intuition** interprets signals from incomplete patterns, and thus involves some kind of completing or interpreting act on your part—even if you don't do it consciously. Here, you will have taken in the *pieces* of an experience, assembled your interpretation of its full pattern, and acted accordingly—even if only cognitively. Some theorized pathways for the different senses are shown in Figure 53-1.

Normal Senses

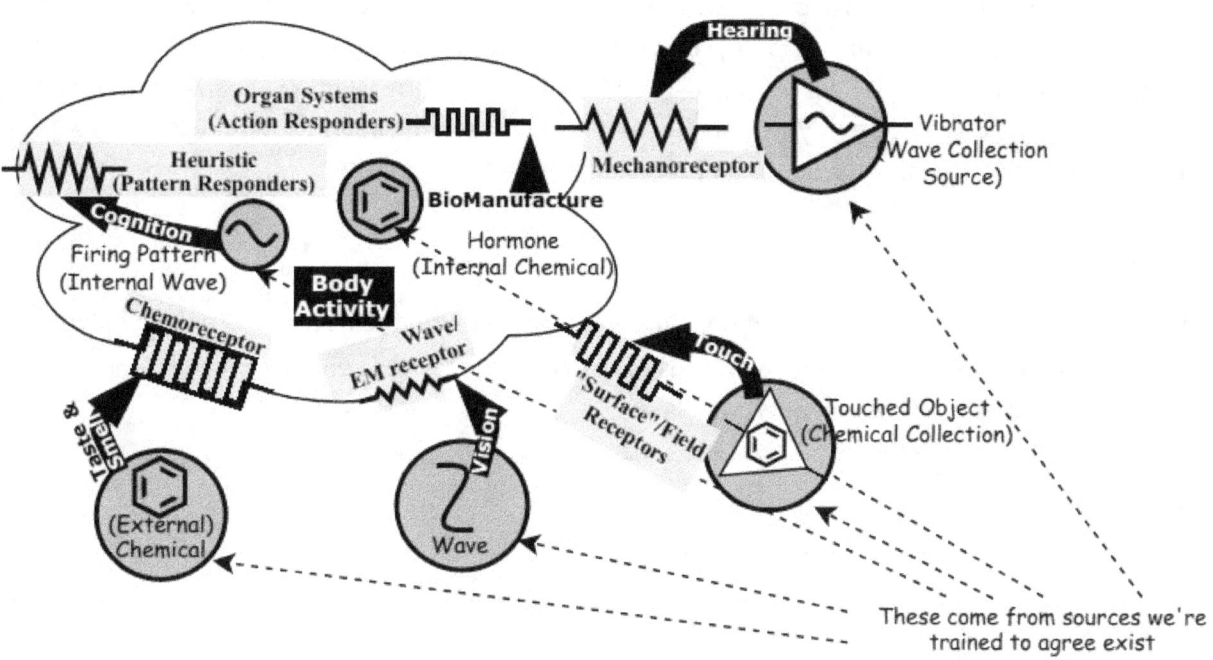

Intuitive / "Psychic" Senses

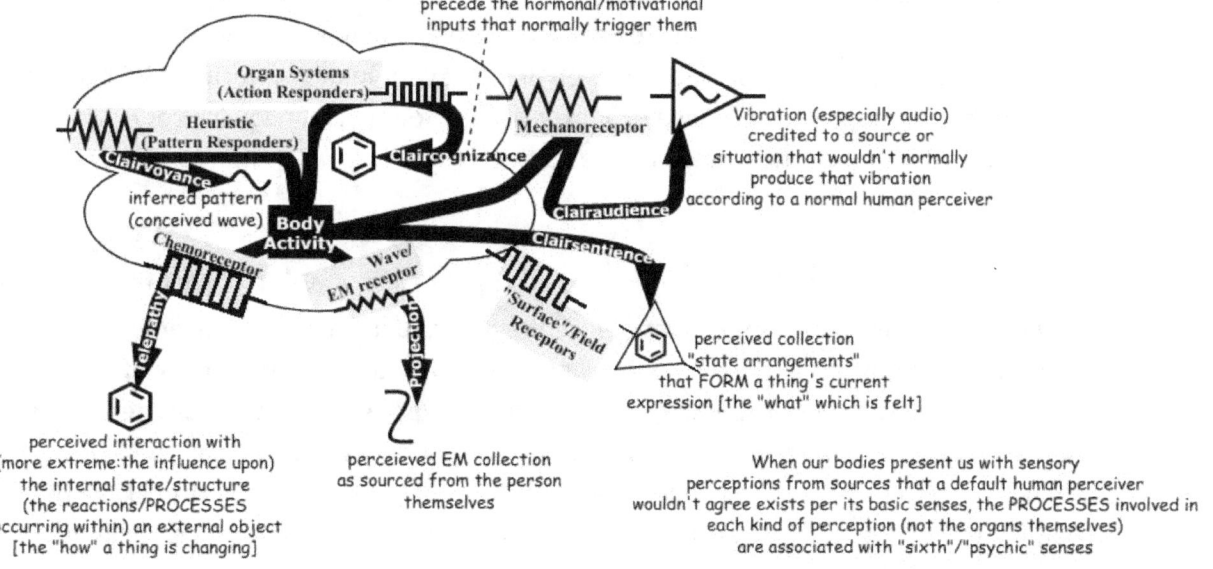

Figure 53-1: A theory of the normal versus intuitive senses. Note that the bold arrows in the second figure don't come from the organs. They all originate in body activity, looping through aa processed *association* with each organ-sensory system.

For the sake of intuition practice, you can think of your friends as being similar to a favorite color or—better yet—a favorite song. Because they are living beings who actively respond to you, however, your friends offer a much broader range of feedback for both your powers of observation and your powers of pattern-making. The ability to understand your friendship dynamics contributes greatly to your ability to understand your own personal rules for taking in and organizing information. Your capacity to maintain your friendships as you evolve tells you more about which characteristics you are more likely to express using the information given. Let's look at an example.

Friends and Clairvoyance

☞ Question 53.13 (The Unknown): **When you are confronted with the new or the unknown (your Approach), you probably have at least two kinds of reactions. How would you describe your positive handling of the unknown? Your negative handling?**

_____
_____
_____
_____

Let's consider your answer to 53.13 to be an indicator of your projective frequency. That is, if you were to feel either the positive or negative versions of the above while you WEREN'T handling the unknown, this would be an indicator of your Approach-ing something regardless of whether there were anything new on the horizon. Your heuristic rule set for a behavior (associated with clairvoyance in Figure 53-1, when you're the one projecting the pattern), can be considered active here even when the thing that triggers the rules (like Approach) isn't observable to everyone. Yet your mind, powerful as it is, can easily "construct" a situation being approached *whenever* it experiences your 53.13. Allowing yourself to construct such [patterned responses to no pattern] marks the beginning of your vision-projective intuition.

☞ Question 53.14 (The friend who trains vision-projection): **Consider any one of your friends, allies, or kindred who has an easy time getting you to approach the new and unknown in a favorable way. You consistently have good experiences of the unknown when you engage this person, with all of the typical kinds of feelings that come with those experiences. This family of experiences can be considered to form a more complete chain of events when your Approach is engaged, and again can be had even when there is no new or unknown thing going on. In the greater context of your sphere, this friend can be considered a kind of trainer for your approach heuristic. The more detail you capture regarding this type of engagement with the friend, the easier it will be to recognize a vision-image which shares both this experience pattern and its unknown trigger combined.**

What is it about your time with the friend which makes the unknown so easy? (Because I want you to give more than just vague answers like "she's fun to be around," I've provided an example.)

	Example
	She's super open, spiritually strong and evolved, well on her path. She's smart creative, and mission focused. (If I'm engaging situations that match these descriptions, my clairvoyant seeing of new Approaches is likely to be higher.)
	In a phrase, she is a Full Warm Intellect.

We'll use vision-projection behavior to evolve your clairvoyance. Recall the sign-skipping, backwards time order discussed in *Laurentia*. According to our earlier Figure 47-4, vision proceeds clairvoyance; this is akin to loading background information (clairvoyance) about the things you are looking at (vision). The reverse would hold when you are the one being looked at (where the places your project into influence your cognition). Ideally, the person you listed above also makes it easy for you to obtain any new information you're seeking from them or from the situation. If clairvoyance is largely a matter of getting new information, a trainer who is tied to your ability to do so by training your patterns of vision will almost certainly help.

Another warning against pre-punishment

The issue with clairvoyance, as I've discussed earlier, is that it is often tied to selfishness. Truly, most of the primary clairvoyants I've met in my own life (with clairvoyance as their strongest intuitive sense) have struggled *mightily* with selfishness and me-centeredness, my-concerns, and my-preferences, and I believe this is largely related to the context-revolves-around-my-construct nature of clairvoyance. The friend who trains this in you also trains the feeling which places your seeing above all others' seeing, even if—especially if—nobody else sees it. This can pose so much of an issue for forming healthy, stable relationships that we also need to learn how to ignore the Approach-ing (and related) heuristics even if what they're telling us is accurate. The unfortunate news is that what you see through trained clairvoyance is very often right...more than half the time because your own actions made it so. I've seen this more times than I can count. All I can say is that it frequently sucks for all involved.

The question we want to ask in our clairvoyance is the same one we would ask in the company of our clairvoyant-trainer friend: "I know where this will probably go if it were entirely up to me, but do I want it to be entirely up to me?" In other words, you know what you're seeing, but have you given the seen thing a chance to respond? That's the way any good feedback loop between two parties should work. In clairvoyance, we can follow the slippery slope all the way down to its mangled end mainly because we never, never EVER, reopen communication with the seen thing between the time the negative impressions start and the time our own screenplay is beyond saving. This is true even for basic relationships that don't appear to have any clairvoyant foresight at play. Still, the rule sets are there, and the rule sets as patterned experiences are the mould through with we give our clairvoyant impressions form. If you can't pause your sculpting to check out your progress—letting the incomplete sculpture speak for itself—you're either boundlessly talented or itching to turn your one-way conversation into a lonely reality. That's clairvoyance applied to relationships. Clairvoyance applied to other kinds of experience besides friend-trainable Approach will depend on the situation whose heuristic you're applying.

A low-scale version of Approach clairvoyance can be seen in the form of suspicion. IF the suspicion you feel resembles the same kind of suspicion that accompanies other events that really have happened, you may be using a clairvoyant-trainable faculty without knowing it. Do you keep your suspicions to yourself? Talk it out? Test the person? That depends on a lot of things, but my advice is to look for your best ending. You can get your heuristic sight under control if you simply ask whether the things you're seeing were even things you wanted to be concerned with. I could see you cheating on me, but do I want that to be a thing? If not, then there are ways to address issues of belonging, security, respect, communication, and being the only one. None of these has to raise my clairvoyant alarm. Your dynamic with your positive trainer friend can arm you with most of the communicative weapons you need in order to fight a negatively self-fulfilling spiral. We've begun our conversation about deep intuition with a conversation about friends mainly because friend-interactions are so positively weighted, in addition to being rich with experiences to which we are tuned.

Fast-forwarding

Much our training in connecting with something that is not us (and possibly not even visible) begins in our connections with friends. Our training in regulating what we sense begins in the things we do to maintain those friendships. The caveat is that not every person is a friend, not every friend is a good heuristic trainer and, analogously, not every clairvoyant pattern is one for which we want a heuristic to even exist. On an A-F scale, my own conscious clairvoyance[36] is about a D-, I can identify all kind of things which I want in my life, but only through dreams. I see basically nothing in waking, and very rarely dream of things that don't want to connect to me. This has everything to do with my priorities in my waking life. Working with data and writing for a living has made me sensitive to informational noise, so I block it as a rule no matter what the form. Should you train your clairvoyance, get used to NOT looking at just any random form simply because it's there. If it threatens to unsettle you or your relationships, change the channel as you would any other unsatisfying movie or post. Unless you're in some kind of high-stakes competition, it often pays more for your clairvoyant situation to never happen than for you to be wrong or right. We call this "fast-forwarding" through certain lessons. We saw an example of this earlier in The Conflict: [Battles Between People].

☞ Question 53.15 (Exercise your clairvoyance with your trainer friend): This exercise is pretty simple. Take some time to envision spending time with the friend you listed in 53.13. During that envisioning, see if the two of you end up having a conversation about your path, their path, yours or their intuition, or anything else associated with the topics in this book. You don't have to force anything, just let the scenario play out naturally. But *do* try to feel the kinds of feelings and perceive the kinds of impressions you listed in 53.14. Write down any observations below. (This activity can be as short as 5 minutes or as long as the time it takes you to fall asleep.)

---

[36] Subconscious waking clairvoyance basically plays out as claircognizance. Non-waking clairvoyance is more like dream projection, which we will talk about later.

_____
_____
_____
_____
_____
_____

(For the record, I did 53.15 before going to sleep and had two pretty interesting dreams about my path. The person I focused on was definitely associated with one of the dreams, and the clairvoyance was definitely active.)

The Talent for Connecting

Each of us has various talents for connecting to various kinds of experience. Our friends animate such experiences and provide us with rich data for training our ability to know what we're connecting to, when, and which of those connections we favor. Though we all have ways of borrowing our own sensory programs to structure nontraditionally sensory events, it is rarely useful to sense whatever you can willy nilly. Unless you're on some kind of special quest, you probably wouldn't make it your goal to see every color or listen to every genre of music; likewise, you shouldn't make it your goal to perceive all kinds of experiences that don't match the makeup of your sphere. You may have heard the cheeky challenge, "if you're psychic then predict this _____ [random stuff]." But that's a lot like saying "If you have friends then connect to this _____ [random person]." In order to see something, you have to have the lens for looking at it. It also helps greatly if you care to pay attention to it at all. Even as we evolve, our friendships train us to manage parts of our sphere that are not physically us—both in what they represent and in how we interact with them. Our friends will almost never mirror our paths exactly, and that's the whole point of them being "not us." They are extensions of our sphere. Mastering how we take care of them means mastering the bridges that occupy our long term road.

There may be times during your evolution where you feel as though good friends are hard to find. Perhaps the ones you have aren't available or don't understand your current interests. Maybe you have begun reevaluating certain parts of your life and your friends have ties to some parts you wish to get rid of. Are your friendships truly something due for review or are you simply revising your own ways of relating? You can usually tell the difference between the former and the latter because in the latter case you'll often find that your friends are still trying to connect with you—in the same way that the messages they train in you would. In the former case they may present you with behaviors that make as much sense as "up = down." The challenge is to know when it's you who is imposing the change and when it's them. If it is you, make sure that the rules you normally use for perceiving the friendships positively have not subtly deteriorated towards being used negatively. You as a broader sphere may still hold the heuristics for processing your friends despite their absence. If you are used to "encountering" or approaching new things with certain among these friends, some of your heuristics may be pre-clairvoyant. Negatively, however, these can manifest as suspicion, irritation, or growing apart. These may be entirely avoidable if you would just communicate more. If you're the one becoming different, how would they know about the changes in your head?

Conclusion: Your Friends Are Your First Test

At the time of this writing, I would be considered a D- clairvoyant. I do get senses about certain situations, but what I get and when I get it is effectively random. Whether I can interpret the information I get in a way that helps anyone is also random. Do I still use what I see to spiral relationships negatively? Unfortunately, when I rely on my ~~D- clairvoyance~~ suspicion, I do. Should you hire me for a clairvoyant job? No way. Even as my friends have paths separate from mine, I still have trouble respecting that fact. I still forget to ask what their views of their own worlds might be, and use my rule sets to judge their actions against my standards alone. I can't speak for you, but if your clairvoyance, clairaudience, cognition, hearing, claircognizance and clairsentience in particular aren't to the point that they are willfully usable in *favor* of the people who support your sphere the most, then you have a starting point for practicing these talents. No matter how intuitive you are already, if your use of your talents doesn't <u>*improve*</u> your **relationships**—beyond merely improving the sweet sound of your "light-positive-friendly" words—then your skills need work. To realistically gauge where you are in your spheremates' eyes, consider your effect on others. Your self-improvement alone will only go so far. In the next chapter we'll finally get the real work started.

Chapter 54. The Foresight

Our web of topics grows more complicated as we absorb our roles, tribes, and conflicts into our sphere. We sit at the center of our sphere as an embodiment which resonates with other people's trained constructs for what they are seeing, yet that embodiment surely evolves beneath the larger window of our full role across time and situation. Our friends are like primary satellites to our own embodiment, where some of our strongest, most obvious, and most natural bonding patterns may be exchanged. Understanding those bonding patterns can be of great use in helping us discover the kinds of experiences we most strongly gravitate towards, and thus can help us begin training our own brand of calculated "magic" one sense at a time.

In this chapter you may find yourself frequently referencing several previous sections. In order of appearance in this book, they are as follows:

- Figure 47-4 summarizes what you do to engage each sense.
- Your answer to Question 53.4 gives you a large selection of experiences for accessing certain senses—including the intuitive ones. It's not always about meditation. When the friends you listed in 53.4 do the things you put in the table, they are reaping the kinds of results that—in the meditative sense—would be associated with the corresponding sense in the first column. This can work for you too. We'll talk more about it later in this chapter.
- Figure 53-1 shows a proposed structure for the senses as bodily experiences.
- Finally (and with odd importance) Question 53.11 shows the conditions which should apply to things you're connecting to if you wish to avoid the assorted negative consequences that come with using your powers. Particularly for clairvoyants who struggle to regulate their seeing and empaths (clairsentients in this book) who find themselves drained by others: If you're looking for ways to control these, you may find more success by keeping yourself around places where the attitudes you wrote in Question 53.11 are the main attitudes that apply. You might avoid situations that don't support such attitudes.

I have a personal definition of learning which I've used in a previous book. **Learning is where we acquire predictable, consistent paths to an outcome in place of the more uncertain space of options that previously existed.** According to this definition, we haven't really shown our learning of something until we've successfully trekked its jungle-for-noobs at least twice (the "consistent" part). Babies have eyes, but until they've trained to differentiate the sights before those eyes, their version of "seeing" isn't the same as what we adults consider "seeing." The same goes for the other senses. The challenge for us is not in using them, but in predictably, consistently, identifying what we've seen. Where the intuitive senses are concerned, we may never convince others that what we perceive is actually there—some senses like clairaudience are specifically defined as anti-perceivable—thus we may need to skip the public agreement step and go straight to the publicly useful action upon our perceptions. The idea here is that, to have learned the use of a sense is not the same as having learned the proof of its inputs. Learning a sense is about taking in its inputs, whatever they are, and consistently, predictably putting together some end result which lines up with a publicly observable reality. Otherwise it's just internal processing. The layers of convolutional neural networks in deep learning work just this way.

It's easy to take for granted why we discussed friendships before discussing the senses. In addition to our friendship behaviors being a convenient source of training, they also provide us with a basic set of boundary conditions for the kinds of inputs we pay attention to. We'll practice the intuitive senses using information we like looking at, using behaviors we like performing—just as we would with friends. And despite anything you may have read which suggests that developing your intuition will require drastic changes in lifestyle, your current lifestyle is actually a good starting place for such development.

☞ Question 54.1 (Paths to knowing): This is a pop quiz. List all the ways you can think of through which a person might exercise their intuition. See if you can think of at least 10 ways.
_____
_____
_____
_____

The easiest way to answer 54.1 is to go back to your 53.4. Anything your friends can do to access advantages that wouldn't be given to others, are things that a person can do to set certain events in motion beyond the more common set of causes.

It should be clear by now that there are many types of intuition, and many subtypes of those types. Telepathy, for example, could refer to bending spoons with your mind, or it could correspond to turning someone on with your intentional impression. Each of these puts you as the means through which another actor's internal dynamics are changed to align with your own inner goals. It turns out that calculated magic like this isn't magic at all, just regular science. The "sixth" sense of it comes when our processes are subject to what others would consider a black box. Projection, for example, is truly accomplished by anything that bounces light, but because we don't usually train ourselves to recognize *where* we're bouncing or *what* we're bouncing towards, we rarely develop any publicly-agreed upon concept of ourselves as projectors. Further still, light isn't the only dimension in which we can project. A sweepingly heinous act can project us onto the cognition of an entire class of media watchers. If we were a food, the form of our existence would make it easy for us to project into the gustatory frame of any creature that experienced us. But we'll need to get beyond the physical forms for this kind of thinking.

This chapter is all about the psychic senses. If you've arrived here without having practiced the previous five chapters, many of the activities won't work. This is because, more than anything, the mastery of intuition—like the mastery of any sense—requires increasing sharpness in your powers of differentiation. One great way to stall your intuitive development, for example, is to dedicate its practice towards the regular space of ego goals. If you were taught that you should have money, you might practice claircognizant action only to the extent that it brings you money. If you're warring with a colleague, your clairvoyant bias against the whole behavioral pattern she represents will simply make you wrong about a significant fraction of impressions related to her. If you haven't found your tribe then your identity toolset for being comfortable with your own patterns of seeing will be incomplete. In other words, the more of an embodiment-centered agenda you have, the harder you can expect it to be to practice receiving impressions as they are. Instead, you're more likely to see them as you want them to be; any impressions you receive will consist of some parts actual, some parts personally-desired. For people to whom a sense does not come naturally, it will be that much more important that you will have graduated past your unnecessary conflicts, tribe searching, role exploration, and narrow friend framing before practicing what's in this chapter. From here on I will assume you've done this. If you have gone through the last five chapters and—despite them—find that The Foresight still isn't working for you, you might take a look at your body wheels from chapter 46 and review what your form suggests you might specialize in. Not everyone prizes visual information. Nor does everyone prize psychic information as a mode worth caring about.

An Important Note about the Psychic Senses

In Chapter 45 we previewed some different dimensions for perceiving. Though we have sometimes referred to engagement of certain dimensional talents as calculated magic, we will assume that any experience that a person can have is rooted in natural laws. Dogs hear frequencies we can't hear. Quarks are energies we can't feel. Half of what we call magic or psychic will be considered a byproduct of our limited windows for taking in (or noticing) certain ranges of energy. The other half of magic will be considered a byproduct of what we're publicly trained to acknowledge. For example, we've always known we had emotions, but not until Skinner were we able to address this (by exclusion) in mainstream science. We all know of that sneaking feeling called intuition, but even now there is no well-established public norm for teaching it. Thus those who are good at using it are more likely to be equated with yahoos or magicians. In the end, however, our worlds are clearly permeated with waves and fields of various kinds, on various scales—a few of which we create ourselves. The psychic senses will amount to those modes of making sense of certain fields, their potentials, and the chains thereof. It's rooted in science, not magic, and will be explored accordingly.

Our goal in learning the intuitive senses should fit with the idea of learning as "navigation through noise." Whatever the information field is, socially trained or not, we should be able to navigate through it towards some goal. The details of that navigation may or may not be observable, and the labels we apply to such navigation may or may not be subject to public agreement. When we study telepathy for example, we'll look at it as navigating the field of internal (often chemical or hormonal) processes within the thing we're interacting with—as in the synchronization of menstrual cycles experienced by some women who live around each other for long stretches. Our end goal for the navigation of another's hormonal space (or an object's chemical reaction space) will be the alignment of *some* of their *publicly observable* conditions with ours. A person who becomes good at this will be considered good at telepathy—even if a person who refused to acknowledge telepathy just called it "rapport." We could just as easily call hearing "mechanoreception." The labels will depend on what people accept as training. The intuitive senses aren't nearly as widely accepted as the normal ones at the time of this writing, so you can expect some people to balk at the idea of "clairs" and projection and all that. It won't matter if they balk. If you can make sense of the information and act upon it in a way that seems to elaborate—

maybe even improve upon—the way you and others live, that's more than enough. This brings us to our first major rule for studying intuition:

> Intuition is not about proving what you perceive (to yourself or others) any more than cognition is about proving what you think. What matters is what you *do* with what you perceive.

Maybe "vision" is just photoreceptivity turned into cognitive heuristics. Perhaps touch is just one kind of cutaneous reception turned into body signaling. So there is no such thing as vision or touch. Just collision or change reception. Yet we package different kinds of reception into in human-simple constructs like vision and touch anyway to aid our conversations about what ultimately happens with this information within and among communicators. So it will be with the intuitive senses. We won't be proving these senses' existence. Just practicing the informational frames behind them.

A Senses Scale

To keep track of our progress, we'll introduce a kind of grading scale for our senses. The scale will be as follows:

- **F** – You can't use the sense.

    0 (0): You don't believe the sense exists.

    1-10 (**FF--**): You can't make sense of what it feels like to use this sense.

    11-20 (**FF-**): You have an idea of how it might feel to use the sense, but haven't successfully experienced it.

    21-30 (**FF**): You have experienced the sense at least once on an occasion you can recall, and remember what it was like. But it was basically a fluke.

    31-40 (**F--**): You've experienced the sense (as we frame it) more than once, but randomly.

    41-50 (**F-**): You've experienced the sense enough times to know your potential for it, and can identify certain situations where it is more likely to happen. But you can't use the sense at will; the situation will have to determine that.

    51-59 (**F**): You can sometimes use the sense on purpose, but it is so biased or unreliable that you might as well not have it.

- **D** – You can trigger the sense, but can't trust it.

    60-63 (**D-**): You can trigger the sense and receive some interesting information, but you know that it is biased or otherwise unreliable.

    64-66 (**D**): You can trigger the sense and receive *useful* information, but the information is biased or otherwise unreliable.

    67-69 (**D+**): You can trigger the sense and receive useful information, but just don't trust what you're receiving.

- **C** – You can use the sense and trust it enough to warn yourself

    70-73 (**C-**): The sense triggers in a way that can warn you of trouble.

74-76 (C): You can purposely use (not just trigger) the sense to get information about your situation. The information mainly benefits you.

77-79 (C+): You can purposely use the sense to get information about others, though that information isn't necessarily useful to them as it comes.

- B – You can use the sense and consistently help others with its results.

    Starting here, "anyone" means any person, thing or situation which <u>allows</u> your connection. Also, it is understood that the information you get will often <u>NOT</u> be related to what you or the other think they are looking for. (If it were, they could get it through the regular senses).

    80-83 (B-): You can receive information about anyone's situation (others' or your own), which is often useful to the person involved. The receipt is occasional.

    84-86 (B): You can trigger information about anyone's situation, the information is useful, and you can present it as you receive it. (You can <u>describe</u> what you're getting.)

    - *Starting here, you know the difference between what you can read and what you can't. You may or may not know this difference for earlier levels, but for B grade and beyond, you certainly do.*

    - *"Presenting" means anything you do to act on the information. It could be telling, behaving, changing an attitude or focus, or deciding on something.*

    87-89 (B+): You can purposely obtain information about anyone's situation, and can present it in a way that is useful for the parties involved. (You can <u>harmonize</u> what you're getting.)

    - *Starting at B+, there is no question you could put this skill on a resume for a job that required it, and be able to handle this skill if hired.*

- A – You can use the sense on purpose and create new, better conditions for others on top of their existing conditions

    90-93 (A-): You are so good at this sense that you could (or do) use it consistently as a part of your day job or daily duties for others.

    94-96 (A): You are so good at this sense that you could (or do) use it consistently as a part of your day job or daily duties for others AND everyone you use it for (including yourself) consistently benefits from its use.

    97-100 (A+): You are so good at this sense that you could (or do) use it consistently as a part of your day job or daily duties for others AND everyone you use it for (including yourself) consistently benefits from its use AND you consistently create brand new things or experiences with its use.

Table 54-1: A Rating Scale for Senses

Critical Exercise
TRACK YOUR DEVELOPMENT OF THE SENSES

Trains: Essential knowledge

☞ **Question 54.2 (Rate your senses):** Referencing Table 54-1, rate your 12 senses in the table below. You can keep coming back to this table over the course of months or even years, but start with today's date. Again, I've put my own ratings in the table as an example, not only because I'm doing every exercise in this book as I write it and am using such things to guide how this book progresses (a combination of cognition and clairaudience), but also to show you how even normal senses like vision might be ranked. My normal senses are all <u>very</u> normal and would basically be considered an A under a normal rating system, but because we're assessing "abnormal" senses alongside these using Table 54-1, they still rate differently depending on how much I *rely* on them to live my life. Similarly, **be sure to rate your senses <u>not</u> based on how "fine" they are, but on how "practical-service-to-the-world-useful" they are** (Table 54-1).

*All senses (like vision) are considered *after* correction. If you normally wear glasses despite being legally blind, the glasses are part of your vision and you should still give yourself an A if an A applies.

Sense	Today's Date	Ex: 3/26/2020											
vision (with glasses+)		C+											
hearing (with aid+)		B+											
smell		D+											
taste		C											
touch (also, precision in handling your body)		B											
biomanufacture (mood reaction)		A-											
cognition (your ideas, thoughts, perspective)		B											
projection (putting yourself into contexts that your physical body shouldn't be able to access at the moment)		B											
clairsentience (empathy, mood or history reading of things that touch you)		B											
clairvoyance (gaining information / scenes you shouldn't be expected to know)		F--											
clairaudience (hearing or thinking communications that didn't come from a common "human- explainable" source)		A+											
claircognizance ("psychic knowing" of the right choices, feelings about what entire places, situations want from you; reckless-looking or odd people often have this, making apparent risks less risky)		A-											
telepathy (compelling things or people to act in line with the way you currently choose to pattern your experience in the moment)		D+											

Now that you've done this, circle any senses you wish to develop further.

Recall your answers to 53.4. Although there are typical notions of abilities like clairaudience, those notions aren't the only ones that exist. Clairaudience, for example, is often associated with receiving *spoken* messages, in a phenomenon called "channeling." But channeling is more like "clairaudient hearing (or speaking)." Other forms might include "clairaudient writing" or "clairaudient cognition" (which are my own modes). A person with a natural, near legendary kinesthetic sense like Fred Astaire might have had something like "claircognizant (active) touch" while a natural composer like Chopin might have claimed "claircognizant hearing" among his senses. A reiki master might excel in "touch telepathy" (which we all have to some degree via others' receipt of our close body heat). Because senses are based on both the reception AND the result, the combinations are wider than they first appear. Sure your eyes respond to electromagnetic energy, but so does your parathyroid gland; such would be the difference between normal vision and a hybrid concept like "biomanufactural vision."

As always, the aim is not to just invent concepts, but to differentiate them in line with what we actually know. Pain reception and pressure reception are different, but "touch" and "proprioception" are as deep as most of us have ever gone in capturing these. As for the over- or under- absorption of certain frequencies in events like sunburn, which sense is that? If it isn't a "scientific" sense despite resulting from absorption of light (just like vision), why not? It affected the evolution of skin color didn't it? You can see how our paradigms for knowledge—though trained as social gospel—can also limit our view. You can specialize in a wide array of senses, but never know—simply because you have no public frames for them. Accordingly, we'll go through the six intuitive senses one by one, establishing a stronger foundation for the development of each one.

A final disclaimer: This isn't a competition. You don't need to achieve an A in every sense. In fact, it may be harmful for you to develop certain senses beyond their current level. A strong empath (clairsentient) who receives his information through vision might open himself to assault by training clairvoyance. A person whose Role it is to produce words cognitively might, ironically, face diminishing returns by taking in too much of what he hears at B+ level or higher. Our bodies are uniquely weighted in the different traits they hold. Sometimes a D- or an FF- is *exactly* what you need in order to perform your Role at its highest in this life, and that's perfect.

Developing Projection

Certain forms of projection come easily. Other forms can be very difficult. The automatic spreading of your reputation on people's minds and phones is among the former. Astral projection is among the latter. Meanwhile, the most basic form of projection—being seen somewhere—is actually in the middle. Why?

The challenge with projection lies *not* with your being perceived, but with your being perceived by things you *want* to perceive you. The chair feels your weight. The spider knows you're there. The stranger across the street has indeed glimpsed the light that bounced off of you. But we don't count these as projection because there will have been very little control over these events. When we project willingly, we often want to see who's seeing us—be it a person, setting, or a situation. To consider ourselves as having been perceived, included in a scene is the overall aim. Yet "seeing" is not the only sense through which others let us know we've been there.

We begin with projection because its simplest form—being on another's mind—can be one of the easiest forms to control. This isn't as far out as pushing a visual hologram of yourself into some room, but instead involves associating yourself with another perceiver's experience of some scenario. Do a thing that will cause others to think of you, or a thing that will leave traces of you in a system, then you can be said to have projected. Some examples of projection include

1. Calling someone on the phone
2. Showing up in someone's dream or thoughts
3. Having your art, writings, music, or ideas experienced by someone
4. Having an electronic assistant do your bidding even when you're not there
5. Having others gossip about you or having media cover your actions
6. Projecting astrally
7. Having a person's body memory keep you through something you did to them physically
8. Leaving a threat or making a promise which ties another's actions to consequences sponsored by you

Granted, some of the above forms of projection are pretty mundane. So is the mere act of opening your eyes is a kind of uninspiring form of vision compared to the eagle eye of a sniper. The senses don't always impress. To the extent that we care only about the psychic senses, only 2 and 6 might move us. But don't discount the other forms of projection. Numbers 3 and 5 can be some of the most effective, most satisfying forms of projection you will ever engage in. 7 may be among the most powerful, 5 the most common, 1 the most important, and 8 the most identity-defining. Where and how you project depends on who you are and, perhaps more importantly, who you want to be.

☞ Question 54.3 (The audience you want): Let's assume you want to be "seen" (heard, talked about, perceived felt, experienced) somewhere. You don't have to have a reason. No one will accuse you of being an attention hound. Each of us is more likely to gravitate towards certain audiences over others, even if that audience is just the trees. What kinds of audiences (people, situations, or settings) do you prefer to be seen by?

	Example
	You could give several different kinds of answers here:
	• I want to be seen in exotic lands
	• By alien creatures, in other dimensions
	• Among friends, as a destroyer of enemies
	• As a champion by people following this field
	• By strangers, by everyone (except people whose seeing would make my life harder)
	• By nature, in a movie, in scenarios that can teach me about the universe

☞ Question 54.4 (How you want to be seen): **You want to be perceived, but how? In what *form*?** One particular note about this question is that it helps determine whether traditional projection is what you're actually after.

	Example
_____	Some examples might include the following:
_____	• As a hero, a good mother, an inspiration
_____	• As physically strong
_____	• As rich, influential, as an expert
_____	
_____	Maybe you want to be seen as all of these, but given your constitution, you should know that some might impede others. Rich Warren Buffett is less likely to have people listen to Sage Warren Buffett for his investment wisdom in its own right. That's just the nature of people. Maya Angelou might travel farther as a collection of words than as a visible face. Benedict Spinoza might travel best as a radical thinker. It would help him survive persecution if he were *not* "famously image projected" in his lifetime though.
_____	
_____	
_____	

If your answer to 54.4 featured something other than a visible form, don't be surprised if visible projections like fame, astral travel, or physical memorability don't come as easily for you. Conversely, if you want to be noted for your ideas or your influence, don't be surprised if you have some physical feature, some odd mannerisms, or some other behavior that often gets you ~~in trouble... noticed...~~ remembered in a "special way" among observers. How you want to be seen is largely related to the form you take in this life. If you wanted to be tasty, you might have been a food. Figuratively speaking. But you get the idea. Take a moment to reflect on your embodiment and its connection to your answer above.

Although we might ask another question regarding what you want to be seen "doing," such a question wouldn't be appropriate, since your long term Role knows more about that than you do. As with your physical appearance, you are more likely to be seen doing whatever is consistent with your sphere-role beyond the body. Creatures in the astral plane will stare at you. Media haters will hate on you. You can pick the where, how, and the what, but rarely all three at the same time without one forcing conditions upon the others. Projection is mainly about your choice of where, with reactions to your what. You could purposely morph the nature of the what, but that wouldn't necessarily be you projecting as yourself. It would be you projecting as a created character. If this is what you prefer, you might be an actor.

Dream projection

Most of the types of projection listed earlier are simple enough to figure out once as soon as you've seen them on a list. Three of those projection types, however—other-dreams, astral, and other-body memory—take more work to pull off consistently. We'll address these in order of difficulty.

Other thoughts and dreams: Them to you

We often show up in other people's thoughts and dreams. Rarely do they tell us when this has occurred. Our main aim then, is not just to project in this way on purpose, but to know when we've done so. Our practice begins with a theory and ends with a friend. Follow me here.

Dreaming is said to have three purposes: as mental prioritization, as an artifact of biological processing, and as memory consolidation. Constructs that serve these ends are more likely to appear in dreams. I'll add that the symbolism in dreams depends heavily on what ideas the dreamer deems to have meaning. I can't tell you how many times I've dreamt of someone by representing them as someone else. That's because I require a lot of information about you until I believe I know you; until that happens, you will be represented as that person I definitely know to be "the coworker," "the clown," or "the lazy one." If you want to show up in someone's dream, it will help if you actually represent something distinct to them. Your reputation precedes you here, so one of the more helpful steps in showing up in another person's dream is to have had a reputation that they can identify. You could try to go straight for the astral broadcast, but obviously this is MUCH harder. Again, think about what you're trying to achieve.

Since being in someone's dream is probably more interesting than being on their plain old thoughts, we'll ignore the latter kind of projection. To get into someone's dream, we'll want to be relevant to them in some way. The bad news is that you can't control this. If they want to block you they will. The good news is that you *can* control whether you have focused your own attention on projection into a scenario which you know is important to them, and you can often control how your own expression aligns with what you think *they* think your role in that scenario would actually be. I know that was complicated. In other words, I can't control whether you think I'm relevant. But, based on my experience of you,

- I can guess what's important to you
- I can guess what you would think of me if I were tied to that important thing
- I can guess how you would react if I did what fit me amidst that tie, and
- I can guess how you would, in waking life, (or *I* would, in the projection itself) let me know that I showed up in your dream.
- To appear in your dreams is to appear in the kinds of scenarios that reflect your subconscious wants. I can read part of this through your prior behaviors.

Now while we would love to practice projection into another's dream, there's some technical training we need to do first: Namely, we need for someone else to try projecting into our dream. The process of projection will be a lot easier to dissect this way. If it is at all possible for you to know the best time of day for seeding your own dreams, that's also the time when you want the other person to try this on you.

☞ Question 54.5 (When is the best time to seed your own dreams?): If you don't already know the best time of day to control what goes into your dreams, try this: Try remembering your dreams for one week. Keep track of what you dream about each time. Recall, if applicable, time of day you were interacting with the kinds of symbols that showed up in the dream. There is a complicated story behind this process, but that's exactly how I learned it. That plus one other way:

> **The second way to determine dream timing.** Go about your normal life until you experience an unusual event. Observe whether that event had a parallel in a smaller, less significant event sometime in the same day (within 24 hours) before it. Note the times of each event. Do this again for a separate event with a different kind of experiential feeling. Ideally, all four events should occur in the same day. Once you have all four times, you can use the time period between the two small events as a miniature version of the time period between the two larger events, and see if you can scale backwards. I discuss this method thoroughly in Chapter 40 of *Laurentia*: "Time in the Astro Wheel." What you're doing here is determining when the seed period begins in your 24-hour cycle. Events that happen for you during the seed period—once you've determined what this period is—have a noticeably higher chance of showing up in a kind of shadow period later on. Yes there is a theory for why this happens, and it's located in the section immediately following, "The Time-Unit Hypothesis" (again in *Laurentia*). If you were to ask another person to try this projection experiment with you, you would want them to do it during that fraction of your day which renders your sleep time a "shadow period." For example, I used this method to determine that my 24-hour seed cycle begins at 5:21pm. I normally sleep from 1am-6am. If I cut my sleep period in half and use 5:21pm as the start point, then between 9:10pm and 11:40pm is when I (or anyone else) would best seed my dreams in my time zone. This really does matter, as the fail rate is very high for dream seeding outside of this window. Again, it's not magic. It's a math cycle (see *Laurentia*).

You'll be asking another person to try projecting into your dreams, but you want them to do so in such a way as to affect your sphere (energy carrying cloud) at the optimum phase of the diurnal/day cycle for intersecting your sleep. Heed this. That said, when is the best time for you to seed your dreams? (You may need to come back to this one later.)

	Example
	between 9:10pm and 11:40pm. The best time to seed the seed is at half of that past 5:21pm: between 7:15pm and 8:30pm. I've found this this consistently, *consistently* works. What I'm doing during these times has a good chance of influencing my dreams.

☞ Question 54.6 (Find someone who has the power to project): **Not everyone is good at projecting,** and not everyone who can project does so through dreams. You're looking for a person who 1) can move you emotionally, 2) is meaningful enough as a character in your life, and 3) is on good enough terms to try this with you. This will usually be a friend, and they will almost certainly need instructions on this process. First, name a person whose projection into your dreams you would want to try out.

☞ Question 54.7.1 (The projection request, part 1): **Ask the person you named in 54.6 something like the following:**

> I'm reading this book about psychic abilities and want to see if you can project into my dreams. Between [the times you listed in Question 54.5] today or tomorrow can you spend at least 10 minutes doing something related to what you think I think is important? But don't tell me about it.

This is similar to what I sent to a friend of mine. You want to give them a couple of days to choose from so that you yourself won't necessarily have fueled your own dreaming of them. (You shouldn't know when to expect them.) You also want to give them a window during which to appear, again so that you yourself won't be able to know when to expect them. Keep track of your experiment below.

	Example
	Day 1 (This actually happened after I wrote the first line of Question 54.7.1, but before I wrote its text box the next day)
	7:03pm: Messaged M the request to try something sometime between 9:10-11:40. She agreed.
	~8:40pm-9:17pm: played Mega Man X 6. Thought Blizzard Wolfang's stage was a $h!tty experience
	9:10-11:40 the window when M. would have done something, if she did it today
	~11:00pm: went to sleep
	~3:00am (15 minutes before waking) had a dream basically about Blizzard Wolfang's stage
	~3:05am had a flash of an appearance from a person who works at another college K., never shows up in dreams, and is not M. Curious.
	~3:15am woke up

After the pair of days has passed, you should tell the person what you experienced, if anything. It's no big deal if nothing happens. This is practice. Just try again.

☞ Question 54.7.2 (The projection request, part 2): **If you had any results from 54.7.1, let the person know what you experienced. Also, ask them what they did. Write down your findings below.**

	Example
	Need to practice again.

☞ Question 54.7.3 (The projection request, part 3): **Did you learn anything about how projection *towards* you might work?**

	Example
	Not yet.

I've found that there are two kinds of people who have an easy time getting into our spheres in general: those with whom we are psychically connected and those who are powerful projectors broadly. I once had a powerful projector cast something in my direction—though I never found out if she did it on purpose—and this raises issues about respecting people's personal space. It might be ethically inappropriate to assault someone psychically, and you enter this territory when you attempt projection knowing that the other party might not like it. But I'll stop just short of warning you not to do this, because in all honesty we do this all the time when we spread our bad attitudes to others in waking. The catch is, psychically intruding on someone is subject to similar rules as other kinds of intrusion you might make. The punishments, if there are any, may be more subtle or more long term; you'll have to measure the limits against the rules of your own conscience. The psychic world *does* tend to be different though, where things that might be taboo in waking will sometimes be perfectly fine, while other things that might be normal in waking will be a kind of failure in dreaming (as in an unenthusiastic, analytical exchange). You'll do as your conscience dictates. In this first projection request, however, we get to see how the system works in a single case from the other side. We're not the projectors here, but we are seeing the kinds of activities and timing that help projection get off the ground.

Now let's reverse it. How do you project into another person's dreams?

Other thoughts and dreams: You to them

Most people will rarely tell you when they've had a dream that included you. Even more rarely will they actually dream *about* you. Most of our dreams are about things that concern us, our memory, our biology, and our preoccupations. If others show up, they are usually part of the topic, but not the focus of the topic themselves. Yet there are times when a dream you've had truly seems to revolve around someone else. I call these "Other-dreams." They are recognizable in that they just don't feel like they come from your world. Instead, their story flow and their emotional familiarity seem to be a part of someone else's house. Other-dreams are also noteworthy in that they often beg to be shared with the Other whom they revolve around. It works this way whether you are the dreamer or the projector. And even though you will rarely know when you've featured in another's dream, sometimes that person will want to tell you about a certain dream they had in particular. They may not know it, but I've found that perhaps 2/3 of the time when a person who normally doesn't tell you about their dreams finally does so, it is typically meant for your ears as well as theirs. Their regular dream becomes your Other-dream, and these are often related to issues which are important for understanding your relationship to them.

It is probably out of human curiosity that we often take an interest in projecting at all. Like going to any store or standing before any audience, projection typically comes with some kind of agenda on the part of the projector. So although you might want to show up in someone else's dream, think about who this serves. Does your showing up do anything for them or their lives? If it's just to indulge your curiosity, is that a good enough reason for you to just appear on their mental couch one day? What if someone whose relationship to you had basically been stably figured out suddenly showed up in your dreams? Would it keep you preoccupied? Would it cause you to reevaluate the relationship? Think of the additional complication it might cause in their lives for you to just "show up" in their worlds unannounced. This is why most of your efforts to project onto someone else—waking or not—will be capped in general. You're typically not thinking of their interests as you do your thing. You would tangle up theirs to advance your own. Furthermore, you probably won't put in enough willed focus to break down that door in the first place. What seems like a game to us—given that we live full-time with ourselves—often has real plot implications for the person we're projecting onto—one who processes us with much greater rarity. For that reason, you might think of casual dream projection as a type of graffiti on another person's wall. It's no surprise that fate would hardly encourage you to do this. Your reasons need to be relevant to them.

Other-dreams are very often relevant to both you and the other person. Why do both of you need to hear this dream? Perhaps because the dreamer/projector has the correct framework which the subject/Other must complete in order for them to understand their own (the Other's) worlds better. My own Other-dreams have had three purposes: Showing me what the Other's backstory is in order to explain their dynamic with me; helping me find out about help that the other is seeking which I can provide; or providing us both information about our dynamic which may be needed in order for us to move forward. These are analogous to *their* biology/history, *their* preoccupation viewed through me, and our *joint* preoccupation respectively. The second class specifically—their preoccupation viewed through me—can be a source of one of the most efficient answers to a problem they're having which vexes them royally. Of course they'll need to be open to communicating with you about that problem. Still, you know when you've been a topic in another's dream when they tell you about it, and you get the sense of yourself as a clear character in that dream. Whatever you did to build up the way they represented you in that dream is the thing you do to project successfully in this way. That seems obvious in hindsight, doesn't it? So why is this kind of projection so challenging to do regularly?

I believe that regular, consistent, reportable-back-to-you projection into other people's dreams is challenging for three reasons:

- It may take years for you to build up enough data regarding what you actually need to do in the waking world to control this.
- You need to build up enough trust and enough disclosure with the person you're projecting onto in order for them to 1) talk to you when they had a dream that concerns you and 2) represent you in a way that allows them to recognize that the dream might concern you in the first place.
- Your role needs to be relevant enough and their own powers of recall strong enough for this type of dream to even occur to them.

And as we've said, projection of this sort isn't the kind of thing you can typically get away with for funsies. Given all this, the next question may take a long time—on the order of years, even—to answer. It assumes that you have kept track of enough Other-dreams to discern a pattern.

(*For technophiles who organize their dreams electronically, I record mine, label them with the word "Other", and keep them in the Dreams folder. I searched in Windows for `other; folder:Dreams` to find them quickly. It turn outs that I only have or hear about one of these every 1 – 1½ years.)

☞ Question 54.7.4 (How you show up in Other-dreams): **Recall where other people have told you about any dreams they have had that seemed related to you. How are you represented? Where do you think the dreams got this representation?**

	Example
	I'm often represented as an assailant, someone in disguise, or in some other way affiliated with crime or investigations.
	These representations come from my mixture of mostly pleasant 1:1 behavior + complex topics of preoccupation + odd/"creepy"/antisocial presentation: a side I use in environments I don't know well enough. Otherwise, among people I know and trust, I present as cheerful but picky, and always working—instantly upsettable if it involves bullies.

If you weren't able to answer 54.7.4, there is another way to find out how people who care enough to represent you go about doing so. Go back to your 52.17—your owned negative traits. Because dreams aid memory consolidation, preoccupation, and biology, you may be most memorable to another where you engage, as a construct, a little bit of all three of these. Namely, your socially threatening characteristics will have an easier time coercing another's, biology, memory, and concern even if they like you a lot. You may be able to put together a persona from these characteristics which better informs your route into another person's subconscious.

☞ Question 54.7.5 (The memorable symbol): Referencing mainly your 52.17, what kinds of forms might you take as a character or object in another person's dream? Be sure to think of yourself as a guest in their worlds, not as a hero in your own. So no, "Robin Hood" shouldn't be your default. "Thief" might be.

List <u>at least 10</u>, including characters, roles, objects, animals, and so on.

	Example
	Antisocial / Weird / Creepy / Not up to the hype / Not what I'm looking for: Possible symbols: <ul><li>an assailant, someone plotting, a dark figure, someone hiding, a very stern commander, a magician, a dangerous little boy, a technical support character from a sci-fi show</li><li>a wolf, a dangerous snake, a tunneling animal like a mole, a watchful and covert animal like anything hiding in a jungle, a praying mantis</li><li>a dark room, an unreasonably complicated computer, a helpful robot, a fortress, or castle</li></ul>

The point of 54.7.5 is not to paint yourself in the most negative light possible, but to turn yourself into the most abstract—yet still most descriptive—version of your most memorable characteristics in the mind of anyone (everyone else) who is NOT you. Don't expect to be Jesus and appear as yourself in a cloud of light. You're more likely to show up as a bicycle, a bird, or a nameless street peddler until the person knows you better. Until they know a lot more about your relevance in their lives. Don't be offended if that happens. From the maze of possible quirks that you could foist onto others, the bike[37] is probably the most concise representation of you that the person can benefit from at the time. Alas, our projections onto others aren't meant to flatter our own egos. They're meant to support the viewer's views of their own journey.

---

[37] One of my favorite acquaintances is associated with dreams about bikes. She's the sweetest person. Bikes and bike dreams remind me of free and open childhood exploration, aligned with welcoming and all-encompassing nature, speed, adventure, and the friends I used to ride with—the times in college where I rode alone and loved it. For her, the bike is a beautiful symbol. On the other hand, when she has appeared as herself in dreams, her appearance has consistently involved more complicated arrangements than this.

Chapter 54: The Foresight

☞ **Question 54.7.6 (What causes you to project?):** It's so easy to think of dream projection as one of the many New Age practices that requires the usual meditation. By now we're starting to know better. Given your answers to 54.7.4 and 54.7.5, what kinds of things have been most effective in helping you project into other's dreams?

I have to:	Example
	I have to: 1. Do something in front of a group they are in (<u>not</u> them specifically), appearing as my usual "odd/creepy/intellectually complicated" self 2. Interact with them 1:1 as my usual charming, polite self 3. Have them know at least a little about my passionate / intense / apparently (but not actually) lusty ways 4. Be at least slightly (or highly) distrusted by them, or get #3 *from them* Usually in that order.

☞ **Question 54.7.7 (Your simple route to projection):** See if you can summarize 54.7.6 in five words or less.

	Example
	Presenting as incubus

☞ **Question 54.7.8 (Efficient projection):** Given your answer to 54.7.7, what would you say is the most efficient route for your projection into other's dreams/subconscious? (Is it actually through meditation and focus, or some other way?)

	Example
	I project best through great one-on-one interaction, alongside a "sinisterized" or suspicious public image, onto other *succubus types. *Though I believe I'm harmless, the demon words were by far the most appropriate. Interestingly, the people whose Other-dreams I've projected into have been all been heavily lusty, unusual, or connected to this themselves. It's not as easy or interesting for me to project onto people who don't display this. Capped exchanges are a dime a dozen. **An interesting note. Once in my meditations I learned that I had a number of succubi around me—especially at night. In their worlds, however, they are just normal feminine beings, I am invisible, and I am an incubus who visits them. Indeed, in this life I do gravitate towards succubus-like personalities much more strongly in general. People interested in demonology may find that kind of world intersection intriguing. I certainly do. (Relax, it's just a stage character—Lon Chaney-style)

You may have realized as I did, that you not only had an optimum route for projection, but also an optimal target. Certain numbers we know how to dial. Of those, only certain recipients will want to pick up. This gets us into the realm of psychic connection—a must for certain kinds of intuitive communication.

☞ Question 54.7.9 (An optimal Other): **You probably have a certain personality which is more likely to receive your projection—not just in dreams, but in general. These people will have stronger reactions to you for better or worse, and will be more concerned with even your smallest deeds than other people. If you were to project, what kinds of people would most likely register your projection?**

	Example
	People with whom I have an electric or emotionally noticeable connection in waking.

What is a psychic connection?

Let's define a **psychic connection** as **a TWO-WAY pattern of emotional (internal) response and acknowledgement between two parties.** The parties could be people, or they could be a person and nature, a pet and an owner, a nationalist and his country. Note that the connection is two-way; one party projecting onto another is not a psychic connection. Note that the pattern involves the <u>internal</u> states of the parties, not just the surface actions. Note finally that the connections entail *response* AND acknowledgement, not just [action-towards] and acknowledgment; if I am to act towards you, it will be a response to what I remember coming from you last. This is a feedback loop in which each party's actions considers the other's last move. Throwing signals at another for one's own release, then throwing out another after the Other's turn has been taken does not constitute a psychic connection. Instead, a psychic connection is essentially a conversation channel between the *inclinations* of two things.

A psychic connection between you and I means that our inclinations are free to exchange, and our inclinations are disposed to us exchanging with each other—for better or worse. I may like you, but not trade my actual inclinations, wishes, wants, deep preferences, hopes, or subconscious aims with you. Even if you traded these with me, we still might not have a psychic connection if it's not two-way. You may hate me, but if you willingly frame your inclinations with respect to me (or against my actions) and I do so with you—if our inclinations nonetheless affect the other in an acknowledged feedback loop—then we do have a psychic connection according to the definition given here. This is often the story of sphere-mates.

- And what if our inclinations loop, but we don't know—let alone acknowledge it? By the definition given here, that's not a psychic connection. There must be (at least internal) acknowledgement.
- What does a psychic connection with a pet or a plant look like? It grows, declines, evolves, or displays "wants" in a pattern consistent with the sum of your general interactions with it. That

is, in the broad sense, it doesn't go in some other direction preference-wise—even if, in the case of plants, it's a preference for light and water.

Remember, you are a sphere. Today a plant is a separate object from you. Tomorrow it will be absorbed into your story as one of the many things you tended to alongside your own health. Right now you think you are you. Yet your past self is you *plus* every significant thing in your story.

- A psychic connection with a space? How does that work? Again, the connection revolves around inclinations. If a place or a situation is developing (elaborating on its potential) in line with your own inclined development, and the place or situation seems to accommodate a role for you—a kind of feedback—in doing so, then this can be considered a psychic connection. This may seem abstract because we're mainly trained to frame ourselves as humans rather than collections of physics-based processes. But places and situations consist of processes too—often sponsored by us as collections of physics on top of their own.

Critical Exercise
FOR DREAM PROJECTORS

Trains: Projection

Rule 1 Before you start this exercise, be sure to select a target to whom you are psychically connected—one who currently evolves along with your Role and who cares to loop inclinations with you. If you cannot find such a person, then don't do this exercise. Not because you'll be committing a psychic crime, but because the mediocre results you get may fool you into thinking you can't project.

Rule 2 Both you and the other person should both be interested in evolving your relationship. No, not necessarily romantically, but in any form your interaction may take. As we discussed before, mere dabbling in another person's affairs reduces your relevance to them, thus the significance of any symbol you take in their dreams. You must be genuinely interested in helping your dynamic with them progress, and vice versa. So much so that even if you weren't projecting, you would still want this. Accordingly, it helps if this person isn't already so close to you that the relationship has already reached an optimum.

Rule 3 The person in this activity needs to be in the middle of a problem. You need to help them solve that problem. Even between the most connected people, if the Other thinks life is just fine while you the projector decide to drop by for a visit, you can expect it to be handled like any waking life visit. "What are you doing here? Can I help you with something?" They may receive you, but will your visit be important enough for them to tell you that it happened?

Rule 4 In this activity, you can't give the Other any warning at all that you're doing this, but you do need to be just close enough for them to contact you if you succeed. This is a tricky balance. And again, if you can't find such a person, then don't do this exercise. It would be a shame if you succeeded on someone who was psychically too far away from you, were never told you succeeded, and gave up on projection early.

Now if you decide to ignore all the rules above and try this exercise anyway, and if you're not already a seasoned projector, I'm telling you now that this exercise probably won't work. Just as surely as you can't just randomly go to someone's house in the middle of the night and expect to be welcomed, you can't project onto just anybody and expect a cordial debriefing afterwards. Only a certain kind of person would greet you in their robes and humor you, and the same goes for the kinds of dream projection for which you expect to receive verification. I know there are a lot of rules here. I also know that this is nowhere near as simple as "sit down and meditate." But we're approaching all of the psychic senses as rooted in believable laws; we want the most predictable steps for increasing our chances of success, and we want proof that it happened. There are ordered rules involved here.

You'll be looking for contact from the Other within one or two days of your attempt, validating the idea that you projected onto them. This contact can be direct, but really consists of anything specifically associated with them that seems to arrive from their sphere if and only if you've attempted the projection. For example, I have many colleagues across my workplace whom I never talk to casually. If I attempted to project towards one and got a project or a mass message sponsored by them within one or two days of the attempt, and if this just doesn't normally happen as an event, then I could consider myself partly successful. Sometimes people really are thinking of you, but have no reasonable reason at all to cross the lines of your waking familiarity to tell you so. Sometimes they *really don't* know your number. Most of the time, even if they did, they would have no idea what to say to you. I knew a person for a while with whom there was a strong mutual attraction, whom I dreamt of as a powerful banshee. Twice. She was the only banshee ever to appear in my entire history of dreaming. What did I tell her when I saw her afterwards? Absolutely nothing. Since you're picking someone who's not super close to you, be prepared for the return communication to not be super close either. Do expect it to arrive though.

☞ Question 54.7.10 (Your projection Other): **List your person here.** _____

And now for the hard part. Some readers may not like this one:

Rule 5
Be prepared to dedicate most of your waking **day** around this person. Just one time. A WHOLE day. As you saw, there are certain time windows where a person's dreams are written. The same act performed in the wrong window can be as good as no act at all. But you almost certainly won't know this person's windows. Nor will you know which acts "project you" as which symbols in their dreams. Neither will they. For brand new projectors, be prepared to consider yourself this individual's personal assistant for a whole 24 hours excluding your sleep. Of course, the longer you sleep, the more hours you lose. I have key windows starting at 2:22am and 3:23am. The other person's time won't stop for you. During your day of projection you'll be keeping track of the different activities you perform, so if/when you do succeed, you'll be able to more easily pinpoint which hour produced the strongest results.

I asked myself and my guardians while developing this activity, "If I don't trust my connection with the person, can I try projecting to two people in the same day." They told me it was complicated, and had to do with what forms a person's strongest connections tended to take. People? Places? Laws? The News? "Do what you think you can handle," they replied, "but do it all as one." In other words, if you want to try projecting to two people, project to the *pair*, not [one and one]. If you want to project onto a city and a pet, project to the pet in the city, not [one and one].

Rule 3 They need to be working on a problem. Help them solve their problem. Be relevant.

Rule 2 Genuinely evolve the exchange.

Got it? Okay.

☞ Question 54.7.11 (Psychic projection): **Towards your person in 54.7.10—without contacting them directly and subject to the rules above**—spend a full 24 hours infusing your activities with the things you listed in 54.7.7 – 54.7.9. This will be utterly exhausting if you're not as into the exchange as Rule 2 required. It will be a full day of thumb twiddling if you're not actually doing anything to solve their problem as Rule 3 required. To help you, here is one more rule: **Rule 6**: If you have any psychic cheats, use them. (My dreams, for example, give me an idea of who will work best for this experiment). Log how you spent your day below, then…

_____
_____
_____
_____
_____
_____
_____
_____
_____
_____
_____
_____
_____
_____
_____

...Allow at least two days for results (for reasons covered in *Laurentia* Chapter 40: "Time Unit Hypothesis").

☞ Question 54.7.12 (Did you succeed?): **If you succeeded, then good for you. Log the contact you got from the other person (or their sphere) here. If you did not succeed, use the space below to log what you learned. If you didn't succeed and didn't learn anything, say so. But if you half-assed the experiment, say that too. One day you may want to try this again. You may open up this book and want to know whether you were really ready to put in the work for training dream projection. It will be greatly helpful to your future self if you don't burn your practice by telling him/her you tried when you really didn't.**

This is one of the few activities in the book I didn't do myself, because at the time of this writing there was no one I cared to try this on. You have to feel motivated to intersect with another sphere on this level, and I just didn't.

Astral projection

You could train to project astrally as your first spiritual priority, but if you are completely new to it you may be climbing uphill. If you have some exposure to the techniques of astral projection but just can't maintain the focus required, one exercise that greatly helped me was Question 53.15. Despite being a natural F- in this kind of projection, I did exercise 53.15 intending to talk to my friend Emily, ended up falling asleep half in visualization of the space where our talk took place, and ended up projecting immediately. Emily is what I would refer to as a "motivator" for spiritual sight (clairvoyance, projection, and claircognizant niche-finding) in the same way that Walmart is a motivator for retail buying and a music video is a motivator for your rhythmic movement. I'll talk more about motivators when we discuss telepathy.

For the most part though, astral projection can be difficult.

An out of body hypothesis

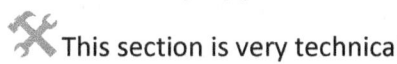This section is very technical.

Part of what makes astral projection difficult is that it requires at least five variations on the senses at once. While there is the broad idea of <u>projecting</u> into some space, there is also the unusual matter of doing so <u>touch/feeling-wise</u> outside of your own body. There is the <u>vision-like perception</u> that you are actually somewhere else. Then you have the <u>cognitive-like processing</u> what is happening as you move around. All of this takes place under some <u>clairvoyant sense of a scene</u> beyond normal accessibility. In this way, astral projection is a more complex equivalent of playing an instrument (where touch, cognition, and hearing typically combine) or dancing. It is a multisensory experience, even if only one sense (likely clairvoyance) is behind it all. To the extent that you perceive yourself elsewhere, astral projection may actually be better described as "sense-rich projective *clairvoyance*." Only if you believe the places you visit are actual places that can actually receive you can you be said to have *projected* there. If you *don't* believe the places were describable as places—coherent or not—you might *say* that you projected, but into where? Did you moonwalk on an invisible dancefloor too?

Many people have had out of body experiences (OOBs or OBEs). I may have one about twice a year. Our question is not *if* they can happen to a person, but *how* they happen. What is the mechanism? In college I recall in my neuropsychiatry class Dr. Bogen telling us all kinds of stories about cortical cats and the separation of the motor system from spatial map, the effects of severing the brain hemispheres—lesions to the cortex and what was—in the UK at the time—known as a bifrontal leukotomy. There we studied all of the usual neurophenomena from phantom limb to ataxias, and the various aphasias, all of which amounted to the results of certain brain functions not talking to others. And then there is sleep paralysis and circadian disruption. Unfortunately, this is not the space to discuss all of that, but I received a good slice of the terrain at the time primarily from three of our textbooks: Oliver Sacks' *The Man Who Mistook His Wife for a Hat*, Eric Kandel and colleagues' *Principles of Neural Science* and, most importantly, Heilmann & Valenstein's *Clinical Neuropsychiatry*. Of course there have been advances in the last 20 years since then, but don't let the new genetics stuff fool you. It's easier for us humans to train against the findings of gross anatomy than it is for us to train against genomic chains and promoters. The basic principles of sensory separation are as old as paralysis itself, and you can still learn from the earlier works. For right now, we'll consider OOB to be something along the lines of a "phantom body" experience: where your brain's firing pattern temporarily forgets that the parts it's firing to aren't accessible.

Yet waves rarely stop *completely* at their physical boundaries. Sound still travels through walls. Neutrinos still travel through the earth. Firing patterns—fields of chemoelectric and thermal potential tied to both their own prior states and the perceived states of environments they respond to—can be described mathematically independently of the specific cells that underlie them (which is why MRI effects, for example, are consistent across different people). Should the brain monitor the body's own holistic fields on top of monitoring the physical organ systems—should the body have its own monitoring system in the form of the distribution of hormones, metabolic needs, and receptor activity whether or not it makes it to the brain—then the gross biologic map can be separated from the brain's various somatic maps—with the brain's maps doing their best to recreate a "body-formed" field from its wide, fuzzy activity despite not having an actual bounded body to talk to. In this way, the cognition can forget both the body's shape and its bounds while simultaneously integrating other special information from the environment that it is interested in.

- My body is lying here, but during this period of paralysis my normal cognitive maps aren't talking to it.
- My endocrine maps—the network of regulatory messengers for connecting brain to body—may or may not be talking to body or cognition in cooperation with either, and might even prefer its own arrangement at this time.
- We can consider there to be at least 3 mapping systems involved in dreaming: the cognition, body, and endocrine/messenger systems. "Messenger" is my shorthand for endocrine, lymphatic, vascular and other cross-body networks that constitute the messenger regulation of the relationship between the first two]). Of these,

    only the body is confined to the familiar shape. This would be the physical body that one "exits" in an OOB.

    The cognition takes the shape of the parts of the body it thinks it's using with respect to the aspects of the containing environment it thinks it's engaging. Naturally, this probably feels more like a "disembody" having an experience populated with symbols which are meaningful to the person. **Out of Body:** This would be the astral traveling body in an OOB before any whole body maps are applied back to it at the end of the experience.

    The messenger system doesn't take any shape beyond for the flow fields of the messengers it normally sends, and knows no such things as "objects" or "body parts." It's just a network of "routes." Yet, to the extent that the person is currently experiencing something to which they are tied emotionally, part of whose own internal response routes are assumed, this system may feel more like a bodyless frequency cloud with no source or destination for its flows—hence no sense of time or space—just the cycle-like wave form itself. **Light travels:** This would be something like a light body in an extended OOB, and might also more accurately explain the form of things like spirits and oversouls.

- Given the above descriptions we can deduce that in order for the messenger system to travel independently, it first has to be a system. The cognition and the body need to already be separate enough for a "messenger" between them to be a thing.

- But now, in order for the mapping systems to have had apparently separate experiences to the knowledge of the traveler themselves, they obviously need to have the systems that connect them—the *cognition-body interface* portion of the messenger system—temporarily disabled.

- With temporary semi-free roam regarding where its messaging focus is directed, the messenger system has a higher probability of reflecting more generic responses to whatever cognitive movie is being played rather than the normal gross body. That is, the messenger system has a higher chance of reflecting the "inclination-space" (something like the derivative or vector field) of the disconnected cognition's movie; with mainly the differences from homeostasis given priority, it has a lower probability of reflecting the conditions of the normal *body* which hosts the movie.

- The body—knowing mainly basic physical interactions—is more likely to produce a chain of would-have-been physical interactions. No special symbolism here—just mundane daily objects and people as exchange recipients.

- We note that only one system, the cognition, has a "memory" in the way that we are familiar with.

- When the cognition is reconnected to the body at the end of the disabling, the current state of the body comes back online. The whole point of the brain is to monitor and regulate the body, so we shouldn't be surprised if the cognition forgets all of its fancy visualizations in favor of the body's distributional reality. The cognitive memory would receive 99%+ of the data it's accustomed to again from the actual state of the body—effectively overwriting any astral journey. But does this mean that the astral journey would be "forgotten?"

- Meanwhile, the messenger's interface would *become* the reconnection. As for the flow of signals all across the body throughout the whole process, half of this signaling will have been involved in the body's story, the other half in the cognition's story. If the traveler forgot either of these, they would almost surely forget the messenger/light body's third story.

By the chain of reasoning above, we probably have coherable "light travels" more often than we think, astral / OOBs more often than light travels, dreams more often than OOBs, and lucid visualizations more often than dreams. Our body, cognition, and messenger systems are always online, but not always disconnected enough for us to perceive them as coherently separate. When they're all communicating, we perceive the same reality that other observers perceive. When we allow the cognition to visualize independent of this normative reality, we enter the lucid state. When we dive so fully into the lucid state that the normative reality is mostly ignored (except for minimal functions), we dream. When our dreams ignore most of our normal physical body collection and engage only the perceptions we're interested in—no unnecessary signals from arms, legs, or the temperature of the room—we disembody in favor of astral travel. When we ignore the worlds of astral travel and pay attention only to the flow of our typical message-carrying frequencies across those worlds, we light-travel...

All that said, however, we have to "save" these experiences to file using the cognition's representations. So after we've done all this, the reconnection process can almost always be expected to write all of these exotic experiences in the form of basic dreams. On the one hand, that might be a letdown. On the other hand, if you're getting 2 or 3 or more dreams at a time back-to-back, and if those dreams are airing apparently different TV shows, you may have all the information you need from each of the astral-cognitive, light-messenger, and real-body dreams after all.

- Part of the reason astral travel may be associated with higher truths is because it deprioritizes the usual maintenance behaviors of the proprioceptive senses in favor of information specifically focused on what we're interested in at the time.

- Light travel may not bring higher truths about the "things" in our world (since, as conceived here, it doesn't engage "things"). It may, however, connect us MUCH more strongly to the frequencies that complement us: our energetic trajectories. The truth would lie in its revelation of the phenomena we're most connected to, but my guess is that without the reconnection of the body and the cognition we wouldn't really be able to translate this into anything actionable in the physical world within our waking reach. My flow may resemble that of Antares, but I won't be going there any time soon.

As for "forgetting" our astral travels, I don't think we do. This is for two reasons. 1) Our whole sphere—the energetic trail of where we've been—does keep a record (a chain of wave functions) of focused experiences beyond our physical bodies; the people who tell our story are more likely to tell of the cognition's journeys than the body's journeys—suggesting that the cognitive subjects remain despite our own disattention to them in resuming our daily physical affairs. This isn't to say that *we* store them, just that they are stored *somewhere* for later recapitulation (probably in the larger composite-wave messaging system of our kindred "sphere" [domain of non near-zero function weighting]). 2) Our waking biases, inspirations, and affinities continue to influence our behaviors, suggesting that although we may add all kinds of physical world symbols on top of our cognitive and messaging journeys, the underlying "~~astral~~" cognitive-object (function set) and "~~light~~" chemoelectric-flow messaging chain (function derivative set) is still there. Dressed up? Yes, in the form of new practical world symbols and expectations. Forgotten? No. The reconnected "body-dream" would act more as the coordinate space over which the function and function derivatives are mapped.

You slept and experienced a messaging cycle that combined the firing and flow of certain neurotransmitters and other energy carriers into a particular waveform—like a song. [This] much GABA plus [this] much serotonin in [these] ratios at [this] rate in [this] region of the field produces [that] composite signal. You "forgot" about it when you pasted dream symbols onto it, and "forgot" about the dream symbols when you pasted the waking state of the body back onto *them*. Yet here you are talking to this person, and it feels like déjà vu. (A hypothesis:) That's because the composite signal of chemical the messengers throughout your body [which is produced by this interaction] strongly mirrors another composite signal you have long covered up in physical references. But you only have so many body systems and so many different kinds of messengers. In one sense, your whole life can be thought of as a constant rearrangement of the flows of NMDA, dopamine, acetylcholine, estrogen,... in the ratios and systems they describe. Your hormonal-emotional-messaging playlist is large, but it's not infinite. You *will* have weighted biases. You *will* have a coherent personality, you can stack these rearrangements in a way that is apparently unbounded to you, but at that point you would be nesting countables (see *Laurentia*: Chapter 36). The reason we can have things like premonitory dreams, déjà vu, and clairvoyance is because our bodies can train themselves to re-assemble physical events from the messaging cycles it always has access to, and the cycles of the other actors it exchanges with (since we can all be exploded into our elemental frequencies. Our affinities dictate where we travel and what we can read. Out of Body is the case of the framework for such being separated from the frame, and perhaps even being more extensively separated from the interface. With that in mind we can study **OOB** as a type of "**pseudophysical perception optimally independent of the physical body**." **Light travel** will be studied as "**simulated perception of biological messaging patterns independent of embodied perception**."⚒

By the above theory, the number one challenge of OOBs lies not in having them, but in remembering them *without* imposing cognitive packages on top of them upon waking reconnection of your motor systems. That is, you may already have them often, but need to work on not rewriting them to look like regular dreams. This will be harder if you can't remember your dreams, so let's start there.

Dream recall

To assist your dream recall, we will begin by letting your subconscious out of jail.

☞ Question 54.8.1 (Imagining in tongues): Set your timer for 10 minutes. Having a timer for this exercise will be absolutely <u>imperative</u> for people who don't trust themselves with what follows. Find a quiet space relatively free of distractions. Start your timer. Over the next 10 minutes, you are allowed to think or envision anything that comes to mind. You might even say it. Do this until the 10 minutes are over. Even if nothing happens, stay there until the 10 minutes ends. You're not focusing on anything in particular, just doing your time.

Now that the time is up, take a few minutes to tell a story about what you experienced. EVEN IF YOU EXPERIENCED NOTHING AT ALL, TELL A STORY ANYWAY. Do this for 5 minutes or until you're until you feel drained of information to put into this story. If you find yourself making things up, the story is over. Don't make things up, just start with the words "I dreamt..." and keep describing on the fly. Pull from things that happened in the 10 minutes, but don't make up things which it doesn't feel like you actually perceived. If you spoke gibberish, tell a story. If you saw nothing, tell a story. It you saw a single image the whole time, tell a story. Write down the general idea of your story (or the whole story) below.

I dreamt...

_____
_____
_____
_____
_____
_____
_____
_____
_____
_____
_____
_____

I had an actual dream when I did this activity, and recorded it as I do all the others. In that process, I recalled the major difference between regular dreaming and lucid dreaming—a distinction with practical implications for OOB.

Controlling your dreams

In lucid dreaming you remain aware of your physical body, environment, or volitional control over events in the dream. In regular dreaming you do not. Lucid dreaming is an exercise in imagination. Regular dreaming is a movie played by your firing patterns. If you can control your dreams, they are probably lucid—less of the subconscious, and more of the conscious will imposed upon the subconscious. Naturally, you will tend to receive a less accurate reflection of your cognition's version of things this way, because your body's historical expectations are still able to override this. The advantage of lucid dreaming lies in its ability to aid us strongly in training visualization. The disadvantage is that the more you depend on it for play calling in the middle of your subconscious work, the less you'll be able to access those experiences for which your conscious has no representation. Where astral travel is concerned, maintaining lucidity is like walking circles in your own back yard. You may see alien worlds, but you will be using your own consciously trained wants (rather than the natural flow of your firing) to script them.

The one thing you do seem to be able to control without disturbing the dream is your *attention* to the different components of the dream. This may not seem like much, but if you think about what dreams are (symbol-infused firing patterns), your attention is to a dream what your action is to waking. In waking you would run from that monster. In a dream you would shift your attention to its "monsterness." How would that help, you say? This is actually how I handle the very rare monster or demon that appears in my dream. The "monster" is a thing. Fear is a pervasive state. If in waking you can train yourself to develop a concept of monsters as being, for the most part, human representations of their own fears instead of just plain animals like yourself, your ability to pay attention to the thing and not the fear can shift the course of a dream. And an OOB.

There is another way of controlling the flow of your dreams, and that is by training their symbols in waking. On the one hand you want your subconscious to reveal its secrets. On the other hand, some of those secrets can be threatening or uncomfortable. The best training against symbols you don't like in a dream is training a waking attitude for handling the threat they represent. To help you resist the urge to put your conscious on top of a subconscious dream or OOB, let's develop a waking attitude for a few threatening situations.

☞ Question 54.8.2 (What would the waking me do?): **Suppose you're awake, and something that only happens normally in a dream has now occurred in real life. What would you do to resolve the problem FULLY? Can you determine what these situations might represent to you?**

I've given only a couple of examples here to get you started, but dreams are highly subjective. Fill out this table as best you can.

	Situation	Your final solution	What does this represent to you
Examples	A monster is coming after you	Not believable. I ask how the hell this monster got made, observe it, then—if it's threatening to others or not otherwise usable for science—I join with the proper authorities to put it down.	a rowdy issue someone else has created which has landed on my plate, and which I have interesting options for dealing with.
	You're arguing with someone close to you	Depending on who it is, I look for what they mean to me in real life and try to avoid the overt fight. If we do actually disagree, I prepare to distance myself beforehand.	diverging paths with the represented person… who may not be the person playing them in the dream.
	A monster is coming after you		
	You're arguing with someone close to you		
	You're falling		
	A problem you're addressing is multiplying		
	You can't turn on a light switch		
	You can't run fast enough		
List your own			
1.			
2.			
3.			

At this point we've taken ownership of our conflicts and major rifts. We've found our tribes and investigated the spirits we gravitate towards. We've also learned our long term Role. Whether we're projecting or dreaming, we likely have more command of the concepts we regularly interact with than we would have otherwise had if we had not explored these deeper levels of self-representation. The concepts we interact with will often have reliable symbols associated with them in our dreams. Let us take a moment to review some of those symbols.

☞ Question 54.8.3 (Stars of the show): **Use the table below to list some of the most frequent characters, places, or other concepts that show up in your dreams. Next to each item, note what you think it represents. List at least 25 of such guests, with the more frequent appearances closer to the top. If you can't complete this question with its interpretations, then you might consider redoing question 54.8.1 several times until you can. Nothing is required of course, but we need for your brain to get used to having and remembering its own symbolic language. If your dictionary of symbols is too small, how sharply you represent your experiences will be limited that much more. Remember, we're treating astral travel as a type of disembodied dreaming. Although you can certainly do it without becoming comfortable with your dreams, our ordered approach for understanding OOB suggests that your skill in the former will help you build a solid foundation for consistently experiencing the latter.**

The 25 most frequent symbols in my dreams (and my guess at their interpretations) are:

Chapter 54: The Foresight

My list looked like this:

The 25 most frequent symbols in my dreams (and my guess at their interpretations) are:		
1. Cousin M. (my 1:1 charming exchanges / popularity)	2. Brother Kwh (my 1:1 charisma / actual interaction with girlfriends / friendships)	3. Brother Kvt (my reputation)
4. Dad (my career purpose/profession)	5. My mother (upbringing for girlfriends / affiliative relationships / romances)	6. A Bright Red / Yellow room (security, a place of friends)
7. My Cousin T. (the daily work life)	8. An argument (something not provided by the symbol I'm arguing with)	9. Buildings (something I must learn or write in order for a relationship to form)
10. My truck (my ideas / philos. writings)	11. A generic mall (a large social space)	12. The little mulatto (the B. slot—any person who occupies the same sphere role as B.)
13. Being naked (having the public see the full me)	14. The "Sand Trap Building" (a specific mall where I have a task to perform)	15. Break-in/Heist (working on something which is ultimately meant for a purpose other than the one commonly assumed)
16. A Blue glass room (place where we heal others [like the Sand Trap Bldg.])	17. Groups of women (the creative potential that exists between me and groups of people I know, male or female)	18. Combat (mastering something)
19. My cat Snow (my Navi/"security camera")	20. Hiding (trying to keep something low key)	21. Houses under construction (another person's goal)
22. MB, SGL, CC, EC, ALG: (themselves)	23. Dogs (loyalties)	24. Wizardry (primary theoretical projects)
25. A performance (someone's public enterprise, business, or broadcast)	26. Kingpin and characters like him (capitalism)	27. Sports games (groups of personal-talent expressers, often at work)

An important note about dream symbols

It's easy to think of the things in your dreams as representing those things. But if you think about it, what sense is there in that cognitively? You don't even know how they actually work on the inside. Yes there will be times when the people or concepts that appear in your dreams actually stand for themselves, but because you're not privy to the inner workings of that which is not you, your interactions with these will tend to be based on yours and their surface responses to each other.

Many times, your dream symbols don't represent themselves, but instead represent the things *you typically do* to interact with what they are. For example, for as long as I've been alive, my cousin Michael has been the most frequent character in my dreams after myself, though I don't interact with him as much now that we're older. Yet I've always thought of my cousin as one of the coolest, most charismatic people in the world. When I interact with him in real life, I'm more aware of what popularity is supposed to look like. So Michael in my dreams represents those exchanges where I'm charming or popular. It would be too much work for my brain to piece actual-Michael's life from information I don't have. That's how symbols work. You don't need to struggle to interpret your dream symbols. It's *your* subconscious. Just interpret them according to your interaction. (I think of Kingpin as a greedy, snorting, ass. But he's clean and cool in his white suit; you could be a lot worse as far as institutional bosses go. My view of capitalism is *exactly* like that. Interpret your symbols based on your response, not on the symbol itself.)

Now that you have some symbols, you might find your dreams more interesting to keep track of. We're helping your brain make some shelf space for the content of your dreams so that we won't just say something like "I just can't remember my dreams, but whatever." If we're planning to get good at astral travel, it's not whatever. We'll need a way to remember what we saw and describe it with some kind of care. If we can't describe basic dream symbols or don't care to remember the nuances, our subconscious will know that overwriting our journeys is okay. We don't want that to be okay. We want to remember what our subconscious was trying to tell us.

Why do *you* dream?

As we learn astral travel, we'll need a reason to stay interested in its development even when it seems we're not getting anywhere. I lost interest in astral travel the first time I encountered it because I wasn't interested in flying through space for no reason. Yet I **love** my dream life, 1) because the dreams are super interesting elaborations upon the normal world, 2) because they show me the future, 3) because I get to see what my subconscious really thinks of all the fluff in my waking life and 4) some of my strongest, most fulfilling relationships with friends and intimates play out there. Accordingly, even when I don't dream, it behooves me to go to sleep with a clear head. It would be such a waste to dedicate that time to dragging daytime worries around once again.

☞ Question 54.8.4 (Dream reasons): **Why do you like dreaming? What makes you want to dream?**

_____
_____
_____
_____

I hope you didn't say "I don't like dreaming." If you did, your astral travel will be a partial extension of this. Nevertheless, you might just need a friendlier set of symbols—things worth seeing in dreams. In any case, astral travel and OOB can further extend your dream life.

Where dreams allow your subconscious to use conscious symbols for making sense of your life, astral travel allows you a much clearer look at what your belief patterns, outlook, Role, and kindred look like. What would you do if you could walk through walls, fly to any scenario, turn a belief into an animal or a situation into a landscape? If you could finally see the kinds of entities that *actually* intersect with your path in this life… Astral travel allows this.

> If you're dreaming of an open field, your astral travel renders brilliant the shimmering warmth of the grass. You don't have a body, so you can sail just above the grass for a closer look at the waves of heat radiating from its blades. The pearl green ribbons cascade unusually upwards like fingers strumming the sky, so you turn upside down in order to make more sense of the view. Clearly this was the underside of an unusual bird's coat—the heat as its breath, the gleam as a ruffle shakes you throughout. And then you wake up. Had this just been dabbling, it may have had no real point other than visual awe. But now you have symbols. The bird and the grass are what your cognition preferred while the body was silent. Accordingly you learn that—at your core—you conceive of the natural environment as a living titan with the ability to soar.

Your travels reveal your frameworks, showing you the language of your own attention. Where you go and on which levels you go there show you what you care about as a fundamental belief, and brings you closer to the basic principles underlying your disembodied thinking. Because I prefer practical results from the things I do, the above description was mainly to convince myself that astral travel wasn't just another form of HDTV. I'll need to know why it's worth putting in all this work to view alien lands. The short answer is, astral travel is to your Role what dreams are to your daily life. Having them may not be of interest for some people. Interpreting them or connecting through them might be.

☞ Question 54.8.5 (OOB reasons): Assume you are already good at astral and/or light travel, and can visit other dimensions at will. What do you like about this? What do you gain after having come back?

	Example
	I learn what certain connections really want from me.

***A VERY INTERESTING NOTE: After finishing my writing for the day at the above section, I had a fascinating experience which surely has implications for how we process astral travel. The result was a more detailed elaboration of the theory we've assembled thus far. Let me tell you a story.

> A Story of Three Selves
>
> Well over 15 years ago while I was still in college I had a dream called "Trinity Shadow" where I walked across a campus with three shadows. Over the course of the next 15 years I learned that almost all of my waking life achievements tended to come in threes. An advancement in work, a new book, and a change in a relationship for example. On days when I learned something, I would learn a theory, learn how that theory helped resolve a personal puzzle, and gain further insight into my path.
>
> Last night, as often happens, I had a 3-section dream called "[Nintendernetarchitect-Coffee-]TCX"—the first part of which (Nintendernet) was about being deployed to a hut in Australia and attempting to write a file there from 0 to F0 for conducting an investigation with a certain colleague. The last part (TCX) featured me watching a dynamic between two women which I assume to be colleagues in waking life (SGL and ALG above). I initially forgot about the section "Coffee," which featured me trying to properly place a tube in a Keurig® and spraying water everywhere. Even now, I don't know whether "Coffee" was the second or the first section of the entire dream.
>
> I've had three-part dreams for well over a decade and already knew them to be a regular occurrence. But this was different. When I woke up and recorded the dream, my commentary afterwards mentioned how "Nintendernet" was related to a certain project I'm currently considering with a colleague, but how I was not at all thrilled about the circumstances surrounding that project (unrelated to her); that is, it showed my opinion. I also realized that TCX was about the real life dynamic between two people I work with, one of whom was likely the same woman (who did not appear, but was only talked to on the phone) in Nintendernet. As I recorded, I became more and more passionate about what additional conditions I would need in order for this project to take place, and how they would entail certain kinds of morale support

that did not seem to be in the queue. It turns out that my emotional and morale needs (associated with water) had everything to do with the third dream section Coffee, its spraying of water everywhere, and the challenges that came with it. Perhaps you can see where this is going.

I noted earlier that flying around just for fun wasn't something some people are into. For experts like Robert Bruce (whom I'm a big fan of), it's not just "flying around." This is their trade and their Role. But some people as we've seen would actually be derailed from their Role if they developed certain senses any farther, such that if they were better at astral travel, for example, they might stray off into a talent field not optimally their own. I can "reputation-project" at a B level, but my astral travel has always been an F. Or so it seems.

Remember what we said about the travels not being forgotten, just buried in the cognitive memory itself? It turns out that you may have flown around to those worlds after all, but when the astral-cognitive body reconnects with the gross biological signaling family, it may—if you've paid enough attention to your dreams for a long enough time—simply be remembered as a related, but separate dream or dream section. Why? Because, like the rest of your biology, your brain *is* part of the body. We may temporarily turn off motor (body-brain) feedback, but motor signaling is still signaling just like the activity going on in the brain. Relatedly, emotional messaging is still signaling just like the activity going on in the brain. We can expect then, that when these functions reconnect at the end of the dream period, it's not as though the brain has to do some fancy work in order to transform "light body" into cognitive history (memory). It just has to store the normal signal trail from the brain-body emotional-messaging network. The astral body can be theorized to work the same way; whatever disembodied experience you may have had, your cognition may want to assign more earthly symbols to it. Thus I concluded that Nintendernet originated as my basic-level dream—cognitive opinion as a world. Stored in symbols, this registered as dream type "Normal Primary." (See Table 54-2.) TCX was my disconnected body response (to the two real-life people) reconnected and stored in dream symbols ("Normal Secondary"). Coffee—whose place in the sequence is still ambiguous—was my light travel (emotional messengers' frequency flow between brain and body) but "file saved" in familiar dream symbols ("Messenger I").

So there it was: astral, real, and messenger patterns recoded in their plain, cognitively symbolized forms.

The TCX trio was funny in that I had to interpret one dream in order to react to all three, whereupon another dream actually predicted my opinion. A third dream (Coffee) ended up predicting my reaction to itself plus the other two. This is consistent with the idea that light travel is more far reaching, astral travel is attention centered, and the state of the stuck body produces what we know as the basic dream that reacts to real life people and their events. Because I was not happy with the implication of the dream, I truly told the recorder that I was sending this dream proposal back for revision, as I wanted a different outcome. But was it too late to control the dream after it ended? Actually, no. It turns out that the best time to control a dream or shift your attention in it is AFTER the dream ends. Weird, I know. Here's why.

Ultimately, dreams do three things: 1) consolidate cognitive memory, 2) process ~~emotional~~ general metabolic preoccupation, and 3) reflect the artifacts of body state. For me these were Nintendernet, Coffee, and TCX respectively. Whatever the form of the original experiences were, they all ended up being saved as (cognitive) dream symbols. Obviously it's harder to remember a disembodied journey when your body is back online, so the astral and light memories can't usually be expected to be "pure" when you recall them. But as this trio illustrates, cognitive opinion and hormonal reactions to things don't tend to change overnight. Your take on these will probably be the same tomorrow as it is today, and one of the trio (if you have trios) may even predict what you will think about itself. This isn't magic. It's how anticipatory hormone flow and the cognitive subconscious work. They precede the knowledge of the overt biology. If you want to control the outcome of a dream then, the best time to do it is not while the dream itself is predicting that you will want to control it, but in waking after the dream is over, where you get to make new decisions in light of the *entire* trio of memories. Shifting attention during the dream is still possible, but this seems like one system—perhaps cognitive—imposing on another system's (perhaps body's) memory writing. The integrity of the three stories to their respective (quasi-independent) systems will not be as strong, but their basic outcome will be written.

I've said this in another book, but a great time to change the outcome of a dream is *after* it finishes, through a waking change in action. The next dream may seem "late" to you, but your opinions and emotions don't really understand lateness the way your body does. Let the dream finish. It will be fine.

One of my primary ways of changing my life trajectory, by the way, is via the games I choose to play. I've learned over years of observation that, if I want to change my situation, I should download a new game whose theme points in that direction. Hence the name Nintendernetarchitect. This will likely be different from how you optimally control your trajectory, but we'll discuss this kind of abstract situational control in the section on telepathy.

 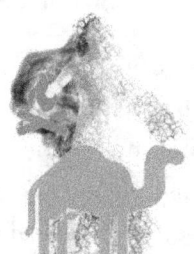 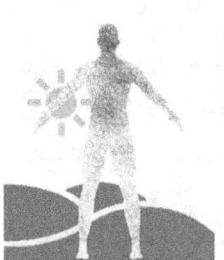  

Cognitive attention / disconnected body dreams (normal dreams; primary): without reliably correlated body feedback, dreams rooted in cognition alone lend themselves to abstract representations; these are "topic preoccupation" dreams that occur separately from less connected body state	**Cognitive save and symbolization of body + flow dreams (normal dreams; back-to-back / secondary)** as cognition's attempt to represent [body + (maybe) flow – (significant) cognitive awareness]; these often show your opinion of the body+flow information, and are semi-real; *hypothesis*: in these the objects *are* the attention; but because cognition is the interpreter, it inserts meaning upon what the body and messaging brought back; these are the "reconnec*tion* dreams"—astral dreams recoded in cognitive terms.	**Cognitive save and symbolization of flow dreams (normal dreams; tertiary)** as cognition's attempt to represent [cognition + body – (significant) flow perception; *hypothesis*: the behaviors *are* the flow; I've found these tend to be dreams about basic deeds and interactions with people you probably recognize (or just you), often currently in your life and within your ability to interact with; they often show your feelings about events; these are "reconnec*ting* dreams" — messenger-light dreams recoded in cognitive terms	**Body state dreams (cognitive save and symbolization of body dreams):** Based in what the body knows how to experience; I've found that dreams rooted mainly in the body state tend to involve health warnings, images of sleeping conditions, and a sense of energy / tingling around the relevant regions. Since we tend to need messaging in order to inform our brain of the body's state, these dreams are rarer, and more likely to show up as the normal (primary) kind. You get them when the body *is* translated into the main topic.	**Astral dream / OOB (Light travel with object awareness)** as cognition's attempt to represent attention + flow – (significant) body boundary; *hypothesis*: the symbols summarize the body's chemical flows and experiential framing; these dreams are most likely to feature non-real world events and symbols	**Messenger dreams (Light travel with abstraction awareness):** Signal flow densities map where hormones, nervous, and other organ system products are going; I've found that dreams rooted in this alone tend to load voices and feelings to match the attention; *hypothesis*: connecting abstract concepts to summarize these gives us "light travel;" these may be the pure form of what happens between normal primary and untranslated body state dreams

Dream Type	Topic	Representation	Behavior	Body	Astral	Messenger
Topic	Whatever issue is currently preoccupying the dreamer	How the body is handling / reacting (conceptually) to the Topic	How the body realistically imagines itself behaving given the Topic	What the body is actually currently experiencing during the dream period	How the cognition understands the body's (incl. its own) various messenger states	How your messenger system states can be represented as abtract worlds in themselves
Dream Owner	Cognition	Messenger+Body (given Cognition)	Body (given Cognition)	Body (given Messenger)	Messenger+Cognition (given Body)	Messenger
Dream Language	Cognitive→ (rewritten as / has its objects determined by) Cognitive	Messenger+Body→ Cognitive	Messenger+Body→ Body doing Messenger (in given background Cognitive Topic)	Messenger+Body→ Cognitive+Body	Messenger+Cognition ← (loads / determines objects from) Cognitive	Messenger ← Cognitive - Body
Feels Like	Basic dreams with more realistically behaving symbols, but a wider selection of symbols than Representation dreams; more likely to be set in real worlds with fictitious characters	Basic dreams with more symbols which behave contrary to reality, but a narrower selection of symbols than Topic dreams; more likely to be set in fictitious worlds with characters real in those worlds	Doing regular things or living regular life, unbothered by the other dreams around it	Definite body startle or feeling / strong sense of emotion upon waking; often a sense of change in / display of some aspect of the body, often (but not always) negative, sometimes a concern that a body-related issue should be addressed	OOB (Out of body experience) / Sleep Paralysis	Talking to higher systems; "high resolution" / "more real than real" encounters

Table 54-2: Some speculation regarding the 3 systems behind dreams. Dream owners correspond to the system most responsible for a dream's content. Hypotheses: 1) We always employ the cognitive in storing any experience; 2) The lower your messenger system awareness, the more difficult it is to regularly have dreams stemming from the gray-boxed combinations

Astral travel as we expect it

If you do wish to experience other dimensions in the disembodied sense then, as always, I highly recommend Robert Bruce's *Astral Dynamics*. His techniques may be summarized as helping you build a body map for your disembodied projection as well as a kind of cognitive-like awareness for your disconnected body. Ultimately you want your body memory—the one which supersedes all others—to develop responses to things like flying, star-skimming, creature encounter, and so on. I won't go over his methods here, but I will present a practice regimen for helping you experience what you're looking for.

Psychologically speaking, traditional astral travel—the disembodied flight kind—might be said to consist of a body-like awareness navigating an imagination-like space. We can think of chores and angels as concepts, but have we trained a biological response to such things? That is, if the astral world consists of all the constructs we know how to "see" arranged in the thematic worlds that unify them, does our body know how to react to an alien, an idea in object from, or a galaxy when it encounters it? Have we trained the feeling of flying, falling, or staring at a unicorn? If we don't have any sense at all of what it's like to walk through walls, chances are our dreams and visualizations won't feature this very often.

I've found that the best way to train the astral sense is to impose a sense of directed encounter on myself when I'm dead tired. When I'm so deliriously tired that my body doesn't want to move any more, I exaggerate the sense of leaning, falling and floating, and couple this with certain experiences that I'm leaning, falling, or floating into. In order to better train the sense of navigation, the direction I move towards is kept consistent with directions I'm used to following:

- Left to right mirrors the English reading direction,
    - Left is what you've thought of (preceding conditions)
    - Right is what you haven't thought of (possibilities)

  I feel a push or pull on either side, and depending on whether I'm tilting, primarily at the top, bottom, or whole side of my body when navigating this way.

- Ahead of and behind me mirrors the approach direction
    - Ahead is something like the future
    - Behind is something like the past

  I feel a push or pull at my chest and back, along with a zoom in or zoom out at my eye and over the shoulder sense when navigating this way.

- Upwards and downwards mirrors the usual scope of vision
    - Upwards sees more things at once in less detail
    - Downwards sees fewer things but in greater detail

  I feel an intensity in my feet pushing up on the rest of my body when flying upwards, and my whole body stretching with a push on the part of me diving first when I descend.

- Moving through walls, I feel a slamming zoom in my eyes followed by a brand new image when moving forward, and a slamming over the shoulder presence followed by a zoom out in my eyes when moving backwards.

Perhaps you can see how training these sensations can help you simulate the feeling of phantom flight.

During astral travel, you could explore this world, or you could explore other worlds. In order to lend a kind of order to the space of worlds, I simulate regular flying when I want to move around in a single world, and simulate a kind of blurred time-based turn or lean when I want to practice moving to other worlds. For what-ifs or what-happeneds I tend to turn behind me, for what should-bes or what will-bes I turn in front of me. A blur for time or dimension navigation across worlds. No blur for navigation within a single world.

In my conception of the astral plane, I rely on my body's regular notion of space to generate a map.

- **Horizon lines** in front of and behind me work like staring down a football field. Time and space are the stacking of experience, so the farther away the horizontal line, the more flying, blurring, or experiencing of the terrain I'll need to go through. I call these "state lines" (as in the state of your progression towards the horizon in either direction.
- **Condition (parallel) lines** pointing towards the horizon, but which I'm not on, feel the same way as parallel roads do while driving. There is a sense of the alternatives I'm not seeing. Again, keeping with left to right reading, I naturally consider parallel lines to my left to be alternatives I've already considered. Parallel lines to my right are paths of what-if. I call these "condition lines."
- **Milestones** are what I call the intersection of a state line and a condition line. Across the larger astral plane, each milestone can have a whole self-contained story play out, and I call these **worlds**. Within a world you have dived into, the milestones are just called **events**.
- As in *Laurentia*, every milestone has a **radius of effect** over which it still counts as happening. Around that radius of effect are six **alternate events or worlds** which progress the milestone forwards and backwards along its possibility/parallel/condition line, and outside of these are six more **potential events or worlds** which shift the milestone sideways along its horizon line. This intersection is just the usual snowflake from Figure 45-2, except turned sideways by -90° so that q180 (the interactant direction) is to the north and q270 (the Saturn/structured things that have already been considered) is to the west. The direction you move away from a milestone into another milestone I call a **decision angle**: the combination of what-if, potential, self-, or interactant-orientation that progresses the event you're currently in.
- Milestones and their alternatives are where things are counted as happening. The empty space not at these intersections are where nothing registers as happening, so from the astral perspective, **the cluster of milestones and their alternatives will have a color**, a feel, an appearance, or a sound. The empty space will be black, dark, invisible, immaterial, or unregistered for their lack of energy sent to you.
- To the extent that you believe you can map a milestone the way you map the whole astral plane (in terms of parallels and horizons), the 12-snowflake and its immediate six **alternate worlds will intersect with a square**: a subset of the grid (on the map you believe can be made).
- Lastly, within a world or event there will be **volumes**—collections of energy that could be animals, trees, blocks of knowledge, planetary dimensions, states of health, or anything else which your cognition can structure—including yourself.

My final conception of the astral plane, based on our daily experience of spatial relationships and in line with both the *Astral Dynamics* account and the dimensional model I proposed in *Laurentia*, is shown in Figure 54-1.

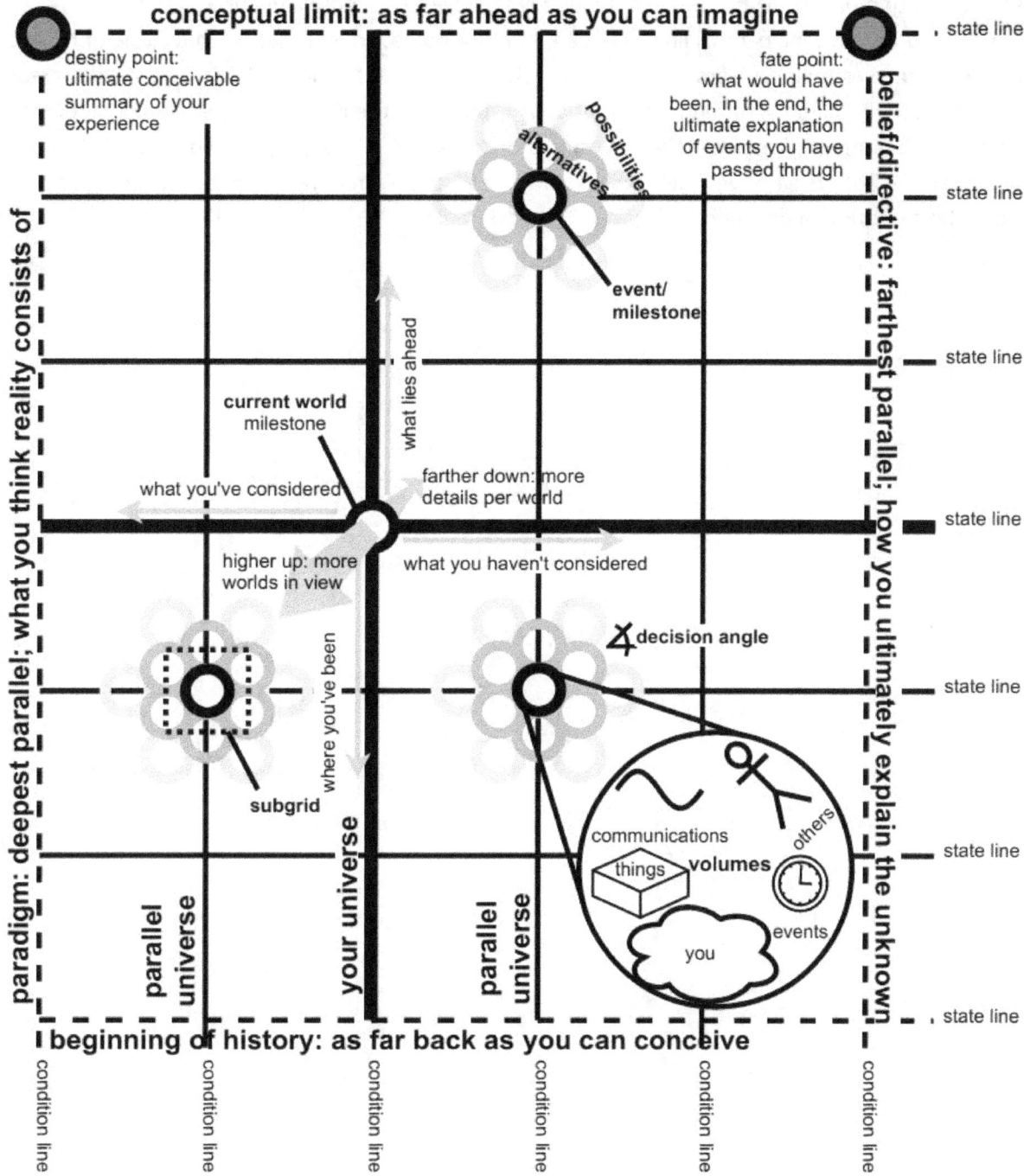

Figure 54-1: A model of alternative state space (a.k.a. the "astral plane")

Clearly Figure 54-1 is not gospel, but in my attempts to understand the structure of the astral plane as Robert Bruce described it, I found the analogies to grid mapping and radii of effect to be fairly clear. I don't actually think of every technical detail of this map during projection practice, but the idea of organizing past versus future and worlds versus events is made easier when I have some spatial explanation for what I'm training my body to feel. As the brain's parietal lobe is more than free to make things up in the absence of full body data, we can—and should—take advantage of existing feelings associated with motor navigation—even the bodily feeling of the known, unknown, and the expected that comes with following parallel lines. We can train our bodies to feel spaces. That's one of the main functions of the vestibular system. A map of the astral plane is less a map of the cosmos and more a map of our own handling of different orientations in space and the different expectations that come with points near and far from us. If we can train our bodies to feel the navigation of such abstractified space, then the body dreams we have which overwrite all others may yet be dreams of that space, making the sensation of disembodied travel that more real.

Chapter 54: The Foresight

☞ **Question 54.8.6 (How to fly):** Once a day for the next 7 days, set aside 10 minutes for constant simulated movement. Set a timer. Use the table below to practice the nine basic sensations shown, then use the rest of the time to simulate the feelings of moving around as you please. Put a ✓ once complete.

Movement type	What experience you start with	Your sight	What feels like it's being pushed	What feels like it's being stretched or pulled	What seems to be panning	What experience you finish with	Day 1	Day 2	Day 3	Day 4	Day 5	Day 6	Day 7
1. flying forward in space (leaning in a little)	your starting location	the distance zooms closer	Your front, especially your chest, slight wind at your legs	your upper back	both sides of your peripheral scroll towards behind you	a location further down the horizon							
2. having the floor drop from under you	a stable position	you quickly survey the surroundings below you	[nothing]	your whole body from below, suddenly	[nothing]	weightlessness							
3. falling	weight-lessness	the surface below zooms closer	the side of you facing the surface below	the side of you away from the surface below	the horizon, upwards	an increasingly fast rise in the scene before you							
4. recovering from a fall by arcing up towards one side (your turning makes this act feel like your choice)	falling	you divert your attention from the surface below to the sky on one side	you, <u>willingly</u> against the air between the surface and yourself	the part of your body that's not pushing	the horizon pans upwards, slowing quickly, then pans downwards	flying diagonally upwards, then basic flying							
5. turning over your shoulder into a different world	the current scene or space of events	you turn over one shoulder with a slight queasy feeling in your chest	a sideways push against the front of your chest	the opposite shoulder	[nothing; as in real life, your vision blurs when this happens]	**the main idea of astral travel:** a new scene or space of events in which different choices were made / different events predominated							
6. visiting a foreign world	events	just observe	[nothing really]	[nothing really]	[only the background of what you yourself pan towards]	events continued							
7. walking through a wall in a particular world	the wall or object	a wall zooms towards you followed by a brief darkness, then a full scene	you, towards the wall, with a noticeable feeling of tension just before (what would have been) impact, then a relief-like drop in tension	[nothing]	a fisheye view of the coming wall, then the new scene doesn't necessarily pan	the view on the other side of the wall or object							
8. blurring upwards, out of one world to see a collection of collection of worlds related to it	the current scene or space of events	the surface below pulls away from you, with a slight queasy feeling in your whole upper body	you, being compressed from below into the fetal position (to simulate light speed), and being pushed relentlessly from above, disorienting	[nothing]	[nothing; blurs don't allow a focused pan]	a grid of colored worlds representing the scene you came from and its alternatives, now made small							
(This one is fun) 9. Following another thing flying with you	focus on the thing	the thing against a blurry, turning, dizzying background	you're pushing your own head in whatever direction helps you follow the moving thing; any parts of your body involved in turning along with it	any parts of your body involved in leaving one position to keep up with the thing	[nothing; in vision we call this "smooth pursuit;" you're not focused enough on the background to process its panning]	still focused on the thing, but dizzy							

The entire sequence in question 54.8.6 can be done in order in under a minute, from flying to falling to exploring. This is shown in Figure 54-2.

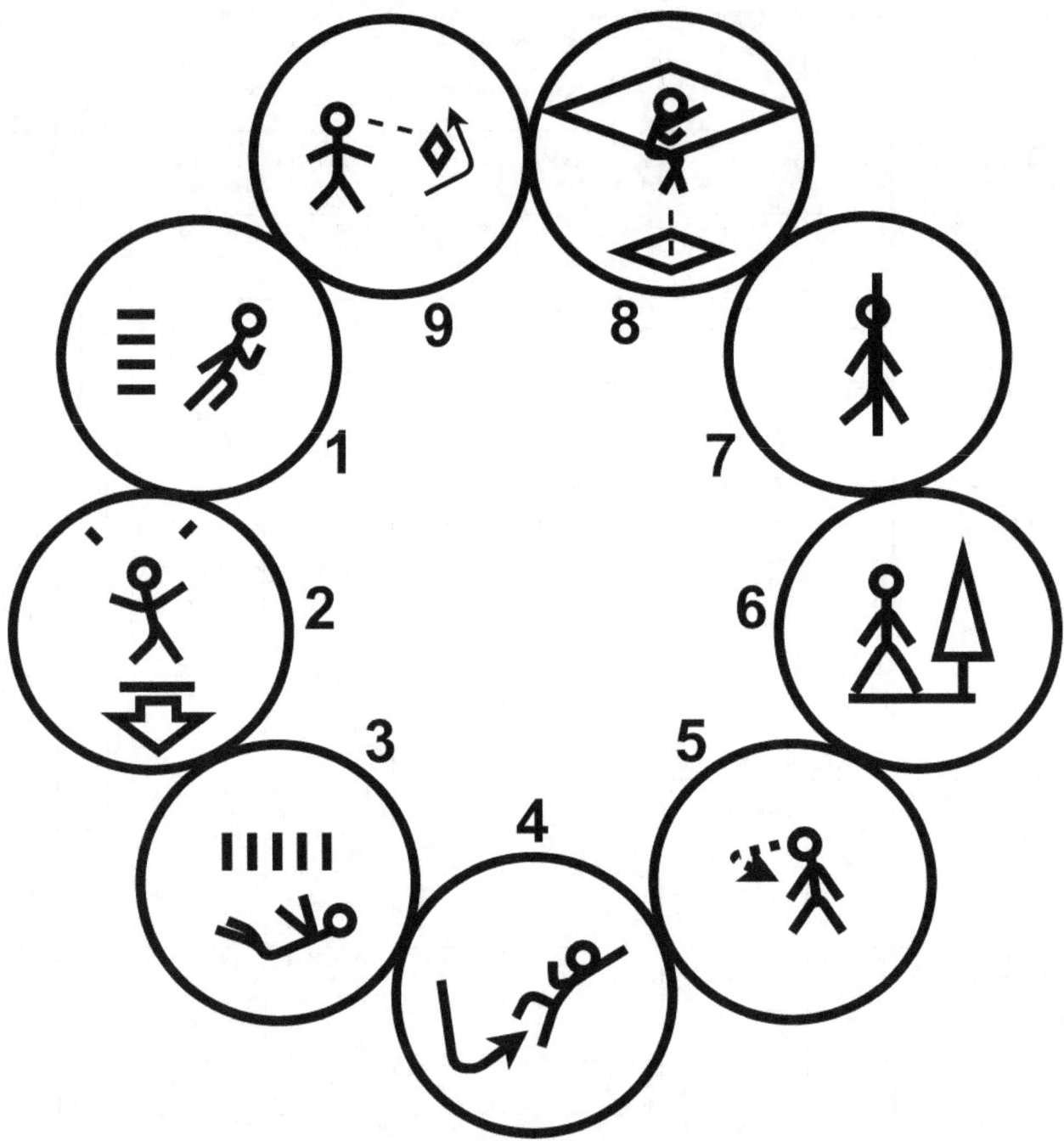

Figure 54-2: Body awareness flight navigation sequence

Exercise 54.8.6 is meant to help you practice feeling all the forces on your body which accompany these moves as you navigate the space of alternative worlds.

For the next few questions, we will be exploring different representations of a particular topic you're interested in, related to your life.

☞ **Question 54.8.7 (Topic space):** What topic related to your life are you most interested in exploring?

_____

☞ **Question 54.8.8 (Forward and backward in your own records):** Imagine you're sitting in a spaceship. Behind you, the chair you rest on is padded with copies of you as far back into history as you can conceive. Ahead of you, the cockpit window displays a kind of football field in space; at each yard line is a movie showing versions of you with more and more history under its belt. This isn't actually a future you, rather it is a *more* detailed biography of your Role. Behind you is a *less* detailed biography. You're interested in exploring this forward-backward line in terms of the topic you picked in 54.8.7—that is, the aspects of your life associated with that topic. You have less experience the further back you lean, and more experience—even the kind of experience that only the life ahead of you knows—the further forward you look. Set a timer for 3 – 7 minutes, and practice blurring back and forth along this "record line" (your current universe; the condition line which you happen to be on right now). When you blur backwards, feel the disorientation, then imagine yourself back in that state where you had far less experience with your chosen topic. When you blur forward, experience the feeling in question 54.8.6:1 (flying forward), then imagine yourself much more familiar with the topic. Blur back and forth, back and forth—taking some time to roam around the two different worlds each time you arrive back in.

Describe what you experience below.

_____
_____
_____
_____
_____
_____
_____
_____

That was fun, but...

The dimensions we've explored (such as [emission x_a versus vacuum z_b], [distance r_b versus system energy β] and [q-magnitude z_a versus mass] in Figure 54-1) aren't actually presented linearly in real life. Clearly we pan in circles and slides, making it nonsensical to think of such pairs as being oriented in this way. In case you were wondering how we represent such dimensions, we do so by feeling *inwardly* and *outwardly* instead.

- Distance r_b goes outward from your sides (that is, distally).
- System <u>energy</u> β goes <u>inwardly</u> from your sides.

Each of these assume you are operating at a fixed energy level (gravitationally or attention-based, for example). Since you're observing things at the same-ish potential accessibility level, these resemble 1-D longitudinal wave behavior.

- Emission x_a comes towards to your attention.
- Vacuum z_b travels away from your attention.

These are framework changes which reset what distances and energies scale to. Thus they resemble 2-D or transverse-introverse spaces.

- Mass pushes towards the big object doing the collecting things on your level (typically what we consider downwards, "mashing" as it were).
- Q-Magnitude resists the pull, and very often feels like leaving much of what is being collected on the level you're comparing it to. (In OOB, the collection is your body mass.)

Each of the up-down energies assume you are changing your energy level—whether or not up or down describes the actual direction. Stacking 1-D worlds into topological sheets, these resemble 3-D wave/surface behavior. (The transforming scales of distance as you move away from old levels automatically introduces a second forward-backward style dimension as you move in fish-eye with respect to the pulling world.

Does the above make sense? Can you imagine the feeling of being pushed in on from all sideways dimensions? Doesn't it feel like collecting energy (β)? Doesn't falling make you more aware of your own mass against gravity?

☞ Question 54.8.9 (~~West and east~~ Inward and outward along the world's timeline): Set your timer for 3 – 7 minutes. Imagine you're sitting in a spaceship. A sense of pressure on your whole body pushes in on you. An awareness of the rest of the ship's interior draws your attention outwards. Recall your 54.8.7 topic. Attending to the space farther and farther beyond the cockpit, your sense of having collected a progressively wider range of happenings related to that topic increases your experience. This is the flow of time with respect to that topic. From here, you feel the information from your 54.8.7 start to decrease. Your attention draws back into the cockpit as you move from what you just foresaw about the topic -> to only what you know right now -> to any assumptions that may not even be correct to begin with. You remember what your life was like before you knew about the topic. On the other hand, you don't know what lies in the empty sky beyond the cockpit, but you *can* perceive something about your topic when you pay attention to what's out there. Practice blurring inwards and outwards between the early stages of your connection to the topic, and the future stages. Feel as though your 54.8.7-related attention is being stretched from the sides then pushed, stretched then pushed again. Also, because the beyond is unknown, you'll need to let your subconscious populate any events you collect from out there; don't be surprised if you see some brand new things in these worlds. Blur inwardly and outwardly. While you're collecting world-versions, take some time to explore them. See if you can gain any insight from how they are structured.

Describe what you experience below.
___
___
___
___
___
___
___
___

> *If you want some advanced practice, try introducing "decision angles." In the same way that we didn't actually move left or right, decision angles won't twist like this either. Instead, consider these to be more like the "interests" you prioritize for exploring any worlds. The Realm of Show? The Realm of The Call? The Realm of [Your Relationship with That Certain Person]? See what kinds of alternative scenarios you can find.
>
> Note that decision angles applied to actual [emission x_a versus vacuum z_b] (more like 54.8.9, not the gimmicky version in 54.8.8) are just the basic visuospatial attention/ignoring we all know and love.
>
> And now for some more non-gimmicky practice...

Let's explore changing energy levels. We shouldn't expect the mass-magnitude astral direction to really be "up-down." To make the projection along this axis-set easier, we'll consider higher worlds to be those where your 54.8.7 topic affects more people and things; lower worlds will be where your topic concerns fewer—but much more specific—interests.

☞ Question 54.8.10: (Higher and lower in world detail): Set your timer for 3 – 7 minutes. Imagine you start off in your spaceship thinking about your 54.8.7 topics, but decide to temporarily forget about how your body feels. If your topic was stressful, don't worry. You'll only be doing this for a couple of seconds at a time. From this position of ignoring your body, you observe more and more collections of multi-world options for prioritizing your next move. Moving even farther beyond even these options, you see even *more* collections of worlds for how everyone/everything *involved* with your 54.8.7 might proceed. Because you're higher up, the little dynamics that normally describe your chosen topic are harder to see, so it's quieter up here, calmer, lit by more events from below. While you're up here, you see a very broad and fuzzy mention of what your chosen topic might have had to do with your Role, but that matters a lot less to anyone. Then you dive back into your own body interests. The further in you go, the more clearly one of the specific concerns related to your topic comes into view. You dive deep into the topic—all the way into the essence of the components that make it up. Dive even further; not every side of you cares about this topic. Zoom only into the side of you that cares. Your Confidence? Your Monologue? Which of your specific "interest particles" are really being pulled towards your 54.8.7? On this very focused level, whatever side of you is most interested in the topic is a side that dominates what you feel. Practice blurring broad-to-focused for a few minutes, making sure that you explore the wide view and the deep view as different worlds entirely. Feel them differently.

Describe what you experience below.
_____
_____
_____
_____
_____
_____
_____
_____

☞ Question 54.8.11 (Parallel universes): **Set your timer for 3 – 7 minutes.** At some point you may want to know what it would have been like had you made different choices with your topic (along an inward history line marker, earlier in time) or if you were able to predict the flow of your history starting at a future date (an outward circumference line). To access a parallel to the past, you'll need to push into your history, forgetting or ignoring much of what you've learned since then. To access a parallel to the future, you'll need to attend beyond your current experience, absorbing the most natural collection of assumptions between now and then. This won't be a new decision point, but rather an "expected future state" from which you may consider things differently. From either of these places, use everything you've learned above to choose a new decision angle. That is, set a *choose a different side of your own interests as the main reason for making the next choice*. One more step: Now, given this choice, "remap" the current kinds of attention you'll pay to things in your sphere <u>right now</u>. Explore this parallel space of universes from where you've landed. And remember, unlike simple inwards-outwards travel in time, "paralleling" requires three steps: 1) changing your reference point, 2) re-prioritizing which interests you want to be your main reason for next steps, then 3) remapping your current attention.

I'll add that remapping is ***a lot*** easier if you choose only one item in your sphere to pay noticeable attention to when checking for differences between the parallel world and the normal one.

Describe what you experience below.
_____
_____
_____
_____
_____
_____
_____
_____

> I expanded greatly on the above section in the final round of edits to this book. The exercises are powerful if you try them even partly. Yet you may be surprised to find that I myself remain fairly weak in imaginative projection as shown above. Why? Because I'm a big fan of the here and now. Alternative worlds don't really interest me. Remember what we said about different people having different talents. How interested you are in a topic will have a major effect on how willing you are to experiment with it.

Final thoughts on astral projection

As I maintained in *Laurentia*, the "directions" for the different dimensions aren't actual directions. They are representations of which kinds of energies must be perceived as perpendicular or potential to other energies (the way accelerometers calculate it). You need to be a perpendicular distance away from a thing in order to perceive its projected pixels (x_a) and the space it obscures (z_b), the perception of its collection (m) of energies (z_a). The dimensions are *conceptually* perpendicular, not physically so. As you get good at astral travel there will be no spaceship, no east-west or timeline distinctions, no forwards-backwards organization, and so on. This is because you won't be working with just one topic, but countless topics and their overlapping orientations at once. Just as surely as each star above emits energy from a different number of light years away, the space of alternate worlds won't be some uniformly flat grid you can push pieces around. The exercises above, despite us sometimes adhering to an imaginary compass, aren't meant to tell you how the astral plane is *actually* shaped. We have applied a shape to it in order to better organize our own conceptual-to-spatial navigation, our own known-versus-unknown framing, and our own general "file system" for representing the symbols in our subconscious from a disembodied perspective. We didn't actually travel astrally, but we gave our bodies a sense of how to impose flight-type movements on a perceptual experience, so that one day, perhaps amidst sleep paralysis, our disconnected motor story might more easily feel the way the spirits would feel.

Developing Clairsentience

Note: In this book, being an "empath" will not be the same as practicing empathy. Empathy trains the <u>receiver's</u> powers of mimicry given input from the giver—a kind of reverse telepathy. Empaths pick up information from the giver, regardless of their training as receivers, and will be considered clairsentient. That is, empathy involves tuning/sharpening the receiver. Being empathic involves receiving from/widening the window from *any giver. Empathy processes what comes in. Being empathic takes in more for processing.

You need to be careful with clairsentience. At least in some forms.

The talent for picking up a thing's energy—be it through touch, nearness, or artifact reading—often brings with it a tendency to fill yourself with tension. This should make sense. Ultimately, energies which are not ours and not a regular part of our sphere (to the extent that they are just foreign vibrations), are much more likely to be broadly irresonant with us. If they were resonant, we might regularly include them in our own patterns. Clearly this is not always the case, but it is often the case. The people and things whose energy you absorb have a good chance of playing a snippet of another song over your personal playlist while the latter is playing. If you are an empath who reads people's emotions or an energy reader of some other kind, one of your best weapons will be greater distance (spatial or otherwise) between you and the energy you don't want to read. Before we even begin discussing clairsentience, know that the ability to keep your distance is an almost necessary part of having this sense active in your life.

A clairsentience hypothesis

Mainstream science at the time of this writing would maintain that clairsentience was nothing more than our emotional rapport mechanisms simulating the inner state of the thing we're interacting with. This is a decent starting point, though incomplete as an explanation, because it doesn't consider those occasions where rapport does not seem to apply, yet the feelings we get arrive spontaneously. If we assume that clairsentience isn't just rapport, but anticipatory response with or without rapport (the same explanation we used in "An Important Note about Dream Symbols"), then that might account for most clairsentience. But this still doesn't account for the feelings we feel when say, reading something related to someone (vision-cognitive clairsentience).

I'm not an empath (one who reads feelings through more direct interaction), but there are two MAJOR things I know about myself. 1) Social media engagement, including responding to posts on my own videos or looking at my own media work, actually makes me feel physically sick. 2) I stopped looking at more than half of the astrology charts I've collected because doing so feels like inviting the chart holder and all their preoccupations into my space. I avoid most news and most popular entertainment for similar reasons, and the effects on how I feel health-wise have gotten more and more pronounced in the last few years—ever since I began making much greater strides in shaping my tribes and Role. What's the explanation for this? We'll say it's psychological. But it's psychological not in response to a particular thing, but in response to my subconscious representation of a class of things. I can tell you that it feels like being given an uncontrollable stimulant as the associated information explodes in, though the content of that information promises nothing once the Pax/Wolfiana-like conflagration has finally been extinguished. Like many emotional empaths, I'm hypersensitive to too much undirected information—but in my case as a learner, the sensitivity comes through excessively exchanged ideas. For readers training empathy, you know this is a thing. It can have direct effects on your health. The ability to strongly regulate what comes in is of the utmost importance.

The firing patterns involved in a cognitive or body representation are describable as frequency (firing-rate and messenger) fields—the same thing we see on an EEG or EKG. So we can argue that clairsentience isn't just about "rapport with" or "anticipation of" experiences, but rapport with or anticipation of *representations* of *frequency fields*. I'll call these **energy resonances** for short even though I know some hard scientists wouldn't like the phrase. (Though they might have followed the logic all the way up to the phrase.) In the end then, clairsentience is energy resonance with the thing you're interacting with or its representation. You can feel it with anything you can conceive of to which your hormonal messaging system allows a strong response. If you don't like radio waves, maybe you'll be sensitive to radio waves. If you don't like the government, maybe you'll be sensitive to its proponents. You can re-represent part of the data field of anything you're sensitive to, for better or worse. You can do this by touching the thing, being near it, or just hearing about it. And your regular senses, as usual, aren't the only channels you'll use. Hormones, heat, increasing or falling stress chemicals or internal activity—by a person, city, or old object... Not only can you simulate the aspects of their processes which are meaningful to your subconscious, you can also simulate the *direction* of such processes. (Is the anger rising or falling?)

When your own internal response has to put in extra metabolic energy to suppress what that re-representation is subtly calling you to respond to, it's like managing the emotional projection of another so that you can continue going about your own. Thus you feel drained.

I believe that we pick up energetic re-representations (partial resonances with the other) not just as humans with senses but as collections of species-organized chemical elements, so you can feel on levels that your basic eyes and ears won't be able to account for. But for the purpose of our practice of clairsentience, you don't need to believe this. All you need to believe is that you can respond emotionally to the idea of something, and biologically prefer to take in such ideas where they occur. Maybe not cognitive preference, but biological preference. We will approach clairsentience this way—with the idea that you can read the emotions or internal processes of or about a thing if only you develop the positive or negative hypersensitivity for it. Let's get started.

In studying clairsentience, it will help greatly if you can think of things as collections of math/wave functions—that is, as their spheres.

Touch clairsentience

Have you ever had someone touch you and pass their emotions onto you? You didn't pick up their emotions before they touched you; after they touched you, you couldn't get their emotions off of you for the next half-hour. This seems to be a form of clairsentience associated with a combination of three things: 1) tension displacement on behalf of the toucher, 2) helping behavior on behalf of the touched, and 3) a longer-term or permanent association between the two. Imagine dropping the barrier of air between the positive pole of a car battery and the negative pole, short circuiting it for longer than a moment of spark. One actor has plenty of tense energy to offload while the other has plenty of interest in addressing tension like that in general. I have touch clairsentience; from what I've seen, this three part cocktail is the best explanation for why it sometimes registers, sometimes doesn't.

Touch clairsentience has consistently registered for me on two kinds of occasions. The first is when I kill bugs or similarly small creatures with a direct body part like my hand or shoeless foot. The second is when another person touches me, they are carrying some personal issue they've displaced onto / blamed on others, AND they are likely to come up again as a significant topic later in my future. I don't always pick up a toucher's energy but when I do the common factors are the other's tension, my wish that I could reduce the situation's (not necessarily the person's) tension, and some kind of permanence or later association. In the case of killing bugs with my hands, I don't like doing it since my whole hand feels like it has permanently served as the death spot for another's life force. Indeed, the sum of the bug's entire frequency story ends at my hand, and if you modeled this mathematically you might see how there would be some falloff time, located at my hand, associated with the bug's total wave. The concept is illustrated in Figure 54-3.

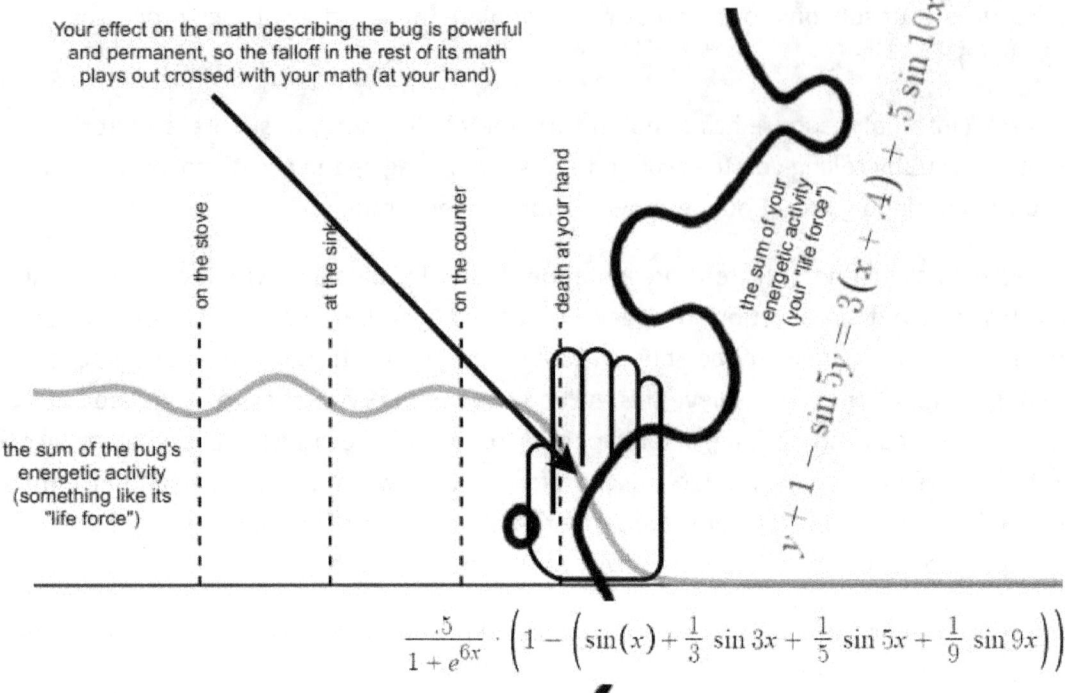

Figure 54-3: A simplified model of what happens when one mathematical representation of a thing's energy terminates at another. For a brief time during the fall off period, the terminated thing's math goes wherever its killer goes. You're not feeling with your senses. Instead the math (composite wave function) associated with your hand temporarily has extra information associated with it from the rest of the character of the thing you killed. Tingling is one result IF you care to pay attention to such information.

Bugs are alright, but I'd rather not kill them and especially don't like killing them with my unshielded body regions. It feels nasty for minutes afterwards. Such is the cocktail for touch clairsentience: their displaced tension + your wish to reduce the tension + a long-standing (sometimes permanent) tie between you and them.

* * *

Most people who touch our shoulders or brush up against us don't leave touch impressions no matter how sensitive we are. We might think of these as two determined math functions contacting each other with no inclination to tangle.

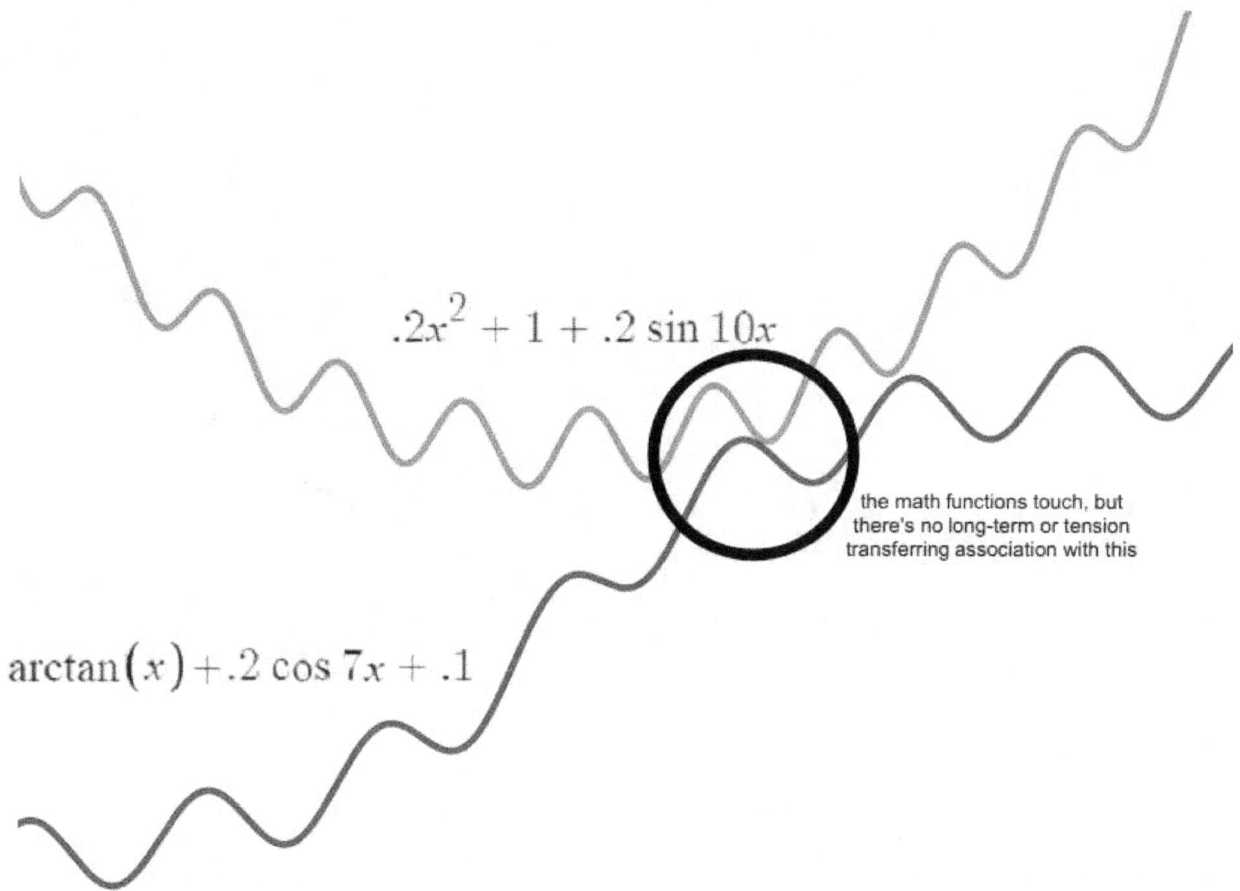

Figure 54-4: Touch without tangle

Suppose, however, that the touch is not the end of it. Suppose one of the parties dies within a few years afterwards and the other party—an apparent stranger—ends up interacting with some aspects of the first person's memory. (I actually had this happen.) Or suppose one of the parties remains a memorable construct in the mind of the other for years after the contact. Now we have "function tangle" as shown in Figure 54-5.

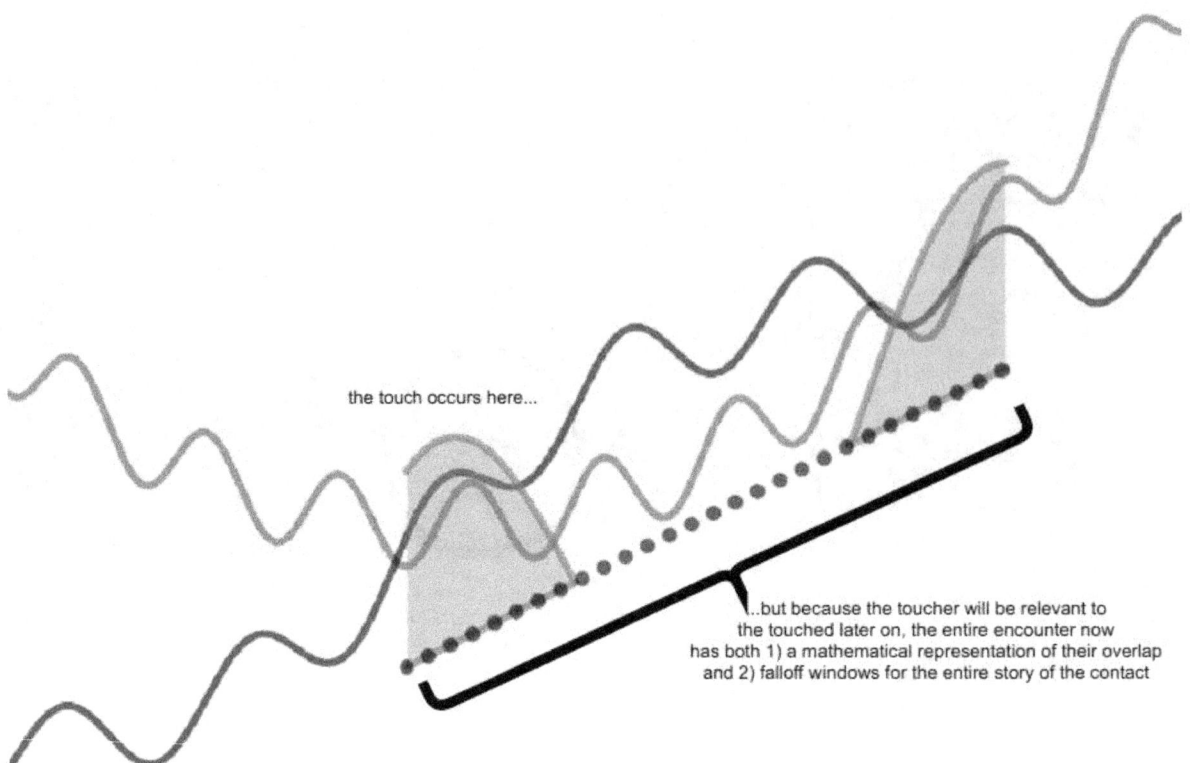

Figure 54-5: Function tangle between touchers

The resurrected relevance of the toucher in the mind of the touched means that the contact between them isn't just a passing moment, but one side of the overlap in a larger function. The representation in the mind, emotions, or physical actions of the touched must be longer-term and behavior-meaningful for this to have a greater chance of occurring. If it isn't longer-term, there is less of a need for an overlap function (as opposed to a quick contact point). If it isn't behaviorally or representationally meaningful, the overlap window will be weaker/smaller.

We can see where there might be a connection between the empathic sense and general empathy. If the clairsentient person cares enough to represent what he contacts for the longer term, he will be more likely to amplify the emotions associated with that contact.

☞ Question 54.9.1 (Touched by a vibration): Actually *practicing* touch-based clairsentience is difficult because, one the one hand, you'll need to reencounter the toucher somehow. On the other hand, you can't reencounter the toucher so often that you simply absorb their math into yours. People who are very close to you won't usually provide the kinds of rich information that episodic semi-strangers will. So if you want to practice touch clairsentience you may need to do it with someone who isn't regularly in your life, but only shows up for something remarkable then leaves again. A physical healer or therapist, a place, or even the vibrations of a particular sound (touch for your ears) can produce this if you strongly associate the toucher with a uniquely-theirs, NOT-ongoing event. You can see a possible connection between sound touch and one's inner feeling in the form of ASMR—likely the only kind of practice in touch clairsentience you can get without imposing on a stranger.

Because sounds are all about windows of vibrations instead of instantaneous moments, they naturally lend themselves to falloff periods in your representation. If you subconsciously associate frequencies such as a cat purring, the clicking teeth of a comb, the hum of a vacuum, or hair brushing with the entrancing focus of an act in progress, you may yet be able to re-represent that entrancing focus yourself. This isn't touch to your skin, but the mechanoreception (micro level touch) of your hearing sense. Training yourself to tie certain vibrations to certain feelings is one part of touch clairsentience. Caring at all to feel the feelings involved is the other part. Take 10 minutes to listen to any steady sound which promotes your spacing out. If you don't know of such sounds, try searching for ASMR on the web. Describe the feeling below.

_____
_____
_____
_____

There is a vast difference between people voluntarily touching you and you touching them. The latter can get into all kinds of issues of personal space, and can greatly change what you read. Accordingly, if you want to practice reading people when they touch you, you should first be aware that they'll need to touch *you*, not the other way around. You should also be aware that what you read on most people will be out of phase with your own energy/math, unless you or they are a healer. Training touch clairsentience is mostly about training yourself to pick up other people's tension. If you would like to do this for the purpose of healing them, however, then you might want to train another skill at the same time such as clairvoyance, telepathy, or basic counseling.

Another reason it's easier to practice touch clairsentience by observing someone's contact with you is because your touching them involves so much of your own motor signaling. Where your sensory pathways are concerned, it's simply harder to register their input when you're busy giving your output.

We've spent some time discussing you as the touched, now we turn to you as the toucher. For this we'll assume that you are something like a healer or some other person whose touch is welcomed enough by the other that it won't disturb the energy they already had. Of course this means you won't be reading the other's default energy, but the brand of their energy which partly receives you. If you'd like to study such contact in detail, then Reiki or other forms of touch therapy may be for you. Here we'll concentrate only on those aspects of touch clairsentience which involve the exchange of sense representations.

Suppose you don't believe in energy. You do not subscribe to tales of Qi or empathicness, or anything like that, but you are interested in using touch to help someone address a problem. You do believe that people are collections of molecules which radiate heat and hormones, and you can believe to a certain extent that we can pick up the emotional changes in another through a combination of microexpressions, stress levels, and other biological tells. Even with a fair amount of skepticism, you can simulate touch clairsentience by doing three things which mimic the three conditions we have discussed so far:

1) As you touch the person, reduce the focus on your own thoughts and your own internal activity, and instead let your mood respond primarily to your perception of the other's mood. This simulates your caring as an emotional receiver of the other's state, even if heartfelt care does not actually apply.

2) Invite the other to release their worries and tension. This sounds cliché, but in order to release tension from a place we typically have to pay attention to that place—at least briefly. If you are receptive enough, you can sometimes observe where you've touched or moved over an area that the other is concerned about. Not only does this mimic the effect of their displacing their tension onto you, but it helps them conceive of your tangle with them. Provided you serve as an outlet for them, you can also observe those subtle reactions where you're getting it right, and this helps you perceive your wider window-tangle with them. Again, however, you'll need to concentrate as fully as you can on *their* feelings, not on your own.

3) Cultivate the sense of memorable ceremony. It's one thing to give a person a random massage or sweep of hands, another thing to sponsor an occasion that they are likely to remember as special. One of the strengths of formalized physical practices like Reiki or yoga is that they stand out as self-contained, labelable experiences. When you associate your touch practices with a more enduring concept, you simulate the perception of a longer term event window both in yourself and in the other. The more one-of-a-kind the event, the stronger your perception as a receiver and their perception as a giver of their tension to you. Having received their tension, you can perform a gesture like flicking your fingers off to the side to throw that tension away. Is this actually a way of dispersing energy, or just you overwriting the perception of tangled tingle with your own overt motor movement? Who knows? Who cares?

The above may not be the most mystical route to touch clairsentience, but it does give us a basis for practical practice regardless of how psychic we think we are.

☞ Question 54.9.2 (Touch to a memory): For this exercise you shouldn't actually touch the person. You only want to sweep your hands over them. Because actual touch will trigger any number of amplified skin signals which we really don't need, hand sweeping will be much better for helping you practice the holistic, steerable observation of the other person's mood. If you touch them, you risk locking their attention on certain areas over others, for better or worse, and may have to go uphill getting them to de-concentrate again on the point of the exercise in general: transferring their tension. Yes this is part of the practice for touch clairsentience, but here we want you train mainly your ability to read another's mood using the space around your hands as an interface.

Find a partner who will let you sweep your hands over them. This person really shouldn't be your spouse, boyfriend, girlfriend, or regular mate because the sense of a rare event will be diminished. A close friend will do. Let them know you're practicing the kind of psychic sense associated with touch, but that you won't be touching them, and see if they will let you try it on them for 12 – 15 minutes (long enough for them to remember that weird thing you did—thus creating an event window for yourself). Ask the person to just relax and imagine all of their tension being absorbed away into your hands.

During the time, sweep your hand over different areas of their body, observing the different impressions you get from them as you proceed. Obviously if it becomes awkward you should stop.

There are a couple of things to note about this exercise. First of all, you may observe different feelings in each hand, so you may want to experiment with the perception of flow into and out of them individually. We don't typically use our hands with equal frequency, and shouldn't expect to feel through them equally either. Second, remember not to focus on what you're getting from them, but rather on what they're giving to the world. This is a lot like the difference between coercing a statement and overhearing a broadcast. You're tuning into them, not shopping for yourself. Your ability to represent *them* clearly depends on this. Lastly, let the warmth in your hands guide you. Pay attention to the other person, but do it in semitrance.

This exercise won't make you a healer, but it will train your focus on reading another's feelings through (near) touch. Describe what you experience below.

_____
_____
_____
_____
_____
_____
_____
_____
_____

Actual touch clairsentience is a lot easier to feel when the other person has an issue on their minds which they feel absolutely must be addressed. In some people this energy is so strong that you'll feel hot, uneasy, or inexplicably warm just being around them. Observe the occasions when you encounter these people. Your own reaction to them constitutes one form of your own clairsentient response in general.

Charged objects

I have a bronze statue of the fire-encircled Shiva Nataraj which is a little over one foot in diameter. I believe my youngest brother got it for me as a Christmas gift, and it has a strange energy to it. For the last decade, whenever I've put it anywhere in the house for at least two weeks, something basically bad happens that leads ultimately to some kind of transformation. Furthermore, it happens in the area of life that seems to correspond to a certain astrological compass with its own version of north, loosely related to the Western Feng Shui directions. Prior to the statue's arrival, I had never had any experience with a "bad luck" object, but the coincidence between when I've placed it, where I've placed it, and for how long is so strong that it actually prompted me to study a little Feng Shui alongside the statue itself to understand its timing. Indeed, on several occasions I have intentionally put the Shiva in certain corners of my house in order to get things to transform (possibly destructively), and all in all he has an honest record of about 15 out of 17. If you leave him there for at least two weeks, there's a good chance that something negative will happen, and the situation will stay negative—getting worse until you move the thing out of casual eyeshot. The statue has a reputation for bringing very bad luck to one's life, which is why we keep it stored in the bottom of an old toy chest at the bottom of a pile of boxes in the back corner of the garage at the family house—not in our own. But why does it do this? One might say it's psychological like other forms of clairsentient projections, but 15 out of 17? The only object in our known family history to sponsor this kind of thing? Resolution of the bad issue within a few days, but only after you move it? A placement-dependent "if and only if"-type coincidence? You need to borrow this statue yourself. It's not psychological. It may be sphere-energetic though. This brings us to a discussion of charged objects.

Remember how killing a bug with your hand might, for some, put the feeling of bug-death around your hand for minutes afterwards? Your hand is still your hand and the bug is…whatever it is, but the event surrounding the intersection of the two is where the tangle of wave functions plays out. Let us assume that a charged object is an item whose *surrounding events* have taken on a certain character regardless of where it is or how it's currently being handled. Where the object is, certain things seem to want to happen, as if the objects themselves are both 1) imbued with their own personality and 2) "telepathic" in projecting their patterned events onto things around them. Indulging the abstract for a moment, you might say that an individual human is the ultimate charged object; as a collection of physics, his appearance and manner compels observers to react in a family of ways peculiar to him. Buildings are charged objects in the sense that we adopt behaviors specific to the buildings' functions when we engage them. Formless patterns of communication frequencies such as the topics of politics and death might also be considered charged for the predictable reactions they elicit. Indeed, clouds of energy of all sorts—material or vibration-based—can "urge" certain events to take place around them. Certain non-living objects like scary houses, viruses, and remarkable artworks can also do this IF the events that happen around them are sharply distinguishable from the normal flow of things in their absence. That is, when the object is there, you get the event; when the object isn't there, you don't get the event. It turns out that the phenomenon of charged objects isn't really rare. What *is* rare is the obvious experience of events connected to things we don't expect to be charged—to the point that such associations become publicly verifiable.

Now rather than thinking about the one-to-one association between object and event as being a property of the object itself, it may help to think of it as the "floating characteristics" of the *event* following the object around. Even this can seem like magic until you think of the entire planet as a giant ball of exploded energy. That is, if you think of every object on the earth as a particle cloud and the events passing around it as various kinds of energy transfer, it's easier to picture the energy *around* an object as forming a kind of activity shell of its own. The object may lie at the core of that shell, but the outer energy itself is a pattern as distinct as the object is. Although we don't think of energies such as fear, love, and happiness as things we can locate in space, clearly our biological representations of these emotions give them at least one location (within us). Objects or buildings which carry a "vibe" about them might be better understood by ignoring the object and thinking only of those attributes most strongly associated with people's behavior *around* the object. An apparently haunted house wouldn't be haunted because of the ghosts in its walls, but because the same energy shell of dark and fearful activity that comes with other topics related to haunting (and the house's inhabitants) would have a center at that house. This idea is illustrated in Figure 54-6.

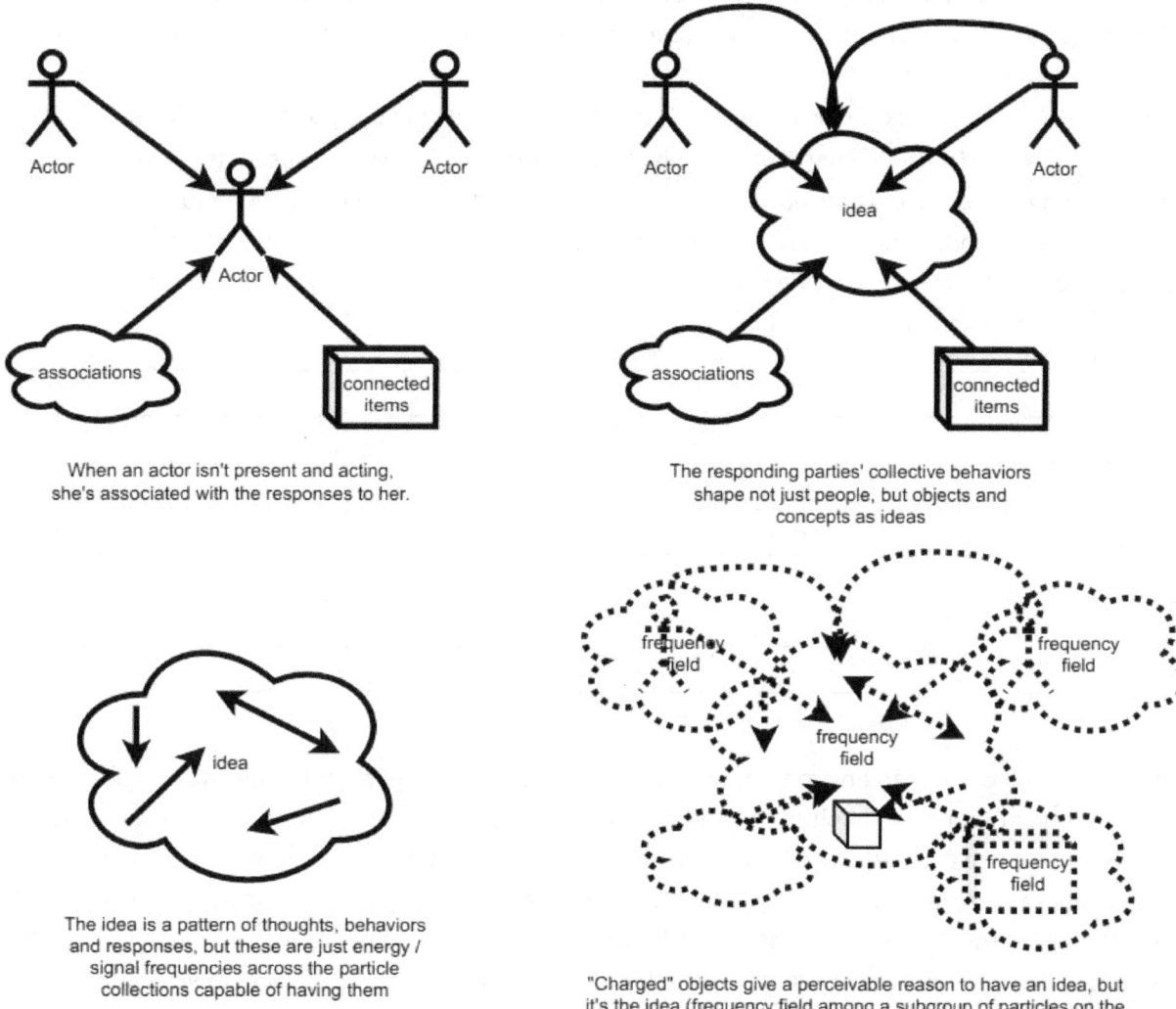

Figure 54-6: When you explode every object on the Earth into its particles, all you have are energy fields. A charged object, building, topic, or person lies at a denser core of such a field. Hypothesis: it's usually the field and not the object people are reacting to. Fields can exist in more than one dimension—not just those perceivable to our senses.

Given the theory advanced above, reading a charged object might be a matter of your own sensitivity to the kinds of events that have taken place in association with an object, but should largely be a matter of how exclusively that object has "owned" the things that have happened around it. Most objects in our consumerist world are quite disposable, and will not have had very distinct occurrences happening around them across their histories. The events would have been a hodgepodge. Yet some objects like computers and furniture—though seemingly personality-less, will have captured a person's "at work" or "at home" behavior more accurately than any other item. Like an object which tends to be used in certain kinds of video games, "energy-coded" things may bring their own niche with them.

You would read objects similarly to the way you read the other person in the hand sweeping activity 54.9.2: Try to ignore your biases; let the image of the item's primary users tell you what to feel.

☞ Question 54.9.3 (Where the activity happens): **Pick an object in your house or workspace which is the <u>only</u> item associated with a particular activity. When this item is not being used, the activity can't happen. When the item is being used, the activity is almost certainly happening. Without touching the item, sweep your hands over it and let your natural response to this special *activity* (not to the object itself) come over you. Relax. Don't be in a hurry to feel anything at all, but if you do feel something, describe the impression(s) you get below.**

_____
_____
_____
_____
_____
_____
_____
_____

Unless you live or work in an environment where the furnishings are each optimally meaningful to you, you may not want to make a habit of reading charged objects. As with empathy, energetic deposits on the things you contact are usually out of phase with your own energy, and even when the object is one you yourself are attached to, the way you've placed it, treated it, maintained it, cleaned it up, ordered its neighbors, or otherwise used it to its potential often leaves much to be desired. Should you read that object clearly enough, you may become aware of your own issues properly tending to your own affairs with respect to it. Don't be so eager to open yourself to the world of random objects. Unless you want to fill your messaging system with an ongoing response to undirected clutter.

Now if, despite the warning above, you feel that touch clairsentience and object reading are key parts of your path, you may find it helpful to train in active reading rather than strictly passive reading. Whereas passive reading foists the object's impressions upon you, active reading is a feedback loop between your impressions of the object and your impressions of your own impressions. By essentially letting your messaging system tell you what it wants to do with your impressions, you can ensure that your object reading does not fall into a one-way conversation bombarding you with information you struggle to shake. Or attracting energy to you that you don't want to carry around.

☞ **Question 54.9.4 (Active object reading):** Find an object which is not yours, which you believe has an energy associated with it. You can touch the object or just sweep your hand over it, but while you're doing so, shift your attention back and forth between the impressions you get from the object, and the feelings you get from the air around yourself. How does the overall environment suggest you respond to the object you're reading? Write down your experiences below.

_____
_____
_____
_____
_____
_____
_____

A final note on charged objects

During the six days I spent writing the "Charged Objects" section above, I was very sick. Once the section was over, I wasn't sick anymore. Early on, I approached the section with an unexplainable sense of dread, and gradually started to feel that it was an invitation for negative fields to attach themselves to me. Upon investigating further, I learned why this was happening. Most people who train in object reading will ultimately train not for the benefit of the energies they encounter, but for their own access to a certain kind of power regardless of the other personalities involved. Just as clairvoyance can foster a kind of "me-centric" world view in the average person, touch clairsentience for *objects* can foster a "who cares if my messing with it disturbs others" outlook. The most charged emotions we install into objects tend to be the negative (noisy, "feelable") ones, where the spirits / energy fields which were interested enough in spreading their frequencies onto an object may be just as interested in spreading their frequencies onto you—this is especially true if you're more interested in the item than the relationship behind the item. This makes charged objects one of the strongest vehicles available for giving negative entities a free ride on your self-indulgent curiosity. Unlike empathy, or person-to-person clairsentience, you won't have another person in front of you saying, "Hey, you're disturbing me," or "This is making me uncomfortable." You can fondle the object to your heart's content, and the types of energies that don't seem to mind—and may even thrive off of this—will often be negative ones with a penchant for spreading themselves everywhere.

I can't tell you how relieved I am to get out of this section. Practitioners of certain kinds of magick and those who engage in summoning rituals might find the above discussion useful, but it is that much more important to keep your own energy field clean. If all you're doing is touching things for the buildup of your own clairsentient resume, don't be surprised if certain opportunistic energies take advantage of your poor screening practices. Touch clairsentience for objects should really be trained alongside another, more actively helpful talent if you are to avoid being a magnet for random, intense energy. Otherwise the spirits you agitate may be more than happy to pull you into their contagious worlds.

Part of the reason I got sick during this section was because of the kind of clairsentience I have related to my writing. If I give a topic page time, I typically manifest it to completion in real life, which is why my books are never exactly about the same thing. The skill is called vision-cognitive clairsentience, and is trained by your level of pickiness regarding the things you experience.

Vision-cognitive clairsentience

If you followed the processes for resolving The Conflict, The Rift, The Spirits, and The Role, you may have already begun developing vision-cognitive clairsentience. As you have stronger and stronger reactions to things you would rather approach or avoid, your messaging system will automatically present you with a story the moment you even look at those things. Vision-cognitive clairsentience might be one of the purest examples of psychosomatics in action, but that doesn't take away from its strongly predictive nature.[38] As shown in Figure 54-6, we can react to the fields around a thing as well as the thing itself, so there really can be this element of psychic reading involved. Where normal people would expect to observe an actual construct as the basis of your reaction, you're actually responding to the exploded field. The stronger your reaction to this field, the stronger this form of clairsentience.

The easiest way to train vision-cognitive clairsentience is to 1) have strong reactions to some thing or some issue and 2) make it a habit of staying far away from that issue. Plenty of people have strong reactions to plenty of things, but then seek out those things again and again for whatever reason. For positive reactions this may be good, but for negative reactions it won't encourage you to develop any predictive messaging if your body knows you're going to dive into the negative anyway. The broader the issue or thing, the stronger your clairsentience can become. Although I like interacting with people one on one, I have strong avoidance reactions to one-sided relationships and noisy social scenarios—so much so that it got to the point where I could feel these far away. Now even when I look at astrology charts, my subconscious immediately starts gathering data on whether my studying the person's chart is helpful, or just a one-sided drain of my energy. The effect is that I load the personality of the individual behind the chart (along with some of their broader energy field), and can reliably feel them by just looking at their wheel. This form of clairsentience is very strong for me, and has only developed in the last four years as the result of reading one too many clients who were also difficult people. My reaction to social media was similarly developed as I engaged it for a moment in my business, only to realize how much I truly, truly hated it. (Something about having to express in a way opposite to the uncensored approach in my writing. Social media puts your ideas before others' scrutiny. As a writer on certain taboo topics for the expression of individuality, I *have* to ignore such scrutiny. Accordingly, I get strong feelings where these two issues become a possibility.)

---

[38] Vision-cognitive clairsentience might be almost entirely explained in terms of biases: you see something, you have a certain feeling towards it. Were you to engage that something, your biases would color the engagement and your initial feeling would come true. Simple as that. And if that is your framework for this kind of sensing then okay. All I'll tell you is that the better you get at it, the more you'll wonder whether cognitive bias is really the end of the story. I myself don't believe that bias is the end of it, especially because you often read things in ways that don't support the information you have—if there is any. But whatever the case, don't let the more rational-sounding explanation discourage you from practicing it. And don't let the idea of "bias" impose itself *as* you practice. This is still a very powerful form of sensing.

☞ **Question 54.9.5 (See it coming):** Name at least one issue you are extremely hesitant to engage, but which comes up so regularly you have to be on guard against it.

_____
_____
_____
_____

☞ **Question 54.9.6 (Gather the warning data):** Given your answer to 54.9.5, what kinds of information must you collect in order to know whether the issue is going to pose problems for you? Is there a certain class of information you have to get good at reading in order to properly warn yourself?

_____
_____
_____
_____

☞ **Question 54.9.7 (Gravitation):** Name at least one issue you can't experience enough of, but for which you must gather more data in order to know if it applies.

_____
_____
_____
_____

☞ **Question 54.9.8 (Gather the validating data):** Given your answer to 54.9.7, what kinds of information must you collect in order to know whether the issue you favor is going to apply? Is there a certain class of information you have to get good at reading in order to properly determine the promise in the scenario?

_____
_____
_____
_____

Your answers to 54.9.6 and 54.9.8 show you the kinds of information you can eventually excel in reading as a clairsentient. Now all we need to determine is the source of your information.

☞ **Question 54.9.9 (Where the information comes from):** Think back to a time before you had such strong preferences for the issues you listed. What kinds of things did you engage indiscriminately for connecting with those issues? These will become your information sources as your powers of discrimination go online. List these sources.

	Example
	Before I was sensitive to social noise and one-sided relationships, I would 1) read astro charts for people's own selfish curiosity—though they had no intention of actually being better to others or themselves, 2) let people commit me to do their work, and 3) go into my own head via writing in order to assess the fairness of these arrangements. Accordingly, I can now read <ul><li>*astrocharts*</li><li>*other people's promises of collaboration*</li><li>*my own writings*</li></ul> clairsentiently in order to read the other person's personality (54.9.8) or the burden they'll put upon me (54.9.6)

☞ Question 54.9.10 (Training vision-cognitive clairsentience): **There is no silver bullet for developing vision-cognitive clairsentience. You'll need to practice it**—which means actually avoiding the thing you said you wished to avoid, and actually gathering data on the thing you think you're being drawn to. For every situation you claim to dislike but end up diving back into anyway, this kind of clairsentience will be delayed for you. On the other side, if you said you were drawn to it, but don't allow your mind to exercise any actionable responses to this draw, vision-cognitive clairsentience will be delayed for you that way as well. In order for the clairsentient data to stick, your having it has to lead to an actual change in your actions, almost every time. Training it works the same as training any other "actionized," reinforceable habit.

Over the next 15 days, make it a habit of actually avoiding the thing you said you needed to avoid, reading the warning source which tells you that you need to avoid it, and reading the kinds of information which helps you piece together this warning. Do the same for the issue you're drawn to. Use the table below to keep track of your progress. You probably won't run into these issues every day, but on the days where each situation applies, be sure to put a check mark. You may also want to fill in your answers to 54.9.5 – 54.9.9 in the blank spaces below each of the six items.

	Did I encounter this today?														
	Day 1	Day 2	Day 3	Day 4	Day 5	Day 6	Day 7	Day 8	Day 9	Day 10	Day 11	Day 12	Day 13	Day 14	Day 15
I prefer to stay away from **54.9.5**															
I am warned about 54.9.5 by reading **54.9.6**-style information															
I read 54.9.6 information through one of my **54.9.9** sources															
I am drawn to **54.9.7**															
I get data about 54.9.7 by reading **54.9.8**-style information															
I read 54.9.8 information through one of my **54.9.9** sources															

You may have thought that the ability to read a thing by looking at its representation required more training through certain special exercises, but not really. Vision-cognitive clairsentience is essentially the "intuition" we've all heard about—the "gut feeling" that people have towards certain topics which are important to them. Thus we tend to develop this sense automatically as a byproduct of our body's natural warning systems. The catch is that, because this kind of clairsentience is rooted in our own intense reactions, it may render us blind to the other kinds of information attached to the issues we observe. Sometimes the other person isn't there to help us play out our pet issue. They are there for something else. We'll need the presence of mind to know when we're seeing only what we know how to see rather than what is there, and the maturity to turn off our intuitive lens in cases where life is really trying to teach us something brand new.

Empathic clairsentience

Even easier than training vision-cognitive clairsentience is training the empathic talent. Empaths pick up the emotions of the room around them, and (not surprisingly) develop this talent through a lifetime of caring how others around them feel. There was a time when you were much more likely to encounter women empaths than men as empaths, not necessarily because men didn't make good empaths, but because men were less likely to be socialized into publicly embracing their emotional caring sides. But that is changing. If your friends or society have forced you to be sensitive to what other people are feeling, and if you have internalized many of the emotional punishments that come with not doing so, then chances are you will develop some level of empathic talent. The principles are the same as other forms of clairsentience. Your own hormonal / emotional messaging system simulates the energy associated with a thing's effect. In this case, however, you're not reading objects or ideas about the thing, but rather the general mood of your current environment which includes that thing.

Interestingly, I've never run into anyone who wanted to train the empathic talent. Never. That's not to say that such people don't exist, it's just that people who have the empathic talent have often developed it as a result of being others' emotional doormat. By and large, chronically caring about a room full of other people's emotions can make you sensitive and distrustful, easily used for other's expressive priorities, and jaded over which situations are actually in your power to fix. I've observed that this tends to remain the case until you develop a more formal gatekeeping system for which emotions people are allowed to saddle you with. And this usually manifests as some kind of "Get yourself together, man…" attitude held by the empath towards the emotional drainers around them. 9 times out of 10 have I seen this apply to the *healthiest* empaths.

If you want to train the empathic talent in the first place, all you need to do is make it an overriding priority to care about the emotions of those around you—so overriding that your own emotions take second place. A leadership position, the role of a parent, being socially isolated, or the role of someone who has been emotionally abused are all routes to a certain level of empathic sense, but again these routes may not be so pleasing to you. To read a room regardless of who's in it says a lot about the kind and magnitude of the burdens you've learned to carry, and may not be something you want to train on purpose beyond some position of responsibility you've actively embraced. In other words, you'd like to read the pulse of rooms you enjoy being responsible for. Not just any room you arrive in (the kind of empathicness often developed by the emotionally abused and isolated).

More than the need to train new empaths, many existing empaths may need help controlling the information that flies at them. As I mentioned earlier, this often involves developing a formal gatekeeping system for which emotions are allowed to visit you, as well as a more official behavioral pattern for processing such emotions. Part of this will be tied to your Role with respect to the larger world.

☞ Question 54.9.11 (What you would tell the room): **Picture yourself in a typical room whose emotions you can easily read. It can be as private as your own house or as public as a subway station. Imagine the other people in the room are doing whatever they usually do, and you have an increasing need to say something to the room as a whole. What do you say?**

	Example
	In a waiting area of any kind, where there is a TV on, ready for my name to be called. Some others in the room are socializing.
	I say to the room, "Nothing against you all, but I prefer my solitude."

Chapter 54: The Foresight

☞ **Question 54.9.12 (Your message, your Role):** Given what you already know about your Role, how does your message in 54.9.11 suggest you best interact with these kinds of rooms full of emotion?

	Example
	I'm more likely to feel imposed upon in rooms I'm unwillingly obligated to be in. Here I'm called upon to respect others' ways while keeping an observer's distance. So room reading forces me to add to my observations of the human experience. It's not meant for me to absorb those experiences myself.

☞ **Question 54.9.13 (Regulate the emotions put upon you):** Given your answers above, suppose someone is throwing emotions at you which you don't want. In your subconscious (though not always openly) what do you tell this person?

	Example
	"You know I'm not your personal shelf. I'll study what you're doing and why you're doing it as part of my scholarship, but other than that, you're wasting energy trying to get me to worry about something that I'm definitely going to reject."

It's easy for an empath to serve as other people's emotional trash can, and especially valuable for an empath to learn how to regulate this. If the rooms bombarding you aren't enabling your Role, they may just be attempting to make their problems into yours.

Developing Clairvoyance

Clairvoyance is where you perceive a scenario as if with the normal senses or cognition despite not having the normal sense or cognitive information for constructing that scenario. Like clairaudience, this is one of the senses which is defined by its abnormality compared to the normal array of senses. As such, the more we can explain it in terms of the normatively observable, the less "psychic" and more basically cognitive it becomes. Normally when we picture a scenario, we draw upon chains of previous mental constructs and sense-input to get a good image of how that scenario works. But as we discussed in a previous chapter, our own mental world is not the end of the information available to us. Just outside of that mental world lies the context which compels it, and to the extent that our hormonal and emotional messaging system can respond to this context—letting the ambient circumstances write images of the scenario for us—we may be able to perceive events based on what appears to be nothing. To develop clairvoyance, then, is to develop a talent for letting the situation *surrounding* the thing you're thinking about provide you the information about that thing. There are two major ways to accomplish this: with assistance and without assistance.

Unassisted clairvoyance

Unassisted clairvoyance is the kind we normally think of where a psychic can simply read an event from seemingly thin air. The talent can be trained, and involves a combination of letting the perceptions enter, then verifying which aspects of the perception were accurate. What people don't tell you about this kind of clairvoyance is the importance of being wrong as you train it. Instead, clairvoyants are among the most likely people to have their skills tested by others, and that's a shame. Like any other form of learning, sharp clairvoyance involves constant refinement of what you feel, constant reduction of those biases that cloud what you feel, and constant evolution of what you know *how* to feel accurately. Unfortunately, because clairvoyants are often discouraged from being wrong, their development of this talent is frequently capped at B-level—where they can warn themselves in light of the strong perception of threats, but can't reliably help others beyond that kind of self-preservation. Maybe they can supplement their clairvoyance with sage-sounding advice, but the faculty itself may not quite be up to the level such supplement suggests. Clearly this won't describe all cases, but the problems of unassisted clairvoyance with no room for error really can create very strong psychics whose stubbornness prohibits the wider use of their talents for other's good. I've discussed this several times throughout the book so far.

Keeping in mind that you'll need to be wrong during your clairvoyant training, we can proceed with less pressure to evolve guru status overnight. Clairvoyant practice begins anywhere you receive seemingly accurate information about a scenario from nowhere, such that you can verify what you've seen against reality. If you can't verify it, it might still be clairvoyance, but can look suspiciously to others like your own superstition.

☞ Question 54.10.1 (Your nowhere source): **Name one type of [scenario information] which you have a talent for receiving from nowhere, as if the details were already worked out in some other world and handed to you in this one.**

_____

_____

_____

_____

Some readers may have been surprised by their own answer. Typically when we think of clairvoyance we assume that the information one gains is about people and their circumstances. This is sometimes the case, but not always. Your clairvoyant scenarios might involve theories, work tasks, special skills you have, or other behavioral stories which you have a special affinity for. Perhaps you had a clairvoyant insight for fixing cars all this time and didn't even know. Lame, you say? Not if fixing cars is your key service to others in this life.

☞ Question 54.10.2 (Verifying what you've gotten): **When you receive the information you mentioned in 54.10.1, what do you do with it? How do you verify its accuracy?**

	Example
	When I get data structures like the astral map, an approach to the asteroid meanings, or the Star from nowhere, I typically work them out exhaustively until I've found a broad formula for these consistent with reality.

☞ Question 54.10.3 (Honing the clairvoyance): **Can you think of anything you do which makes it even more likely for you to receive such clairvoyant information?**

	Example
	Drinking coffee around 9am, receiving the "flood" of information around 10:34am. Setting a particular theoretical problem as my next goal. The solve-rate for any theoretical questions I pose in the course of self-teaching is very high. For my questions involving specific people and relationships, very low.

You can see from my example above that your clairvoyance can be helped by any number of things: dietary practices, timing, the kinds of questions you ask or don't ask, and your overall Role. Since writing spiritual books is a major part of my work in this life, my clairvoyance revolves almost entirely around the structures I write about. This brings us to a major point. Although you may want to train yourself to see a specific kind of event, this will only be easy to the extent that such an event aligns with what you're naturally here for.

If your role is to advance local law, you may have a clairvoyant talent for perceiving law-related scenarios. You may *want* to train yourself to perceive distant events involving people, but unless these events are related to law, you may be in for some hard work trying to tune your law energy to the frequency of people energy. Clairvoyance involves gaining information from your context, remember? Imagine how difficult it must be to gain information from a context you're not usually in.

Your greatest talent for clairvoyance will be in the areas associated with your long-term Role. Recall how we stretched ourselves out far across time in order to summarize ourselves as a trail of effect. Here again we see how that trail stores information which we-by-the-moment could not know. It turns out then, that training clairvoyance is less about what you want to see and more about what you're "destined" to see—hence the source of the information's accuracy. As you grow into the acceptance of your Role you'll find it easier to take the otherworldly flood of information as it's given, sharpening your view of that information the more you put it to practice in the normal sense world.

☞ Question 54.10.4 (further clairvoyance): **If you wish to develop your clairvoyance but don't yet know where to start, go back to Question 52.30, the Critical Exercise. If you didn't do it, make plans to do it. Once you've done it, use the space below to note the kinds of expressive tools most valuable to your long-term work in the world.**

_____

_____

_____

_____

Your unassisted clairvoyant sense is strongest when focused on events that actually fit your Role in the long-term. You train it not by putting in hours and hours of visualization practice, but by continually using a talent which comes so natural to you it's as if it were handed down by the gods. As you apply that talent in the real world, the accuracy of what you receive will be tested automatically—not for the sake of testing for testing's sake, but as a way of translating the language of your far-reaching vision into something that other people around you can use. Keep in mind that clairvoyance is tied to your context. Other people are a part of that context. Like your other senses, clairvoyance is a means of connecting you to inputs from the world around you, and as long as you remain interested in receiving those inputs and putting them to use, you'll likely find this skill far easier to develop than you might have first thought.

Don't forget: If you prefer the easiest route to this sense, what you learn to see does need to align with your overall path, though.

Assisted clairvoyance

Let me share something intriguing with you. As I write this, I'm about to open up my book of traditional Chinese characters—as I've done every day for the past year and a half. Let's see what today's random word from a random corner of a random page is:

Chapter 54: The Foresight

[qǐ] how can it be that...?
Used in: 岂有此理 [qǐ yǒu cǐ lǐ] (saying) outrageous; ridiculous; absurd

Amazing. It still amazes me how the thing I now know as "The Mandarin Oracle" has a near perfect record for describing where my day is going. It is so consistent that I knew it would work even now. And it did. Indeed, I am about to address that very question: *How can it be that* divination tools like tarot and the I-ching are able to consistently give us answers to questions despite being apparently unrelated to our individual problems? As I realized that my normal daily Mandarin practice had evolved into a kind of fortune teller, I asked just what it is that makes something into a good divination tool. Here's what I came up with:

Think back to the bug-death example. When you explode our particles, everything everywhere can be described as an elaborate math function, whether it is as small as an amoeba or as large as a star. As our math functions evolve in time, they are typically very smooth (continuous), barring any violent events that may take us by surprise. Because our math functions are basically smooth, even the non-smooth discontinuities we introduce into those functions ultimately—in the aggregate—fill in the holes in our experience smoothly IF two conditions hold: 1) the thing we're filling in the holes with can cover almost any possible outcome and 2) our use of that hole-filler *feels* like just a regular continuation of our day. The idea is illustrated in Figure 54-7.

The flow of the function that describes you (with a hole)

Any system you use which covers all options and feels continuous will BE continuous

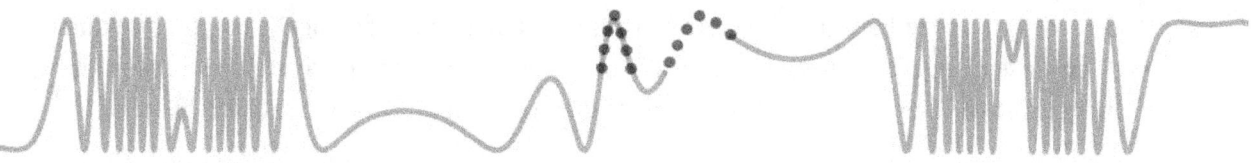

The results of the tool are absorbed smoothly into your larger function, aligning them with reality

Figure 54-7: Hypothesis regarding how divination tools work. Systems like Tarot and I-ching insert continuous sections into our overall energy function, but only to the extent that they cover all possible outcomes, and can thus offer all believable continuations of what we're doing. Our use of them needs to feel like a regular continuation of our day. I actually used two *different math formulas above: the main wobbly one (a sinusoid) and a separate, nonequal one (a polynomial) to serve as the dotted fill-in. Hypothesis: Divination tools work on "continuity fill-in" principles like this.

As we've seen so many times before, if we want to make sense of the esoteric sides of our experience, it pays to think of ourselves as fields of math.

Whereas unassisted clairvoyance helps us tap into our own paths, assisted clairvoyance helps us tap into events we're interested in. This is not necessarily the same as tapping into others' actual paths, and not necessarily the same as tapping into the truth of things around us. As I noted in *FSA*, divination tools each have their own personalities, whether those tools come in the form of cards, wheels, deities to whom we pray, or a book of foreign characters. While the Tarot may show you the state of things you ask about, it can also act as a kind of addictive "devil on your shoulder," indulging any fears you already have about anything. The kind of deck you use matters A LOT.[39] If you have any suspicions about the topic at hand, rarely will the Tarot help alleviate those suspicions. The I-ching on the other hand gives flatter advice, and says a lot less about the specific personalities involved in an issue. My "Mandarin Oracle" operates like a basic to-do list, and doesn't so much give me advice as it provides a summary of what's coming up next. Astrology provides you a general map of the personality components making up the person or event you're asking about but almost never will it tell you how to manifest the best version of the chart (though you can often see what that best version is). Aside from the basic divination tools, you can also invoke any number of gods and goddesses to give you insight—as long as your belief in them comes so naturally to you that you can reference them with a casual, functionally-continuous ease. Even though others might say that your gods don't exist, it isn't really a matter of whether they "exist" to others or not. It's more a matter of whether your own math function remains continuous as you reference ANY energy, field, or concept for filling in the holes in your experience. You're just putting one energy field on top of another as a way of keeping the whole of your experience smooth.

☞ Question 54.10.5 (A tour of three tools): **Over the course of the next several days, go on line and experiment with the following three major divination tools: Tarot, I-Ching, and Astrology. Try asking questions and see what kinds of answers you get. Be warned,**

- it may be easier to read something in the I-ching that wasn't actually said. Indeed, you basically *have to* read it this way.
- The Tarot, with its quick visual answers can get very addictive very quickly. If you find yourself suddenly asking question after question after question in order to navigate an increasingly complex web of things you're more and more unsure of, put it down. That kind of spiral is

---

[39] **A note on selecting a tarot deck:** I briefly studied tarot over a decade ago, and still have my deck—the Fey Tarot. At the time, the classic Rider-Waite deck (which many of us are familiar with) struck me as having more judgement, calamity, and medieval Christian-looking images in it than my life actually contained. (Nothing wrong with Christianity, but it wasn't my belief system.) Imagine that you really never experience the kind of ill-fortune shown on the Rider-Waite 10 of swords, or even the kind of crash indicated by the Tower? What if you don't believe in the Devil really? People who specialize in Tarot know that these cards need not always indicate what the pictures seem to show. But as we've seen throughout this book, framing is everything. Rather than subject yourself to the extra level of translation required to turn *a* deck's language into *your* language, you may do better to pick a deck whose theme matches your basic outlook in the first place. Don't feel obligated to go with the defaults. Like any message-bearer, your choice of deck will have a great deal of say over how you understand the story it's conveying.

almost certain to cause you perspective problems later on. Be sure to read the previous footnote on deck selection if you're in a position to choose your deck.

- Astrology has more of a learning curve and is not likely to give you as many answers early on, but the longer you work with it the more you'll see that it offers more long-term stable answers than the above two tools combined.

Write your impressions of the three tools below. How did it feel using them? Was any tool more natural to you than the others?

_____
_____
_____
_____

It is possible to use divination tools to answer almost any question you can think of, provided you've tested a tool enough to be convinced of its merit. The Tarot is especially powerful in this regard. The biggest problem with the Tarot is that it tells you what the outcome would be like *if* it happened, not whether the outcome is actually likely to happen. The I-Ching is more realistic in this regard, but doesn't give you much detail as to how you would bring certain results about. Instead, if you want the ultimate answer regarding that burning question, astrology can show you the full picture of a thing's potential. Let's use all three tools to accurately answer the single most important question we're interested in asking.

Critical Exercise
HOW TO ASK THE MOST IMPORTANT QUESTIONS
Trains: Clairvoyance

This exercise is extra important in that it presents the "correct way" to ask questions under assisted clairvoyance. If you've ever worked with clients before, you know they are constantly asking the kinds of questions that don't really have answers you can help them with. "Will I ever find [such and such]?" "Can you [basically predict my whatever]?" "Can you give me [some clue regarding my own something I haven't started myself yet]?" While these questions may make for informative conversation, they are ultimately not good questions to ask because they put such a heavy, HEAVY weight on you the reader to resolve their entire life's worth of dilemma in a single clean answer. As if anything you told them would suddenly produce some kind of epiphany that the client is going to miraculously act on. Of course, *you* know this is not the case. "Show me my path" questions and "Tell me what I *will* do" questions are as good as worthless in most cases; if the person hasn't put in enough work to start answering these questions for themselves, it's highly likely that you won't be able to do their homework for them either. This doesn't just apply to questions asked *of* you, but also to questions asked *by* you.

In this exercise, you'll pose a burning question that has been on your mind, but it CANNOT BE IN THE FORM OF A "WILL I..." (future question) and CANNOT BE IN THE FORM OF A "SHOW ME..." (road map question). Instead, we'll pose your question in the three ways most conducive to honest, less biased answers from astrology, I-Ching, and the Tarot. We'll begin with astrology, since it provides the best overall summary of what energies are actually possible in your life.

☞ Question 54.10.6 (Your burning question): For now, put your burning question here:
_____
_____

If your question above is in the wrong form, we'll alter it shortly.

Part of the reason that future questions don't work is because the answer to such questions is almost always "yes," albeit in an expressive form rather than an overt form. If you want to know whether you'll ever find your dream job, you've probably already found your dream job except for the little pieces of your own attitude which stop you from seeing it. If you don't believe this, you may need to go back through the Conflict, The Rift, The Spirits, and The Role again. Those old attitude problems should be long taken care of. A rather sarcastic answer to the "will I..." question might be, "I don't know, will you?... That's a matter of your own willingness to take steps in that direction. Don't expect Fate to indulge your laziness with a short cure-all reply."

Before we get to the heart of our burning question, we first need to know how the issue we're asking about is structured in our lives. Anything you can conceive of will be represented in some way in your astrology chart; *how* it's represented will make all the difference. Below are some of the most important astrological bodies related to some of our most important topics.

Table 54-3: Some asteroids for key topics

MPC Number	Name	Interpretation	Topics Related to this Body
		Bad Habits	
709	Fringilla	where you can be critical and bullying to your partners	your mistreatment of others
834	Burnhamia	where you endure a tragic event or exit, alternatively, the circumstance which writes your name in stone in everyone's minds	events you can't seem to end correctly
679	Pax	where your inconstant delivery makes people angry or else incites their passions	your own high stress levels
448	Natalie	the thing which—should you allow to play out negatively, will ruin what you've built; the area whose proper functioning you must preserve no matter what	your self-sabotage
827	Wolfiana	where you spend energy in excess	burning yourself out
351	Yrsa	strong trait for which you are 1:1 sought after	addiction
		Being Used by Others	
801	Helwerthia	where you are receptive to command by those who pressure you despite your strength	where you are a pushover
134340	Pluto-Charon	societal power standard and the pressure to meet it	how friends' friends assess you; the rumor mill; general social pressure
238	Hypatia	where you are bombarded or burdened as the price of being skilled	where others use you up
36	Atalante	where you put yourself on sale for others; consumption; where others suspect that you prostitute yourself—trading your primal instincts for various forms of material approval	selling yourself out
126	Velleda	where sexual exploitation [or sometimes more material forms of corruption] is more likely to be an issue	abuses committed by you
459	Signe	where others fancy you as a source of fulfillment for their own dark desires	abuses committed against you
	White Moon/Selene + Mercury	precocious talent	childhood abuses committed against you
		Career	
962	Aslog	what you seem to be on a quest to perfect through your career	the point of your career
993	Moultona	money-making trade	the nature of your career
		Creative Works	
4580	Child	where your creations must reflect you properly; what you wish for your creations to build up	what you're trying to express creatively
202	Chryseis	where you have an affinity for girls and girly things—feminine and softer versions of things	things you crystallize as collections
946	Poesia	your unsatisfiable vision, never ending quest	your obsessions
		Friendships	
258	Tyche	where you're never without friends	where supporters are always available
2212	Hephaistos	emotional home base	where you are emotionally most comfortable
858	El Djezair	how family and friends are expected to reinforce their connectedness with you [very important for others to know if they want to be in your life])	the things people do to solidify themselves as being like family to you
15760	1992 QB1/ Albion	support attractor	where you are a magnet for support
2063	Bacchus	your friends, cliques, and groups who will always promote your interests	the kinds of people who will always have your back (usually regardless of any dirty secrets you carry)

		Influence Over Others	
497	Iva	excessive extracting from others	where you drain others (the other side of Hypatia)
550	Senta	where you can lead leaders	your top-level leadership potential
952	Caia	where your imagination becomes doctrine	giving form to your creative will
	Mars	steering others	how you easily steer others
72	Feronia	where your style is irresistible to others	where you attract the favor of the world (silver platter)
		Long-Term Issues	
	Saturn	restrictions, boundaries	limits you either own yourself or which own you
269	Justitia	that side of you which suffers if you make wrong decisions	where you must stay in the right
997	Priska	where you are the charismatic second-place to a primary personality, but you are the more stable and more powerful of the two	where you always feel second place or take a support role to another
383	Janina	where you are attractively tempting, but often passed over for more favorable choices; it is often easier to make your own way with the first dedicated partner or opportunity you can find until another comes along; advancement tends to be consistently, but reliably in someone else's hands no matter what your own efforts entail	where you're not picked, despite being qualified; being un(der)impressed (by others with you or by you with something else)
879	Ricarda	where your progress is hampered by larger factors: where you must seek someone else to aid your advancement or else actively resist the very progress you seek	where you cannot advance AT ALL without someone else's help
897	Lysistrata	where you are associated with unconsummated or incomplete relationships [often romance]	where relationships generally are not supposed to work for you
2060	Chiron	therapy, doctor-patient context	chronic health or psychological issues
		Notoriety	
663	Gerlinde	means through which you sponsor followers and fan clubs	where you are popular
626	Notburga	your eccentricity and eccentric tastes; where you shock others constantly	where you surprise others, even by being normal
476	Hedwig	your potentially famous behavior	what you could be famous for
845	Naema	what your name comes to be associated with	what your name is almost guaranteed to be synonymous with in the long run
		Relationships	
103	Hera	deep bonds	the interaction style that fosters your deepest bonds
3	Juno	commitment in the eyes of the world	the types of energy you commit to / marry yourself to
		Spirituality	
734	Benda	where a higher imaginative or spiritual directive seems to shadow your actions	where you seem guided by a higher force
20000	Varuna	giving form to	how you manifest things in your world
519	Sylvania	what you use in order to make your wishes come to pass	behavior you display to bring about your wants (shorter term)
775	Lumiere	where you express a desire for some grand wish to be fulfilled—one that seems outrageous, but may come true; a big wish granted long before you realize it	how you make your longer-term, bigger dreams come true
79	Eurynome	where people expect you to be successful based on your surface characteristics	the role that the world pushes you to be successful in as a person
490	Veritas	where you carry abilities that are bigger than you are; the synecdoche asteroid	where your actions—no matter how odd—align with a greater rightness for those connected to you
195	Eurykleia	where spiritual fortunes are made grandly evident	others' clearest view of your spiritual gifts in action
	White Moon/Selene	your blessed talent	your strongest gift in this life
	Anti-Neptune (the point opposite Neptune)	your spiritual weapon	how you tackle the environment around you

		Status	
585	Bilkis	where you accept only events of value	where only the highest class of things will do for you
302	Clarissa	an accepted role, a place of acceptance in the world	where you are accepted as a person in the world
752	Sulamitis	worldly advancement-enabling gains	how you get ahead in the world
640	Brambilla	what the build-up of money or other kinds of value entails the use of	how you gradually build up value
1688	Wilkens	where extreme wealth comes to you with almost no effort on your part	things you inherit from life / others
		Your Path	
	ASCENDANT	your approach to new situations	why you would get involved in anything
162	Laurentia	the reason you have jobs and opportunities handed to you	where it is possible for you to win nonstop
332	Siri	where you express your unhappiness with established systems	what you are always determined to improve
473	Nolli	where people see you as being in your right element	where you are right at home
423	Diotima	where you appear to strike an ideal balance between two extremes of expression	contradictions you must live with
773	Irmintraud	where you act as a life change agent for others	where you can change other's lives
	Moon	emotions and inclinations	what must be stable and working for you to feel emotionally well
890	Waltraut	perfect ideal acceptance, the best above all else you could ask for	area where—if others have planets here—those planets can do no wrong in your eyes
	VERTEX	susceptibility to life change	how you can force instant change on your life
	mean Node	destiny summarized	your optimal style of *journey* through life (not a "destination")

When you want to know about any of the non-standard bodies in your astro chart, you typically go online and enter the MPC number to add the bodies to your regular chart display. By reading the sign and house where those bodies are located, along with any other bodies next to them, you can get a good sense of how these bodies actually play out in your life. I talk about this throughout the first four books in this series, and won't go over chart reading here. The idea, though, is that you might have a body such as `890 Waltraut` next to `Mars` in your `sixth house`, and if you were asking questions about your potential for happiness in this life, it would tell you that one route to [perfect acceptance] would be `influencing people through work`. Given Table 54-3, let's rephrase our question 54.10.6 in a way that astrology can answer.

☞ Question 54.10.7 (Your burning question as a "capacity" issue): Take your question from 54.10.6 and rephrase it like this: "What is my capacity for..." My own question might have been something naïve like "Will I ever find my perfect partners?" So I would rephrase that as "What is my capacity for interacting with my perfect partners?" Astrology can't answer a "Will I..." question, but it can answer a "What is my pattern for..." question. Once you've rephrased your 54.10.6, try to identify at least one asteroid from Table 54.2 that can help you answer your question. (Mine would have been Juno, Nolli, & Diotima).

_____

_____

_____

☞ **Question 54.10.8 (What does the chart tell you?):** Using Table 54-3 along with what you gather online, describe what your chart says about your question. If you have access to *Full Spectrum Astrology*, you can also use the basic planetary and house combinations in there to help you read your chart.

	Example
	My Nolli & Diotima are close together, so I'm right at home with two extremes. But they are 90° (square/want) away from my Juno, making it unlikely that I can be right at home and be committed at the same time. There would need to be some ongoing quest (want) involved.

Your 54.10.8 may not be what you want to hear, but will be an honest explanation of how your life has arranged certain things to come easily or with difficulty. I already knew the answer to my partners question, and at least won't be fooling myself into thinking there's some happily ever after just around the corner. When you ask certain questions about your life, the answers you get will hopefully be consistent with everything you've lived up to that point. If you're getting answers that make it seem like a major change could arrive in a matter of minutes, you may be deceiving yourself. It doesn't mean that what you're seeking is impossible. It does mean that what you're seeking needs to come in a way that respects the rest of how you've chosen to live up to now. Rarely does this involve a quick fix.

Now we'll turn to the I-ching. You know a little more about the capacity for your question, now we need to know the most helpful attitude for meeting that capacity.

☞ **Question 54.10.9 (How should you approach your question?):** Now, rephrase your 54.10.6 like this: "What is the best attitude or outlook I should take for…" The I-ching is very good at telling you how to view things in order to resolve them smoothly. We want to take your 54.10.8 results and help them work out as favorably as possible.

☞ **Question 54.10.10 (Consult the I-Ching):** Go online and pose your question 54.10.9 to the I-ching. (There are several free sites; just explore them.) Write down your results below. What are your thoughts about those results?

My example question would have been "What is the best attitude I should take for interacting with my ideal partners?" The I-ching gave me a realistic (if not a downer of an) answer. But that's not the end of the inquiry. We still need to know how Fate itself wants us to handle things.

☞ Question 54.10.11 (What does life want?): Rather than using the Tarot to card ourselves into a frenzy, we'll use it to learn what Fate or Life itself wants us to do about our situation. Rephrase your 54.10.6 in the form of "How does Life want me to approach…"

☞ Question 54.10.12 (Consult the Tarot): Go online and pose your 54.10.11 to the Tarot. Write down your results and your thoughts about those results below.

You've asked your burning question and received three related answers regarding your ability to handle your own question. The answers you received didn't provide any instant fixes, but they did present you with some of the best directions possible for properly framing the issue at hand. Normally when we ask the higher realms for insight, we count on the answers we receive to help us overcome our own spinning about the issue. But if we were inclined to spin in the first place, it typically means that we had at least two paths worth traveling in our dilemma, and our best answer may be the one which best supports the comparison of paths itself. Rarely will one perspective be definitively favored over the other. In the end it may be far more valuable learning to live with our contradictions than clinging to a divination tool to make them go away.

*

Assisted Clairvoyance can be as easy to learn as your level of interest in the divination tool of your choosing. Certainly your practice will train a level of insight and problem framing that you may not have otherwise gotten through unassisted clairvoyance or regular interaction. The main problem with assisted clairvoyance lies in the idea that you can get so wrapped up in the images, symbols, and asteroids of it that you forget to ask whether people are *actually* being helped by your counsel, or just feeling a placebo-like relief from having their problem articulated by someone other than them. Not to pass my own skepticism onto you, but after you've seen enough psychics in action—and perhaps been one yourself—you know that most people who regularly consult clairvoyants are the same as people who regularly consult any other kind of counselor: We gain from the conversation itself, though the reading may not be very actionable. This isn't to say that the clairvoyant sense isn't legitimate—not at all. But it is to say that the kinds of questions we typically ask in the clairvoyant vein are more of the "Can I... Will I... Please reassure me..." kind than the "How do I actually solve this..." kind. I recently went online and saw the usual array of questions about soulmates (you can have several), destined careers (which are multi-dimensional) and success (which is relative to all, closer to meaningless if you don't define your own). These all make for entertaining questions, but will it really make a difference to get a psychic answer to these? Or a psychiatric answer? Or a regular conversational answer? While the real value in a clairvoyant answer lies in what normal senses can't show you, a clairvoyant answer doesn't mean very much when all your questions are gee whiz fantasy-based. *Will I ever find that pearl unicorn atop the golden hills?* The clairvoyant may answer you earnestly, but the question is impractical.

I've noted several times throughout this book that clairvoyance is one of the senses which needs to be most heavily tempered with a dose of reality. Just because we can draw on other worlds like second nature, there is this tendency to think that what we've drawn is that much more relevant to the querent's life. Yet most querents don't know what they want and wouldn't know how to ask even if they did know. Many querents who come to us looking for answers will have stopped short of actively seeking those answers on their own. And most answers we offer are more like conversation pieces than actual answers. We humans love our quick fixes; the assumption is that a clairvoyant fix will be even quicker. But that assumption is almost always wrong. Because it invites details from an entire scenario, the clairvoyant answer—when it is accurate—tends to lay out a more complicated, multi-faceted, paradoxical picture than the easy black and white versions our simplifying brains prefer. Your clairvoyant skills will become stronger the more you are able to appreciate the richer world of options available through this dimension without reducing that richness to something flat and easy.

Developing Clairaudience

Clairaudience is where you host words or thoughts which don't seem to come from you. No, it's not like schizophrenia, but instead feels more like reading a book—the kind of book where much of the content is as surprising to you as it is to anyone listening to you. One of the most overt forms of clairaudience is that of spoken channeling, though this isn't the only form. There is also channeled writing, clairaudient narrative, and channeled thoughts. These four forms of clairaudience are basically developed the same way, except that your own way of handling bias and harnessing concentration will steer you towards certain methods over others.

Whereas some senses like projection and clairsentience connect you to the external world, clairaudience connects you to your own internal monologue. As such, there is much less risk of tangling up someone else's business with your otherworldly insights, and a much greater chance of you collecting a lot more information about your own life. Of course, you can always go public with your channels, but this doesn't have to be the default.

Clairaudient messages are more likely to occur in people who value auditory information, conversation, and internal reflection as a means of working out problems, and tend to be clearer where the flow of ideas is comparatively unmoderated. If you're someone who is naturally very careful with her spoken words, you may find that your spoken channels keep wanting to edit themselves unless or until you can determine how to let them pass through more naturally. If you're someone whose thoughts go all over the place, you may channel clairaudient information full of biases unless or until you learn how to direct your thoughts.

My first major psychic experience came in the form of a fascinating spoken channel in which I told myself about my past lives, yet spoken channeling and channeled thoughts have been hit and miss for me ever since (for the reasons I listed above). In order to direct my thoughts, I've found it extremely useful to either 1) write towards an overall point or 2) pose a specific spoken scenario into my recorder. The first method, channeled writing, relies on the writing's objective to keep the clairaudient information from wandering. The second method, clairaudient narrative, uses a focused conversation between two characters to achieve this same goal. If, for example, I wanted to ask my guardians how this book was coming along, I would say something like "The Student goes to the Teacher and asks, 'Okay, how'm I doing?'" The "Teacher" would give his typical reply, "Doing in what?" and the rest of the spoken conversation would flow from there. I must have hundreds of recorded conversations like this, and it is by far one of my clearest routes to any of the psychic senses. Channeled writing comes in a close second. How do you learn to do something like this? Just find some way—any way—to order your thoughts about things for which you have very little information and almost no conversation plan. Then start thinking or talking.

As with the other psychic senses, you do want to verify your clairaudience against reality. The general rule is, if it gives you clarity and makes you better as a person—the same way a good counseling session would—then that's good enough. If you're able to gain insight into things that should have been hidden to you, that's also good, but not the main point of clairaudience. Your insights are for your conscious explorations, not necessarily your channels. Your channels are more about ordering your own understanding of "truth," not defining what that truth is. You can order that understanding best by keeping track of your clairaudient input through writing, recording, or having another listen, then seeing how the message sounds when played back to you later on.

☞ **Question 54.11.1 (A talk with your guardians):** As an introduction to clairaudient messaging, see if you can narrate a conversation with your guardians. Instead of talking to them directly however, tell a story of someone in a position like yours talking to someone like one of your guardians. (I call these the Student and Teacher respectively, but you can call these two whatever you want.) Imagine that the person in your position has some questions for the person in the guardian's position, even if it's just a basic introduction. Write down your experience below.

☞ **Question 54.11.2 (A short story of you):** Imagine looking into a mirror and staring at your reflection. Gradually your vision blurs, and suddenly your reflection begins living its own life. In the space below, describe what your reflection is doing, perhaps why it is doing it, perhaps what it wants or what it cares about. <u>Be sure to fill up as much of the space as possible</u>.

Questions 54.11.1 and 54.11.2 provide early practice in clairaudient narrative and channeled writing respectively. Channeled thoughts and spoken channels are trickier since you'll need to get around your biases in order to receive messages clearly.

☞ Question 54.11.3 (Spoken channel): Find a quiet place where you won't be disturbed for a while. Set your timer for 15 minutes. Now just relax. If at any point you start talking, go ahead and allow yourself to keep talking. If your words aren't in English,[40] you can say "English please" and just keep going. Try to stay with the exercise until the full 15 minutes is over. You may actually want to record the whole thing on audio if you can, since these kinds of spoken channel are often very interesting. Write your experiences below.

_____
_____
_____
_____
_____
_____
_____
_____

Clairaudient channeling is one of those skills which a person either takes to or doesn't, much like projection. For some, the production of words during relaxation may seem like a giant burden while, for others, it may be a phenomenon that refuses to be turned off. The more interested you are in learning new things via the messages you channel, the more likely you are to keep channeling. It should also be noted that you'll tend to channel personalities which are compatible with yours—another reason why, once you've started channeling, you may be less likely to stop the habit. Certain energies will automatically prefer talking through you, probably because you have certain characteristics which align your views more easily with theirs. Once you've made that initial connection, the rest is usually a matter of your own willingness to hear from them again.

Channeled thoughts feel as though someone is running a movie in your head even while your own thoughts continue. You won't necessarily hear voices or even feel like someone is interrupting you, but you may feel as though there are other people in your mental room having a casual conversation about anything they care to talk about. You can practice observing these conversations by practicing regular clairaudient narrative. The only difference between the two modes is that, in clairaudient narrative, you actively participate in the topic creation while, in channeled thoughts, you are a more passive agent.

---

[40] There's a good chance your words won't be in English, for reasons related to the beginning of Chapter 41 in *Laurentia*; when we disconnect the socialized regulation of speech from the need to speak in the first place, we are more likely to get utterances that match our animal gestures than our K-12 ruleset. "Speaking in tongues," as it were, isn't so different from having your Broca's Area, Wernicke's Area, and the rest of your brain's speech arc partly disconnected in the way that some aphasics or sleep paralyzed people have. It's just communication without the lookup table. Don't worry about it.

Depending on the topic of your channeled thoughts, you may experience the messaging more as a stream of inspired ideas than an actual conversation.

That's about all there is to clairaudience. As long as you're not forcing yourself to be the spokesperson for some famous angel[41], biasing your messages with some ego need to enlighten the world, clairaudience works about the same as regular thought. You say, think, or write whatever is on your mind and try not to insert your own edits during the process. If you have the discipline to stay focused on the topic at hand, you may find clairaudience to be among the smoothest of the six intuitive senses to work with, with very little pressure to put on a performance for anyone but yourself.

Developing Claircognizance

Since claircognizance is that sense of automatically knowing which decisions are right for oneself, you won't be surprised to learn that training claircognizance begins with a strong sense of your own feeling about the situations you've gotten into. Through years of simply living your life, learning what you can get away with and what you should stay away from, you develop a kind of hormonal preview for the next best step. The clearer your framing of your next options in terms that the preview deems familiar, the more automatic your decision making can be. What would seem like luck to a bystander ends up being basic energy alignment on your part—between your messaging system and the early-evolving situation. All it takes is your own history of observing what works. That and a genuine lack of interest in pursuing routes that don't work.

We all possess at least some degree of active claircognizance; it is the faculty that guides us towards certain hobbies over others, and certain strong desires to get involved with specific things in the world. I recently read about how the actress Vivien Leigh just "knew" she needed to play Scarlett O'Hara in *Gone with the Wind*, and indeed this iconic role ended up being one with which she is now most strongly associated in film history. Was it destiny that she gravitated so strongly to this character? Or was it a key piece of her long-term Role in American cinema? I believe these are basically the same question. Where certain things may seem like a lottery to everyone else, when they are meant for you, you will be able to read your own name on them from miles away. This is as true for jobs and favorite hobbies as it is for mates and music preferences. When a particular event is meant to be a part of your ultimate sphere, you will have known the connection to it long before it became a viable option. Your tangle with it forms a Role wave long, long, long past the brief window of years where you actually lived. *If*, that is, you haven't let more distracting options get in your way.

☞ Question 54.12.1 (Gravity): Use the space below to list some things throughout your life to which you just gravitated easily. Noted how you've ended up interacting with those things in the time since then.

---

[41] Some people can do this. But don't *force* it.

Claircognizance is all about following your gravity. No matter where life leads you, it will lead you somewhere. But claircognizance doesn't mean just taking whatever events are handed to you. It's more like being given a certain box of drawing tools along with general instructions for the picture you are to produce, then relying on your own talent for the rest. Most of the skill in claircognizance comes from knowing when to ignore what others suggest as safe and go with your own abilities instead. Of course it helps to know what those abilities are. It also helps to be fairly confident in the final product you end up producing.

☞ **Question 54.12.2 (Your creation):** List some of the best decisions you've made even though it meant going against what other people suggested. Also list some of the best decisions you've made which agreed with others' suggestion, but which you pursued for your own reasons.

Recognizing a good claircognizant path is often a matter of seeing the resources which are available to you which aren't available to anyone else. If, for example, you wanted to be a musician despite others' advice, could you see where you had the talent for music which those others didn't have? Perhaps you have the urge and the means to spontaneously travel while others would convince you to wait for retirement. Where you have the ability, where it makes you a better person to yourself and others, and where the door seems to open easily, you may be looking at a path which Fate has made easy for you to follow, not necessarily for everyone else to do so.

In many ways, your Tribe and your Role have an easier time appearing under claircognizance. The people and the paths which are most suited to you are often essential for pushing you forward along the course that is most yours. Resources alone are rarely enough to make a decision path worthwhile, but you'll also need the right environment for facilitating that path. Accordingly, much of claircognizance begins before you have even perceived any decision options at all—as early the mood you're in to go somewhere or do something which doesn't seem to fit the current schedule.

Do you have certain groups or activities which seem to call you spontaneously?

☞ **Question 54.12.3 (The rounds):** You can practice claircognizance by making the rounds between the tribes and activities from several chapters ago. Throughout a full day, <u>practice going from one favored activity to another, to another</u>, depending on what you are scheduled to be doing at the time—whether that's work on the job, house chores, or getting ready to head out. The rounds establish every activity as the correct one, and further reinforce the idea that you already have an intuitive sense of your best direction in life. See if you can keep this going all day, for five days in a row. Keep track of your progress below.

Day 1 Activities:
Day 2 Activities:
Day 3 Activities:
Day 4 Activities:
Day 5 Activities:

It won't be until you've developed a dedicated creative hobby that you'll be able to fully practice claircognizance in a way that allows you to actively produce single creative works or behaviors. Prior to this, your claircognizance might be limited to the task families you've inherited. That's okay. But once you've found your special creative niche for generating original events in the world, the efficient use of this sense will become more obvious—especially as a source of behaviors for better serving your fellow human.

Pursue your rounds and follow the talents that are yours. As usual, it isn't magic, but it is one route to knowing your correct way long before any way has ever presented itself.

Developing Telepathy

The last of the six senses, telepathy, is a lot easier to see in action when used by others rather than yourself. Specifically, telepathy is most obvious in people whom I call "motivators." Clearly we've all met someone who brings out certain characteristics in us that wouldn't otherwise be brought out among other people. You may have asked yourself, "Why do I act this way around this person and not around anyone else?" The behavior brought out of you may be positive or negative, and is typically reinforced by certain attitudes and communicative patterns that the other person displays. Normally when we think of telepathy we might think of the more overt cases of someone staring you in the eye and hypnotizing you into doing their bidding. Perhaps we think of a person trying to move a paper cup with their mind, but most telepathy isn't so dramatic. Instead, the ability of one person to steer the internal actions of another is a lot more common (and often more nefarious) than we would expect. Once again, we see how your energy field can overlap with another energy field in ways that encourage you to place heavier weight on certain among your own behaviors than others. Telepathy, much like clairsentience, can be one of those areas where you really have to practice controlling your space if you are to avoid letting others influence you wrongly—their energy bringing out patterns in everyone they interact with as a way of aligning their own worlds with what they've been taught to expect.

My first major experience with telepathy was with a person I had known for years who had a talent for getting me (and anyone else) to share their complaints with her. You might make an honest decision to start being as positive as possible, but when you got around this person all you did was complain again—mostly about other people. It was a very negative effect that she brought out of others, and the longer I observed it the more I realized that this was partly a byproduct of her conversation style, but mostly a byproduct of her inner attitude towards others in general. She was one of those people who needed to knock others down in order to build herself up, and this wasn't something you emulated with your rapport so much as it was something you automatically averaged into your own sphere-bond with her. Only by refusing to connect with this person in basic conversation could you nullify the effects of her personality on yours, and this is pretty much how all telepathy works. With this sense, it isn't a matter of giving someone the eye in order to force them to do your will. It's more a matter of letting your contagious pattern of relating spread itself to anyone interested in relating to you.

Over the last two years I acquired several cheats that I learned how to use for motivating exercise, writing, and productive work. There are certain people, certain kinds of music, and a certain deliriously tired mood which, if I interact with them, will automatically motivate the above three actions regardless how I feel at the moment. For instance, there are three specific people who appear in some portraits I have, and just by looking at any one of these three people I will go from 0 mode to full on exercise mode in just under a minute. In another example, my friend Emily is one of the only people with whom I prefer visiting new places over old. The list goes on. While you might think that issuing telepathy or serving as a motivator required a lot of focus on your part, it actually doesn't. You can send driving messages to others just by being yourself, to people who will never meet you but will only hear about you or see you in an image. The trick is knowing what kinds of messages you naturally send.

☞ Question 54.13.1 (What they motivate): **Before we get into the kinds of messages you send, let's see if we can better understand the messages that others send to you.** In the space below, list at least four things or people who are THE ONLY ones you behave a certain way around. They can have that effect on people besides you, but *you* won't typically behave in this unique way with others besides them. To give yourself an idea of how strong these others are as motivators, estimate the percentage of the time they are able to successfully evoke this behavior in you.

	Example
	E: I am driven to explore ANY new settings, no matter what I think of those settings on a normal day (80%)
	F: I am instantly driven to exercise (strength), even if I was in no mood at all minutes earlier (90%)
	Akino Arai – Unknown Vision / Maaya Sakamoto – Inori: I am driven to get lost in eccentric creativity (70%)
	Elise Gulan – Elements Ballet Conditioning: I follow the exercises (tone & flexibility) all the way through, with the necessary discipline (80%)

☞ Question 54.13.2 (The unique energy of the motivators [Challenging]): **In the space below, write what you think is the quality held by each of the four things you listed which is THE reason why they serve as such strong motivators. You'll really need to sharpen your powers of description for this one, since you'll basically be describing each thing's energy. You'll want to describe the energies so precisely that it should be clear to you that no other thing you encounter shares this effect. I've given example of my exercise motivator F in the box.**

	Example
	F: is in excellent shape, with a rare top to bottom flow which, in graphic design, would be referred to as a strong visual hierarchy. Whereas we typically focus on one area or another in observing images of beauty, F has a holistic balance of features which draw the eye equally—much like a statue. You would describe her more in the way you described a sweeping landscape or a gallery of an artist's work more than you would describe any singular features she had—where every portion of her draws you to any of the adjacent portions. You won't get stuck on any single feature. So she obeys a kind of aesthetic law that not even the most stereotypically attractive sight obeys—motivating you yourself to also participate in the whole construction of an experience. In this case, your own fitness. There are other things that also trigger instant exercise for me. All of them have this same property: "aesthetic expanse."

☞ **Question 54.13.3 (The energy that calls you):** Take your descriptions from 54.13.2 and summarize them using a single phrase. That phrase should not only describe the thing's energy, but also {who that energy affects and how it affects them}. Definitely look at my examples if you want a preview of how this is done.

	Example
	E: Acceptance of the other person's most open creative flow {people who want to release their full creativity}
	F: Far-reaching aesthetic expanse which converts a local person into a full situation {those who want to experience the full situation, not just a surface}
	UV / I: A person's relentless dream backed by an enduringly stretched intensity; you can't say they didn't put everything they had into it {those who value the maximum put into one's work}
	Gulan Ballet: Guided, graceful mastery {those who, when not pursuing flowing mastery under their own power, are pursuing it under someone else}

It won't surprise you to learn that your 54.13.3 resonates with energies in your own sphere. Part of the reason you would be so deeply affected by certain telepathic messages is because those messages are stronger outsourcings of your own full energy. Note however that these energies are exactly that: energies. They are patterns of signals and patterns of attention rather than static traits or deeds you like having done. As telepathic messages they are more like modes of broadcast which transform one level of attention into another, at one level of intensity or another, against one style of frequency background or another. In that regard, you may find it easier to draw the energies you're getting than to describe them. But we won't do that here. Instead we'll look at your own major effect on other people, and see if we can decipher the kinds of telepathic messages you yourself are best at sending.

☞ **Question 54.13.4 (Resonant others):** Imagine there is a particular type of want-style out there which you are very strong at compelling. That is, if a person has this particular kind of want-style, there is a high percentage chance that you will be able to motivate them. You may not be able to attract them as allies, but you will definitely be able to compel their reaction. Think about the kinds of people you have affected in your life even when you weren't trying to do so. These people may have declared themselves your ally, enemy, fan, or simply someone who reacted strongly to you. Describe these want styles in the same way that you did in the {} of 54.13.3.

	Example
	{those who love being the center of attention / commanding others' ceaseless interest}
	{those who have a unique, pioneering, possibly unusual message which they will advance completely solo if they have to}
	{those who fight for those who can't fight for themselves}
	{those who have a passionate genius about them}

☞ **Question 54.13.5 (Theme messages):** Now we'll try reverse-engineering your answers to 54.13.4. For each of the want-styles you listed in the previous question, see if you can list a song which enables that energy. Consider it to be the case that, if a person likes that song, there's a decent chance they'll like you, and perhaps even resonate with much of your music (frequency) tastes for that category in general. Try to pick songs which best capture your overall music preferences. We're investigating your general energy pattern here.

	Example
	Digital Underground – Kiss U Back, Sarah Vaughan – Doodlin' (fun / shameless center of attention)
	Aoife O-Donovan – King of All Birds, Steve Winwood – Higher Love (acoustic friendship & love/pioneering solo message)
	Mountain Heart – Another Day, Cream – White Room (bluegrass & classic rock/ those who fight for those who can't fight for themselves)
	Jeffrey Smith – Afro Blues, Ekaj – Super Metroid Zebes Rising, Kirby Superstar – Marx's Theme, Mesmerizer - Like a Machine (Brain Attack), (maze jazz, intellectually intricate / passionate genius)

☞ **Question 54.13.6 (Hypnotize them):** Given your answers to 54.13.5, perhaps you can see how it's possible for you to purposely send certain messages to people with your energy—keeping in mind the kinds of people they are and whether or not they seem to resonate with you or simply squirm under your presence. If you've ever noticed certain intriguing patterns with the personalities you attract it may be because of the combination of energy patterns you naturally broadcast. You may, for example, send a natural combination of messages which is so mixed that only another complex personality like your own would be able to withstand it. Or maybe you send the kinds of signals that everyone likes, so that you have to beat people off of you with a stick. While your mind might be interested in sending specific messages to others, your broad energy has probably decided on this issue long before you knew how to address it. The kinds of messages available to you for telepathic sending will more likely align with your 54.13.5, and will be more likely received by people who already prefer to hear those messages. In the space below, rephrase your 54.13.5 responses as if they were commands or strong suggestions instead—to be issued only to the kinds of people receptive to such commands.

	Example
	{I want you to be the shameless center of attention; so much so that you might make people uncomfortable.}
	{Your message of love, openness and honesty is right. Don't let anyone tell you it isn't.}
	{Your difficult background will be used for other's benefit far beyond yourself. You can handle what they couldn't.}
	{Your brilliance will produce works that are out of this world. People may not be able to keep up today, but they will know who you are tomorrow.}

☞ **Question 54.13.7 (Messages of encouragement):** Now imagine that the people who need to hear those messages above also need some encouragement from you, since it's not always easily living with characteristics that the norming world tries to silence. Imagine that the other person might be asking, "Why do I have to live with [this characteristic]?" And it's your job to give them a reason. For each of the telepathic messages you've been listing, use the space below to give someone else a reason why the trait is so important. Tell them why their unique possession of the trait is so important for everyone else (as well as themselves).

	Example
_____	Without people at the center, no one would feel safe being themselves. But *everyone* has a unique self. Your way is critical for a less judgmental, more fun world.
_____	People learned to stop expressing genuine love because it wasn't professional, practical, or money-making enough, or because it was seen as weak. But more than ever we need people to be brave enough to build bridges across people's safe status crutches. You're among the truly brave.
_____	Your story—both the negative beginning and its important resolution—will give so many people something to hold onto. Without you, the way forward for them will be lost as it was generations before this. Your story is a beacon.
_____	I know you don't want to be isolated, but everyone in their uniqueness is automatically isolated in some corner of vision which only they have. You turning your isolation into a singularly brilliant work lets people know just how special this side of life really is.
_____	
_____	
_____	

See how telepathic messages don't just exist for our own manipulation of others. They are energetic messages tied to people's identities—including our own. Because they tend to be connected to only a few people, however, there is often an element of isolation that comes with being a telepathic motivator. Often you or they will be the only one in people's lives who provides the kind of energy in question, so that the same energy that outsiders see as some kind of special talent will appear to the bearer as a burden that must simply be endured. When you yourself are a telepathic sender, the recipient of your messages may also face a different kind of isolation, and may depend on you as the rare motivator for whatever kind of energy they need to draw upon at the time. Once in the realm of the telepathic, it may be safe to assume that you're working with people's subsurface inclinations, so this is not the time to be rough with the contents of other's subconscious. You too as a sender of messages will want to do more than just toy with others' wants. Here we've practiced handling the wants of others with care: the same way we would want our own inclinations handled by another.

Conclusion

And so we've made it through all six of the psychic senses. We've theorized regarding how they work and practiced developing them on a basic level within ourselves. We've discussed a few trouble spots in our work with those senses and seen how they don't necessarily need to look like magic in order for us to use them properly.

Most importantly, we've seen how the psychic senses rely heavily on the idea of people as energy fields, and how resonances among those fields are the key to clear sending and receiving of information. When we engage in energy exchange, it's important to protect ourselves from energy that would drain us or otherwise cost us, and much of this is a matter of diverting our attention away from influences we don't want. Particularly with forms of clairsentience, it can be very easy to be bombarded by other people's issues, so the more practice we get keeping negative others out of our space the better for all of our senses across the board.

While we're still new to the psychic senses, there is a tendency to think of all the cool things we would do in only we could tap into alien worlds, gain all kinds of knowledge from the cosmos, or summon all manner of upper level entity for inclusion in our spiritual playgrounds. As we progress in our psychic development, however, a lot of these ideas yield to the basic realities of continued human life. If we weren't past our conflicts before developing these new senses, we probably won't be afterwards. If we weren't inclined to listen to spiritual advice for making ourselves better before developing the new senses, we probably won't be afterwards. While there are surely some advantages to having the psychic senses available (namely a certain style of warning before we make foolish decisions), most of the advantages of the psychic senses lie in the steps we must take to develop them. Knowing ourselves and what we resonate with, knowing how to defend our energy and where our energy is encouraged to serve as a guest… To practice these is to reap the benefits of the psychic senses regardless of whether or not the senses ever come online in a way that we would appreciate. Hopefully throughout this chapter though, you have found a sense or two which you might be interested in further developing, and whose benefits you will be able to reap accordingly. Keep practicing, and try to avoid weighing yourself down with all of the sparkly promises of psychic ability. It's just science, and you're still you. Your abilities may amplify who you already are, but they won't miraculously solve problems you were unwilling to look at beforehand.

Chapter 55. The Asteroid

We have officially reached a turning point in our journey. Now that we have been exposed to the psychic senses, possibly even using them to augment our understanding of our Role, it is possible to introduce certain things in our lives that formerly would have been "nice to haves." While you were still learning your path, certain experiences like money or fame may have eluded you as being in the way of your spiritual priorities. Had you made all the money you wanted, you might not have asked the kinds of questions you needed to in order to become who you are. Or maybe you had plenty of money, but couldn't find the friendship security. But had you acquired all the friend security you wanted, you might not have explored all of the issues of personal worth needed to become who you are. Now that's all over and done with. You've resolved your conflicts, determined your Role, understood your friends, and glimpsed the different senses for learning even more about your perfect path. Now we can go about the business of manifesting all of the riches and relationships and success we ever wanted, right?

But not so fast. While it may be true that we've entered the realm of the "nice to haves," that doesn't mean that every advertised thing we can think of will suddenly become something that fits us. Graduating in your spirituality doesn't automatically give you access to every conceivable treasure there is. All it means is that you've cleared the period of uncertainty regarding where you are supposed to go in life. There will be nice-to-haves from this point forward, but nice for whom? The old treasures didn't fit your old ego, do you think they'll fit you now? Maybe they will. Maybe they won't. That will depend on your energetic setup. In this chapter, we'll investigate how to read that setup in your astrology chart, with a very, very brief crash course in the astrology of manifestation.

The aim of this chapter is to give you a general overview of how to read the potential in your astrology chart. The treatment here will be nowhere near as detailed as the treatment in *FSA* or *HBS*, won't have nearly as many asteroids as *Laurentia*, and won't have the advanced methods of *144*, but should give you an idea of how to pull the information you're looking for out of your chart.

A Review of the Chart

Let's briefly review some astrology basics as provided in *HBS* Chapter 16:

- Astrology involves the study of space objects at a particular time and from a particular viewpoint. The position of each object captures the state of an "event" that occurs at that point. Planets and signs don't really mean anything, but their orbits and angles mean <u>everything</u> in determining what each planet and sign is about.

- The **signs** (like Capricorn and Aquarius) are **sections of the <u>universal</u> sky which give a certain character to the objects in them**. But they don't have any real meaning by themselves. Instead, signs are like tilt directions in the gravitational "field" of our solar system, within the gravitational field of our galaxy, within our cluster of space dust flying off of the Big Bang. The signs spin around the chart throughout the day as different stars rise and set against the Earth's horizon.

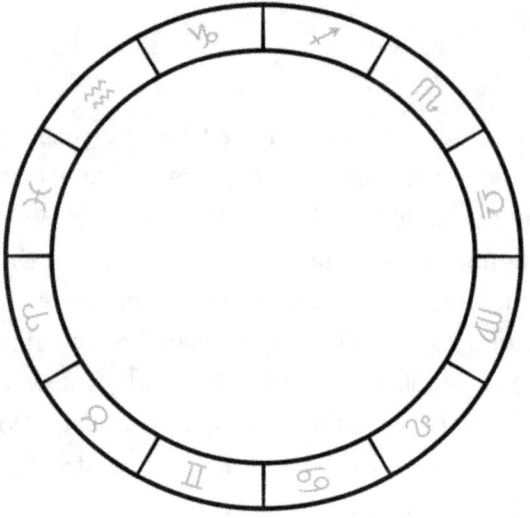

♈	Aries
♉	Taurus
♊	Gemini
♋	Cancer
♌	Leo
♍	Virgo
♎	Libra
♏	Scorpio
♐	Sagittarius
♑	Capricorn
♒	Aquarius
♓	Pisces

Figure 55-1 [16-1]: The signs divide the sky into sections against the background of the <u>universe</u>. These spin around the wheel throughout the day (which is why you need an accurate birth time to read most charts).

Also, in what is the most obvious turn of all, the turn of the Earth with respect to the Sun gives us night and day. Divide up the sky into 12 sections starting with the rising eastern horizon and you get the **houses**: regions of the <u>local</u> sky which tell you the areas of life your various planets are most comfortable expressing in.

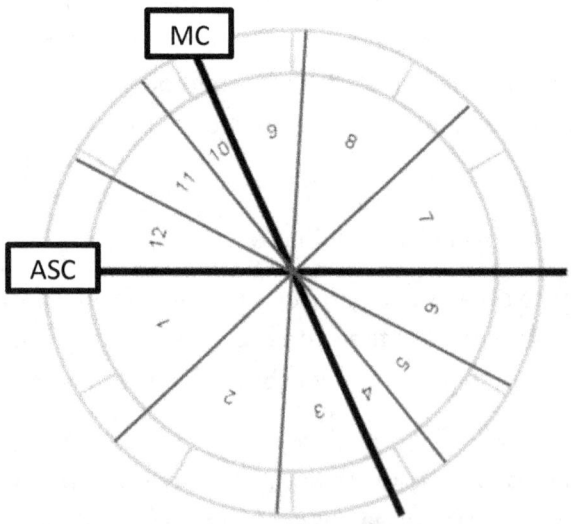

House 1.	Personal approach to new things
House 2.	Personal value, identity
House 3.	Personal internal monologue and close communication
House 4.	Personal home and family
House 5.	1:1 interaction (to another); hobbies, fun, personal expression process
House 6.	1:1 meaning making and common ground with another; fitness, analysis, service, daily work
House 7.	1:1 communication (back and forth with another); friends and open enemies
House 8.	1:1 steering of another; sex, death, the occult, psychology
House 9.	Higher learning, long journeys, marriage: image projection in the world
House 10.	Reputation, career: structure making in the world
House 11.	Social groups, surrounding talk, public aspirations: information-bathing in the world
House 12.	Secrets, institutions, creativity, spirituality: mood-making in the world

Figure 55-2 [16-2]: The houses divide the sky into sections against the background of the <u>local sky</u>. Although their widths change depending on latitude and time of day, they don't rotate around the wheel the way the signs do.

Since the Earth is tilted, the sections of its local sky are usually unequal. There are several **ways to slice the sky into sections**, and these different ways are called **house systems**. I use Topocentric/Polich-Page houses, but this is a personal preference. Placidus house and Koch house systems are also popular. The start of a house (going counterclockwise from house 1) is called a cusp, where the **start of the 1st house** (the **Ascendant (ASC)** / rising sign) and the start of the 10th house (the **Midheaven (MC)**) are the most important.

- If you look at **the Earth's tilt with respect to the background of the Sun, the signs will be based on seasons**. This is the **tropical system** we're all familiar with—where a new sign starts around the 21st or 22nd of every month. But if you look at the Earth's tilt against the background of the rest of the universe (and hence the actual stars, you get the **sidereal system**—where all of the signs are moved backwards by 1° for every 72-ish years past the year 285 c.e. or so. Under this system, the sign of Aries in 2021 actually has its first 25° taken up by the stars of Pisces, other constellations like Ophiucus squeeze into the picture, all the constellations defy "30° neatness," and if you're doing real astronomy like NASA, this is what you rely on. But we regular people don't care about this because it's all the modern Aries anyway. So we assume the tropical system...even if today's egotistical Leo would have been considered an attention-needy Cancer 2000 years ago.

Table 55-1 [17-3]: What the signs do (simple)

Signs and their common associations		
Aries	**Leo**	**Sagittarius (Saj)**
Instinct, assertion, bravery, pressure to BE, spontaneity, creation, existence	ego, attention, good standing, leadership, reliability, pride	fun, exploration, journey, success, importance, luck, politics, fame, expansiveness
Taurus	**Virgo**	**Capricorn**
self-image, money, confidence, body, sensation, self-value (ideas that you build your identity against)	meaning, comparative health, analytical nature, rules of order	rules, karma, old age, time, built structures, wealth as security, law, history, authority, respect
Gemini	**Libra**	**Aquarius**
Internal thoughts, ideas, dexterity, driving, talking	fairness, affinity, friendship, sharing, manners	sociable detachment, society, rumors, peer groups, technology, humane ideals, renown
Cancer	**Scorpio**	**Pisces**
subconscious, feeling, dreaming, wants, connection, emotionality, the home, mothery-ness	sex, death, others' money, psychology, power, the occult	humane feeling, intuition, illusion, escape, the hidden, art, abstraction

Table 55-1 [17-3]: Basic sign characteristics

- All cycles that we'll use in basic astrology are divided into 12 sections for three reasons.
  - First, 12 can be divided into a **beginning, middle, and end—three sections of four. Section 1 shows how we interact with ourselves, section 2 shows how we interact with others or objects right in front of us, and section 3 shows how we interact with the faceless world around us**. I call these the **self-other-world** levels. The first four signs, Aries through Cancer, are all about what you feel

like doing from within. The next four, Leo through Scorpio, concern your 1:1 interactions with others. The last four (Sagittarius through Pisces) are all about how you interact with the world beyond your direct influence.

- o Secondly, 12 can be divided into four key points on a cycle: rising, sitting at peak, falling, and sitting at minimum. These four points also correspond nicely to the **elements**: [a **family of labels which describe 1)** a process *without* an apparent background context (action; **Fire**), **2)** a finished process turned into an object *with* context (object; **Earth**), **3)** a finished object turned into a process *with* context (thoughts; **Air**)**, and 4)** a finished thought turned into an object *without* context (the inclination to do the next action; **Water**)]. Here, "context" is just the surrounding stuff which gives a thing its shape. The elements aren't actually elements, but metaphors for how "tangible" an experience is.

- o ⚒ Third, to make a very complicated story short, 12 divisions is trigonometrically favorable, since it enables the existence of halfway points on a 2-dimensional graph depicting real versus "imaginary" (potential) energy. It also allows us to easily form planes within planes—triangles within triangles which build up new combinations of real-imaginary energy from similar, older ones. Lay out a bunch of pennies together as tightly as possible to see what I mean.

- The planets/bodies in an astrochart all have angles between each other. The angle of separation between bodies (from Earth's viewpoint) is called an **aspect**. Although astrology traditionally assigns meaning only to major aspects like 0° of separation (conjunct, 0°), $1/3$ of a circle (trine, 120°), $1/4$ of a circle (square, 90°), and a few others, all angles of separation actually have meaning depending on how many times you have to loop them to make a whole circle. For example, you need 4 repeats of a square (90°) to make 360°, so squares give a meaning similar to orbit #4. But you need 35 repeats of a III-undecile ($1/35$ of a circle 10°17′), so it behaves like orbit #35. **Families of angles which require the same number of repeats to make a whole circle** are called **harmonics**. So 72° and 144° are both part of the "quintile" (5th) harmonic because they both need to repeat 5 times in order to line up with a full circle of 360°, 720°, 1080°… In *FSA* I did the statistics on these to determine what angles like $1/35$ of a circle mean, and repeat the findings in *Table 55-2 [16-6]*. Lastly, every time we start **a new layer of 12 harmonics**, we go up one **level**. 0° through $1/12$ of a circle constitute **level I**. $1/13$ through $1/24$ of a circle form **level II**. $1/25$ through $1/36$ of a circle form **level III**.

Table 55-2 [16-6]: The harmonics (angle families) 1-36

The angles of separation (aspects) between bodies constitute the main thing that gives you all of the combinations of characteristics in astrology, so you should try to get familiar with these.

Harmonic	Name	Symbol	Degrees	Meaning	How to use
1	conjunct	☌	0°	natural trait	do something, be yourself
2	opposition	☍	180°	natural value	feel something, value something
3	trine	△	120°	easy thought	think about something

4	square	□	90°	wanting, having an inclination	want something
5	quintile	★ or Q	72°, 144°	projecting your way 1:1 with another	notice how you promote yourself to others
6	sextile	✱	60°	finding common ground with another	serve, work, or analyze
7	septile	✵	51°26', 102°51', 154°17'	share ideas under a common topic with another	notice how you share ideas with others; notice what kinds of games you prefer to play
8	octile	∠ or ⚹	45°, 135°	overriding other's intent	manipulate another's actions
9	novile	九 or N	40°, 80°, 160°	declaring one's identity in the world	notice how you declare your identity
10	decile	+	36°, 108°	forming a reputation	consistently perform actions which others can see
11	undecile	U	32°44', 65°27', 98°11', 130°55', 163°38'	gaining popularity	perform unique actions which few can copy
12	inconjunct	⊼	30°, 150°	leaving an impression without doing the actual deed	notice how others treat you in light of things you haven't done
13	II-conjunct	σ^2	27°42', 55°23', 83°05', 110°46', 138°28', 166°09'	your expressive style	note the tools you use to promote your values. These could be objects or tactics
14	II-opposition	σ^{o2}	25°43', 77°09', 128°34'	what your values are intended to accomplish	let others interact with your socially (ethnically) trained ideas or respond to your physical presence
15	II-trine	$\triangle^2$	24°, 48°, 96°, 168°	what you strongly extract from others simply by being around	show up and give your unqualified opinion
16	II-square	$\square^2$	22°30', 67°30', 112°30', 157°30'	what you wish to be respected for	develop an expert's intuition for subjects related to this angle family
17	II-quintile	★² or Q²	21°11', 42°21', 63°32', 84°42', 105°53', 127°04', 148°14', 169°25'	what you brag about, complain on behalf of, and are personally proud of	let others praise you regarding planets separated by this angle family
18	II-sextile	✱	20°, 100°, 140°	your goal-oriented work efforts	investigate, then practice the most important ideas you seek to build up in others
19	II-septile	✵	18°57', 37°54', 56°51', 75°47', 94°44', 113°41', 132°38', 151°35', 170°32'	how you present compelling ideas to others	imagine yourself in an idealized conversation with someone over an issue you think is important; note how that image relates to the planet pair
20	II-octile	∠² or ⚹²	18°, 54°, 126°, 162°	unstated, but well-known magnetism, causes of jealousy in others	publicly display those values, material possessions, and tokens of self-worth which are intended to manipulate viewers' feelings
21	II-novile	九² or N²	17°09', 34°17', 68°34', 85°43', 137°09', 171°25'	overadherence to rules, excessive zeal for proving you've met a standard	think about what you believe to be the most important ideas in your world, then consider the values you hold and behaviors you adopt concerning those ideas; learn to convince others of the importance of those ideas through actions, not words alone
22	II-decile	+²	16°22', 49°05', 81°49', 114°33', 147°16'	the standards against which you measure a proper reputation; the reputation you earn by structuring things	combine all pairs in +² into a single ideal career; investigate how you would pursue that career

23	II-undecile	U²	15°39', 31°18', 46°57', 78°16', 93°55', 125°13', 140°52', 172°10'	standalone individualism, values that get you talked about in the world	collect items, ideas, or people you believe to be unique
24	II-inconjunct	⊼²	15°, 75°, 105°, 165° (tao)	works of the imagination which are likely to manifest in the real world	pay attention to those things which you are inclined to stick with through thick and thin; reinforce this dedication
25	III-conjunct	☌³	14°24', 28°48', 43°12', 100°48', 115°12', 172°48'	your vehicles for expression; your deeds which align with mass psychology	ask what characteristics people tend to come to you for and what characteristics cause people to stay away from you; what about you as a person makes others jealous?
26	III-opposition	☍³	13°51', 69°14', 96°55'	your tendency to check your actions against your values; fans and supporters	notice where and how you publicly question decisions you've made; when do fans follow you?
27	III-trine	△³	13°20', 26°40', 66°40', 106°40'	your ability to broadcast your ideas without remorse; forward confidence; insight	locate the △³s in your chart and do more of what the pairs suggest; exercise where you have insight
28	III-square	□³	12°51', 157°09'	your ability to deliver measured cooperation while still maintaining your own perspective; morals	look at those areas where you don't care what others have to say about your choices; stay with those choices
29	III-quintile	⋆³ or Q³	12°25', 24°50', 37°14', 62°04', 86°54', 124°08', 148°58', 173°48'	your ability to use humor and hold a self-contented sense of prosperity	look at areas in which others don't take you seriously; master them by not taking yourself so seriously in those same areas
30	III-sextile	⋆	12°, 84°, 132°, 156°	your ability to deliver expert criticism	look at areas in which most other groups of people defer to your judgment; learn to deliver your criticism in ways that don't violate others' sense of self-respect
31	III-septile	✲	11°37', 23°14', 34°50', 58°04', 92°54', 116°08'	your ability to engage a task all the way through; spreading doctrines and beliefs through speech	look at areas in which you are attentive to detail in every aspect, every time; practice engaging those areas without getting drained
32	III-octile	∠³ or ⊡³	11°15', 78°45', 146°15	your ability to delve beneath the surface of an event and break your relationship with it if necessary; an interest in mysteries	think about the things you love doing, where interactants are less enthusiastic than you are; learn to read cues for when you've dwelled too long on those things
33	III-novile	九³ or N³	10°55', 21°49', 76°22', 109°05', 141°49'	your ability to get a group fired up	channel your influence over receptive groups towards a useful cause which others are inclined to support
34	III-decile	+³	10°35', 52°56', 74°07', 158°49'	your ability to elevate yourself above others; your ideas regarding authority	behave as you believe a true authority would
35	III-undecile	U³	10°17', 30°51', 41°09', 113°09', 174°51'	your ability to follow your unique curiosity	indulge your curiosity regarding planets in this harmonic
36	III-inconjunct	⊼³	10°, 50°, 70°, 110°, 130°, 170°	your ability to promote an idea despite the secret impression behind it	investigate why you present your ideas as you do; admit areas where you lack focus and develop workarounds

Table 55-2 [16-6]: the first 36 of 144 possible angle families in a 12 cycle cut in to 12 more pieces.

Chapter 55: The Asteroid

Table 55-3 [16-2]: What the houses do

Time frame	Scope	House	What is represented	Types of experience associated with the house
Night	Self	1 ASC	An internal action or event …	First impressions; appearances, attitude towards confronted world; characteristic means of expression
		2	Yields to a bodily state or identity context…	Self-worth; body image; ideas about worth in general which are built on self-worth; characteristic means for assigning value to the self; feelings about who one is;
		3	Which exchanges energy with existing physiology…	Voice; means of expression; how one talks to regular familiar people when conveying personal thoughts (thus sibling relationships); how one decides to present internal ideas to others; conveyances (like cars / how one sends his ideas around);
		4	Leaving a new dyadic inclination for…	Home; subconscious; feelings about what one is doing (not the same as self-worth); memory; dreams; emotional training; stereotypical mother
	Other	5	An interaction-centered action or event…	Voluntary, fun relationships, friendship groups and hobbies; how one gets attention from things he wants
		6	That becomes practical context…	Daily routine; health; kind of effort one puts into his work; job tasks and what one's daily doings look like
Day		7	Which exchanges communication with others…	Who we voluntarily socialize with (even if it means fighting) the type of people who generally surround us; people to whom we are attracted and the characteristics which sponsor this; how we best communicate with the people
		8	Leaving a new (us-centered inclination) for a…	Anything which involves us using things that people wouldn't normally share willingly; steering others' emotions, physical response, and psychology; others' money; knowing their secrets; keeping our own
	World	9	Circumstance-aimed action or event…	Anything which involves the desire to project something in the world without actually limiting it with structure; marriage association; parties; exploration of the unknown; unbounded (higher) education; nationality
		10 MC	That becomes a circumstance-defining context…	Anything which involves limits too big for us to directly influence; institutions; our long-term reputation (our categorization in the eyes of the world); fatherly discipline; discipline in general; time; consequences of our actions (where we end up in order to pay for what we broke)
		11	Which contextualizes groups of ideas…	Groups we want to be a part of; information we surround ourselves with; the kind of talk which follows us; social cliques and information fields associated with us
		12	Leaving a new internal inclination for …	Any feelings whose source we can't identify; intuition; what our spirituality looks like; sickness; the vibe that we impress others with and hence, the kind of people we attract who like that vibe; any behaviors which create unidentifiable impressions in others; art; acting; music; other entertainment; Any public impressions which inspire us to individual action; service of others (often health or illusion based); containment of others (through imprisonment); containment of ourselves (unstable responses in light of excessive negative impressions)

- I've used the term "**asteroid**" in this book **to refer to anything that can show up in an astrochart which represents a particular kind of experience**. As I've noted before, however, "asteroids" don't have to be actual asteroids, but can be planets, locations, or even imaginary points. The main planets and asteroids we have been using are summed up in *table 16-3*.

Table 55-4 [16-3]: What the main planets, asteroids, and points do

Planet	Body type	General meaning
Main Bodies		
Moon	Planet	Inner emotional world
Sun	Star	How your motivation to interact with others plays out
Mercury	Planet	Meaning making, what you show you value with another
Venus	Planet	Willing socialization with another
Mars	Planet	How you steer interactants' inner emotional worlds
Jupiter	Planet	How your instinct to interact with the world plays out
Saturn	Planet	Structures set in place by the world at large (not you, not other individuals) with which you interact; institutions
Uranus	Planet	The information that floats around you; thus social talk, friends, hang-out groups you wish you were like, technology
Neptune	Planet	Your generation's socio-emotional tendency; group emotional vibe on average
Pluto	Dwarf Planet	Your generation's instinctual urge or priority; what the collective pressures its members to value
Other bodies and calculated points		
Ascendant (1st house cusp)	Calculated Point/cusp	How you approach the world
Midheaven (10th house cusp)	Calculated Point/cusp	Your reputation and career
Ceres	Dwarf Planet (1)	Where you take care of others
Chiron	Centaur (2060)	Where you need to be validated
Selene (White Moon)	Calculated Point	Gifts you are super-blessed with
Lilith (Lunar Apogee/ Black Moon)	Calculated Point	The point where you are most defiant or most contrary against the usual norms
Vertex	Calculated Point	Where others can change your life easily and drastically
North Node	Calculated Point	"Destiny" (but not really); more like the focal point around which your emotions are targeted
Part of Fortune	Calculated Point	Where you are in your element
Vesta	Asteroid (4)	Your focus backed with action
Pallas	Asteroid (2)	Your intellectual contribution to the greater good
Juno	Asteroid (3)	Your formally committed relationships in the eyes of the world
Hera	Asteroid (103)	Who you actually bond with
Eros	Amor asteroid (433)	What turns you on
Bacchus	Apollo asteroid (2063)	Where you make the best host for others; groups you actually serve

Table 55-4 [16-3]: Planets and locations of interest in a chart. Minor planet designations are listed in () where they apply—just in case you need their numbers to look up online.

- Additionally, there are many other asteroids we have covered so far throughout this book.

Chapter 55: The Asteroid

Table 55-5 [54-2] Additional bodies

Name	MPC Number	Interpretation
Fringilla	709	where you can be critical and bullying to your partners
Burnhamia	834	where you endure a tragic event or exit, alternatively, the circumstance which writes your name in stone in everyone's minds
Pax	679	where your inconstant delivery makes people angry or else incites their passions
Natalie	448	the thing which—should you allow to play out negatively, will ruin what you've built; the area whose proper functioning you must reserve no matter what
Wolfiana	827	where you spend energy in excess
Yrsa	351	strong trait for which you are 1:1 sought after
Helwerthia	801	where you are receptive to command by those who pressure you despite your strength
Hypatia	238	where you are bombarded or burdened as the price of being skilled
Atalante	36	where you put yourself on sale for others; consumption; where others suspect that you prostitute yourself—trading your primal instincts for various forms of material approval
Velleda	126	where sexual exploitation [or sometimes more material forms of corruption] is more likely to be an issue
Signe	459	where others fancy you as a source of fulfillment for their own dark desires
Aslog	962	what you seem to be on a quest to perfect through your career
Moultona	993	money-making trade
Child	4580	where your creations must reflect you properly; what you wish for your creations to build up
Chryseis	202	where you have an affinity for girls and girly things—feminine and softer versions of things
Poesia	946	your unsatisfiable vision, never-ending quest
Tyche	258	where you're never without friends
Hephaistos	2212	emotional home base
El Djezair	858	how family and friends are expected to reinforce their connectedness with you [very important for others to know if they want to be in your life])
1992 QB1/Albion	15760	support attractor
Iva	497	excessive extracting from others
Senta	550	where you can lead leaders
Caia	952	where your imagination becomes doctrine
Feronia	72	where your style is irresistible to others
Justitia	269	that side of you which suffers if you make wrong decisions
Priska	997	where you are the charismatic second-place to a primary personality, but you are the more stable and more powerful of the two
Janina	383	where you are attractively tempting, but often passed over for more favorable choices; it is often easier to make your own way with the first dedicated partner or opportunity you can find until another comes along; advancement tends to be consistently, but reliably in someone else's hands no matter what your own efforts entail
Ricarda	879	where your progress is hampered by larger factors: where you must seek someone else to aid your advancement or else actively resist the very progress you seek
Lysistrata	897	where you are associated with unconsummated or incomplete relationships [often romance]
Gerlinde	663	means through which you sponsor followers and fan clubs
Notburga	626	your eccentricity and eccentric tastes; where you shock others constantly
Hedwig	476	your potentially famous behavior
Naema	845	what your name comes to be associated with
Benda	734	where a higher imaginative or spiritual directive seems to shadow your actions
Varuna	20000	giving form to

Sylvania	519	what you use in order to make your wishes come to pass
Eurynome	79	where people expect you to be successful based on your surface characteristics
Veritas	490	where you carry abilities that are bigger than you are; the synecdoche asteroid
Eurykleia	195	where spiritual fortunes are made grandly evident
Anti-Neptune		your spiritual weapon
Bilkis	585	where you accept only events of value
Clarissa	302	an accepted role, a place of acceptance in the world
Sulamitis	752	worldly advancement-enabling gains
Brambilla	640	what the build-up of money or other kinds of value entails the use of
Wilkens	1688	where extreme wealth comes to you with almost no effort on your part
Laurentia	162	the reason you have jobs and opportunities handed to you
Siri	332	where you express your unhappiness with established systems
Nolli	473	where people see you as being in your right element
Diotima	423	where you appear to strike an ideal balance between two extremes of expression
Irmintraud	773	where you act as a life change agent for others
Waltraut	890	perfect ideal acceptance, the best above all else you could ask for

All in all, a complete astrology chart looks like Figure 55-3 below.

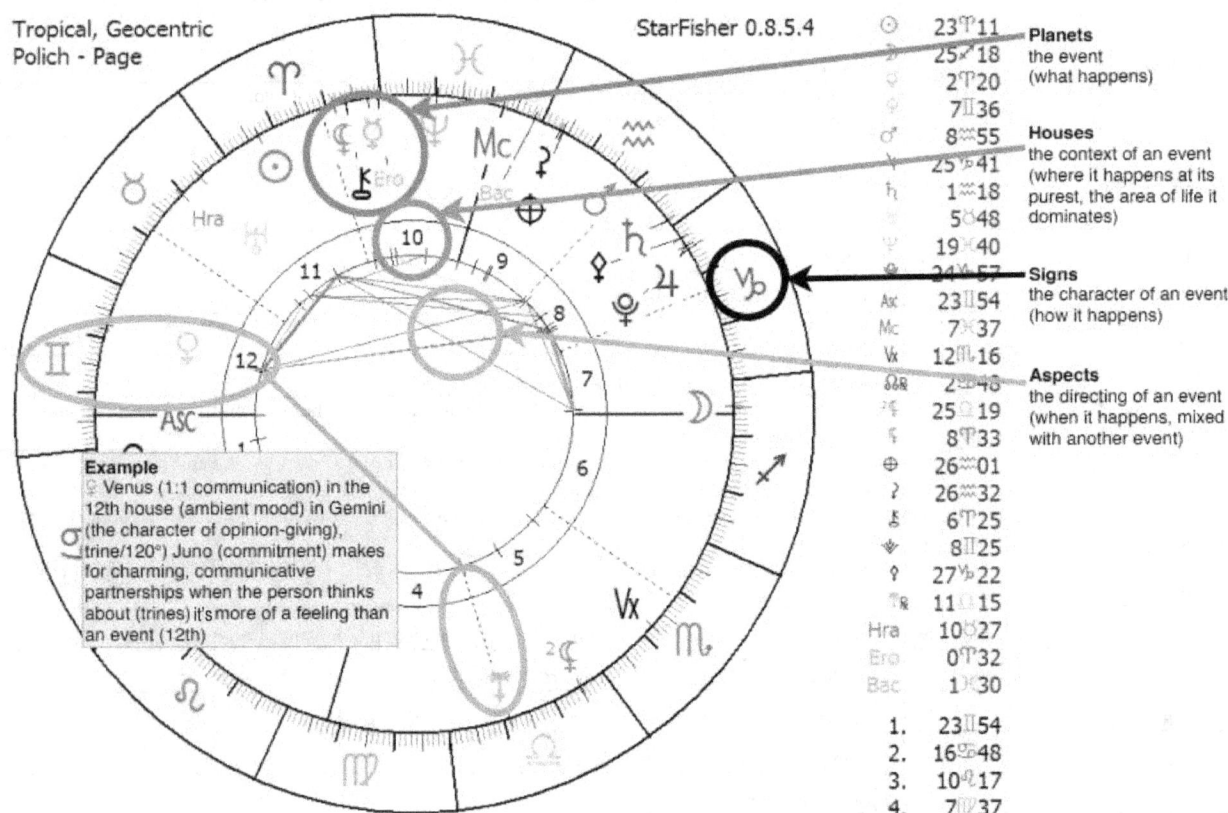

Figure 55-3: Components of an astrology chart

Typically in order to read an astrology chart, you look at which planets are in which houses and signs around the wheel, and interpret their placements with respect to each other. But it turns out that reading an astro chart for its potential is not the same as reading it regularly. In many ways it's easier to do, but the wheel is not what you want. Instead, you want all of your asteroids listed in table form as shown in Table 55-6. I typically get this table from serennu.com and select the first 1000 asteroids to appear in the display. (You need an account for this). The result will be a list that you can sort in excel all you want. More importantly, if you arrange the table by sign and degree, it will also allow you to see which asteroids and planets sit next to each other in your chart. This is what we will be using for the rest of this chapter.

204	227	Philosophia	4 cn 52'23"	Rx	33°34'1"	-0.0388543	Asteroid	3.004423497
205	142	Polana	4 cn 55'57"	Rx	25°2'49"	-0.0132182	Asteroid	1.983079035
206	82	Alkmene	5 cn 21'9"		26°24'31"	0.059893	Asteroid	1.65970669
207	623	Chimaera	5 cn 33'55"		40°46'28"	0.046572	Asteroid	1.477572639
208	99	Dike	6 cn 5'44"	Rx	34°26'45"	-0.027624	Asteroid	2.457469132
209	790	Pretoria	7 cn 21'53"	Rx	17°40'15"	-0.0386629	Asteroid	3.218821547
210	795	Fini	8 cn 27'31"		45°4'4"	0.0109595	Asteroid	2.270187871
211	65	Cybele	8 cn 30'32"	Rx	19°11'27"	-0.0203658	Asteroid	3.193021871
212	390	Alma	8 cn 33'22"		35°33'24"	0.0546803	Asteroid	1.779329324
213	737	Arequipa	8 cn 46'17"	Rx	7°37'30"	-0.0196239	Asteroid	2.171190644
214	852	Wladilena	9 cn 19'56"	Rx	47°18'9"	-0.0264042	Asteroid	2.07799156
215	215	Oenone	9 cn 45'11"		24°54'47"	0.0202665	Asteroid	2.147628778

Table 55-6: Snapshot of an asteroid list arranged by sign & degree.

☞ **Question 55.1 (Question 49.10/Your full asteroid list again):** If you didn't obtain a list of the first 1000 Minor Planet Center Asteroids, you should do so now. You can go online and search for a site with an "ephemeris" or "ephemerides" or you can go to a site that lets you produce your chart plus additional asteroids, where you will enter the numbers of each asteroid you want. Once you've obtained your list, save it in Excel or some other spreadsheet program, and put a check here: _____

There is a very long chapter in *Laurentia* which contains nothing but interpretations for each of the first 1000 MPC bodies plus a few more. That chapter is far too long to include in this book, but you can consult *Laurentia* or any other online source if you want more information on asteroids not defined here in *Alma Mater*. Tables 55-4, 55-5, and 49-2 should give you plenty to begin with though.

The Two Rules of Astrological Potential (Individual)

My undergraduate degree was in cognition/computational neural science. While I was attending school back in 1999, astrology was still a bit away from the statistical approaches available to us now. The only reason for believing that it worked lie in a certain kind of connection you had to make: 1) There would be events that you knew to be true in waking life and 2) (given how you thought astrology was supposed to work) you would *later* learn that the chart told that same story. If you knew yourself to be picky, you might find a picky planet like Mercury in a publicly displayed sign like Sagittarius. If you knew yourself to feel most at home making art, you might find a "most at home planet" like Sun, North Node, or the Part of Fortune tied to Pisces or the 5th house, Neptune, or something similar. After a while you would develop a kind of pseudo hypothesis test for what it made sense to see in a chart, and from there you basically learned not only how to read one, but also how to classify certain experiences into organized astroboxes. Thus, learning astrology before the age of data allowed you to build up a real intuition for distinguishing, say, Sun-ego from Midheaven-notability. Not just in a chart, but in regular interactions.

Once you could distinguish various categories of experience, you could also perceive two kinds of basic energy within those experiences: the harmonious want-more-of-it kind and the tense two-objectives-opposed kind. As in normal geometry, these correspond to parallel and perpendicular forces respectively. Astrologically, bodies in conjunct (0° separation) are next to each other and basically act as though parallel, supporting each other's effect upon the place where they eventually arrive. Meanwhile, bodies in square (90° separation) are strongly intersected "at cross purposes" with each other, so that it's harder to get them to influence each other directly. (No matter how sideways you slide, it won't raise you any higher or lower.) What does this mean?

- Bodies next to each other or in the same space tend to support each other. The sharper the closeness, the stronger the reinforcement.

- Bodies square each other are more likely to show tension or frustration in the chart holder, simply because using one of the bodies does nothing (apparent) in getting the other body to change. This is the key which never fits the lock. The closer to exact 90°, the more independent the bodies are.

This brings us to the two most basic rules of astrological potential:

1. If you want to know how a chartholder looks at their best and easiest, look at their conjuncts.

2. If you want to know a chartholder's strongest potential effect on their worlds or most pronounced journey towards the thing they want, look at their squares.

    - Because we tend to dislike failing to get what we want, "strongest potential effect" often means tension, strife or disharmony with the self or others.

    - By learning to be okay with the want, minus the having, we master areas even stronger than conjuncts. This is what makes gods, goals, and journeys—things we will never fully realize until death—among the strongest companions of all.

Conjuncts: Easy for you to do (as long as the squares to it aren't stronger)
Squares: Easy for you to direct your efforts towards (as long as you're okay with the tension/not having)

It's interesting to note how different a thing looks when you like it versus when you don't like it. When you like something, you tend to see its conjuncts. When you dislike it or are tense over it, you tend to see its squares. If, for example, Moe has Venus and Mercury conjunct, both square Mars, people who like him will see him as charming (Venus 0° Mercury), but people who don't like him will see him as bossy (Mercury 90° Mars) or pushy-dominating (Venus 90° Mars). Same person, different lens. He has the potential for both. But if Moe has worked on his own brand of conflict thoroughly enough, his tension may not come out as tension at all, perhaps only an ongoing, incomplete quest to make something work (Mercury easy-90° Mars) or a lingering attractiveness (Venus easy-90° Mars). Regardless of how intricate our personalities are, our squares and our conjuncts remain among the easiest trait for readers of our chart to observe.

☞ Question 55.1.1 (Astro at a glance, easy): If you don't have astrology software of your own, visit astro.com and create a free horoscope/chart wheel for yourself. While you're there, enter the numbers of these three strong asteroids: 845, 993, and 162. These asteroids (Naema, Moultona, and Laurentia), show 1) how you're ultimately known by others, 2) how you gather others towards coherent action (your fitting career), and 3) where you have an easy time winning, winning and winning again. Next, look for any planets or bodies that are less than 5° apart. These traits tend to go together with you. Be sure to look at the example if you need help doing this. Using the symbol interpretations in your program, this book, or from anywhere else, note which traits are the absolute easiest for you to display together.

	Example
	Tropical, Geocentric, Polich - Page StarFisher 0.8.5.4
	[chart wheel diagram]
	Laurentia-Vesta: Winning+Focus
	Bacchus-Ceres: Permanent Friends+Caretakers (Carefriends)
	Uranus-Mercury: Social talk+Meaning making (Intellect)
	Pallas-MC: Social Justice+Public Reputation
	Venus-Chiron: Conversation+Healing
	Juno-Pluto: Commitment+Social Pressure

☞ **Question 55.1.2 (Astro at a glance, hard):** Still looking at your chart, now note any bodies which are 90° to each other. Look only at the really sharp squares, less than 2°-3° apart.

	Example
	Tropical, Geocentric, Polich - Page — StarFisher 0.8.5.4
	Laurentia-(Mercury, Uranus): Building Intellect plants the seeds for winning Vesta-Naema: Focus plants the seeds for Name-Legacy (Bacchus-Ceres)-Node: Carefriends plant the seeds for destiny Vertex-Node: Life changes facilitate destiny (I listed these in arbitrary order—Vertex-Node as opposed to Node-Vertex. There is actually an order to it, but I cover this is *All 144 aspects*: "Squidalgo")

☞ **Question 55.1.3 (Astro at a glance, summary):** Given what you noted in the previous two questions, see if you can come up with a very basic interpretation of your chart which is very likely to apply to you, even if you never did anything but eat, sleep, gyrate, and cry.

	Example
	Conjuncts: Focus gets this one praised or rewarded; people who take care of others tend to be permanently attached to this one. They are intellectual, interact with others in a therapy-like relationship, and have commitment partners or relationships which are constantly under pressure or which fill witnesses with a sense of pressure. **Squares:** This one probably won't be known for their focus, but their focus is exactly what shapes how they are known. Using their intellect today helps foster wins tomorrow. The changes this one goes through may not seem conducive to destiny/the right path, but once the changes are over, the right path will simply apply. It's the carefriends who bring this about. (This was actually the chart of an organization, not a person.)

The working of squares is exactly the reason why we sometimes need to do things that don't appear to pay off, just because we want to. The future that will be is just as real as the present which *is*—only with a different timestamp. Putting new asteroids into old charts is a good way to gain some further details about that future. It's all really just one repetitive pattern.

If you're even a little experienced with astrology, you know we've ignored a host of other angles, asteroids, and additional details that could be read in a chart. We didn't even consider trines (120°) or house placement, for example. The reason for that is simple. This book is not focused on practicing astrology; it's focused on training intuition. The parts of astro chart reading most conducive to intuition are the parts that involve detecting tension and harmony, at a glance, against whatever experiential background (body) you're considering. The goal is to be able to read many strange charts quickly and simply—quantity over quality for the sake of practice—so that you can develop a "feeling" for the constructs these astro bodies represent in the normal, non-astrological world. Let me give you an example.

Chapter 55: The Asteroid

At the time of this writing I am working with a certain business partner. Together, we seem to walk on water—with success after success. We respond to new issues with solidarity (commitment) and, when we're not being seen in public, we have great conversations. The (relative) chart depicting our interaction is among the four below. Additionally, one of these below is the chart of my relationship to our business, where I respond to new issues as the data guy. Another shows the relationship between two people who are attached enough to never leave each other completely, but tend to limit each other when they respond to things as a pair. The last is a basic friendship which has little obvious maintenance, but triggers talk in response to the friends' unusual arrival in places. Can you tell which chart is which? (Hint: Response = the Descendant—the rightmost horizontal line in every chart. Being seen is the Midheaven or MC. "Not being seen" is the lower heavy line opposite the MC.)

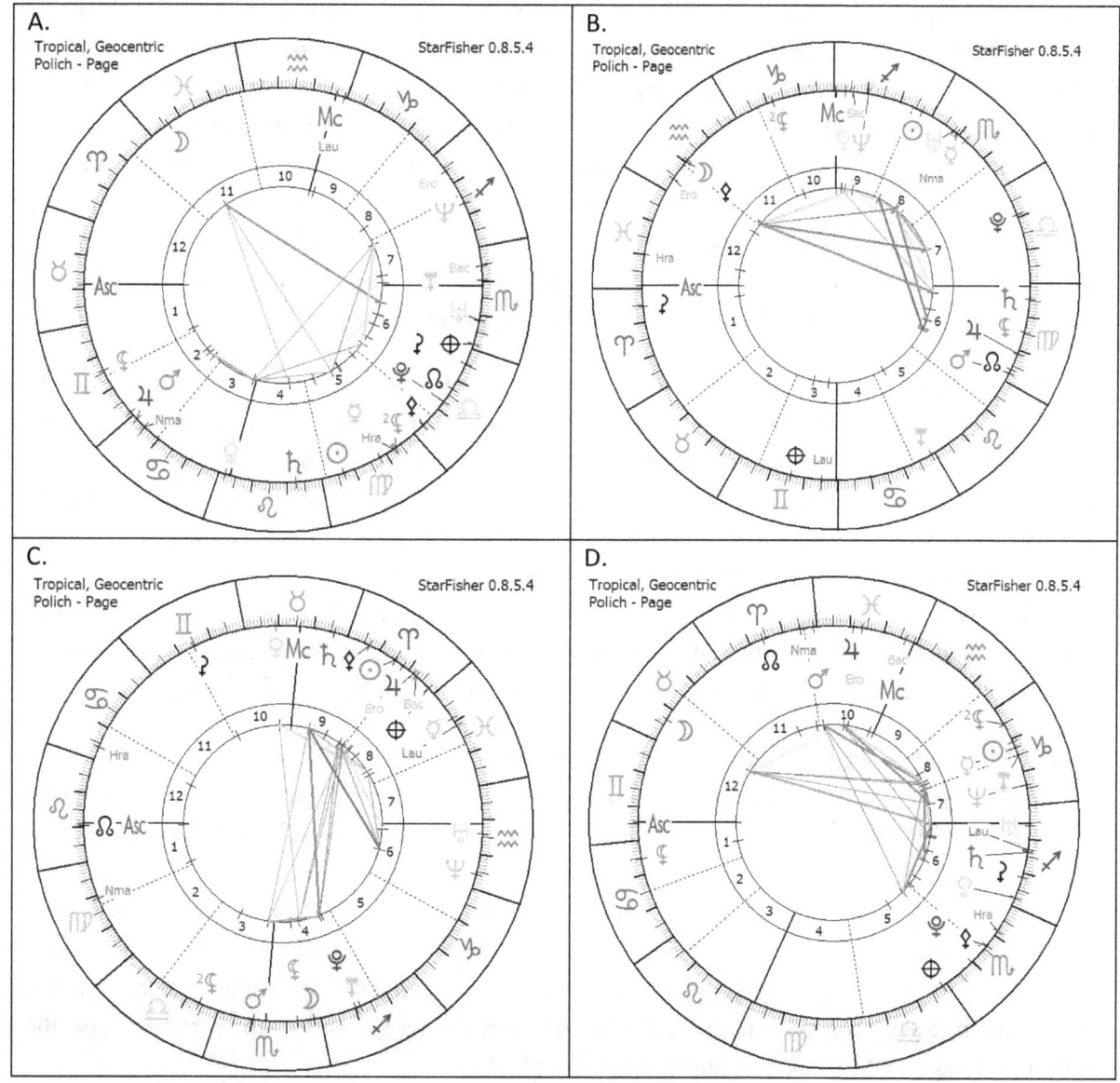

Figure 55-1: Select relationship charts

Answers: The great partnership is A. The business relationship is C. The semi-connected relationship is B. The basic friendship is D.

Answers (from the previous page): The great partnership is A. The business relationship is C. The semi-connected relationship is B. The basic friendship is D.

A Clock for all Wheels

Because all things which have begun will (as far as we know) eventually end, there is a [life]cycle that all things have which resemble a circle: from nothing, back to nothing. Recall that we argued in *Laurentia* that every cycle has at least four key points: 1) rising, 2) peak, 3) falling, and 4) trough. If the beginning of a lifecycle can be thought of as a kind of rising, we might be able to make a case for an event's astrowheel having some kind of "clock" automatically associated with it. The clock 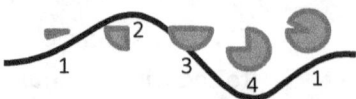 would be set in motion at the ASC/Ascendant—where the total swept-through arc at birth is 0°—then would come the progressive unfolding of the full set of experiences that chartholder will ever have. From 1) development to 2) peak potential to 3) midlife to 4) legacy making. At 360°, the lifecycle ends. Meanwhile, as with any reasonably flowing system, the chartholder's clock might be thought of as moving from high-difference, high-density frequency coverage (compared to the background context; the integral) to low-difference, almost-completely-merged frequency coverage (blending back into the background context). If you followed the arguments in *FSA*, *144* and *Laurentia*, all of this might be familiar to you. We're making a case for the LSRI (lifespan revolution indicator)—the mythical calculated point which flows like a single clock hand over all 360 degrees of a chartholder's chart. It starts at the highest energy/1st house/rising degree, and makes its way around the whole circle over the course of your life. Once it gets back to 0°/360°, the show's over. You're done.

For shaman-types who like to know more or less when they're going to die, the LSRI provides the ultimate means of calculation. I, for example, plan to die in my sleep, at sunset, preferably away from loved ones, around age 83-84 (like a typical Uranus/science type). All I had to do was look at my chart, line up the milestone events, and find the location of the LSRI at each point. This book, maybe my most important one thus far, is being written right around the 175°/360° ♎ mark in that plan, right where my Mars is located. More interesting than its uses for reading living progressions, though, the LSRI can be *extremely* useful for reading 1) creative works, 2) organizations and 3) relationships. Armed with additional asteroids, we can now put the concept to use for studying the nature of our connections with other people, as well as the most important energies involved in those connections. ⚒

The Two Rules of Astrological Potential (Relationships)

Since we've already thoroughly covered synastry (trait interplay) and composite charts (the relationship in the minds of the people in it) in *HBS*, we won't revisit those here. Instead we'll take a quick but informative glance at relative/Davison charts between you and another party. This is the chart which is formed at the average of yours and their birth time and birthplace, also known as "the way your relationship looks to the rest of the world—actually, the rest of the galaxy for that matter; where you and the other are nothing but interacting particles." These read just like regular birth charts, the way we read them in *FSA*, with one basic caveat: Relative charts should be read as abstractions—specifically, without all the houses or super high-level aspects of *144*.

Unlike you, your relationships don't have brains for working through all kinds of intricate details or self-monitoring. Because they don't "think," you don't even need to bother with the basic trine (unless you yourself want to reflect on similar moments on the relationship's timeline). Because your relationships don't think of themselves as having identities in the way that you do, you don't need to bother with oppositions either. With relative charts, the most efficient thing you can do is read conjuncts, squares, and the general flow of objects around the circle. That's it. Here we arrive at the two basic rules for reading relative charts:

1) Object flow: Look at the four major axes (Ascendant, Descendant, Midheaven, Imum Coeli) (and perhaps the Part of Fortune) to see the payoff that comes with you and the other party's investment. From strongest to weakest:

    a. The Imum Coeli (IC, the bottom of the chart) shows what you and the other are doing in the background to maintain the exchange when it's not being seen in public
    b. The Descendant shows how your pair responds to the events it encounters—you and them together.
    c. The Midheaven shows how the world identifies your pair if the two of you should ever be publicly associated.
    d. The Ascendant shows how your pair seeks out new events
    e. The Part of Fortune is something like the character of the circumstances where your pair does its natural work.

2) Timeline: Trace around your pair's wheel from Ascendant through IC, then Descendant, then MC, back to Ascendant, to view a rough story of your relationship from start to finish.

    a. As discussed previously, it is possible for a relationship to end completely, then start again. In cases like that, you hope that the same cycle you repeat gets better with each subsequent pass through.

If you just want the basic, most likely potential in a relationship, those are the rules.

For reasons that have everything to do with the level of control each party holds in writing a relationship, we're going to do something unusual; we'll learn how to assess your relationship with a non-living object first, then talk about how to translate this for living people. Trust me, doing it this way will be healthier for you in the future.

Is this relationship legit?

Figure 55-2 shows the relative chart between [me] and [my business with my partner]. One of the first things you'll notice is that the four axes—Asc, IC (Anti-MC), Desc (Anti-Asc), and MC—each have a major planet on them, as does the Part of Fortune. The placements are a little wide (less insistent), but all four are there. This is what you want in a vested relationship. Together you

- do something (Asc) (North Node in the example)
- are seen as something (MC) (Venus in the example)
- respond as a pair (Desc) (Uranus in the example) and

- maintain the relationship (IC) (Mars in the example)

With the Part of Fortune you may even have a reliable niche during your efforts (Jupiter and Bacchus in the example). Figure 55-2 has a classic heavy hitter on all five of our regions. Because these are major planets—except for Bacchus—it means that the pair's expression is less likely to be deactivated. The majors are more likely to be the behaviors you have to employ if you're doing anything. Compare this to Figure 55-3, the semi-exchange.

In 55-3, there's nothing major on the Ascendant, so there's no "critical behavior" compelling the partnership to move towards anything. There's nothing on the IC, so there's no pressing drive to maintain the exchange. Nor is there any particular niche near the Part of Fortune ⊕. Perhaps interestingly, the relationship responds with information, data, or social talk on the Descendant and a publicly unshakeable attachment with Bacchus on the MC. Looks utilitarian doesn't it? Actually, the real-life relationship is better described as "low maintenance." I can tell you that these two people's actual communication pattern tends to play away from public eyes. Does this show up in the chart? Yep. Look at Venus-90°-MC. Now that's a pretty sharp square. 55-2 also has a couple of sharp squares, but each planet that lives on each axis forces the whole setup to adopt better turn-taking.

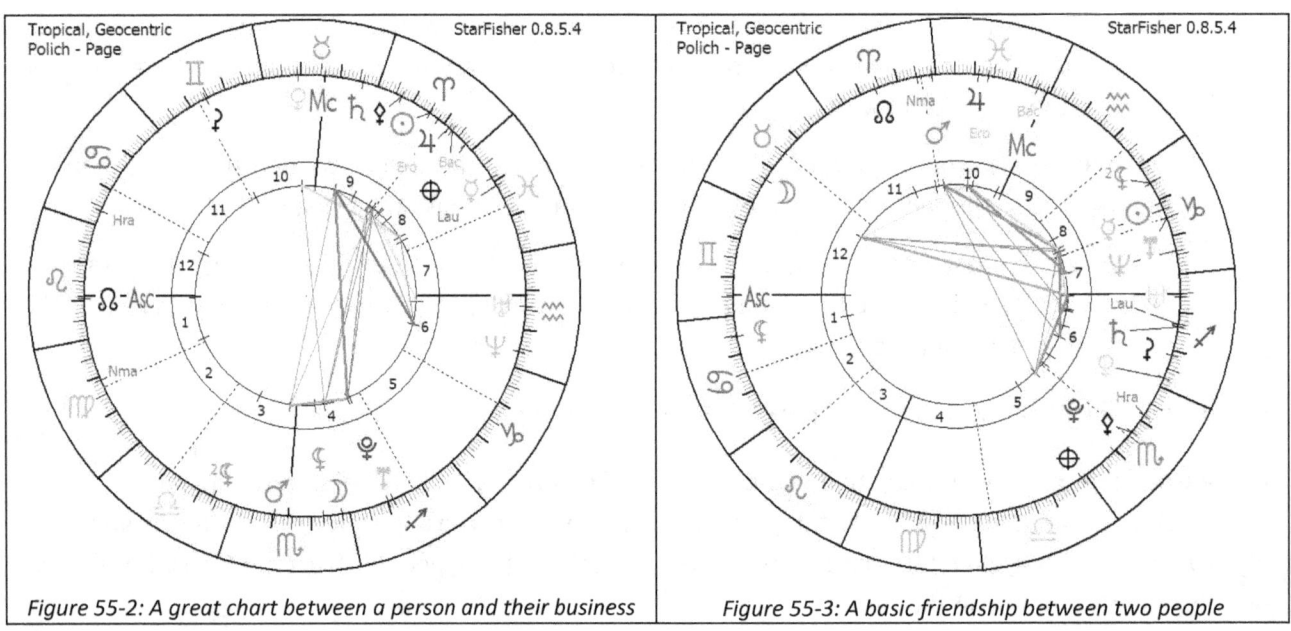

Figure 55-2: A great chart between a person and their business   Figure 55-3: A basic friendship between two people

Now, if you don't have any major planets on the axes, that's not necessarily cause for alarm. There are thousands of asteroids out there. Surely all four of your pair's axes will have *something* on them. In fact, whatever those somethings are will tell you what the public point of the relationship is. Remember how I said my partner and I have a tendency to win? Figure 55-1A shows the asteroid Laurentia on the MC. Had I not chosen to display it on the wheel, it would look like nothing was there. But where our business goals are concerned, having the asteroid of winning at the top is definitely *not* nothing. Who knows what interesting bodies are actually on the seemingly empty Ascendant? If only I knew which ones to display.

Question 55.2.1 (Create a relative chart): If you don't already have a relative chart available, use any of the previous pieces of software for generating such a chart now. After entering yours and the other's birth information, take a quick glance at the four axes. If you don't see anything, you may want to try displaying any of the asteroids listed in Tables 55-4 or 55-5.

	What's on your Midheaven/MC? How does the public see your pair?	
What's on your Ascendant/ASC? How does your pair approach new situations?	What's on your Part of Fortune? Do you have a niche?	What's on your Descendant/Desc? Do the two of you respond jointly to events in some coherent way?
	What's on your Imum Coeli? How do you maintain the relationship when it's not being publicly seen?	

Consistently, relationship charts with Juno, Hera, or Bacchus on the axes are charts which compel the two parties to be friends in all the ways you would expect. Juno on the Ascendant or Midheaven is especially associated with partnerships which are considered official in some way—official marriages, friends, or formal duo mates. Hera is associated with parties who basically adore each other or each other's company. Bacchus is associated with parties who can't detach from each other, regardless of whether they love or hate every minute of it. Other asteroids not featured in this book (but perhaps covered in *Laurentia*) can sometimes make excellent substitutes even for the major planets. Again, there is no need to worry if you don't see anything on the axes. There's almost certainly something there. You just have to know which asteroids to select.

How will this relationship play out?
Although you can't predict what will happen in a relationship, you can predict the *character* of the various themes that will greet it. If you are interested in shaping yours and the other's response to those themes, a quick trip around the circle will help. Figure 55-2 shows that my initial association with the business (initially founded by my friend a year earlier) feels like destiny—the North Node. Sometime later something happens which essentially shows how the business and I will be commonly co-associated for the rest of time—Naema. Later still, the use of our blessed talent will be a theme (Selene), and so on. I believe that all chartable events, including relationships, are like this. Follow the wheel like a table of contents. For creative works like books or movies, tracing the LSRI like this can work like an *actual* table of contents. You can read more about this in *FSA* and *HBS*.

For some people, it can be fun to use the LSRI cycle to fully map a relationship. The first time I did this was with a person whom I knew wasn't going to last, where I estimated us to be at the 120°/360° mark after a mere 1-2 months. Sure enough the association was pretty much dead by month 5. Good riddance, I said. More importantly, the kind of milestone matching you do in order to measure a relationship can give you an excellent sense of what you and the other party are jointly building. If you can spot the punchline early enough, you can save yourself a lot of needless trouble.

I can't tell you how to do milestone mapping for measuring the duration of a relationship, though I can give you a general process for it:

1) Create the relative chart for you and the other party. Start at the Ascendant.
2) Consider any significant events that have happened in the relationship thus far, and see if you can spot those events, in order, flowing counterclockwise from the Ascendant.
3) Stop at where you think you are in the relationship. This is the fraction of the pairing you have already completed before it all ends.
4) Take the length of time you've been in the relationship ÷ the percentage of the wheel you've completed.

That's the broad process. Now here's why we can't get any more specific than that:

> Lifecycles are HEAVILY dependent on what you *want* to happen—how long you *want* the relationship to last.

For example, the 5-month pairing I just mentioned above actually could have lasted up to six years. It could have been considered "started" earlier than the start date I eventually stuck with. But I purposely shortened the relationship simply because I didn't trust the person. In cases like that, little events can be promoted to big milestones, effectively speeding up the relationship's clock. Furthermore, when the pair is between you and a non-living thing, you typically have several options for choosing a start date. It depends on what you consider an official birth to look like. If you've read some of my more recent books for example, you know that I typically include the book's birth date somewhere in the book itself. *FSA*, *HBS*, and their siblings each have a birthday in Starfisher (for me, the date of creation for the initial Word document), and this is essential for me studying the books' effects on others later on. Do you choose the day you first met or the day you were published, the first date, or the first great conversation to be the official beginning? It depends on which maneuver holds the most authority in defining the event. As for milestones, the story is similar. Do you plan for the relationship to last until you die or just until you move? For geometric reasons buried in *Laurentia*, the same milestones can predict different arcs of the wheel, such that mapping where you are in a relationship is half dependent on math, half dependent on your own interest in continuing.

If you want more options for how you scale the lifespan of a relationship, just dump a lot of asteroids into the chart wheel. Doing so will provide you with a more varied set of bodies to attach milestones to.

Sign and house changes, by the way, are just like planets in a relationship chart. They spell different phases in the pair's maturation process, and can also be used to trace where you are on the timeline.

Chapter 55: The Asteroid

☞ Question 55.2.2 (Doorway to the past): **If you have the birth date AND birth time of someone with whom your relationship has already ended, create a relative chart for you and them. In the blanks below, log the milestones that occurred in the relationship, alongside any planets or sign changes that correspond to them. Be sure to begin with a rough estimate of how long the exchange lasted.**

	Example
_____ _____ _____ _____ _____ _____ _____ _____ _____ _____ _____ _____ _____ _____ _____ _____ _____ _____ _____	Duration: about 3.5-4 years (active mainly during years 2-3.5) 0yr: met, worked together; mostly me popping into her work area for things ~1yr: co-hosted exciting event ~ 1.9yr: worked on special assignment. very different. complicated. One memorable event a *major* turnoff. ~2-2.8yr: kept working, pretty friendly exchange. contemplated talking more, but never did. Somewhere in here, she made a comment which ruined my view of her. super selfish. ~2.8yr: had lunch once. good. emerged as friends. ~2.9yr: second lunch. okay. Then texted for 3 days. started well. Instantly turned very bad. blocked her. no more communication after that. ~3.5yr: months later discovered nicer texts I hadn't answered. Note: I remember this exchange as being marred by Other's reckless, groundlessly snippy, hazardous communication, and their very wrong conclusions about me

☞ Question 55.2.3 (Revisiting the potential): **Given your response to the above, was there any point in hindsight where you could have changed the trajectory of the relationship? Even if you are perfectly happy with the way everything went, was there any fork in the road where you could have made things turn out better for all parties involved? If so, 1) when was it and 2) what section of your own chart does this correspond to?** (You may need to generate your normal birth chart to remind yourself of what's in there.)

*When you answer this question, keep in mind that the other person or event must retain their normal ways. You can't make them any more understanding, more patient, or anything like that. This is all about how you might have changed your own behavior and yours alone.

	Example
_____ _____	Negative as it was, I definitely needed to experience the event at year 1.9/3.5 in order to know Other's full personality. After that, nothing else should have surprised me. If I had paid more attention to that event, the super selfish event between year 2 and 2.8 wouldn't have been such a shock. Nor would the conversation at 2.9. Instead, I would have never entertained her as a long-standing friend in the first place. So if I could go back, I would probably have decided at year **1.9**/3.5—after the first negative event—that we should not associate past colleague level. The whole relationship would have played out more smoothly that way. Based on what I know about us both, though, the ending would have been the same. Less sudden and more cordially gradual, though. Year 1.9 is somewhere between Node/Vertex/Naema and Pluto. Knowing my own chart, I have the asteroids Siri, Zelia and Saturn on the relationship's Naema/Vertex/Node— indicating that I should have blocked more instead of leaving the door open. (If the event had been more positive, blocking wouldn't have been necessary—just joint structuring. Like a business venture.)

The best of all worlds in your 55.2.2 may not have been achievable if you and the other party weren't *both* willing to change your ways leading up to defining event you chose in 55.2.3. This is why we started by looking at one's relationship to a non-living thing first. The you+thing case doesn't have any personal motives involved besides your own, and gives you the space to evaluate your own part without tangling up the decisions or efforts of another person. Reviewing the relationship as a series of milestones matchable to asteroids on a wheel also allows you a 30,000 ft view of what certain energies look like in a relationship. Thus you can sharpen your intuition for recognizing these patterns in future relationships, not just to people. It took me about a decade to recognize two particular patterns I have which ALWAYS spell the coming death of a relationship if I don't personally change course. It won't matter who's at fault. It's my sphere. If I want the thing to continue, I'll stay off such paths. This brings us back to a topic we discussed earlier in the series.

☞ Question 55.2.4 (The last thing): **What is the last major thing you tend to do before you get written out of people's stories? To find out, generate your regular birth chart, and include all of the majors, as well as any other asteroids which you think are central to who you are.** For your particular life, these extra asteroids, no matter how obscure, are just as good as major planets. Once you have this chart, take a look at the last body right above (coming back around to) the Ascendant. Think about how you've ended partnerships. How does the last body correspond to this pattern?

	Example
	(Tropical, Geocentric, Polich - Page; StarFisher 0.8.5.4 birth chart)
	My ending pattern is something I call the "Final Reach." It's one last caring, passionate, or otherwise intense push for justice before I disappear, as indicated by Eros-Pallas in 16 Aquarius. Now that I'm older it almost always looks friendly, though formerly it was basically a temper tantrum. Behind the friendliness though, the resolution to end the exchange with nondestructive finality is definitely there.
	Interestingly, my Ninina (Nnn), the asteroid of being turned on, has often served as the precursor to an end. 3 of my 5 major personal[ity] planets (*Sun, *Mercury, *Venus, Moon, Mars) have "lust asteroids" on them and those same three also live in the actual constellation Scorpio (hence the source of *S12*), but their role in my life is almost entirely intellectual. Still, if the person felt I was being inappropriate and reacted as such, then my dial—in their lives—is basically set to Nnn and we're nearing my end in their story. I can always spot this, and Eros-Pallas is my way of correcting for when I've felt I've been treated unfairly. If, however, they don't react this way, my dial could be on Hera (Hra) Moon, Velleda (Vel), Juno, or Melusina (Mlzn) depending on what was communicated. In those cases the lifespan of the exchange is greatly extended. This an example of how relationships can be scaled depending on the parties' responses to each other.

Question 55.2.5 (Maybe not the last thing): **Take a look at the example that comes with the previous question.** In line with common sense, it turns out that you actually have several ways to end a relationship. (I hope this was obvious.) The last major thing is actually one of at least six potential candidates for how you write yourself out of others' worlds. In order of increasing familiarity, you have

1. the broad sign (if you just don't want the person to come any closer)
2. the last major/important asteroid (the default; for relationships that aren't worth further effort to perfect)
3. the actual last asteroid that you are aware of (limited by your familiarity with the asteroids in general)
4. the actual *actual* last asteroid which you are not aware of which is even closer to the Ascendant (Future researchers will have to find this for you. At the time of this writing there are over 750,000 of them available to download.)

For people who don't actually experience you directly, you also have at least two fixed star options:

5. the tropically projected star which clusters of strangers may assign to you. You can look these up in *FSA*.
6. the sidereal star which summarizes your generic effect on strangers regardless of how they interpret your actions. You'll need an actual astronomy program to see the stars actually parked on the eastern horizon.

Using the space below, write down your Ascendant location. Then see if you can find bodies 1-3, 5 and 6 in your chart: the last bodies just before you return to the Ascendant. You'll likely need to do some web searching, but what you find should prove insightful.

	Example
	Ascendant: 24.6 Aquarius Last bodies: 1. Sign: Aquarius: informational background 2. Main body: Eros+Pallas conjunct / passionate justice 3. Any body: Mirielle / welcome and respect, mainly in career 4. [don't know] 5. Projected star: Sadalsuud / luck and fortune granter 6. Horizon star: Nashira / lucky, cheerful, benevolent

☞ Question 55.2.6 (Doubts): **Take a moment to think about a family of relationships which you have entered, that have not ended so well.** At what point in this type of exchange have you begun to have your doubts? Once the doubts have set in, how long has it taken for the relationship to die? Having answered these questions, see if you can locate the moment in your birth chart where your exit plans tend to appear. Following this, look at the next major bodies (going counterclockwise). Assuming your task is to drop the tension you're holding, what do those bodies suggest you do?

	Example
	Tropical, Geocentric / Polich - Page StarFisher 0.8.5.4
	Doubts: after I gave something to the relationship that didn't seem to be received. This comes as part of an incomplete conversation, and is definitely a Libra thing. Even if I didn't know that, it comes around the 2/3 mark. Pluto ♇ is the obvious culprit. (And actually, the asteroid Marlu—greatest riches you can possibly share—is also located right there. Apparently the moment where I try giving the main gift tends to present a crossroads for the relationship.
	Next is Nolli-Diotima, whatever happens, I'm tasked to be comfortable (Nolli) with two options (Diotima). For negative outcomes above, this would be a more comfortable backup. Don't get mad, Ajani. Get a backup. More specifically, feel comfortable anyway (Nolli), the backup often arrives (then Diotima going counterclockwise). And this has proven consistently true.

How do I get the most out of this relationship, given the doubts have begun? A hypothesis.

In *HBS* we asked a similar question to the above, with one major difference: our *HBS* cocktail assumed no information about your exchange as it has already played out. In this case we actually have a sense of the preferences of the other party behind the relative chart. If you did the previous exercises, you have some practice sensing the end of an exchange. You also know a little bit more about where the exit plan occurs. This gives you enough to work with where milestone mapping the exchange is concerned. Have you hit the doubt point yet? (My Pluto was at 235°/360°, roughly 2/3. So I would ask whether our relative chart has hit the 2/3 mark.) If you haven't hit the doubt point, there may be no need to think about any of this. If you have hit the doubt point and see the end coming, it may be time to start mining the relationship for salvageable treasure. I have a hypothesis for how to do this, which people besides me might want to test: All you do is create an overlay chart which scales your Doubt-Ascendant arc onto the relative chart's current milestone-Ascendant arc. There is a good reason for doing this.

We're assuming that the other party's relationship with you is a kind of story, and that your life in that story follows your regular LSRI—in that particular story, that is. As the relationship winds down, so will your personal pattern for maintaining it. The arc overlay allows you to say, "from here we close out." Yet it also considers the idea that you may have known the other person before or after your clock as a character began ticking. Furthermore, unless your doubts lead to the immediate dissolution of the relationship, you will likely have several degrees to travel before it's actually over. You could just quit the thing cold turkey, but your thoughts will linger on it until the relative chart has run its course (like my "months later…" texts in the earlier example). While the relationship is still active, it is as though you are still under contract for the lesson at hand (the relative chart) even if you have no further business with the other individual birth chart that contributed to it. The relationship is half you, so it doesn't pay to hate it even if you've come to hate the other person. As long as you're stuck for the rest of the relative clock progression, you might as well get something good out of it. You don't have to bother with the other person's synastry anymore if you don't want to. This is all about learning from the event so that your own brain doesn't set you up to do it this way with this kind of person again.

Suppose, for example, I see the writing on the wall regarding relationship 55-1B. The doubts have begun, but I know more or less where our relative chart is milestone-wise. Figure 55-4 shows what this looks like.

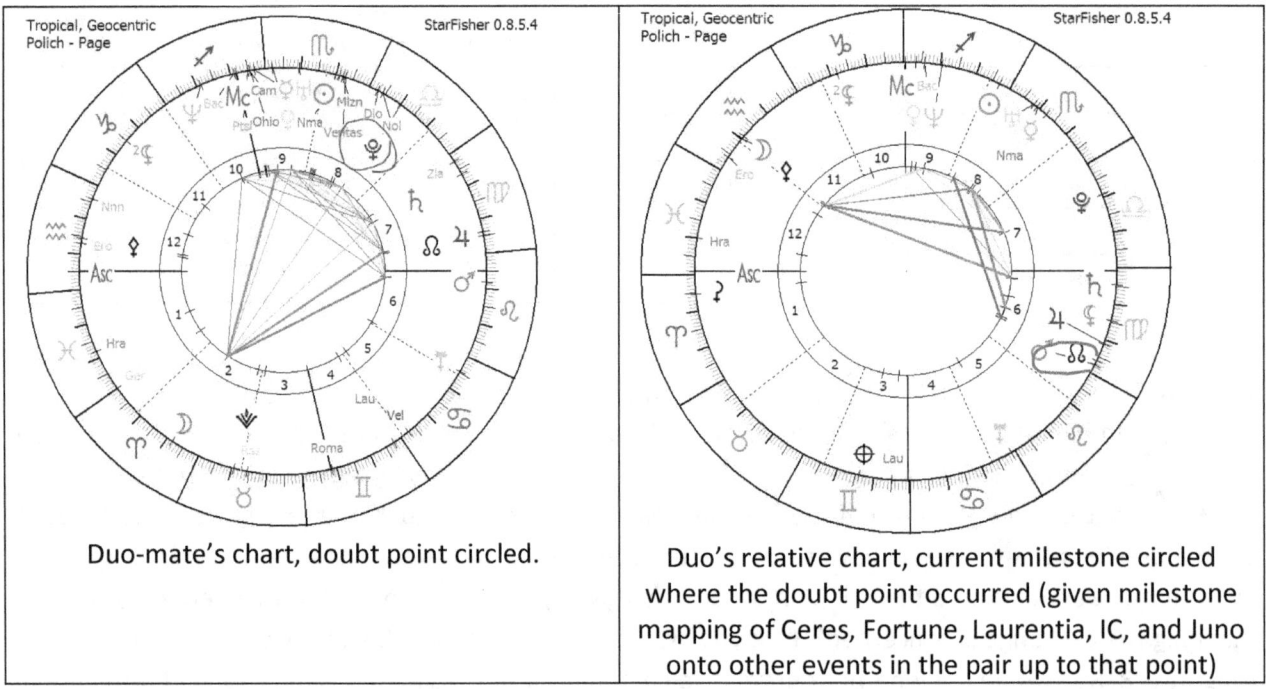

| Duo-mate's chart, doubt point circled. | Duo's relative chart, current milestone circled where the doubt point occurred (given milestone mapping of Ceres, Fortune, Laurentia, IC, and Juno onto other events in the pair up to that point) |

Figure 55-4: A non-promising pair

Notice that the left chart has 120° remaining at the time of doubt. The pair has about 210° left. To mine the relationship (according to this hypothesis), you would find the point in *your own* chart which you want to build up. Let's say it's my Sulamitis/rising in the world at 29.5° Sagittarius (not shown). This asteroid is 55° away from my Ascendant, so it would correspond to 55 (my desired asteroid distance from ASC) x 210 (relative chart milestone to ASC distance) ÷ 120 (my chart milestone to ASC distance) =

96.25° (relative chart asteroid distance from ASC). Looks like Neptune-Bacchus in the duo chart. If I want the -55° mark in my pattern to be HELPED EVENTWISE by the duo, I'll make the most of Neptune-Bacchus in the duo when the time arrives to show some kind of dedication (Bacchus)-imagination (Neptune). If I want my Sulamitis at the -55° mark to be REINFORCED CHARACTERWISE by the duo, I'll make the most of the duo's Venus which actually sits in that same spot. The first method is an arc stretch. The second is basic synastry.

By sheer coincidence, the arc stretch at Duo Ascendant-96.5° (~24° Sagittarius) isn't far from where my Sulamitis actually lives in this example. When we're only looking at character reinforcement, basic synastry—signs on top of signs—works fine. But if we actually want to pull energy from whatever random source the relationship is ready to provide at the time, we can hardly expect the other or our duo to be as interested in each of our own quirky priorities as we are. It's not about making lemonade from lemons. It's about buying lemonade while the store is still open. Alas, different parties operate on different time scales. Here we've proposed a method for hopping the right train at the right time, when we know there won't be another (we may not *want* to see another) for a while. ⚒

Now if the above section confused you, it may be helpful to think of everything in terms of love languages. There are things you get from the person and things you get from your relationship with the person. Although it is true that you, the other, and the relationship may have some sense of [giving gifts], that doesn't necessarily mean that your having gift giving as your favorite is going to automatically afford you the opportunities to do so. Your partner may require [words of affirmation] before they allow you to give anything. These are akin to two different signs in basic chart-chart synastry. Relative charts combine you and partner to form an average duo chart. If, for example, your gifts and your partner's words make for a happy [acts of service] duo, then your focus on the relationship's ability to sponsor general acts of service may be a better route to you doing whatever you need to do for the partner to stay happy. Ultimately that may mean more gift giving from you, even if the behavior looked unrelated. But it wasn't unrelated. It was the "arena" in which the things you were used to doing could actually get done. In the end, sign-sign synastry only lines up character. Timeline-timeline arc stretch synastry with the relative chart lines you up with the opportunity inherent in the relationship's actual events. It pays to consider both the right energy and the right time.

A Brief Recap of Three Kinds of Relationship Astrology

Throughout the series we've discussed three kinds of relationship astrology.

- **Synastry** puts one chart wheel outside of another or arranges all of their bodies into a single list. The result is a pair of charts overlayed, so you can see **which of Party A's planets connect to those of Party B**.
- **Composite charts** take the average position of each body from both charts, giving you a single chart which reflects the **character of the relationship in each party's mind**. It's kind of like morphing two bodies into an average, regardless of sex, cavemanism, or anything like that. Is it physics-possible? Maybe, but not likely.

- **Relative charts** average the birth time and birth place of both actors first, then read that average "person" as their own chart. This provides **a picture of the duo as a general, standalone entity** born in the middle as seen through the eyes of the world. It is possible for the physics of orbits to produce this.

We covered the first two kinds of chart thoroughly in *HBS*, and have covered the third kind here.

- You look at synastry when you want to know how the other party's sign character interacts with yours.

- You look at relative charts when you want to know what the *combination of you and the other produces, where you care less about the details of how that combination works.

- You look at composites when you want to know the middle-of-the-road aims of you and the other coming together. Composite charts reflect the result of prior planets' joint efforts, possibly because of the exponential orbits involved, so that a composite Venus built on two people for example tells you more about the single Mercuries (the planet prior) of each one of them.

> *When in doubt, use synastry. When curious about the union/combination, use relative charts. When reading motivations behind the combination, use composites.*

When you want to build up a trait of your own using someone else as fuel, DEFINITELY use relative charts. That's the whole point of this chapter. The actual person may not be willing to play with you, but your ability to summon the thought of them means that the thought itself is yours to engage.

Telepathy and the Asteroid

If you were wondering why we spent so much time on reading astrological potential, the reason is twofold. First, practicing the ability to distinguish harmony and dissonance in your interactants' charts will go a long way in affirming your general intuition for such things. Secondly, training yourself to see your interactions clearly—not through rose colored glasses or bias, but for their actual endings, investment levels, and so on—will help you uncover a talent that we all have: You specialize in calling certain things into existence, as long as your sphere is tuned to them. What you can't call on your own you can have your interactants call for you. In this section we will practice more with calling certain nice-to-haves into existence using the skills we have already addressed.

☞ **Question 55.3.1 (Easy summons):** Before we revisit telepathy, take a moment to think about three people whom you know personally who have the unique ability to trigger specific urges in you. It could be the urge to go shopping, to watch a certain show, to exercise, feel love, or whatever. Think of three people who, when you think about them, have an easy time motivating you towards a specific action. For each person, write down what that action is.

	Example
	I. creative muse
	E. role group maturity
	K. obligation to work

☞ **Question 55.3.2 (Easy summons chart):** It would be really nice if you had the birth charts of the people you listed, but chances are you don't. Try to find at least one person in answer to 55.3.1 for whom you have an accurate birth day, time, and place. This person should be reasonably good at triggering a particular urge in you. For this activity, you may need to actually ask them. They need their birth date, place, <u>and time</u>. Add them to your answer to 55.3.1, along with any other birth information you have for the people listed there.

Although people definitely donate traits to you and draw traits out of you through synastry (especially via the North Node and Imum Coeli as the draw-er), I've found over the years that they are less likely to do this with any constancy. That would require that they express their drawing planets towards you *all the time*. Instead, whenever you feel a constant vibe triggered by someone, I've found that is its more likely to be you, not them, keeping the vibe alive through your interaction with them—the relative chart relationship which obeys your attention much more consistently than the person themselves. This is good news, as it basically means that you can (and often should) summon the benefits of a *relationship* with a person rather than invading the sphere of the person themselves when you want to build an attribute in your world using them as the catalyst.

For years I wrestled with the idea of calling someone into my life just to mine them for attributes. By the time I wrote *Non-capital Wealth*, however, I had gotten over this dilemma. Not only are relationship energies akin to the kind of psychological and emotional capital that are *supposed* to be shared (unlike dollars), but in the case of positive attributes for the summoner, the summoned person's energy has its beneficial reach amplified. On an even more basic level, we do such summon-mining all the time when we read a person's success book, follow their posts, or even think about them while indulging our own trains of thought. Instead of taking in their energy visually, auditorily, or cognitively, we'll just be taking it in emotionally.

At the beginning of this book I talked about the idea of calculated magic. Granted, there's nothing particularly magical about amplifying your own traits through targeted thoughts about your interactions, but because our mainstream science in the early 21st century doesn't respect psychic invisible energy the way it respects gravitational or magnetic invisible energy, your frequency attunement to a particular concept as if you were your own MRI might as well be like magic. Here we'll practice thinking of others in order to build up our capacity for the traits they foster, but we'll also be using astrology to study why those others have such effects. By the time we're done you should have some sense of how to pick summon targets on purpose using birthday information in a systematic way.

An example of three triggers

In the example for 55.3.1 I listed three people who have had definite effects on my own attributes over the long run. Where the "long run" means identifying a significant corner of your world with them for anywhere from 2-3 years, I've found that thinking of these people in particular has led to permanent changes in how I operate. Figures 55-5 through 7 show my relative charts with them. I've circled the key axes. (If the cluster was big enough/in "stellium," wider separations were okay.)

	Figure 55-5: Ajani & Irene (Creative Muse) Great long-term increase in creativity and in the ability to be devoted to something	Figure 55-6: Ajani & Emily (Homegirl) Great long-term increase in stability of social circle & role group	Figure 55-7: Ajani & Keith (Brother) Great long-term increase in the drive to keep perfecting my work to a high level
ASC: Association goes forward	(weak) Fabiola: explosive creativity Eros: passion Bacchus: friends who'll never leave you	Ceraskia: work effort	Sun: projected natural behavior Ceraskia: work effort North Node: destiny
IC: Behind the scenes	Ceraskia: work effort Moon: intuitive want	Sun: projected natural behavior Eros: passion	Hera: deep bonding; Eros: passion Moultona: career; Pallas: social justice Saturn: structure; Mars: influence
DESC: together response	Klio: expert's store of creative power	Juno: BFF	Laurentia: ceaseless winning
MC: publicly seen	Laurentia: ceaseless winning Ceres: carebullying Saturn: age/restriction/limits	Fabiola: explosive creativity Marlu: greatest richest you can give	
Fortune: where the pair's main effect "lives"	Lilith: rebelliousness	Lilith: rebelliousness Camelia: overpowered influence tool	Moon: intuition
Vertex: The special activity accomplished		Bacchus: friends who'll never leave you	Uranus: social talk

While creating the chart above, I investigated the further pattern that people with Ceraskia were easier for me to channel and permanently learn from. This is probably because Ceraskia is near my Selene; I use that area of my birth chart heavily. **It raises the question, if there's some area of your chart that you spend a lifetime building, and there happens to be an asteroid in that area which strongly aligns with the priorities there, does that make people with that asteroid on the axes easier to summon?** It seems so. All six of my strongest summons—people who show up when I think of them, have parallel events, facilitate next steps when I actively recall their role in my life—have Ceraskia on the axes.

I also noted that Vertex (Vx) shows the "special thing" that the duo does together. My brother Keith and I, for example, publish books (Uranus). Emily and I are the gold standard in my expiration-resistant friendships (Bacchus). Because relative charts are rooted in real physics, hybrid points like Antivertex and Squidalgo (discussed in *144*) still work.

We'll get to an activity in a moment, but first there are two important things to note about summoning:

1. Even if you can summon someone easily, you can't just call them up for any willy nilly purpose. I've highlighted in the above charts the areas each person is most effective for in my waking life. If you try to invoke someone for going forward in something (ASC) when they are really stronger at supporting your behind the scenes effort (IC), you may come up with nothing. You have to call people through the thoughts they actually help you become good at. I think of Irene when I'm stuck starting (ASC) a creative project, and sometimes while working on it (IC). It doesn't happen often, but that's where the duo idea with her is most effective. After meeting Emily I never lamented the quality of my social circle and role group again (Vertex). You call by the specific specialty, not by the general person.

2. To get good at summoning someone in the six areas above, you have to tie your own identity to them in that area of performance. It pays mightily if you are grateful for them. If you are not grateful to have them as a thought, you'll be far less likely to keep them for the months required to build them into your life reliably.

☞ Question 55.3.3 (Determine their powers): Generate relative charts between yourself and each of the people listed in your 55.3.1 table. You can display any asteroids you think are relevant to each relationship. Try to do this for at least three charts. Note that you're really looking for people whose lives seem to intersect strongly with yours—whose presence in your life has helped change you over the course of at least 1-2 years, maybe longer. Parents, spouses, siblings and children won't (normally) count, or anyone else to whom you are stuck living closely. You want the charts of people with whom your continued relationship is completely voluntary. (I chose my brother because we're both grown men living in two different states with separate family lives). Once you have the charts, gather the axis details and fill in the table below with the bodies you find, as you saw in 55-5 through 55-7 above.

	Relative Chart 1 Bodies/Meaning	Relative Chart 2 Bodies/Meaning	Relative Chart 3 Bodies/Meaning
ASC: Association goes forward			
IC: Behind the scenes			
DESC: together response			
MC: publicly seen			
Fortune: where the pair's main effect "lives"			
Vertex: The special activity accomplished			

Did you notice any interesting patterns? More importantly, could you see which axes constituted the core of these relationships?

Almost everyone with whom we are in contact for any prolonged amount of time will bring some of their specialized brand of frequencies out of us. If you just think of yourself as a sphere of energy overlapping with their sphere—a big atom bonded to their atom, you can see the bond and the blend as some average of the two of you. This is the relative chart. No matter how geographically separate you are, as long as you have enough of your perceptual frequencies tied up in their impressions on you, you can effectively use your relationship to them as a source of furniture for the expressive world you occupy. It is not always reasonable to actually live with them, date them, or even talk to them—unless you're willing to take on all of the responsibilities that come with managing the entire furniture store that is their daily waking life. But you can certainly benefit from targeted, grateful thoughts of your exchange with them. Of your *exchange* with them. Not necessarily them. When it comes to the world of wanting certain experiences in your life, the feeling of having is better than the feeling of craving; the feeling of gratitude is the pleasantly reinforceable feeling of having. Or having had. Reinforce the experience, receive its axes. It's fairly simple. (Too many people reinforce the negative, unfortunately.)

Sometimes you get people you feel have good traits for absorbing, but whom you just can't stick with energywise. I've found that this often occurs when that other person's life priorities are so distant from yours that the little corner you're paying attention to is but a blip on their radar. When you are consciously or subconsciously aware that you won't have much to connect to anytime soon, your radio station won't bother. This is like trying to tune to a station in Portland from a radio in Seattle. Remember, your life circumstances/sphere has put you among certain accessible people for the stage you're in right now. Tuning into someone who's energetically too far away from you may sound like fun at first... just ask yourself whether you're willing to move back to the kind of person you were when you first knew them, or are willing to work to become the kind of person to actually meet them.

There is one exception to the above warning. This is the person who feels far away, but whose memory affects you deeply.

Critical Exercise
THE ONE THAT GOT AWAY

Training: Critical (challenging) practice for training the "summoning" component of telepathy

Question 55.3.4 (The One that Got Away): This activity will only work if you have the birth information (including time) for someone who fell out of your life, whose interaction you still greatly value. If you don't have their birth time, you may need to spend some effort guessing. In this case, however, you would guess based on the most reasonable population of axes in your relative chart with them, not based on their chart alone. Assuming you have this, you can proceed.

This person you will be looking at will need to fit a specific set of characteristics:

- They were once in your life, now they are not.
- YOU ended the exchange. Not a move. Not a job change. Not them. It was almost entirely you.
- In hindsight you are very grateful for what they brought into your life.
- Even if you still couldn't work things out with them in real life, the exchange is still very valuable.
- You can forgive both them and yourself for how it ended.

1 Create your relative chart with them. Be sure to display any asteroids related to the trait you're going to build by summoning them.

2 Start bragging to yourself, celebrating, or otherwise expressing gratitude for what they brought to any of the six areas of your life which we've covered. Make sure you consider the asteroids tied to those locations on the relative chart.

3 Do this for one month. Remember all those rules about being grateful? Your responsibility for ending it? You're going to need stamina to see this activity through. It needs to be easy to sustain, with a believable sense that it was truly up to you whether the relationship persisted. It is going to be MUCH more difficult to try this activity if those conditions don't hold.

Use this 30-day grid to help yourself stay on track.

1	2	3	4	5	6	7	8	9	10
11	12	13	14	15	16	17	18	19	20
21	22	23	24	25	26	27	28	29	30

Only after you've finished the challenge, write down any changes in your life which you think are related to this activity.

_____
_____
_____
_____
_____

We've spent some time practicing the cursory read of other people's charts. Now, despite all the complex details we've applied to our own chart reading throughout this book series, it's time to use our quick reading skills on ourselves.

I've often mentioned Robert Bruce's *Astral Dynamics*, but one thing I haven't mentioned is the book's nigh magical effect on me as a reader. Truly, between 8-9 times out of 10 when I read a section of the book, I have a dream or a vision that same night involving the astral world. This is no exaggeration. I would be curious to know what he considers the birthdate of this book, as the work itself must have an interesting chart. But the work is in many ways the child of its author. When you experience it, you are channeling some combination of the author's will, the world he was responding to in writing it, and the perspectives of any editors or other contributors who helped bring the book to the public. Accordingly, Bruce and his book can be said to have relative charts with me as a reader, allowing me to summon them when I want to grow in the astral travel skill.

Though I'm not particularly lucky to myself, I'm consistently lucky to certain people who pull me into their lives, very unlucky to certain others. Thinking of myself as a relative chart with almost no inner existence, my cursory read would look like this in your life:

Figure 55-8: The author's chart as a relative summary

(In line with the next activity you'll be doing, only asteroids that affect others are displayed)

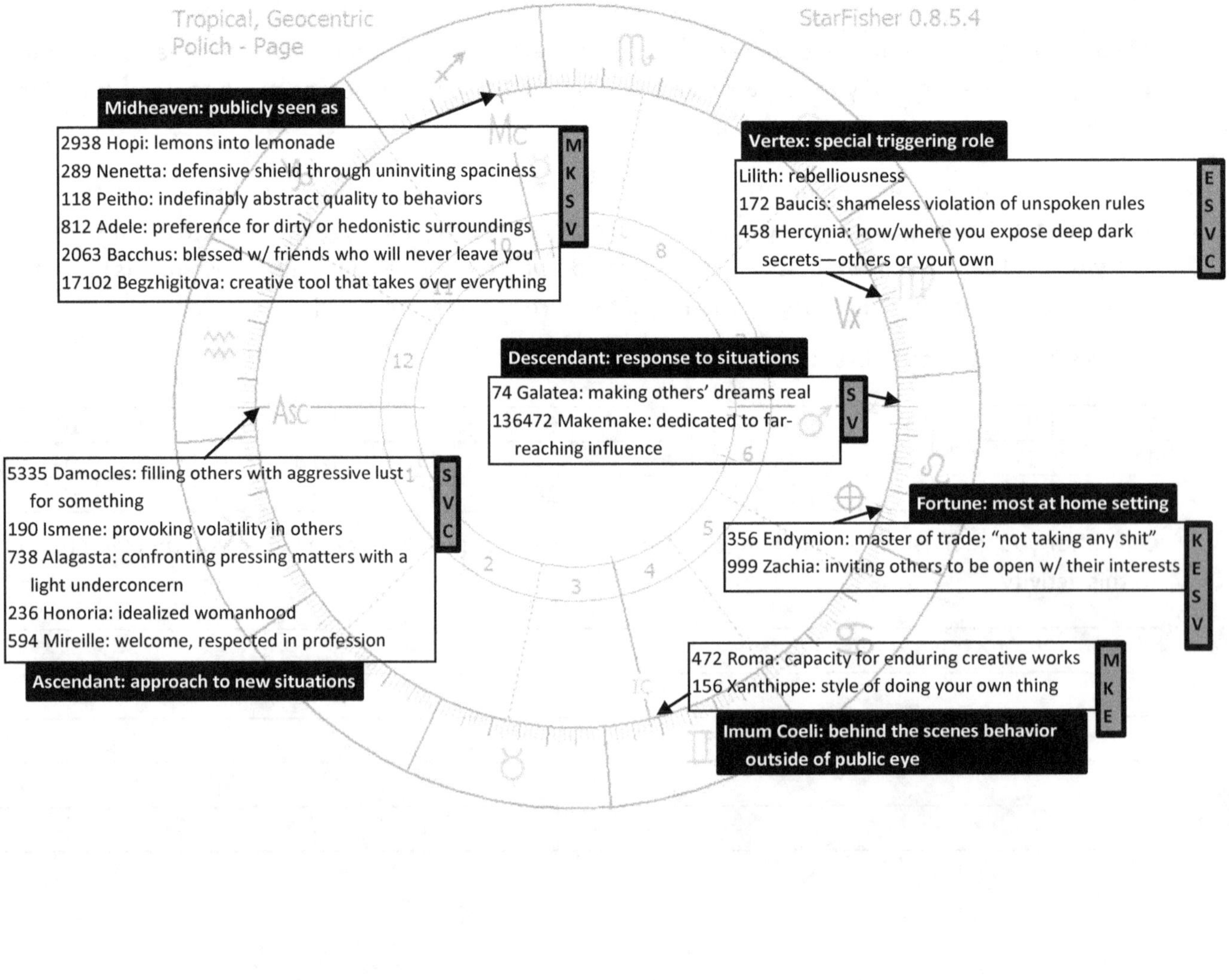
Tropical, Geocentric
Polich - Page
StarFisher 0.8.5.4
Midheaven: publicly seen as
2938 Hopi: lemons into lemonade
289 Nenetta: defensive shield through uninviting spaciness
118 Peitho: indefinably abstract quality to behaviors
812 Adele: preference for dirty or hedonistic surroundings
2063 Bacchus: blessed w/ friends who will never leave you
17102 Begzhigitova: creative tool that takes over everything
M K S V
Vertex: special triggering role
Lilith: rebelliousness
172 Baucis: shameless violation of unspoken rules
458 Hercynia: how/where you expose deep dark secrets—others or your own
E S V C
Descendant: response to situations
74 Galatea: making others' dreams real
136472 Makemake: dedicated to far-reaching influence
S V
5335 Damocles: filling others with aggressive lust for something
190 Ismene: provoking volatility in others
738 Alagasta: confronting pressing matters with a light underconcern
236 Honoria: idealized womanhood
594 Mireille: welcome, respected in profession
S V C
Ascendant: approach to new situations
Fortune: most at home setting
356 Endymion: master of trade; "not taking any shit"
999 Zachia: inviting others to be open w/ their interests
K E S V
472 Roma: capacity for enduring creative works
156 Xanthippe: style of doing your own thing
M K E
Imum Coeli: behind the scenes behavior outside of public eye
Mc
Asc
Vx
IC

Don't worry about the letters on the side of each box. We'll get to those.

Just as a relationship can be subject to a quick read for its effects on the participants, a regular birth chart can also be treated this way. But when you read a birth chart is if it were a relationship among multiple parties, you are no longer concerned with what it "thinks" of itself, only with its influence on those interacting with it. If someone should attempt to describe you as a type of event in the world, the bodies on your axes would constitute the different dimensions of that event. Broadly speaking, the people you meet who reinforce your various dimensions in the same area can be considered a part of your sphere—enough to be thought of as "channeling you" there. These folks have a way of summoning you/mining you for traits just as you can them. For example, for me to meet [people who produce creative works behind the scenes] (Imum Coeli)) or [people who are both publicly popular and hedonistic] (Midheaven) is for me to have seen people with an easy time summoning me—with a telepathic channel to them already built in.

In other words, reading yourself as a relative chart makes it VERY easy to spot people with whom you are psychically connected.

By behavior, character, and situation, your frequency will simply align with theirs—like characteristic orbitals of the same chemical elements, despite their spatial separation. Want to know how psychically connected you are (or could be to someone)? Want to know if you could send them messages... if not through words or dreams, then through life events? Ask yourself if they express themselves in any of the ways shown among your six axes. Then ask yourself whether they have gotten stronger in these ways since meeting you, and if you have at least expressed these same areas consistently without squashing them (not necessarily openly with the other). The formal science behind this is not yet established at the time of this writing, but it makes sense doesn't it? I suspect that all of this is nothing more than frequency amplification—turning up the volume on your various stations of interest. The more people you have tuning into each axis, the more widespread that frequency across and through the empty space you all occupy. It imparts a kind of gravity to that particular energy throughout the environment.

Critical Exercise
THE BROADCASTER

Training: Critical practice for the "being summoned" component of telepathy.

Question 55.3.5(On Being Summoned): It's fairly simple to know when another person can send messages to you, more complicated to know when you've successfully sent messages to them. Without going into more detail about telepathy, we'll try an activity first. After that, we'll return to the theory.

If you haven't done it already, go to serennu.com[42], get a subscription, and generate the first 1000 asteroids for your birth date. Be sure you get the time zone offset right by checking your houses against a more traditional chart wheel program. It will be extra important to have an accurate birth time here, since houses and calculated points are the main basis for the kind of reading we'll be doing. If you have some other way of generating the first 1000 or more asteroids, then you can use that instead of serennu.

Next, you'll need interpretations of the asteroids. I have these in *Laurentia*, but you can use such interpretations wherever you find them. Now if you don't want to spend the money or put in the side effort to get an exhaustive list of asteroids (you can even calculate 21,000 of them on serennu) then I can understand that. I think you'll be missing out on some fascinating finds about yourself, but it's up to you. You can still get a decent start from the numerous asteroids listed in this book. You'll just need to add them separately to your chart instead of having them all calculated at once by a website. The main objective here is to obtain an entire wheel full of asteroids, then to easily note all of the ones that cluster around your six axes.

Generate a regular birth chart for yourself, but this time only pay attention to bodies at or near the ASC, DSC, IC, MC, Fortune, and Vertex. Note these as I did in Figure 55-8.

Be sure to spend some time with the asteroids and interpretations you encounter. You'll note that many of them will be more personal to you while others will apply mainly to outsiders. For the purpose of telepathic messaging, we want to consider only those bodies which you think others would be able to reliably use for themselves. For example, an asteroid like Wolfiana/"where you spend energy in excess" may be more reflective of you personally than others, so you wouldn't put it in the final list unless you noticed some version of this in people you've actually encountered. I dropped about half of the asteroids that were actually on my axes in Figure 55-8 for this reason. Think of yourself as an ego-less event.*See note below

Once you've determined which asteroids to keep on your axes for the sake of your users, label them on your chart list or wheel.

---

[42] I have no connection to the folks at serennu. It's just what I use. If you can find another site that generates asteroids then have at it.

After I did this activity myself, I instantly became interested in identifying specific people who reinforced these axes. As stated earlier, these are the people who

- express themselves in any of the ways shown among your six axes
- have gotten stronger in these ways since meeting you, and
- have helped you express these same areas consistently or more, whether or not they are aware

Put the names of these people—as long as you are reasonably interested in connecting with them—next to your axes' notes (I put initials in 55-8). These are the people who can "hear" you psychically. Remember, words and dreams aren't the only routes to this.

An important note about the asteroid interpretations in Laurentia. Many of the asteroid interpretations in *Laurentia* reflect other people's characteristics rather than reflecting 1) broad events or 2) inner, personal experiences. I talk about why this is in different places throughout the series, but the short reason is that almost all of the charts I used were (not surprisingly) birth charts. There were far fewer books, businesses, and natural event charts in the sampled collection. So most of the asteroids are described in terms of personality. As mostly Mars-Jupiter Belt asteroids, they also lean towards a Scorpio flavor—where bodies like Chiron, Damocles, and Eris are among the exceptions covered. Furthermore, since I interpreted the asteroids primarily on the basis of their major aspects to the two most publicly unavoidable points (the North Node and the MC/Midheaven), every asteroid interpretation is more likely to be the public one. That's good in that it gives you a fair sense of the asteroid's behavior in a generic person's chart, but what about your own internal experience? That's a lot harder to observe. Reference Table 20-4 in *HBS* to see what I mean.

Surely there is more behind asteroids like 485 Genua (bossy women) and 189 Phthia (talking good game), but without being able to get into the heads of hundreds chartholders, all we have is the most easily viewable, publicly common trait as a starting point. As far as the above activity is concerned, you'll have more than enough to proceed.

But here's something interesting...

※Since the publication of *Laurentia*, I went back and applied some newly learned text analysis on not 800, but 62000 Wikipedia and astro-databank articles, pulled out frequent words, kept only [p-values < .01 (subject to document frequency) on Chi-square keywords (10 per major part of speech), Kruskal-Wallis ($p<.0001$), ANOVA] (statistics jargon), and produced some super-informative tables like this one below for 485 Genua. ※

	A	B	C	D	E	F	G
1	Document body text	Test	Second column name	Document	Correlation value	p-value	H-Value
2	[noun.possess] - cut , pea	Pearson r	[[noun.possession] - cu	3	-0.11304	0.010127	
3	social	Kruskal-Wallis	[social,social]	2		0.0014005	10.35403
4	formal	Kruskal-Wallis	[formal,formally]	2		0.0031149	9.227669
5	train	Kruskal-Wallis	[train,training]	2		0.003997	8.403098
6	[WP] - banjo , comet	Pearson r	[[WP] - banjo, cometic,	2	0.252434	0.0044369	
7	real	Kruskal-Wallis	[real,real]	2		0.0097046	6.874216
8	mutual	Kruskal-Wallis	[mutual,mutual]	2		0.0109552	6.54541
9	[UH] - man , pleas , rowdi	Pearson r	[[UH] - man, please, rov	2	0.115468	0.0134463	
10	left	Kruskal-Wallis	[left,left]	2		0.0174044	5.664831
11	bui	Kruskal-Wallis	[buy,buy]	2		0.0176699	5.640322
12	die	Kruskal-Wallis	[die,die]	2		0.0181778	0.05184
13	presid	Kruskal-Wallis	[president]	1		0.0001824	14.00412
14	off	Kruskal-Wallis	[off]	1		0.0001998	13.83285
15	ministri	Kruskal-Wallis	[ministry]	1		0.0006087	11.74915

Here, bossy women -> "unpossessor"(₍₁₎) of social formal training [who₍WP₎] [makes real] a mutual [instinctual expression₍UH₎] left to pay for a "death"… -> <u>authority-unsponsored loss reaction</u>):

An unexpected interpretation like Kressida, the breasts—becomes…

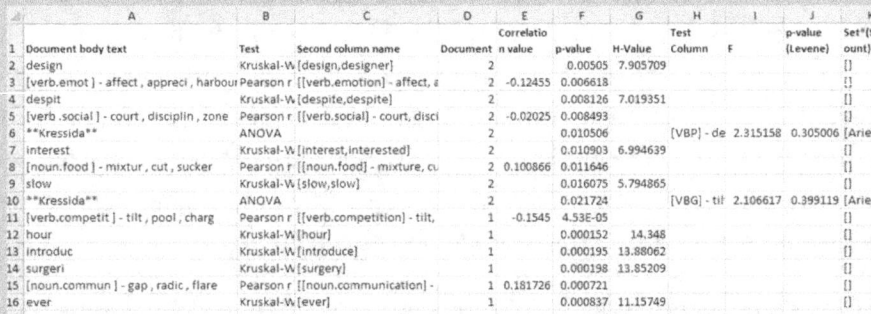

…designer of [being an emotional target₍verb. -0.12₎] despite socialization₍-.02₎ for interest in food, slowly competed with₍-.15₎ for time. To me, this looks like a less embodied version of feeding. That is, when you remove the physical body, you get the abstraction. Overall, the text mining on the first 2000 asteroids has been fascinating, but since I don't currently have a good bot for putting every coherent sentence together from the significant words, it may be a while before I finish it.

Here's a final random one for you which I've never heard of until right now, buried among my 22,000 output files. 1963 Bezovec…

	A	B	C	D	E	F	G	H	I	J	K
1	Document body text	Test	Second column na	Document	Correlation value	p-value	H-Value	Test Column	F	p-value (L Set*	
2	**Bezovec**	ANOVA		3		0.022294		[noun.act] - fl	2.182737	0.584609	[Gen
3	**Bezovec**	ANOVA		2		0.002932		[VBN] - refine	2.76446	0.278887	[Arie
4	[feel] - harden , thickli , l	Pearson r	[[feel] - hardened,	2	0.126934	0.003469					[]
5	[anx] - distract , strain , d	Pearson r	[[anx] - distraction	2	0.161389	0.006404					[]
6	[certain] - distinct , posit	Pearson r	[[certain] - distinct	2	0.117321	0.007679					[]
7	historian	Kruskal-Wal	[historian,historiar	2		0.011984	6.314745				[]
8	plai	Kruskal-Wal	[play,playing]	2		0.012106	6.569011				[]
9	group	Kruskal-Wal	[group,group]	2		0.012125	6.449436				[]
10	travel	Kruskal-Wal	[traveler,travels]	2		0.012771	6.449955				[]
11	**Bezovec**	ANOVA		2		0.042489		[RB] - dark, gr	1.864909	0.178597	[Pisc
12	[death] - lynch , sorrow ,	Pearson r	[[death] - lynching	1	0.207887	0.000105					[]
13	stori - young_man	Kruskal-Wal	[story - young_mar	1		0.000427	12.41139				[]
14	[noun.Top] - thing , unit ,	Pearson r	[[noun.Tops] - thir	1	-0.1615	0.000744					[]
15	societi	Kruskal-Wal	[society]	1		0.000771	11.31018				[]
16	where	Kruskal-Wal	[where]	1		0.000841	11.14782				[]
17	controversi	Kruskal-Wal	[controversial]	1		0.000962	10.89937				[]

```
...the feeling of anxious certainty that historians are playing group
travelers, ending the account of nothings(-.16) where controversial.
``` Sounds like "where you're concerned with having negative accounts spread about or around you." Only a thorough observation of this asteroid in charts can validate this interpretation, though. I've never seen it in action.

For people familiar with statistics, the tables above are standard fare for harder scientific reporting. The complicated theory scattered across *Laurentia* wasn't just for fun. It was meant to offer a starting point for why actual stats on the asteroids really do produce not just probabilistically meaningful results, but also results consistent with the kinds of broad observations we can make from groups emphasizing the relevant astro-item in their charts.

I've been somewhat cloak and dagger about my "statistics" in previous books, mainly because the process has been very complicated. But as a little extra, here is a slice of my beloved program which I ran for months (Knime) through 62000 charts x 15000 words x 1100 asteroids x 18 major aspects (Sun, Node...). Some parameters (like the *p*-values) are set lower than their labels indicate.

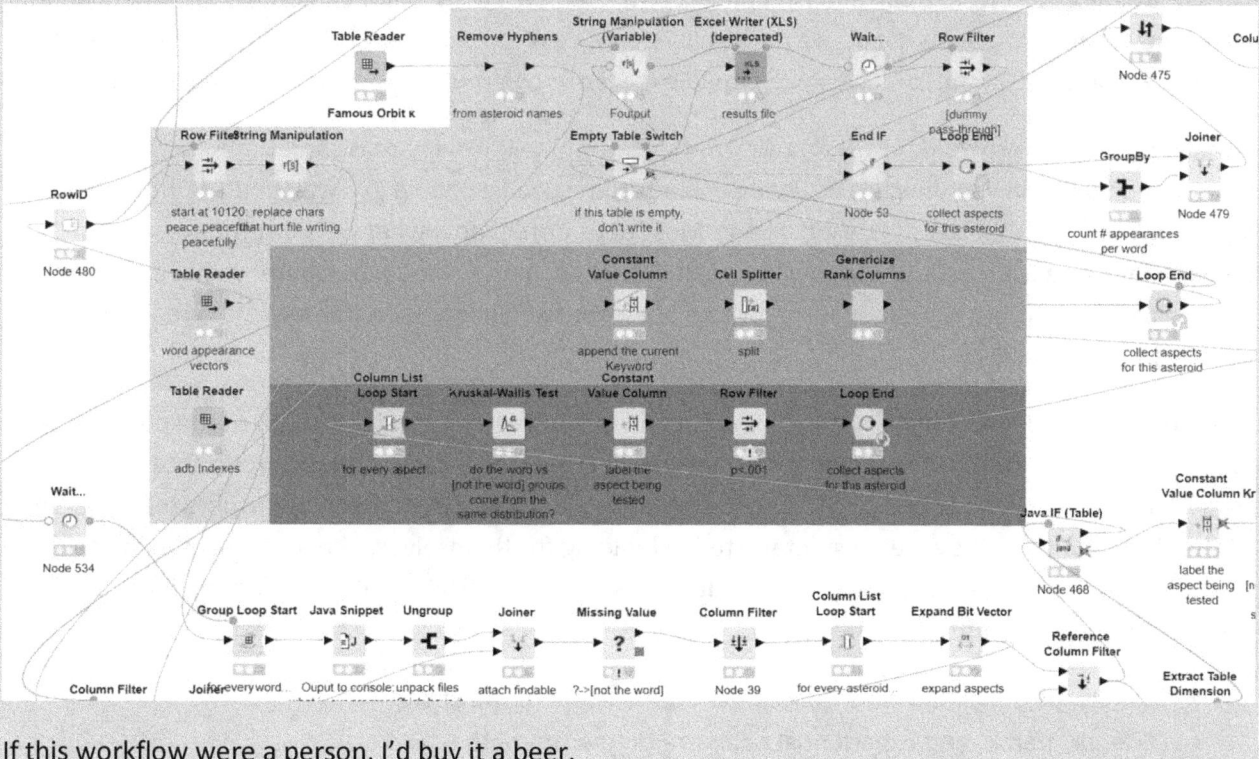

If this workflow were a person, I'd buy it a beer.

\*

We've used asteroids as a kind of filing system for reading energy with much sharper clarity. Gone are the days when eating the whole soup was your only option. Now you can buy the carrots separately, and eat only those if you like. The separation of energies allows us to really focus on only the most effective energy packets tradeable between us and our compatible friends, temporarily setting aside those constructs and behaviors which no one in our sphere uses. Dreams, events, and frequency calls will be clearer from them to us and vice versa. Yet some pressing questions still remain. Is there any point to these calls? How do either of us know what the other person wants? Is there some practical *reason* for calling someone psychically instead of in person?

## What waking humans couldn't say

I've learned two profound lessons over the last few years when it comes to close relationships. We don't always say or do what's on our minds. And we don't always know what we want, let alone what we need… from ourselves or from the other person. In a skittish, cancel-culture 21st century US, there are so many ways to upset the wrong person, break the heart of some poster, or invite a deluge of corrective opinion from even trusted ingroups that it becomes more and more difficult to be honest without some level of callousness towards the triggery subgroup that might hear you. We can have an opinion… as long as it is the popular one. We MUST have an opinion… which validates the bias of the current listener. What can be gained from the organization of so many personality traits through astrology or the telepathic communication among friends? Perhaps a level of truth we are otherwise discouraged from following, just because it's not simple or reducible to a short comment.

The communication we've discussed isn't magic, but resembles it. We can read others' axes and identify when they've read us. But what do we do with what we've read? To answer this, we need a better idea of what we ourselves want, and what we would expect our communication partner to do about it.

Question 55.3.6 (Know what YOU would want… from them): **Now here is something we think we do but don't actually do very much: ask what we want from specific people <u>in a way that fits what they know how to give</u>.** That last part is important. Most of us don't know what we want for ourselves in general, let alone from each of our most important friends. In the rare cases where we have thought about this second topic, the thoughts may have been too fixed in our own framework to really be actionable by the other.

Again using astrology as a filing system, create regular birth charts for at least three of the people you identified in 55.3.3 or 55.3.5 (assuming you can "hear" them psychically; it's less important that they hear you). You MUST have their birth time. Given what you know about them, determine the 1-3 areas of the chart you think they are most interested in building for themselves. The area might be an axis or might not be. If you need help figuring this out or aren't so comfortable with astrological diagnosis, here are some rules of thumb:

- Family, personal and work goals are on the bottom of the chart
- Friends, public, and experiential goals are on the top of the chart
- Things they want to have happen are on the right side of the chart
- Things they want to do or express are on the left side
- If they want to feel it, it's a water sign; to do it is fire; to communicate or have it communicated is air; to identify themselves with it, against it, own it, or control it is an earth sign

For the extra ambitious, you may try using synastry between the person's birth chart and their relative chart with you. (Their chart on the inside, the relative chart between the two of you on the outside—

which you'll need to generate and get the average birth information for first. See if any planets line up between both charts AND seem to match the person's priorities.)

Use the basic interpretations throughout this book or from any other source to pinpoint their main aim. Make sure the aim is one you can actually do something about. You can't usually fix their marriage if you're not married to them, their finances if you're not financially tied to them. If you just can't find anything, maybe they are actually interested in a trait from *your* chart. Referencing this as a last resort, you might use the trait from your chart to find the associated trait in theirs. Maybe it's something trine, conjunct, opposite, or sextile your planet.

For each person, list the body they are most interested in building up (at least in your interaction with them).

|  | Example |
|---|---|
|  | M. Neptune in 22.9 Capricorn, House 5 (with relative Selene): insightful impression; Jupiter in 14.1 Scorpio, House 3 (with relative Vertex): image for influence; Selene in 4.5 Aquarius: blessed talent for uniqueness |
|  | K. Jupiter in 7.5, Fortune in 10.3 Aquarius (with relative Moon, Fortune): comfortable image making among social realms |
|  | S. Pallas, MC in 5 Aries opposite Pluto, Eros in 5 Libra (with relative Pallas): passion for social justice |

**The next sequence of exercises is arguably one of the most important groups in this entire book for [calculated magic: telepathy] that we've encountered thus far. PLEASE obtain a list of your first 1000 asteroids if you haven't done so. It will be essential.**

☞ Question 55.3.7 (How you amplify): The positions you listed above should correspond to very obvious priorities in each person's life. That is, these will be traits that anyone could observe in each person without using any astrology at all. In some cases, you may even spot a common thread among the people you listed (mine had an affinity for 5°-10° air signs), and this will tell you a lot about what binds you to this cluster of people as a whole. Given the positions you identified in 55.3.6, go back to your 1000 asteroid list from 55.3.5 and locate the bodies in your chart which line up (are conjunct; not trine, opposite, etc....) accordingly. You will likely have several asteroids for each point, so only pick those which seem to fit with behaviors you express towards your chosen people in real life. (For example, I have 15 asteroids on my brother Keith's Jupiter-Fortune, but have DEFINITELY seen how a certain three of them from me during COVID have corresponded to a strong increase in Jupiter-Fortune from him; you could even look up the effects of this online [*Cereus & Limnic* and *Alma Mater* are being written at the same time]. Where you can spot the other's "most important asteroid cluster" [for your specific relationship to them], you can essentially spot what they "want" from you. This is "want" in the sphere-frequency/role-group sense; rarely will either of you know this without using tools like astrology—at least not until you've practiced this kind of intuition for a while.)

In the lines below, write down not only your corresponding (relevant) asteroids to the other people's items you listed in 55.3.6, but also note the real-world behavior you believe they correspond to.

|  | Example |
|---|---|
| _____ | M. Neptune in 22.9 Capricorn, House 5 (with relative Selene): insightful impression <Aj: 934 Thuringia-other bearing, 735 Marghanna-agitated environments; *preoccupations talk*>... |
| _____ | K. Jupiter in 7.5, Fortune in 10.3 Aquarius (with relative Moon, Fortune): comfortable image making among social realms <Aj: 78 Diana-being above the little people; 474 Prudentia-super busyness with creative ideas; 704 Interamnia-greedy chasing; *artist conversations, book structure*> |
| _____ | S. Pallas, MC in 5 Aries opposite Pluto <Aj: 234 Barbara-how you make others obey you; *didn't know this*>, Eros in 5 Libra (with relative Pallas): passion for social justice <Aj: 940 Kordula, 774 Armor-*high status, dynamic duos*> |
| _____ |  |
| _____ |  |

Hopefully your *corresponding behaviors* above make so much sense that you already recognize yourself as doing them, and just need to aim them more sharply to fit your chosen people's needs. Notice how you probably could have figured these behaviors out on your own, but over the span of the whole sky, how would you have known where to focus your efforts?

☞ Question 55.3.8 (What you want from them...to you)(part 1): **Now be honest.** There are probably behaviors which you sense your people are capable of, which they aren't quite displaying towards you. Suppose you want them to start displaying that behavior now. This is actually a two-part problem: 1) It won't pay to manipulate them, since all you'll get is their tension. From there, you can expect your whole chart full of conjuncts to take a back seat and your chart full of squares to kick in. Do no harm. Follow the golden rule. You can ignore this advice if you like, but get ready to pay for it... They have to *want* to be ready to give you what you're psychically asking for. 2) You have to know what you're ready for. You want love? Are you ready to date them or live with them? Share time and space with them? You want money? Are you ready to work for or with them in ways that they require in order to compensate you? Will you compromise your own interests to take on theirs as if it were your *job*? That forest may be darker than you expect.

Before asking for something you'll regret, do this: Take a look at the birth chart of someone who's currently within your zone of easy communication/influence, from whom you want something they've yet to give you. The assumption here is that on a soul level we all know what's up. Your spiritual contact list is changing as your frequencies store the information in this book, such that people and events who are ready to respond to you will be within your reach *right around now*. If you have to work to pull them into your world in fulfilling the coming requests, consider them busy. No manipulation. Respect their current priorities as you would want yours respected. Only people within your communicative reach are eligible for this particular question. List those people below.

|  | Example |
|---|---|
|  | E., M., K. S. |

Question 55.3.9 (What you want from them...to you)(part 2): How can you tell when someone wants to give you something, for better or worse? In previous books, we had a definition for **want**: **A person wants what he or she turns their actions towards the experience of**. We can think of those actions as corresponding to a background frequency involving you, so when you think of them you may feel certain attributes they bring getting amplified once you open the door. Some people, though you are close, won't have this at the moment. As I write this, for example, both of my brothers are close to me, but when I think of them, I don't really feel any inertia pushing me to stay with the thought of any energy they might want to hand me. Goings on in their worlds, yes. Impulse for me to act or express in a certain direction, no. So Keith comes off my list as he is busy with his own tasks. (Don't take someone's busyness personally. It's no different from them being on the other line when you call. It'll be fine. But do ☞ note when your thought of them seems to compel your reinforced attention towards them, though you yourself don't otherwise have much of a reason to reinforce the type of feeling you're getting. As I write this, I have a particular song in my head telling me my homegirl Emily probably wants something from me, though it could be anything from support, to a stronger business, to getting my shit together, or whatever. Maybe she wants me to go to hell. You never know with this kind of feeling, and since your framework is not theirs, you can't assume. What you can do is keep them on your list from the previous question. We'll work out the details for mutual benefit shortly.

Given your inertial attention, who stays on your list from 55.3.8?

|  | Example |
|---|---|
|  | E., M. |

Question 55.3.10 (What you want from them...to you)(part 3): Pick at least one of the people from the previous question. Generate their birth chart, then note all of the areas of their chart which they seem beneficially open to displaying towards you. Here, you should stick mainly with the major planets, and possibly the axes (unless you have reason to investigate the more obscure asteroids).

|  | Example |
|---|---|
|  | M. |
|  | Moon in 11 Gem, Saturn in 5 Pis, Mercury in 1 Pis, MC & 858 El Djezair (super strong) in 1 Aqu, Neptune in 22.9 Cap, Bacchus in 14.1 Cap, Uranus in 25.5 Cap, Node in 27 Sco, Pluto in 27.9 Sco, Descendant in 6.9 Pis |
|  | (Lots of areas expressed beneficially in this chart means I know or get along with this person well enough.) |

The people who survived filtering in 55.3.9, and the points which you listed for those people above in 55.3.10 will yield the only degrees you should choose from when psychically requesting from them. Otherwise you'll sow the seeds of tension all over both your charts. Heed what I say. Consider that someone might also learn how to extract certain behaviors from you. Would you take kindly to being drained through responses you weren't interested in giving?

Interestingly, as you do this exercise you may naturally find out what the other person wants from you in exchange. We have a separate activity for that, but you may find it interesting that between the writing of the previous paragraph and this one, about a day has passed, I talked to M., and it was obvious which of the above areas we were most interested in. Rather than boring you with what they were, I'll tell you what to look for:

1) After having narrowed down some areas which are safe to request from the other person,

2) pay attention to any direct or indirect interactions with them in the couple of days following. Especially if you *get a chance* to interact with them after you've done an activity like 55.3.10, you'll know that their sphere is as interested in letting you know what they want as yours is the other way around.

3) Interactions or conversations which go something like, "Man, I didn't know ___ about you. Here's ___ about me" are a dead giveaway as to what you might want to focus on.

Whatever the case, you'll settle on one of the above areas.

Question 55.3.11 (Showtime): You now know the area of their chart which you are going to request the other person amplify in your life. Now you just need to look at the corresponding asteroids in your own chart which you are willing to express to their benefit in exchange. This next part will be as hard or as easy as your own willingness to trade fairly. 1) Express your own cluster in ways that benefit the other person. 2) In whatever way you can, let them know you're doing it for them. It's more important that you set up the habit than set up the calendar, so all you need to do is "accept the trade as fact." I know that's vague. Sorry. Some people will need to do something every day, others only twice in a month. Some will be able to talk to their person directly, others not. Some activities are done with the other person, others independently. Your only goal is to survive the month under your new trade agreement, whatever you decide and however often. Color in the boxes below as you make it through the next month, trading your own cluster for the thing you're asking the other person to give more of.

| Week 1 | Week 2 | Week 3 | Week 4 |
|---|---|---|---|
| | | | |

(In case it wasn't clear, trading clusters works like this: Suppose you want the other person to give more Saturn/organization to the relationship, and your asteroid 997 Priska is located in the same place. You'll need to adopt second-placedness in the other person's favor and try to let them know you're doing so. This should happen in such a way as to benefit you both, not obligate you both.)

This will be obvious in hindsight, but here goes: The other person wants whatever you seem to be giving. That's it. More specifically, if there is a particular behavior which your interaction with the person is extracting from you, that is at least part of what they want. Obvious, right? Now sometimes—a lot of times, actually—people will extract behavior A from you because they don't know behavior B is an option. Additionally, they may also extract tension from you instead of harmonious giving. Where the other person doesn't know enough about you to extract what you're actually willing to give, they'll just have to wait until you're ready to show them such options, if ever. But if a person is extracting tension from you, and you can identify the culprit area being activated in your chart, don't display the culprit area. Display either of its two squares.

> There is a particular person in my sphere who has the ability to easily extract tension from me. I like her, but the headache is no good. Let's look at how I determine what to do about this.

Square process

> - I ask myself if the tension is related to myself, my interaction with her, or with some property of my larger world. Since it involves my status in the world and ability to encounter certain people and networks, it's a world issue. Sagittarius, Capricorn, Aquarius, or Pisces.
>
> - Is the issue tied to my projection (fire), my structure (earth), my information (air), or my inclinations (water)? It's structure with a little bit of projected image as an excuse: Capricorn and Aquarius.
>
> - I then look at her birth chart for the thing this person projects tensely onto me which also lives in these areas. In the chart of this person, there are only two obvious culprits—Selene in 29 Aquarius and Midheaven in 27 Capricorn.
>
> - Next, I verify that the corresponding areas of my own chart were afflicted by the above. Indeed, my 47 Aglaja (breaking new ground) and 438 Zeuxo (becoming indispensable) were diminished by her. Not hindered, but discouragingly downgraded at the time. As for the Midheaven, there didn't seem to be any problems after all.
>
> - Having verified the person's inharmonious area, I stop looking at its home in 29 Aquarius and start looking at the squares to it. These are 29 Taurus and 29 Scorpio. I know she is defensive regarding my 29 Scorpio planets, so I'll look a 29 Taurus instead. Bingo. I see the cluster of asteroids she wanted me to display instead, and those clusters make sense given the nature of our exchange. Will I do those things on her behalf? No. And that about wraps it up. We have a dead end here, and probably won't be interacting any time soon.

As you can see, not all requests are met with a yes, from you or them. This is why we went through the trouble to find "safe clusters" in the first place. Other clusters have a good chance of wasting one or both of your energies.

☞ Question 55.3.12 (What they want from you...to them)(part 1): If you've ever had a person in your life who just didn't seem to go away, no matter how hard you tried to dump them, you'll be familiar with the energy of someone wanting something for their own life goals. Rarely is this want directed at you personally; instead is typically more of a general mojo aimed at a particular role in their lives. In cases where you feel you are being pulled by some larger force to stay with a particular person—where the force doesn't seem to consider your own priorities, do you give the person the energy they are demanding of people like you? Maybe, but I would be wary. Some people have an insatiable appetite for select experiences. Even if it feels like they only have eyes for you, spheres aren't typically so exclusive. If another person has managed to stay in your life or on your mind despite causing you tension as they do so, you are more likely to be facing a general feature of their personality or your relative chart with them, not a specific request to you. **Perhaps there is someone out there who would be a more cheerful giver to them?** So that you may avoid considering these people in the coming calculations, write their names down in the blanks below…

_____
_____
_____

…these are people who seem to want something from you, but haven't cleared the way for you to give it. Instead, their sphere has left your tension exactly where it is. Don't bother trying to fulfill these people's requests right now. Maybe some other time.

☞ **Question 55.3.13 (What they want from you...to them)(part 2):** Now suppose you have someone who's stuck on you mind, they cause you tension, but you're not trying to get rid of them or bring their role in your life to some closure. People like this may be worth investing in. After all, you too probably have tense lessons you need to reconcile. Using the Square Process from a couple of pages ago, try to locate the problem area of their chart (with respect to you), then check that degree location against your chart to verify that the location is consistent with an area you yourself struggle to apply with them. Once you've determined that you've located the problem area, look at both sections of your chart which are 90° square to it. Confirm that there are asteroids in either or both of these areas which you know could be used to fix the issue. When it comes to a tension provider, consider that the square to the problem area is the *real* energy they compel you to express <u>beneficially</u> towards them.

| Question | | Example |
|---|---|---|
| 1. Is the problem area related to<br>   a. Self (Aries, Taurus, Gemini, Cancer; things you personally are allowed to do)<br>   b. Other (Leo, Virgo, Libra, Scorpio; interactions with the person/event)<br>   c. World (Sagittarius, Capricorn, Aquarius, Pisces; opportunities you can have in the bigger context) | | T (One of my businesses. You can also do these with events, not just people):<br><br>There are some specific things I don't do well in running this business, though there is no shortage of opportunity (c.), and having it helps me do what I want(a.). Interaction (b.) is the problem. |
| 2. Is the problem area tied to<br>   a. How you project in the world (Aries, Leo, Sagittarius; fire)<br>   b. How you structure or are structured by things (Taurus, Virgo, Capricorn; earth)<br>   c. Information passage (Gemini, Libra, Aquarius; air)<br>   d. Your inclinations (Cancer, Scorpio, Pisces; water) | | Marketing (c.) is my weakness, as are some administrative duties (b.) |
| 3. Make a birth chart for the person/event. | | [Done] |
| 4. Given your answers to 1. and 2., what areas of *their* chart to you think are behind the issue (square-problem degrees)? | | Jupiter 15.6 Libra, IC 8.75 Libra? Node 0 Virgo.<br><br>Maybe also Juno & Pluto 18-19 Capricorn<br>(There's no rule confining your answers to 1. & 2. If you spot it, go with it.) |
| 5. Check your own chart (using 1000 asteroids) for any bodies that sit on the degrees you are about to blame. Do you have problems with these bodies in your interaction with the other? | | 8.75 Libra: fine.<br>15.9 Libra: 25143 Itokawa – processing massive amounts of info. 965 Angelica – giving up control to partner, 125 Liberatrix – sudden termination of partnership. Quite the pickle.<br>18-19 Capricorn: 294 Felicia – Difficult women/feminine energy as harassers, 144 Vibilia – being objectified, 26 Proserpina – primal urge responses from others |
| 6. Summarize your findings from 5. in a way that makes sense with your experience of the other. | | My business partners in T have always been better at marketing, but the price I've paid is exactly as 5. suggests. |
| 7. Look at the squares to the problem points you settled on (square-solution degrees). Do any asteroids look familiar as potential fixes? | | 15.9 Libra->15.9 Cancer: fine.<br>15.9 Libra->15.9 Capricorn: 418 Alemannia – hindered expansion given inner maintenance, 98 Ianthe – sex as social currency, Selene – blessed talent<br>18.5 Capricorn->18.5 Libra: 604 Tekmessa – under pressure to perform professionally; 178 Belisana – women who are meant to be followed, 895 Helio – friendly but demanding<br>18.5 Capricorn->18.5 Aries: 476 Hedwig – potentially famous behavior, 569 Misa – magnet for |

| | | |
|---|---|---|
| | | the opposite sex (I don't feel I know what this cluster is saying. We'll need to wait for the next chapter to learn more about this region of Aries on The Star.) |
| 8. Summarize what the squares "want" from you. | | (Recall from *Laurentia*-"Time Unit Hypothesis" that later signs tend to "cause" earlier ones in the default flow of time.<br><br>15.9 Cap->15.9 Lib: Hindered expansion, still using talent causes the marketer to appear. I may need to accept what I just can't do, and BE PREPARED TO DEAL WITH 15.9 LIBRA-OTHER PERSON HEAD ON.<br><br>18.5 Ari->18.5 Cap->18.5 Lib: [doing The Star of 18.5 Aries (discussed next chapter)] causes administrative needs which causes pressure to perform professionally which I NEED TO ACCEPT. (Haven't yet.) |
| 9. Are you willing to do what you concluded in 8. for the other person/event's benefit? | | I have no plans to abandon my business, so I suppose so. Yes. Eventually. |

☞ Question 55.3.14 (What you both need from some other): **What if you and the other person/event** *want* to get along, but just don't have it in you to do what is required? In the example to 55.3.12, I can see the problem with my other (the business), can see that the solution is to accept a certain level of difficulty in the exchange, but just don't have the ammo to survive that kind of difficultly for the long term. When this happens, what do you do? The answer: You find someone who's happy to do it—who MUST do it (that is, they have a major planet there)—to engage the square for you. Be ready to go back to 55.3.11 and trade with them. If you have the discipline to get what you need from the *relationship* to the other (your relative chart with them) rather than some third party, then that's good. But if that relationship doesn't have the axes you need (major planets are hard to pinpoint in relative charts, remember?) then you may just need to find another human or something to keep you and the other together.

| Question | | Example |
|---|---|---|
| 1. Using your basic intuition/gut feeling/common sense about it, who (or what event) do you think could help you with any squares you can't tackle from 55.3.12? Remember, they should be within your easy communicative reach if possible. That is, they time with your reading of this book as you seek solutions right now. | | I'm not engaged enough with T itself to rely on the relative chart with it. K., M., relative-M., or relative-E., W. (another business) might also work. |
| 2. Take a look at the charts of everyone you listed in 1. Look for people and event charts with *major planets* on your square-solution degrees from 55.3.12. Look for relative/ relationship/ event charts with *axes* (ASC, Desc, IC, MC, Fortune, maybe Vertex) on your square-solution degrees. See if any of them have ALL solution-degrees occupied. | | 18.5 Aries: M.'s Vesta, W.'s IC<br>18.5 Libra: W.'s MC<br><br>15.9 Capricorn: [not found]/my Selene |
| 3. Are you willing to trade with this third party to improve your exchange with the second party? Consider doing 55.3.11 again with this third party and the relevant degree. | | Maybe. |

## Conclusion

We can think of planets/asteroids and their signs as being like songs and radio stations respectively. Songs are packages of frequencies; radio stations take up windows of frequency space. You can have a Neptune/spiritual song played on an Aries/igniting station or a Neptune/spiritual song played on a Pisces/spiritual station. Although the song won't change its fundamental energy, it's effect on you will vary against the greater context of what you expect to hear on the station that plays it. The asteroids, then, act like a bigger music collection beyond the basic major planets of astrology, adding much greater precision to how you classify the various frequency packets out there. In this chapter we used the asteroids to really focus our reading of our own and others' needs. We built up a set of rules for "tuning in" to others in the process.

I've had an interesting two weeks writing this chapter. Three people whom I hadn't spoken to in a long while showed up just in time for the next phase of a major project I'm working on and, as is the case with most of the activities in this book, I got to practice the examples as I was writing them—again using the results of each one to let myself know what questions you might have next, as I had those same questions. I learned over the weeks that it becomes easier and easier to read situations intuitively the more you practice filing the right experiences into the right places...and the less time you dedicate to things that won't receive your call.

More than anything, we need to consider our *entire* set of circumstances when making connections with others. Just because our minds may want something, doesn't mean our goal structures or our current life setup wants the same thing. I began the second half of this chapter thinking I was going to reconnect with some long-lost person or people from the past, but quickly found out that this came at a high price; do you *de*volve in order to go back? Or do you just leave your path as you have built it up to now? The latter is almost always better.

We've looked around the wheel, but we don't really know what its various sections mean. Sure Leo is Leo, but how is 0° Leo different from 29° Leo? There's a big difference between Christmas and New Year's, though they are only a week apart. Shouldn't the signs themselves have more detailed subsections than just "more Aries" versus "less Aries?" It sure would be nice in cases where we land somewhere in the chart, but don't find any planets there. That kind of general dissection of the wheel—minus any planets or asteroids—will be the focus of our next chapter, The Star. Once we've seen it we'll have a means to fully query frequency space for certain kinds of answers, adding even further to our library for classifying the various forms of intuition.

# Chapter 56. The Star

As part of my day job at the time of this writing, I work heavily with text analysis and mining. In attempts to reduce words to the two dimensions of communion and agency discussed earlier in this book, I used a group of databases and a body of assorted documents to examine interchangeability among the various parts of speech. I also completed a massive mining project after the one mentioned in last chapter's side box, where I used something I called pseudo-ARIMA to smooth out themes on the four critical numbers used in Chapter 38 for the asteroid meaning formula.

It is customary to report your methods for any kind of major science, and I would gladly elaborate elsewhere. But between lemmatizing, averaging bags of words, correlating predicates, non-parametric tests on bit vectors, and merging sentiment columns, it's a story way too long and too complicated for this book. Accordingly, these two paragraphs, along with last chapter's diagram are as far as we'll go towards explaining the topic which forms the center of this chapter. When 12 signs and their basic meanings are not enough, when we need more specific details for knowing not only what the signs within signs do, but more importantly when we should care... When we need a very general, very communion-agency reclassification of the astrowheel that can be more easily used to solve practical problems, the basic 12-wheel will not be enough. Instead we'll need an astro circle with the kinds of questions built-in that each of the signs within signs (144 duodecanates) is able to answer. The astrowheel with 144 addressable situations attached to it will be called "The Star," and we'll spend the rest of this chapter talking about it.

The Star comes from five basic sources:

- Predecessor and successor mining on the SUSANNE corpus[43]
- The 144 asteroids work in *144*
- Aphelion, perihelion, semimajor axis, and axis-span ranking and smoothing on 1100 of the Minor Planet Center bodies
- ANOVAs, Kruskal-Wallis tests and some term and document frequency formulas on the keywords featured in astrodatabank articles and category attributes
- A circular addition system meant to preserve aspects around the wheel (for example, where any pair of sections 23, 13, 124, etc. duodecanates apart will always have the same relationship to each other, no matter which sections they are).

---

[43] Sampson, G. R. (1995). English for the computer: The SUSANNE corpus and analytic scheme. Clarendon Press (Oxford University Press); Sampson, G. R. (2001). Empirical linguistics. Continuum International.

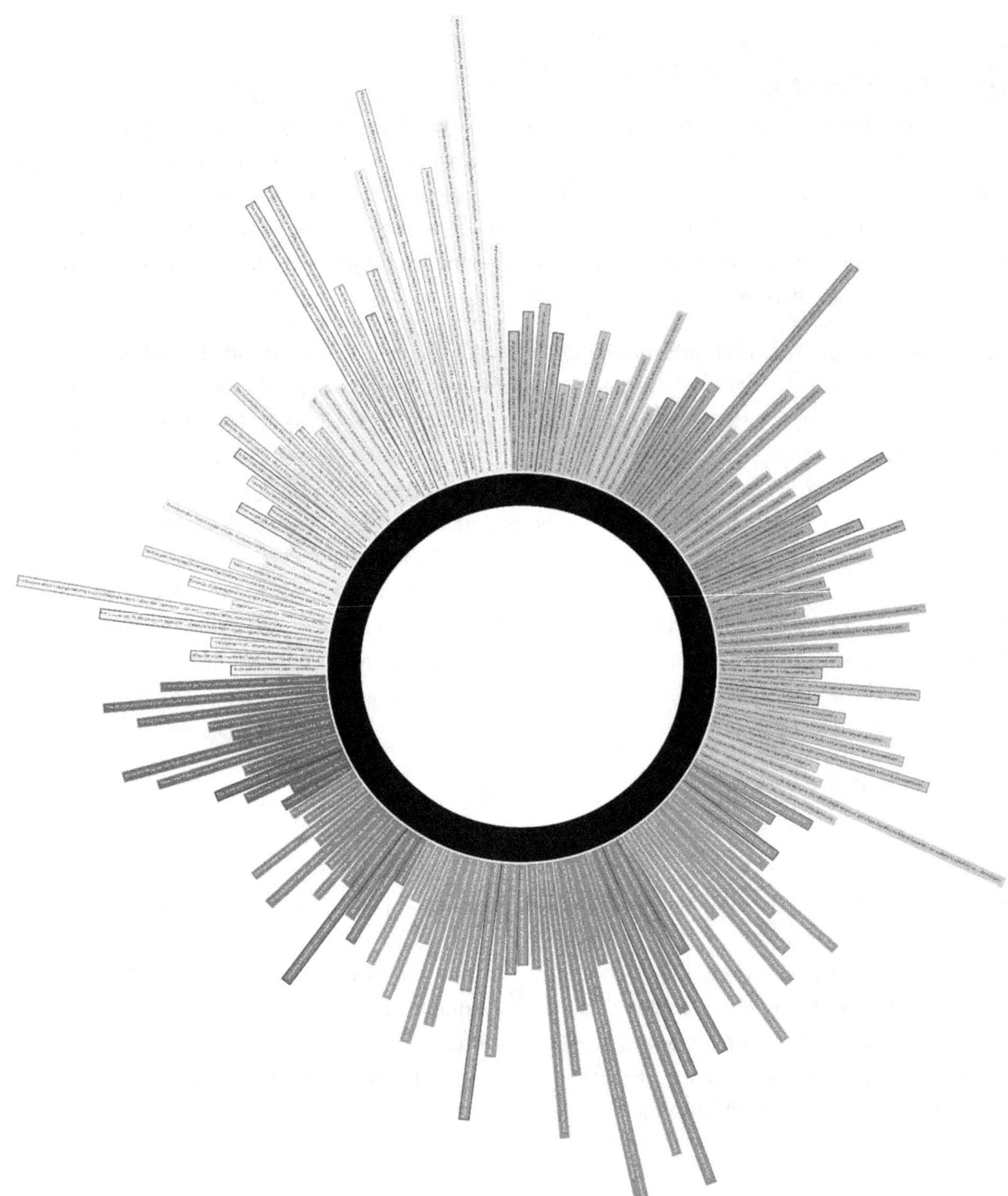

*Figure 56-1: The Star*

## How to Read the Following Sections

In each of the following sections, you will find a table which shows you what each sign within a sign (duodecanate) tends to correspond to. When you have planets or asteroids in the corresponding section, those bodies will tell you how you do the thing that the duodecanate is in charge of. If, for example, you want to know what status-related money means to you (not whether you have it), you can look at duodecanate 37-wrapping and read the asteroids there. If your Sun is there, that kind of money is more likely synonymous with ego or expressive right. If your Yrsa is there, it may be synonymous with addiction or indulgence. And if you had, say, one of the "extreme asteroids" like Feronia, Helena, or Laurentia there, that would indicate an easy capacity for a lot of such wrappable stranger-value. All in all, each duodecanate has a particular frequency which is related to, but not the same as, that of its neighbors. If you've printed your 1000 asteroids, you can have a field day learning how you do almost anything.

Not only does each duodecanate listed have a name and a meaning, it also has a number. One of the first things you'll notice is that, following the practice in *All 144 Aspects*, I've listed the sections backwards. There is a very important reason for this: As in real life, higher frequencies are typically harder to get to from lower ones. When you're studying intuition through the lens of frequency-based astrology, you repeatedly return to fundamental, easy, lowest-level behaviors like the conjunct (0, 1/1, or 100% movement on a circle) and the opposition (1/2 of a circle). These correspond to duodecanates 1 and 2 (what I've called the level-1s), and are located in Pisces. Sextiles correspond to Pisces-6. Squares correspond to Pisces-4. It works like this because duodecanates are actually a second-level cycle of the main wheel. Virgo represents sextiles when you're just "joining" generally. The [dash]6 duodecanates represent when you're "joining within (another sign level's) context." To give another example, when you are under tension and showing your square/90° behavior, for example, you will tend to play out whatever asteroids are in your 20°-22.5° Pisces by default. If your tension is related to image projection or foreign places, you'll focus on your 20°-22.5° Sagittarius instead. The thing is, later signs in context are A LOT more likely to describe your default behaviors than earlier ones, and as you progress in your intuition practice you'll see this time and again. Aries…Pisces is good for astrology. Pisces…Aries is better for actual energy-consuming behaviors. The latter goes from the generic to the specialized in terms of how you respond to things.

*Tables 56-1 – 56-12: Astrowheel specific subsection interpretations*

Suppose you have 518 Halawe and 762 Pulcova in this degree. You would read them as "In my native environment, when I start things, I have a style of veiled conquest (518) in my asserting despite the crowd (762)."

The asteroids you have in a particular degree correspond roughly to your method for playing out this theme. If, for example, you had 573 Recha in 21° Pisces, playfulness would be a part of how you insert new behaviors into situations.

## 56-1 Pisces

| # | Sign Degree | Duodecanate Name | Theme | Character |
|---|---|---|---|---|
| 1 | 27.5°-29.9° | Pisces-1 | proceeding | In my native environment, when I start things, I… |
| 2 | 25°-27.5° | Pisces-2 | identification | When I'm where I want to be, I would surround myself with things that… |
| 3 | 22.5°-25° | Pisces-3 | transmission | The experience of… inspires me to new thoughts and ideas |
| 4 | 20°-22.5° | Pisces-4 | insertion | Everywhere I go, I'm always on the lookout for… (paranoia or distrust in negative cases, opportunity-radar in positive cases) |
| 5 | 17.5°-20° | Pisces-5 | reception | In situations where I strongly desire to show something to others, I also often experience… (longing in negative cases, immersion / further engagement in positive cases) |
| 6 | 15°-17.5° | Pisces-6 | agreement | In stabilized surroundings, I make myself useful by… |
| 7 | 12.5°-15° | Pisces-7 | participation | The kinds of conversations I would have (if allowed to simply vibe out) involve… |
| 8 | 10°-12.5° | Pisces-8 | consideration | My flow gets interrupted / I interrupt the flow of others interacting with me through situations that look like… |
| 9 | 7.5°-10° | Pisces-9 | shop | Seen in the emotional space I create, people see me as… |

| # | Sign Degree | Duodecanate Name | Theme | Character |
|---|---|---|---|---|
| 10 | 5°-7.5° | Pisces-10 | demand | The things I use to protect my space are… |
| 11 | 2.5°-5° | Pisces-11 | production | The information I use to sustain my vibe, my music / entertainment / preferred social surroundings are… |
| 12 | 0°-2.5° | Pisces-12 | pattern | The nature of my fantasy life is… |

Master of the ambient vibe, Pisces describes all the things you do when you're not in any specific context. Even if someone irked you at work (Virgo) or wowed you with their ego (Leo), you will eventually go back home and ruminate in your own "what's-next" space. Your basic conjuncts will all be colored with the priorities of your asteroids located in 27.5°-29.9° Pisces and its nearby neighbors from around 5° Aries to 23°-ish Pisces. Your oppositions—your style of viewing one thing against the backdrop of another—will all be colored with the priorities of your planets located in 25°-27.5° Pisces, with some input from other bodies between 2°-ish Aries to around 20° Pisces. Vital to the practice of intuition is your increased familiarity with how it feels to express these energies. Pay attention to the character of each duodecanate and use that character to amplify the kinds of experiences you seek the most. You might benefit from doing something similar to the visualization exercises in "The Worlds" chapter at the beginning of this book.

## 56-2 Aquarius

| # | Sign Degree | Duodecanate Name | Theme | Character |
|---|---|---|---|---|
| 13 | 27.5°-29.9° | Aquarius-1 | percept | When people talk about how I naturally do things, these topics arise: |
| 14 | 25°-27.5° | Aquarius-2 | pull | People associate me with identity labels related to… |
| 15 | 22.5°-25° | Aquarius-3 | inclusion | I express my views amidst others' talk, taking over the floor in this way: |
| 16 | 20°-22.5° | Aquarius-4 | rules | In light of the information around me, I tend to feel… (my role in family-like structures) |
| 17 | 17.5°-20° | Aquarius-5 | choices | Given the information around me, I tend to show…, reacting to things or declaring my way nonetheless |
| 18 | 15°-17.5° | Aquarius-6 | comprehension | My problem solving amidst the social information around me involves… |
| 19 | 12.5°-15° | Aquarius-7 | knowledge | The conversations I have amidst the social information around me—my friend groups—are associated with… |
| 20 | 10°-12.5° | Aquarius-8 | translation | Amidst the information around me, I compel others' action through… |
| 21 | 7.5°-10° | Aquarius-9 | attention | I easily project a gossipable public image associated with… |
| 22 | 5°-7.5° | Aquarius-10 | scope | My control or authority is expressed against others' talk in ways that involve… |
| 23 | 2.5°-5° | Aquarius-11 | frame | People talk about how I'm talked about, making me exceptionally unique in… |
| 24 | 0°-2.5° | Aquarius-12 | space | The ongoing information about /around me is associated with an air of… |

Whereas Pisces mostly operates alone, your Aquarius describes your interface with other frequency-generating people or events. These are the types of existential noise you surround yourself with just beyond your default solitude, which explains A LOT about how you believe the world to work in terms of energy and influence exchange. The character of your very basic friendships are in Aquarius-7, the defining emotional climate of those whom you count as family are in Aquarius-4. Your mob-mates with whom you tear up the enemy's stuff are in Aquarius-8, while your rule set for understanding the effect of physical company are in Aquarius-2. This section is all about what you believe the rules of interaction are—given how you were socialized, that is. Even your training in behaviors that go beyond training—your uniqueness—can be found here.

## 56-3 Capricorn

| # | Sign Degree | Duodecanate Name | Theme | Character |
|---|---|---|---|---|
| 25 | 27.5°-29.9° | Capricorn-1 | group | The identity systems, constructs, or groups most associated with how I am known and formally labeled by the world involve… (the systems I rally). In such groups, how I naturally do new things |
| 26 | 25°-27.5° | Capricorn-2 | agenda | The types of expressive structures or groups against which I identify are associated with… (outside those groups, where I'm most likely to gain fans and followers who like this kind of thing) |
| 27 | 22.5°-25° | Capricorn-3 | priority | Amidst the groups I identify with, I communicate my ideas in this way… (outside those groups, this is how I deliver insight) |
| 28 | 20°-22.5° | Capricorn-4 | acceptance | The emotional disposition typical of the group that best describes me / my principles are related to… |
| 29 | 17.5°-20° | Capricorn-5 | subordination | The style of showing most typical of the group / rules that best describe me—where I am comfortable declaring myself is… (Powerful personalities often live here. To the extent that they value things like rulership or money in your life, this section is associated with rulership or money, mostly forced via the character described.) |
| 30 | 15°-17.5° | Capricorn-6 | model | At home in the group which best describes me, where I make myself useful is associated with… This is also the method of meaning that I model for others outside of that group. |
| 31 | 12.5°-15° | Capricorn-7 | framework | At home in the group that best describes me, the kinds of conversations I have are… (my natural friend-network in that group, my governing doctrine or belief system outside of that group; my "major" in the college of life) |
| 32 | 10°-12.5° | Capricorn-8 | kinesis | I handle power and steer others in accordance with the rules of the group that best describes me. Those rules involve… (Like Capricorn-5, this area is associated with powerful people. Unlike Capricorn-5, this section is a magnet for followers rather than a magnet for attention. In my experience this section is less imposing, more sweeping-influential than Cap-5.) |
| 33 | 7.5°-10° | Capricorn-9 | function | Outside of the rules that govern me, I project those rules onto others as a "type"-exemplar / group leader easily associated with… (within those rules, where I stand out) |
| 34 | 5°-7.5° | Capricorn-10 | designer | … shows where I belong in the inner circle among the groups that best describe me; the group among groups; where I am a boss and/or master; the overarching nature of my native group itself |
| 35 | 2.5°-5° | Capricorn-11 | uniqueness | Within my native groups, the social information around me / the agenda most easily reflected is associated with… Outside of those groups, where my inner group's agenda seems more like an alien language—where I am considered a genius is… |
| 36 | 0°-2.5° | Capricorn-12 | presence | Within my native rule set or groups, the air about me is related to… Outside of those groups, where I am easily memorable |

The energy requirements keep increasing as we move from groups that swirl around us, to groups that park around us imposing their structures. Here we put in the extra effort to control our behavior amidst external structures such as our morality (Capricorn-4), our coerced shows of personality (Capricorn-5), those whom we believe have true power (Capricorn-8), and those we believe to be masters in their realms (Capricorn-10). In all cases, throughout the wheel, we have at least three options for expressing anything that arises: we can hold the trait ourselves, outsource the trait to others, or roam the trait as a surrounding situation. Additionally, we can display the harmonious or dissonant versions of each of these. We can see them as a thing to be given or a thing to be received by whoever holds them. Truly there are many options. The catch is, we almost never have the level of neutrality required to show all of these traits with equal favor. Unless you've done some miraculous personal and circumstance-setting development work, you will almost certainly have to choose some priorities over others. The Capricorn section is one of the more insistent realms in this respect.

## 56-4 Sagittarius

| # | Sign Degree | Duodecanate Name | Theme | Character |
|---|---|---|---|---|
| 37 | 27.5°-29.9° | Sagittarius-1 | wrapping | When I'm headed out to make a public impression, I think of myself as… (this region is strongly associated with money as status) |
| 38 | 25°-27.5° | Sagittarius-2 | contact | As an impression maker in public, I best describe myself as / my stage persona is… |
| 39 | 22.5°-25° | Sagittarius-3 | presentation | My outlook among crowds of foreigners and the public, my ice-breaking commentary is… |
| 40 | 20°-22.5° | Sagittarius-4 | amplification | This is how I feel about being out in public or making a public impression: |
| 41 | 17.5°-20° | Sagittarius-5 | convenience | My way of demonstrating for an audience is… |
| 42 | 15°-17.5° | Sagittarius-6 | purpose | I lecture, teach, or host panels with the effect of… |
| 43 | 12.5°-15° | Sagittarius-7 | reason | On a date or some other notably public adventure with a partner, I experience… |
| 44 | 10°-12.5° | Sagittarius-8 | involvement | I call out or challenge audience members by… |
| 45 | 7.5°-10° | Sagittarius-9 | administration | …describes how audiences tend to receive me overall |
| 46 | 5°-7.5° | Sagittarius-10 | region | …is how I most strongly correct or control my image in front of audiences |
| 47 | 2.5°-5° | Sagittarius-11 | center | The public spaces I tend to naturally frequent are characterized by this kind of information or social talk: |
| 48 | 0°-2.5° | Sagittarius-12 | category | My entry into a new public place brings an air of… |

Sagittarius holds, for the most part, your energies related to projected actions among groups beyond you. Unlike Pisces, Aquarius, and even Capricorn, this is the first sign where either you or the stranger *has* to do something with respect to you. (Capricorn was more about what you couldn't do; Aquarius was more about what socialized doing consists of.) So this sign requires more energy than the previous three groups. Because it is focused on actions passing between you and faceless strangers, the Sagittarius group feels a lot like status, stature, and other differentiating means you might employ for being somebody in the broad world. Both Sagittarius-1 and Sagittarius-4 are associated with your prerogative in the world, while other sections describe various forms of recognizability—whether as an individual or as an occupant on someone else's scene. Look to this group for insight regarding the kinds of strange worlds you are actually interested in visiting. Not everyone longs to travel or be rich as their way of showing that they've made it in the world. There are many other options for affirmation among strangers.

## 56-5 Scorpio

| # | Sign Degree | Duodecanate Name | Theme | Character |
|---|---|---|---|---|
| 49 | 27.5°-29.9° | Scorpio-1 | pacifying | …is associated with how I naturally begin steering others |
| 50 | 25°-27.5° | Scorpio-2 | lure | …summarizes what I'm typically trying to get to happen when I steer others |
| 51 | 22.5°-25° | Scorpio-3 | acquisition | As I steer others, I communicate my thoughts in line with the framework of… |
| 52 | 20°-22.5° | Scorpio-4 | absorption | I tend to feel concerned with… when compelled to steer others |
| 53 | 17.5°-20° | Scorpio-5 | displacement | …is how I show where I stand while I'm steering another (negatively where the standards aren't met, how I patronize; positively where the standards are met, how I sweet talk) |
| 54 | 15°-17.5° | Scorpio-6 | inculcation | I analyze things I wish to influence or do research in line with… |
| 55 | 12.5°-15° | Scorpio-7 | separation | I easily enter arguments through… (positively, these are discussions of how to attack a joint issue) |
| 56 | 10°-12.5° | Scorpio-8 | appraisal | I use… to compound my dissatisfaction with things. Also, how I show obsessive perfectionism, micromanaging |
| 57 | 7.5°-10° | Scorpio-9 | market | …is the impression I leave when I steer others |

| #  | Sign Degree | Duodecanate Name | Theme | Character |
|----|-------------|------------------|----------------|-----------|
| 58 | 5°-7.5°     | Scorpio-10       | disruption     | …: How I want things done when I demand that they get done |
| 59 | 2.5°-5°     | Scorpio-11       | development    | …shows how others around me talk when I use force or coercion, or otherwise steer things |
| 60 | 0°-2.5°     | Scorpio-12       | transformation | The mood around me changes to… when I steer or coerce things |

When you want things to be other than they are, foreign worlds get squished into the affairs of a single interactant—the same energy level as Sagittarius, but compressed as well as drawn out with more focus. Plus you're likely to be dissatisfied with something. Thus Scorpio takes more energy still. This is the sign containing your methods for making your interactants do what you want. Steering your circumstances with someone is the purview of Scorpio-1, steering how worlds project is the goal of Scorpio-9. And then there are the classic steering through conversation and argument (Scorpio-7) as well as picking things apart piece by piece (Scorpio-8). Despite its occasionally negative reputation, Scorpio is the place where we exert our effects on others. Those effects are not always for the worst. We just need to work on maintaining harmony for as many parties as is feasible when we use the asteroids in this sign.

## 56-6 Libra

| #  | Sign Degree | Duodecanate Name | Theme | Character |
|----|-------------|------------------|----------------|-----------|
| 61 | 27.5°-29.9° | Libra-1          | clarification  | I start relationships and conversations with… Also, how I am summoned to participate in things; where I am surprised |
| 62 | 25°-27.5°   | Libra-2          | standout       | I measure whether I am in a real relationship or conversation based on… |
| 63 | 22.5°-25°   | Libra-3          | resembling     | Being in a relationship changes my outlook in ways related to… |
| 64 | 20°-22.5°   | Libra-4          | gesture        | In a relationship or conversation, I show a new style of basic wanting which is related to… |
| 65 | 17.5°-20°   | Libra-5          | animation      | …are the set of qualities I like to show off to others from within the context of a relationship or good conversation |
| 66 | 15°-17.5°   | Libra-6          | role           | When I start to see issues that need to be solved in a relationship, this is what happens… |
| 67 | 12.5°-15°   | Libra-7          | information    | …reflects the way I talk to people about how I relate to people |
| 68 | 10°-12.5°   | Libra-8          | count          | In conversation, I convince, persuade, or push others using… |
| 69 | 7.5°-10°    | Libra-9          | monopolizing   | In a relationship, I give off a public image of… |
| 70 | 5°-7.5°     | Libra-10         | validation     | The must have rules for me to "do" 1:1 communication or a relationship with someone are best described as… |
| 71 | 2.5°-5°     | Libra-11         | frequency      | The information that comes along with 1:1 communication / relationships for me is associated with… |
| 72 | 0°-2.5°     | Libra-12         | energy         | …describes how others feel around me in relationship mode. |

If you're like me, you've probably been inclined to read mainly those degrees so far where you have major planets. "My Sun is in degree X," you've said. "My Moon is in degree Y." But that's what you would do if you were studying astrology. Remember, we're not here to study astrology; we're here to develop our intuition for certain behaviors. It's better to read these tables for their themes and characters. "I define what it means for a relationship to stand out when I feel…(what are those obscure 1000 asteroids again?)" Along the way you'll, start seeing things less in terms of the "popular songs" that comprise the major and familiar planets and more in terms of the "radio stations"/frequency regions you're good at tuning into…regardless of how popular their songs are.

☞ **Question 56.1 (Check-in):** Of all the regions you've seen so far, are there any in particular which have interested you the most?

_____
_____
_____
_____
_____

The Libra regions encapsulate your motivations to keep trading behaviors with something. Trading ideas you identify with forms the basis of a conversation or long-term relationship, even if it's via argument (Libra-8). Trading shows of personality forms the basis of normal engagement—animating your dynamic (Libra-5). You'll note that Libra is associated with Venus, and Venus is traditionally considered a positive planet. That's because it does not behoove most of us to have negative feedback interactions most (or even often) times. Feedback loops—Libra's specialty—take A LOT of energy and are best when they're stable and at least non-harmful.

So we dwell on the positive here. Yet there is a dark side to Venus and Libra in the form of "othering." The Libra sections become problematic not for what they do, but for what they don't do. If it isn't represented here, there's a decent chance it won't have nearly as much social value to you. You may like it or appreciate it, but you won't engage it as if equal. This is especially true for the signs square to Libra. We may be too busy looking up to the Capricorn section to ever claim its laws for power or success as our own. We may be too busy wanting the Cancer section to admit that we already have it. In order to overcome the blind spots introduced by the Libra section—the comfort zones as it were—we need to be ready to see certain things we desire to engage as NOT being our communicative equals. This is perhaps the hardest lesson you can learn from this region (and one I'm only learning now as I type this): If you've ever wished for that perfect relationship with something, that authority, or that wished object...only to fail countless times to achieve it, it may be because you're expecting the relationship to be in the trenches with you, feedback for feedback. But sometimes our lives aren't set up like that. We have children (Cancer) or bosses (Capricorn) play roles we thought would be reserved for spouses. We have likes and favorites (Libra) eat up the dedication we would spend on things we claim to want (Cancer). The Libra duodecanates show where you are communicatively equal enough with some things to keep them going for a long time. Yet, to master Libra is to know when certain favored and equal exchanges need to be put aside for unequal ones. It doesn't have to be painful. Just know that your role model (Capricorn) or intuitional ideals (Cancer) aren't supposed to play happily-ever-after. They WILL involve one-sided bias. If you want these non-Libra things to work, be ready to drop the expectation for a completely balanced exchange.

Relationship quirks and the squares to Libra
Before we continue, remember this: SQUARES AREN'T BAD! One angle reaps what the other angle sows More of one means more of the other, just not at the same time. That said, let's continue.

> Right after writing the previous section, I realized something that will ultimately turn into an activity for you in a couple of paragraphs. If you've read some of my previous books you know that I'm strict-polyamorous and tend to get into unbalanced relationships if I'm in one at all. Two of the most salient features of my chart are {[Juno (commitment/marriage) in Cancer-2 (collection)] 90° [Nolli-Diotima (perfect comfort-extreme pairs) in Libra-2 (standout relationship)]}. And then there is {[Padua-Fredegundis-Aspasia plus 10 more very colorful asteroids in Libra-11 (relationship's social scene)] 90° [Velleda-Merxia-Sila-Nunam plus 7 more (another colorful cluster) in Cancer-11 (compeller)]}. As I've gotten older, I've lost most of my initial training in monogamy and gained a lot more "taboo" exchanges instead. I've also gravitated much more strongly towards celibacy where the existing options are unacceptable. With the asteroid of commitment Juno 90° one of the strongest duodecanates of commitment—Libra-2—my relationships have taken on a two-sidedness as their only stable means of playing out for the long-term. Additionally, I'm almost always in a kind of parental/boss dynamic with the other person. In 20 years of exchanges, it has NEVER been balanced. Never. (In case you wondered how it just doesn't seem to work out for some people... in the expected ways at least.)

Libra shows how you comfortably relate. Square to it, Cancer shows what you want. We've seen several times throughout the series how wanting=not having, yet having=narrowing of other dimensions for interaction. The good news is that the squares in your chart will build together. The uncomfortable news is that, the more you have in some favored Libra relationship, the more you tend to want from its Cancer/mother/intuitive square (recall the first paragraphs of this book). Depending on how you're gender-socialized, you may also find that the more you have in Libra relating, the more you'll have to deal with authority/father/institutional matters in Capricorn. In cases where you encounter contradictions—where two energies that should go together are a square each other—you'll tend to set up camp in multiple places. Where those contradictions are related to Libra relationships, you'll tend to adopt dominance dynamics with Capricorn, dissatisfaction dynamics with Cancer. We're generally trained to accept these consequences as a part of relationship's natural compromise. But in people where the consequences are reinforced heavily enough, such compromise won't be an option. This is where quirky relationship dynamics enter the picture.

In *Sex in 12 Dimensions* I talk a lot about the things we do to re-balance our exchanges when they get of order. Particularly in the Dimension 10 chapter, I list many of the practices people engage in as they search for healthier outlets both for partners and for themselves. Not to corrupt you, but if the regular ways don't work then they just don't work. For the longest time I thought that my relationships were cursed, but it was more like my sphere was built on certain contradictions. Throwing in the towel doesn't have to be your only choice in situations like that. You may just need to develop a particular acceptance of where your contradictions lie, and relate accordingly.

Most of this is inner work. It takes place *outside* of your partners' reach. But once you've done it, you'll find that the nature of your partners and partnerships changes for the better.

☞ **Question 56.2 (Relationship quirks, dissatisfaction):** Have you had issues relating successfully in partnerships? If you haven't, are there areas where you are chronically dissatisfied even within a successful partnership? Something you just seem to always want? Take a look at the asteroids of Libra and Cancer. Is there any square contradiction which stands out?

_____
_____
_____
_____

☞ **Question 56.3 (Relationship quirks, authority):** Have your relationships presented you with authority issues? Is the other person always too immature or too overbearing? Do you prefer it that way? Are they abusive? Are you? It may be better to look at it here than right in front of your partner. Take a look at your Libra versus Capricorn asteroids. Do you notice any 90° squares which favor unbalanced authority?

_____
_____
_____
_____

### A note for your intuition training

There is a difference, by the way, between authority (Capricorn), and power (Scorpio). This is a difference many of us need to train ourselves to feel: Authority is your right to determine how something works or what it does. Power is your impulse to change a thing's direction even when you don't necessarily have such rights. To feel the difference, ask yourself if you or your support tools are in a position to write a thing's rules. That's authority. If you are not in a position to write the thing's rules, but just want it to behave differently, more, or deferentially, then that's where you're inclined to apply power. A knack for rule-writing is more strongly related to claircognizance. A talent for pushing things not subject to your rules is associated with telepathy.

☞ **Question 56.4 (Feel the difference: power vs authority):** Get a timer and set it for 2 minutes. Take half the time to feel the places where you have authority—the ability to determine the rules. Spend the other half of the time feeling the places where things exist outside of your rules, but where you have (or wish you had) the ability to push them. Write down any observations below.

_____
_____
_____
_____

In case it wasn't evident, issues of power (Scorpio) are 90°/square issues of undifferentiated blending (Aquarius) and 90°/square issues of display without other-steering (Leo). You can investigate these relationships in your chart accordingly.

## 56-7 Virgo

| # | Sign Degree | Duodecanate Name | Theme | Character |
|---|---|---|---|---|
| 73 | 27.5°-29.9° | Virgo-1 | reflection | The start of a new problem to solve, for me, is associated with… |
| 74 | 25°-27.5° | Virgo-2 | proxy | My worth as a problem solver is measured through… |
| 75 | 22.5°-25° | Virgo-3 | basis | I communicate the details of a problem using… the things against which I most naturally form my opinions |
| 76 | 20°-22.5° | Virgo-4 | component | My general attitude during work is associated with… |
| 77 | 17.5°-20° | Virgo-5 | operation | The way I convey discoveries or accomplishments during work is… |
| 78 | 15°-17.5° | Virgo-6 | training | I police my own problem-solving efforts, employing the tools to solve the task at hand using… |
| 79 | 12.5°-15° | Virgo-7 | search | My default coworkers, colleagues, and the nature of the tools I use at work are all best associated with… |
| 80 | 10°-12.5° | Virgo-8 | exploration | How I do research / force facts (or people's roles) to align with my framework while problem-solving is associated with… |
| 81 | 7.5°-10° | Virgo-9 | method | As a worker or daily task performer I give off the image of… |
| 82 | 5°-7.5° | Virgo-10 | perspective | The nature of the services I perform for others has the effect of… |
| 83 | 2.5°-5° | Virgo-11 | summary | The kinds of external information that surrounds me as I work, the nature of high-stressors and chaos (but also the kind of demands I am working to address) are… (Pax-stress) |
| 84 | 0°-2.5° | Virgo-12 | alternative | Ideally, I belong in a work environment of… Also, the prime topic of my fantasy life |

With Virgo we officially step out of the influence of others and into our own complexity. The energy demands are often lower per unit time spent, but last for a much much longer, ongoing window. So ultimately they cost a lot more. Your day job is a good example of this. The Virgo duodecanates describe how you reconcile the different things you experience, blending them into a coherent singleness. How you search and find (Virgo-7), how you compress the complex or have it compressed into you (Virgo-11), and how you explain moving from one attitude to another (Virgo-4) are all contained in this region of the wheel. If Sagittarius shows the concepts we wish to expand before strangers for no particular reason, then Virgo shows where we want expand before strangers because we're preoccupied with squeezing those strangers into the familiar. You can't get famous before an audience you're shrinking into yourself. But what if you have a contradiction like 101 Helena in Virgo? Then you'll do the reconciling first, be noted for it later.

## 56-8 Leo

| #  | Sign Degree  | Duodecanate Name | Theme        | Character |
|----|--------------|------------------|--------------|-----------|
| 85 | 27.5°-29.9°  | Leo-1            | intersection | When I'm with somebody, the way I wish to initiate new directions is… |
| 86 | 25°-27.5°    | Leo-2            | transfer     | As company to another, I am best described as… |
| 87 | 22.5°-25°    | Leo-3            | gift         | In preferred company, I express my views by… |
| 88 | 20°-22.5°    | Leo-4            | suggestion   | Being around preferred company, I generally have the urge to… |
| 89 | 17.5°-20°    | Leo-5            | assumption   | When I'm with somebody, I really prefer the theme to involve… |
| 90 | 15°-17.5°    | Leo-6            | opening      | An issue I like to bring up in preferred company is that of… the kinds of topics I draw from my long-range vision of things |
| 91 | 12.5°-15°    | Leo-7            | aim          | In preferred company, my conversational context tends to have… happen around it |
| 92 | 10°-12.5°    | Leo-8            | hunger       | When I'm with somebody, I like to make the other person do… for my satisfaction (or to override them) |
| 93 | 7.5°-10°     | Leo-9            | fulfillment  | When I am with preferred company, the rest of the world sees me (or I see myself projecting towards the world) as… |
| 94 | 5°-7.5°      | Leo-10           | fixation     | With somebody, I show my ability to enforce order, control by… |
| 95 | 2.5°-5°      | Leo-11           | update       | I am more likely to do things with somebody / enjoy preferred company in social settings which involve… Also, how I play out my uniqueness |
| 96 | 0°-2.5°      | Leo-12           | pathway      | Being with somebody adds an air of… This is how I go questing with them. The nature of what I create for fun. |

Leo is traditionally associated with ego, leadership, and charisma, mainly because this region is concerned with the things we show. Behind the show lie a thousand reasons for what led us to what we're currently projecting, where Leo packages the results of those reasons for the people and events that deal with us in detail. The strangers of Sagittarius are too zoomed-out for this. Leo demonstrates who we are amidst direct one-on-one interactions, regardless of the interactant's immediate input.

Take a moment to think about the visual world. Behind its superficial appearance, every object you observe—every event you encounter—originated in some prior trail of events. Some individual, some system, or some chain of laws led that cup to sit where it is or that engine to squeak as it does. When you engage the visible or (more broadly) the experiential world, you are interacting with a snapshot of countless histories all frozen into a single scene. The duodecanates of Leo divide up these histories into categories based on the types of stories that went into making them.

※ Although the characters of Leo are probably not surprising, I found the themes to be very surprising. In order to generate the themes for these duodecanates, I took the four main values of each of the 1100 asteroids in *Laurentia*, used each as a sort column, summarized their cluster families of interpretations, re-summarized them principal components-style across all four values (semimajor axis, aphelion, perihelion, and span), then selected a word which best summarized the duodecanate as well as the two neighboring duodecanates on either side. I did this for 144 clusters, but it could have just as easily been done for 60, 500, or a million groups. It's the fraction of the circle (not the number itself) that matters. The process works like something called an ARIMA (auto-regressive integrated moving average) in time series analysis, but since it was based on words and not numbers, I called the method "pseudo-ARIMA." Leo-7 (aim), for example, is a reflection of all of the asteroid interpretations which were about 91/144 of the way between one major planet band and the next—grouped four times for the four planetary values, then smoothed to consider measures 90/144 and 92/144 of the way (with 89/144 and 93/144 less so) to account for any imprecision in the Minor Planet Center values or my own interpretations in the first place. (Take a look at themes 84–86 for an example of how the sections flow into each other across signs.) Accordingly, the themes in each table are much more stable reflections of what the sign divisions actually do than the traditionally sharp astrological divisions of say, Scorpio versus Libra imply. The Leo themes are particularly counterintuitive, but only where we forget about the underlying backstory that drives an ego to project as it does in the first place. ✹

Leo comes across as how you show yourself, but we should think of it more as the sum of what you've sought (Leo-7), what you've eaten (Leo-8), what environments you've spent your time hanging around (Leo-12), how you've informed yourself or taken in new information (Leo-11), your biological imperative for starting new interactions in general (Leo-1), the limits you've faced (Leo-10), how you've built your identity (Leo-2), and five other broad realms. As practice, you might consider what those other realms might be.

Suppose you're going for a certain image in your exchanges. You want to be a certain kind of person (in front of thorough exchangers, not strangers). You can build up that image by doing the things square to Leo, eating and steering Scorpio-style, being consumed and subsumed identitywise Taurus-style. My oft-cited identification as an oldest brother, for example, is a Taurus-3, 4, 5, and 8 summary of my identity dynamics, and influences how I make requests of people. Squares are how you build up potential. Once the potential is built, trines show the logical path strangers follow in each dimension as they get to know you better, then as you get to know yourself with respect to them. While planting your own interactional seeds via square acts, it pays to welcome others (or yourself) differently via trine acts. There's rarely a need to spray the entire library of success books in order to change something. Just focus. Do your squares. Welcome through your trines.

☞ Question 56.5 (If you were to change yourself...): Even if you're happy the way you are, take a moment to imagine one of the Leo duodecanates in which you would change yourself. The asteroids in there will already tell you *how* you would change yourself, so pick any section with a nice-to-have. Once you have picked, list the asteroids square to the Leo section which you think are related to your building up the region you chose. Then list any asteroids trine to the Leo section which you, when you treat others or yourself better, feel would be associated with your improvement there.

| Question | Your Answer | Example |
|---|---|---|
| 1. What section of Leo would it be nice to improve in? | | Leo-8 |
| 2. Are there any specific asteroids you're looking to address? | | 1688 Wilkens – inherited value<br>3671 Dionysus – audacity<br>9 Metis – socially idealized company |
| 3. Looking at your squares to this region, do you see any concepts which seem to have a seed-planting effect here? | | Scorpio-8<br>911 Agamemnon – ruthless pursuit of ends<br>603 Timandra – physical presence as topic |
| 4. What do you think the relationship is? | | More determined insistence on standards →better chances of inherited social ideal |

| 5. Looking at your trines to the Leo region, do you see any concepts that are analogous in the world or in yourself which, when you treat these accordingly, feel connected to your Leo section improvement? | | Sagittarius-8<br>54598 Bienor – women of singularly unique accomplishments<br>40 Harmonia – talent which takes you to far off terrains |
|---|---|---|
| 6. What do you think this implies for your interactants? | | more talent-oriented plans+accomplished women as circle→better chances of inherited social ideal |

Do the connections you made align with life as you've experienced it thus far? Hopefully they do.

## 56-9 Cancer

| # | Sign Degree | Duodecanate Name | Theme | Character |
|---|---|---|---|---|
| 97 | 27.5°-29.9° | Cancer-1 | preference | My intuition for new situations comes most sharply through… |
| 98 | 25°-27.5° | Cancer-2 | collection | … in my life reflect how well I honor my instincts and act on my wants appropriately (the reward for achieving emotional stability) |
| 99 | 22.5°-25° | Cancer-3 | progression | Themes of… accompany situations where I feel I need to speak up / something needs to be said |
| 100 | 20°-22.5° | Cancer-4 | arrival | I assess my own feelings in terms of… People can tell I'm really evaluating things when they see me do this. (Warning before a boil) |
| 101 | 17.5°-20° | Cancer-5 | following | In the course of wanting something, I feel inclined to show others where I stand in light of… This is also the group of behaviors I use when my feelings about something have come to a boil |
| 102 | 15°-17.5° | Cancer-6 | holding | I am great at assessing what needs to be done / how to best progress forward when… (how and where I receive good guidance regarding issues that need to be solved) |
| 103 | 12.5°-15° | Cancer-7 | reinforcement | …describes how I am drawn to interact with certain things |
| 104 | 10°-12.5° | Cancer-8 | value | …is what I tend to dwell on while waiting for others do as I would want. This is also the kind of thing which I will hesitate to tell people I'm close to unless I'm ready to blow up the relationship—what they need to bring to light themselves. The potential event which I hold inside, waiting for others to give to me. When they give it to me favorably it comes out as inheritance. (This region roughly corresponds to your ACTUAL definition of riches: the things you want for the purpose of influencing others. Even if you had a bunch of money, it wouldn't matter nearly as much if you couldn't use it to access this region.) |
| 105 | 7.5°-10° | Cancer-9 | culture | I come across as… in the eyes of the world when in a state of deep assessment |
| 106 | 5°-7.5° | Cancer-10 | dilemma | …is what I use to resolve a pressing urge I've had. Also the groups where I am most likely to view myself as a master |
| 107 | 2.5°-5° | Cancer-11 | compeller | As I consider my wants, the nature of the information around me is… (the kind of talk, music, or entertainment associated with my style of desiring) |
| 108 | 0°-2.5° | Cancer-12 | continuation | I engage my intuition / wants best in an environment of… |

**\*\*This next paragraph is EXTRA important for understanding dissatisfaction in your life\*\***

Cancer describes your approach to things which are potentially rather than (currently) actual in nature—things which are conceivable in your life but which you are not quite engaging (Libra- or Aries-style) at the moment. Opposite Cancer's sections are the Capricorn limits which circumscribe your intentions towards these goals. Your potential actions (Cancer-1), potential power (Cancer-8), potential identification (Cancer-2), potential stranger-environments (Cancer-9) and other feelings that something should happen all live in here, making this the group most associated with your styles of dissatisfaction.

At the heart of the Cancer family lies the concept of "progression" (Cancer-3). On the one hand, we could spend our lives wanting. On the other hand, we could spend it journeying. For every duodecanate here which manifests through dissatisfaction, there is another perspective wherein the same duodecanate manifests as a stream of experiences towards perfection. I have to say that, after years of going back and forth on how to handle Cancer and its associated super-angle (the square), I've found that intuition may not actually be the best or highest use of this energy. Journeying is likely better. That's because intuition is just another form of sight, much like Leo visibility or Gemini expression. (Zooming out, there's a reason these signs are next to each other.) Once you go beyond the realm of your own perspective or your own need to have things happen in your own language, however, your intuition may not be so useful for aligning the worlds you share with others. Sometimes it is, sometimes it isn't. Instead, embracing the journey in things seems to be a more practical, more ongoing alternative to plain intuition, while plain intuition seems to be generally healthier than the plain insatiable want which describes our socially-trained Cancer by default. We've been practicing intuition, and certainly the asteroids in Cancer show you what you have an intuition for. But once you've developed that capacity to a certain level, putting it to use becomes the thing.

☞ Question 56.6 (A sense of where. A sense of what. A sense of how): **The routes to intuition are plentiful, but most of us are more familiar with intuition as "feeling." Pisces, Scorpio, and Cancer are all concerned with feeling, but whereas Pisces tells you *where* you're going next, Scorpio tells you *what* the other's inclination is, and Cancer tells you *how* you yourself will process the next thing emotionally.** Scorpio energy is harder for most of us to work with—at least when it concerns people—because other people's behaviors are a moving target. Scorpio energy, however, is much easier to work with in matters of research, major exits, or other areas where the interactant is not so changeable. Beyond this, the Pisces and Cancer forms of intuitive feeling are far more accessible through means like dreams and compelled responses respectively. It can be useful to differentiate these kinds of intuition, but before we practice let's remind ourselves of two fundamental differences between these energies:

- Pisces is what you sense when there is no major objective. Cancer is what you sense against some specific object, an end you're moving towards. The former seems to have no identifiable home when it comes to whoever delivered it to you. The latter is more strongly connected to your active mental assessment of targets of your choosing.

- Pisces shares seed planting with events in the world. Cancer shares seed planting with your behavioral choices.

Take 1 minute to sit silently, with no thoughts in your head except for this feeling: you're responding to something and it's responding to you, over and over until the time ends. Write down your observations below.

_____
_____
_____
_____

Now take 1 minute to think about a scenario where you are responding back and forth with something you really want in your life. Write down your observations.

_____
_____
_____
_____

Did you notice any differences in feeling? For the first minute (Pisces-7) I felt my stomach tingling, with more of a desirous edge. For my second minute (Cancer-7), I clearly felt a kind of happiness associated with some data projects I'm working on. Having not memorized all 1100 asteroids in my chart, I look up the bodies around both these areas...Kallisto and Xanthe in Pisces-7, Berkeley and Urda in Cancer-7 Sounds about right.[44] Did you observe any asteroids that might explain the feelings you just had?

_____
_____
_____
_____

These bodies would form the characters of these kinds of intuition for you.

If you believe that time is like a movie, then there's nothing stopping us from running the movie backwards. The good thing about things happening together—correlation—is that you don't automatically have causation with it. Energywise and astrowise, you can have a feeling for something before that something occurs, simply because the feeling and the occurrence travel together. All it takes is the temporary suspension of the ordering mind. Now imagine that you're tired of living in dreamland, and want to turn these kinds of feelings into a more practical journey. How do you do it?

For reasons discussed back in *Laurentia*, the sextiles (60°) are the default "frame rate" for our experiential movie. This may be related to the two levels of the snowflake model discussed in that book, but whatever the explanation, the forward and backward sextile from any point on the wheel show that which naturally occurs before or after that point when there is no pressure to change foci. Where Cancer shows nurturance, Taurus shows food. Where Cancer shows progression, Taurus shows reconciliation. It's no coincidence that the sextiles to [reinforcement/Cancer-7] are [search/Virgo-7] and [treatment/Taurus-7], putting the strict definitions aside, perhaps you can see a common story related to objective-making here. Given your intuition for expressive reinforcement, it is possible to turn any dissatisfaction here into a satisfied search/journey or treatment/ongoing dynamic. We feel the want and immediately move on, thus turning our dissatisfaction into a source of positive identity.

## On Cancer and riches

What does it mean to be rich? One esoteric definition might be "having the means to trade for (a lot of?) what you want." Dollars and Euros are one route to this. Credit, holdings, and favors owed may be others. Favors owed, however, get us into much cloudier territory. Are you rich if you can afford a

---

[44] The second time I did this activity, my targets were more abstract: Pisces-11 and Cancer-11 in hindsight. Yours may be different as well.

$100,000 car with your $500,000 salary, or rich if you can buy that same car at 1/3 the price on half the salary? Now the notion of broad comparative worth enters the picture. The astro chart doesn't really look at currency, but at broad comparative worth on the whole. Thus the sections most associated with riches are those that combine certain concepts of want with certain indicators of the (extra) ability to compel that want. "Want" itself is the purview of Cancer. The power to interact as you wish is the purview of Cancer through Scorpio. Accordingly, Cancer-4 through Cancer-8 tell a large part of the story of what actual riches looks like to us. You may think it's about money because that's what the broad world—knowing little about your preferences—uses to enable your desires later down the line. But if you had all the money you ever wanted you would surely buy the kinds of things that move your fancy. Cancer-1 through Cancer-3 show how you would prefer to think while Cancer-9 through Cancer-12 show where, emotionally, you would prefer to have externally-facilitated experiences (neither of which you need money for). Cancer-4 through Cancer-8, however, show the kinds of *interactions* you wish you could have. You probably have these anyway, but somehow you know that the shinier versions of these interactions require more cash for you to access. And so it is, the middle sections of Cancer show the various senses in which you would compel others to vote **your** way. Specifically, Cancer-8 describes something like the ultimate form of other-coercive power in a person's chart. It's opposite, Capricorn-8, shows the kinds of groups which wield that power. To understand your Cancer-8 is to get to the heart of steering-riches as you might conceive it, though this is not the only section of the chart dedicated to such things. (Sagittarius-1, Taurus-11, and any section of the chart which aligns with the will of your local power holder are also related to riches.[45])

☞ Question 56.7 (The quest for riches): **Let's build up a journey towards expressive riches.**

| Question | Your Answer | Example |
|---|---|---|
| 1. Do you have any interesting asteroids in Cancer-8? | | 153 Hilda – critical improvement advice<br>662 Newtonia – glued to a system's proper function<br>32532 Thereus – unusual standout |
| 2. Do either of the sextiles (60° angles) to this section have asteroids which naturally lead to the cluster you just listed? | | Virgo-8<br>50 Virginia – noob behavior<br>448 Natalie – perfection, or else ruin |
| 3. Do either of the sextiles (60° angles) to this section have asteroids which naturally follow from your Cancer-8? | | Taurus-8<br>265 Anna – others obey your suggestion<br>3200 Phaeton – skillful innovation |
| 4. Complete the following cocktail: "My ultimate riches are in the form of [having lots of 1], which I build up through [lots of 2]. With it, I show my influence through [lots of 3]."<br><br>(Be sure to write this in the present tense. Don't be shy. You may find yourself successful in this already!) | | My ultimate riches are in the form of [being a unique an indispensable contributor to a system], which I build up through [the perfected expression of things I'm new to]. With it, I show my influence through [skillful innovation that gets listened to]. No wonder I build up better value through smaller projects and mini-puzzles. |

---

[45] As we saw in *FSA*, the United States' Moon is located in 18° Aquarius. To the extent that they relate to the country as a whole, individuals have a better chance of aligning with the wants of the nation when they use their asteroids located here in the country's favor. Such alignment makes it easier for them to advance as Americans. This isn't riches, but it presents a kind of connection which favors one's expressive right. Take a look at Aquarius-5 to see what's involved. I use July 4, 1776, 2:32am in Philadelphia as the US birth chart because that chart's interpretations tended to make more sense, aligning more with how we actually experience the country than other alternatives.

☞ **Question 56.8 (The quest for social mobility): While we're here, let's put together a formula for expressive mobility.**

| Question | Your Answer | Example |
|---|---|---|
| 1. Do you have any interesting asteroids in Sagittarius-1? | | Sagittarius-1<br>560 Delila, 752 Sulamitis, 806 Gyldenia, 515 Athalia, *188 Menippe |
| 2. Do either of the sextiles (60° angles) to this section have asteroids which naturally lead to the cluster you just listed? | | Libra-1<br>457 Alleghenia, 726 Joella, 2254 Requiem |
| 3. Do either of the sextiles (60° angles) to this section have asteroids which naturally follow from your Sagittarius-1? | | Aquarius-1<br>427 Galene, 438 Zeuxo, 23 Thalia |
| 4. Write down a cocktail that reads something like: "I become socially mobile in the form of [1], resulting in my [lifestyle doing 3]. I need [2] in order for this to happen.<br><br>(Be sure to write this in the present tense. Don't be shy. You may find yourself successful in this already!) | | I become socially mobile consummate with my [unapologetic (perhaps primal) role in the entertainment field], resulting in my [lifestyle of boisterous, groundbreaking environments]. I need [to be called on (I can't or shouldn't initiate), and should keep a measured distance with the caller] for this to happen. |

☞ **Question 56.9 (The quest for whatever): You get the idea by now. Let's do one more.**

| Question | Your Answer |
|---|---|
| 1. Do you have any interesting asteroids in *any* duodecanate you've seen thus far? Be sure to write which one it is.) | |
| 2. Do either of the sextiles (60° angles) to this section have asteroids which naturally lead to the cluster you just listed? | |
| 3. Do either of the sextiles (60° angles) to this section have asteroids which naturally follow from your chosen cluster? | |
| 4. See if you can follow the formulas from prior questions to produce a cocktail of your own: "I build up my [1] based on [2]. It leads to [3]." | |

(Be sure to write this in the present tense. Don't be shy. You may find yourself successful in this already!)

## Easier said than done?

What if you created the cocktails above but didn't like the causes you got? "A will give me B, but I can't do A." Sometimes it happens. There are many routes to making a thing happen via the astro chart, and we've discussed most of these ways in previous books. Here, though, I'd like to add one more method related to the notion of anti-planets discussed in *144*.

For everything that happens, there is a context for it happening. A planet of speaking would have a complementary point for being spoken. A planet for emotions would have a complementary planet for being felt. For your causes in the cocktails above, there will also be complements; these complements show you the context (and often the person) you interact against when you're bringing something about. The complement to social wrapping (Sagittarius-1) is truth (Gemini-1), since both involve the recognition of a foreign entrant and their standardized value system, but one is the entrant while the other is the assigner of meaning—the native of the world being entered, the declarer of truth. The complement to Aquarius-1 (percept) would be Leo-1 (intersection). And if you chose to outsource one of these you could expect another person to appear in your life for carrying it—provided you have *truly* decided not to strive for it on your own.

The points opposite any degree will show you not only the context for that degree's occurrence, but also part of the character of a typical person or thing which embodies that degree. If you are in mystery regarding who might help you bring the degree about, the opposition to it may shed some light on things.

Note, though, that we've come a long way in this book when it comes to owning our current position. You should know by now that, although there are plenty of ways to fight the circumstances that have brought you where you are, you may still want to think twice before ushering in something you're not actually ready for.

## Breaking into a sign

There is one final, useful note worth mentioning regarding Cancer. Suppose you've got a lot of good asteroids sitting in a particular *sign* which you're not good at intentionally accessing—not without conscious effort at least. (Sagittarius and Leo are like this for me.) Because of the way you assign priority to certain behaviors, you may find that certain chart regions tend to come in second place to... everything—such that you just can't get these regions started. The Cancer duodecanates, taken together, provide one of the best examples of the difference between whole signs and whole bodies versus sections of signs; you can use this to get a good idea of the actual whole-sign context that might better fit you by looking at its Cancer microcosm. We'll explore this in a moment, but first I'll need to address something which may be (unfortunately) confusing given everything we've addressed since *144*:

**Signlettes (mini decans) go forward in a sign. Duodecanates (mini signs/aspects) go backwards.**
If you want a sign's "opinion" of a behavior, you read backwards (what we've been doing).
If you want a sign's "opinion" of its own effect, you read forward (useful for broad subjects with no direct object).

For example, the Aries-Taurus-Gemini sections of Cancer correspond to Cancer-1, 2, and 3 respectively when you do them energywise, but have a Cancer:Pisces decan feel to the people looking at you. Although it should make sense that behaviors occurring within you (Cancer-1…4) are occurring outside of everyone else (Cancer-[World]), it reintroduces a monkey wrench which we thought we'd disposed of at the beginning of *All 144 Aspects*. We won't spend long on this topic because, frankly, it's very easy to overcomplicate if you think too hard about it. Instead, I'll give you a pair of statements to summarize the issue:

| | |
|---|---|
| Cancer-1 to you is more like Cancer:Pisces to everyone else because your self-motivation is a world (beyond reach) abstraction to them.<br><br>Relatedly, Cancer-2 to you *would be* something like Cancer:Aquarius to everyone else; Cancer-3 to you *would be* like Cancer:Capricorn to everyone else and so on…, **BUT** | Elon Musk may be rich to himself, but your observation of him makes you poorer by comparison. |
| since the world can't normally distinguish sub-motivations in you like this, it's neither statistically nor practically useful to divide the wheel into 144ths based on outsiders' observation of an object/event/you. The data (in previous books) don't support this. Instead, the outside observer-system can say broadly that your Self is its World, your World is its Self, and your Other is its Other, giving us the traditional *decan*—forward order—mentioned briefly in *FSA*. Since then we've defined *duo*decanates in terms of the backwards order since the forward order didn't correspond to people's actual choices in *144*; the backwards order did. This same issue is relatedly to the earlier comment on how the asteroid interpretations were a lot easier to generate from the outside looking in (simplistic grouping perspective), not the other way around. | Reading his chart, you might see his Sagittarius-1/ wrapping as a strong region. But very broadly, this would be something like the Sagittarius:Pisces-ish effect on you. But you as a stranger wouldn't be privy to his "Sagittarius:Pisces" through his "Sagittarius:Sagittarius" for lack of experiential detail. Thus you could only bundle these as your Sagittarius:[World] (measured against his actual behavioral Sagittarius-1…4) as a broad interactional section of his personal motivation in your experience. Sagittarius:[World] would be Sagittarius:Leo with respect to the Sagittarius sign itself (since Saj:[Self] would actually be equal to Saj:Saj in the forward order.) |

And why do you care about the above? Why talk about this NOW?

**To make a long story short: If you're doing something <u>to be interpreted by someone else</u>, you'll need to do it as you do it, but consider that it will be interpreted as the mirrored sub-region of the same sign.**

I know it's confusing. There's nothing we can do about it.

Say, for example, you really :want: more Taurus (self-worth) riches in your life broadly, but you know you're not very good at optimizing your Taurus asteroids. Your Cancer-2 shows your "want for Taurus/2" experiences, so you might look at :Cancer:-2 and find that your own *actual* approach to *wanting* worth lies with the asteroids that live there. So you try exercising this quirky cluster; it kind of works; you know you've achieved inner satisfaction with your choices… but where's the cash? This is where the issue above comes in: The world won't see your Cancer-2 as wanted identity; it will see it broadly as a part of your wanted:[World] (Cancer:Pisces traditional decan). You'll need to address the *mirror* to Cancer-2 in this sign: Cancer-11, and even then—because it's "want" we're talking about—you'll only be planting seeds for what the world views as the Cancer:Cancer traditional decan. Square to this will be the

Libra:Libra and Aries:Aries traditional decans in which the world views you as broadly sociable or expressively forceful respectively. But ultimately you didn't actually do either of these in order to get the identity riches going. You exercised the asteroids in Cancer-11 **AND** Cancer-2... Because if you had only done the former *instead* of the latter, you will have had the opposite problem as the one that brought us here: the external *image* of wanted riches achieved *without the feeling.

So it turns out that, if you want something to manifest fully and it doesn't depend on sharing power with [sign]:Other, you'll need to exercise both [sign]:Self and [sign]:World in order to achieve both the inner feeling and the outer recognition. This will allow you to break into signs you perhaps haven't been so good at, mainly through others' acknowledgement of the results of endeavors seed-planted/SQUARE those signs. Even after you've done everything right, expect to be misinterpreted or oversimplified by the rest of the world which sponsored the frameworks you were seeking. 🛠

That was rough, wasn't it? But if you've used astrology long enough to experiment with it, you know it doesn't get any cleaner than this. It goes to show why you can't just pick up a chart and make things happen. Yes, your Cancer in particular will give you entry access to whole regions of your chart which you're not so good at, but if you're looking at those regions in order to experience certain effects, you'll need to tackle the issue on multiple fronts, keeping in mind that your own inner priorities are the LAST facets of you that everyone else will have access to. The world-affecting people become known as notable individuals. The self-affecting people become known more for their contributions to everyone else's—the world's—mood. You can do this for other aspects of your life besides that of "want," as long as you keep these same principles in mind.

## 56-10 Gemini

| # | Sign Degree | Duodecanate Name | Theme | Character |
|---|---|---|---|---|
| 109 | 27.5°-29.9° | Gemini-1 | truth | I begin offering my opinion of things in a way that naturally emphasizes… |
| 110 | 25°-27.5° | Gemini-2 | connection | My style of communication is… |
| 111 | 22.5°-25° | Gemini-3 | other | Ideally, I try to communicate my ideas in a way that stresses these kinds of mannerisms: |
| 112 | 20°-22.5° | Gemini-4 | rights | My default attitude while communicating is that of… |
| 113 | 17.5°-20° | Gemini-5 | enjoyment | I'm inclined to think of my myself as leaving this kind of impression on interactants when I communicate: |
| 114 | 15°-17.5° | Gemini-6 | relation | As a communicator, I consider failures of… to be unacceptable in making myself understood |
| 115 | 12.5°-15° | Gemini-7 | representation | …is a feature of how I retell the story of my interactions with others |
| 116 | 10°-12.5° | Gemini-8 | difference | I justify to myself the use of power or coercion by paying attention to… |
| 117 | 7.5°-10° | Gemini-9 | self-image | I gain an easy public reputation related to… based on how I give out my opinions. Also, the kinds of publics most likely to receive me overall |
| 118 | 5°-7.5° | Gemini-10 | insistence | My style of communication is especially useful for controlling or bringing order to… (in myself or others) |
| 119 | 2.5°-5° | Gemini-11 | context | My communication naturally elicits surrounding talk about… |
| 120 | 0°-2.5° | Gemini-12 | audience | As a communicator I leave a notable impression of… |

Now here's something interesting. Way back in chapter 17 we introduced a table that outlined different levels for the same aspect. Typically we think of communication as just being verbal or mental in nature, but the duodecanates of Gemini show us that there is far more to how we express our own internal informational processes. Sure you have the standard thought processes (Gemini-1 through 4). But you also have preferred listeners (Gemini-11 and 12), natural objects of attention (Gemini-7 and 8), as well as certain concepts you insist on considering (Gemini-6 and 10). This area of your wheel tends to be automatic, takes up untold amounts of metabolic energy compared to the signs before it, and is very difficult to reshape consciously, yet it plants the seeds for both your daily duties and your basic feelings in Virgo and Pisces respectively. So it is well worth honing if you have trouble in these areas.

More than anything, your Gemini divisions show your basic attitude towards things you encounter— where you're free to unload your opinion without any consequences... or without any *apparent* consequences. I'll bet you the consequences are there, though. Let's see how negative "opinionation" (as we've called it) really can affect you in other, more public areas of life not too far down the line.

☞ Question 56.10 (Because of negative opinionation...): **Take a look at the Gemini table above and ask yourself "is there anything towards which I have a strongly negative opinion? Not negative communication or interaction, but a negative opinion in my own head? If so, what is it and what asteroids/duodecanate might be reflecting this? Being tense, does it have square consequences for something else I might encounter?"**

| Question | Your Answer | Example |
|---|---|---|
| 1. Do you have a very basic negative opinion of anything in particular? | | Social media, mobs, and web noise. My attitude towards these things is contemptuous, pissy, and intolerant |
| 2. If you answered yes, what Gemini duodecanate and asteroids may be behind this? | | 87 Sylvia – where polished order is important, Gemini-10; 995 Sternberga – "area in which, when others attempt to influence you, you become stern [and often coldly] uncooperative" Gemini-6. True facts. |
| 3. Are any squares to this negatively affected? | | Yes. Pisces-10 maintains a bubble around me: South Node – irritation, 897 Lysistrata – unconsummated exchanges Pisces-6 and its asteroids make a certain level of isolation necessary |
| 4. Is this something you'll need to work on? | | Nope. Looks like my anti-mob gene/need to order information makes my *Virgo* asteroids very strong. Things like these books get produced. |

Maybe your negative opinion hurts your opportunities elsewhere. Maybe it actually helps. We're all different.

## 56-11 Taurus

| #   | Sign Degree | Duodecanate Name | Theme        | Character                                                                                          |
|-----|-------------|------------------|--------------|----------------------------------------------------------------------------------------------------|
| 121 | 27.5°-29.9° | Taurus-1         | individual   | Above all, I am a natural…                                                                         |
| 122 | 25°-27.5°   | Taurus-2         | instance     | People/things who measure their worth against me are naturally…                                    |
| 123 | 22.5°-25°   | Taurus-3         | membership   | My most natural way of thinking / giving my opinion is…                                            |
| 124 | 20°-22.5°   | Taurus-4         | food         | Left alone without pressure, my general attitude towards life / the way I spend unhurried leisure time is… |
| 125 | 17.5°-20°   | Taurus-5         | nurturance   | Ideally, I prefer interactions which let me…                                                       |
| 126 | 15°-17.5°   | Taurus-6         | promotion    | I'm great at putting things together / making things work in…                                      |
| 127 | 12.5°-15°   | Taurus-7         | treatment    | My best conversations are described by…                                                            |
| 128 | 10°-12.5°   | Taurus-8         | work         | As an influencer of people or situations, I am… Also, where I am a perfectionist                   |
| 129 | 7.5°-10°    | Taurus-9         | material     | My overall public image is that of a…                                                              |
| 130 | 5°-7.5°     | Taurus-10        | construction | I demand order and control in…, adopting it as my stance in the larger world                       |
| 131 | 2.5°-5°     | Taurus-11        | source       | I easily get myself talked about for…                                                              |
| 132 | 0°-2.5°     | Taurus-12        | effect       | The spirit of those around me is that of…                                                          |

In perhaps my favorite surprise of all 144 duodecanates, Taurus-4 is associated with, of all things, food. Not the food you eat, but *you* as food for others. Almost all duodecanates from 123 through 135, in fact, describe who you are as an energy to be consumed by various other energies. Taurus describes the nurturance class you belong to (Taurus-4), the processes you enable after being consumed (Taurus-5), the phenomena for which you are a building block (Taurus-6), the afflictions/deficits you help fix (Taurus-7), and several other neat roles you play among others and in society at large. Personally, I've found Taurus-9 to be a decent reflection of the culture I live in. And in one of the strongest (and perhaps weirdest) indicators of popularity, Taurus-11 shows where you are passed around like a plain old object for sale. If you ever wanted to know what you'd look like if you were a thing to be sold on eBay, Taurus-11 shows you this. Scorpio-11 shows you what kinds of characters pass you around (when you've outsourced this). Pay close attention to these Scorpio-11 types, as they have a natural talent for putting you on center stage before the world.

We often celebrate leaders and dominance, but there is a strong case to be made for letting yourself get passed around. Such is the story of branding, referral, and other people's transmission of your value, such that it won't always help you to have an ego about these things. For people wishing to know their place in the world, Taurus-6 is good for you, but Taurus-7 through 11 are better for the systems that deploy you. Be warned that the themes here are far more philosophical than they look, so you'll need to put some thought into how you tackle them. Taurus-9, for example, shows your "definition" of what it means for something to be considered a material. Its asteroids have implications for the types of energy you can actually work with in doing your thing for the world. One of my asteroids, 523 Ada, involves power and 1:1 exploratory behavior—an attitude I'm compelled to take in anything I write that actually gets published. Things that lack your Taurus-9 are far less likely to make it to production where your natural, popularly tradeable expression is concerned. You put them together in the style of your Taurus-10, and have Taurus-7 effects on the people who are actually benefitting from what you sponsor. Perhaps being objectified isn't always a bad thing.

## 56-12 Aries

| # | Sign Degree | Duodecanate Name | Theme | Character |
|---|---|---|---|---|
| 133 | 27.5°-29.9° | Aries-1 | infiltration | I motivate myself to start something by… |
| 134 | 25°-27.5° | Aries-2 | harmonizing | I approach new projects like a… |
| 135 | 22.5°-25° | Aries-3 | excitement | The message I convey when I start something is that of… |
| 136 | 20°-22.5° | Aries-4 | recruitment | This is the way I feel about the things I start (or while I am starting them): |
| 137 | 17.5°-20° | Aries-5 | mobilization | As I start things, I am compelled to show… to others |
| 138 | 15°-17.5° | Aries-6 | behavior | When I start things, the nature of the problem that confronts me tends (in my eyes) to involve… |
| 139 | 12.5°-15° | Aries-7 | imposition | My starting things typically begins with conversations revolving around… Also, the kind of relationship partner I attract |
| 140 | 10°-12.5° | Aries-8 | co-creation | When I start things, I push others along with me by… |
| 141 | 7.5°-10° | Aries-9 | ideal | When I start things it's easy for me to provoke an impression of… |
| 142 | 5°-7.5° | Aries-10 | stability | Starting things, the first thing I seek to get under control / the first place I look to an authority source is… |
| 143 | 2.5°-5° | Aries-11 | activity | The informational context most conducive to me starting things (also, my fired up music / entertainment) is one where… |
| 144 or 0 | 0°-2.5° | Aries-12 | atmosphere | I'm more likely to get things started / make spontaneous decisions in an environment of… |

Aries is, for all intents and purposes, the story of the birthing process. The way you start things (Aries-6), the environments you come into (Aries-12), what you help (Aries-2), what you disrupt (Aries-1 and 3), the energies you mix with (Aries-7, 10, and 11), and how you steer others when you're starting things (Aries-8) are all described here. Because this is all about initiation and not about continuation, it doesn't say much about how you sustain things. It *does*, however, say a lot about who you sustain things with and *where* you do so: You sustain around the things that help you start more things. Does that make sense?

One of the strongest indicators of your relationship partner, Aries-7 is a great example of an outsourced opposition in action. Libra-7 provides conversation about your conversations, and is often reserved for only the most interested parties. Aries-7s are those parties. It's also the mode in which you say, "Hey, guess what? Yack, yack, yack, yack, yack..." Again, like Taurus, Aries has themes which can get very philosophical, such that the asteroids in each section truly are likely to be your practiced definition of that theme.

I recall double-checking my results when it seemed that one's definition of a generic "ideal" lie in Aries-9. Why not in Pisces? Why not in Libra or Cancer? But ideals aren't really known for our conversations with them. The ongoingness would rob them of their impression-making luster. Instead, ideals are more like generative backdrops (Sagittarius-style worlds) against which we are motivated to express at our most satisfied. Asteroids in Aries-9 constitute key features of such backdrops, in what amounts to a surprise turn away from the wants of Cancer. If you thought ideals would be located in a water or earth sign, you're not alone. Their place in the fire sign of initiation may be unexpected, but makes sense the more you think about it. True ideals are often immediately evocative of your effort to reach them—if only through conception. They trigger the "journey towards," for a brief moment diminishing all dissatisfaction associated with their actual attainment.

## Universal Access

In previous books I've claimed that all cycles have at least four dimensions: real, anti-real, potential, and anti-potential. In both 2D and 3D space, we can argue further that 12 dimensions is yet another stable value for a base number of dimensions since the four cyclical dimensions can be directed towards self, other, or world. The 12 dimensions themselves can be further divided, but it doesn't really matter whether you use 144 or 10,004. As the grades of angles move around the wheel, we still get divisions forming categories that look something like the old cycle of real and potential. Figure 56-2 below shows the actual theme names for the duodecanates before I simplified them in the charts above. You may find many of the section names intriguing. In many cases they are far more complex (yet far more precise) than I cared to bog the reader down with in the initial tables.

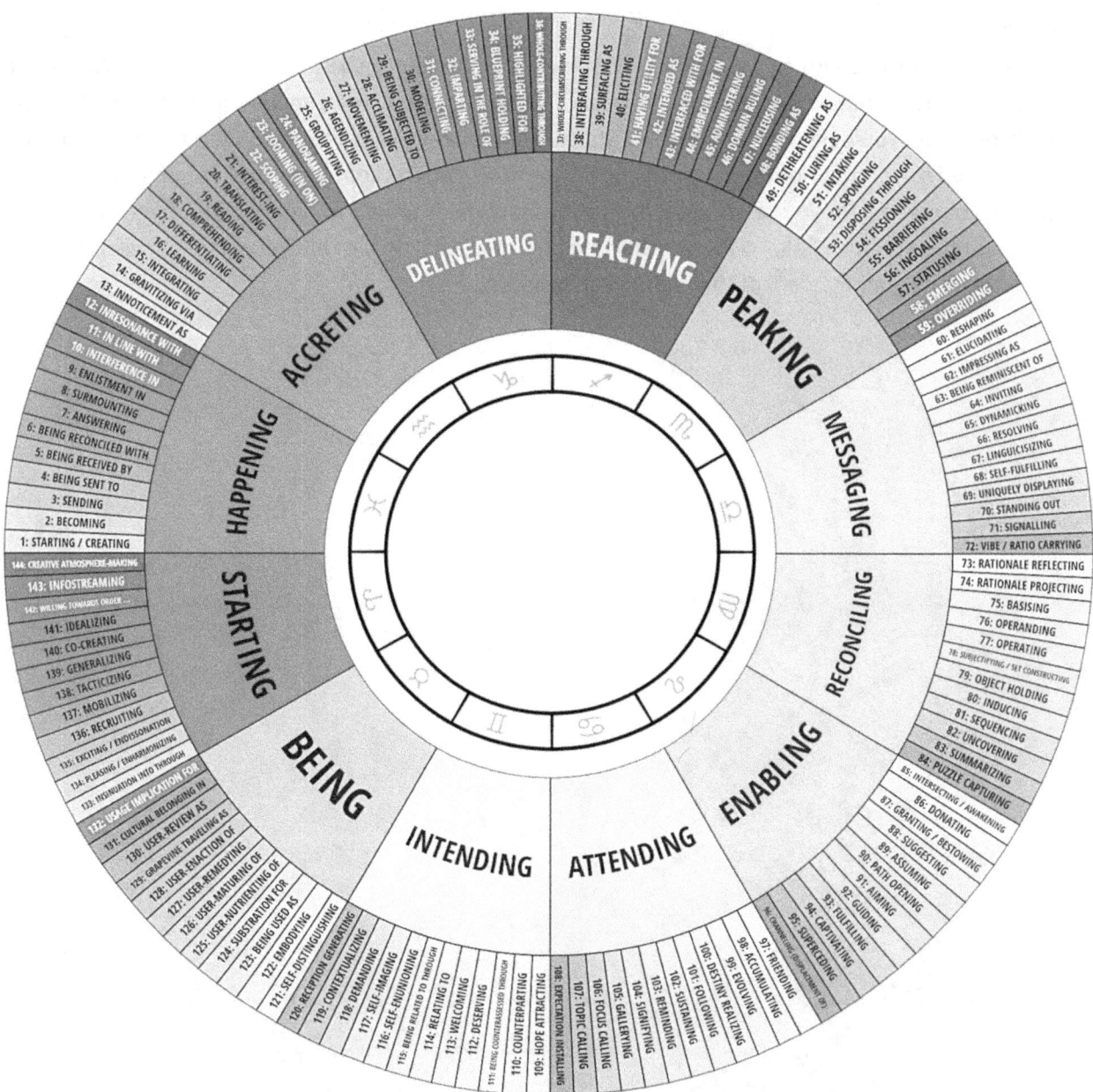

*Figure 56-2: Advanced theme circle. Use these for a more precise look at the Star.*

Given the relative cyclicality of our behaviors, almost every healthy person can be expected to have access to every theme in the astromap. The themes are agnostic when it comes to our cultural details, but well-delineated in their capture of the regions in which they lie. We may not all have official status, but we all have stat*ure*/wrapping. We won't all live by logic, but we'll employ some form of reason—even if that reason is randomness. Accordingly, there is no area of the wheel disallowed to us, if only we knew when to outsource or world-delegate versus expressing it ourselves. Closely related is the idea that anything you can conceive of lives somewhere in your chart. You already have it even if it's limited to some celeb on TV. That you perceive it means it can be yours more closely. But there are paths you are better equipped to follow in bringing it near. Make room for those paths and the things that enable them in order to proceed.

## Conclusion

We all have notions of anything we've assigned meaning to, including the things others have. You could be as rich as Warren Buffett, but would you live as Warren Buffett lives? If you wouldn't live as Warren Buffett lives, could you be as rich as Warren Buffett? Your wheel will provide you with the opportunity, but it will be up to you to prioritize accordingly. Better than living as someone else, you might investigate your wheel for your own versions of the ideals we're taught to worship in others. The characters of the Star may help you with a starting point for each area of life you wish to investigate, further enhancing your mastery of the talents you're given.

# Chapter 57. The Nickname

When I first began writing this book, I imagined the last major chapter, The Nickname, to convey the highest lesson I had learned at the time. This was the idea that we have certain archetypes which repeatedly appear and disappear in our lives, and those archetypes can be given names which reflect our interactions with them as "slot fillers." By giving names to certain recurring personalities, you could better understand (and eventually perfect) your dynamic with them until they no longer split or merged into newer forms. Does this all sound familiar? It should. We actually covered this as early as nine chapters ago, and it's nowhere near the highest lesson we've learned. So much for this chapter's original plan.

Instead, I'd like to conclude the book with a kind of puzzle I'm facing right now. Suppose you've found your tribe. You know what you're here for and more or less what each of them is here for. You know who they are, who's on the fringes, and where everyone is in terms of their readiness to do the shared work of the role group. You know yourself and your nice-to-haves. You can even use some of the six non-standard senses and some astrology to calculate how to make it all go. There's just one problem. The cast is set, but there is no play; it seems your role group's schedules don't line up; collectively, you can't get off the ground. What do you do?

It might go without saying that all of your role members might need to meet each other, or at least get a chance to operate in the same space. It *might* go without saying, but we'll say it anyway: you'll need a unifying space. A cause, a location, a forum,... a shared *something* that all members of the role group belong to. If you don't have this, don't be surprised if your people don't speak the same language, don't seem to know each other, or don't have much of a reason to concentrate their efforts. Let's start there.

*You may be a member of several role groups. For the following questions, pick only one.

☞ Question 57.1 (The unifying front – cast of characters): **So you've mastered nearly every chapter before this. Now you're ready to do what you were put here to do, with a full team beside you. List the people whom you currently consider to be a part of your role group. (As with any team, this roster may change periodically.)**

_____

_____

_____

☞ Question 57.2 (The unifying front – common cause): **What is the common skill, cause, or circumstance which unites the people you listed in 57.1?**

|  | Example |
|---|---|
| 1. Common circumstance: | 1. Common circumstance: <br> Writing (positive, spiritual, creative, learning) |

| | |
|---|---|
| 2. Does a person have to meet in/do the above in order for you to consider them a part of your role group? | 2. Does a person have to meet in/do the above in order for you to consider them a part of your role group?<br>Yes. |
| 3. If you answered yes to the above, why? If you answered no, how did you determine that this was the group? | 3. If you answered yes to the above, why? If you answered no, how did you determine that this was the group?<br>Yes, because even though we know a lot of positive, talented people, there's a certain combination of discipline, diplomacy, and communicative bridge-building that our family of favorite issues requires. |

☞ **Question 57.3 (The unifying front – end goal): Recall this definition: "A person wants what they turn their actions towards the experience of."** Consider what your group of people, as a <u>collective</u> (not as separate individuals), are turning their actions towards. In other words, what is the end goal for your role group as a whole? Asked differently, if you all formed your own state, what issue would that state be most interested in addressing?

| | Example |
|---|---|
| | We want to leave a permanent record for inspiring others beyond their boxes |

☞ **Question 57.4 (Question 57.1 revisited): You may have people on the fringes who support your role work, but are basically on the sidelines.** Maybe they share the skill but won't use it, or use it with a different end in mind. Maybe they kind-of use it but don't follow through. Nothing against them, but if the goal is to mobilize this particular group, it may help (greatly) to know who *not* to wait for. The key people who are available to you right now who share the cause and *do* follow through can be considered your "prime role group." Who are they?

_____

_____

☞ **Question 57.5 (The Nickname): If you had to give your role group a nickname, referencing that name whenever you thought of your collective work, what would it be?**

| | Example |
|---|---|
| | Miranda (after the Uranian moon; a colonizable satellite of the social world; balancer of Shakespeare's *The Tempest*; and a reminder of the rights that all people have) |

While the nicknames you assign to your slot fillers will fade as their associated personalities stop rotating in and out, the nickname you give to your role group will have special power as it compels you to pay attention to your larger work.

☞ Question 57.6 (Advancing the individuals): **The members of your prime role group each probably need something in order to easily do their part in the group. Including yourself, what does everyone need to be at their most effective? If you don't know the answer to this, ASK THEM.**

_____
_____
_____
_____
_____
_____

☞ Question 57.7 (Unblocking the individuals): **You're in a group for a reason. The members of your prime role group probably have complementary skills and weaknesses which need to be traded with each other. What are these complements and how are they traded?**

|  | Example |
|--|--|
|  | 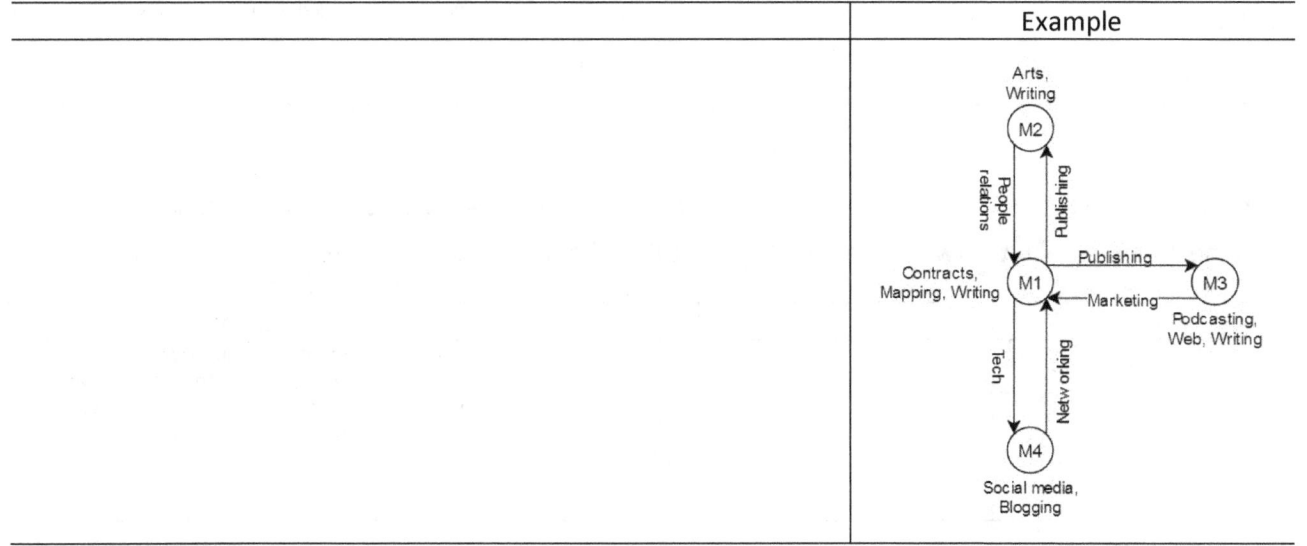 |

Great. Assuming you've connected your role group sufficiently, your collective should be on track. So why are you still dissatisfied? (That's what I asked myself.) If you've followed the major steps throughout this book and done enough connecting with the people you listed above, you should be good to go. But then again…

## Challenge: The *Other* Role Group

The questions above made me realize something: My role group *is* moving exactly as it should. Did you notice this for yours? But remember how we live in at least two spaces, real and potential? If you have one role group dedicated to all things real, is it possible that you have another group which lives in potential?

After all of your main evolution has been structured and you've assembled your principle tribe towards its sought end, it is possible that you still have aims that live outside of that tribe. Astrologically, you yourself may have more than one main family of energies active in your chart. You may have a mode for work only, then friends only. Perhaps these additional modes live outside of your first role group, by necessity—for whatever reason aims which the first role group is *not allowed* to tackle. Like Bruce Wayne and Batman. If you are to build your second role group, you first need to know how to identify its components. Then you'll need to master one last skill which the first role group doesn't require: becoming friends with environments instead of people.

☞ Question 57.8 (Your shadow): Consider that your first role group will be completely successful one day. There, your collective would have done everything necessary to fulfill its mission. Yet you still have dreams of living your life in a certain way. There are preferences you have which you feel your main role group wouldn't really have room for. What are they? Can you summarize these under a single theme?

|  | Example |
|---|---|
|  | Form-response theory: the body as fashion worn by souls |

☞ Question 57.9 (Shadow connection): Since both role groups are yours, you probably see a connection between the two where others wouldn't. What is that connection?

|  | Example |
|---|---|
|  | My interest in this physical life (shadow role) motivates the writings meant to accept everyone—especially under common energy structures (main role); Role 2 is my reason for role 1 |

## Chapter 57: The Nickname

☞ Question 57.10 (The story of the shadow role): **Use the space below to envision your life under your shadow role.**

|  | Example |
|---|---|
|  | I elaborate form-response theory in something called the book of contours, which doubles as a full, uncensored dataset for anywhere from 2-75 data-savable humans. The work generates a kind of building-block system for human social actors. Need to study behavioral sims, more neuro, and have in the role group at least one other person who loves this same work. I'll be in the book—to see how my data would behave under alternate worlds. |

☞ Question 57.11 (Why wait): **If you haven't started building this role group, why not? (If you have you can skip this question.)**

|  | Example |
|---|---|
|  | I need to feel that we've evolved to "phenomenal" level before my (potential) second group begins its exposition. We need full, clear data free of regrets and free of unresolved issues. |

☞ Question 57.12 (Silent participants): **Referring back to Figure 56-2 and the tables before it, which duodecanates do you think are most involved with this alternate role group? Which asteroids?**

|  | Example |
|---|---|
|  | 37, 45, 47, 56, 61, 96, 98, 104, 107, 137; where Velleda, Melusina, Naema, and Diotima live |

☞ Question 57.13 (Initiation): **If you wanted to start building this role group today, what do you think you'd need to do? Why?**

|  | Example |
|---|---|
|  | Move. This isn't the right culture for role 2. It's the perfect culture for encountering obstructions to individuality and writing about how to get past them. |

Assuming your supports for this new role live in the realm of want, potential, information, or some other intangible, you'll need a way to make them real while accepting that they are not real enough. There are several ways of doing this, but taking up a journey towards fulfillment or perfection may do the trick. Your mind may be heavily wired to see yourself as not having what you want, but having a kind of fantasy or wish list of it instead. The secret to reifying these lies in acknowledging what you want as already existing (lightly) in what you have, then continuing to seek more. If you can fool your brain into thinking there's no such thing as "not having," you can start to build new versions of wish and want rooted in refining the current, not chasing the future.

> Factoid: About a month has passed between the paragraph above and the one below. In that time I actually began plans move out of San Antonio, where all of these books have been written, and bought some land in Arizona. Whatever your answer to 57.13, you might actually begin taking steps towards doing it. Money and time, though they are often real barriers, for many of us are only an excuse. Courage is needed.

## Square Roles (Ajani's Observations)

*This section is an extrapolation from some side work I'm doing. It should not be taken as gospel, but has proven immensely useful to me.

We live our lives in patterns of behavior. From homeostasis, away from homeostasis, peaking in the distance our bodies and minds allow, then coming back to homeostasis. This is the standard 4-cycle of real, anti-potential, anti-real, potential, and applies broadly to every repeating thing we do or think (with some additional factors for evolving the cycles in time). Given this, it makes sense to think about the personas we adopt as existing in "grand crosses" (See *FSA* and *HBS*)—that is, families of points 90° apart from each other. For every behavior we adopt on the cycle of potential-space, there are three other behaviors which represent the other alternatives against which the behavior is compared.

<u>Again, you'll need a list of several hundred of your asteroid positions in order to follow along below.</u>

Since *144*, we've divided the 12 signs in to 12 mini signs, for a total of 144 duodecanates. Prior to that, I looked only at the first 36. This turns out to be fortunate, because the first 36 lay out everything you need to explain the other ¾ of your options for behaving. When you behave in ways that emphasize a specific duodecanate, the asteroids there broadly describe your personality. My Midheaven is in 8°15' Sagittarius (duodecanate 45), for example, so my basic public image to people looks like this:

2938 Hopi: lemons into lemonade
289 Nenetta: defensive shield through uninviting spaciness
118 Peitho: indefinably abstract quality to behaviors
812 Adele: preference for dirty/hedonistic surroundings
2063 Bacchus: blessed w/ friends who will never leave you
17102 Begzhigitova: creative tool that takes over everything

But while the above describes me, there has to be a "viewer" to perceive this. Whether a person, situation, or reference interactor, that viewer will be described by the asteroids of 8°15 Gemini. Furthermore, when I don't have the energy to bother with my public reputation or its viewers at all, these two opposed points are converted into pure potential. So 8° Virgo and 8° Pisces, a secondary pair, will take over—one as the behavior and the other as *its* viewer. (This was the same logic that motivated the discussion of antiplanets and square points in *144*.) All in all, we can be said to gravitate towards one of four grand cross points of our chart whenever we pay attention to that particular one of the first 36 harmonics. 8°15 Sagittarius (duo 45), Virgo (duo 81), Gemini (duo 117), and Pisces (duo 9) are all related to duodecanate 9, which—according to Table 56-1—is associated with how we frame standard "shops"—the emotional spaces we create. This raises an interesting question though: What does it mean for a person to behave like a "shop?" Is there a predictability to the kind of human-like personality role played by people in our lives which emphasize this region? I've found that there is.

I went down the list of my asteroids and asked two questions:

1) Does this duodecanate cluster describe any person or *kind of person* that I tend to have in my life?

2) When I arrange these duodecanates into their grand cross (1/36th) families, do I have a main and a secondary preference for which cluster describes me vs the clusters that describe who I'm interacting with?

At the end of the above investigation, I had a list of roles for all 144 duodecanates, along with my primary and secondary preferences for most clusters. Because everyone generally frames people differently (some people consider "bandits" to be a category while others consider "Chileans" to be a category), I doubt that my list of role types will match yours. I have, however, included my chart full of personality roles—a cast of characters in my own life's game if you will—in Appendix VI so you can see what the final list may look like.

## Critical Exercise
GRAND CROSS ROLES

**Trains: Manifestation, Life path**

This exercise may take a while, but I've found it to be one of the strongest in the book for performing calculated magic in general. If you assume that we are nothing but energy patterns, then calling certain events into your life is more a matter of playing certain psychological roles than it is actually passing through the human-trained hoops associated with those roles. The idea here is that we all have a kind of causal filing system telling us when it pays to be hungry, when it's worth it to dominate someone else, what makes a powerful person powerful,... and what the effects of such displays may be. It turns out that you too can do as Mega Man—stealing the powers of anyone you imagine IF only you are willing to put your favorite corner of the appropriate grand cross aside for a while. But first you need to know the four characters involved in each setup in the first place—1) and 2) the first and second choices for your part, and 3) and 4) the standard viewers of each.

☞ **Question 57.14 (Grand Cross Cast):** The asteroids around your chart can be thought of as behavior packets infused with the character of the signs they are in. Those sign regions, however, follow from relationships to each other along a standard repeating cycle. (0° Aries, 29° Pisces represent the start of a cycle while 0° Sagittarius, 29° Scorpio represent the start of a cycle's effects on the larger context; every "sign" region of the wheel tells a kind of story about the complete cycle in the same way that every time of day on the clock corresponds to a certain set of events which is more likely to happen in the day.) In this book we've divided the circle into 144 smaller regions, so that there are 144/4 or 36 different rotations of the same inscribed real-imaginary axis square that we can consider. Using the table below, fill in the closest personality type you've consistently encountered in your life which fits the summarized character of your asteroids in that cluster.

| Grand Cross Group | Duo (#) Private Rising | Duo (#) Private Setting | Duo (#) Public Setting | Duo (#) Public Rising |
|---|---|---|---|---|
| 36 | 0°-2.5° Aries-12 (144 or 0) | 0°-2.5° Cancer-12 (108) | 0°-2.5° Libra-12 (72) | 0°-2.5° Capricorn-12 (36) |
| | | | | |
| 35 | 2.5°-5° Aries-11 (143) | 2.5°-5° Cancer-11 (107) | 2.5°-5° Libra-11 (71) | 2.5°-5° Capricorn-11 (35) |
| | | | | |
| 34 | 5°-7.5° Aries-10 (142) | 5°-7.5° Cancer-10 (106) | 5°-7.5° Libra-10 (70) | 5°-7.5° Capricorn-10 (34) |
| | | | | |
| 33 | 7.5°-10° Aries-9 (141) | 7.5°-10° Cancer-9 (105) | 7.5°-10° Libra-9 (69) | 7.5°-10° Capricorn-9 (33) |
| | | | | |
| 32 | 10°-12.5° Aries-8 (140) | 10°-12.5° Cancer-8 (104) | 10°-12.5° Libra-8 (68) | 10°-12.5° Capricorn-8 (32) |
| | | | | |
| 31 | 12.5°-15° Aries-7 (139) | 12.5°-15° Cancer-7 (103) | 12.5°-15° Libra-7 (67) | 12.5°-15° Capricorn-7 (31) |
| | | | | |
| 30 | 15°-17.5° Aries-6 (138) | 15°-17.5° Cancer-6 (102) | 15°-17.5° Libra-6 (66) | 15°-17.5° Capricorn-6 (30) |
| | | | | |
| 29 | 17.5°-20° Aries-5 (137) | 17.5°-20° Cancer-5 (101) | 17.5°-20° Libra-5 (65) | 17.5°-20° Capricorn-5 (29) |
| | | | | |
| 28 | 20°-22.5° Aries-4 (136) | 20°-22.5° Cancer-4 (100) | 20°-22.5° Libra-4 (64) | 20°-22.5° Capricorn-4 (28) |
| | | | | |
| 27 | 22.5°-25° Aries-3 (135) | 22.5°-25° Cancer-3 (99) | 22.5°-25° Libra-3 (63) | 22.5°-25° Capricorn-3 (27) |
| | | | | |

| | | | | |
|---|---|---|---|---|
| 26 | 25°-27.5° Aries-2 (134) | 25°-27.5° Cancer-2 (98) | 25°-27.5° Libra-2 (62) | 25°-27.5° Capricorn-2 (26) |
| 25 | 27.5°-29.9° Aries-1 (133) | 27.5°-29.9° Cancer-1 (97) | 27.5°-29.9° Libra-1 (61) | 27.5°-29.9° Capricorn-1 (25) |
| 24 | 0°-2.5° Taurus-12 (132) | 0°-2.5° Leo-12 (96) | 0°-2.5° Scorpio-12 (60) | 0°-2.5° Aquarius-12 (24) |
| 23 | 2.5°-5° Taurus-11 (131) | 2.5°-5° Leo-11 (95) | 2.5°-5° Scorpio-11 (59) | 2.5°-5° Aquarius-11 (23) |
| 22 | 5°-7.5° Taurus-10 (130) | 5°-7.5° Leo-10 (94) | 5°-7.5° Scorpio-10 (58) | 5°-7.5° Aquarius-10 (22) |
| 21 | 7.5°-10° Taurus-9 (129) | 7.5°-10° Leo-9 (93) | 7.5°-10° Scorpio-9 (57) | 7.5°-10° Aquarius-9 (21) |
| 20 | 10°-12.5° Taurus-8 (128) | 10°-12.5° Leo-8 (92) | 10°-12.5° Scorpio-8 (56) | 10°-12.5° Aquarius-8 (20) |
| 19 | 12.5°-15° Taurus-7 (127) | 12.5°-15° Leo-7 (91) | 12.5°-15° Scorpio-7 (55) | 12.5°-15° Aquarius-7 (19) |
| 18 | 15°-17.5° Taurus-6 (126) | 15°-17.5° Leo-6 (90) | 15°-17.5° Scorpio-6 (54) | 15°-17.5° Aquarius-6 (18) |
| 17 | 17.5°-20° Taurus-5 (125) | 17.5°-20° Leo-5 (89) | 17.5°-20° Scorpio-5 (53) | 17.5°-20° Aquarius-5 (17) |
| 16 | 20°-22.5° Taurus-4 (124) | 20°-22.5° Leo-4 (88) | 20°-22.5° Scorpio-4 (52) | 20°-22.5° Aquarius-4 (16) |
| 15 | 22.5°-25° Taurus-3 (123) | 22.5°-25° Leo-3 (87) | 22.5°-25° Scorpio-3 (51) | 22.5°-25° Aquarius-3 (15) |
| 14 | 25°-27.5° Taurus-2 (122) | 25°-27.5° Leo-2 (86) | 25°-27.5° Scorpio-2 (50) | 25°-27.5° Aquarius-2 (14) |
| 13 | 27.5°-29.9° Taurus-1 (121) | 27.5°-29.9° Leo-1 (85) | 27.5°-29.9° Scorpio-1 (49) | 27.5°-29.9° Aquarius-1 (13) |

| | | | | |
|---|---|---|---|---|
| 12 | 0°-2.5° Gemini-12 (120) | 0°-2.5° Virgo-12 (84) | 0°-2.5° Sagittarius-12 (48) | 0°-2.5° Pisces-12 (12) |
| 11 | 2.5°-5° Gemini-11 (119) | 2.5°-5° Virgo-11 (83) | 2.5°-5° Sagittarius-11 (47) | 2.5°-5° Pisces-11 (11) |
| 10 | 5°-7.5° Gemini-10 (118) | 5°-7.5° Virgo-10 (82) | 5°-7.5° Sagittarius-10 (46) | 5°-7.5° Pisces-10 (10) |
| 9 | 7.5°-10° Gemini-9 (117) | 7.5°-10° Virgo-9 (81) | 7.5°-10° Sagittarius-9 (45) | 7.5°-10° Pisces-9 (9) |
| 8 | 10°-12.5° Gemini-8 (116) | 10°-12.5° Virgo-8 (80) | 10°-12.5° Sagittarius-8 (44) | 10°-12.5° Pisces-8 (8) |
| 7 | 12.5°-15° Gemini-7 (115) | 12.5°-15° Virgo-7 (79) | 12.5°-15° Sagittarius-7 (43) | 12.5°-15° Pisces-7 (7) |
| 6 | 15°-17.5° Gemini-6 (114) | 15°-17.5° Virgo-6 (78) | 15°-17.5° Sagittarius-6 (42) | 15°-17.5° Pisces-6 (6) |
| 5 | 17.5°-20° Gemini-5 (113) | 17.5°-20° Virgo-5 (77) | 17.5°-20° Sagittarius-5 (41) | 17.5°-20° Pisces-5 (5) |
| 4 | 20°-22.5° Gemini-4 (112) | 20°-22.5° Virgo-4 (76) | 20°-22.5° Sagittarius-4 (40) | 20°-22.5° Pisces-4 (4) |
| 3 | 22.5°-25° Gemini-3 (111) | 22.5°-25° Virgo-3 (75) | 22.5°-25° Sagittarius-3 (39) | 22.5°-25° Pisces-3 (3) |
| 2 | 25°-27.5° Gemini-2 (110) | 25°-27.5° Virgo-2 (74) | 25°-27.5° Sagittarius-2 (38) | 25°-27.5° Pisces-2 (2) |
| 1 | 27.5°-29.9° Gemini-1 (109) | 27.5°-29.9° Virgo-1 (73) | 27.5°-29.9° Sagittarius-1 (37) | 27.5°-29.9° Pisces-1 (1) |

☞ Question 57.15 (Your favorite roles): **Now that you've filled in the different roles in 57.14's table, go back and mark which of the four roles in each row you prefer above the others in the same row. You'll need to pick one in *every* row (all 36), because there will be cases in life where that particular duodecanate cross group is just something you'll be pushed to pay attention to. When you do, which mode do you tend to choose? Once you have picked a primary, you'll need to go back again and pick a *secondary* behavior when the first one you picked in a row is not available to you. THE RULE:** your secondary **has to be** next to your primary. It cannot be opposite. For example, if your row 1 primary was Gemini-1, your secondary has to be either Virgo-1 or Pisces-1; it cannot be Sagittarius 1. Usually. Try not to do it, at least.

If you've done most of the activities in this book, this one can serve as the best "final exam" in your journey towards directed intuition. Knowing the roles of the key characters in your life gives you more conscious control over how and when they appear. If you're not sure of how to do 57.14 and 57.15, definitely take a look at Appendix VI for an example of what these questions are asking for as well as some extra things you can look at to explain yourself to yourself.

## A Master Plan

Although I can't give you a silver bullet for finding everlasting happiness in your wheel, I can tell you a couple of things I've learned about the astrocycle and its nicknamed sections:

- Sometimes your worst asteroids turn out to be your highest talents. My Lysistrata-Berolina blocks a lot of connections because of where it is placed, but in so doing is also the indicator of my spiritual role models like the Buddha, St. Catherine, and Ashoka. You see things like this when you do activity 57.14.

- There are MANY asteroids which are meant to protect you from subpar interactions. Zelia, Sauer, Saturn, Endymion, Agathe, Bilkis, Agamemnon and Amphitrite are just a few. Additionally, bodies like Ricarda, Natalie, Pax, Wolfiana, Hypatia and Pluto may bring you stress and pressure, but also call for you to be very sharp in the kinds of pressures you take on. Mastering these often amounts to your conscious decision to control an event within very specific bounds. The sharper you are, the more these work in your favor.

- On the other hand, some bodies like Neptune and Naema, some regions like Capricon-12 and Pisces-3 and 4, are notoriously amorphous. Try not to let the amorphousness bring chaos to others, but take these as places where your imagination can influence everyone around you.

- If you want something, take on its role in your chart. If the role does not fit you, make plans to become friends with the kind of person whom it does fit. So you don't like capitalists but want to be rich? Don't like "care free" poor people but want to be care free yourself? Get ready to get over it. No one's asking you to stop calling a fool a fool or a jerk a jerk, but even if they're both a fool and a jerk, get ready to keep *someone* like them in your sphere if you want what they have to be yours too.

- Happiness comes in all forms, but much of your happiness will depend on your ability to bring the same to those you expect to keep you happy. The second half of this book—assuming you made it through the first half—has a number of exercises designed to help you see what other people (or events) want outside of your own bias. Half the battle in achieving happiness in the magic sense, lies with dropping the popular templates for what happiness should be. You may need to give up a dream, only to provide a seemingly small thing to someone who can grant that dream tenfold for the both of you. The practices in this book won't make you into a god. For basic geometric reasons, when it comes to the great potential in your chart, the most you'll be able to cover is *half*...

- ...the other half will depend on the settings you create for your interactants.

## Moving On

After I wrote The Rift, I did end up rifting with all three people mentioned. It gave me the space I needed from old versions of myself, and within 9 months, all three exchanges were stabilized. They weren't as dead as I'd first rendered them, but were rewritten on newer, wiser terms. Following the repair of the last one, I actually entered into a brand new conflict which began, ended, then proceeded as though the whole first half of the exchange had never happened—like the other and I had simply been actors in a movie. It was an intriguing experience, but one that taught me an important final lesson. Life truly can be a game if you surround yourself with—consuming a spiritual diet of—fun people. You don't always need to fight, but if you like fighting you might as well make it enjoyable. You don't always need to strive for something shinier than what you have, but if striving suits you, you might take it as a testament to the miles you've already covered. It helps greatly to understand the roles played by the various hurdles you encounter; once you've organized those roles it becomes much easier to trade them out as casting demands. Given that you'll never be able to see the back of your own eyeball, you'll just need to choose one of the roles and accept some other party as your counterpart. Society often trains us to hate and whine about the counterparts we inherit, but all that does is trap us in smaller and smaller corners of our own psychological framing. If you want to see more and be more, you'll eventually need to forgive your co-stars for completing your movie—even if the current script calls for some short-lived combat.

This is as true of life in general as it is with people.

# Chapter 58. Some Background on This Book

My first experience with clairaudience occurred in March of 2001 in my apartment when, during semi-sleep, my mouth suddenly wanted to move. It said, "Who am I?" It then proceeded to go through a list of past lives and the alleged spirit names of people I knew, outlining my generic purpose in the world. Up to then, I had done nothing but listen to chakra music, having never been very good at actual meditation. From then on, my roommate Kevin and I studied angels, demons, and all kinds of things, I discovered sacred-texts.com, gravitated towards astrology and generally learned to auto-talk more. Later that year in October, while I was stupid drunk off of Amaretto, I received a channeled message from someone I knew who had come to say goodbye. My dad died unexpectedly of a stroke about 2 months later, at 48. It's noteworthy that, because I had been warned, and because I was out of state when I got the news, I found it a lot easier to make the trip back home and be an anchor for the rest of the family.

In the ensuing years, I used my love of order to take note of super predictable coincidences which were so predictable as to follow several levels of hourly, daily, through yearly schedules. I've had premonitory dreams since then on a very steady schedule, learned more or less when I'll die and how that corresponds to the timing of some (but not all) of my cycles, and have generally come to view this whole life thing as nothing but a program. It's as predictable as any software creation you can name or any chemical reaction you can orchestrate. But you have to think of everything as energy-code in order to appreciate it. It is as if the elements of the periodic table were the musicians in a multitrillion-member concert… There may be a lot of them, but they still obey ever-repeating, natural law.

Until about two years ago, I was fascinated by astrology and all of its psychological packages. Once finished with *Laurentia*, however, I had said everything I'd wanted to say about the subject. Also, I had grown tired of reading charts for people and their same old drama. My interest in the subject returned only after I got a new job as a data analyst and was able to ask more complicated questions for putting the chart to use. Here I found that astrology was no longer interesting for its own sake, but was VITAL for framing the space of the interpersonal human in a time where the best we could do was predict sights and sounds.

Even as I worked with algorithms and bots, they hardly compared to thrice-weekly dreams telling me about the year ahead. I wanted to study humanity as an existential wrapper around patterned energy, where all the computers in the world couldn't answer what social norms wouldn't allow us to investigate. For the full space of emotional expression and expectation, there needed to be a book which attempted to order the occult senses and their training. I couldn't find one that captured the kind of repetitious ordering of my own experiences. At the same time, I kept running into these highly intuitive people who punished others for things that hadn't happened yet. As of late 2019, after waking from a dream about unnecessary psychic pre-punishment (see the section "Unassisted Clairvoyance"), it felt as though people really needed some standards for training and using their intuition wisely[46], thus I

---

[46] Fun fact: This is the official reason *Alma* was written.

received the map in Figure 54-1 in connection with a dream called "State Line Mandeville" and *Alma Mater* was born.

Today I can, for the most part, call anything I want into my life within a couple of months, provided it aligns with some basic overarching priorities. As you'll find out in your 57.14, some of the classics like money, romance, status, and certain kinds of security aren't actually worth calling until you've straightened out the values opposite them… or negative opinions conjunct them, so applying calculated magic wouldn't be worth using in these cases. Instead, much of your calculated magic will ultimately need application in your relationships to others and the broader world, since you're probably fine with most of who you are already. As such, calling things into your life via calculation is much more about practicing attunement to your favorite energies, getting nicer-behaving versions of the difficult ones to stay in your sphere, then saddling up with the rest of your role group to do some cool stuff. Most of us can call many things into our lives alone, but we can't call *most* things without the aid of at least a couple of others.

Once you've found those others, it pays to consider their needs just as you would consider your own. Selfishness is a call unanswered.

Between the above paragraph and this one, I used "role-selection" of Capricorn-5 in the previous chapter (see Appendix VI) to manifest a new job with considerably higher pay and broader horizons for the next phase of our group's work. I used Sagittarius-1 to advance some other areas, and my Role group set off on a professional and creative winning streak which, ~~two~~ six months later, is still going strong. The first and last chapters of this book may not be the most exciting, but they are, for the most part, the most practical. The following section explains how you "hack" like this in detail.

Be warned, my tone below is slightly different from other parts of the book, as you'll basically be getting a glimpse of the very Capricorn-5 attitude switch I used to accomplish the hack.

## Using This Book for Calculated Life Path Hacking

I took two half-year breaks during the writing of this book. One involved a series of failed endeavors and a handful of rifts with some people close to me (the latter replaced with much stronger exchanges). The other involved the application of a hack using my Capricorn-5 and Sagittarius-1. Here's exactly what I did, and what resulted. This isn't just autobiography. If you do **these things**, you too will be poised to accomplish similar kinds of miraculous turns in your own life.

- I had been doing several of the exercises here in *Alma* while writing the book—as I mentioned, as a way of knowing better which steps a reader really needed to follow. Among these was the **Critical Exercise 2 of 2 in Chapter 46: Flow of the Body Type: Recap 2**. That exercise is very complicated, and in order to do it **you need a solid understanding of how the signs differ**. Some

- people may not like that the exercise is so complicated, but if you're going to intentionally play out signs, you really need to know what the roles are and know them well. That well.
- While writing under Dimension 12 as usual (from *Sex in 12 Dimensions*), I unexpectedly wrote **Chapter 47 - The Resonance and paid A LOT of attention to what came out of it**. Actually, I kept it in my head for so long that it would eventually be elaborated upon as **Chapter 54 - The Foresight. The activities in that chapter also contributed specifically to the hack.**
- **I put GENUINE effort into Critical Exercise 48.6 and GAVE HONEST ANSWERS to Question 49.13**. My score on 49.13 was good enough to continue, but I knew I still had some work to do…
- …I claimed to have these big dreams, but was letting several things slide in my sphere—almost all of them stemming from my own laziness, pride, or whatever. **Your sphere is your choice—at least that's how I saw it. I decided to settle some longstanding blocks to my growth—starting by cutting the amount of say held by people whose ways would always keep me stuck.** Accordingly, Chapter 50 – The Rift was written. Why did I keep such a chapter in this book? Because if you're serious about cleaning up your influences and you, like most people, have some strongly entrenched blocking relationships to address, you'll need to handle those relationships with no flowery bullshit getting in your way. Not all of the decisions you'll need to make will be pretty. If those relationships stand to eat away at months—or even years—of anything you could have become, however, I urge you to consider making some changes…
    - o   To help you clean up your circles, **Read Chapter 51: 100%+ Relationships and apply it to yourself.** The idea had arisen in my life a couple of chapters earlier.
- I stopped working on *Alma Mater* for 6 months while addressing the above. Magic is hard to pull off if you know you're watering down your own formula. **You will almost certainly need to stop the book at least once while going through it.** I hope this is obvious, but there is no value in getting to the last page just to say you got there. It's more important to practice the intuition, to do the cleanup, and strengthen your sphere than it is to simply "clock-in." **Don't speed past the topics your guardians (or your own intuition) want you to stay with**… just because some trained urge towards the quick finish is ramming you through. What a way to waste your talent.
- I resumed the book while doing some new asteroid mining on bodies 1001-2000. With my original 1000 asteroids, I produced the table in Appendix VI (Question 57.14). This table, along with **anything you can learn about handling squares** (90°; which I talk about throughout this book) is essential—ESSENTIAL for showing you what the menu options are for any roles you wish to trigger. Consider it your command center for selecting all your hacks. **You MUST do activities 57.14 and 57.15.** Once you've done them and gotten through the steps above, you'll be ready to hack in earnest.

    READ THIS NEXT PART CAREFULLY.

- Right around the time of elections, I began telling friends that I was "putting on my Donald Trump hat" to be the self-assured, unmovable character which—on normal days basically corresponded to my definition of a bully. I've talked about how I feel about bullies, but if you've read my books you know that I believe that reckless judgment others is a no-no. The former

President, a contentious figure? It doesn't matter. If you see it, frame it, or package it as a construct in any way, that could be you. It often doesn't occur to us that, because we live our lives in our own comfortable frameworks, the perspectives we oppose are the same ones we need to take on in order to have what those others have. In my astrological setup, my Capricorn-5 slot is where the bully energy lives, but also where the worldly power lives. Sagittarius-1 is where the getting-over-at-another's-expense energy lives, but also where the perks come from the sky. How do you suddenly adopt the behaviors of an energy you typically misalign with? Answer: You see your own lens for its role in setting up the problem to look as it does—your own refusal to stand in the misaligned party's shoes—put on your big person's pants, and grow past your own lens. If you can do questions 45.9.4 – 45.9.6 without any tricks, at all, then you can apply it to the duodecanate you wish to adopt. This is what I did.

My friends will tell you that I adopted a looking-down-on-the-little-people perspective as well as an I'm-not-doing-any-more-work (effectively stealing) perspective in my business and job respectively. HOWEVER, I took on the reasoning that I would have had if I had been raised to think that way while *still doing what I could to help everyone* everywhere. Same underlying principles—different standpoint for what constituted realism. From thief to Robin Hood, from bully to decision-maker for people who couldn't—I truly tried to stand in the viewpoint of people outside my own framework. Refer back to Appendix VI: When it came time to use my preferred Aries-5 from that particular cluster (29), I just didn't. **Once you have your 57.15 completed, use the kind of reasoning from 45.9.4 – 45.9.6 to switch any of your 36 duodecanates to whatever you want. But you have to <u>really believe it</u> in order to do it without messing up your current life setup. Open-mindedness is the key.**

- **I kept the above going for about 2 months.** You need to give your spheremates / job / homelife / etc. time to re-split and remerge around your new style.

- Lastly, I did the most important thing to set the life changes in motion. One of my three big dreams is to build a city, so—even having failed to get the raises or jobs—I did what is shown in the Factoid box under **57.13**. That is, **with your switched attitude firmly in place, you take a tangible, irreversible step in the direction of your dream for that particular duodecanate**.

And here are the results:

- I found land in mid-September 2019, bought it before the end of the month.

- Between finding the land and closing, I got a call from a recruiter who saw an old resume of mine floating out there. By October I had a lot of land…

- …and later got the job, its 70% raise, and the next phase of learning I was seeking (a full machine learning position and NOT the same job I've referenced throughout the book. This one is better.)[47]

---

[47] Some people might ask (as I would), "Don't you want to be a writer who doesn't have to work a day job?" No. I have two other big dreams, and my day jobs teach me the very complex things I need to accomplish them. Don't frown on your optimum Role.

- I made an AWESOME first-time trip to visit (and had all kinds of new experiences with) my brother Keith Hayden and his wife as we finalized the publication steps for his first novel *Cereus & Limnic*. We know it's a top quality work—better than anything I've ever written.

- My business partner and I received a *major* boost to our other business, bringing several more good events.

- A long-time friend of mine and I have reestablished contact on yet another endeavor, and it's picking up a new kind of momentum.

- I discovered the biggest next-level read in my spiritual growth since the *Dao De Jing* and a biography I read about Srinivasa Ramanujan: It was Jacob Boehem's *Signatura Rerum*. For my own path, the text is the most advanced course in spirituality I've taken yet.

All of the above happened within a 4-month span after years of much sparser support for all of the above. I'll tell you it was definitely my Capricorn-5 decision that flipped on the switch, and the decision to actually *do* what came out of 57.13 which gave it the final push.

And now about you…

We're taught that no one likes a braggart. But goddammit, how do you ever develop your own power by listening to a world full of others' collective put-down? **Do exercise 53.5 again. Read through The Foresight again. Do 49.13 again** and get those downers out of your way. Get out of your own way. Find people who really believe in your crazy ideas—who'll put up with your earnest attempts to grow past yourself even as you wear that weirdly-fitting new hat. Find people who will accept your best, and who will encourage you to share that best with all the world.

*   *   *

I don't have a better way of showing you how the acts in this book can work for you besides giving you the recap of how they worked for me—even after 20 years of "knowing this stuff already." It didn't really start moving until I came closer to finishing this book for you. It contains everything I know and every event I've passed through—including the ugly ones—so that you'll have a tool in every world for any spiritual task ahead of you. I've read over *Alma* so many times before releasing it, knowing full well that it has plenty of moments that might make you squirm. Yet there is one final secret to high-powered spirituality that I've yet to mention which will make all the difference in your studies. I'll say it only once:

> If you intend to take full control of your sphere in accordance with your truest design, YOU CAN'T HAVE SKELETONS.

…maybe hidden from others, but not from yourself. You can't be afraid of demons, darkness, truths you failed to acknowledge, people you've failed to re-position, arrangements you've yet to do your part in, evils you curse yet secretly anchor yourself to, vices you rest your comfy little head on, greatness you're afraid to claim, debts you won't admit never intending to pay, perks you'd rather steal than earn, or unknowns you cover up in social buzz. We all have parts of ourselves that could be used to shame us or hold us back—not least of which is the openness to other spaces to begin with, things we're taught to fervently, wholeheartedly distrust by people who have no courage to even ask. But I don't know what to tell you about that… You probably know of your own box if you're in one. *Alma* has chapters for getting you out of any part of that box if you choose to do so. I sincerely hope the content didn't make you too uncomfortable. For some, it may be the only place you ever see these kinds of things purposefully addressed by another for the sake of *your* own path.

I hope this book will help you find the courage and the means to unlock your highest role.

## Final Thoughts

For the last few years I've joked to my friends, "It's a good thing nobody believes in astrology. We can keep these spells to ourselves and nobody will know how we did it." As I continue reading through *Signatura Rerum*, it's clear how certain knowledge becomes secret or heretical: People just don't take the time to look past the simplest summary. I imagine that in 20 or so years, however, astrology will be a respected science again. It will be called *astronomy*, while "astrology" will forever be a bad word like "ether" or "phrenology." In that future, we'll use machine learning to accurately align packets of psychology with the paths of things and people who embody their dynamics—conveniently replacing asteroids with something called "modalities" or whatever. By then, the systems out there will be better and finding most people's ideal life paths than the people themselves are—the heavens' ultimate "gotcha" as our guardians tell us what to do through some company's python code. That's okay I suppose. Our noisy world probably needs it. But for now you have it in your hands to decide that path on your own before the doodly cutesiness because your primary means of exposure to it. Although I truly respect the innovators out there advancing the knowledge of everything, we can't *really* know what we eternally block. The doodle won't show you your own stuff. It's your job to address that.

As always, I wish you well in your travels. My tone might seem a little different this time—the level of disclosure greater (so you too will be that honest with yourself)—but I'm as optimistic as ever. This book wasn't really the place to play nice with the material… since we were effectively uncovering pages and pages of issues you probably learned to hide and hide well. Now that I think about it, we've gone through it in the same way we would have gone through a doctoral residency in spirituality. The training wheels stopped some time ago, and our assumption has been that you the reader are ready for game time. Of course you are. When you go back to the chapter on The Foresight and practice your specific sense—when you catch yourself applying it and seeing its uncanny function in your life, you'll know what it is to see past the skeletons—yours and those imposed on you. Across multiple layers of experience you'll start to master your own control panel for directing events as you would really have them. As always, the more you benefit others, the more you'll be allowed to play with that control panel without interruption.

As always, for astrologers:

The print version of this book was born June 4, 2019, 8:58 PM (CDT), in San Antonio, TX. This is the date of first file creation, and my default birth marker.

## Chapter 58: Some Background on This Book

The e-version—different in a few key ways—was born April 28, 2021, 9:00 AM, (CDT), in San Antonio, TX. This is when the final publish button was clicked, because *Alma*-e required too many specialized data edits to be considered complete any earlier.

# Appendix I: True Signs

A major realization occurred to me which resulted in almost a year delay in releasing this book. After finally building some strong statistical tests into *Laurentia's* asteroid mining process as well as completing the pseudo-ARIMA in building The Star, the truth became increasingly obvious: Tropical astrology will eventually have to come to an end—at least in its status as Western astrology's gold standard. As the field inches steadily back to its proper home in astronomy—indeed, as you begin to encounter more and more discrepancies in explanations of topics like the Sabian Symbols, the Star's actual asteroid mining, and the design of the body itself—I think you'll be more likely to see that tropical astrology's moving backdrop of signs has strong implications for longer-term phenomena. Those implications aren't very promising.

To summarize briefly, tropical astrology measures signs against the Earth's seasons as our solar system progresses around the center of the Milky Way. Sidereal astrology and its partner Right Ascension don't do this. The stars stay where they belong. At the time of this writing, for example, the fixed star Antares—the heart of the *constellation* Scorpio—is actually around 8°-9° in the *tropical* sign Sagittarius. Most of the tropical sign Aries is actually taken up by the real constellation Pisces. In a couple of hundred years the real constellation Aquarius' (somewhat contrived) 30° window will start to officially encroach on tropical Aries—bringing us into the fabled "Age of Aquarius." All of this happens because our whole solar system and its orientation has a spin of its own against the greater universe. What I've said before is that it doesn't matter though "because it's all the modern Aries anyway." Remember that?

But maybe you also remember a few other things:

- The Sabian Symbols seemed to be "off" by about 3°. Why?
- The regions of the body sometimes fail to logically correspond to the sign allegedly associated with them. Hmm...
- The psychic talents, though broadly mappable to the astrowheel, seem to rely on some counterintuitive mechanics—telepathy, for example, is related to Scorpio influence but also seems to rely heavily on a Libra-like communicative channel between you and the receiver. You may or may not have noticed this in your practice, but give it time. Telepathy has a lot less to do with forcing your will and a lot more to do with another's willingness to hear you.

The above points weren't so surprising. We maintained in an earlier book that tropical astrology was for measuring events against the current times, while sidereal astrology measures them against the universal dynamic. In this book, however, we've introduced two MAJOR concepts that now call into question the appropriateness of the tropical currentness. One is the use of the (*evolved* body) to exercise the psychic senses. The other are the actual patterns among the asteroids themselves against the solar system at large.

Here's why they matter.

Recall that, in tropical astrology, the signs creep backward 1° about every 70 years because that's the rate which corresponds to the earth's own seasonal meander. That means that an early 20th century doctor studying, say, 50-100 year old astrological records might correctly associate body regions with symbolic degrees given his research, but about 100-200 years after his research material might be shown to have produced symbols about 2°-3° off. Such would be the case for the Sabian Symbols (discussed further in *FSA*). That's not necessarily a problem until you attempt to train a sense which requires specific biology. Cognition requires the brain. Biomanufacture roughly requires the parathyroid and other related organs. Given that everything we've talked about in this book was rooted in some sort of actual science, it's no longer acceptable to think that today tropical Aries (sidereal Pisces) rules the head but 2000 years from now tropical Pisces (sidereal Aquarius) will. It won't make sense that the cognitive skill is Geminan in nature but 2000 years from now it will be Taurean. Since the publication of *Laurentia* I've gathered A LOT more data on orbital elements, wiki bios, 1000 more asteroids, and other information you may see in the future; the patterns are clear. But if they're clear, they must align with actual evolution. Our legs have the same function they've always had. The tropical precession would have us believe that our legs will have served *every* function over the course of a couple of thousand years. But that doesn't make sense. The evolved body associations shouldn't creep like this. The locomotion and manipulation of our arms and legs—typically Saj-Gemini in the tropical sense—need to stay stable in how we understand their energy-moving role.

That bothered me.

But nothing bothered me more than this single particular duodecanate: hunger. The mining on actual asteroids put it in Leo-8. But why? Many readers will be familiar enough with astrology; cooking and nurturance is the purview of Cancer—Leo's *sidereal* sign (as of 2021).

And then there is one more somewhat technical point. Recall that back in *All 144 Aspects* we made the case that Sedna, orbit-wise, should be associated with Cancer (Table 29-1). Assume that our solar system is a giant ball whose "cycle" of influence starts at the center and ends at the Oort Cloud. Given the arguments in *Laurentia* and *144*, we might divide the imaginary radius of the solar system into 12 base-2 logarithmic regions, with the Sun and Sedna roughly representing two Earth-relevant critical nodes on our giant string. Following this logic along with the math we used in our scaling formula, Mercury would be associated with Leo-Virgo, Venus with Virgo-Libra, Mars with Libra-Scorpio and so on. Neptune would go with Pisces, Eris with Aries-Taurus, Sedna with Cancer-Leo, all the way back to Sun/Sedna around Summer/Cancer-Leo. Buried elsewhere in *Laurentia* we might find the idea that, because the Moon is too small to be orbit-significant in the solar system's major band—yet it is the next strongest object influencing the Earth after the major band setup, to the extent that we are geo-centric measuring the Earth against the Sun, the Moon can act as a lower octave of whatever the "note" below Sun (anti-Earth)/Sedna is. Thus the Moon can be considered a "micro" ruler of Cancer. Truly, before exploring beyond the Kuiper belt, the Moon as Cancer-associate was all we knew. On the scale of the solar system, though, we now have other options.

To accommodate the scale of our own energies on this planet, we may always do better to use things like latitude-longitude, overt characteristics, and genetics as proxies for the energy of Aries-Gemini. Not knowing how to chart these though, I used the fictitious Points of Action, Worth, and Internal Monologue as a kind of "choose your own ruler" option. You can and should still do this in order to cut the obligated marriage to double rulers and other arrangements (like Pluto governing Scorpio) which don't make any spatial or statistical sense. Whatever the case, though, we gradually come to see that maybe the Sun should be associated with the hottest sign region. Sedna should represent that same energy one octave lower. Everything else should scale accordingly, including our evolved bodies as this same scale of possible 2-logarithmic frequencies shifted one or more octaves higher.

The snowflake model proposed in *Laurentia* can be thought of as a "folding out" of the 3D 12-sphere onto a flat plane in accordance with the compression shown in Figure 36-18 as well as the surface area-to-disk $2^n$ transformation in general.

If you picture the arguments in the 3 paragraphs above you might be able to see the very basic geometry of it all. I won't go into more detail than this, but present all of it as a way of getting us to think about the following: We evolved via the same chemistry as everything else and should—if we know how to accurately map our correspondence—be able to be able to see where even our basic body plan is a replay of basic phases in any dynamic system. There are real and anti-real, potential and anti-potential, and the 8 halfway points along each of these. In the space of the body—almost *any* body—there is what it does and what it does it against, what it could be doing and what it could be doing it against. Call these activity-versus-interaction and structural capability-versus-the lineage which cultivated that structure. If these sound like Aries-Libra and Capricorn-Cancer, that shouldn't be surprising. We always claimed that the signs were just analogies for *any* generic cycle, remember?

Halfway between the unregistered state and full activity is the inclination phase versus the state to be reconciled (Pisces-Virgo), the aftermath perception versus the thing perceived as replacing your activity (Taurus-Scorpio). Lastly, halfway between unregistered structure and full structure is metabolic elaboration versus byproduct offload (Aquarius-Leo) and structural erosion/absorption into the environment versus the environment or activity doing the absorbing (Sagittarius-Gemini). The signs don't actually matter anymore, we're only keeping them in order to maintain reference to the analogy.

Imagine now that a certain collection of chemistries gathers into a self-preserving package, evolving various components to perform the above 12 health-cyclical functions:

| Activity; hierarchical role; environment attraction | Evolution towards structural capability | Being acted against; processing the interactant | Structural capability; genetic, chemical, or structural composition |
|---|---|---|---|
| After-act perception; self-monitoring and reinforcement | Released/displayed byproducts of metabolism | Things that replace one's acts in order to have themselves be perceived; domain and niche awareness; instinct | Metabolic elaboration |
| Energy-consumptive experience | States to be reconciled; seeking behavior | Having one's structure consumed or responded to; habitat and adaptive body features | inclination to act; environmental awareness |

*Table I-1: Cycle phases for a self-preserving actor*

Can you see the correspondences with both the signs and the body plan? These are one way of dividing the basic energetic cycles of living (and by analogy, non-living) things. We won't go into much detail regarding specific structural components here, just know that there is an evolutionarily aligned connection between the frames we carry around, the behaviors required for a thing to self-preserve, and a more general allegory for energy cycling. The functions of our body components won't change very quickly, so it pays to assign their phases correctly.

## The General 12-Cycle, Senses, and the True Signs

If we imagine developing strong abilities in any of the cyclical activities listed, we may also imagine the associated sense or physical faculty we need in order to practice such abilities. But before we go guessing what such faculties might look like, let's get some help from a source we can actually rely on: the asteroid patterns themselves as they played out in people's lives.

It turns out that doing sidereal astrology isn't difficult in the technical sense. All you do is tell your chart program to produce a sidereal chart instead of a tropical one. At the time of this writing, all the signs will move backwards about 20°-25° and that's it. You're done. The hardest part about making the switch lies in changing your constructs against everything that you and almost everyone else in the West has probably been doing all this time. I've been the proud owner of a Scorpio 9°52' Sun forever. All of a sudden under the sidereal chart I have a Libra 17° Sun. It honestly feels weird. Yet, as I've spent the time trying to perfect my hacks, I know full well that the 9-duodecanate shift lines up better with my asteroid patterns and intuitive practice. Let's revisit Tables 56-1 – 56.12, sidereal-style, so you can see what I mean.

Table I-2: Sidereal Duodecanates

| s# | Sidereal Sign Degree | Sidereal Decan Region | State | Body | and its AU | $2^k$ exponent AU from the Sun[48] | | | Bodies in this Duodc. are how you accomplish: | Body A + [s# to get Body B] means Body A _____ Body B |
|---|---|---|---|---|---|---|---|---|---|
| 0, 144 | 27.5°-29.9° | | | | | 45.25 | 5.5 | harmonizing | is synonymous with |
| 1 | 25°-27.5° | | | Kuiper Belt[49] | | 42.71 | 5.4 | excitement | implies |
| 2 | 22.5°-25° | Pisces-Scorpio | | | | 40.32 | 5.3 | recruitment | presents a state of |
| 3 | 20°-22.5° | | Engagement In | | | 38.05 | 5.3 | mobilization | intends expression of |
| 4 | 17.5°-20° | | | | | 35.92 | 5.2 | behavior | a tense form of |
| 5 | 15°-17.5° | | | | | 33.90 | 5.1 | imposition | holds as its base unit |
| 6 | 12.5°-15° | Pisces-Cancer | | | | 32.00 | 5.0 | co-creation | processes collections of |
| 7 | 10°-12.5° | | | Neptune | | 30.20 | 4.9 | ideal | is the process employed during |

---

[48] Using the end of Pisces as duodecanate 1 to keep things simple, I slid the fraction of 144 over and took the base 2 log as was done in previous books. The actual formula for the exponent column is 12-(s#)/12 – 6.5 (+12 past Mercury) in a formula very similar to the tropical asteroid meaning formula in *Laurentia* and earlier in this book. We've scooted the tropical duodecanates over by 11 though, so the 6.5 is has changed from 7.5 as well.

[49] Pluto's orbit is almost synonymous with the span of the Kuiper belt, but to discourage you from assigning it rulership of anything, I've left its name out of the table in favor of (what I think is) a better choice at the end. What we can say about Pluto and the Kuiper belt is they reflect transitions between engagement in something and constructing something from it. Perhaps Pluto's association with social pressure is not too far off.

| # | Range | Sign Pair | Phase | Planet | Value | Value2 | Term | Definition |
|---|---|---|---|---|---|---|---|---|
| 8 | 7.5°-10° | | | | 28.51 | 4.8 | stability | is accomplished by a |
| 9 | 5°-7.5° | | | | 26.91 | 4.8 | activity | recruits, from the outside, a |
| 10 | 2.5°-5° | Pisces-Pisces | | | 25.40 | 4.7 | atmosphere | is the event demanded by a |
| 11 | 0°-2.5° | | | | 23.97 | 4.6 | proceeding | receives, from the surrounding context, a |
| 12 | 27.5°-29.9° | | | | 22.63 | 4.5 | identification | as part of its function, requires |
| 13 | 25°-27.5° | Aquarius-Libra | | | 21.36 | 4.4 | transmission | has a higher likelihood of exerting, on another, a |
| 14 | 22.5°-25° | | | | 20.16 | 4.3 | insertion | is built up through exhaustive |
| 15 | 20°-22.5° | Aquarius-Gemini | | Uranus | 19.03 | 4.3 | reception | is distinguished among its environment mates as the chief aggregator of |
| 16 | 17.5°-20° | | | | 17.96 | 4.2 | agreement | resists outside |
| 17 | 15°-17.5° | | Transfer | | 16.95 | 4.1 | participation | to those subject to it, exerts a |
| 18 | 12.5°-15° | | | | 16.00 | 4.0 | consideration | is exited via |
| 19 | 10°-12.5° | Aquarius-Aquarius | | | 15.10 | 3.9 | shop | is the impulse/imaginary optimization/third derivative of |
| 20 | 7.5°-10° | | | | 14.25 | 3.8 | demand | is built by panning across |
| 21 | 5°-7.5° | | | | 13.45 | 3.8 | production | is selected into via |
| 22 | 2.5°-5° | | | | 12.70 | 3.7 | pattern | is expansively granted under |
| 23 | 0°-2.5° | | | | 11.99 | 3.6 | percept | of each respective target implies a |
| 24 | 27.5°-29.9° | | | | 11.31 | 3.5 | pull | of an other is exposed through their |
| 25 | 25°-27.5° | Capricorn-Virgo | | | 10.68 | 3.4 | inclusion | draws on a pool of |
| 26 | 22.5°-25° | | | | 10.08 | 3.3 | rules | , spread over a field, constitutes |
| 27 | 20°-22.5° | | | Saturn | 9.51 | 3.3 | choices | strengthens the reception of |
| 28 | 17.5°-20° | Capricorn-Taurus | | | 8.98 | 3.2 | comprehension | when its newness is finally accumulated, becomes |
| 29 | 15°-17.5° | | Grouping and Framing | | 8.48 | 3.1 | knowledge | obscures the source of |
| 30 | 12.5°-15° | | | | 8.00 | 3.0 | translation | sent into a system is allowed via |
| 31 | 10°-12.5° | | | | 7.55 | 2.9 | attention | consists of an assembly of |
| 32 | 7.5°-10° | | | | 7.13 | 2.8 | scope | is a borrowed slice of |
| 33 | 5°-7.5° | Capricorn-Capricorn | | | 6.73 | 2.8 | frame | is a transformation / rearrangement on |
| 34 | 2.5°-5° | | | | 6.35 | 2.7 | space | enacts towards a purpose, |
| 35 | 0°-2.5° | | | | 5.99 | 2.6 | group | culminates in a particular \ having filed through certain |
| 36 | 27.5°-29.9° | Sagittarius-Leo | | | 5.66 | 2.5 | agenda | once completely expressed, yields to |
| 37 | 25°-27.5° | | | Jupiter | 5.34 | 2.4 | priority | is intentionally shaped through the right |
| 38 | 22.5°-25° | | | | 5.04 | 2.3 | acceptance | is determined as effective against a stream of |
| 39 | 20°-22.5° | | | | 4.76 | 2.3 | subordination | consists of a statically contained volume of |
| 40 | 17.5°-20° | | | | 4.49 | 2.2 | model | is the underlying thematic basis of |
| 41 | 15°-17.5° | Sagittarius-Aries | | | 4.24 | 2.1 | framework | is a stranger-bridging form of |
| 42 | 12.5°-15° | | | | 4.00 | 2.0 | kinesis | equates the target and the interactants |
| 43 | 10°-12.5° | | Circumscribing | | 3.78 | 1.9 | function | knows its extent via |
| 44 | 7.5°-10° | | | | 3.56 | 1.8 | designer | commands in high fidelity, a view of |
| 45 | 5°-7.5° | | | | 3.36 | 1.8 | uniqueness | confers among its interactant pieces, alignment of |
| 46 | 2.5°-5° | | | | 3.17 | 1.7 | presence | has members / components who share, as a common bond, |
| 47 | 0°-2.5° | Sagittarius-Sagittarius | | | 3.00 | 1.6 | wrapping | encapsulates component pieces within the same |
| 48 | 27.5°-29.9° | | — | | 2.83 | 1.5 | contact | is a component of |

# Appendix I: The Shape of the Human Body

| # | Degrees | Sign Pair | Category | Body | Val1 | Val2 | Term | Description |
|---|---|---|---|---|---|---|---|---|
| 49 | 25°-27.5° | | | Main Belt | 2.67 | 1.4 | presentation | requires attention to |
| 50 | 22.5°-25° | | | | 2.52 | 1.3 | amplification | reveals a thing's local mode of |
| 51 | 20°-22.5° | | | | 2.38 | 1.3 | convenience | fosters the receiver's powers of |
| 52 | 17.5°-20° | Scorpio-Cancer | | | 2.24 | 1.2 | purpose | holds an insistence on receiving |
| 53 | 15°-17.5° | | | | 2.12 | 1.1 | reason | consists of many |
| 54 | 12.5°-15° | | | | 2.00 | 1.0 | involvement | culminates in or is shipped away via |
| 55 | 10°-12.5° | Scorpio-Pisces | | | 1.89 | 0.9 | administration | has, as its ultimate complement, |
| 56 | 7.5°-10° | | | | 1.78 | 0.8 | region | prohibits |
| 57 | 5°-7.5° | Scorpio-Scorpio | | | 1.68 | 0.8 | center | affirms, among outsiders, one's |
| 58 | 2.5°-5° | | | | 1.59 | 0.7 | category | towards the surrounding context, exhibits a |
| 59 | 0°-2.5° | | | Mars | 1.50 | 0.6 | pacifying | to the witnessing space of viewers, accomplishes a |
| 60 | 27.5°-29.9° | | | | 1.41 | 0.5 | lure | is a sneaky method of |
| 61 | 25°-27.5° | | | | 1.33 | 0.4 | acquisition | is a reward conferred by the witnessing context among those who |
| 62 | 22.5°-25° | Libra-Gemini | Impressing and Absorbing Against | | 1.26 | 0.3 | absorption | exerts, compared to all things outside it, a singularly unique, internal mode of |
| 63 | 20°-22.5° | | | | 1.19 | 0.3 | displacement | is bounded to its less distinct category mates by |
| 64 | 17.5°-20° | | | | 1.12 | 0.2 | inculcation | sets, as its existential goal, to achieve like itself |
| 65 | 15°-17.5° | | | | 1.06 | 0.1 | separation | to those subject to it, is the superior source of |
| 66 | 12.5°-15° | Libra-Aquarius | | Earth / (geocntrc) anti-Sun | 1.00 | 0.0 | appraisal | manifests, one on one, as a |
| 67 | 10°-12.5° | | | | 0.94 | -0.1 | market | manifests as its target's expression of |
| 68 | 7.5°-10° | | | | 0.89 | -0.2 | disruption | enacts against others' press for |
| 69 | 5°-7.5° | Libra-Libra | | | 0.84 | -0.3 | development | of the whole is served by |
| 70 | 2.5°-5° | | | | 0.79 | -0.3 | transformation | of the actor is the definition of |
| 71 | 0°-2.5° | | | Venus | 0.75 | -0.4 | clarification | of the actor, assumes the actor, among others, has a |
| 72 | 27.5°-29.9° | | | | 0.71 | -0.5 | standout | collected, are processed as |
| 73 | 25°-27.5° | Virgo-Taurus | | | 0.67 | -0.6 | resembling | is fueled by |
| 74 | 22.5°-25° | | | | 0.63 | -0.7 | gesture | is a questionable, though useful-for-incompleteness substitute for |
| 75 | 20°-22.5° | | Class Likeness and Similarizing | | 0.59 | -0.8 | animation | is accomplished by passing, onto an external, more |
| 76 | 17.5°-20° | | | | 0.56 | -0.8 | role | can be infinitely conferred through a stream of |
| 77 | 15°-17.5° | | | | 0.53 | -0.9 | information | creates reconciliation between actor and target when applied to |
| 78 | 12.5°-15° | Virgo-Capricorn | | | 0.50 | -1.0 | count | , overlapped and stored, constitutes |
| 79 | 10°-12.5° | | | | 0.47 | -1.1 | monopolizing | are more easily known / familiarized through an increase in |
| 80 | 7.5°-10° | | | | 0.45 | -1.2 | validation | is a most-important reduction of |
| 81 | 5°-7.5° | | | | 0.42 | -1.3 | frequency | alters the usefulness of a body of |
| 82 | 2.5°-5° | | | Mercury | 0.40 | -1.3 | energy | freezes the traded dynamics of |
| 83 | 0°-2.5° | Virgo-Virgo | | | 0.37 | -1.4 | reflection | adds precision to the field of |
| 84 | 27.5°-29.9° | | | | 0.35 | -1.5 | proxy | seeks the actor's capacity for / attainment of |
| 85 | 25°-27.5° | Leo-Aries | | | 0.33 | -1.6 | basis | is tested for mastery or correctness against the target's |
| 86 | 22.5°-25° | | Choices Among | | 0.31 | -1.7 | component | is put together on the basis of the actor's cooperative |
| 87 | 20°-22.5° | | | | 0.30 | -1.8 | operation | is assembled using collections of |
| 88 | 17.5°-20° | | | | 0.28 | -1.8 | training | is aggregated around by |

| # | Degrees | Sign Pair | Phase | Object | $2^k$ | k | Term | Definition |
|---|---|---|---|---|---|---|---|---|
| 89 | 15°-17.5° | Leo-Sagittarius | | [No reliable Object][50] | 0.26 | -1.9 | search | is only as effective as its enactor's use of |
| 90 | 12.5°-15° | | | | 1024.00 | 10.0 | exploration[51] | is a distinguishable unit of |
| 91 | 10°-12.5° | | | | 966.53 | 9.9 | method | is the alternative mode of passing through compared to |
| 92 | 7.5°-10° | | | | 912.28 | 9.8 | perspective | is the mirror against which one perceives his casing's |
| 93 | 5°-7.5° | | | | 861.08 | 9.8 | summary | is surface-circumscribed by |
| 94 | 2.5°-5° | Leo-Leo | | | 812.75 | 9.7 | alternative | homogenizes the bounds of a |
| 95 | 0°-2.5° | | | | 767.13 | 9.6 | intersection | consists of component pieces threaded by volumes of the medium |
| 96 | 27.5°-29.9° | | | | 724.08 | 9.5 | transfer | entails |
| 97 | 25°-27.5° | | | | 683.44 | 9.4 | gift | has its expressive agenda set via |
| 98 | 22.5°-25° | Cancer-Pisces | | | 645.08 | 9.3 | suggestion | forces a surface field, from the interactant, of |
| 99 | 20°-22.5° | | | | 608.87 | 9.3 | assumption | is a collectivized sponsor of |
| 100 | 17.5°-20° | | | | 574.70 | 9.2 | opening | subjects an interactant to its contents upon expression of the interactant's |
| 101 | 15°-17.5° | | Intake | | 542.45 | 9.1 | aim | displaces the energy / focus from an initial |
| 102 | 12.5°-15° | Cancer-Scorpio | | Sedna | 512.00 | 9.0 | hunger | bounces from one component (of the) actor to another, permeating |
| 103 | 10°-12.5° | | | | 483.26 | 8.9 | fulfillment | is the actual result of an interaction initiated in |
| 104 | 7.5°-10° | | | | 456.14 | 8.8 | fixation | is the cooperative allowance of |
| 105 | 5°-7.5° | | | | 430.54 | 8.8 | update | is a non-actor / stranger / alien version of |
| 106 | 2.5°-5° | | | | 406.37 | 8.7 | pathway | is an effect inverted / negative space version of |
| 107 | 0°-2.5° | Cancer-Cancer | | | 383.57 | 8.6 | preference | is the work intentionally put in against the stability of |
| 108 | 27.5°-29.9° | | | | 362.04 | 8.5 | collection | is the parent set, other actor complement to |
| 109 | 25°-27.5° | | | | 341.72 | 8.4 | progression | is rammed into permanence by a reinforcing, noncontingent, input-ignoring body of |
| 110 | 22.5°-25° | | | | 322.54 | 8.3 | arrival | is the permuted stacking / aggregation of |
| 111 | 20°-22.5° | Gemini-Aquarius | | | 304.44 | 8.3 | following | is the process run askew to the space of |
| 112 | 17.5°-20° | | | | 287.35 | 8.2 | holding | reinterprets with a new expresser as basis |
| 113 | 15°-17.5° | | Sequencing | | 271.22 | 8.1 | reinforcement | corrals efforts around a common |
| 114 | 12.5°-15° | | | 2012 VP 113 | 256.00 | 8.0 | value | is the end state of the target (towards the actor?) sought by |
| 115 | 10°-12.5° | Gemini-Libra | | | 241.63 | 7.9 | culture | has, as its circumscribing activity (counterambience), |
| 116 | 7.5°-10° | | | | 228.07 | 7.8 | dilemma | is achieved on the basis of some underlying |
| 117 | 5°-7.5° | Gemini-Gemini | | | 215.27 | 7.8 | compeller | is required of, in order to keep it possible, |
| 118 | 2.5°-5° | | | | 203.19 | 7.7 | continuation | has its enforcement upon others constrained by |
| 119 | 0°-2.5° | | | | 191.78 | 7.6 | truth | can't be fittingly applied without the existence of |
| 120 | 27.5°-29.9° | | | | 181.02 | 7.5 | connection | exists where there is a gathering of |
| 121 | 25°-27.5° | | | | 170.86 | 7.4 | other | is a nonnegotiable side effect of |
| 122 | 22.5°-25° | Taurus-Capricorn | | | 161.27 | 7.3 | rights | is the prime object of security under a state of |
| 123 | 20°-22.5° | | Association | | 152.22 | 7.3 | enjoyment | is an expression of interest to those under the spell of |
| 124 | 17.5°-20° | | | | 143.68 | 7.2 | relation | has its effects (largely) annulled under |
| 125 | 15°-17.5° | | | | 135.61 | 7.1 | representation | absorbs a foreigner into a field of |

---

[50] Going by powers of 2 and considering the most stable, reliable orbits we currently know, alas there is no corresponding band for mid-Leo in 2021. This is convenient, though, as it allows us to designate the end of our 12-cycle string as the beginning.

[51] Notice that we wrap around at Mercury/Sedna, given there are no major planets closer than Mercury's perihelion at ~ .3 AU. The wrap fits nicely doesn't it? .3 AU is about = $2^{-1.8}$, which explains Mercury's $2^k$ column

# Appendix I: The Shape of the Human Body

| | | | | | | | | |
|---|---|---|---|---|---|---|---|---|
| 126 | 12.5°-15° | Taurus-Virgo | | | 128.00 | 7.0 | distinguishing | is properly mapped against encounters with |
| 127 | 10°-12.5° | | | | 120.82 | 6.9 | self-image | offers a compounded array, towards the same goal, of |
| 128 | 7.5°-10° | | | | 114.04 | 6.8 | insistence | are known by their directed focus of |
| 129 | 5°-7.5° | Taurus-Taurus | | 2008 ST 229 | 107.63 | 6.8 | context | is an unsolicited expression of |
| 130 | 2.5°-5° | | | | 101.59 | 6.7 | audience | collects onto its space of effect, |
| 131 | 0°-2.5° | | | | 95.89 | 6.6 | individual | in its occurrence, takes count of |
| 132 | 27.5°-29.9° | | | | 90.51 | 6.5 | instance | is a patterned extension of |
| 133 | 25°-27.5° | Aries-Sagittarius | | | 85.43 | 6.4 | membership | is one of the noteworthy benefits of |
| 134 | 22.5°-25° | | | | 80.63 | 6.3 | food | is more apt to be pursued given |
| 135 | 20°-22.5° | | | | 76.11 | 6.3 | nurturance | is advanced by passing through a |
| 136 | 17.5°-20° | | Construction | | 71.84 | 6.2 | promotion | presents to the prior space of interactants before it as a |
| 137 | 15°-17.5° | Aries-Leo | | Eris | 67.81 | 6.1 | treatment | expects of itself across contexts, |
| 138 | 12.5°-15° | | | | 64.00 | 6.0 | work | seeks to receive from its participant(s) |
| 139 | 10°-12.5° | | | | 60.41 | 5.9 | material | is taken advantage of via an interactor's [use of] |
| 140 | 7.5°-10° | | | | 57.02 | 5.8 | construction | puts on top of an existing subset of itself, |
| 141 | 5°-7.5° | | | | 53.82 | 5.8 | source | when immediately sought, compels its actor to look for |
| 142 | 2.5°-5° | Aries-Aries | | | 50.80 | 5.7 | effect | has its reach declared as limited by |
| 143 | 0°-2.5° | | | | 47.95 | 5.6 | infiltration | is determined as real by the actor from which it accepts |
| 144 | 27.5°-29.9° Pisces | | Engagement in | Quaoar[52,53] | 45.25 | 5.5 | harmonizing | is synonymous with |

The bottom line is this:

- If you plan to stay with tropical astrology, use the Tables 56-1 through 56-12 to describe what the planets in your chart are doing in each section.
- If you plan to try out sidereal astrology, the degrees and the general division descriptions will shift, but you'll gain the ability to do stable math on the sections. Try generating your sidereal chart, then interpreting aspects by adding the number of duodecanates they are apart. Going forward in the wheel (0° Aries to 2.5° Aries for example) adds one duodecanate for every 2.5°. So if you had Mars in 25° Leo and Venus in 27.5° Leo, then you'd get [Mars implies Venus] and [Venus is determined as real by the actor from which it accepts Mars]. When the "implying" is happening, it will have the flavor of the objects you have in 25°-27.5° SIDEREAL Pisces. When the

---

[52] You might say that I cheated by wrapping around the table, but as you can see from the decan labels, actual space doesn't care about our love of even divisions. The cycle does repeat.

[53] If you recall what we said about 50000 Quaoar in *144*, the sense of creativity that comes from nowhere fits the beginning of sidereal Aries perfectly. As with the discussion of astrology and evolution earlier, our best indicators of what an orbit band truly does is the body which is both big and moves around the least. Unlike Pluto with its orbital span of ~20 AU, Quaoar has a span of about 4 AU (an eccentricity of .04). As you probably know, there are many fairly large Trans-Neptunian objects out there; in order to find the best one to put my money on, I divided the distance across (size) by the eccentricity. Although objects like 136472 Makemake are bigger, their eccentricity drops this value. It probably isn't coincidence, however, that Quaoar, Pluto, and Makemake are all related to influential pressures in some way.

"determining as real..." is happening, it will have the flavor of your asteroids in 0°-2.5° sidereal Aries. Give or take some wiggle room.

Can you see how the creeping signs of tropical astro will slowly shove all the angles out of their original cycle levels? You can't do this kind of fixed-value math with the tropical signs you're used to. But if our evolution keeps things stable for epochs at a time, the energy flow levels for each point on the astronomical cycle *must* stay fixed.

Perhaps in a future book I will explain what I did to produce the chart above. The story isn't long, but it is complicated. It also coexists with the aspect math in *144*, but again is a bit too complicated for this appendix. (*144's* aspects preserve the sign, Table I-2's preserves the cycle.) In order to sharpen your powers of differentiation between the tropical and sidereal, sidereal and sign addition systems, the best thing you can do is practice with both versions of your chart. Compare the Star to how you make decisions in the world; compare I-2 to how your motivations and effects on your environment tend to chain together. Both systems will feel right, but I've found that sidereal somehow feels more long-term, more "aftermathy."

## So What Does Each Sidereal Signs Actually Represent?

Although it is possible to summarize the various columns in I-2 to produce some kind of overall label for each sign, we won't do it in this book. There is an entire third column's worth of even newer information which has more to do with the evolved body than it does the senses or interaction, making the subject a much bigger topic than we can currently tackle here. To get a hint as to what that third column entails, you might look at one odd difference between the Body (planet) column in I-2 and the Sidereal Decan Region column: In the former the cycle starts at Leo, in the latter it starts in Aries. Why? I asked this while making the chart above, and had an interesting experience over the course of four nights. What I learned has formed the basis of a later project which will not be part of this series, but the successor to *Sex in 12 Dimensions*: *The Book of Contours*. It will take a few years to collect all the research for it though. Until then, I-2 and its duodecanate addition will be all there is.

# Appendix II: Completed Sample of the Body Wheels

The Body Wheels are based on the octants from the circumplexes below. I've included a compass on each just in case you want to rotate each circumplex to line up with the familiar human measures. North indicates dominance:

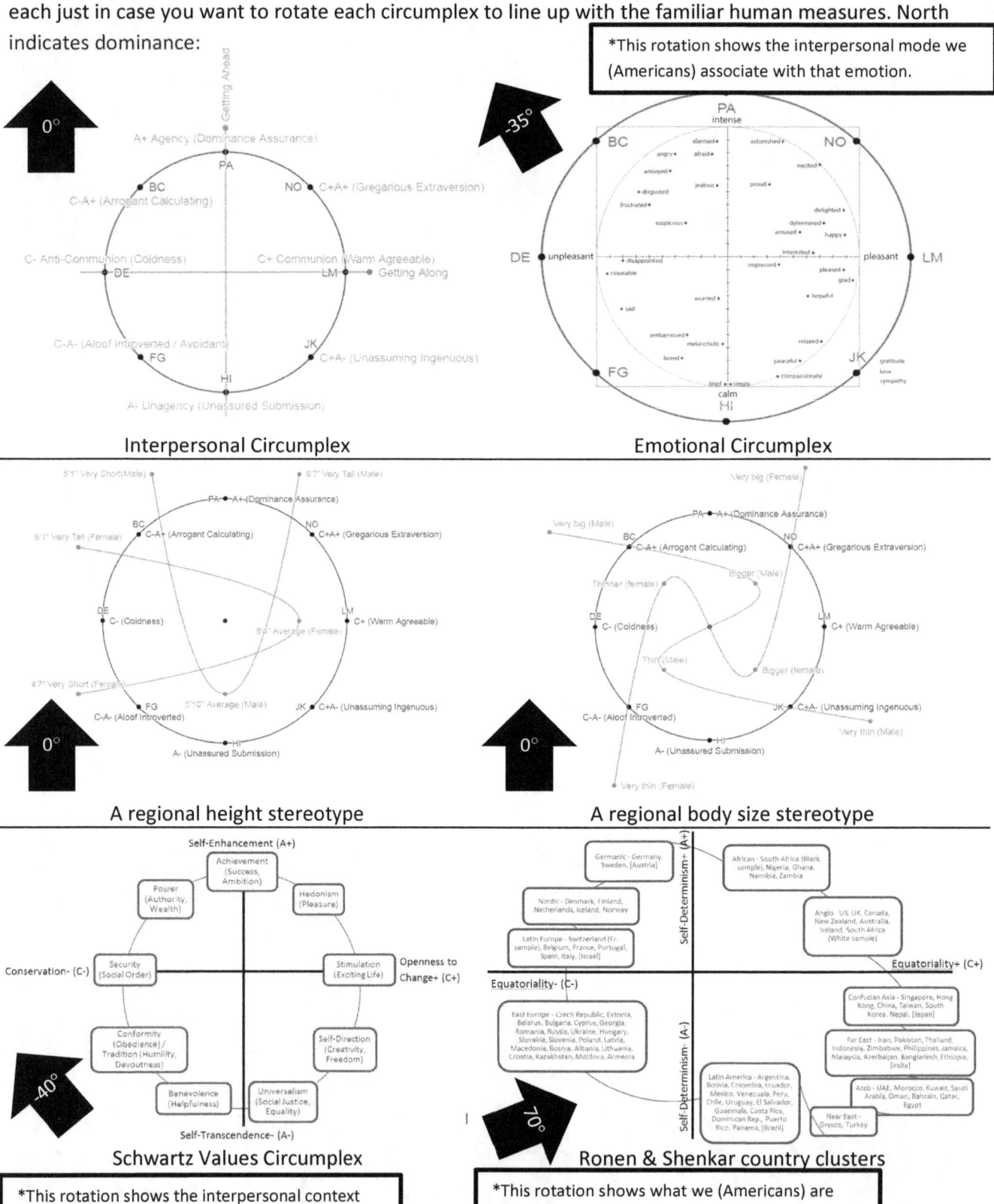

| External Region | Map | Question Number | Your Octant Answer(s) | Internal System | Any health issues or special notes about columns y or b? | Your description of this sign level | Is there anything you would cha about this a, b, or this sign level general? |
|---|---|---|---|---|---|---|---|
| y | z | a | A | b | B | C | D |
| face, head | | 46.1 | CD (Cold-Calculating) | the face, **muscular system** | | a "keep away from me" bearing regarding most strangers | |
| neck (throat) | | 46.2 | BC | the **upper digestive system**, | | I eat and breathe data and actual calculations (arrogant-calculating) | |
| arms | | 46.3 | BC | mannerisms, the **respiratory system** | shortness of breath during "theory flood" | are often misread: arms and ideas, quick energy | would love to not have mood dr after arm exercises |
| upper chest | | 46.5 | CD (frus-tration) | **endocrine system (hormones)**, | | intellectual fuel = taboo, "dirty" things, women; pre-sleep intensity | |
| beneath the chest heart | | 46.8 | BC | **circulatory system** | | refusal to be stopped; picky about eating any artery cloggers | |
| umbilical region | | 46.18 | HI, KL, NO, BC | reasoning, the **lower digestive system** | | will try almost anything once, can combine any idea with any other | |
| (love handles) | | 46.6 | JK | voluntary com. **lymph urinary /excretory sys** | | friends must contribute to peace, path, and creativity | |
| reproducive organs | | 46.7 | NO | output of the **urinary/excretory, reproductive** | | co-creators want to change the whole world, extraversion | universal reach = information → c creator should be a global huma |
| gluteals and thighs | | 46.16 | NO | **(hair skin & nails)**, outward appearance | "tiger stripes" birthmark on right leg | disheveled but out there anyway, lion's mane hair, exhibitionistic | |
| knees to lower legs | | 46.10, 46.11 | FG, JK | **skeletal system**, the general body plan, body size | | non-dominant but not HI-submissive either | |
| lower legs to ankles | | 46.4 | JK | the social structure and **nervous system** | naturally high strung nerves | inner world full of ideas, remains hidden from most | |
| feet | | 46.13←, 46.17 | DE←OP,M, H, women | memory, **senses brain, central nervous system** | | building better social structure, every waking minute, enabled by determined women | |

## Ajani's Summary

| Topic | Element | Chosen Sign | Embodiment | Summary |
|---|---|---|---|---|
| Purpose | Water 1 | ♓ Pisces | extensive, positive dream life | I am called to build better social structures as a nonstop, ongoing focus in my life. |
| | Air | ♎ Libra | efficient immune system | As I do this, I am fueled mainly by my exchanges with determined contributors to peace, path, and creativity |
| | Water 2 | ♋ Cancer | naturally attract ♀ who are ultramagnetic, desirous, social assets; bullying if I'm not careful | (which I associate with women), the taboo, |
| | Water 3 | ♏ Scorpio ♓ Pisces | charge/bi/info turn on; dreams | and use my encounters with these people's complex dynamics to inspire even further social structuring. |
| Identity | Water | ♏ Scorpio | easily turned on by charged or bi-women, or certain information; ongoing need to add a 2nd partner in every creative undertaking | The people I create things in this world with are almost always erratic or noisy; this suggests that I might actually do more by partnering with interactions between people—groups of more than one—than partnering with an individual. |
| | Earth 1 | ♑ Capricorn | small build, but athletic shape | In engaging these co-creators, I am not designed to dominate, but should not let myself be completely submissive either. I should resist feeling stepped on. |
| | Earth 2 | ♉ Taurus | chronic coffee, tea, junk food eater | My worth alongside my co-creators depends on my heavy use of data where, |
| | Earth 3 | ♍ Virgo ♏ Scorpio | non-stop eating; charge/bi/info turn on | in my work with them, I will try almost anything once; also I have a skill for combining any one idea with any other. I am not to dominate, but to assemble structures on behalf of those who can do so cooperatively. (I'm a Scorpio Sun. Venus & Uranus are also there) |
| Forms of Communication | Air 1 | ♊ Gemini | high metabolism, low socialization tolerance, introvert | I am easily misread and often seen as unpredictable—with an instant mood and mentality drop when asked to visit new individuals (voluntarily), |
| | Air 2 | ♎ Libra | "instant" lymphatic, strong immune system. Prefer food & drink combinations that don't always match; a snacker | and so I've learned to select friends who contribute to peace, path, and creativity—that is, friends who understand what I'm trying to communicate. As a straight male, I find the greatest peace through creative women. |
| | Air 3 | ♒ Aquarius | super high nerve activity as baseline (but it's not stressful); don't like people behind me, secrets, or closets with doors still on them. For real for real. | These people act as a kind of shield between me and the rest of the world, which I keep far away from me most of the time. I have a high strung nervous system despite being pretty relaxed most of the time, so I need for the information passing through me to be thoroughly good for the sake of my basic health maintenance. |
| | Fire | ♈ Aries ♊ Gemini | mean resting face; new person mood drop (strangers) | No misreaders allowed. My "keep away from me" bearing in new situations is a primary tool for this. |
| Projection | Fire 1 | ♌ Leo | happy mood (non-strangers), quick to vacate a bad sitn.; hobbies need a 3rd person as a back-up. Very highly self-accepting. | Despite anything described above, I approach my goals with a refusal to be stopped. I am designed to be extremely picky about accepting anything that might clog my energy flow |
| | Fire 2 | ♐ Sagittarius | crazy hair, instantly mess up new clothes, backwards regimen, black; dislikes public spaces, but if it's a duty, exhibitionistic | and may, as a result, make a wild or uncooperative impression on the "accept everything" world outside. There is at least some level of disregard for what that world expects. The stripes on my leg remind me of proceeding like a hunter, a good enough analogy, |
| | Fire 3 | ♈ Aries | unwelcoming resting face | and although there is nothing in my energy that suggests I should ever have to fight anything, there is a lot in my surface |
| | Earth | ♑ Capricorn ♌ Leo | small athletic quick vacate | that suggests others should be prepared for one. |
| Recap | Water | ♓ Pisces | great, detailed dream life | I am here to build better emotional systems |
| | Air | ♎ Libra | good immune system | alongside determined contributors to peace, path, and creativity. |
| | Earth | ♍ Virgo | nonstop eating | I do so by joining diverse communications, |
| | Fire | ♌ Leo | stay happy, quick vacate | employing only positive support (no hardship, friction, or frustration) in the process |

**Recap 2:** The frictionless emotional world-building of peace & path-creating groups

# Appendix III: Ajani's Answer to Question 48.3

Your circle will include various experiences which have proved most memorable across your life history. I've anonymized some things in this activity but you should complete your version in full.

| ♈ | ♉ | ♊ | ♋ | ♌ | ♍ |
|---|---|---|---|---|---|
| Aries | Taurus | Gemini | Cancer | Leo | Virgo |
| spontaneous behaving | experiencing things you value or identify yourself against | communicating your ideas or instinctual movement; thinking or talking to or for yourself | paying attention to how you feel or how you're reacting to things | playing, enjoying leisure time, having fun, broadcasting yourself | working, making meaning, doing daily duties and maintenance tasks |
| ♎ | ♏ | ♐ | ♑ | ♒ | ♓ |
| Libra | Scorpio | Sagittarius | Capricorn | Aquarius | Pisces |
| socializing, friends, conversation with others, engaging in 1:1 feedback activities like playing instruments or video games | using your power over others, over information, or over situations broadly | leaving an impression among strangers | being associated with certain formal classes of people | being talked about | performing default actions |

# Appendix IV: Ajani's Answer to Question 49.3

For question 49.3 you are challenged to come clean and explain to yourself, as much as possible, the kinds of fights you pick, the ones you avoid, and the ones you naturally enjoy. When you close this book and open it back up years later, you'll see what you thought of your penchant for self-created drama of both the good and bad kind, so it's important that your answer be long, elaborate, and all-encompassing. I didn't think twice about putting my own answer in here, not to convince you that I was vain, but to write the same kind of off-the-dome self-assessment I'm asking you to write. But if, after reading this you feel that you're not quite up to owning your conflict style, or think you need more of some other form of preparation in order to answer this question, don't hesitate to skip it until you're ready to unfold the whole truth about your own assaults on your own sphere. As the answer below shows, your response should not only explain your conflict style, but also your views on how that style relates to your larger personality. There will be much in it about your identity and why, sometimes, the fights you enter may truly seem like a matter of your survival as a coherent personality.

My dad told me sometime in middle school, "When you fight you fight to end it. Never sleep with one eye open." The aim was, fight to kill or don't fight at all. Go figure that Dad was one of the most peaceful people I've ever known.

Naturally high-strung, I'm very sensitive to things in general. I startle easily, but don't scare easily, instead getting agitated, irritated, or fortress-like defensive, with trust dropping to 0 if you surprise me negatively without some kind of olive branch attached. I have no sense of humor for jokes made at others' expense, judgment, or any other kind of high and mighty garbage, and this extends to my view of higher forces. As a child I had a major temper, was a wall-puncher, and gradually learned that being black with this kind of temper cost me more than it did others. Yet society expects me to misbehave in the face of injustice, and when I don't do this, some people are tempted to use the label "passive aggressive"—the American insult for people who don't burn their own house down when provoked. As a black male I learned early not to fall for that kind of ego insult, lest I let somebody's *else's* flapping mouth get *me* in trouble.

On the other hand, as a teacher and an oldest brother, I've always been protective of others' value—even "enemies." There is no one I wouldn't forgive, whose aid I wouldn't come to if they asked it—including my five worst relationship and business partners. I pride myself in being too focused on greater things to let the Joneses get to me. I find energy burn-off more reminiscent of the times I was distrusted for no reason other than gossip, and accordingly don't trust cliques, family weigh-in, or anyone trying to tell me how to be "better" when they've made no attempt to understand "normal" for people other than themselves. Patronization of others gets you kicked out of my circle.

I'm a sore loser in general and an even worse winner since, in most kinds of actual competition, I won't rest until I feel you've been permanently erased. I'll never sleep with one eye open just to stay in the octagon with you. In a struggle for control, close wins are dissatisfying. Only slaughters count. My nervous system goes into overdrive while I'm pursuing this, and the feeling is horrible. Accordingly, I want everyone to win, want to pick up every person who was called a loser, and want everyone to have the second chance (or first) that many never gave me. It's my empowerment over little judges. And although I like group dynamics, I don't have the heart to be a part of one for very long. Mobs are full of fools. Most conflict is not worth getting arrested, fired, or dragged around the grapevine for, but when you respond as the mob tells you, you sign up for stuff like that. So I try to keep peace. Many people have seen this as weakness, but they've always learned otherwise, sooner than later. I have nothing to prove. I have no fear. I have no regret. I'm here to do a job I believe only I can do. The conflict must be worth it, easy, and unquestionably winnable in order for me to bother with it, otherwise I've got better things to do.

No one will ever compel me to step backwards, but as a result I've had difficulty maintaining long term stable relationships because I end them at the first sign of entrenched misalignment, and still possess the very quick defensive impatience I dislike in others. My main weapon against most opponents is total devaluation, where I render even the closest years-long exchange permanently worthless over the course of a few minutes. It remains one of my worst traits as a human. My protection against this is to avoid starting relationships with others unless they come to me first. The other way around makes me feel weak (by my own standards) from the very beginning, and has often ended badly. My circles include only people who keep my spirits very high at all times. Otherwise my matter-of-fact dismissal of the other's value can be cruel. It's a defense I try to use less and less as I get older, quieted by picking the right circles. But it's also my only true protection as a Daoist-Buddhist.

# Appendix V: Ajani's Answer to Question 49.7

Here is an example (with anonymized names, of course).

| # | Question | Answer | bad- | bad | neutral | good | good+ |
|---|---|---|---|---|---|---|---|
| | | | | | | | How would you rate this outcome? |
| 1. | Who were those people? | Aida, Janice, Clara | | | | | |
| 2. | What was the general overview of the conflict? | An apparently good exchange, but frustratingly unreliable | | | | | |
| 3. | (Interaction before) What was the in-the-moment conflict about? | I won't tell them no if they need me, but their word is absolutely no good | | -1 | | | |
| 4. | (Interaction after) How did the conflict ultimately end? | I made one last friendly reach, exch stops there | | -1 | | | |
| 5. | (Your weapon before) During the conflict, how did you respond to them? | became increasingly, visibly skeptical -> them | | -1 | | | |
| 6. | (Your weapon after) How do you respond to that kind of challenge now | assign no real worth to them | | -1 | | | |
| 7. | (Their weapon before) How did they respond to you during the conflict? | flaked | | -1 | | | |
| 8. | (Their weapon after) How has that response changed in your occupant(s) now that you've had the conflict a few times?[54] | they flake more | | -1 | | | |
| 9. | (Your view before) How did you generally view this kind of occupant before? | fun, interesting | | | | | 2 |
| 10. | (Your view after) How do you generally view this kind of occupant now? | as a flake | | -1 | | | |
| 11. | (Their view before) How did this type of occupant view you before? | admiration, as an escape maybe? | | | | 1 | |
| 12. | (Their view after) How does this kind of occupant view you now? | arrogant, better than everyone else | | -1 | | | |
| 13. | (Yourself before) How did you generally view yourself in this situation before? | hopeful for romance | | | | 1 | |
| 14. | (Yourself after) How do you generally view yourself in this situation now? | bothered and mystified by their continued appearance | | | 0 | | |
| 15. | (Your wants from them before) What would you have wanted from this type of occupant in this situation before? | romance, supportive friendship | | | | 1 | |
| 16. | (Your wants from them after) What do you want from this type of occupant in this situation now? | nothing. Maybe to know why this kind of person keeps finding me. I'm not looking for them. | | | 0 | | |
| 17. | (Whole relationship before) On the whole, what did you formerly think of this style of pairing of you and the occupant-type? | ego flattering, fun | | | | | 2 |
| 18. | (Whole relationship after) On the whole, what do you think of this style of pairing of you and the occupant-type now? | I'm indifferent. It's still oddly positive though. | | | 0.5 | | |

19. Take a look at your ratings and note which parts of your sphere improved under the conflict versus those which didn't. Overall, what would you say was the point of this kind of "battle?"

The only outcome that went up was a drop in my need to pursue romance from everything. I guess that was good. Then again, no it wasn't.

Actually…it looks like I've gotten better at staying with a person who needed me even though there was nothing at all in it for me.

---

[54] This is a forced answer to the question, *What did you want to happen?* Rather than asking what you wanted in your head, it asks what your *deeds* wanted, and ultimately got.

# Appendix VI: Ajani's Answer to Question 57.14

The object of this activity is for you to describe the personality type which you normally encounter that best describes each cluster of asteroids in the duodecanates of your chart. I believe that, as long as your brain groups such attributes together, it will also tend to set up a family of behaviors for you to adopt when you focus those attributes in your life. If those attributes tell a story you would rather not claim for yourself, they will describe someone else or a situation instead. HOWEVER, 57.14 asks you to try your best to identify a personality first, a situation only as a last resort.

57.15 asks you to pick a **primary** behavior which you favor above the other members in a grand cross. When you're behaving this way, you tend to do so against a **primary interactant** person or situation. You also need to pick a *secondary behavior* you prefer when you don't have the energy or interest in engaging the primary pair. It occurs against a *secondary interactant*.

There are a couple of extras I have added to this chart which were not asked for in the scenario, but which I found very useful.

1. In general, the energy preferences in my chart tended to be smooth. You can see this in the flow of shaded areas. The exception occurred in two places where the preferences wanted to jump around. In both cases, I found that I tended to prefer both the 0° and the 90° behavior to it equally, rendering that section of my chart a kind of a) "always on" feature AND b) place where another person was required, since I effectively needed to be part of a binary setup in order to move energy constantly across my sphere in this way.
2. In some cases, to remind myself of my own life priorities, I noted the **[asteroids]** I'm most interested in building up. This helps with an at-a-glance understanding of the actual character of these roles. You can think of these asteroids as the bosses of their region, circumscribing the duodecanate's priorities. In particular, [asteroids] which appear in unshaded regions (e.g. Pauly) show characteristics I would look for in my partners, interactants, and contexts I put myself in; they are less likely to be behaviors which I adopt for myself.

   I found the unshaded role in the grand cross to be one of the strongest indicators of something you will never have or will rarely have for yourself in life; you'll need to tie yourself to another in order to get it. Formal committed partnerships (Juno)—part of the holy grail of American socialization—are an example of something I have less of. This activity made it clear why: I value its opposition cluster (12.5° Capricorn through 2.5° Aquarius) MUCH more strongly. As mentioned in bullet 1 above, I've found that you often need the help of another person in order to sustain a sudden spiked change in energy flow around the behavior wheel. In the case of things like money, partnerships, or status, you may find that you need a yet another partner in order to obtain a first shot at these areas. I've talked about this topic in several books prior, but this activity lets you see exactly where something like that occurs in your chart.)

# Appendix VI: Ajani's Answer to Question 57.14

| Grand Cross Group | Duo (#) Private Rising | Duo (#) Private Setting | Duo (#) Public Setting | Duo (#) Public Rising |
|---|---|---|---|---|
| 36 | 0°-2.5° Aries-12 (144 or 0) | 0°-2.5° Cancer-12 (108) | 0°-2.5° Libra-12 (72) | 0°-2.5° Capricorn-12 (36) |
| 36 | *interface: how people access your story* | social darlings, private | sexual-creative submissives, private standards | respected ones |
| 35 | 2.5°-5° Aries-11 (143) | 2.5°-5° Cancer-11 (107) | 2.5°-5° Libra-11 (71) | 2.5°-5° Capricorn-11 (35) |
| 35 | *music and media mood bridgers, the artists who produce this; creatives I am a fan of* | **[Velleda]** physical prowess, public | **[Padua]** *exhibitionists, co-creative open books & body models, public* | purposeful manipulators |
| 34 | 5°-7.5° Aries-10 (142) | 5°-7.5° Cancer-10 (106) | 5°-7.5° Libra-10 (70) | 5°-7.5° Capricorn-10 (34) |
| 34 | good trainers and instructors - mode | physical prowess, private | *exhibitionists, co-creative open books & body models, private* | **[Pauly]** experts |
| 33 | 7.5°-10° Aries-9 (141) | 7.5°-10° Cancer-9 (105) | 7.5°-10° Libra-9 (69) | 7.5°-10° Capricorn-9 (33) |
| 33 | professional athletes and other competitors | definition of a leader, public | *event hosts, public* | those singularly familiar with a particular topic, monopoly knowledge holders |
| 32 | 10°-12.5° Aries-8 (140) | 10°-12.5° Cancer-8 (104) | 10°-12.5° Libra-8 (68) | 10°-12.5° Capricorn-8 (32) |
| 32 | *life-changers, influencers, great coaches* | definition of a leader, context | event hosts, private life | driven perfectionists who often form fragile alliances; mercenary types |
| 31 | 12.5°-15° Aries-7 (139) | 12.5°-15° Cancer-7 (103) | 12.5°-15° Libra-7 (67) | 12.5°-15° Capricorn-7 (31) |
| 31 | *people who are satisfied and want to show it now* | masculine definition, public | socialites & trophies, public | language and culture-exclusive groups |
| 30 | 15°-17.5° Aries-6 (138) | 15°-17.5° Cancer-6 (102) | 15°-17.5° Libra-6 (66) | 15°-17.5° Capricorn-6 (30) |
| 30 | *the nature of sudden decisions, people choosing a new direction* | masculine definition, motivation | socialites & trophies, end effect | **[Selene (White Moon)]** individuals who are a template for an idea, models |
| 29 | 17.5°-20° Aries-5 (137) | 17.5°-20° Cancer-5 (101) | 17.5°-20° Libra-5 (65) | 17.5°-20° Capricorn-5 (29) |
| 29 | *holders of intuitive skill* | feminine definition, public | **[Pluto, Marlu]** *iconic stars, public reputation* | typecast representatives of a value-defined system |
| 28 | 20°-22.5° Aries-4 (136) | 20°-22.5° Cancer-4 (100) | 20°-22.5° Libra-4 (64) | 20°-22.5° Capricorn-4 (28) |
| 28 | **[Moon]** *singular enterprises, good mysteries* | feminine definition, what fulfills | pop-culture beloveds, humor, emotional appeal, and end effect | instillers of want |
| 27 | 22.5°-25° Aries-3 (135) | 22.5°-25° Cancer-3 (99) | 22.5°-25° Libra-3 (63) | 22.5°-25° Capricorn-3 (27) |
| 27 | *admission requirements* | advertising machine, pedestal personality, public | talents and career artists | intruders & disruptors |
| 26 | 25°-27.5° Aries-2 (134) | 25°-27.5° Cancer-2 (98) | 25°-27.5° Libra-2 (62) | 25°-27.5° Capricorn-2 (26) |
| 26 | party maker | **[Juno]** advertising machine, pedestal personality, promotable | **[Nolli, Diotima]** *invited guests* | **[Borasisi, Ophelia]** spokespeople, announcers, broadcasters |
| 25 | 27.5°-29.9° Aries-1 (133) | 27.5°-29.9° Cancer-1 (97) | 27.5°-29.9° Libra-1 (61) | 27.5°-29.9° Capricorn-1 (25) |
| 25 | visionary | rock stars, public | *watchable authorities* | system emperors, mob bosses, system admins |
| 24 | 0°-2.5° Taurus-12 (132) | 0°-2.5° Leo-12 (96) | 0°-2.5° Scorpio-12 (60) | 0°-2.5° Aquarius-12 (24) |
| 24 | ideal partner-friend power riser | **[Nuwa]** rock stars, home life [...Westphalia, Orcus] | **[America]** *top bosses* | **[Bilkis]** VIP organizations, snobs, entitled people |
| 23 | 2.5°-5° Taurus-11 (131) | 2.5°-5° Leo-11 (95) | 2.5°-5° Scorpio-11 (59) | 2.5°-5° Aquarius-11 (23) |
| 23 | mom, public | **[Siwa...]**: (my chain of cats) objectified associate; pet, impression | stepdad, mom's second man, journeyer no one can locate | **[Ninina]** power usurpers, elite clubs |
| 22 | 5°-7.5° Taurus-10 (130) | 5°-7.5° Leo-10 (94) | 5°-7.5° Scorpio-10 (58) | 5°-7.5° Aquarius-10 (22) |
| 22 | the mom, private | **[P.Fortune, Endymion]** objectified associate; pet, other-trigger | **[Veritas, Hidalgo, Agathe]** *the mom's ideal man, who* | managers of power systems |

| | | | she trains her sons to be, the brothers | |
|---|---|---|---|---|
| 21 | 7.5°-10° Taurus-9 (129) | 7.5°-10° Leo-9 (93) | 7.5°-10° Scorpio-9 (57) | 7.5°-10° Aquarius-9 (21) |
| 21 | the dad, public | self-broadcasters, towards the public | [Sun, Naema] people drawn to you; step-mom, dad's second woman, one who shows interest in you for inexplicable reasons, possibly despite themselves | popular people, hometown heroes, college jock, beauty queen |
| 20 | 10°-12.5° Taurus-8 (128) | 10°-12.5° Leo-8 (92) | 10°-12.5° Scorpio-8 (56) | 10°-12.5° Aquarius-8 (20) |
| 20 | dad, private | [Wilkens] self-broadcasters, end effect | [Agamemnon] dad's ideal woman, who he trains his daughters to be | [Interamnia] prolific artist / creative / intellect |
| 19 | 12.5°-15° Taurus-7 (127) | 12.5°-15° Leo-7 (91) | 12.5°-15° Scorpio-7 (55) | 12.5°-15° Aquarius-7 (19) |
| 19 | younger sibling, public | association commodity, public | what the younger sibling is asked to do in the world | viral personality, thought leaders, influencers |
| 18 | 15°-17.5° Taurus-6 (126) | 15°-17.5° Leo-6 (90) | 15°-17.5° Scorpio-6 (54) | 15°-17.5° Aquarius-6 (18) |
| 18 | younger sibling, private | association commodity, private | younger's bf/gf, committer, private life | governments, judges, referees |
| 17 | 17.5°-20° Taurus-5 (125) | 17.5°-20° Leo-5 (89) | 17.5°-20° Scorpio-5 (53) | 17.5°-20° Aquarius-5 (17) |
| 17 | older sibling, public | king of field, public | what the older sibling is asked to do in the world | masculine revolutionaries, secessionists, cult founders |
| 16 | 20°-22.5° Taurus-4 (124) | 20°-22.5° Leo-4 (88) | 20°-22.5° Scorpio-4 (52) | 20°-22.5° Aquarius-4 (16) |
| 16 | older sibling, private | [Mars] king of field, behind the scenes | [Uranus] older's bf/gf, committer, private life | feminine revolutionary & counterculture communication patterned groups |
| 15 | 22.5°-25° Taurus-3 (123) | 22.5°-25° Leo-3 (87) | 22.5°-25° Scorpio-3 (51) | 22.5°-25° Aquarius-3 (15) |
| 15 | partner, public | [Descendant] people who launch opportunity for others, public | what the partner is asked to do in the world | [Ascendant] masculine-dominated endeavors; professional opinionators |
| 14 | 25°-27.5° Taurus-2 (122) | 25°-27.5° Leo-2 (86) | 25°-27.5° Scorpio-2 (50) | 25°-27.5° Aquarius-2 (14) |
| 14 | partner, private | people who launch opportunity for others, expectations | what the partner is preoccupied with | feminine-dominated enterprises |
| 13 | 27.5°-29.9° Taurus-1 (121) | 27.5°-29.9° Leo-1 (85) | 27.5°-29.9° Scorpio-1 (49) | 27.5°-29.9° Aquarius-1 (13) |
| 13 | friends, public | [Augusta, Fortuna, Hooveria, Epyaxa]: (α male feminism...); transgender, intersex, public | [Venus, Priska] realm which the friends belong in, representing a movement; role group work | royal, star couples, masculine-feminine combination endeavors |
| 12 | 0°-2.5° Gemini-12 (120) | 0°-2.5° Virgo-12 (84) | 0°-2.5° Sagittarius-12 (48) | 0°-2.5° Pisces-12 (12) |
| 12 | friends, private | [Kastalia, Ute, Hybris]: (...bi-gender favoring); transgender, intersex, private | how you support your friends, your favored teachers | aspired-to lifestyle holders |
| 11 | 2.5°-5° Gemini-11 (119) | 2.5°-5° Virgo-11 (83) | 2.5°-5° Sagittarius-11 (47) | 2.5°-5° Pisces-11 (11) |
| 11 | [May, Crescentia] most valuable supporter, public | celibates & nonsexuals, public | [Ohio, Franziska, Tirza, Camelia, Signe, Mercury] what and how you learn, lessons you absorb, most valuable supporter's context; who they strive to please; insistent influence | non-domesticatable beasts |
| 10 | 5°-7.5° Gemini-10 (118) | 5°-7.5° Virgo-10 (82) | 5°-7.5° Sagittarius-10 (46) | 5°-7.5° Pisces-10 (10) |
| 10 | most valuable supporter, private | [North Node, Triberga] celibates & nonsexuals, private | most valuable supporter's interests, friend-dynamics | [Berolina, Lysistrata]: (Dao/Buddhism) impossibilities, mythical personas, spiritual rule makers |

# Appendix VI: Ajani's Answer to Question 57.14

| | | | | |
|---|---|---|---|---|
| 9 | 7.5°-10° Gemini-9 (117) | 7.5°-10° Virgo-9 (81) | 7.5°-10° Sagittarius-9 (45) | 7.5°-10° Pisces-9 (9) |
| 9 | **[Imum Coeli, Roma]** bf/gf co-creative consort, public | *gays, public & social* | **[Midheaven, Bacchus, Antares (fixed star), Begzhigitova]** the world you provide for bf/gf, a phenomenon which has fans, your version of a cult figure | *questers* |
| 8 | 10°-12.5° Gemini-8 (116) | 10°-12.5° Virgo-8 (80) | 10°-12.5° Sagittarius-8 (44) | 10°-12.5° Pisces-8 (8) |
| 8 | bf/gf co-creative consort, private | *gays, personal life & private* | what bf/gf/co-creator seeks from you, founders you pay attention to | **[Poesia]** *bequeathers, quest assigners and initiators* |
| 7 | 12.5°-15° Gemini-7 (115) | 12.5°-15° Virgo-7 (79) | 12.5°-15° Sagittarius-7 (43) | 12.5°-15° Pisces-7 (7) |
| 7 | **[Varuna, Roswitha, Hypatia]: (recording)** assistant/right hand, public | **[Vertex, Lilith, Hertha]: (frequent interactant)** *countersexuals, deviants, public* | **[Brambilla]:(writing)** assistant's context, your clients; those you need a system for engaging | **[Zubaida, Xanthe]: (unsatisfiability)** *power-hungry people, villains* |
| 6 | 15°-17.5° Gemini-6 (114) | 15°-17.5° Virgo-6 (78) | 15°-17.5° Sagittarius-6 (42) | 15°-17.5° Pisces-6 (6) |
| 6 | *assistant/right hand, private* | *countersexuals, deviants, private* | your assistant's fuel source, preoccupation; what you need assistance with; what you can only do through them | the land where the adventure takes place, quest context |
| 5 | 17.5°-20° Gemini-5 (113) | 17.5°-20° Virgo-5 (77) | 17.5°-20° Sagittarius-5 (41) | 17.5°-20° Pisces-5 (5) |
| 5 | role model, public | **[Zeus, Kreusa]: (ASMR maintenance duties soundmaker)** *multipartners & poly, public* | **[Neptune]** the role model's public; your desired public | **[Hera]** the ultimate power which may be conceivably wielded, especially in an imagined setting |
| 4 | 20°-22.5° Gemini-4 (112) | 20°-22.5° Virgo-4 (76) | 20°-22.5° Sagittarius-4 (40) | 20°-22.5° Pisces-4 (4) |
| 4 | *role model, private* | promiscuous wanters, end effect | *fuel originators, role model's driver, teacher's teacher who can also teach you* | **[Moultona]** work of the mad scientist or singularly dedicated builder |
| 3 | 22.5°-25° Gemini-3 (111) | 22.5°-25° Virgo-3 (75) | 22.5°-25° Sagittarius-3 (39) | 22.5°-25° Pisces-3 (3) |
| 3 | *admired strangers, public* | **[Saturn, Neally]** sexual-creative dominants, public | *inventors* | retirement, post-achievement communication pattern; one who has completed the mission |
| 2 | 25°-27.5° Gemini-2 (110) | 25°-27.5° Virgo-2 (74) | 25°-27.5° Sagittarius-2 (38) | 25°-27.5° Pisces-2 (2) |
| 2 | *admired strangers, private* | **[Berbericia, Hohensteina]** sexual-creative dominants, private | *champions* | **[Philippa, Bouzareah, Nysa]** ultimate entity, highest embodiment of spiritual aspiration |
| 1 | 27.5°-29.9° Gemini-1 (109) | 27.5°-29.9° Virgo-1 (73) | 27.5°-29.9° Sagittarius-1 (37) | 27.5°-29.9° Pisces-1 (1) |
| 1 | **[Laurentia]** *social darlings, public* | **[Siri, Zelia]** sexual-creative submissives, public | **[Sulamitis, Delila]** *those elevated above others* | your story, the lesson it ultimately conveys; favorite stories and quests |

# Index

100%+ relationship ............................................ 209, 236
1992 QB1/Albion ........................... 67, 177, 353, 381
4-cycle ................................................................... 23, 85
active object reading ................................................ 338
activity
    45.01.01 (Instinctual starter) ............................... 13
    45.01.02 (Major starts) ........................................ 14
    45.01.03 (Involved in the start) ........................... 14
    45.01.04 (Evolved from the start) ....................... 14
    45.01.05 (Start reaction) ..................................... 15
    45.01.06 (Start's aftermath) ................................ 15
    45.01.07 (Why you begin) ................................... 15
    45.02.01 (Self-description) ................................. 17
    45.02.02 (A key partner) ..................................... 17
    45.02.03 (Do you complement?) ......................... 18
    45.03.01 (The once disrespected) ........................ 22
    45.03.02 (Respected words) ................................ 23
    45.03.03 (A respected person) ............................ 23
    45.03.04 (Transition words) ................................ 24
    45.04.01 (Places you "live" in) ............................ 26
    45.04.02 (Central plot-advancing characters) 27
    45.04.03 (Central plot activities) ......................... 27
    45.04.04 (Good call reception) ............................ 29
    45.05.01 (How did I get here?) ............................ 33
    45.05.02 (Reasons for the summon) ................... 33
    45.05.03 (You've been briefed, they haven't) . 34
    45.05.04 (Providing for the one who doesn't know) ............................................................... 34
    45.05.05 (Why the summoner called) ................ 35
    45.05.06 (Other motivations for summoning) 35
    45.05.07 (Other uses for the summoned) .......... 35
    45.05.08 (Summoned one's best task completion ....................................................... 35
    45.06.01 (The fixation) ........................................ 37
    45.06.02 (The problem statement) ..................... 37
    45.06.03 (Room for the calling) .......................... 37
    45.06.04 (Aligned actions) .................................. 38
    45.06.05 (Align THIS week!) ............................... 38
    45.06.06 (Do 45.6.5) ............................................ 38
    45.07.01 (Patterns you like) ................................ 40
    45.07.02 (Directed patterns) ............................... 40
    45.07.03 (Pattern heights) ................................... 40
    45.07.04 (Favored senses) ................................... 40
    45.07.05 (Abstract) (You as an instrument) .... 40
    45.07.06 (Them as a musician) ........................... 40
    45.07.07 (Your music) ......................................... 40
    45.07.08 (The sounds made) ............................... 40
    45.07.09 (Your overall best "instrument") ....... 40
    45.08.01 (Where you would faithfully serve) .. 42
    45.08.02 (Uneasy service) ................................... 43
    45.08.03 (The rewards of service) ...................... 44
    45.08.04 (Service extractors) .............................. 44
    45.08.05 (Time to bring out your power) ......... 45
    45.09.01 (The upsetters) ..................................... 47
    45.09.02 (The upsetters who actually exist) .... 50
    45.09.03 (Transitioning from the nonexistent upsetters) ........................................................... 50
    45.09.04 (What makes a nonexistent upsetter?) ............................................................................ 51
    45.09.05 (YOU as the upsetter) .......................... 51
    45.09.06 (Your summary as an upsetter) ......... 51
    45.10.01 (Government job match) ..................... 54
    45.10.02 (Piecing together a career-like field)54
    45.10.03 (The real issue with government) ..... 56
    45.10.04 (You are the remedy) ............................ 56
    45.10.05 (The fixer) ............................................. 57
    45.11.01 (Information sources) ........................... 58
    45.11.02 (Informational themes) ........................ 59
    45.11.03 (Thumbs down products) .................... 60
    45.11.04 (Informational blurb) ........................... 60
    45.11.05 (Information source abbreviation) ... 61
    45.11.06 (Paint the picture) ................................ 62
    45.11.07 (Spirit picture analysis) ........................ 64
    45.11.08 (Bonus) (Informational shields) ........ 65
    45.11.09 (Informational health foods) .............. 65
    45.12.01 (The senses, one by one) ..................... 70
    45.12.02 (Sense weighting) ................................. 70
    45.12.03 (Sense pipelines) ................................... 71
    45.12.04 (Primary intuition gateway) ............... 71
    45.12.05 (The senses one by one, narrated) .... 72
    45.13 (Sign quiz) .................................................. 76
    46.01 (Head region) ............................................. 86
    46.02 (Torso region) ............................................ 86
    46.03 (Overall body plan) ................................... 86
    46.04 (Surrounding information) ....................... 87
    46.05 (How you display want) ........................... 88
    46.06 (Close friends) ............................................ 88
    46.07 (Co-influencers) ......................................... 88
    46.08 (Follow up influence question) ................ 88
    46.09 (Your sex) .................................................... 88
    46.10 (A rough height effect) ............................. 89
    46.11 (A rough body size effect) ........................ 91
    46.12 (Follow up) ................................................. 92
    46.13 (A universal value) .................................... 93

| Entry | Page |
|---|---|
| 46.14 (Important follow up) | 93 |
| 46.15 (Important follow up 2) | 94 |
| 46.16 (Your [Foreign Worlds] heritage) | 95 |
| 46.17 (Your supporters) | 96 |
| 46.18 (Your supporters 2) | 96 |
| 46.19 (Focused areas) | 97 |
| 47.01 (The tuning list) | 108 |
| 47.02 (The unattuned list) | 109 |
| 47.03 (Chords) | 110 |
| 47.04 (Name the column) | 110 |
| 47.05 (Reaction direction) | 110 |
| 47.06 (Reaction intensity) | 110 |
| 47.07 (Reaction sense modality) | 111 |
| 47.08 (Critical clairaudience practice) | 115 |
| 47.09 (Clairaudient conversation practice) | 116 |
| 47.10 (Bodily feeling survey) | 117 |
| 47.11 (Feel the history of an object) | 118 |
| 47.12 (Read a common object) | 119 |
| 47.13 (Seeing an invisible message source) | 123 |
| 47.14 (Commonly projected dream roles) | 124 |
| 47.15 (Commonly projected waking roles) | 125 |
| 47.16 (Reaction wheel assignments) | 126 |
| 47.17 (Identify the real events) | 127 |
| 47.18 (Future reference) | 127 |
| 47.19 (You just know) | 128 |
| 47.20 (You just don't know) | 129 |
| 47.21 (Claircognizance practice) | 129 |
| 47.22 (Your clairvoyant indicators) | 133 |
| 47.23 (Your clairvoyant bases) | 133 |
| 47.24 (The Clairvoyant Oath) | 134 |
| 47.25 (Your highest empathy) | 137 |
| 47.26 (Determining which emotions you should want more of) | 138 |
| 47.27 (Empathy practice for emotions you want more of) | 139 |
| 47.28 (Telepathic receivers) | 139 |
| 47.29 (Easier telepathic messaging) | 139 |
| 47.30 (Easier sources of intuitive practice) | 141 |
| 48.01 (Confirmation of multidimensionality) | 143 |
| 48.02 (The Sphere) | 145 |
| 48.03 (The history of your sphere) | 149 |
| 48.04 (Packages with holes) | 151 |
| 48.05 (The main actors in your current scene) | 153 |
| 48.06 (Past this point) | 154 |
| 48.07 (Targeting the right dimension) | 157 |
| 48.08 (Accepting the right help) | 157 |
| 48.09 (Remove a hole) | 160 |
| 49.01 (Your favorite and least favorite conflicts) | 163 |
| 49.02 (Your overall conflict approach) | 164 |
| 49.03 (Summary of your conflict preferences) | 164 |
| 49.04 (Optional conflict read) | 165 |
| 49.05 (Where is Chiron?) | 170 |
| 49.06 (Where is your Moon?) | 172 |
| 49.07 (Conflict analysis) | 176 |
| 49.08 (Conflict reduction) | 177 |
| 49.09 (Open another's door) | 177 |
| 49.10 (Your full asteroid list) | 180 |
| 49.11 (Recasting an Anti-Principle) | 191 |
| 49.12 (Your top obstacle) | 192 |
| 49.13 (Have you graduated past basic conflict?) | 195 |
| 50.01 (Your better endings) | 199 |
| 50.02 (Catharsis 1) | 202 |
| 50.03 (Empowered helpers) | 202 |
| 50.04 (A repeatable statement) | 203 |
| 50.05 (Testing purposes) | 203 |
| 51.01 (The place you grow the most) | 211 |
| 51.02 (Separating the growth from the challenge) | 211 |
| 51.03 (Moving the challenge outside of the growth place) | 212 |
| 51.04 (A piece of heaven) | 212 |
| 51.05 (The perfect activity) | 213 |
| 51.06 (Who's who of the tribe) | 213 |
| 51.07 (The mastery continues) | 213 |
| 51.08 (I love being here…) | 215 |
| 51.09 (3 slots) | 217 |
| 51.10 (What the slot characteristic represents to me) | 218 |
| 51.11 (What are these slots telling me?) | 219 |
| 51.12 (What kind of attitude am I encouraged to have for each slot?) | 220 |
| 51.13 (What's my existential language?) | 225 |
| 51.14 (Observations from the phenomenon table) | 225 |
| 51.15 (An hour in the language, abstract) | 229 |
| 52.01 (What's your sphere?) | 238 |
| 52.02 (What are your conflicts?) | 238 |
| 52.03 (If there is conflict, why?) | 238 |
| 52.04 (Conflict resolution) | 238 |
| 52.05 (Necessary rifts) | 238 |
| 52.06 (Have you pulled the trigger?) | 239 |
| 52.07 (Have you found most or all of your tribe-spaces?) | 239 |
| 52.08 (Are you free to be a master?) | 239 |
| 52.09 (Top seed) | 239 |
| 52.10 (The person others wish you were) | 241 |
| 52.11 (The critic in a few sentences) | 243 |
| 52.12 (The general grapevine) | 243 |
| 52.13 (Your first line) | 244 |
| 52.14 (Tied to the times) | 244 |
| 52.15 (You as the skeptical stranger) | 244 |
| 52.16 (The catalyst) | 244 |
| 52.17 (The purposeful faults) | 245 |
| 52.18 (What kinds of tension are you prone to?) | 246 |
| 52.19 (Tension paths) | 248 |

- 52.20 (Your kind of tension) .............................. 249
- 52.21 (You're immune to that, part 1) ............. 249
- 52.22 (You're immune to that, part 2) ............. 250
- 52.23 (Your interest groups) ............................ 252
- 52.24 (Edge of the curve) ................................. 253
- 52.25 (Width of the window) ........................... 253
- 52.26 (Your beneficiaries) ................................ 253
- 52.27 (Those who hoped for you) .................... 254
- 52.28 (What were your senses again?) ........... 254
- 52.29 (Insights from your senses) ................... 255
- 52.30 (Your bio) ................................................ 256
- 53.01 (They don't even know their friends, part 1) ................................................................. 259
- 53.02 (They don't even know their friends, part 2) ................................................................. 259
- 53.03 ("Better" friends) .................................... 261
- 53.04 (Qualities of a good friend) .................... 262
- 53.05 (Kindred and your Role) ......................... 264
- 53.06 (Observations of Kindred) ...................... 266
- 53.07 (Our friend dynamics rearranged) ........ 267
- 53.08 (Observations from the friend table) .. 268
- 53.09 (A smaller source of friend interactions) .......................................................................... 268
- 53.10 (Other priorities) .................................... 269
- 53.11 (The attitude that gains you good friends) .......................................................................... 273
- 53.12 (Friendship fuel) ..................................... 274
- 53.13 (The Unknown) ....................................... 276
- 53.14 (The friend who trains vision-projection) .......................................................................... 276
- 53.15 (Exercise your clairvoyance with your trainer friend) ............................................... 278
- 54.01 (Paths to knowing) .................................. 282
- 54.02 (Rate your senses) .................................. 286
- 54.03 (The audience you want) ........................ 288
- 54.04 (How you want to be seen) ..................... 289
- 54.05 (When is the best time to seed your own dreams?) ....................................................... 290
- 54.06 (Find someone who has the power to project) .......................................................... 291
- 54.07.01 (The projection request, part 1) ..... 292
- 54.07.02 (The projection request, part 2) ..... 293
- 54.07.03 (The projection request, part 3) ..... 293
- 54.07.04 (How you show up in Other-dreams) .......................................................................... 295
- 54.07.05 (The memorable symbol) .................. 296
- 54.07.06 (What causes you to project?) ......... 297
- 54.07.07 (Your simple route to projection) .. 297
- 54.07.08 (Efficient projection) ......................... 297
- 54.07.09 (An optimal Other) .............................. 298
- 54.07.10 (Your projection Other) ..................... 300
- 54.07.11 (Psychic projection) ............................ 301
- 54.07.12 (Did you succeed?) ............................. 302
- 54.08.01 (Imagining in tongues) ....................... 307
- 54.08.02 (What would The Waking Me do?) 309
- 54.08.03 (Stars of the show) .............................. 310
- 54.08.04 (Dream reasons) .................................. 312
- 54.08.05 (OOB reasons) ..................................... 313
- 54.08.06 (How to fly) .......................................... 321
- 54.08.07 (Topic space) ....................................... 323
- 54.08.08 (Forward and backward in your own records) ......................................................... 323
- 54.08.09 (Inward and outward along the world's timeline) ......................................... 324
- 54.08.10 (Higher and lower in world detail) 325
- 54.08.11 (Parallel universes) ............................ 326
- 54.09.01 (Touched by a vibration) ................... 332
- 54.09.02 (Touch to a memory) .......................... 334
- 54.09.03 (Where the activity happens) ........... 338
- 54.09.04 (Active object reading ........................ 339
- 54.09.05 (See it coming) .................................... 341
- 54.09.06 (Gather the warning data) ................ 341
- 54.09.07 (Gravitation) ........................................ 341
- 54.09.08 (Gather the validating data) ............. 341
- 54.09.09 (Where the information comes from) .......................................................................... 341
- 54.09.10 (Training vision-cognitive clairsentience) ............................................. 342
- 54.09.11 (What you would tell the room) ...... 344
- 54.09.12 (Your message, your Role) ................ 345
- 54.09.13 (Regulate the emotions put upon you) .......................................................................... 345
- 54.10.01 (Your nowhere source) ...................... 347
- 54.10.02 (Verifying what you've gotten) ........ 347
- 54.10.03 (Honing the clairvoyance) ................. 347
- 54.10.04 (further clairvoyance) ........................ 348
- 54.10.05 (A tour of three tools) ........................ 350
- 54.10.06 (Your burning question) .................... 352
- 54.10.07 (Your burning question as a "capacity" issue) ............................................................. 355
- 54.10.08 (What does the chart tell you?) ....... 356
- 54.10.09 (How should you approach your question?) ..................................................... 356
- 54.10.10 (Consult the I-Ching) .......................... 356
- 54.10.11 (What does life want?) ....................... 357
- 54.10.12 (Consult the Tarot) .............................. 357
- 54.11.01 (A talk with your guardians) ............. 360
- 54.11.02 (A short story of you) ......................... 360
- 54.11.03 (Spoken channel) ................................ 361
- 54.12.01 (Gravity) ................................................ 362
- 54.12.02 (Your creation) .................................... 363
- 54.12.03 (The rounds) ........................................ 363
- 54.13.01 (What they motivate) ......................... 365
- 54.13.02 (The unique energy of the motivators [Challenging]) .............................................. 366
- 54.13.03 (The energy that calls you) ............... 367
- 54.13.04 (Resonant others) ............................... 368
- 54.13.05 (Theme messages) .............................. 368
- 54.13.06 (Hypnotize them) ................................ 369
- 54.13.07 (Messages of encouragement) ......... 370

# Index

55.01 (Question 49.10/Your full asteroid list again) .................................................. 383
55.01.01 (Astro at a glance, easy) ............... 386
55.01.02 (Astro at a glance, hard) .............. 387
55.01.03 (Astro at a glance, summary) ...... 387
55.02.01 (Create a relative chart) ............... 393
55.02.02 (Doorway to the past) .................. 395
55.02.03 (Revisiting the potential) .............. 396
55.02.04 (The last thing) ............................. 397
55.02.05 (Maybe not the last thing) ........... 398
55.02.06 (Doubts) ........................................ 398
55.03.01 (Easy summons) ............................ 403
55.03.02 (Easy summons chart) .................. 403
55.03.03 (Determine their powers) ............ 405
55.03.04 (The One that Got Away) ............. 407
55.03.05 (On Being Summmoned) .............. 410
55.03.06 (Know what YOU would want... from them) ................................................. 414
55.03.07 (How you amplify) ........................ 415
55.03.08 (What you want from them...to you)(part 1) ............................................ 416
55.03.09 (What you want from them...to you)(part 2) ............................................ 417
55.03.10 (What you want from them...to you)(part 3) ............................................ 417
55.03.11 (Showtime) ................................... 418
55.03.12 (What they want from you...to them)(part 1) ......................................... 419
55.03.13 (What they want from you...to them)(part 2) ......................................... 421
55.03.14 (What you both need from some other) .................................................... 422
56.01 (Check-in) .......................................... 432
56.02 (relationship quirks, dissatisfaction) .. 434
56.03 (relationship quirks, authority) ......... 434
56.04 (Feel the difference power vs authority) ...................................................... 434
56.05 (If you were to change yourself...) ... 437
56.06 (A sense of where. A sense of what. A sense of how) ....................................... 439
56.07 (The quest for riches) ....................... 441
56.08 (The quest for social mobility) ......... 442
56.09 (The quest for whatever) .................. 442
56.10 (Because of negative opinionation...) . 446
57.01 (The unifying front – cast of characters) ................................................................ 451
57.02 (The unifying front – common cause) 451
57.03 (The unifying front – end goal) ........ 452
57.04 (Question 57.1 revisited) .................. 452
57.05 (The Nickname) ................................. 452
57.06 (Advancing the individuals) ............... 453
57.07 (Unblocking the individuals) ............. 453
57.08 (Your shadow) .................................... 454
57.09 (Shadow connection) ......................... 454
57.10 (The story of the shadow role) ......... 455
57.11 (Why wait) .......................................... 455
57.12 (Silent participants) ........................... 455
57.13 (Initiation) .......................................... 455
57.14 (Grand Cross Cast) ............................. 458
57.15 (Your favorite roles) ........................... 460
Critical Exercise (51.9 – 51.12) ................... 217
Critical Exercise (Part 1 of 2), BODY WHEELS 98
Critical Exercise (Part 1 of 3), CONFLICT ANALYSIS ............................................... 176
Critical Exercise (Part 2 of 2), FLOW OF THE BODY TYPE ............................................ 102
Critical Exercise (Part 2 of 3), CONFLICT RESULT SHORTCUT ................................ 177
Critical Exercise (Part 3 of 3), CONFLICT REWRITING ............................................ 177
Critical Exercise, 7-DAY HOLE CHALLENGE . 160
Critical Exercise, AN HOUR IN THE LANGUAGE ................................................................ 229
Critical Exercise, ASTROLOGICAL SIGN QUIZ .. 76
Critical Exercise, BEGIN TO SERVE ............. 45
Critical Exercise, FOR DREAM PROJECTORS . 299
Critical Exercise, GRAND CROSS ROLES ..... 457
Critical Exercise, HOW TO ASK THE MOST IMPORTANT QUESTIONS ........................ 352
Critical Exercise, OBSTACLE REWRITING CHALLENGE ............................................ 191
Critical Exercise, SPHERE TIMELINE .......... 149
Critical Exercise, SPIRIT PICTURE ............... 61
Critical Exercise, THE BELIEF ABOUT GOOD FRIENDSHIPS .......................................... 270
Critical Exercise, THE BROADCASTER ........ 410
Critical Exercise, THE ONE THAT GOT AWAY ................................................................ 407
Critical Exercise, THE PLAYLIST ................... 29
Critical Exercise, THE ROLE ........................ 256
Critical Exercise, TOWARDS AN ANSWER ... 38
Critical Exercise, TRACK YOUR DEVELOPMENT OF THE SENSES ..................................... 286
get an astrology chart .................................. 31
great to serve ............................................... 42
introduction, Cancer ................................... 26
introduction, dimension Aries .................... 13
introduction, dimension Gemini .............. 3, 20
introduction, dimension Leo ........................ 2
introduction, dimension Taurus ................. 16
Other's other conflicts ............................... 199
sharable idea ............................................... 68
Adele ......................................................... 456
Agamemnon .......................... 166, 184, 189, 437
Agathe ............................................... 184, 189
Aglaja ........................................................ 419
Albion ............................... See 1992 QB1/Albion
*All 144 Aspects* ........................ 128, 166, 443
allies .......................................................... 261
Alma ............................................................ 41

Amalia ..................................................... 179
Anna ........................................................ 441
Anti-Neptune ................................... 354, 382
Aquarius ............................................ 32, 375
    duodecanates .................................... 428
    realm ..................................................... 58
Aries ................................................... 32, 375
    duodecanates .................................... 448
    realm ..................................................... 12
Ascendant ................................ 355, 375, 380
    relative chart ..................................... 391
Aslog ................................................. 353, 381
ASMR ...................................................... 332
aspects ................................................... 376
    01 conjunct ........................................ 376
    02 opposition .................................... 376
    03 trine ............................................... 376
    04 square .................................... 376, 377
    05 quintile .......................................... 377
    06 sextile ............................................ 377
    07 septile ........................................... 377
    08 octile .............................................. 377
    09 novile ............................................. 377
    10 decile ............................................. 377
    11 undecile ......................................... 377
    12 inconjunct ..................................... 377
    13 II-conjunct .................................... 377
    14 II-opposition ................................. 377
    15 II-trine ........................................... 377
    16 II-square ........................................ 377
    17 II-quintile ...................................... 377
    18 II-sextile ........................................ 377
    19 II-septile ....................................... 377
    20 II-octile ......................................... 377
    21 II-novile ........................................ 377
    22 II-decile ........................................ 377
    23 II-undecile .................................... 378
    24 II-inconjunct ................................. 378
    25 III-conjunct ................................... 378
    26 III-opposition ................................ 378
    27 III-trine ......................................... 378
    28 III-square ...................................... 378
    29 III-quintile .................................... 378
    30 III-sextile ...................................... 378
    31 III-septile ..................................... 378
    32 III-octile ....................................... 378
    33 III-novile ...................................... 378
    34 III-decile ....................................... 378
    35 III-undecile ............................ 376, 378
    36 III-inconjunct ............................... 378
assisted clairvoyance ....... *See* clairvoyance, assisted
astral navigation ..................................... 322
astral plane (map) .................................... 319
astral projection ............................... 303–22
astral travel

    forgetting ........................................... 306
    levels of ............................................. 305
    navigation .................................. 317–22
    overwriting ....................................... 305
astral traveling body ............................... 304
astrology chart
    reading .............................................. 383
Atalante ........................................... 353, 381
Ate ............................................................ 67
Athalia ..................................................... 190
attention ................................................. 112
authority .................................................. 52
authority versus power ........................... 434
Bacchus ................................... 353, 380, 456
    in the relative chart .......................... 393
Barcelona ................................................ 184
Beatrix ..................................................... 190
Begzhigitova ........................................... 456
behavior
    ally-like .............................................. 264
    kindred-like ....................................... 264
    personal friend-like .......................... 264
being summoned
    training .............................................. 410
Benda .............................................. 354, 381
beneficiaries .................................... 251–57
Berolina .................................................... 67
Bethgea ................................................... 179
Bezovec ................................................... 412
Bienor ..................................................... 438
Big Bang ................................................. 373
Bilkis ................................................ 355, 382
biomanufacture ............................... 112, 128
*Black Male Feminism* ............................. 179
blame ...................................................... 156
blessed talent ......................................... 354
body ............................................. *See* planet
    geographic origin ............................... 94
    geometry ............................................ 83
    height .................................................. 89
    race ..................................................... 92
    sex ............................................... 88, 102
    weight ................................................. 90
Bohemia ................................................... 67
Brambilla ......................................... 355, 382
Brendelia ................................................ 179
Burnhamia ...................................... 353, 381
Caia ................................................. 354, 381
calculated magic ........................ 9, 283, 404
calling ...................................................... 37
Cancer .............................................. 32, 375
    and riches ......................................... 440
    duodecanates .................................... 438
    realm ................................................... 25
capital ..................................................... 231

# Index

Capricorn .................................................. 32, 375
   duodecanates ........................................ 429
   realm ..................................................... 52
career ...................................... 53, 54, 57, 353
Ceres ............................................................ 380
channeled writing ..................................... 359
channeling ................................................. 359
charged objects ................................... 335–40
Child ................................................... 353, 381
Chiron ...................... 169, 184, 189, 354, 380
   formula ................................................ 169
Chryseis .............................................. 353, 381
circumplex .................................................... 87
clairaudience .............................................. 115
   developing ..................................... 358–62
   speaking in tongues .............................. 361
   training ............................................. 29, 229
clairaudient narrative ................................ 359
claircognizance ........................................... 127
   developing ..................................... 362–64
   training ............... 38, 45, 61, 149, 176, 191, 256
clairgustance .............................................. 140
clairsentience ............................................. 116
   developing ..................................... 323–45
   empathic ......................................... 343–45
   touch-based .................................... 329–35
   training ............................................. 61, 229
   vision-cognitive .............................. 340–43
clairvoyance ............................................... 130
   approach .............................................. 278
   assisted ............................................ 348–58
   developing ............................... 132, 346–58
   hypothesis ............................................ 131
   training ....................... 61, 98, 149, 160, 352
   unassisted ...................................... 346–48
Clara ............................................................ 190
Clarissa ............................................ 166, 355, 382
cognition ..................................................... 112
collections .................................................. 353
color ............................................................. 121
communion and agency ............................... 85
complementary points ............................... 443
composite chart .......................................... 401
conflict ............................................... 163, 184
   and character combinations .............. 179
   cutting ties with friends and family .... 197
   opponent ............................................. 177
   rift and possessions ........................ 204–6
conjunct energies ....................................... 385
conjuncts ........................................... 184, 195
contextual memory ...................................... 21
creative expression .................................... 353
creative works ............................................ 353
cusp ............................................................. 375
Damocles ..................................................... 184
dark spirits .................................................. 228
Davida ................................................. 184, 189
Davison charts ........................... *See* relative chart
decanates .................................................... 443
deception .................................................... 189
Delila ................................................... 184, 189, 190
demons ....................................................... 228
Descendant
   relative chart ....................................... 391
Desiderata .................................................. 189
Dido ............................................................... 67
Dionysus ..................................................... 437
Diotima ............................................... 171, 355, 382
divination tools .......................................... 350
Dodona .......................................................... 67
dream interpretability
   training ................................................ 149
dream interpretation
   training .................................................. 76
dream recall ............................................... 307
dream representation ................................ 296
dream symbols .................................. 126, 311
dreams ................................... 107, 124, 290
   controlling ...................................... 308–11
   lucid versus regular ............................ 308
   seeding and timing ............................. 290
duodecanates ..................................... 67, 427
El Djezair ............................................ 353, 381
elements ..................................................... 376
   air ......................................................... 376
   earth .................................................... 376
   fire ....................................................... 376
   water ................................................... 376
embodiment ....................................... 92, 106
emotional capital ............................... 231, 233
emotions .................................................... 137
empathic clairsentience ........ *See* clairsentience, empathic
empathicness
   and information control ..................... 328
empathy ............................................. 134, 137
   training ............................... 29, 191, 270
Endymion ........................................... 184, 189
energy resonances ..................................... 328
Eros ............................................................. 380
essential knowledge
   training ......................... 76, 102, 160, 286
Eurykleia ............................................ 354, 382
Eurynome ................................... 41, 354, 382
Fabiola ........................................................ 185
familial dynamics ....................................... 267
fast-forwarding .......................................... 278
father role ............................................. 52, 54
Feronia ............................................... 354, 381
foreign audiences ........................................ 48

friends ............................................................. 261
friendship ........................................................ 353
   and attitude ............................................ 271
   types ........................................................... 260
Fringilla .................................................. 353, 381
*Full Spectrum Astrology* ...................... 180, 356
function tangle ............................................. 331
Gemini ...................................................... 32, 375
   duodecanates ............................................ 445
   realm ............................................................. 19
Genua .............................................................. 411
Gerlinde .......................................................... 354
government ............................................... 53, 55
grand cross roles ........................................ 457
gravitational field ....................................... 373
group soul ..................................................... 244
growing apart .............................................. 260
guardians ...................................................... 219
Gutemberga .................................................. 190
Gyldenia ........................................................ 190
Hamiltonia ............................................ 185, 189
happiness ........................................................ 66
Harmonia ...................................................... 438
harmonic levels ........................................... 376
harmonics .............................................. 376–78
Harvard .................................................. 168, 171
*Hayden's Book of Synastry* ........................ 402
hearing ................................................... 111, 115
Hedwig .................................................. 354, 381
Helwerthia ............................................ 189, 353, 381
Hephaistos ........................................... 353, 381
Hera ................................................. 67, 354, 380
   in the relative chart ................................. 393
Hilda ............................................................... 441
holes ....................................................... 151, 159
honor ................................................................ 21
Hopi ................................................................ 456
house systems ............................................. 375
houses ............................................................ 374
Hygiea .............................................................. 67
Hypatia ............................................ 185, 189, 353, 381
Hypsipyle ........................................................ 67
I-ching ............................................................ 350
identity ............................................................ 16
identity mirrors ............................................. 18
Imum Coeli .................................................. 403
   relative chart ............................................ 391
Industria ....................................................... 190
inertial attention ......................................... 417
influence .......................................................... 41
influence over others ................................ 354
inheritance .................................................. 355
Inna ................................................................. 179
internal monologue ..................................... 19
interpersonal circumplex ....................... 85, 92

intuition ................................................... 71, 274
   Pisces vs Scorpio vs Cancer styles of ........ 439
intuition, a theory of ..................................... 73
intuitive development .............................. 192
Irmintraud ........................................ 177, 355, 382
Iva .......................................................... 354, 381
Janina ............................... 166, 185, 189, 354, 381
Juno ........................................................ 171, 354, 380
   in the relative chart ................................. 393
Jupiter ............................................................ 380
Justitia ................................................... 354, 381
kindred ........................................................... 261
Kressida ......................................................... 412
last body (in an astro chart) ................... 398
*Laurentia* . 5, 28, 180, 291, 318, 355, 361, 382, 384,
   390, 440
leadership potential ................................... 354
learning ......................................................... 281
Leo ............................................................ 32, 375
   duodecanates ............................................ 436
   realm ............................................................. 30
Leonisis ......................................................... 189
Liberatrix ............................................... 185, 189
Libra ......................................................... 32, 375
   duodecanates ............................................ 431
   realm ............................................................. 39
   squares to ............................................ 432–35
life path ......................................................... 355
   training ... 102, 149, 160, 176, 191, 217, 256, 457
light body ..................................................... 305
light travel .................................................... 307
Lilith ............................................................... 380
Lipperta ......................................................... 185
LSRI ................................................................ 390
lucid dreaming ............................................ 308
Lucina .............................................................. 67
Lumiere ......................................................... 354
Lysistrata ....................................... 67, 185, 354, 446
manifestation
   training ......................................................... 457
manifestation of forms of things ............ 354
Mars ..................................................... 185, 189, 354, 380
Massalia ........................................................... 67
mastery ......................................................... 213
Melitta ........................................................... 179
Melusina ............................................... 179, 185
Menippe ........................................................ 190
Mercury ................................................ 353, 380
Mercury-Selene .......................................... 189
merges .................................................... 216–23
   purpose of .................................................. 222
Metis .............................................................. 437
Midheaven .......................................... 375, 380
   relative chart ............................................ 391

milestone mapping ....... *See* relative chart, milestone mapping
monetary capital .................................................. 233
Moon ............................................................. 355, 380
mother role .......................................................... 52
motivators, telepathic ...................................... 365
Moultona ................................................... 353, 381
multidimensionality ........................................ 143
musical instrument ............................................ 39
Naema ................................... 179, 354, 381, 393
Natalie .................................. 186, 353, 381, 441
negative spirits ................................................. 227
negativity ............................................................. 22
Nenetta ............................................................. 456
Nephele ............................................................ 109
Neptune ................................................... 189, 380
Newtonia .......................................................... 441
Nolli ................................... 168, 171, 355, 382
*Non-Capital Wealth* ................................ 152, 201
North Node ........................................ 355, 380, 403
Notburga .......................................................... 354
notoriety .......................................................... 354
Nymphe ............................................................. 67
object reading, warning ................................. 339
obsession ........................................................ 353
octiles ...................................................... 184, 195
OOB ........................... *See* out of body experience
Ophiucus ......................................................... 375
other-dreams .................................................. 294
othering ........................................................... 432
out of body experience ....................... 303, 307
outgroups .......................................................... 49
Pallas ....................................................... 186, 380
Part of Fortune .............................................. 380
  relative chart ............................................ 391
partnership ................................... 39, 174, 181
  as merge .................................................... 222
Pax .................................... 182, 186, 189, 353, 381
Peitho ............................................................... 456
Phaeton ........................................................... 441
Phthia ............................................................... 411
Pierretta ............................................................ 67
Pisces ........................................................ 32, 375
  duodecanates ........................................... 427
  realm ............................................................ 66
planetary orbits .............................................. 373
Pluto ........................................................ 186, 353, 380
Poesia ............................................ 67, 189, 353, 381
power versus authority ................................. 434
premonitory dreams ..................................... 260
pre-punishment ................................... 132, 277
Priska ..................................................... 186, 354, 381
problem areas
  abuse ................................................... 187, 353
  abuse, childhood ..................................... 353

addiction ................................................ 189, 353
Agamemnon ................................................... 195
Agathe .............................................................. 195
attracting others' corruption ...................... 187
attracting people or situations with negative effects ....................................................... 189
attracting unseemly influences ................... 185
bad habits ........................................................ 353
Barcelona ......................................................... 195
barriers for friends ........................................ 188
being a pushover .......................................... 353
being abused ................................................. 353
being domineering ....................................... 186
being ignored or passed by ........................ 185
being used up, drained ............................... 353
blocking influences ...................................... 188
boundaries ..................................................... 186
burdens ................................................... 184, 185
burnout ........................................................... 353
chaining something down ......................... 186
Chiron .............................................................. 195
coming in second ......................................... 186
constantly complaining .............................. 187
corruption ............................................. 187, 189
costly leadership ........................................... 185
costly skill ........................................................ 185
crusading ........................................................ 186
Damocles ........................................................ 195
Davida .............................................................. 195
Delila ................................................................. 195
devaluation ..................................................... 189
diminishing partner worth ......................... 185
dissatisfaction ................................................ 438
elimination ..................................................... 184
Endymion ....................................................... 195
enslavement .................................................. 189
excessive projection .................................... 185
Fabiola .............................................................. 195
feeling second placed .................................. 354
filing through options ................................. 187
Hamiltonia ...................................................... 195
hurt .................................................................. 184
Hypatia ............................................................. 195
irritating or frustrating others ................... 184
isolation .......................................................... 184
Janina ............................................................... 195
lack of validation .......................................... 185
leaving a relationship .................................. 185
Liberatrix ........................................................ 195
Lipperta ........................................................... 195
loneliness ....................................................... 184
Lysistrata ........................................................ 195
Mars .................................................................. 195
Melusina ......................................................... 195
mistreatment of others ............................... 353

Natalie................................................................. 195
needing to be perfect....................................... 186
needing to force something............................ 185
oppression ......................................................... 189
overspending energy....................................... 187
Pallas ................................................................... 195
Pax ....................................................................... 195
pervasive situational stress............................. 186
Pluto..................................................................... 195
pressure to produce......................................... 186
Priska................................................................... 195
relationship stress ............................................ 188
relationship walls ............................................. 185
Ricarda................................................................. 195
Rockefellia.......................................................... 195
rumor mill .......................................................... 353
ruthlessness ...................................................... 184
Saturn.................................................................. 195
Sauer.................................................................... 195
self-sabotage ..................................................... 353
selling yourself out........................................... 353
sexual exploitation .......................................... 189
Signe ................................................................... 195
Siri........................................................................ 195
stealing ............................................................... 184
stress ............................................. 186, 188, 353
struggling uphill .............................................. 186
suicide................................................................. 189
suppression of others ..................................... 184
susceptibility to influences............................. 188
suspicion............................................................. 278
tension as you interact with a certain side of
      another................................................... 184
tension as you try to use one trait but keep
      getting the other................................... 184
tension as you want certain results............... 184
tension as you want something..................... 184
theft..................................................................... 189
torture................................................................. 189
trauma.......................................................184, 189
unending events .............................................. 353
Velleda ................................................................ 195
Wolfiana.............................................................. 195
Xanthe................................................................. 195
Yrsa ..................................................................... 195
Zelia..................................................................... 195
projection....................................... 120, 127, 282
    astral............................................... 303–22
    dream............................................289–303
    dreams, them to you..............................290–94
    dreams, you to them...............................294–98
    further development..............................287–322
    training ........................... 61, 98, 102, 256, 299
proprioception........................................................ 112
Protogeneia.......................................................... 179

pseudo-ARIMA................................................. 436
psychic calls...................................................... 414
psychic communication ............................ 27, 30
psychic connection.......................................... 298
psychic senses.................................................. 282
psychicism ..........................................................71
psychological capital ................................231, 233
public assessment...................................... 241–51
reactions, replacing......................................... 190
reflection partner............................... 18, 19, 181
relationship astrology..................................... 401
relationship types........................................... 152
relationships..................................................... 354
    doubts................................................... 399
    nonstandard ................................... 432–35
relative chart............................................390, 402
    and psychic connection ...................... 409
    Ascendant, Midheaven, and other axes ...........391
    how to read ...................................390–401
    milestone mapping.............................. 394
    relationship scan ........................... 391–93
Requiem.............................................................. 189
resonance ........................................................... 107
    hypothesis ............................................ 135
resonating partner............................................ 181
respect ..................................................................21
Ricarda................................................. 186, 189, 354, 381
riches................................................................... 440
Rockefellia.......................................................... 186
Role groups........................................................ 454
Sagittarius.................................................... 32, 375
    duodecanates....................................... 430
    realm........................................................46
Salacia................................................................. 189
Saturn.................................................. 166, 186, 354, 380
Sauer..................................................... 67, 166, 186
Scorpio.......................................................... 32, 375
    duodecanates....................................... 430
    realm........................................................41
Selene (asteroid)..................................................67
Selene (White Moon)..... 41, 177, 353, 354, 380, 393
self-other-world ......................................... 75, 375
senses.................................... 111, 113, 140, 255, 274
    hybrid.................................................... 287
    normal versus intuitive ...................... 275
    scale....................................................... 284
Senta............................................................354, 381
service...................................................................42
*Sex in 12 Dimensions*........................... 36, 89, 214
shadow Role group........................................... 454
sidereal system................................................. 375
Signe ................................................... 187, 189, 353, 381
signs..............................................................32, **373**
    breaking into................................. 443–45
Siri........................................................ 166, 187, 355, 382

# Index

slot holders .................................................. 152
smell .......................................................... 111
snowflake model ........................................... 11
social capital ............................................... 233
South Node .................................................. 446
speaking in tongues .................................... 361
sphere ....................................... 27, 144, 214
   occupants .............................................. 148
   under conflict ........................................ 174
spirit domains ............................................. 226
spirits .................................................. 219, 220
   messages from ..................................... 220
   types ....................................................... 224
spirituality ................................................... 354
splits ..................................................... 216–23
   purpose of ............................................. 222
square energies ........................................... 385
Square Process ............................................ 419
squares .................................... 170, 184, 195
   and judgment ........................................ 172
Squidalgo ............................................ 128, 170
status .......................................................... 355
Sternberga .................................................. 446
stress ..................................................... 181–83
Sulamitis ......................................... 190, 355, 382
summoning ............................. 32, 33, 34, 405
   training .................................................. 407
Sun ...................................................... 179, 380
Sylvania ................................................ 354, 382
Sylvia ........................................................... 446
synastry ....................................................... 401
Tanete ........................................................... 67
Tantalus ....................................................... 190
tarot ..................................................... 350, 351
taste ............................................................. 111
Taurus .................................................. 32, 375
   duodecanates ...................................... 447
   realm ........................................................ 16
Taurus and objectification ........................ 447
telekinesis ................................................... 134
telepathy .............................................. 134, 283
   developing ....................................... 364–71
   training ........... 38, 45, 98, 154, 229, 270, 407, 410
   using the astro chart ........................ 402–22
tension .............................. 248, 246–49, 385
tension map ................................................ 247
theoretical astrology
   elements ............................................... 376
   signs ...................................................... 373
Theresia ........................................................ 67
Thereus ....................................................... 441
Timandra ..................................................... 437
touch ........................................................... 111
trading asteroid clusters ............................ 418
training

being summoned ........................................ 410
clairaudience ........................................ 29, 229
claircognizance ...... 38, 45, 61, 149, 176, 191, 256
clairsentience ....................................... 61, 229
clairvoyance ................... 61, 98, 149, 160, 352
   dream interpretability ........................ 149
   dream interpretation ............................. 76
   empathy ................................. 29, 191, 270
   essential knowledge ........ 76, 102, 160, 286
   life path .. 102, 149, 160, 176, 191, 217, 256, 457
   manifestation ....................................... 457
   projection ................ 61, 98, 102, 256, 299
   summoning .......................................... 407
   telepathy ........ 38, 45, 98, 154, 229, 270, 407, 410
tribe ....................................... 213, 214, 235
   connecting ............................................ 236
   multiple ................................................ 215
tropical system ............................................ 375
Tyche ................................................... 353, 381
unassisted clairvoyance ............ *See* clairvoyance, unassisted
Under 100% relationship ............................ 209
Uranus ......................................................... 380
Varda ........................................................... 179
Varuna .................................................. 354, 381
Velleda ........................................ 187, 189, 353, 381
Venus .................................................... 169, 380
Veritas .............................................. 41, 354, 382
Vertex .................................................. 355, 380
   relative chart ....................................... 405
Vesta .................................................... 189, 380
Virginia ........................................................ 441
Virgo .................................................... 32, 375
   duodecanates ...................................... 435
   realm ....................................................... 36
vision .................................................... 111, 120
vision-cognitive clairsentience ... *See* clairsentience, vision-cognitive
Waltraut ............................................... 355, 382
want (working definition) ........................... 417
wants .................................................. 26, 32, 151
waves ........................................................... 140
   introverse ............................................. 122
   longitudinal .......................................... 113
   postlongitudinal .................................. 119
   surface .................................................. 113
   transverse ............................................. 113
Wilkens ........................................ 355, 382, 437
Winchester .................................................. 189
wishes come true ........................................ 354
Wolfiana ...................................... 187, 189, 353, 381
words
   disrespect ................................................ 22
   negative .................................................. 23
   positive ................................................... 23

| | |
|---|---|
| respect ................................................. 23 | Yrsa ................................ 188, 189, 353, 381 |
| transition ........................................... 24 | Zelia ............................................................ 188 |
| work ......................................................... 37 | Zeuxo ......................................................... 419 |
| Xanthe ................................................... 187 | |

## About the Author

My name is Ajani Abdul-Khaliq, a data artist and the oldest of three brothers. I received my B.S. in a self-designed [Biology + Education + Psychology + Computational Neuroscience] major—4 parts—from the California Institute of Technology in 2003.[55] I obtained my M.A. in Sociology (2006), and PhD in Leadership Studies (2017) both from Our Lady of the Lake University—the latter in a study involving circular statistics, canonical correlation, and a lot of code. I own an angel co-operating company called Social Arts & Technical Alliance which lends operations assistance to creators' projects and businesses, and have an indie publishing imprint attached to it called i&ℝ (imaginary & real) for lending a voice to isolated perspectives. I have three big dreams:

1. *The City.* To establish a forward-thinking city. Books like *Black Male Feminism* and *Non-capital Wealth* focus on progressive social policy.
2. *Talking Trees.* To contribute to the machine learning technology for having image-recognized objects tell us their human-like stories. *Alma Mater*, *The Sphere,* and my study of astro-categories serve this goal.
3. *Form-Response.* To build a globally useful theory for translating physical things into their interactions—ultimately for saving humans as data and broadcasting them to other places. To save a whole human, though, you have to save the *whole* human—even the taboo areas. I also plan to have my own data saved[56], my books roughly tracking my evolution as a person whose life-path might be useful to the world. *Gamified Spirit* and *Sex in 12 Dimensions* are all about options for representing ourselves and co-creating with others respectively, given that our ways may not match how everyone else trains us to be.

Throughout *Alma Mater* I've referenced several other books which may be new to readers of the *Full Spectrum Astrology* series. What all of those books have in common is that they revolve around the three dreams above, where I believe that knowing ourselves as connected stories instead of separable objects is key to making the world a happier place. As a data artist, I find a beauty in our interactions, our physical bodies translated against physics potentials, and believe that capturing the magic of this through laws can produce worlds more rewarding than even the unexplainable kind. My works may sometimes seem disparate, but they are all aimed at tolerance as we reassess our individual value against the digital future. Everything everywhere has a value. All should be given a chance to show it.

---

[55] This route was also known as "the hard road." The major, {Cognition} for short, didn't exist at Caltech in 2003 and I had to put together a detailed submission and appear before the academics committee to get it officially approved by the University. I was booted out twice on academic probation and had to covertly sign up for biology classes despite the major I was stuck with (physics) while all this was being built. Caltech, in general, is a very hard school, but it forces you to stand on your own as a thinker. In late 2003 I was banned from Caltech after a run-in with a security guard and a one-way hearing I didn't know had happened until the ban message itself came. I don't know what kind of story the guard and his administrator friend told, but it convinced enough people at least. Weird. Unjust. To this day the school doesn't know what *actually* occurred—mainly because they didn't ask—but this is typical of how "othering" works. They'll obviously never get the apology from me that they demanded. Yet they still send me alumni requests every year asking for money. That experience and a number of other interesting soap operas have motivated my creations for voices that aren't allowed to be heard, and I wouldn't change any of it as a part of my path. (As an extra fun fact, the asteroid 2906 Caltech, late blooming brilliance and (film) noir, are on my Midheaven.) It's all good though. Without events like the one above, this series surely wouldn't exist: Ironically, I was introduced to astrology while at Caltech by a fellow student Olga R. Why weren't the star interpretations as random as our skeptical peers "knew" they should be? They hadn't even run the tests. Thus began a lifelong relationship with the field. We now know that the relationships are there, but as with object recognition, we didn't have the machine learning to investigate this complex multicollinear space properly at the time. Now you might say that the correct way to test astrology is through a process called "non-parametric topic embedding on {chartholders, text descriptions, orbital elements, object aspects}," something like what I do here following Question 55.3.5. That and the "blind method" discussed before composite Pluto-Selene in *HBS*. These would have been much more difficult to do before big data and machine learning.

[56] Hence the shaded boxes throughout *Alma*. All of my books were written as part of my journey, so these boxes more or less explain why the sections that contain them exist.